TO DAN

With my special and fondest love
for my beautiful and caring
fiancée, and all my good wishes for
the future.

John. Charles
XXXXXX.
Xmas 1992.

# The Ultimate Humour Book

# The Ultimate Humour Book

CHANCELLOR PRESS

First published in Great Britain in 1988 as
*Humorous Stories*

This revised edition published in 1991 by
Chancellor Press an imprint of
Reed International Books Limited
Michelin House
81 Fulham Road
London SW3 6RB

Reprinted 1992.

Copyright © introduction and arrangement 1988, 1991,
Reed International Books Limited

ISBN 1 85152 144 5

Printed in The United Kingdom by
William Clowes Limited, Beccles and London

# Introduction

Collecting funny stories should be a national pastime in this country. We spend far too much time hanging over bridges wondering what's happened to the 11.23 from Rippingbourne, or catching cold while waiting for a particularly rare starling to dash out of the bushes, or comparing matchboxes at seaside conferences. Not me. I'd rather sit in a comfy chair, having had just a little too much Christmas turkey, but safe in the knowledge that I'm going to laugh it all off anyway. I'd rather have an after-dinner titter than a mint. And yet, when I tell people that I collect funny stories, they look at me as if I've got feathers. I can assure you I haven't, so don't worry about that. Like everyone else, I have them clipped so that they don't get caught in car doors.

I'm not cross about that, though. I'm not even upset that these stories have cost me quite a lot of money in extra purchases. Firstly I've had to buy a torch so that I can read them in bed under the sheets. I've also invested in a pair of rubber gloves so that I can read them in the bath. That worked a treat until I got roped into doing the washing-up as well. And I've also bought one of those marker pens – 'Barker's markers' I call them – so that I can highlight my favourite lines. I chose a lime-green colour. The only trouble is, I've marked so many pages I no longer need the torch after all: the book glows in the dark! They're jolly useful, those pens. I can now put my finger on a funny line at a moment's notice. This is particularly helpful when you need to be funny in a great hurry: when making a carefully prepared, spontaneous after-dinner speech, for example, or opening a garden fête under a cloudburst, or trying to get the Gas Board to come round.

Humour anthologies are fun to read, because they catch a particular writer at his or her best. Maybe there were times when Geoffrey Willans's Molesworth or Richmal Crompton's William behaved like angels, scurrying off to do their homework and prepare for the church fête, or washing twice before coming down to supper. Well, I don't know about you, but I'd rather have them at their rebellious worst. And, maybe, somewhere, there lurks a 'Beginner's Guide to the Dutch Language' in a dusty library, written by a very young P. G. Wodehouse, or a book of Victoria Wood's favourite pasta recipes. All very well, I'm sure, and most useful if that's what you need, but not much use in a book of humorous stories. So I'm very grateful to the publishers of this book for choosing an absolutely 'top-hole' selection of talented writers at their very best.

Of course, you don't have to look very far to find something funny written by the many names in the contents list. They are all dedicated professionals, ready to drop anything – except their pens – when the chance to write something hilarious comes along. People like James Thurber and O. Henry wrote all the time, that's why they were so good. No matter what they were doing, they always made time in the day to compose. I'm following their example right now, as a matter of fact. Even though I'm on holiday, I've chosen this moment to write this introduction. Naturally, I have been getting some pretty funny looks (I wrote down some of the funnier ones). I'm not surprised. You'd stare too if you saw a man writing a humorous introduction while water-skiing. But I'm sure if James Thurber were here today, he'd probably have his typewriter with him as well. Time for another jump. Here goes . . .

The humorous stories in this book are remarkable because they are so unlike any other entertainment. You've got to do it all yourself. No one's reciting the story to you. You'll have to bring your own accents when required, read it at your own pace, picture it in your mind – and laugh when you yourself judge that it's funny. It's very different from television comedy, but it does seem to work. Perhaps they should write a new television comedy show where the audience is given the script and left to read it on their own. Every now and then the writers or the producer could wander on to the stage, chuckle quietly to let them know how funny it is, and then walk off.

Now, I prefer to read comedy while sitting down. Call me old-fashioned if you like, but I'll bet you a shilling that you do, too. I'm not laying down any rules about it. You're very welcome to read it in whatever position suits you, so long as it helps you to laugh harder and longer. It must be something to do with the circulation. That's why you find stand-up comics and sit-down audiences, rather than vice versa. Let them do the work. After all, that's what they're paid for. And you take the weight off your legs – you'll need it to preserve your strength if you want to keep up with Clive James or David Niven. You might be lying down after a hard day's night. If so, a couple of stories each night should send you off to sleep with a smile on your lips. On the other hand, you might be lying down *during* a hard day's work. In that case, I don't think reading will be on your mind, but let's not get into that now!

At this stage, I should issue some advice. It's true what they say: Humour can be contagious. If you bump into someone in the washroom having a quiet chuckle, they're probably remembering a line from the wonderful *Diary of a Nobody*. And if they tell it to you, and you start chuckling too, chances are just about everyone will be in there before long, so for goodness' sake make sure that someone's left behind to answer the phone, as the coffee break might take a bit longer than ten minutes!

Then again, if you see someone on the train tomorrow with a big smile on her face, don't nudge her on the elbow and say: 'I know what you were getting up to last night!' I know that they probably *were* reading the story by Evelyn Waugh, as you suspected, but there is just a chance that they were doing something else (and I don't mean reading one of Barry Pain's 'Eliza' stories). So be prepared.

If, on the other hand, the prospect of buying a plant is making you wilt, or if the thought of winding yourself up to buy a digital clock for Christmas is making you see red – be of good cheer! I know you know what time it is even without a clock (i.e. five minutes later than you thought it was), but cast dull cares aside. Pack a couple of extracts of Fran Lebowitz into your shopping basket and you'll sweep through the stores with a huge grin on your face, looking like you've just won the Pools.

The best thing about reading this book, though, is that you won't get fined by the police for laughing yourself silly. No officer is going to wave you down and breathalyse you because you've been mixing your J. M. Barrie and your Leslie Thomas. 'Now come on, officer, there's a good fellow, I'm only halfway through this story.' 'One minute, sir. When was the last time you read this extract from *The Ascent of Rum Doodle*?' 'Half an hour ago, officer.' 'I see, sir. But your eyes look a little glazed and your cheeks are flushed. Can you explain that?' 'Yes, that's because I'm reading a short story by Woody Allen.' Light will then break out all over his face. 'Woody Allen, sir? One of my favourites! I don't normally read on duty, but in this case . . . after you if you don't mind, sir.' And a few minutes later, you'd be back into the book, ready for some more choice comedy.

People ask me why some Humour works and some doesn't, but I'm not terribly good at all that analytical hocus pocus. Someone once said to me at a party, 'Ronnie, Humour is like a doughnut: It's covered in sugar, shaped like a ring, fried in oil, and sometimes it contains jam in the middle.' Obviously you can quibble with the details, but I think that by and large that sums up my attitude to Humour. Ever since then, whenever anyone asks me to analyse it, I just reach for the doughnuts!

I think it's about time I left you to the stories. I've been once round the lake behind this boat, and it's beginning to slow down, so it's probably time to change hands. I'll just say Farewell! Adieu! Keep smiling, but above all, keep reading. And don't forget: The soldier kills with a sword, the lover with a kiss but the humorist falls flat on his face after an encounter with a banana-skin and then goes home to write a story about it!

# CONTENTS

# The Grand Design

## Jonathan Lynn and Anthony Jay

### JANUARY 23RD

The last few days have been overwhelmingly exciting. I went to the Palace and kissed hands. The next morning I moved into Number Ten. I'd read in the memoirs of past Prime Ministers that the staff line up in the front lobby, and in the long corridor inside it that leads down to the grand central staircase, and applaud the incoming Prime Minister. I wonder why they didn't applaud me. [*This accolade is only granted, traditionally, to a Prime Minister who had just won a general election – Ed.*] I hope this does not bode ill.

It took a day or two to move in. The PM lives in the flat 'above the shop', and the whole building is extremely confusing. From the outside it looks like an average size Georgian terrace house – but inside it is absolutely huge, a small stately home, a mini palace.

This is because it is, in reality, two houses. Not two houses side by side (the Chancellor of the Exchequer lives in Number Eleven), but two houses that almost back on to each other, joined by corridors, stairwells and courtyards. Each house has five or six floors, and the house at the back has large elegant staterooms for entertaining my subjects. [*Hacker was plainly suffering from delusions of grandeur, and was confusing himself with the monarch – Ed.*]

The main problem in finding one's way around Number Ten is that, because it is two different houses, because of subsidence during the war,[1] and because the ground slopes away towards the back, it's almost impossible to know what floor you're on once you're upstairs.

But my confusion on moving in was like nothing compared to my state of mind today, my fifth day in office, on being taken into the top-

[1] World War II.

secret operations room below the MOD.[2]

It looked just like you'd expect: maps of the five continents, girls at video terminals, officers at desks. I was shown around by the Chief of the General Staff, General Sir Geoffrey Howard, a tall dapper chap with sandy hair, bushy eyebrows and a brisk commanding voice. Sir Humphrey and Bernard were hovering about, as always.

Naturally, my first question was about the Hot Line. The General looked puzzled.

'Which one?'

'To Russia.'

'Ah. That's in Downing Street,' the General told me. I glanced at Bernard. Why hadn't I been shown it? He looked surprised – perhaps he hasn't been shown it, either.

I continued: 'So if there's an emergency, can I get straight through to the Soviet President?'

'Theoretically, yes,' General Howard replied cautiously.

'Does that mean no?'

'Well, it's what we tell journalists. In fact, we did once get through to the Kremlin, but only to a switchboard operator.'

'Couldn't the operator put you through?'

'We couldn't find out, she didn't seem to speak much English.'

'How often is it tested?'

The General looked blank. Testing had clearly not occurred to him.

'They try not to test it too often,' Humphrey intervened smoothly. 'It tends to create unnecessary panic at the other end. And panic is always a good thing to avoid where nuclear weapons are concerned, don't you think?' I certainly do.

The General walked me over to a telex machine.

'Now this –' he said meaningfully, '*is it*!'

'Is it?' I asked.

'Yes,' he said.

'Good,' I replied, encouragingly. Then I realised that I was going to get no further clue as to what he was talking about. 'Er . . . *what* is it, exactly?' I inquired casually, with what I hoped was a knowledgeable air.

'It's the trigger, Prime Minister,' Sir Humphrey murmured.

[2] Ministry of Defence.

I felt a sudden chill. 'The trigger?'

'Yes. The nuclear trigger . . . the button.'

'This?' I couldn't believe it. I stared at the innocent-looking telex machine.

'Indirectly, yes.' The General could see my concern. 'It's simply a telex link to HMS Northwood. You would send a coded signal, you see. Then the telex operator at Northwood sends out an authentication signal.'

'So he knows it's from you, you see,' added Sir Humphrey softly.

'And when the instruction has been authenticated, and a target indication been made, Northwood would sent the command to one of our Polaris submarines, and they'd actually press the button.' The General seemed quite satisfied with all this.

It all seemed so simple, so cut and dried. I give the order, they carry it out. My mouth felt all dry, but I had to find out more.

'They'd do it . . . just like that?'

'Just like that.' General Howard was visibly proud.

'When I say so?'

'When you say so.'

'But wouldn't anyone . . . *argue* with me?'

General Howard was shocked. 'Of course not. Serving officers obey orders without question, Prime Minister.'

I swallowed. 'But supposing I get drunk?' I asked, jokingly. Humphrey replied, rather too seriously: 'On the whole, it would be safer if you didn't get drunk.'

'Yes, but . . . seriously,' I asked, 'what happens if I go off my rocker?'

'I think the Cabinet might notice.' Sir Humphrey was trying to sound reassuring.

I wasn't reassured. I don't think one can count on the Cabinet noticing that kind of thing. For a start, half of them, if not exactly off their rockers themselves, are not exactly what you'd call well-balanced.

I had to know more. 'Supposing I gave the order to press the button, and then changed my mind?'

'That's all right,' said the General with a chuckle, 'no one would ever know, would they?' Everyone else chuckled appreciatively.

I tried to chuckle too, but somehow I just couldn't. Instead, I asked how many actual bombs we have.

'Four Polaris submarines,' said the General. 'Sixteen missiles on each. Three warheads per missile.'

Mental arithmetic has never been my strong point and I didn't like to fish out my pocket calculator. Bernard saw my problem and spoke up. 'One hundred and ninety-two actual bombs, Prime Minister.' Obviously he'd been told before.

One hundred and ninety-two nuclear bombs! It doesn't bear thinking about! And Humphrey piled on the pressure, pointing out that each has at least five times the power of the Hiroshima bomb.

They all waited for me to speak. But I felt quite overwhelmed by the horror and the insanity of my new responsibilities.

The General looked at me with sympathy and understanding. 'I know what you're thinking,' he said. 'Not very many.'

That wasn't *at all* what I was thinking! I told him sharply that one hundred and ninety-two bombs seemed plenty to me. He didn't agree. 'Not with twelve hundred Soviet missiles trained on Britain, waiting to retaliate instantly.'

Twelve hundred? I felt I should assume a stiff upper lip. 'Ah well,' I remarked, 'Britain's always fought against the odds, haven't we? The Armada, the Battle of Britain . . .'

Even as I spoke I realised that the notion of fighting bravely against the odds is completely irrelevant in the context of nuclear war.

But General Howard saw this as an opportunity to put in a plug for Trident. He pointed out that we would have much more fire power at our disposal when it is delivered. And therefore we'd have a much greater deterrent.

'Meanwhile,' I said, 'thank God we've got our conventional forces.'

They all looked at me, slightly sceptically.

'Prime Minister,' said the General stiffly, 'our conventional forces could hold the Russians for seventy-two hours at most.'

'At most?'

'At most.'

The General was standing at attention. It looked most odd in his civilian suit. As a matter of fact, I thought irrelevantly, all these men around me were unmistakably soldiers, even though none of them were in uniform. Unless you call baggy blue pinstripe suits a uniform.

I forced myself to consider the ghastly implications of the latest piece of information that I'd just taken on board. 'So, in the event of a Russian attack, I would have to make an instant decision, would I?'

General Howard shook his head and smiled. 'No, Prime Minister. You'd probably have twelve hours.'

Twelve hours? That's what *I* call instant. I asked him if we shouldn't do something about that.

The General agreed emphatically. He thinks we certainly should do something about it. But, he informed me bitterly, the military has been told by the politicians for thirty years that this country can't afford the conventional forces to do the job.

Sir Humphrey, at my shoulder, nodded.

'Conventional forces are terribly expensive, Prime Minister,' he explained. 'Much cheaper just to press a button.'

JANUARY 24TH

I had a sleepless night last night. My visit to the MOD had unsettled me quite profoundly. I couldn't get those figures out of my head. My powers of concentration are pretty remarkable [*we believe Hacker intended no irony here – Ed.*] but today I found it hard to keep my mind on my work.

'Seventy-two hours,' I found myself murmuring in the middle of a meeting with Bernard.

'Um, Prime Minister?' He was trying to bring me back to what we'd been discussing. 'Isn't seventy-two hours a bit generous for a meeting with the New Zealand High Commissioner?'

He was being facetious, I suppose. He could see I was thinking about the length of time that NATO forces could hold the Russians. I asked him if we could persuade the Americans to strengthen *their* conventional forces.

Bernard felt that it wouldn't really help. 'Apparently the American troops in Germany are all so drug-ridden that they don't know which side they're on anyway. And on the last NATO exercise the US troops dispersed and picknicked in the woods with lady soldiers.'

I asked him about the other NATO armies. He said they were all right on weekdays. I asked him to make himself clear.

'The Dutch, Danish and Belgian armies all go home for the weekend.'

This was the most extraordinary thing I'd heard yet. 'So,' I followed through with my usual relentless logic, 'if the Russians are going to invade we'd prefer them, on the whole, to do it between Monday and

Friday.'

He nodded.

[*In fact, even if Warsaw Pact forces had invaded between Monday and Friday it would hardly have helped the NATO forces. The NATO barracks were so far behind their forward positions that the invaders would have, in any case, reached those positions first – Ed.*]

'Is this widely known?' I asked, amazed.

He could see I was thinking of the Russians. He explained that if he knew it, the Russians certainly do. 'The Kremlin usually gets NATO defence information before it filters through to us at Number Ten.'

I summed up. 'So it all comes back to Trident.'

'When it comes,' he agreed.

'When it comes,' I mused, wondering when that would really be.

'If it works,' Bernard added.

*If it works?* What did he mean?

Casually, he told me. 'Frequently, Prime Minister, when new weapons are delivered the warheads don't fit the end of the rockets. That's what happened with Polaris. You know the sort of thing. It's all in the files.' He flipped through a file. 'Wiring faults, microchip failure. Ground-control transmitter on a different frequency from the receiver on the missile.' He looked up at me apologetically. 'We didn't have the means of delivering Polaris for some years. Cruise is probably the same. Trident might be too.'

I told him that I considered this absolutely intolerable, that we should take the manufacturers to court.

Bernard shook his head sadly, and explained that it is impossible for us to risk the publicity. And he's right of course. Security makes it impossible. And the manufacturers know it.

I asked him about changing manufacturers.

'Oh we do.' He sighed. 'All the time. But the trouble is that all the manufacturers know it too. That's why that torpedo landed on Sandwich Golf Course.'

I thought I'd misheard him. A torpedo on Sandwich Golf Course? Why hadn't we seen that in the papers?

Bernard knew all about it. 'There was a cover-up. The members just found a new bunker on the seventh fairway the next morning.'

I didn't know whether I was more concerned about the cover-up or the malfunctioning torpedoes. I asked Bernard why even our torpedoes

don't work. He reassured me. Apparently it's only the *new* ones that
don't work. All the others are working fine – the ones that were
designed during World War II.

But these are forty years old. Why, I wanted to know, do they work
better than our latest weapons? The answer was so obvious that I
should have thought of it myself: the old torpedoes had lots of testing.
We can't afford to test modern weapons properly – partly because it's
too expensive and partly because if there *is* a nuclear war it won't last
long enough for weapons tests.

I wondered what other revelations lay in store, now that I was
entitled to know all our military secrets. I decided I'd better find out.
'What else don't I know about the defence of the United Kingdom?' I
asked Bernard.

'I don't know, Prime Minister. I don't know what you don't know.'

I don't think he was being insolent because he went on to give me
some useful advice. If I want another view, I might find it valuable to
have a word with the Government's Chief Scientific Adviser.
Apparently he sees the problem rather differently from the MOD.

I told Bernard to get him in at once. Bernard was hesitant. 'A late
drink may be better,' he advised. 'Better not to let the Cabinet Office
know. Sir Humphrey gets rather upset – he doesn't regard the Chief
Scientific Adviser as one of us.'

I looked up the Chief Scientific Adviser in *Who's Who*. Professor Isaac
Rosenblum. DSO at Arnhem. How could Humphrey not trust a man
who fought on our side at Arnhem, and who was decorated by His
Majesty for bravery?

'I'm afraid that it doesn't make up for his speaking with an Austrian
accent,' Bernard remarked. 'And he certainly didn't go to Oxford or
Cambridge. He didn't even go to the LSE.'

One of Bernard's little jokes. I think.


JANUARY 25TH

Tonight I asked Professor Isaac Rosenblum up to my flat for a late
drink. And now my mind is reeling. It's not very often in politics that
you meet, and talk to, a genuine intellectual. I used to be a polytechnic
lecturer, and you don't get very many intelligent conversations in

academic life either. [*Hacker, it seems, regarded polytechnics as part of academic life – Ed.*] There are a *few* intellectuals in both walks of life, of course, but politicians never dare own up to it and academics prefer gossip anyway.

Professor Rosenblum is a small wiry elderly man. He is in his mid-seventies, lean, bright-eyed, and with a mind like a steel trap. I felt like an undergraduate at a tutorial. But I certainly learned a thing or two, and I believe that tonight's discussion will have a decisive effect on the future of my government and of this country. There will be changes made. [*Hacker was so excited when dictating this entry into his diary that he completely forgot about the Civil Service – Ed.*]

He popped in to Number Ten this evening, long after Humphrey had gone home.[1] I arranged with the security people that he should be allowed in through the back door, as there's always press watching the front.

He began by asking me if I believed in the nuclear deterrent.

'Yes,' I said.

'Why?' he asked.

I didn't quite know what to say. I mean, everyone believes in the nuclear deterrent. I asked him to repeat his question.

'Why?' he asked again.

'Because . . . it deters,' I replied, weakly.

'Whom?'

I'd never before met anyone who spoke in such short sentences. You never find *them* in politics, nor in academic life either. But I couldn't see quite what he was driving at.

'I beg your pardon?' I asked.

'Whom?' he asked again. He could see I didn't understand. He clarified his question. '*Whom* does it deter?'

It seemed obvious to me. 'The Russians. From attacking us.'

'Why?' There it was again, that irritating little word. Why *what*? I played for time. 'I beg your pardon?' I asked.

'Why?'

Why does the deterrent deter the Russians from attacking us, that's what he was asking. 'Because,' I replied firmly, 'they know that if they launch an attack I'd press the button.'

[1] 6 pm.

'You would?' He sounded surprised.

'Well . . .' I hesitated, 'wouldn't I?'

'Well . . . *would* you?'

'In the last resort, yes. Definitely.' I thought again. 'At least I *think* I definitely would.'

His questions continued relentlessly. I had to think carefully. [*Hacker was out of practice at this – Ed.*]

'And what is the last resort?'

'If the Russians invade Western Europe.' That at least seemed quite obvious.

Professor Rosenblum smiled. 'But you would only have twelve hours to decide. So the last resort is also the first response, is that what you're saying?'

*Was* that what I was saying? It seemed crazy.

The Chief Scientific Adviser stared at me critically. 'Well, you don't need to worry. Why should the Russians try to annex the whole of Europe? They can't even control Afghanistan.' He shook his head. 'No. If they try anything it will be salami tactics.'

[*Salami tactics was the description customarily given to 'slice by slice' manoeuvres, i.e. not a full scale invasion of the West, but the annexation of one small piece at a time. More often than not, the first steps would not be annexation of land but small treaty infringements, road closures, etc – Ed.*]

Rosenblum stood up. He paced enthusiastically up and down my living-room, a glass of orange juice in hand, expounding an assortment of defence scenarios. First, he postulated riots in West Berlin, with buildings in flames, and the East German fire brigade crossing the border to help. He stopped pacing, stared at me, and asked me if I'd press the button in such circumstances.

*Obviously* the answer was no. Rosenblum nodded. He seemed to agree. Then he asked me if I'd press the button if the East German *police* came with the fire brigade. Again I shook my head. How could I start a nuclear war because of such a small territorial infringement?

Rosenblum started pacing again. A little smile was now visible around the corners of his mouth. 'Suppose the East Germans send some *troops*. Then more troops – just for riot control, they say. And then the East German troops are replaced by Russian troops. You press the button?'

Russian troops replacing East German troops in West Berlin? Would

I start a nuclear war? I don't see how I could. I shook my head again.

The Chief Scientific Adviser smiled, and suggested cheerfully that the next 'slice' would be that the Russian troops don't go. They would be 'invited' to stay, to support the civilian administration. Then the civilian administration might close the roads and Tempelhof Airport. West Berlin would now be cut off. [*West Berlin was an island of the West German Federal Republic, sixty miles inside the border of the German Democratic Republic. 'Democratic' in this context, naturally means communist – Ed.*] Would I *now* press the button? he inquired.

I didn't know. I told him I needed time to think.

'You have twelve hours!' he barked.

I felt totally panicked. Then I reminded myself, and him, that he was inventing all this, and I relaxed.

He shrugged. 'You are Prime Minister today. The phone might ring now, from NATO Headquarters.'

The phone rang! It shook me to the core. Bernard hurried across my study and answered it. 'Hello. Yes?' He turned to me. 'NATO Headquarters, Prime Minister.'

Was a nightmare coming true? Then Bernard went on. 'Are you willing to address NATO's annual conference in April?'

I *thought* I was – but by then I was no longer sure of anything. I couldn't reply.

'Yes,' said Bernard into the phone, and rang off.

Professor Rosenblum turned to me again. 'Right,' he began. 'Scenario Two. Russian army manoeuvres take them "accidentally" on purpose across the West German frontier . . . is *that* the last resort?'

'No,' I replied. It didn't seem to be.

'All right,' he continued with great enthusiasm. 'Scenario Three. Suppose the Russians *have* invaded and occupied West Germany, Belgium, Holland and France. Suppose their tanks and troops have reached the English Channel. Suppose they are poised for an invasion, is *that* the last resort?'

I stonewalled. 'No.'

'Why not?' he demanded. '*Why not?*'

My mind was a fog. I was trying to see sense in all this. 'Because,' I fumbled, 'because . . . we would only fight a war to defend ourselves. And how can we defend ourselves by committing suicide?'

'So what *is* the last resort?' smiled the little old Professor. He shrugged, sat down and settled back into the overstuffed chintz armchair by the fire. 'Piccadilly? Watford Gap Service Station? The Reform Club?'

I stared at him, trying to put my thoughts in order. 'If you put it like that,' I said to him, 'the nuclear deterrent makes no sense. Is that what you're saying?'

Professor Rosenblum shook his head. 'No – I'm not saying that. If either the Russians or the Americans have the bomb, the other side must have it too. And we might as well keep Polaris, just in case.'

I didn't yet understand what exactly he was proposing.

He spelt it out to me. 'Cancel Trident. Spend the £15 billion you will save on conventional forces. Because you wouldn't really press the button, would you?'

'I might,' I said carefully, 'if I had no choice.'

He sighed. 'But we've been through this. They'll never put you into a situation where you have no choice. They'll stick to their salami tactics, remember?'

'So,' I took a deep breath, 'what happens if we divert £15 billion from Trident. What do we spend it on – tanks?'

'No. We spend it on ET.'

What on earth could he mean? Extra-terrestrials?

He saw what I was thinking, and smiled. 'ET stands for Emergent Technology. Smart missiles. Target finding. Infra-Red. The ET needs to be operated by a large conventional army.'

And then I got my inspiration! I suddenly saw what to do. Everything fell into place. It is ridiculously simple, but *completely workable*. First, we cancel Trident. We don't buy Cruise either. Then we introduce conscription, which will not only solve our defence problems by giving us a large conventional army, it also solves our unemployment problem! Excited, I explained my thoughts and Bernard raised a worry. 'Isn't conscription a rather courageous policy, Prime Minister?'

Bernard was quite wrong. Conscription would certainly be a courageous policy in times of full employment – but nowadays it would give young people something to do.

In fact, there are other definite plusses. Conscripted young people would be learning trades and skills. They'd even learn to read – the army never discharged anyone who was illiterate. In fact, we will be able to give our young people a comprehensive education, to make up for their Comprehensive Education.

We shall call the whole thing National Service, just like they used to – to remind everyone that the young people will be out in the country, serving the community and the nation.

It's a great policy. A new deal for Britain. I shall call it my Grand Design. Hacker's Grand Design. I already have notes for my House of Commons speech in which I shall outline the whole concept: 'From time to time, in our great island story, it falls to one man to lead his people out of the valley of the shadows and into the broad sunlit uplands of peace and prosperity.'

I wonder why I never thought of all this till tonight.

[*One reason, perhaps, was that Hacker and Professor Rosenblum had only just met – Ed.*]

### JANUARY 26TH

Things have really got to change round here, and I'm the man so see that those changes happen. [*After only a week in office Hacker appears to have slightly lost touch with reality – Ed.*]

A very busy morning was spent in Cabinet Committee and in appointing the remaining members of my government including some junior ministers. Then I went upstairs to the flat for lunch.

But there was none. As I came in Annie was putting on her raincoat. And she wasn't in too good a mood. When I asked her in a tone of only mild surprise if she was going off somewhere she reminded me that she was late for her Voluntary Services Committee. Whatever that is.

I asked her if there was any chance of some scrambled eggs or something. *Anything* really. She told me that there were eggs in the fridge.

I couldn't believe it. She wanted me to make lunch. I mean, it's not that I'm a male chauvinist or anything, but I am the Prime Minister and I do have plenty of other things to do. And as a politician I'm not really eligible to eat with all the Downing Street civil servants in the Cabinet mess.[1]

I can see her point. We did agree that she could carry on with her work if I became PM and we moved to Number Ten. She had been very

---

[1] Attached to the Cabinet Office.

opposed to the move here anyway, and I begin to see why. There's not much privacy. We were just discussing the eggs and I was fairly unhappy at finding myself cast as Mother Hubbard when there was a knock on the open door and a young woman messenger marched in with a Foreign Office Green Box.

'Foreign Office telegrams, Prime Minister,' she explained.

Annie was absolutely fed up. 'See what I mean?' she complained. 'It's bad enough living in this goldfish bowl anyway. I've got to be able to get out and live my own life. Every time I want to step out for some cigarettes I have to walk past a dozen journalists, a TV film crew, a bunch of messengers, housekeepers and policemen in the lobby, and fifty gawping tourists at the bottom of the street. There's no privacy *anywhere*!'

I pointed out that there is a back door. She thinks it makes virtually no difference which door we use. And there's total privacy up here in the flat. Or nearly total privacy. Well, *some* privacy, anyway.

'Our life's not our own any more.' She hammered home the point. 'What about the President ringing you in bed from the White House at two o'clock this morning?'

Rather foolishly I replied that it was only nine p.m. in Washington, which, I agree, hardly makes it any better from her point of view. I was about to explain that it was an important call to discuss my forth-coming visit to Washington when there was another knock on the door and in burst two sniffer dogs with tongues hanging out dragging a couple of police dog-handlers behind them. Apparently there was a bomb scare, and they had to search the place.

Annie looked at me and asked, 'Privacy?'

She wasn't being very reasonable, in my opinion. Surely she'd rather have security checks than be blown up. I told her that she could always have privacy if she went for a walk in the garden. I've never seen anyone out there at all.

'I've tried that,' she answered with defiance. 'About sixty people stare at you from the windows of Number Ten, Number Eleven, Number Twelve *and* the Cabinet Office. It's like exercising in a prison yard and being watched by the inmates and the warders. To think we actually have to pay rent for this place. They should pay us to live here.'

I must admit I share her resentment about the rent. I should have thought – *I did* think – that we would be given the place to live in, in view of the great personal sacrifice one makes for one's service to the nation. [*Many non-politicans do not see the acquisition of the greatest political power and patronage in the land solely in terms of 'great personal sacrifice'. And many others may wonder why Hacker imagined that, on attaining power, he should be entitled to live rent-free – Ed.*]

The dogs and dog-handlers left. I said to Annie: 'Look, it's actually a pretty nice place to live, at least it's quiet.' It was an idiotic think to say – no sooner had I uttered it than the bloody brass band started playing on Horse Guards Parade, right outside the window.

She snarled at me. 'That's been going on since seven o'clock this morning.' True, but it *is* Horse Guards Parade out there, and they are the Horse Guards – they have to rehearse somewhere. Of course, I'm lucky, because I'm always up by 7 a.m. in any case.

I tried to calm her down. 'Be reasonable, Annie. A career of public service inevitably involves some sacrifice.'

She buttoned her coat up. 'Fine. I sacrifice my sleep. You sacrifice your lunch.' And off she went.

I ran after her. 'What did *you* have for lunch?' I called down the staircase.

'Half a Yorkie bar.'

Seething, I returned to the flat to look for the other half. I couldn't even find it. There were indeed some eggs in the fridge but I just couldn't face cooking. So I meandered gloomily down the stairs and mooched into my study. Hungrily I stood at the window, watching the military band marching up and down. I left a message in the private office that Bernard should pop up to see me as soon as he returned from lunch.

Forty-five minutes later he bounced in, cheerful and well-fed. I turned and asked him if he'd had a good lunch.

He was slightly surprised. 'Quite good, yes.'

'Where did you have it?'

'In the Cabinet mess.'

'Three courses?'

'Yes.'

'Wine?'

'A glass of claret, yes.' He paused, trying to understand what I was driving at. 'Um ... if you're interested, Prime Minister, I had mulligatawny soup, followed by a veal chop with sauté potatoes and . . .'

'I'm not interested, Bernard,' I snapped. 'Do you want to know what *I* had for lunch?'

He sensed that I was upset, but still couldn't quite see why. 'Um . . . do you want to tell me?' he asked.

I smiled unpleasantly. 'Yes,' I snapped. 'Nothing.'

'Are you dieting, Prime Minister?'

I explained succinctly that I was not dieting. I expressed my total astonishment that there are facilities at Number Ten for feeding Bernard, and all the private secretaries, the whole of the Cabinet office, the press office, the garden-room girls,[1] the messengers . . . but not me. And I bloody live here!

Bernard asked if Mrs Hacker could cook for me. I reminded him that she has her own job. Then he offered to get me a cook. It looked a good offer – until closer examination revealed that I would have to pay for it. And, according to Bernard, the cost of a full-time cook would be between eight and ten thousands a year. I can't afford that. Trying to get himself off the hook, he suggested that I talk to the Cabinet Secretary – obviously he didn't want to get involved in a discussion when it wasn't in his power to change the system.

But I was very irritated. Still am, come to that. I turned back to the window and fumed silently.

Bernard cleared his throat. 'I think the Cabinet Secretary's due here in a few moments anyway. So shall we get on with the affairs of the nation?'

'Stuff the affairs of the nation,' I replied. 'I want a cook.'

Bernard promised that the matter would be looked into, and ushered in Malcolm Warren, the Number Ten press officer. He's a big bluff Yorkshireman, a career civil servant but with a sense of the way things are done in the real world. He was appointed by my predecessor in Number Ten, but I've kept him on because he has an iron grip on the lobby correspondents and the whole Whitehall public relations machine.

I asked him to be brief, as I was due to meet the Cabinet Secretary any moment.

---

[1] The name given to the very high-class ladies of the registry and typing pool at Number Ten, who worked in a basement room that leads out on to the garden.

'Certainly, Prime Minister. Two things. First, and most important, we should discuss your first TV appearance as Prime Minister.'

This is such a big and important subject that I asked him to postpone discussion of it for a day or two, until we have time to go into it thoroughly.

The other thing he wanted to discuss was my official Washington visit. Of course, that's much less important than my first TV appearance.

The one urgent point he wanted to raise was that an awful lot of press want to come with us to Washington. I think that's good. Malcolm was worried about the expense. But I explained to him that this would be a terribly important occasion. I shall be standing there, on the White House lawn, side by side with the President of the United States. There will be national anthems. Photographs of two world leaders together. He will tell the world about our happy relationship, our unity and resolve. He'll probably say a word or two about my own courage and wisdom and statesmanship. And it is essential that, if so, it is fully reported back here in Britain. This sort of publicity is vital to Britain. [*Hacker meant that it was vital to him – Ed.*] Vital to our prestige. [*His prestige – Ed.*] Our place in the world. [*His place in the history books – Ed.*]

Malcolm readily agreed, especially when I told him that, as a matter of policy, I intended that we should have no secrets from the press about this country's successes. I told him that we must be absolutely frank about my government's achievements. I want fearless honesty about every government triumph.

He understood. He raised the nit-picking point that, as I have only been in office for seven days, there aren't all that many triumphs yet. Perfectly true. But there will be.

I also gave him an idea for a good press story: I told him that I had had to make my own lunch today. I asked him if he knew. It appeared that he hadn't been informed of this. So I told him all about it. How there's no cook or housekeeper for the flat upstairs, how Annie has her own job, we can't afford staff, and that it looked as though I'd be washing the dishes and washing my socks.

He was a bit slow on the uptake. He couldn't see that there was a good press story in all this. I explained that he could do one along the lines of 'Jim Hacker's not stuck up. He can identify with the problems of ordinary people.' That sort of thing.

Malcolm wanted to think about it. 'We don't want you to seem *too* ordinary, Prime Minister, even though you are.'

Did he mean that the way it sounded? I don't think so, because he continued: 'What I mean is, that sort of publicity can be counter-productive. You remember when Jimmy Carter was attacked by a rabbit?'

I did vaguely remember. He looked a bit of a fool. Also there was that photo of him out jogging, looking as though he was on the point of total collapse. He probably thought it was a good idea to be photographed taking exercise – but it made the voters think that he was not long for this world. Lost him a lot of support. Maybe Malcolm's right to be cautious.

Malcolm amplified his point of view. 'Perhaps it's better that we build you up a bit – photos of you doing the washing might make you look a bit wet.'

I sent him out and Bernard brought Humphrey in. I told him I'd been thinking.

'Good,' he said encouragingly.

'I've been Prime Minister for a week now,' I said.

'And a very good Prime Minister you are too, if I may say so.'

I was pleased. It's always nice to have the approval of one's colleagues, especially if they are as hard-bitten as Humphrey. I told him that I wasn't fishing for compliments. But it *has* been going well, and I'm glad he recognised it.

However, we immediately uncovered our first mistake, or rather *their* first mistake, and a pretty serious mistake it is too. I remarked, casually, that it's nice to be able to reward one's old allies. 'Was Ron Jones pleased about his peerage?' I inquired.

'Oh yes,' said Bernard. 'He said his members would be delighted.'

I couldn't think what Bernard meant. 'Members?'

'The Members of his Union. The National Federation of . . .'

I suddenly saw what had happened. I was livid. 'Not *him*!' I yelled. 'I meant our backbencher. I wanted to offer the peerage to Ron Jones, not *Ron Jones*.'

'Ah,' said Bernard. A rather inadequate response, I thought.

We all sat and stared at each other. There was no going back on it now. Bernard tried to make the best of it. 'If it's any consolation to you, Prime Minister, I gather he was awfully pleased.'

I bet he was! Pleased – and amazed! I asked Humphrey what we could do about *Ron Jones's* peerage – could we give him one too? Humphrey thought not. 'With respect, Prime Minister, we can't send *two* Lord Ron Jones to the Upper House – it'll look like a job lot.'

But I've promised him an honour of some sort. We scratched our heads for a bit. Then Humphrey had an idea. As Ron isn't remotely interested in television, hasn't even got a TV set, we're going to make him a Governor of the BBC.

Then we passed on to important matters. I explained to Humphrey that we need a cook-housekeeper in the flat upstairs.

He suggested that I advertise. He was missing the point. I explained that we need a *government* cook-housekeeper.

Humphrey, as I expected after my talk with Bernard, was not entirely helpful. He said that it could be difficult to get a government cook-housekeeper as Number Ten is a private home which just happens to be in a government building.

I pointed out that I happen to live in it. And therefore – surprise, surprise! – happen to eat in it too. 'It is not unreasonable to want someone to cook my lunch.'

'No. But it's not possible,' said Humphrey categorically.

I've never heard anything so ridiculous. Humphrey was asking me to accept that I have the power to blow up the world but not to ask for scrambled eggs. [*It was not in dispute that Hacker had the power to* ask *for scrambled eggs – Ed.*]

I explored this nonsense a little further, taking it to its logical conclusion. 'Suppose I invited the German Ambassador to lunch?' I asked.

'That would be all right,' reflected Humphrey. 'Official engagement. Government hospitality will gladly provide five courses, with three wines and brandy. No problem.'

So what Humphrey was saying was that the German Ambassador's lunch is government business, but my lunch isn't. And not just the German Ambassador's, of course – *any* ambassador's.

So, there and then I told Bernard to get the diary out. Then I ordered him to arrange for me to have lunch with the German Ambassador on Monday, with the French Ambassador on Tuesday, and on Wednesday the American Ambassador. Then, not forgetting the Commonwealth, on Thursday I would lunch with the New Zealand High

Commissioner. 'Bernard, how many countries are there in the United Nations?'

He knew the answer, of course. 'One hundred and fifty-eight.'

'Good,' I beamed at Humphrey. 'That'll keep me in lunches for about six months. Then we'll go round again.'

Bernard was hurriedly leafing through the diary. 'Prime Minister, you're not free for lunches with ambassadors every day. Sometimes you will have other official lunches.'

'Good news,' I replied. 'So much the better. We can just use ambassadors to fill up the blank spaces.'

Humphrey was looking worried, and remarked that the Foreign and Commonwealth Office might have views on this matter. [*This would undoubtedly have been the case. It has always been said that one Prime Minister's lunch with an ambassador destroys two years of patient diplomacy. The Foreign Office would have been unlikely to react favourably to such lunches – Ed.*]

I didn't much care what the Foreign Office would say. 'It's quite absurd that there's no one to cater for me and my family.'

Humphrey couldn't see why. But then he wouldn't, would he? He gets his lunch in the Cabinet mess too. 'Prime Minister, it's the way things have been done for two and a half centuries.'

'Is that the clinching argument?' I demanded.

'It has been for two and a half centuries.'

Bernard, bless his heart, intervened in his usual pedantic and obsessive fashion, 'Um . . . with respect, Sir Humphrey,' he began disrespectfully, 'it can't have been the clinching argument for two and a half centuries, because half a century ago it had only been the clinching argument for two centuries, and a century ago only for one and a half centuries, and one and a half . . .' Humphrey was staring malevolently at him and he ground to a halt. But Bernard's logic was both as impeccable and irrelevant as always.

I stepped in hurriedly, to distract Humphrey and direct his wrath away from my loyal Private Secretary. 'Humphrey, I am not convinced. I want a cook and I want you to see that it's paid for.'

Humphrey was stony-faced. Stubbornly he turned to me. 'Then let me put it like this. How would you like the press to announce that your first act as Prime Minister was to give yourself an effective salary increase of eight to ten thousand pounds a year?'

I hadn't thought of that. But I couldn't see why we should tell them.

Nobody would ever know.

Humphrey read my thoughts. 'We must tell them, by the way. We have no alternative. The Prime Minister's salary and expenses have to be published.'

'Isn't there any way we can . . . not refer to it?' I asked hopefully.

'Open Government, Prime Minister. Freedom of Information. We should always tell the press, freely and frankly, *anything* that they can easily find out some other way.'

I simply do not believe that there is no way to solve this problem. But I had to let it drop for today. Humphrey's position is that ever since Number Ten was first used as the PM's official residence, two hundred and fifty years ago, there has been no solution to this problem. And therefore, according to Civil Service reasoning, there never will be.

Humphrey changed the subject. 'Prime Minister, you said you had been thinking.'

'Yes, Humphrey,' I replied. 'We have agreed that things have been going well ever since I've been Prime Minister. So I have been asking myself: "How do I ensure that this run of success continues?"'

Humphrey gazed at me hopefully. 'Have you considered . . . masterly inactivity?'

Ridiculous. But I was patient with him. 'No, Humphrey, a Prime Minister should be firm.'

'Indeed!' he agreed. 'How about *firm* masterly inactivity?'

I could afford to be nice – after all, I'm in the driving seat now. 'No,' I smiled, 'but I *shall* be firm.'

'Good,' said Sir Humphrey.

'And decisive,' I went on.

'Absolutely,' agreed Sir Humphrey.

'And imaginative,' I added provocatively.

'I'm not so sure about imaginative.' I *bet* he's not!

'And above all,' I finished up, 'I must offer leadership.'

'Leadership.' He was at his most encouraging. 'Leadership, above all.'

'And as I'm the Prime Minister I have the power to do so, don't I?'

'Indeed, Prime Minister, you are the Prime Minister, and wherever you lead we shall obediently follow.'

So I told him my new policy. My Grand Design. 'I've decided to cancel Trident, spend the £15 billion on conventional forces and the

ET,[1] bringing in conscription, and thus solve our defence, balance of payments, education and unemployment problems at a stroke.'

He gaped at me. I glanced at Bernard, who was watching his old boss with considerable interest.

I waited for Humphrey's response. But answer came there none. Not at first, anyway. He seemed absolutely poleaxed. I gave him a few moments to pull himself together and then, as I was getting bored with waiting, I told him to say something.

'I . . . er . . . where did this idea come from?' Not a very flattering question. But I reminded him that I'd been thinking.

'You can't do that!' he said with desperation.

At first I thought he was telling me that I can't think. Or mustn't think. But he went on to say that what I was proposing was completely revolutionary, an unprecedented innovation.

So the gloves were off! He meant that I could not pursue my policy. Well, in my opinion it is not up to him to say.

He clearly thinks it is. 'Prime Minister, you can't simply reorganise the entire defence of the realm, just like that!'

My answer was simple. 'I'm the Prime Minister.' Besides, he had said he would follow me. He had agreed that I should be decisive. He had agreed that I should offer leadership. So what was he complaining about? [*Presumably Sir Humphrey wanted Hacker to be decisive only if he took decisions of which Sir Humphrey approved. And leadership was only welcome if it went in the approved direction – Ed.*] 'Furthermore,' I added, 'I have the power.'

He didn't like that one bit. 'Yes – but only within the law and the constitution and the constraints of administrative precedent, budgetary feasibility and Cabinet government. What about your Cabinet colleagues, what do they think?'

I was obliged to admit that I hadn't told them yet. But I know they'll love it. They'll love anything that cuts unemployment. Half of them would even welcome inflation on those grounds. And I know that the Cabinet will be only too happy to have an extra £15 billion of Trident cash available for other public spending. Anyway, I'm the Prime Minister, what does it matter what they think?

'I appoint the Cabinet,' I said simply.

[1] Emergent Technology.

Humphrey smiled coldly. 'I'm sure you don't want to *dis*appoint them.'

Very droll, as he used to say so patronisingly to me. I didn't laugh. I didn't say anything. I just waited for him to capitulate. Unfortunately he didn't say anything either.

'Humphrey, you're very silent.'

'You've given me a lot to be silent about.'

'You mean, *you* think we should keep Trident?'

He could only answer that one way. 'It is not for me to say, Prime Minister.' Quite right. He's only a civil servant.

'Fine,' I agreed magnanimously, 'that's agreed then.'

Humphrey couldn't let it go. 'But since you ask my opinion . . .'

I was enjoying myself. 'Go on then.'

'Yes,' he said grimly, 'I do think we should keep it.'

I told him I couldn't see the sense in it. Humphrey, groping for my reasoning, asked if I was therefore going to buy Cruise missiles instead.

I told him that I intended that the UK should buy no more nuclear weapons.

He blanched. 'But Prime Minister – you're not a secret unilateralist, are you?'

I explained that I was nothing of the sort, that we still have Polaris, and that I have no intention of getting rid of that.

He relaxed a little. At least (in his view) I was not a security risk, just a loony. He tried to tell me Polaris is not good enough, that it's a ramshackle old system, whereas Trident is superb – faster, more warheads, independently targeted. According to Humphrey, Trident is almost impossible to intercept whereas the Soviets might easily develop a multi-layered ballistic missile defence system that can intercept Polaris.

'By when?' I asked.

'In strategic terms, any day now.'

I can spot an evasive answer at fifty paces. [*The more so since Hacker was himself a master of the evasive answer – Ed.*] I asked him by what year, precisely, this might happen.

'Well . . . 2020.' I smiled. 'But that's sooner than you think,' he added hastily.

'And you're saying that such a missile defence system could intercept all 192 Polaris missiles?'

'Not *all*, no. But virtually all – ninety-seven per cent.

I took out my pocket calculator and did a few quick sums. I looked up at him. 'That would still leave five Polaris bombs which could get through the defences.'

Humphrey was triumphant. 'Precisely – a mere five.'

'Enough,' I reminded him gently, 'to obliterate Moscow, Leningrad and Minsk.'

'Yes,' he sneered, 'but that's about all.'

I wasn't sure I was understanding him correctly. 'I would have thought that that's enough to make the Russians stop and think.'

Humphrey's enthusiasm for Trident knows no bounds. 'But don't you *see*, Prime Minister – with Trident we could obliterate the whole of Eastern Europe!'

I don't want to obliterate the whole of Eastern Europe. I told him so. He nodded impatiently. He knew that. He thought I was missing the point. 'It has to be an effective deterrent, Prime Minister.'

'But it's a bluff,' I told him, 'I probably wouldn't use it.'

'They don't *know* that you probably wouldn't use it,' he argued.

'They probably do,' I said.

He was forced to agree. 'Yes . . . they *probably* know that you probably wouldn't. But they can't *certainly* know.'

He's right about that. But they don't have to certainly know. 'They *probably* certainly know that I probably wouldn't,' I said.

'Yes,' he agreed, 'but even though they *probably* certainly know that you probably wouldn't, they don't *certainly* know that although you *probably* wouldn't, there is *no probability* that you certainly would.'

Bernard was taking careful minutes. It's lucky he does shorthand and was able to reconstruct this conversation for me in writing by the end of the day.

But Humphrey could see that he was making no headway with his deterrent argument. So he made one attempt to persuade me to keep Trident, this time by flattering me and playing on my vanity. I can't imagine why he thought that would have any effect!

'Look, Prime Minister, it all boils down to one simple issue. You are Prime Minister, Prime Minister of Great Britain. Don't you believe that Britain should have the best?'

'Of course.'

'Very well.' He took that as a cue to rhapsodise. 'If you walked into a nuclear-missile showroom you would buy Trident – it's lovely, it's elegant, it's beautiful, it is – quite simply – the best. And Britain should have the best. In the world of the nuclear missile it is the Savile Row suit, the Rolls-Royce Corniche, the Château Lafite 1945. It is the nuclear missile Harrods would sell you! What more can I say?'

'Only,' I replied calmly, 'that it costs £15 billion and we don't need it.'

Humphrey shook his head sadly. In his view I had completely missed the point. 'You could say that about anything at Harrods,' he replied reasonably.

JANUARY 30TH

Tonight we had a reception at Number Ten. Six-thirty to eight. My first party since I became Prime Minister, though many of the guests were hangovers from the previous regime.[1] As we were members of the same party, it didn't matter much.

I wasn't looking forward to it much, after a long and trying day. But, as so often happens, something truly unexpected emerged from a chance conversation. Among the guests was General Howard, who had showed me over the MOD a week or so ago. I buttonholed him. I told him that I had to sound him out on something, and that he was not going to like it.

'Tell me the worst, Prime Minister,' he said stiffly.

So I did. I said that even though it would doubtless come as a severe blow to the services and would be most unpopular, I intended to cancel Trident.

He muttered something that I only half heard. 'Now hold on,' I said, 'don't jump on it too quickly, it's no use arguing, I . . .' And I stopped. I realised what I'd half heard. 'What did you say?' I asked, in case I was fantasising.

'Good idea.' Terse and to the point, as always. I wasn't sure I understood him correctly.

'You mean, you're in favour? Of cancelling Trident?'

'Of course.'

[1] And a few *had* hangovers from the previous regime.

For the second time in just over a week, all my preconceptions about defence were stood on their head.

I stood there, gazing up at this imposing, sandy-haired, beetle-browed, six-foot-four giant. 'Why are you in favour?'

'We don't need it,' he replied briefly. 'It's a complete waste of money. Totally unnecessary.'

I could hardly believe my ears. The most senior army officer in the country agrees with me that Trident is a complete waste of money. I told him that I hoped to keep Polaris, keep the American bases, and strengthen our conventional forces.

'You're right.'

I wondered if he were a tame eccentric. 'Does the whole Defence Staff agree?'

He shook his head. 'No. The Navy want to keep it. It's launched from their submarines. Take away Trident and they've hardly got a role left.'

'So they'll resist it?'

'Yes, but the Navy resist everything. They nearly lost us World War I by resisting convoys.'

'And the RAF?' I asked.

'Well,' he replied dismissively, 'you can ask them. If you're interested in the opinions of garage mechanics. But I'm afraid they'd want Trident. Only they want it in the form of a missile launched from the air, like an Exocet.'

Suddenly it was all making sense to me. Why had I ever thought the Services would have a joint view of the matter?

General Howard continued to explain the RAF mentality as he sees it. 'They want the Bomb to be carried around in an aeroplane, you see. All they're really interested in is flying around dropping things on people. Not that they're any good at it – I mean, they couldn't even close the runway at Port Stanley. They'd probably never even find Moscow. If they did, they'd probably miss.'

The problem is clear. How do I get the policy past the MOD if only the army is in favour of it? I put this to the general and he had a ready-made solution. 'The Chief of Defence Staff job is shortly becoming vacant. Technically it's the navy's turn. But it's your decision. If you appoint a soldier . . .'

Delicately, he let his sentence remain unfinished. I already knew that he is the most senior soldier. So if I appoint him, I'll have the Chief of

Defence Staff on my side. I don't know whether that'll be enough, or how the Navy will respond if I overlook their man, but it's obviously something I have to consider in due course.

[*Sir Humphrey Appleby also had a few words with General Howard at the reception at 10 Downing Street that evening. And their conversation, unlike General Howard's conversation with the Prime Minister, apparently changed the course of events. Sir Humphrey's recollections of that conversation are to be found in his private papers – Ed.*]

The General seemed unusually relaxed after a short talk with the Prime Minister, which I had been observing. When in due course I spoke to him, he remarked that he was pleased to have come across a Prime Minister with a bit of sense.

I asked which country was so blessed with such a leader. I knew, of course, that he was referring to Hacker, and my guess was that Hacker had not put him fully in the picture.

I was right, of course. The PM had spoken to General Howard about cancelling Trident, but *not* about reintroducing conscription. When I mentioned all the details the General was horrified, as I knew he would be.

Hacker wants conscription because it helps unemployment and therefore wins votes. The army does *not* want conscription, and has never wanted it. They are very proud of their élite, professional army. It is tough, disciplined, possibly the best in the world. The Chiefs of Staff do not want a conscripted mob of punks, freaks, junkies and riff-raff, a quarter of a million hooligans on its hands with nothing to do except peel potatoes at Aldershot. The generals are afraid that this would turn it into an ordinary army. [*Like the one that won World Wars I and II – Ed.*]

They are also worried about the new equal-opportunity legislation. In America it is well known that the NATO commanders don't know if the troops being posted to them are men or women. Not until they arrive. Sometimes not even then.

In view of the potential conscription General Howard felt that it would be better to keep Trident, with all its faults. He urged me to find some method of 'stopping' the Prime Minister from pursuing this unfortunate policy.

I explained that, unfortunately, Prime Ministers cannot be 'stopped'. But they can be slowed down. In fact, they almost invariably are – after a few months most new Prime Ministers have more or less ground to a halt.

My idea is to have a quiet word with the American Ambassador. General Howard approved.


[*Hacker's diary continues – Ed.*]


### JANUARY 31ST

Today there was good news and bad news. The bad news came first.

In my morning meeting with Humphrey, Bernard and Malcolm we went over the final preparations for my American visit. Malcolm is to make sure that the BBC News and ITN get really good positions on the White House lawn, so that they can get a close two-shot of me and the President.

I've also told him to ensure that there are good photo opportunities inside the White House as well. Shots of me and the President alone together.

I've given him a list of all the photo ideas that I've had: coverage of the start of the talks on the second day, coverage of the President saying goodbye to me, hopefully grasping my elbow with his left hand, the way he did with the West German Chancellor, it looked frightfully chummy.

I wanted him to arrange all of this with our Embassy, but Malcolm felt that it could be difficult. I must say, I don't know what we have all these embassies for. Any time we need anything important for Britain [*i.e. for Hacker – Ed.*] they always make trouble.

It's not that I'm concerned with political advantage or vote winning, or anything like that. It's good for Britain to be seen by the rest of the world as an equal partner of the United States, that's all.

Humphrey was unwilling to discuss the publicity aspects any further. I wondered why. Instead, he showed me the Cabinet agenda.

You didn't have to be Hercule Poirot to see that the agenda had been tampered with. The discussion of the cancellation of Trident was conspicuous by its absence. I questioned Humphrey about this – after all, as Cabinet Secretary it's his job to draw it up.

'We were indeed going to discuss Trident, Prime Minister, but I thought perhaps it might be wiser to leave it a little longer. Go into it thoroughly, closer scrutiny, think through the implications, produce some papers, have some inter-departmental discussions, make contingency plans. We are discussing the defence of the realm.'

I can't believe that he still thinks these old devices will fool me. I challenged him, and he protested innocence. 'No, indeed, Prime Minister, but the Cabinet must have all the facts.'

I grinned. 'That's a novel idea.'

He was not amused. 'Important decisions take time, Prime Minister.'

I could see immediately what he was playing at: delaying tactics, the oldest trick in the book. The longer you leave things, the harder it is to get them off the ground.

But then came the bad news. It was a real bombshell. Apparently Humphrey has learned from the American Ambassador – informally – that the Americans would be very unhappy if we cancelled Trident unless we ordered another of their nuclear missiles instead.

At first I was defiant about it. After all, I have to think of what's best for Britain. But it seems they claim to have two reasons for their disquiet: the first is that they feel that they need our partnership and do not want to carry the nuclear burden alone. This is perfectly reasonable, but as we would still have Polaris they wouldn't be doing so. So the second reason is the real one: the little matter of losing billions of dollars of business and tens of thousands of jobs in the American aerospace industry.

The question is what – if anything – I can do about this American opposition to my Grand Design. I told Humphrey that I have no intention of changing my policy. The Americans will have to learn to live with it.

'As you wish, Prime Minister,' he said, 'but I thought if we kept your Trident proposal secret until after your American visit, it might save some embarrassment.'

I replied sharply that I didn't agree. 'If there has to be some tough talking, I might as well have it out with the American President when we meet.'

He shook his head sadly. 'Ah, well, that's the point. As you know, the agenda of your meeting must be agreed in advance. You can't just go all the way there for a chat.'

'Why not?'

'Well . . . you might not think of anything to say. And, if your Trident proposal were put to the Americans in advance, I understand there would be a slight change of plan.'

'What change of plan?'

'You would not be met by the President. You would be entertained by the Vice-President.'

I was thunderstruck. The Vice-President? I could hardly believe my ears. I thought he wasn't serious. But he *was*!

It's absurd. It's ludicrous. It's a total insult. Even Botswana was met by the President [*Botswana had not just cancelled an order for Trident – Ed.*]

Humphrey tried to put it as nicely as he could. 'I'm sure they'd do it gracefully, Prime Minister. He'd have a diplomatic toothache, like Krushchev's. Or they'd explain that the President had catarrh, or bruised his thumb or something. Fallen asleep, perhaps.'

Humphrey knew as well as I that the whole point of the visit to the States was the PR value of being seen meeting the President. I asked him what choices we had. He advised me that in practice I have no choice at all. And that if I want to be entertained by the President I must leave Trident off the agenda.

This is a terrible blow. I have to raise it with the United States sometime. When better than while I'm there? But what must be, must be.

There remained the question of whether or not I should raise the Trident question in Cabinet. Humphrey advised me to leave it until my return, in case the discussion leaked to the US Ambassador. He could be right. Clearly someone has been leaking to him already on this subject. I wonder who.

'Anyway, Humphrey,' I said miserably, 'a new Prime Minister must show that he has arrived, show that there's a new mind and a firm hand in Number Ten. I must make my mark.'

And then Humphrey revealed the good news. It seems that I have accomplished something that none of my predecessors ever accomplished. A cook, no less! Seconded from the Cabinet Office canteen, to do our lunch in the flat when required. Except for weekends and bank holidays, of course.

This was gratifying. A place in the history books. I think that this shows that I have started the way I mean to go on. I am in charge, and the Civil Service can clearly see that there is a new mind and a firm hand in Number Ten.

I told Humphrey that, as far as Trident's concerned, I am not changing my policy and I am not changing my mind. In due course I shall lose it. [*Hacker presumably meant that he would lose Trident, not his mind – Ed.*] But in the meantime I see no harm in postponing the Trident discussion till I return from America, and I gave Humphrey my firm decision to leave Trident off the agenda for tomorrow.

He tood it like a lamb. 'Yes Prime Minister,' he replied deferentially.

# Phogey!

## *Malcolm Bradbury*

One of the things that we English like to tell foreigners (if we speak to them at all) is that our society is democratic; but how miserable we should all be if it were. We do, in this country, affirm the principle that Everyone's Opinion Is as Good as Anyone Else's; our qualification is that some people need to be told what are the best opinions to have. The difference between the English and American patterns of democracy can be simply summed up; while America is broadly speaking a permissive society, England is authoritarian, by consent. Visiting Americans always notice how easily we fall into postures of command or submission. We are dragooned in teashops, post offices, buses, by people who have, always, something better to do, and say so. Likewise we are dragooned by our government, the Inland Revenue, the National Health Service. The reason that we accept it is that it seems to us always to have been like that, and if it always was, it must be right.

As Freud ('that psychology nonsense') would say, we are looking for our fathers or, alternatively, for our sons – because, in matters of authority, it takes, as with the tango, two to do it (a phogeyarch and phogeysite, let us call them). In fact neither is lost for long. Observe our respect for law and order, our desire not to cause trouble, our fondness for keeping ourselves to ourselves, our lack of complaint when we are obviously being lied to, or cheated. And indeed how else can one explain the fact that retired army generals are considered natural choices for the high management posts in nationalized industry – and the even stranger fact that retired railwaymen are almost never made generals? It is all, of course, because army generals are trained in authoritarianism. Why can't we be like the Americans, and put our generals in positions where they can do no harm whatsoever – like the Presidency?

Democracy affirms that all men are rightly equal, and equally right.

Since this is manifestly untrue, and since certain things are plainly and by divine plan morally right and others morally wrong, the phogey is in a firm position. Thus it is morally right that drain-pipes should be on the outside of houses. *I was there* when an American asked an Englishman: 'But why do you have your drain-pipes on the *outside* of your houses?' 'Well, obviously,' said the Englishman, with, in our direction, that amused smile that people have when they are asked silly questions, 'so that we can get at them more easily when they freeze.' (I do not deny the grain of truth here; English houses are so badly heated, by the same divine law, that the pipes might very well freeze indoors as well; after all, comfort isn't everything, and if bedrooms were not cold in England there'd probably be no sex here at all.)

Whence springs the phogey mentality? It doubtless derives from the ancient picture of the Englishman, that national character which is the product of history, or rather, what phogeys have taught, and learned, as history. Summarizing this stock figure's virtues and vices, we get something like this:

(A) STIFF UPPER LIPPERY, or steadiness under fire. Bertrand Russell says that people imitate their national heroes, and surely Drake was ours. The scholar was hero to the old Chinese; this could not happen in England.

(B) NON-OSTENTATION. What the English most dislike about the Americans is their celebration of their skills. Englishmen, never seeming to enjoy anything, never display either their talents or their wealth. English guidebooks say: 'Looking above your head, you will see a somewhat imperfect hammerbeam roof, marred by the fact that the chimney is placed somewhat to the left of where it should be. There are far better examples of this type of architecture at . . .' It is a proper modesty and since the other places cited are usually too far away to reach (since there are, in England, no roads), it costs nothing. In America, though, it would always be the best, and perfect. This attitude depends, of course, on the other persons present being informed enough to disagree with you. It has its roots, one suspects, in the conditions of the early nineteenth century, when the only way for the rich to avoid social revolution was to make it seem that it was enjoyable to be poor.

(C) SELECTIVE IGNORANCE. This is the theory that there are certain things it is better not to know. Most of these things are foreign anyway. The argument leads of course to an empirical view of the universe – try what was done before and, if it doesn't work, muddle through. The world is full of information, but most of it the British prefer to ignore. Associated with this view is the notion of the gentleman amateur, who is not expert at anything, but contrives, when necessary, to know people who are.

(D) SUPERIORITY TO FOREIGNERS. This is because, once, we were. It is now impossible for an Englishman to believe that Americans have a superior material standard of life, or that Russia has a superior educational system, any more than it is possible for him to believe that women are intelligent.

(E) MUDDLING THROUGH. The twentieth century has done some strange things to England. Of course, it has not got off scot-free; England has done some strange things to the twentieth century. Yet somehow the new age has made its mark; it may even be making us adaptable. But we doubt it. Muddling through once did ring true, and was part of a Victorian modesty which cloaked flexibility, initiative and the capacity for brilliant improvisation. The fact now is that the new industrial age is upon us, and it requires planning; and planning is suspect, because THEY plan. So we continue to muddle through. Consider that in England there are no roads.* The real reason why England has been proof against invasion for so long is that it is impossible to get inland. There are only lanes, clogged with motionless traffic and blocked by herds of cows wandering home to be milked. In any case, if invaders did land, they would never get anywhere, because no one knows where anywhere is. They would ask their way of old men and be misdirected, or told: 'If I was you I wouldn't start from here.' Frustrated and muddled, they would go back where they came from, leaving a dotard or two to speculate in the village snug about the snow on their boots.

These cannot be said to be undesirable traits. But since physical courage is now outmoded (there are no more victories), modesty inhibiting, ignorance fatal, superiority dangerous, and muddling through completely ineffectual, the British have responded to the

---

* There is now one, but it stops before it gets there.

challenge with their usual phlegm; in adversity, the traits have become *heightened*. Being improved by adversity is in fact

(F)  THE LAST TRAIT, and much the most important. An Englishman arranges systems of manners and institutions which are, to him, unchallengeable. He admits there are two sides to every question (his, and one that no right-thinking person in full possession of his senses could possibly hold) and yet he will maintain for ever that certain things are manifestly true. This is the essence of phogey. The phogey is the man who maintains his equilibrium, under all circumstances, by the use of *protocol*. For the phogey, there are no new situations; everything has happened before. He is concerned with Institutionalizing Things, and Living by Rote. He depends on a *voluntary* authoritarian structure in which everyone knows his place, from high to low, and perceives this condition as essentially unchangeable; it was *God* who pointed out that, with tea, some social classes put milk in first, and others last, and that one way is *inherently* better than another.

Yes, there are certain characteristics of the English spirit which occur in both reactionaries and radicals, and make Englishmen different from any other race of men anywhere else on earth. It is in these residual, permanently nineteenth-century qualities that our society maintains itself; and herein lies *phogey*.

'Our car costs so much to run now, we live in it.' Things are in a pretty pass, I found, talking to the m.c. (middle class) young phogey whose comments culminated in the above admission; the old pretences are increasingly hard to keep up. The phogey is, to some extent, at bay. This is inevitable, of course; it is increasingly difficult, in this age of equality and relativism, to convey even *valid* notions of superiority. The phogey is oriented to values that no longer survive in their pure state. Essentially inner-directed and tradition-bound, he is the product of a society tooled up, so to speak, for Empire building. The building, however, has stopped, and he has no real place to exercise his talents. One foresees the end of all this in some small colony named, let us say, Umbala, in the heart of Africa. It is the last surviving colony and here they are all gathered – the hundreds of governors and the thousands of administrators, packed together in a few square miles, clutching the

Colonial Office set of Kipling, governing and admi̶n̶, and dressing each night for dinner. A sad but likely r̶

The phogey's values are inculcated in him from an ea̶r̶, nanny or his public school or even his elementary (in phoge̶, you sit on straight-backed chairs, good for the spine, and on w̶ ̶ ̶e̶n̶ benches, chastening to the rump, and you play team games, because there is something *moral* about rugger). The author can remember the days when schools were grim buildings, with few toilets, and self-expression and finger painting had never been heard of. However, the Dewey-eyed system of permissive education, where children learn how to have well-rounded personalities and get on well with the group, has never caught on in England and one doubts if it ever will. Phogeys have ill-rounded personalities and are proud of it; they suspect that people who get on well at parties and can Influence Friends and Make People are up to no good; they are usually right. The true phogey, in any case, has nothing to celebrate, and is much more at home at a funeral than at a party.

The phogey spends his life testing the universe against English institutions and if it isn't somehow right, he asks for something to be done about it; after all, obviously, God is English. These days, it is less easy to convince foreigners that England is the centre of the world (because it isn't) and that to behave in ways unlike the English is an aberration. The fact is that foreigners are learning that you get by more easily if you are less like the English, for the phogey, being stringently moral, lacks fluidity. Understand, I am not saying anything against foreigners; some of my best friends are foreigners and remember – they have not had our advantages.

The phogey is, then, Phineas Fogg; he expects foreign climes to give him special dispensation; Englishmen go out in the midday sun in the firm knowledge that, in a day or two, the sun will *catch on*. Climbing a very high mountain in remote America with an English phogey girl, author Bradbury was not surprised to hear her say, when they reached the top, sucking hard for oxygen, while black specks hovered menacingly in the sky above them, and nature seemed red in tooth and claw: 'Looook, I say, look at that bird; isn't that an English blackbird?' Cut off from Ovaltine, life in America had been a hard fight for her, but with the stout English capacity for transmogrifying all American situations (and birds) into English ones, she had not felt the pinch at all. (The same girl once accompanied the same Bradbury to the film of *Lady Chatterley's Lover*, and at the point where Lady Chatterley's head – all of her that was visible on screen – was expressing the highest access of bliss at what had happened to her when she and the gamekeeper had been caught by a rainstorn in a secluded hut, the girl turned with a distraught expression on her face: 'Her horse is getting wet,' she said.)

Phogey values come completely from inside, and are internalized by the age of eleven. Americans change their characters with their clothes, and whenever they go from one room to another; they will join a discussion condemning dirty jokes, go through a door, and tell dirty jokes. Phogeys are stuck with their characters all the time, and like it. Americans believe in being nice, and they do it by being whatever the majority of people want them to be; their view of character is that it's a nice place to visit but you wouldn't want to live there. Phogeys dislike being nice, in case they are nice to someone who doesn't deserve it. And, as the phogey says, if you are odious, why lie about it? Ask Americans what they believe in, and they say: 'It depends who I'm with.' English people don't care whom they are with, and prefer not to be, anyway.

A nineteenth-century figure, then, the phogey survives into the twentieth and finds that his code no longer quite fits, and that people are doing things in other ways and getting away with it, even though it must be apparent that his way is best. The phogey is inner-directed – which means doing unto others because they did it unto you; and in these days of relativism, when you can't blame anyone for anything because it was the fault of his environment or his toilet-training, the inner-directed man is an anachronism. Inner-directed people make fine generals, managing directors and sado-masochists; they depend, however, on a society in which one code of values is universal. In short, they need no public relations men, because who needs relations with the public anyway? English government and American government is much the same, but the Americans explain why they do what they do; and this gives the public the illusion that they can interfere.

'We're bringing up Garth to be inner-directed,' an American academic couple explained to me one day, when I found them flogging their child, in a most un-American way, with a carpet beater. 'The next generation's going to need a few of them.' But this is no good, for if you don't have a phogey-speaking society there's nothing you can do. 'It's no use,' I told this couple, 'if you're going to understand him as well.' They looked upset. 'The trouble is, we understand him already. We wouldn't have if we'd known . . . but well, I guess once you've read Spock you've read Spock, and that's all there is to it.' Other-direction is bringing up your children to be happy; in inner-directed England happiness is looked upon, quite properly, with universal distrust. I take these two categories from an American sociologist named David Riesman, who in his book *The Lonely Crowd* defined the two life-styles in order that people could choose which brand they preferred. To sum it up simply, the difference between them is this; the inner-directed man says, 'I don't know anything about art, but I know what I like,' while the other-directed man says: 'I know all about art, but I don't know what I like.' With other-directed persons, you can never get through a door, because they all want to go through it last.

Think of Etonians. When you meet an Etonian in the street, you walking in one direction, he walking in the other, you will stop (if he cares to recognize you) and chat, and he will take you by the arm and you will walk on, chatting, both in the direction in which he was going; it can take you as much as half an hour to get away, by which time you are probably a good bus-ride out of your route. This is inner-direction, and is, to the phogey, as important as inner cleanliness. There are certain inherent truths about the universe which the phogey takes for granted, as common to all men, or all who matter. One, for example, is that everyone who needs to know knows where the Athenaeum is, so that it is wholly unnecessary to label it.

Visitors run into this difficulty constantly; thus, 'It's a wonder she didn't call a bobby,' said an American, describing a misadventure in an English fishmonger's, when he went in to ask for some of the snails in the window. 'There are,' said the girl indignantly, 'no snails in *our* shop.' Aware that he had stepped on an obscure English prejudice, the American went carefully. 'Snails to eat,' he said. 'People don't eat snails,' said the girl with a laugh. 'In France . . .' 'Oh,' said the girl, 'don't talk to me about *France*. You can't even find a clean toilet . . .' 'Then what do you call those things over there?' asked the American. 'They're winkles,' said the girl. 'Can I have some?' asked the American. 'They're not snails, you know,' said the girl. 'That's all right,' said the American. 'Those *happen*,' said the girl, 'to come out of the *sea*.' 'I'd like some,' said the American. 'What do you want them for?' asked the girl.

'To eat,' said the American, and he added, too casually, 'tell me – how do you eat these winkles?' 'Well, how *do* people eat winkles?' cried the girl. 'I don't know,' admitted the American. 'How do you think?' cried the girl, 'With a pin, of course.' 'Of course,' said the American.

By inner-directedness we mean that the phogey is a man with a response to situations that don't even *exist* yet. This is because he will not admit the principle of change. All situations are commonplaces and the phogey lives by sleep-walking; thus in railway carriages a dry clearing of the throat and a piercing stare and slight re-arrangement of clothing will suffice for any eventuality, from complaints about smoking, down to persons who want to talk. I have been in railway carriages with phogeys and tried to tell them that their clothes are on fire ('I say, I believe your clothes are on fire') only to be withered by this treatment, so that I sat there uneasily while the man's clothing smouldered all the way to Crewe. It seemed heartless, but I knew he would have wanted it that way. The symptoms of the sleepwalking manner are broadly those of drunkenness – loss of critical faculty and a sense of cosiness (*gemütlich*). It is the mood of the completely self-centred and assured, confident that things are always as they were. Observe a phogey faced, for the *first time*, by one of those contemporary chairs into which you insert your bum deeply and then, as it were, peer out over your kneecaps to spy out the land; he will find it absurd. He will find modern poetry absurd, and modern art. He cannot understand why people are not writing good poetry, like that fellow Tennyson, who really understood tears, idle tears, and why Edward Marsh ever stopped publishing *Georgian Poetry*. Yet notice the young phogey who has grown up with the new. He will not find the contemporaneous ridiculous (contemporary furnishing, which is in fact ten years out of date, is a phogey style; however, the idea behind it, that articles can be appreciated SIMULTANEOUSLY with their creation, is new and anti-phogey) – but he *will* be amused, like Gilbert Pinfold, by things that are changed during his own lifetime. Thus to the phogey things are starting to go wrong just around now. Phogeys are not makers, and chart no new ways; they are too involved with the old ones, and know them to be right.

For phogeys are the instruments of tradition. (Tradition is a key phogey word, and here is how tradition works: 'The Manor and most of the soil are the property of Captain Philip Bennett, MP, of *Rougham Hall*, a handsome castellated Tudor Mansion which was erected by his father.' *History, Gazetteer and Directory of Suffolk*.) Tradition is also Joe Higgs, seconded from his dustcart during the summer months in order to act as town-crier for the American tourists. The phogey's survival depends on the extent to which inherited manners and conventions remain unchallenged from outside. But his solidified tradition is in fact a recent one, and phogeyness a recent phenomenon, characteristic of a late stage in society when institutionalization and emphasis on manners become substitutes for active adjustments to new conditions. This is known as taking the long view, and depends on the doubtful proposition that the world will, at some point, take up again where it left off in 1914, and the sun will come out again. Phogeys hark back, back to the Good Old Days. This is a phrase used by phogeys without thought, because old days were all good, much gooder than the days they try to fob people off with now. You could have a good meal at the Savoy and a girl for the night, and still get change out of a bob, whatever that might be. Even working-class life was better; people starved, but they enjoyed it much more than they do now. British summers were always long and hot and filled with cucumber sand-wiches; indeed it is quite clear that it is climatic change that has made the twentieth century since 1914 the miserable and chaotic affair it has so obviously been. And all this is why the favourite British sport is archaeology, a form of extended reminiscence, and why the high point of British sentiment is a garden with a *sundial* in it.

And so, the phogey tells us, 'In my opinion all human affairs get worse as time goes on.' From his point of view this is true, and it is not an entirely improper view of history to take, given what history gives us in return. Hence people who get involved with things like change are by definition unreliable; and the phogey naturally distrusts the young, and intellectuals, because they are principles of inquiry, and people who inquire about things tend to be articulate. And articulate is one thing phogeys are not. After all, there is little to articulate about, because one knows instinctively when things are as they should be. The way you know this is by *experience*, which is what the young and the intellectuals do not have. 'I think one of the purposes of us old fogeys in life is to stop the young from being silly,' said one phogey MP lately, representing a large constituency. 'When I was young . . .,' says the old phogey; when he was young he was, of course, a young phogey, a class of which there is never any lack. Faced by the mysterious phenomenon of the 'Angry

Young Men', a new young phogey, a Mr Plantagenet Somerset Fry, spoke up for young phogeys everywhere: 'Frankly, the "angry young man" never cut any ice at all, and it is ignored rather than reviled, as it ought to be in London.' Clearly what was so irritating about the angry young men was not that they were angry but that they were *young*; it is, after all, the old who are entitled to be angry. And it must be said that there is quite a lot of phogey even in the angry young men themselves – angry, after all, either because their fathers were not at Oxford, or because they were; angry, too, both because their protest was not understood, and because it was so immediately accepted. Not by everyone, of course: Mr. Christopher Sykes, who is 'tall, broad, ebulliently aristocratic in manner,' says the press, accused them of being full of belly-aching and self-pity. But it could be, it could just possibly be, that it is the phogey spirit that has made them so.

Phogeys are of all age-groups, all social classes, all political and religious persuasions, all sexes. They can equally be top people who read the *Daily Sketch* (once you get to the top, you can stop reading *The Times*; that chore is over) and go beagling; or lib-labs who live on wheat germ and have petitions to sign whenever you go and see them. What they all possess is assurance, the assurance that they are superior to, or inferior to, someone else.

Let us note some of the characteristics of the phogey, that he be recognized. Throughout society he is ubiquitous, from the henna-haired harridans in teashops, for whom customers are an imposition, to those at the top – the Phogeyarchs, let us call them, in official power positions (members of Watch Committees, Lord Chamberlains, Hanging Judges, Diplomats, Dons, Scoutmasters, Youth Leaders, and the like). Below the phogeyarchs and existing in far greater numbers are the phogeysites. While the former is a phogey because he is in a phogey job, and is known to be such even before he acts or speaks, the latter have to work for years to attain general recognition. By their indifference to their fellows and their insistence on the letter (no juniors in the senior men's washroom) they are marked. Their long wait has often made them morose . . . and afraid. Always they are careful but *are they careful enough*?

Phogeys are proper, orderly and well-mannered. 'There should be a law . . .' says the phogey. Actually there almost always is. The

Americans distrust and resent their policemen; the English respect theirs, because they know they are looking after them. There is a story told of the philosopher T. E. Hulme, which shows how this respect is returned. Hulme was found by a policeman one night in Soho Square, urinating against a tree. 'You'll have to move on, sir,' said the policeman. Hulme protested, 'But I'm a member of the middle classes.' 'I'm sorry, sir,' said the policeman, retiring in embarrassment.

The English treat life as they do their washrooms; they believe that you should leave society as you would wish to find it. For this reason even the most revolutionary persons cannot conceive of too much change, nor of fighting for it if it is going to disturb people. When people suggest change in England, the reply is always: 'It wouldn't work.' Phogeydom is thus preserved by law and institutions even as it withers away in persons. This is in the cause of order and control, two principles of phogey *gemütlichkeit*, which holds that life is really nice, if you did but know it. Much of the famed English tolerance and respect for persons is because it's too much trouble to go on about the thing. Argument only exposes the divisions. The thing to do is to shut one's eyes. Thus many of the hostilities implicit in society are hidden in institutions that conceal behind an apparent relationship a fundamental indifference, or antipathy, or class-hostility on either side. The great English kewing system is just such a pretence, as in this example:

BUS CONDUCTOR (*collecting fares*): Kew? Kew?
PASSENGER: Thrupny, please.
BUS CONDUCTOR: Kew (*Taking money.*) Kew.
PASSENGER: Kew.
CONDUCTOR (*handing ticket*): Kew.
PASSENGER: Kew.
CONDUCTOR (*handing change*): Kew.
PASSENGER: Kew.
CONDUCTOR: Kew. (*Going on down bus.*) Kew? Kew?

This is made even more difficult if the passenger is going to Kew. This is pervasive politeness, and the present author was able to score as many as fifteen kews in the course of one transaction, the purchase of a packet of cigarettes.

'You are liable . . .' say the phogey notices; is there anywhere in the world where you are liable for so much, so often? Nowadays there are so many traffic police that motorists have to go about in pairs; and government by notice is rife – NO DANCING, NO SINGING, NO GRINNING. The story is even recorded of a notice, a phogey notice, which said: DO NOT THROW STONES AT THIS NOTICE. One young phogey of my acquaintance was driving through Bury St. Edmunds where he lives and *keeps a diary*, when his car licence became unstuck from the windscreen. Rather than offend, he drove with one hand and held it up to view with the other. People ran for cover as he zig-zagged down the street. 'You're liable, you know,' he said. It is my contention that if he had hit someone and been taken to court, he would have got off because he was obeying the law.

And every Englishman knows the feeling of guilt that washes over him when he has trespassed against some institution, even when it is some petty sin like having used it while the train was standing in the station or stamping on the top deck of a Nottingham bus. (DRIVER BELOW: PLEASE DO NOT STAMP FEET, say the notices. Nottingham residents are lucky in having, as far as we know, the only city council go-ahead enough to clamp down on the great foot-stamping menace, even though, in this case as with so many others, no one would have thought of the offence, until the notice suggested it.) The author and his friend Orsler were once caught together in a guilt-situation of this kind; it was unauthorised pea-shelling. They were caught by a guard in a railway train at Dawlish, shelling peas in preparation for their dinner that evening. Though they were creating no litter (Orsler, ever meticulous, was actually swallowing the empty shells) and there was no law against it, it was apparent enough that this was morally wrong and that, unless something were done about it, pea-podding might run rife on British Railways. Therefore, with supreme aplomb, 'Sorry, sir, no pea-podding,' said the guard. In such a situation, how deep the soul is seared. And that is *it*, the phogey in all of us.

One of the classic forms of phogeydom is the phogey pooh-pooh. In America, when an idea is suggested, people criticize the person who suggested it but then set about trying to do it; in England, when an idea is suggested, people praise the person who suggested it, regarding him as a useful man to have around, but never do anything about it. Americans do not like people who have ideas, because it's hostile to the group (if one has an idea, one never says, as in Europe, 'I happen to be an expert on this . . .'; one says, 'Well, I don't know anything about this, and this is just off the top of my head, but let's put this one out on the step and see if the cat licks it . . .'); however, they do tend to use the ideas. In England it is possible to get to the top by having ideas that no one has ever done anything about. Americans are pragmatists, and the great American phrase is 'So what?' – meaning all right, it's an idea, but what can you do with it?

In England the phogey pooh-pooh works like this. Let us suppose that a weekend trip to Scotland has been suggested, or the building of a garage: the English reply is, 'Good idea, old boy, but can't be done. Who'll look after the cat?' or 'Splendid thought, but we don't know enough about alignment, do we?' An Englishman's first response to any suggestion is that it cannot, in any circumstances, be done. Like *the* regulations ('Passengers are not allowed to stand if there are more than seven seats in the vehicle immediately following, in which case not more than four passengers are allowed to sit with the driver'), the phogey pooh-pooh adds to the strange sense of perpetual fog that one has in England. 'Sorry, sir, the bar's closed'; 'Sorry, sir, no eating in the library'; 'Sorry, can't sweep a chimney under six months.'

One of the illuminating differences between England and America lies in the words used to describe the service that in America is called INFORMATION and in England is called INQUIRIES. The English notice is descriptive of the people on one side of the counter, the American of those on the other. In England, that is, you are entitled to *ask*; in America you are entitled to be *told*. These are two very different freedoms descriptive of two very different kinds of democracy. For while American democracy is going towards something, ours seems to be coming away from something.

As an Englishman, one only comes to understand the pooh-pooh when one has visited America or has been visited by Americans in England. Americans think that anything is possible; they are swiftly disabused when they visit the English shore.

Englishmen, with their sense of propriety and order, know that there are God-given laws that say that shops should close at six in the evening and that it is morally improper to drink beer in public places between three and six in the afternoon and after eleven at night; they know that most things are impossible and that there is nothing to be done about them. It is only when they have American guests and run out of potatoes at ten o'clock at night, or want to buy a toothbrush on a Sunday, when the shops are allowed, by law, to be open but are not allowed, by law, *to sell anything* (or perhaps, one thing, like toothpaste), that they realize that their lives are bounded by an intrinsic sense of the limitations of the world. Only an American would dream of running out of potatoes at night in England, or suppose that there is a mechanical solution to the problem of switching off your television set without rising from your chair. Thus Englishmen, like myself, go to America simply in order to be able to find a place to eat at two in the morning.

# The Amazing Hat Mystery

## *P. G. Wodehouse*

A Bean was in a nursing-home with a broken leg as a result of trying to drive his sports-model Poppenheim through the Marble Arch instead of round it, and a kindly Crumpet had looked in to give him the gossip of the town. He found him playing halma with the nurse, and he sat down on the bed and took a grape, and the Bean asked what was going on in the great world.

'Well,' said the Crumpet, taking another grape, 'the finest minds in the Drones are still wrestling with the great Hat mystery.'

'What's that?'

'You don't mean you haven't heard about it?'

'Not a word.'

The Crumpet was astounded. He swallowed two grapes at once in surprise.

'Why, London's seething with it. The general consensus of opinion is that it has something to do with the Fourth Dimension. You know how things do. I mean to say, something rummy occurs and you consult some big-brained bird and he wags his head and says "Ah! The Fourth Dimension!" Extraordinary nobody's told you about the great Hat mystery.'

'You're the first visitor I've had. What is it, anyway? What hat?'

'Well, there were two hats. Reading from left to right, Percy Wimbolt's and Nelson Cork's.'

The Bean nodded intelligently.

'I see what you mean. Percy had one, and Nelson had the other.'

'Exactly. Two hats in all. Top hats.'

'What was mysterious about them?'

'Why, Elizabeth Bottsworth and Diana Punter said they didn't fit.'

'Well, hats don't sometimes.'

'But these came from Bodmin's.'

The Bean shot up in bed.

'What?'

'You mustn't excite the patient,' said the nurse, who up to this point had taken no part in the conversation.

'But dash it, nurse,' cried the Bean, 'you can't have caught what he said. If we are to give credence to his story, Percy Wimbolt and Nelson Cork bought a couple of hats at Bodmin's – at *Bodmin's*, I'll trouble you – and they didn't fit. It isn't possible.'

He spoke with strong emotion, and the Crumpet nodded understandingly. People can say what they please about the modern young man believing in nothing nowadays, but there is one thing every right-minded young man believes in, and that is the infallibility of Bodmin's hats. It is one of the eternal verities. Once admit that it is possible for a Bodmin hat not to fit, and you leave the door open for Doubt, Schism and Chaos generally.

'That's exactly how Percy and Nelson felt, and it was for that reason that they were compelled to take the strong line and they did with E. Bottsworth and D. Punter.'

'They took a strong line, did they?'

'A very strong line.'

'Won't you tell us the whole story from the beginning?' said the nurse.

'Right ho,' said the Crumpet, taking a grape. 'It'll make your head swim.'

'So mysterious?'

'So absolutely dashed uncanny from start to finish.'

You must know, to begin with, my dear old nurse (said the Crumpet), that these two blokes, Percy Wimbolt and Nelson Cork, are fellows who have to exercise the most watchful care about their lids, because they are so situated that in their case there can be none of that business of just charging into any old hattery and grabbing the first thing in sight. Percy is one of those large stout, outsize chaps with a head like a water-melon, while Nelson is built more on the lines of a minor jockey and has a head like a peanut.

You will readily appreciate, therefore, that it requires an artist hand to fit them properly, and that is why they have always gone to Bodmin. I have heard Percy say that his trust in Bodmin is like the unspotted faith of a young curate in his Bishop and I have no doubt that Nelson would have said the same, if he had thought of it.

It was at Bodmin's door that they ran into each other on the morning when my story begins.

'Hullo,' said Percy. 'You come to buy a hat?'

'Yes,' said Nelson. 'You come to buy a hat?'

'Yes.' Percy glanced cautiously about him, saw that he was alone (except for Nelson, of course) and unobserved, and drew closer and lowered his voice. 'There's a reason!'

'That's rummy,' said Nelson. He, also, spoke in a hushed tone. 'I have a special reason, too.'

Percy looked warily at him again, and lowered his voice another notch.

'Nelson,' he said, 'you know Elizabeth Bottsworth?'

'Intimately,' said Nelson.

'Rather a sound young potato, what?'

'Very much so.'

'Pretty?'

'I've noticed it.'

'Me, too. She is so small, so sweet, so dainty, so lively, so viv—, what's-the-word? – that a fellow wouldn't be far out in calling her an angel in human shape.'

'Aren't all angels in human shape?'

'Are they?' said Percy, who was a bit foggy on angels. 'Well, be that as it may,' he went on, his cheeks suffused to a certain extent, 'I love that girl, Nelson, and she's coming with me to the first day of Ascot, and I'm relying on this new hat of mine to do just that extra bit that's needed in the way of making her reciprocate my passion. Having only met her so far at country houses, I've never yet flashed upon her in a topper.'

Nelson Cork was staring.

'Well, if that isn't the most remarkable coincidence I ever came across in my puff!' he exclaimed, amazed. 'I'm buying my new hat for exactly the same reason.'

A convulsive start shook Percy's massive frame. His eyes bulged.

'To fascinate Elizabeth Bottsworth?' he cried, beginning to writhe.

'No, no,' said Nelson, soothingly. 'Of course not. Elizabeth and I have always been great friends, but nothing more. What I meant was that I, like you, am counting on this forthcoming topper of mine to put me across with the girl I love.'

Percy stopped writhing.

'Who is she?' he asked, interested.

'Diana Punter, the niece of my godmother, old Ma Punter. It's an odd thing, I've known her all my life – brought up as kids together and so forth – but it's only recently that passion has burgeoned. I now worship that girl, Percy, from the top of her head to the soles of her divine feet.'

Percy looked dubious.

'That's a pretty longish distance, isn't it? Diana Punter is one of my closest friends, and a charming girl in every respect, but isn't she a bit tall for you, old man?'

'My dear chap, that's just what I admire so much about her, her superb statuesqueness. More like a Greek goddess than anything I've struck for years. Besides, she isn't any taller for me than you are for Elizabeth Bottsworth.'

'True,' admitted Percy.

'And, anyway, I love her, blast it, and I don't propose to argue the point. I love her, I love her, I love her, and we are lunching together the first day of Ascot.'

'At Ascot?'

'No. She isn't keen on racing so I shall have to give Ascot a miss.'

'That's Love,' said Percy, awed.

'The binge will take place at my godmother's house in Berkeley Square, and it won't be long after that, I feel, before you see an interesting announcement in the *Morning Post*.'

Percy extended his hand. Nelson grasped it warmly.

'These new hats are pretty well bound to do the trick, I should say, wouldn't you?'

'Infallibly. Where girls are concerned, there is nothing that brings home the gravy like a well-fitting topper.'

'Bodmin must extend himself as never before,' said Percy.

'He certainly must,' said Nelson.

They entered the shop. And Bodmin, having measured them with his own hands, promised that two of his very finest efforts should be at their respective addresses in the course of the next few days.

Now, Percy Wimbolt isn't a chap you would suspect of having nerves, but there is no doubt that in the interval which elapsed before Bodmin was scheduled to deliver he got pretty twittery. He kept having awful visions of some great disaster happening to his new hat: and, as things turned out, these visions came jolly near being fulfilled. It has made Percy feel that he is psychic.

What occurred was this. Owing to these jitters of his, he hadn't been sleeping any too well, and on the morning before Ascot he was up as early as ten-thirty, and he went to his sitting-room window to see what sort of a day it was, and the sight he beheld from that window absolutely froze the blood in his veins.

For there below him, strutting up and down the pavement, were a uniformed little blighter whom he recognized as Bodmin's errand-boy and an equally foul kid in mufti. And balanced on each child's loathsome head was a top hat. Against the railings were leaning a couple of cardboard hat-boxes.

Now, considering that Percy had only just woken from a dream in which he had been standing outside the Guildhall in his new hat, receiving the Freedom of the City from the Lord Mayor, and the Lord Mayor had suddenly taken a terrific swipe at the hat with his mace, knocking it into hash, you might have supposed that he would have been hardened to anything. But he wasn't. His reaction was terrific. There was a moment of sort of paralysis, during which he was telling himself that he had always suspected this beastly little boy of Bodmin's of having a low and frivolous outlook and being temperamentally unfitted for his high office: and then he came alive with a jerk and let out probably the juiciest yell the neighbourhood had heard for years.

It stopped the striplings like a high-powered shell. One moment, they had been swanking up and down in a mincing and affected sort of way: the next, the second kid had legged it like a streak and Bodmin's boy was shoving the hats back in the boxes and trying to do it quickly enough to enable him to be elsewhere when Percy should arrive.

And in this he was successful. By the time Percy had got to the front door and opened it, there was nothing to be seen but a hat-box standing on the steps. He took it up to his flat and removed the contents with a gingerly and reverent hand, holding his breath for fear the nap should have got rubbed the wrong way or a dent of any nature been made in the gleaming surface; but apparently all was well. Bodmin's boy might sink to taking hats out of their boxes and fooling about with them, but at least he hadn't gone to the last awful extreme of dropping them.

The lid was OK absolutely: and on the following morning Percy, having spent the interval polishing it with stout, assembled the boots, the spats, the trousers, the coat, the flowered waistcoat, the collar, the shirt, the quiet grey tie, and the good old gardenia and set off in a taxi for the house where Elizabeth was staying. And presently he was ringing the bell and being told she would be down in a minute, and eventually down she came, looking perfectly marvellous.

'What ho, what ho!' said Percy.

'Hullo, Percy,' said Elizabeth.

Now, naturally, up to this moment Percy had been standing with bared head. At this point, he put the hat on. He wanted her to get the full effect suddenly in a good light. And very strategic, too. I mean to say, it would have been the act of a juggins to have waited till they were in the taxi, because in a taxi all toppers look much alike.

So Percy popped the hat on his head with a meaning glance and stood waiting for the uncontrollable round of applause.

And instead of clapping her little hands in girlish ecstasy and doing Spring dances round him, this young Bottsworth gave a sort of gurgling scream not unlike a coloratura soprano choking on a fish-bone.

Then she blinked and became calmer.

'It's all right,' she said. 'The momentary weakness has passed. Tell me, Percy, when do you open?'

'Open?' said Percy, not having the remotest.

'On the Halls. Aren't you going to sing comic songs on the Music Halls?'

Percy's perplexity deepened.

'Me? No. How? Why? What do you mean?'

'I thought that hat must be part of the make-up and that you were trying it on the dog. I couldn't think of any other reason why you should wear one six sizes too small.'

Percy gasped.

'You aren't suggesting this hat doesn't fit me?'

'It doesn't fit you by a mile.'

'But it's a Bodmin.'

'Call it that if you like. I call it a public outrage.'

Percy was appalled. I mean, naturally. A nice thing for a chap to give his heart to a girl and then find her talking in this hideous, flippant way of sacred subjects.

Then it occurred to him that, living all the time in the country, she might not have learned to appreciate the holy significance of the name Bodmin.

'Listen,' he said gently. 'Let me explain. This hat was made by Bodmin, the world-famous hatter of Vigo Street. He measured me in person and guaranteed a fit.'

'And I nearly had one.'

'And if Bodmin guarantees that a hat shall fit,' proceeded Percy, trying to fight against a sickening sort of feeling that he had been all wrong about this girl, 'it fits. I mean, saying a Bodmin hat doesn't fit is like saying . . . well, I can't think of anything awful enough.'

'That hat's awful enough. It's like something out of a two-reel comedy. Pure Chas. Chaplin. I know a joke's a joke, Percy, and I'm as fond of a laugh as anyone, but there is such a thing as cruelty to animals. Imagine the feelings of the horses at Ascot when they see that hat.'

Poets and other literary blokes talk a lot about falling in love at first sight, but it's equally possible to fall out of love just as quickly. One moment, this girl was the be-all and the end-all, as you might say, of Percy Wimbolt's life. The next, she was just a regrettable young blister with whom he wished to hold no further communication. He could stand a good deal from the sex. Insults directed to himself left him unmoved. But he was not prepared to countenance destructive criticism of a Bodmin hat.

'Possibly,' he said, coldly, 'you would prefer to go to this bally race-meeting alone?'

'You bet I'm going alone. You don't suppose I mean to be seen in broad daylight in the paddock at Ascot with a hat like that?'

Percy stepped back and bowed formally.

'Drive on, driver,' he said to the driver, and the driver drove on.

Now, you would say that that was rummy enough. A full-size mystery in itself, you might call it. But wait. Mark the sequel. You haven't heard anything yet.

We now turn to Nelson Cork. Shortly before one-thirty, Nelson had shoved over to Berkeley Square and had lunch with his godmother and Diana Punter, and Diana's manner and deportment had been absolutely all that could have been desired. In fact, so chummy had she been over the cutlets and fruit salad that it seemed to Nelson that, if she was like this now, imagination boggled at the thought of how utterly all over him she would be when he sprang his new hat on her.

So when the meal was concluded and coffee had been drunk and old Lady Punter had gone up to her boudoir with a digestive tablet and a sex-novel, he thought it would be a sound move to invite her to come for a stroll along Bond Street. There was the chance, of course, that she would fall into his arms right in the middle of the pavement: but if that happened, he told himself, they could always get into a cab. So he mooted the saunter, and she checked up, and presently they started off.

And you will scarcely believe this, but they hadn't gone more than half-way along Bruton Street when she suddenly stopped and looked at him in an odd manner.

'I don't want to be personal, Nelson,' she said, 'but really I do think you ought to take the trouble to get measured for your hats.'

If a gas main had exploded beneath Nelson's feet, he could hardly have been more taken aback.

'M-m-m-m . . .' he gasped. He could scarcely believe that he had heard aright.

'It's the only way with a head like yours. I know it's a temptation for a lazy man to go into a shop and just take whatever is offered him, but the result is so sloppy. That thing you're wearing now looks like an extinguisher.'

Nelson was telling himself that he must be strong.

'Are you endeavouring to intimate that this hat does not fit?'

'Can't you feel that it doesn't fit?'

'But it's a Bodmin.'

'I don't know what you mean. It's just an ordinary silk hat.'

'Not at all. It's a Bodmin.'

'I don't know what you are talking about.'

'The point I am trying to drive home,' said Nelson, stiffly, 'is that this hat was constructed under the personal auspices of Jno. Bodmin of Vigo Street.'

'Well, it's too big.'

'It is not too big.'

'I say it's too big.'

'And I say a Bodmin hat cannot be too big.'

'Well, I've got eyes, and I say it is.'

Nelson controlled himself with an effort.

'I would be the last person,' he said, 'to criticize your eyesight, but on the present occasion you will permit me to say that it has let you down with a considerable bump. Myopia is indicated. Allow me,' said Nelson, hot under the collar, but still dignified, 'to tell you something about Jno. Bodmin, as the name appears new to you. Jno. is the last of a long line of Bodmins, all of whom have made hats assiduously for the nobility and gentry all their lives. Hats are in Jno. Bodmin's blood.'

'I don't . . .'

Nelson held up a restraining hand.

'Over the door of his emporium in Vigo Street the passer-by may read a significant legend. It runs: "Bespoke Hatter To The Royal Family." That means, in simple language adapted to the lay intelligence, that if the King wants a new topper he simply ankles round to Bodmin's and says: "Good morning, Bodmin, we want a topper." He does not ask if it will fit. He takes it for granted that it will fit. He has bespoken Jno. Bodmin, and he trusts him blindly. You don't suppose His Gracious Majesty would bespeak a hatter whose hats did not fit. The whole essence of being a hatter is to make hats that fit, and it is to this end that Jno. Bodmin has strained every nerve for years. And that is why I say again – simply and without heat – This hat is a Bodmin.'

Diana was beginning to get a bit peeved. The blood of the Punters is hot, and very little is required to steam it up. She tapped Bruton Street with a testy foot.

'You always were an obstinate, pig-headed little fiend, Nelson, even as a child. I tell you once more, for the last time, that that hat is too big. If it were not for the fact that I can see a pair of boots and part of a pair of trousers, I should not know that there was a human being under it. I don't care how much you argue. I still think you ought to be ashamed of yourself for coming out in the thing. Even if you don't mind for your own sake, you might have considered the feelings of the pedestrians and traffic.'

Nelson quivered.

'You do, do you?'

'Yes, I do.'

'Oh, you do?'

'I said I did. Didn't you hear me? No, I suppose you could hardly be expected to, with an enormous great hat coming down over your ears.'

'You say this hat comes down over my ears?'

'Right over your ears. It's a mystery to me why you think it worth while to deny it.'

I fear that what follows does not show Nelson Cork in the role of a parfait gentil knight, but in extenuation of his behaviour I must remind you that he and Diana Punter had been brought up as children together, and a dispute between a couple who have shared the same nursery is always liable to degenerate into an exchange of personalities and innuendoes. What starts as an academic discussion on hats turns only too swiftly into a raking up of old sores and a grand parade of family skeletons.

It was so in this case. At the word 'mystery,' Nelson uttered a nasty laugh.

'A mystery, eh? As much a mystery, I suppose, as why your uncle George suddenly left England in the year 1920 without stopping to pack up?'

Diana's eyes flashed. Her foot struck the pavement another shrewd wallop.

'Uncle George,' she said haughtily, 'went abroad for his health.'

'You bet he did,' retorted Nelson. 'He knew what was good for him.'

'Anyway, he wouldn't have worn a hat like that.'

'Where they would have put him if he hadn't been off like a scalded kitten, he wouldn't have worn a hat at all.'

A small groove was now beginning to appear in the paving-stone on which Diana Punter stood.

'Well, Uncle George escaped one thing by going abroad, at any rate,' she said. 'He missed the big scandal about your aunt Clarissa in 1922.'

Nelson clenched his fists.

'The jury gave Aunt Clarissa the benefit of the doubt,' he said hoarsely.

'Well, we all know what that means. It was accompanied, if you recollect, by some very strong remarks from the Bench.'

There was a pause.

'I may be wrong,' said Nelson, 'but I should have thought it ill beseemed a girl whose brother Cyril was warned off the Turf in 1923 to haul up her slacks about other people's Aunt Clarissas.'

'Passing lightly over my brother Cyril in 1924,' rejoined Diana, 'what price your cousin Fred in 1927?'

They glared at one another in silence for a space, each realizing with a pang that the supply of erring relatives had now given out. Diana was still pawing the paving-stone, and Nelson was wondering what on earth he could ever have seen in a girl who, in addition to talking subversive drivel about hats, was eight feet tall and ungainly, to boot.

'While as for your brother-in-law's niece's sister-in-law Muriel . . .' began Diana, suddenly brightening.

Nelson checked her with a gesture.

'I prefer not to continue this discussion,' he said, frigidly.

'It is no pleasure to me,' replied Diana, with equal coldness, 'to have to listen to your vapid gibberings. That's the worst of a man who wears his hat over his mouth – he will talk through it.'

'I bid you a very hearty good afternoon, Miss Punter,' said Nelson.

He strode off without a backward glance.

Now, one advantage of having a row with a girl in Bruton Street is that the Drones is only just round the corner, so that you can pop in and restore the old nervous system with the minimum of trouble. Nelson was round there in what practically amounted to a trice, and the first person he saw was Percy, hunched up over a double and splash.

'Hullo,' said Percy.

'Hullo,' said Nelson.

There was a silence, broken only by the sound of Nelson ordering a mixed vermouth. Percy continued to stare before him like a man who has drained the wine-cup of life to its lees, only to discover a dead mouse at the bottom.

'Nelson,' he said at length, 'what are your views on the Modern Girl?'

'I think she's a mess.'

'I thoroughly agree with you,' said Percy. 'Of course, Diana Punter is a rare exception, but, apart from Diana, I wouldn't give you twopence for the modern girl. She lacks depth and reverence and has no sense of what is fitting. Hats, for example.'

'Exactly. But what do you mean Diana Punter is an exception? She's one of the ring-leaders – the spearhead of the movement, if you like to put it that way. Think,' said Nelson, sipping his vermouth, 'of all the unpleasant qualities of the Modern Girl, add them up, double them, and what have you got? Diana Punter. Let me tell you what took place between me and this Punter only a few minutes ago.'

'No,' said Percy. 'Let me tell you what transpired between me and Elizabeth Bottsworth this morning. Nelson, old man, she said my hat – my Bodmin hat – was too small.'

'You don't mean that?'

'Those were her very words.'

'Well, I'm dashed. Listen. Diana Punter told me my equally Bodmin hat was too large.'

They stared at one another.

'It's the Spirit of something,' said Nelson. 'I don't know what quite, but of something. You see it on all sides. Something very serious has gone wrong with girls nowadays. There is lawlessness and licence abroad.'

'And here in England, too.'

'Well, naturally, you silly ass,' said Nelson, with some asperity. 'When I said abroad, I didn't mean abroad, I meant abroad.'

He mused for a moment.

'I must say, though,' he continued, 'I am surprised at what you tell me about Elizabeth Bottsworth, and am inclined to think there must have been some mistake. I have always been a warm admirer of Elizabeth.'

'And I have always thought Diana one of the best, and I find it hard to believe that she should have shown up in such a dubious light as you suggest. Probably there was a misunderstanding of some kind.'

'Well, I ticked her off properly, anyway.'

Percy Wimbolt shook his head.

'You shouldn't have done that, Nelson. You may have wounded her feelings. In my case, of course, I had no alternative but to be pretty crisp with Elizabeth.'

Nelson Cork clicked his tongue.

'A pity,' he said. 'Elizabeth is sensitive.'

'So is Diana.'

'Not so sensitive as Elizabeth.'

'I should say, at a venture, about five times as sensitive as Elizabeth. However, we must not quarrel about a point like that, old man. The fact that emerges is that we seem both to have been dashed badly treated. I think I shall toddle home and take an aspirin.'

'Me, too.'

They went off to the cloak-room, where their hats were, and Percy put his on.

'Surely,' he said, 'nobody but a half-witted little pipsqueak who can't see straight would say this was too small?'

'It isn't a bit too small,' said Nelson. 'And take a look at this one. Am I not right in supposing that only a female giantess with straws in her hair and astigmatism in both eyes could say it was too large?'

'It's a lovely fit.'

And the cloak-room waiter, a knowledgeable chap of the name of Robinson, said the same.

'So there you are,' said Nelson.

'Ah, well,' said Percy.

They left the club, and parted at the top of Dover Street.

Now, though he had not said so in so many words, Nelson Cork's heart bled for Percy Wimbolt. He knew the other's fine sensibilities and he could guess how deeply he must have been gashed by this unfortunate breaking-off of diplomatic relations with the girl he loved. For, whatever might have happened, however sorely he might have been wounded, the way Nelson Cork looked at it was that Percy loved Elizabeth Bottsworth in spite of everything. What was required here, felt Nelson, was a tactful mediator – a kindly, sensible friend of both parties who would hitch up his socks and plunge in and heal the breach.

So the moment he had got rid of Percy outside the club he hared round to the house where Elizabeth was staying and was lucky enough to catch her on the front door steps. For, naturally, Elizabeth hadn't gone off to Ascot by herself. Directly Percy was out of sight, she had told the taxi-man to drive her home, and she had been occupying the interval since the painful scene in thinking of things she wished she had said to him and taking her hostess's dog for a run – a Pekinese called Clarkson.

She seemed very pleased to see Nelson, and started to prattle of this and that, her whole demeanour that of a girl who, after having been compelled to associate for a while with the Underworld, has at last found a kindred soul. And the more he listened, the more he wanted to go on listening. And the more he looked at her, the more he felt that a lifetime spent in gazing at Elizabeth Bottsworth would be a lifetime dashed well spent.

There was something about the girl's exquisite petiteness and fragility that appealed to Nelson Cork's depths. After having wasted so much time looking at a female Carnera like Diana Punter, it was a genuine treat to him to be privileged to feast the eyes on one so small and dainty. And, what with one thing and another, he found the most extraordinary difficulty in lugging Percy into the conversation.

They strolled along, chatting. And, mark you, Elizabeth Bottsworth was a girl a fellow could chat with without getting a crick in the neck from goggling up at her, the way you had to do when you took the air with Diana Punter. Nelson realized now that talking to Diana Punter had been like trying to exchange thoughts with a flag-pole sitter. He was surprised that this had never occurred to him before.

'You know, you're looking perfectly ripping, Elizabeth,' he said.

'How funny!' said the girl. 'I was just going to say the same thing about you.'

'Not really?'

'Yes, I was. After some of the gargoyles I've seen today – Percy Wimbolt is an example that springs to the mind – it's such a relief to be with a man who really knows how to turn himself out.'

Now that the Percy *motif* had been introduced, it should have been a simple task for Nelson to turn the talk to the subject of his absent friend. But somehow he didn't. Instead, he just simpered a bit and said: 'Oh, no, I say, really, do you mean that?'

'I do, indeed,' said Elizabeth earnestly. 'It's your hat, principally, I think. I don't know why it is, but ever since a child I have been intensely sensitive to hats, and it has always been a pleasure to me to remember that at the age of five I dropped a pot of jam out of the nursery window on to my Uncle Alexander when he came to visit us in a deerstalker cap with earflaps, as worn by Sherlock Holmes. I consider the hat the final test of a man. Now, yours is perfect. I never saw such a beautiful fit. I can't tell you how much I admire that hat. It gives you quite an ambassadorial look.'

Nelson Cork drew a deep breath. He was tingling from head to foot. It was as if the scales had fallen from his eyes and a new life begun for him.

'I say,' he said, trembling with emotion, 'I wonder if you would mind if I pressed your little hand?'

'Do,' said Elizabeth cordially.

'I will,' said Nelson, and did so. 'And now,' he went on, clinging to the fin like glue and hiccoughing a bit, 'how about buzzing off somewhere for a quiet cup of tea? I have a feeling that we have much to say to one another.'

It is odd how often it happens in this world that when there are two chaps and one chap's heart is bleeding for the other chap you find that all the while the second chap's heart is bleeding just as much for the first chap. Both bleeding, I mean to say, not only one. It was so in the case of Nelson Cork and Percy Wimbolt. The moment he had left Nelson, Percy charged straight off in search of Diana Punter with the intention of putting everything right with a few well-chosen words.

Because what he felt was that, although at the actual moment of going to press pique might be putting Nelson off Diana, this would pass off and love come into its own again. All that was required, he considered, was a suave go-between, a genial mutual pal who would pour oil on the troubled w's and generally fix things up.

He found Diana walking round and round Berkeley Square with her chin up, breathing tensely through the nostrils. He drew up alongside and what-hoed, and as she beheld him the cold, hard gleam in her eyes changed to a light of cordiality. She appeared charmed to see him and at once embarked on an animated conversation. And with every word she spoke his conviction deepened that of all the ways of passing a summer afternoon there were none fruitier than having a friendly hike with Diana Punter.

And it was not only her talk that enchanted him. He was equally fascinated by that wonderful physique of hers. When he considered that he had actually wasted several valuable minutes that day conversing with a young shrimp like Elizabeth Bottsworth, he could have kicked himself.

Here, he reflected, as they walked round the square, was a girl whose ear was more or less on a level with a fellow's mouth, so that such observations as he might make were enabled to get from point to point with the least possible delay. Talking to Elizabeth Bottsworth had always been like bellowing down a well in the hope of attracting the attention of one of the smaller infusoria at the bottom. It surprised him that he had been so long in coming to this conclusion.

He was awakened from this reverie by hearing his companion utter the name of Nelson Cork.

'I beg your pardon?' he said.

'I was saying,' said Diana, 'that Nelson Cork is a wretched little undersized blob who, if he were not too lazy to work, would long since have signed up with some good troupe of midgets.'

'Oh, would you say that?'

'I would say more than that,' said Diana firmly. 'I tell you, Percy, that what makes life so ghastly for girls, what causes girls to get grey hair and go into convents, is the fact that it is not always possible for them to avoid being seen in public with men like Nelson Cork. I trust I am not uncharitable. I try to view these things in a broad-minded way, saying to myself that if a man looks like something that has come out from under a flat stone it is his misfortune rather than his fault and that he is more to be pitied than censured. But on one thing I do insist, that such a man does not wantonly aggravate the natural unpleasantness of his appearance by prancing about London in a hat that reaches down to this ankles. I cannot and will not endure being escorted along Bruton Street by a sort of human bacillus the brim of whose hat bumps on the pavement with every step he takes. What I have always said and what I shall always say is that the hat is the acid test. A man who cannot buy the right-sized hat is a man one could never like or trust. Your hat, now, Percy, is exactly right. I have seen a good many hats in my time, but I really do not think that I have ever come across a more perfect specimen of all that a hat should be. Not too large, not too small, fitting snugly to the head like the skin on a sausage. And you have just the kind of head that a silk hat shows off. It gives you a sort of look . . . how shall I describe it? . . . it conveys the idea of a master of men. Leonine is the word I want. There is something about the way it rests on the brow and the almost imperceptible tilt towards the south-east . . .'

Percy Wimbolt was quivering like an Oriental muscle-dancer. Soft music seemed to be playing from the direction of Hay Hill, and Berkeley Square had begun to skip round him on one foot.

He drew a deep breath.

'I say,' he said, 'stop me if you've heard this before, but what I feel we ought to do at this juncture is to dash off somewhere where it's quiet and there aren't so many houses dancing the "Blue Danube" and shove some tea into ourselves. And over the pot and muffins I shall have something very important to say to you.'

'So that,' concluded the Crumpet, taking a grape, 'is how the thing stands; and, in a sense, of course, you could say that it is a satisfactory ending.

'The announcement of Elizabeth's engagement to Nelson Cork appeared in the Press on the same day as that of Diana's projected hitching-up with Percy Wimbolt: and it is pleasant that the happy couples should be so well matched as regards size.

'I mean to say, there will be none of that business of a six-foot girl tripping down the aisle with a five-foot-four man, or a six-feet-two man trying to keep step along the sacred edifice with a four-foot-three girl. This is always good for a laugh from the ringside pews, but it does not make for wedded bliss.

'No, as far as the principals are concerned, we may say that all has ended well. But that doesn't seem to me the important point. What seems to me the important point is this extraordinary baffling mystery of those hats.'

'Absolutely,' said the Bean.

'I mean to say, if Percy's hat really didn't fit, as Elizabeth Bottsworth contended, why should it have registered as a winner with Diana Punter?'

'Absolutely,' said the Bean.

'And, conversely, if Nelson's hat was the total loss which Diana Punter considered it, why, only a brief while later, was it going like a breeze with Elizabeth Bottsworth?'

'Absolutely,' said the Bean.

'The whole thing is utterly inscrutable.'

It was at this point that the nurse gave signs of wishing to catch the Speaker's eye.

'Shall I tell you what I think?'

'Say on, my dear young pillow-smoother.'

'I believe Bodmin's boy must have got those hats mixed. When he was putting them back in the boxes, I mean.'

The Crumpet shook his head, and took a grape.

'And then at the club they got the right ones again.'

The Crumpet smiled indulgently.

'Ingenious,' he said, taking a grape. 'Quite ingenious. But a little far-fetched. No, I prefer to think the whole thing, as I say, has something to do with the Fourth Dimension. I am convinced that that is the true explanation, if our minds could only grasp it.'

'Absolutely,' said the Bean.

# How I Edited an Agricultural Paper

## *Mark Twain*

I did not take temporary editorship of an agricultural paper without misgivings. Neither would a landsman take command of a ship without misgivings. But I was in circumstances that made the salary an object. The regular editor of the paper was going off for a holiday, and I accepted the terms he offered, and took his place.

The sensation of being at work again was luxurious, and I wrought all the week with unflagging pleasure. We went to press, and I waited a day with some solicitude to see whether my effort was going to attract any notice. As I left the office, toward sundown, a group of men and boys at the foot of the stairs dispersed with one impulse, and gave me passage-way, and I heard one or two of them say, 'That's him!' I was naturally pleased by the incident. The next morning I found a similar group at the foot of the stairs, and scattering couples and individuals standing here and there in the street, and over the way, watching me with interest. The group separated and fell back as I approached, and I heard a man say, 'Look at his eye!' I pretended not to observe the notice I was attracting, but secretly I was pleased with it, and was purposing to write an account of it to my aunt. I went up a short flight of stairs, and heard cheery voices and a ringing laugh as I drew near the door, which I opened, and caught a glimpse of two young rural-looking men, whose faces blanched and lengthened when they saw me, and then they both plunged through the window with a great crash. I was surprised.

In about half an hour an old gentleman, with a flowing beard and a fine but rather austere face, entered, and sat down at my invitation. He seemed to have something on his mind. He took off his hat and set it on the floor, and got out of it a red silk handkerchief and a copy of our paper.

He put the paper on his lap, and while he polished his spectacles with his handkerchief, he said, 'Are you the new editor?'

I said I was.

'Have you ever edited an agricultural paper before?'

'No,' I said; 'this is my first attempt.'

'Very likely. Have you had any experience in agriculture practically?'

'No; I believe I have not.'

'Some instinct told me so,' said the old gentleman, putting on his spectacles, and looking over them at me with asperity, while he folded his paper into a convenient shape. 'I wish to read you what must have made me have that instinct. It was this editorial. Listen, and see if it was you that wrote it:

*'Turnips should never be pulled; it injures them. It is much better to send a boy up and let him shake the tree.'*

'Now, what do you think of that? – for I really suppose you wrote it?'

'Think of it? Why, I think it is good. I think it is sense. I have no doubt that every year millions and millions of bushels of turnips are spoiled in this township alone by being pulled in a half-ripe condition, when, if they had sent a boy up to shake the tree – '

'Shake your grandmother! Turnips don't grow on trees!'

'Oh, they don't, don't they? Well, who said they did? The language was intended to be figurative – wholly figurative. Anybody that knows anything will know that I meant that the boy should shake the vine.'

Then this old person got up, and tore his paper all into small shreds, and stamped on them, and broke several things with his cane, and said I did not know as much as a cow, and then went out and banged the door after him; and, in short, acted in such a way that I fancied he was displeased about something. But not knowing what the trouble was, I could not be any help to him.

Pretty soon after this a long, cadaverous creature, with lanky locks hanging down to his shoulders, and a week's stubble bristling from the hills and valleys of his face, darted within the door and halted, motionless, with finger on lip, and head and body bent in listening attitude. No sound was heard. Still he listened. No sound. Then he turned the key in the door, and came elaborately tiptoeing toward me till he was within long reaching distance of me, when he stopped, and after scanning my face with intense interest for a while, drew a folded copy of our paper from his bosom, and said:

'There, you wrote that! Read it to me – quick! Relieve me! I suffer!'

I read as follows; and as the sentences fell from my lips I could see the relief come; I could see the drawn muscles relax, and the anxiety go out of the face, and rest and peace steal over the features like the merciful moonlight over a desolate landscape:

> *'The guano is a fine bird, but great care is necessary in rearing it. It should not be imported earlier than June or later than September. In the winter it should be kept in a warm place, where it can hatch out its young.*
>
> *'It is evident that we are to have a backward season for grain. Therefore it will be well for the farmer to begin setting out his cornstalks and planting his buckwheat cakes in July instead of August.*
>
> *'Concerning the pumpkin. – This berry is a favorite with the natives of the interior of New England, who prefer it to the gooseberry for the making of fruit-cake, and who likewise give it the preference over the raspberry for feeding cows, as being more filling and fully as satisfying. The pumpkin is the only esculent of the orange family that will thrive in the North, except the gourd and one or two varieties of the squash. But the custom of planting it in the front yard with the shrubbery is fast going out of vogue, for it is now generally conceded that the pumpkin as a shade tree is a failure.*
>
> *'Now, as the warm weather approaches, and the ganders begin to spawn – .'*

The excited listener sprang toward me to shake hands, and said:

'There, there – that will do! I know I am all right now, because you have read it just as I did, word for word. But, stranger, when I first read it this morning, I said to myself, I never, never believed it before, notwithstanding my friends kept me under watch so strict, but now I believe I *am* crazy; and with that I fetched a howl that you might have heard two miles, and started out to kill somebody – because, you know, I knew it would come to that sooner or later, and so I might as well begin. I read one of them paragraphs over again, so as to be certain, and then I burned my house down and started. I have crippled several people, and have got one fellow up a tree, where I can get him if I want him. But I thought I would call in here as I passed along and make the thing perfectly certain; and now it *is* certain, and I tell you it is lucky for the chap that is in the tree. I should have killed him, sure, as I went back. Good-bye, sir, good-bye; you have taken a great load off my mind. My reason has stood the strain of one of your agricultural articles, and I know that nothing can ever unseat it now. *Good*-bye, sir.'

I felt a little uncomfortable about the cripplings and arsons this person had been entertaining himself with, for I could not help feeling remotely accessory to them. But these thoughts were quickly banished, for the regular editor walked in! [I thought to myself, Now if you had gone to Egypt, as I recommended you to, I might have had a chance to get my hand in; but you wouldn't do it, and here you are. I sort of expected you.]

The editor was looking sad and perplexed and dejected.

He surveyed the wreck which that old rioter and these two young farmers had made, and then said, 'This is a sad business – a very sad business. There is the mucilage bottle broken, and six panes of glass, and a spittoon and two candlesticks. But that is not the worst. The reputation of the paper is injured – and permanently, I fear. True, there never was such a call for the paper before, and it never sold such a large edition or soared to such celebrity, – but does one want to be famous for lunacy, and prosper upon the infirmities of his mind? My friend, as I am an honest man, the street out here is full of people, and others are roosting on the fences, waiting to get a glimpse of you, because they think you are crazy. And well they might, after reading your editorials. They are a disgrace to journalism. Why, what put it into your head that you could edit a paper of this nature. You do not seem to know the first rudiments of agriculture. You speak of a furrow and a harrow as being the same thing; you talk of the moulting season for cows; and you recommend the domestication of the pole-cat on account of its playfulness and its excellence as a ratter? Your remark that clams will lie quiet if music be played to them was superfluous – entirely superfluous. Nothing disturbs clams. Clams *always* lie quiet. Clams care nothing whatever about music. Ah, heavens and earth, friend! if you had made the acquiring of ignorance the study of your life, you could not have graduated with higher honor than you could today. I never saw anything like it. Your observation that the horse-chestnut as an article of commerce is steadily gaining in favor, is simply calculated to destroy this journal. I want you to throw up your situation and go. I want no more holiday – I could not enjoy it if I had it. Certainly not with you in my chair. I would always stand in dread of what you might be going to recommend next. It makes me lose all patience every time I think of your discussing oyster-beds under the head of 'Landscape Gardening.' I want you to go. Nothing on earth could persuade me to take another holiday. Oh! why didn't you *tell* me you didn't know anything about agriculture?'

'*Tell* you, you cornstalk, you cabbage, you son of a cauliflower? It's the first time I ever heard such an unfeeling remark. I tell you I have been in the editorial business going on fourteen years, and it is the first time I ever heard of a man's having to know anything in order to edit a newspaper. You turnip! Who write the dramatic critiques for the second-rate papers? Why, a parcel of promoted shoemakers and apprentice apothecaries, who know just as much about good acting as I do about good farming, and no more. Who review the books? People who never wrote one. Who do up the heavy leaders on finance? Parties who have had the largest opportunities for knowing nothing about it. Who criticise the Indian campaigns? Gentlemen who do not know a war-whoop from a wigwam, and who never have had to run a footrace with a tomahawk, or pluck arrows out of the several members of their families to build the evening camp-fire with. Who write the temperance appeals, and clamor about the flowing bowl? Folks who will never draw another sober breath till they do it in the grave. Who edit the agricultural papers, you – yam? Men, as a general thing, who fail in the poetry line, yellow-covered novel line, sensation-drama line, city-editor line, and finally fall back on agriculture as a temporary reprieve from the poor-house. *You* try to tell *me* anything about the newspaper business! Sir, I have been through it from Alpha to Omaha, and I tell you that the less a man knows, the bigger the noise he makes and the higher the salary he commands. Heaven knows if I had but been ignorant instead of cultivated, and impudent instead of diffident, I could have made a name for myself in this cold, selfish world. I take my leave, sir. Since I have been treated as you have treated me, I am perfectly willing to go. But I have done my duty. I have fulfilled my contract as far as I was permitted to do it. I said I could make your paper of interest to all classes – and I have. I said I could run your circulation up to twenty thousand copies, and if I had had two more weeks I'd have done it. And I'd have given you the best class of readers that ever an agricultural paper had – not a farmer in it, nor a solitary

individual who could tell a water-melon tree from a peach-vine to save
his life. *You* are the loser by this rupture, not me, Pie-plant! Adios.'

  I then left.

# Examining Psychic Phenomena

## Woody Allen

There is no question that there is an unseen world. The problem is, how far is it from midtown and how late is it open? Unexplainable events occur constantly. One man will see spirits. Another will hear voices. A third will wake up and find himself running in the Preakness. How many of us have not at one time or another felt an ice-cold hand on the back of our neck while we were home alone? (Not me, thank God, but some have.) What is behind these experiences? Or in front of them, for that matter? Is it true that some men can foresee the future or communicate with ghosts? And after death is it still possible to take showers?

Fortunately, these questions about psychic phenomena are answered in a soon to be published book, *Boo!*, by Dr. Osgood Mulford Twelge, the noted parapsychologist and professor of ectoplasm at Columbia University. Dr. Twelge has assembled a remarkable history of supernatural incidents that covers the whole range of psychic phenomena, from thought transference to the bizarre experience of two brothers on opposite parts of the globe, one of whom took a bath while the other suddenly got clean. What follows is but a sampling of Dr. Twelge's most celebrated cases, with his comments.

### APPARITIONS

On March 16, 1882, Mr J. C. Dubbs awoke in the middle of the night and saw his brother Amos, who had been dead for fourteen years, sitting at the foot of his bed flicking chickens. Dubbs asked his brother what he was doing there, and his brother said not to worry, he was dead and was only in town for the weekend. Dubbs asked his brother what it was like in 'the other world,' and his brother said it was not unlike

Cleveland. He said he had returned to give Dubbs a message, which was that a dark-blue suit and Argyle socks are a big mistake.

At that point, Dubbs's servant girl entered and saw Dubbs talking to 'a shapeless, milky haze,' which she said reminded her of Amos Dubbs but was a little better-looking. Finally, the ghost asked Dubbs to join him in an aria from *Faust*, which the two sang with great fervor. As dawn rose, the ghost walked through the wall, and Dubbs, trying to follow, broke his nose.

This appears to be a classic case of the apparition phenomenon, and if Dubbs is to be believed, the ghost returned again and caused Mrs Dubbs to rise out of a chair and hover over the dinner table for twenty minutes until she dropped into some gravy. It is interesting to note that spirits have a tendency to be mischievous, which A. F. Childe, the British mystic, attributes to a marked feeling of inferiority they have over being dead. 'Apparitions' are often associated with individuals who have suffered an unusual demise. Amos Dubbs, for instance, had died under mysterious circumstances when a farmer accidentally planted him along with some turnips.

### SPIRIT DEPARTURE

Mr Albert Sykes reports the following experience: 'I was sitting having biscuits with some friends when I felt my spirit leave my body and go make a telephone call. For some reason, it called the Moscowitz Fiber Glass Company. My spirit then returned to my body and sat for another twenty minutes or so, hoping nobody would suggest charades. When the conversation turned to mutual funds, it left again and began wandering around the city. I am convinced that it visited the Statue of Liberty and then saw the stage show at Radio City Music Hall. Following that, it went to Benny's Steak House and ran up a tab of sixty-eight dollars. My spirit then decided to return to my body, but it was impossible to get a cab. Finally, it walked up Fifth Avenue and rejoined me just in time to catch the late news. I could tell that it was reentering my body, because I felt a sudden chill, and a voice said, "I'm back. You want to pass me those raisins?"'

'This phenomenon has happened to me several times since. Once, my spirit went to Miami for a weekend, and once it was arrested for trying to leave Macy's without paying for a tie. The fourth time, it was actually my body that left my spirit, although all it did was get a rubdown and come right back.'

Spirit departure was very common around 1910, when many 'spirits' were reported wandering aimlessly around India searching for the American Consulate. The phenomenon is quite similar to transubstantiation, the process whereby a person will suddenly dematerialize and rematerialize somewhere else in the world. This is not a bad way to travel, although there is usually a half-hour wait for luggage. The most astonishing case of transubstantiation was that of Sir Arthur Nurney, who vanished with an audible *pop* while he was taking a bath and suddenly appeared in the string section of the Vienna Symphony Orchestra. He stayed on as the first violinist for twenty-seven years, although he could only play 'Three Blind Mice,' and vanished abruptly one day during Mozart's Jupiter Symphony, turning up in bed with Winston Churchill.

### PRECOGNITION

Mr Fenton Allentuck describes the following precognitive dream: 'I went to sleep at midnight and dreamed that I was playing whist with a plate of chives. Suddenly the dream shifted, and I saw my grandfather about to be run over by a truck in the middle of the street, where he was waltzing with a clothing dummy. I tried to scream, but when I opened my mouth the only sound that came out was chimes, and my grandfather was run over.

'I awoke in a sweat and ran to my grandfather's house and asked him if he had plans to go waltzing with a clothing dummy. He said of course not, although he had contemplated posing as a shepherd to fool his enemies. Relieved, I walked home, but learned later that the old man had slipped on a chicken-salad sandwich and fallen off the Chrysler Building.'

Precognitive dreams are too common to be dismissed as pure coincidence. Here a man dreams of a relative's death, and it occurs. Not everyone is so lucky. J. Martinez, of Kennebunkport, Maine, dreamed he won the Irish Sweepstakes. When he awoke, his bed had floated out to sea.

TRANCES

Sir Hugh Swiggles, the skeptic, reports an interesting séance experience:

We attended the home of Madame Reynaud, the noted medium, where we were all told to sit around the table and join hands. Mr Weeks couldn't stop giggling, and Madame Reynaud smashed him on the head with a Ouija board. The lights were turned out, and Madame Reynaud attempted to contact Mrs Marple's husband, who had died at the opera when his beard caught fire. The following is an exact transcript:

MRS MARPLE: What do you see?

MEDIUM: I see a man with blue eyes and a pinwheel hat.

MRS MARPLE: That's my husband!

MEDIUM: His name is . . . Robert. No . . . Richard . . .

MRS MARPLE: Quincy.

MEDIUM: Quincy! Yes, that's it!

MRS MARPLE: What else about him?

MEDIUM: He is bald but usually keeps some leaves on his head so nobody will notice.

MRS MARPLE: Yes! Exactly!

MEDIUM: For some reason, he has an object . . . a loin of pork.

MRS MARPLE: My anniversary present to him! Can you make him speak?

MEDIUM: Speak, spirit. Speak.

QUINCY: Claire, this is Quincy.

MRS MARPLE: Oh, Quincy! Quincy!

QUINCY: How long do you keep the chicken in when you're trying to broil it?

MRS MARPLE: That voice! It's him!

MEDIUM: Everybody concentrate.

MRS MARPLE: Quincy, are they treating you okay?

QUINCY: Not bad, except it takes four days to get your cleaning back.

MRS MARPLE: Quincy, do you miss me?

QUINCY: Huh? Oh, er, sure. Sure, kid. I got to be going . . .

MEDIUM: I'm losing it. He's fading . . .

I found this séance to pass the most stringent tests of credulity, with the minor exception of a phonograph, which was found under Madame Reynaud's dress.

There is no doubt that certain events recorded at séances are genuine. Who does not recall the famous incident at Sybil Seretsky's, when her goldfish sang 'I Got Rhythm' – a favorite tune of her recently deceased nephew? But contacting the dead is at best difficult, since most deceased are reluctant to speak up, and those that do seem to hem and haw before getting to the point. The author has actually seen a table rise, and Dr. Joshua Fleagle, of Harvard, attended a séance in which a table not only rose but excused itself and went upstairs to sleep.

### CLAIRVOYANCE

One of the most astounding cases of clairvoyance is that of the noted Greek psychic, Achille Londos. Londos realised he had 'unusual powers' by the age of ten, when he could lie in bed and, by concentrating, make his father's false teeth jump out of his mouth. After a neighbor's husband had been missing for three weeks, Londos told them to look in the stove, where the man was found knitting. Londos could concentrate on a person's face and force the image to come out on a roll of ordinary Kodak film, although he could never seem to get anybody to smile.

In 1964, he was called in to aid police in capturing the Düsseldorf Strangler, a fiend who always left a baked Alaska on the chests of his victims. Merely by sniffing a handkerchief, Londos led police to Siegfried Lenz, handyman at a school for deaf turkeys, who said he was the strangler and could he please have his handkerchief back.

Londos is just one of many people with psychic powers. C. N. Jerome, the psychic, of Newport, Rhode Island, claims he can guess any card being thought of by a squirrel.

### PROGNOSTICATION

Finally, we come to Aristonidis, the sixteenth-century count whose predictions continue to dazzle and perplex even the most skeptical. Typical examples are:

'Two nations will go to war, but only one will win.'

(Experts feel this probably refers to the Russo-Japanese War of 1904-05 – an outstanding feat of prognostication, considering the fact that it was made in 1540.)

'A man in Istanbul will have his hat blocked, and it will be ruined.'

(In 1860, Abu Hamid, Ottoman warrior, sent his cap out to be cleaned, and it came back with spots.)

'I see a great person, who one day will invent for mankind a garment to be worn over his trousers for protection while cooking. It will be called an "abron" or "aprone." '

(Aristonidis meant the apron, of course.)

'A leader will emerge in France. He will be very short and will cause great calamity.'

(This is a reference either to Napoleon or to Marcel Lumet, an eighteenth-century midget who instigated a plot to rub béarnaise sauce on Voltaire.)

# Plants: The Roots of All Evil

*Fran Lebowitz*

The Unabridged Second Edition of Webster's Dictionary – a volume of no small repute – gives the following as the second definition of the word *plant*: 'any living thing that cannot move voluntarily, has no sense organs and generally makes its own food . . .' I have chosen the second definition in favor of the first because it better serves my purpose, which is to prove once and for all that, except in extremely rare instances, a plant is really not the sort of thing that one ought to have around the house. That this might be accomplished in an orderly manner, I have elected to consider each aspect of the above definition individually. Let us begin at the beginning:

ANY LIVING THING
In furnishing one's place of residence one seeks to acquire those things which will provide the utmost in beauty, comfort, and usefulness. In the beauty department one is invariably drawn to such fixtures as Cocteau drawings, Ming vases, and Aubusson rugs. Comfort is, of course, assured by the ability to possess these objects. Usefulness is something best left to those trained in such matters.

It should, then, be apparent that at no time does Any Living Thing enter the picture except in the past tense. In other words, it is perfectly acceptable to surround oneself with objects composed of that which while alive may have been Any Living Thing but in death has achieved dignity by becoming a nice white linen sheet.

THAT CANNOT MOVE VOLUNTARILY
Here one is confronted with the problem that arises when Any Living Thing takes the form of an extra person. An extra person is quite simply a person other than oneself. Living things of this nature undoubtedly have their place in both town and country, as they usually prove to be

the most adept at typing, kissing, and conversing in an amusing
fashion. It must be pointed out, however, that moving voluntarily is the
very key to their success in performing these functions; the necessity of
having to actually operate them would quite eliminate their appeal.

I have previously stated my contention that plants are acceptable in
extremely rare instances. This type of extremely rare instance occurs
when one is presented with a leaf-ridden token of affection by an extra
person who has provided valuable service. Refusal of a plant thus
offered will almost certainly result in the termination of this bond.
Therefore, while the decision as to who exactly should be allowed to
burden one with such a memento is, of course, a matter of personal
conscience, one is wise to remember that talk is cheap, a kiss is just a
kiss, but manuscripts do not type themselves.

### HAS NO SENSE ORGANS

It is necessary to remember that, although No Sense Organs does most
assuredly guarantee no meaningful glances, no snorting derisively, and
no little tastes, it also, alas, guarantees no listening spellbound.

### AND GENERALLY MAKES ITS OWN FOOD

There is, I believe, something just the tiniest bit smug in that statement. And Generally Makes Its Own Food, does it? Well, bully for It. I
do not generally make my own food, nor do I apologise for it in the least.
New York City is fairly bristling with restaurants of every description
and I cannot help but assume that they are there for a reason.
Furthermore, it is hard to cherish the notion of a cuisine based on
photosynthesis. Thus, since I have yet to detect the aroma of Fettuccine
Alfredo emanating from a Boston fern, I do not consider And Generally
Makes Its Own Food to be a trait of any consequence whatsoever.
When you run across one that Generally Makes Its Own Money, give
me a call.

# The Brigadier Down Under

*Peter Tinniswood*

Well, we have arrived Down Under, the lady wife and I.

Oh, woe is me.

Oh, misery beyond redemption.

Oh, wretchedness beyond compare.

Dear, dear Witney Scrotum – how my heart yearns for you wrapped now in the raiments of English winter, cold mists coiling round the massive summit of Botham's Gut, wild geese wailing in the frost-chapped water meadows at Cowdrey's Bottom and icy dewdrops clanking from the tip of old Granny Swanton's ancient nose.

Ah, the pain of exile!

Ah, the cruelties inflicted on a sensitive soul from noble Albion by this godforsaken hell-hole of a country with its weak, tepid beer, foul Antarctic gales, ugly women with hairy chests and fat bottoms and sun-addled men with no lead in their pencils.

Vileness surrounds on all sides.

Every prospect displeases.

The ghastly sun beats down out of a relentlessly blue and cloudless sky.

Our nostrils are most brutally assaulted by the scents of stale meat pies and fetid armpits.

All we hear is the drone of mosquito, the flip and flop of shuffling feet, the screech of cockatoo, the rattle of beer can, the long-drawn, snivelling winge and whine of the Australian native tongue, and, most vile of all, the cricket commentaries of Richie Benaud.

So why are we here?

Well may you ask, dear readers, well may you ask.

There is only one person on the face of this earth who could have reduced me to such depths of misery and despair.

Of course, dear readers, of course – it is the lady wife.

And why has she dragged me here?

Is it punishment for some dire sin I committed during the summer long since gone?

Did I forget to pull the chain in the ablutions offices 'during company?'

Did I knock my pipe out in the goldfish bowl 'once too often?'

Did I commit an 'error of judgement' by wearing ginger plus fours in the presence of the Pope on the occasion of the Holy Father's personal pilgrimage to Witney Scrotum to pay homage to the tomb of the unknown leg spinner?

No.

The answer is more hideous by far.

We are here Down Under in order to visit the lady wife's unmarried spinster brother, Naunton.

Dear God, in my innocence I had thought I was forever free of his rampant loathsomeness when the beast was banished from the Mother Country following 'an incident' in his regiment involving a trench mortar, half a bar of nougat and a well-known Wiltshire occasional seamer.

This, however, was not the case.

During the late summer, to my profound distress, the lady wife received intelligence that the vileness was 'alive and kicking' in some Australian outback town, the name of which, as is the case with most other towns in this godforsaken country, sounds like some highly-contagious disease of the private parts.

Apparently he was 'earning his crust' selling marsupial underpants to incontinent wicket keepers and bringing succour and comfort to lonely cricketers through the medium of life-sized, inflatable rubber dolls in the shape of Messrs Rodney Marsh and Dennis Lillee.

The lady wife, with the typical impetuosity of her gender, which is female, had to see him at once.

In vain did I plead for mercy.

If we were away for winter, who, I said, would feed and water old Granny Swanton, who would man the hot Bovril kiosk at the golf ball museum, who would run the Christmas raffle for defrocked umpires at the Baxter Arms?

The lady wife was adamant.

She fixed me with those pink and piggy little eyes of hers and boomed in those familiar hectoring tones:

'I don't know what you're making such a fuss about. You can watch the cricket, can't you?'

Watch the cricket?

Watch the cricket, did she say?

Good God, one doesn't watch cricket in Australia.

One listens to it.

On the talking wireless.

In the depths of an English winter.

At the crack of cold, grey dawn.

In the Commodore's summer house, wrapped in Vick-impregnated I Zingari mufflers and fortified by flasks of Instant Possum and whisky-flavoured cream crackers.

One sits 'glued' to the talking wireless, preening with pleasure, crooning with delight, as 'over the ether' ring the sweet and dulcet tones of Lord Henry Blofeld, the profound and majestic sermons of Cardinal Bailey and the sharp, barked commands of the leader of the BBC Blackshirt Brigade, Don 'Sir Oswald' Mosey.

But of these matters, I fear, the 'opposite gender' is ignorant, every man jack of them.

Scum!

What do they know of the 'finer things of life?'

Have they ever worn spats?

No.

Have they ever driven a snorting, snarling steam locomotive up Lickey Bank or gone twelve rounds with Randolph Turpin?

No.

Have they ever edited Wisden's Almanack, smelled the inside of Mr. Ian Botham's socks, kissed the chaste and pure Mr. David Gower, sandpapered the toenails of an Airedale terrier, held the post of Prime Minister of the United Kingdom?

Of course not.

I am not a prejudiced man, but, if I had my way, I should . . .

No matter.

No matter, dear readers.

Suffice it to say that on a dour and sullen November morn we set forth for Australia.

Farewell Witney Scrotum.

The villagers lined the streets wailing and wringing their hands.

The church bells tolled.

The sightscreens on the village green were blackened and turned inwards and the flag flew at half mast on the roof of Squire Brearley's Indoor Knitting School.

Outside the Baxter Arms poor old doddery Arlott shuffled forwards and touched his grizzled forelock.

'Promise me one thing, sir,' he said. 'Don't touch the Aussie claret. If you wants a good tipple, sir, take my advice and only drink the Château Trumper Spaetauslese, 1967. He be a noble drink, sir. A noble drink.'

I slipped the poor wretch a 20p Peter Dominic gift voucher, and he seemed well-pleased.

The Commodore insisted on driving us to the rail-head, from which we were to embark for London.

He wept copiously throughout the journey, and at the station buildings he gripped my hand firmly and said:

'Shall I buy a platform ticket?'

I lowered my eyes.

'No,' I said. 'No.'

He shook with emotion.

And so did I.

Of such moments is the stock of friendship forged.

I watched him depart the station yard, and as his dear, familiar, bottle-green Humber disappeared from view with half old Squire Brearley's cattle grid and the corpses of three of Grannie Swanton's Buff Orpingtons dangling from its rear bumper I confess I blubbed shamelessly.

I was still in a state of 'high emotion' when, fifteen hours later, we reached the landing strip at Heathrow, and boarded the moving aeroplane.

We travelled under conditions of extreme squalor, throughout which the lady wife viewed me with icy disdain.

I tried to make conversation.

'Look,' I said, pointing out of the window. 'That must be Iceland.'

'Humph,' said the lady wife.

'Jolly decent of the chaps to live there, don't you think?' I said.

'Humph.'

I looked out of the window again and examined more closely the bleak, icy, gale-ravaged wasteland.

'Of course it could always be Old Trafford,' I said.

'Humph,' said the lady wife and immersed herself once more in her paperback library book entitled 'The Official War Office Biography of Sir Geoffrey Boycott – *Volume Seven* – The Years of Destiny, Aged Three to Six and a Half.'

Hell.

Sheer, unadulterated hell.

Admit it, dear readers, travel by moving aeroplane is as stimulating as sitting in the middle of a jumbo-sized packet of medicated catarrh pastilles.

The hours dragged by interminably.

Vast legions of infants in arms howled and puked endlessly, for all the world like spectators on the Hill at Sydney Cricket Ground.

I could stand it no longer.

I poked the lady wife in the ribs with the handle of my stumper's mallet and said:

'Well, it can't be long now till we pole up in Australia.'

'Australia?' said the lady wife. 'Australia? We haven't even landed in America yet.'

Oh God, another nail in the coffin.

To my horror it transpired that the lady wife had arranged for us to break our journey at a hell-hole, name of Los Angeles, which in my ignorance I had always assumed was the title of some obscure rhumba band on Workers' Playtime of blessed memory.

Would that it had been, dear readers, would that it had been.

Can you imagine my chagrin when I discovered the name of our night's lodgings?

The Beverly Wiltshire!

How typical of the lady wife's atavistic miserliness – the bloody place wasn't even first class.

The Beverly Derbyshire or the Beverly Worcestershire – that might have been acceptable to a lover of our 'summer game'.

But the Beverly Wiltshire!

Good God, it's only Minor Counties.

I spent a thoroughly wretched night.

What the Yanks don't realise is that the only requirements the true red-blooded Englishman needs for an overnight stay in an hotel is a dry and level space for his palliasse, ample supplies of standing water for his ablutions activities and sufficient bookshelf space for his Wisden's Almanacks.

What he does not need are two bathrooms, twenty-seven multi-coloured telephones, uncountable numbers of shower caps, shoe horns, darning kits, unstrikeable paper matches and a bed the size of Twickenham rugby football pitch.

What a scandalous waste of space and resources.

Dear Lord, in our room I could have accommodated the whole of Fred Rumsey's hindparts and 'made a good show' of staging the World Welterweight Boxing Championship.

If there is one race upon this earth I detest above all others it is the Yanks with their ill-fitting shirts and their air-conditioned handshakes.

I am not a prejudiced man, but . . .

We spent the rest of our stay in Los Angeles in a smog-bound torpor.

The lady wife averred that it was 'worth it' because she had seen in the foyer of the hotel some starlet of the moving kinematograph screen, name of Ann Hefflin.

I myself did not see the swine.

I did, however, see Sir C. Aubrey Smith, who was looking 'in the pink'.

And thus did we enplane once more for the 'final leg' of our journey to Australia.

The langorous torpor of Los Angeles mixed pleasurably with a state of semi-intoxication induced by the fumes from the whisky-sodden breaths of the swarms of Australian surfers who boarded the plane at Honolulu and entertained themselves for the rest of the journey by eating the blankets of their fellow travellers.

The lady wife kept the scum at bay with liberal squirtings from her linseed oil anti-mugger spray, and I 'did my bit' with the handle of my portable cricket bat.

And so, dear readers, we find ourselves in our winter quarters in Adelaide.

I have passed on the personal regards of Lady Falklander, The Ink Monitor at Number Ten, to Colonel 'Mad' Bob Willis and the troops.

As requested I have brought for them a trunkful of Phyllosan for Mr Bob Taylor, a fresh selection of Rupert annuals for Master Derek Pringle and a letter of consolation for the lugubrious Innersole from Sir

Geoffrey Boycott.

And now in the dead of the tropic night I sit on the balcony of the hotel launderette and look out on moon-bleached hills, whispering, hissing palms ruffled by the sighs and screams of small birds of the night, and I have only one thing to say:

'I want to go home.'

'I want to go home.'

# My Brother Henry

## J. M. Barrie

Strictly speaking I never had a brother Henry, and yet I cannot say that Henry was an impostor. He came into existence in a curious way, and I can think of him now without malice as a child of smoke. The first I heard of Henry was at Pettigrew's house, which is in a London suburb, so conveniently situated that I can go there and back in one day. I was testing some new Cabanas, I remember, when Pettigrew remarked that he had been lunching with a man who knew my brother Henry. Not having any brother but Alexander I felt that Pettigrew had mistaken the name. 'Oh no,' Pettigrew said; 'he spoke of Alexander too.' Even this did not convince me, and I asked my host for his friend's name. Scudamour was the name of the man, and he had met my brothers Alexander and Henry years before in Paris. Then I remembered Scudamour, and I probably frowned, for I myself was my own brother Henry. I distinctly recalled Scudamour meeting Alexander and me in Paris, and calling me Henry, though my name begins with J. I explained the mistake to Pettigrew, and there, for the time being, the matter rested. However, I had by no means heard the last of Henry.

Several times afterwards I heard from various persons that Scudamour wanted to meet me because he knew my brother Henry. At last we did meet, in Jimmy's chambers; and, almost as soon as he saw me, Scudamour asked where Henry was now. This was precisely what I feared. I am a man who always looks like a boy. There are few persons of my age in London who retain their boyish appearance as long as I have done; indeed, this is the curse of my life. Though I am approaching the age of thirty, I pass for twenty; and I have observed old gentlemen frown at my precocity when I said a good thing or helped myself to a second glass of wine. There was, therefore, nothing surprising in Scudamour's remark, that, when he had the pleasure of meeting Henry, Henry must have been about the age that I had now reached. All would have been well had I explained the real state of affairs to this annoying man; but, unfortunately for myself, I loathe entering upon explanations to anybody about anything. This it is to smoke the Arcadia. When I ring for a time-table and William John brings coals instead I accept the coals as a substitute. Much, then, did I dread a discussion with Scudamour, his surprise when he heard that I was Henry, and his comments on my youthful appearance. Besides, I was smoking the best of all mixtures. There was no likelihood of my meeting Scudamour again, so the easiest way to get rid of him seemed to be to humour him. I therefore told him that Henry was in India, married, and doing well. 'Remember me to Henry when you write him,' was Scudamour's last remark to me that evening.

A few weeks later some one tapped me on the shoulder in Oxford Street. It was Scudamour. 'Heard from Henry?' he asked. I said I had heard by the last mail. 'Anything particular in the letter?' I felt it would not do to say that there was nothing particular in a letter which had come all the way from India, so I hinted that Henry was having trouble with his wife. By this I meant that her health was bad; but he took it up in another way, and I did not set him right. 'Ah, ah!' he said, shaking his head sagaciously, 'I'm sorry to hear that. Poor Henry!' 'Poor old boy!' was all I could think of replying. 'How about the children?' Scudamour asked. 'Oh, the children,' I said, with what I thought presence of mind, 'are coming to England.' 'To stay with Alexander?' he asked. My answer was that Alexander was expecting them by the middle of next month; and eventually Scudamour went away muttering, 'Poor Henry!' In a month or so we met again. 'No word of Henry's getting leave of absence?' asked Scudamour. I replied shortly that Henry had gone to live in Bombay, and would not be home for years. He saw that I was brusque, so what does he do but draw me aside for a quiet explanation. 'I suppose,' he said, 'you are annoyed because I told Pettigrew that Henry's wife had run away from him. The fact is, I did it for your good. You see I happened to make a remark to Pettigrew about your brother Henry, and he said that there was no such person. Of course I laughed at that, and pointed out not only that I had the pleasure of Henry's acquaintance but that you and I had a talk about the old fellow every time we met. "Well," Pettigrew said, "this is a most remarkable thing; for he," meaning you, "said to me in this very room, sitting in that very chair, that Alexander was his only brother." I saw

that Pettigrew resented your concealing the existence of your brother
Henry from him, so I thought the most friendly thing I could do was to
tell him that your reticence was doubtless due to the unhappy state of
poor Henry's private affairs. Naturally in the circumstances you did
not want to talk about Henry.' I shook Scudamour by the hand, telling
him that he had acted judiciously; but if I could have stabbed him in the
back at that moment I dare say I would have done it.

   I did not see Scudamour again for a long time, for I took care to keep
out of his way; but I heard first from him and then of him. One day he
wrote to me saying that his nephew was going to Bombay, and would I
be so good as to give the youth an introduction to my brother Henry?
He also asked me to dine with him and his nephew. I declined the
dinner, but I sent the nephew the required note of introduction to
Henry. The next I heard of Scudamour was from Pettigrew. 'By the
way,' said Pettigrew, 'Scudamour is in Edinburgh at present.' I
trembled, for Edinburgh is where Alexander lives. 'What has taken him
there?' I asked, with assumed carelessness. Pettigrew believed it was
business; 'but,' he added, 'Scudamour asked me to tell you that he
meant to call on Alexander, as he was anxious to see Henry's children.'
A few days afterwards I had a telegram from Alexander, who generally
uses this means of communication when he corresponds with me. 'Do
you know a man Scudamour? Reply,' was what Alexander said. I
thought of answering that we had met a man of that name when we
were in Paris; but, after consideration, I replied boldly: 'Know no one
of name of Scudamour.'

   About two months ago I passed Scudamour in Regent Street, and he
scowled at me. This I could have borne if there had been no more of
Henry; but I knew that Scudamour was now telling everybody about
Henry's wife. By and by I got a letter from an old friend of Alexander's
asking me if there was any truth in a report that Alexander was going to
Bombay. Soon afterwards Alexander wrote to me saying he had been
told by several persons that I was going to Bombay. In short, I saw that
the time had come for killing Henry. So I told Pettigrew that Henry had
died of fever, deeply regretted; and asked him to be sure to tell
Scudamour, who had always been interested in the deceased's welfare.
Pettigrew afterwards told me that he had communicated the sad
intelligence to Scudamour. 'How did he take it?' I asked. 'Well,'
Pettigrew said, reluctantly, 'he told me that when he was up in

Edinburgh he did not get on well with Alexander. But he expressed great curiosity as to Henry's children.' 'Ah,' I said, 'the children were both drowned in the Forth; a sad affair – we can't bear to talk of it.' I am not likely to see much of Scudamour again, nor is Alexander. Scudamour now goes about saying that Henry was the only one of us he really liked.

# Match Wits with Inspector Ford

*Woody Allen*

### THE CASE OF THE MURDERED SOCIALITE

Inspector Ford burst into the study. On the floor was the body of Clifford Wheel, who apparently had been struck from behind with a croquet mallet. The position of the body indicated that the victim had been surprised in the act of singing 'Sorrento' to his goldfish. Evidence showed there had been a terrible struggle that had twice been interrupted by phone calls, one a wrong number and one asking if the victim was interested in dance lessons.

Before Wheel had died, he had dipped his finger into the inkwell and scrawled out a message: 'Fall Sale Prices Drastically Reduced – Everything Must Go!'

'A businessman to the end,' mused Ives, his manservant, whose elevator shoes, curiously enough, made him two inches shorter.

The door to the terrace was open and footprints led from there, down the hall and into a drawer.

'Where were you when it happened, Ives?'

'In the kitchen. Doing the dishes.' Ives produced some suds from his wallet to corroborate his story.

'Did you hear anything?'

'He was in there with some men. They were arguing over who was tallest. I thought I heard Mr Wheel start yodeling and Mosley, his business partner, began yelling, "My God, I'm going bald!" Next thing I knew, there was a harp glissando and Mr Wheel's head came rolling out onto the lawn. I heard Mr Mosley threaten him. He said if Mr Wheel touched his grapefruit again, he would not cosign a bank loan for him. I think he killed him.'

'Does the terrace door open from the inside or from the outside?' Inspector Ford asked Ives.

'From the outside. Why?'

'Exactly as I suspected. I now realize it was you, not Mosley, who killed Clifford Wheel.'

### How Did Inspector Ford Know?

Because of the layout of the house, Ives could not have sneaked up behind his employer. He would have had to sneak up in front of him, at which time Mr Wheel would have stopped singing 'Sorrento' and used the mallet on Ives, a ritual they had gone through many times.

#### A CURIOUS RIDDLE

Apparently, Walker was a suicide. Overdose of sleeping pills. Still, something seemed amiss to Inspector Ford. Perhaps it was the position of the body. Inside the TV set, looking out. On the floor was a cryptic suicide note. 'Dear Edna, My woolen suit itches me, and so I have decided to take my own life. See that our son finishes all his push-ups. I leave you my entire fortune, with the exception of my porkpie hat, which I hereby donate to the planetarium. Please don't feel sorry for me, as I enjoy being dead and much prefer it to paying rent. Goodbye, Henry. PS This may not be the time to bring it up, but I have every reason to believe that your brother is dating a Cornish hen.'

Edna Walker bit her lower lip nervously. 'What do you make of it, Inspector?'

Inspector Ford looked at the bottle of sleeping pills on the night table. 'How long had your husband been an insomniac?'

'For years. It was psychological. He was afraid that if he closed his eyes, the city would paint a white line down him.'

'I see. Did he have any enemies?'

'Not really. Except for some gypsies who ran a tearoom on the outskirts of town. He insulted them once by putting on a pair of earmuffs and hopping up and down in place on their sabbath.'

Inspector Ford noticed a half-finished glass of milk on the desk. It was still warm. 'Mrs. Walker, is your son away at college?'

'I'm afraid not. He was expelled last week for immoral conduct. It came as quite a surprise. They caught him trying to immerse a dwarf in tartar sauce. That's one thing they won't tolerate at an Ivy League school.'

'And one thing I won't tolerate is murder. Your son is under arrest.'

### Why Did Inspector Ford Suspect Walker's Son Had Killed Him?

Mr. Walker's body was found with cash in his pockets. A man who was going to commit suicide would be sure to take a credit card and sign for everything.

### THE STOLEN GEM

The glass case was shattered and the Bellini Sapphire was missing. The only clues left behind at the museum were a blond hair and a dozen fingerprints, all pinkies. The guard explained that he had been standing there when a blackclad figure crept up behind him and struck him over the head with some notes for a speech. Just before losing consciousness, he thought he had heard a man's voice say, 'Jerry, call your mother,' but he could not be sure. Apparently, the thief had entered through the skylight and walked down the wall with suction shoes, like a human fly. The museum guards always kept an enormous fly swatter for just such occasions, but this time they had been fooled.

'Why would anyone want the Bellini Sapphire?' the museum curator asked. 'Don't they know it's cursed?'

'What's this about a curse?' Inspector Ford was quick to ask.

'The sapphire was originally owned by a sultan who died under mysterious circumstances when a hand reached out of a bowl of soup he was eating and strangled him. The next owner was an English lord who was found one day by his wife growing upside down in a window box. Nothing was heard of the stone for a while; then it turned up years later in the possession of a Texas millionaire, who was brushing his teeth when he suddenly caught fire. We purchased the sapphire only last month, but the curse seemed to be working still, because shortly after we obtained it, the entire board of trustees at the museum formed a conga line and danced off a cliff.'

'Well, Inspector Ford said, 'it may be an unlucky jewel, but it's valuable, and if you want it back, go to Handleman's Delicatessen and arrest Leonard Handleman. You'll find that the sapphire is in his pocket.'

### How Did Inspector Ford Know
### Who the Jewel Thief Was?

The previous day, Leonard Handleman had remarked, 'Boy, if I only had a large sapphire, I could get out of the delicatessen business.'

### THE MACABRE ACCIDENT

'I just shot my husband,' wept Cynthia Freem as she stood over the body of the burly man in the snow.

'How did it happen?' asked Inspector Ford, getting right to the point.

'We were hunting. Quincy loved to hunt, as did I. We got separated momentarily. The bushes were overgrown. I guess I thought he was a woodchuck. I blasted away. It was too late. As I was removing his pelt, I realized we were married.'

'Hmm,' mused Inspector Ford, glancing at the footprints in the snow. 'You must be a very good shot. You managed to lug him right between the eyebrows.'

'Oh, no, it was lucky. I'm really quite an amateur at that sort of thing.'

'I see.' Inspector Ford examined the dead man's possessions. In his pocket there was some string, also an apple from 1904 and instructions on what to do if you wake up next to an Armenian.

'Mrs Freem, was this your husband's first hunting accident?'

'His first fatal one, yes. Although once in the Canadian Rockies, an eagle carried off his birth certificate.'

'Did your husband always wear a toupee?'

'Not really. He would usually carry it with him and produce it if challenged in an argument. Why?'

'He sounds eccentric.'

'He was.'

'Is that why you killed him?'

## How Did Inspector Ford Know
## It Was No Accident?

An experienced hunter like Quincy Freem would never have stalked deer in his underwear. Actually, Mrs Freem had bludgeoned him to death at home while he was playing the spoons and had tried to make it look like a hunting accident by dragging his body to the woods and leaving a copy of *Field & Stream* nearby. In her haste, she had forgotten to dress him. Why he had been playing the spoons in his underwear remains a mystery.

### THE BIZARRE KIDNAPPING

Half-starved, Kermit Kroll staggered into the living room of his parents' home, where they waited anxiously with Inspector Ford.

'Thanks for paying the ransom, folks,' Kermit said. 'I never thought I'd get out of there alive.'

'Tell me about it,' the inspector said.

'I was on my way downtown to have my hat blocked when a sedan pulled up and two men asked me if I wanted to see a horse that could recite the Gettysburg Address. I said sure and got in. Next thing, I'm chloroformed and wake up somewhere tied to a chair and blindfolded.'

Inspector Ford examined the ransom note. 'Dear Mom and Dad, Leave $50,000 in a bag under the bridge on Decatur Street. If there is no bridge on Decatur Street, please build one. I am being treated well, given shelter and good food, although last night the clams casino were overcooked. Send the money quickly, because if they don't hear from you within several days, the man who now makes up my bed will strangle me. Yours, Kermit. PS This is no joke. I am enclosing a joke so you will be able to tell the difference.'

'Do you have any idea at all as to where you were being held?'

'No, I just kept hearing an odd noise outside the window.'

'Odd?'

'Yes. You know the sound a herring makes when you lie to it?'

'Hmm,' reflected Inspector Ford. 'And how did you finally escape?'

'I told them I wanted to go to the football game but I only had a single ticket. They said okay, as long as I kept the blindfold on and promised to return by midnight. I complied, but during the third quarter, the Bears had a big lead, so I left and made my way back here.'

'Very interesting,' Inspector Ford said. 'Now I know this kidnapping was a put-up job. I believe you're in on it and are splitting the money.'

### How Did Inspector Ford Know?

Although Kermit Kroll did still live with his parents, they were eighty and he was sixty. Actual kidnappers would never abduct a sixty-year-old child, as it makes no sense.

# The Ransom of Red Chief

## *O. Henry*

It looked like a good thing: but wait till I tell you. We were down in South, in Alabama – Bill Driscoll and myself – when this kidnapping idea struck us. It was, as Bill afterward expressed it, 'during a moment of temporary mental apparition'; but we didn't find that out till later.

There was a town down there, as flat as a flannel-cake, and called Summit, of course. It contained inhabitants of as undeleterious and self-satisfied a class of peasantry as ever clustered around a Maypole.

Bill and me had a joint capital of about six hundred dollars, and we needed just two thousand dollars more to pull off a fraudulent town-lot scheme in Western Illinois with. We talked it over on the front steps of the hotel. Philoprogenitiveness, says we, is strong in semi-rural communities; therefore, and for other reasons, a kidnapping project ought to do better there than in the radius of newspapers that send reporters out in plain clothes to stir up talk about such things. We knew that Summit couldn't get after us with anything stronger than constables and, maybe, some lackadaisical bloodhounds and a diatribe or two in the *Weekly Farmers' Budget*. So, it looked good.

We selected for our victim the only child of a prominent citizen named Ebenezer Dorset. The father was respectable and tight, a mortgage fancier and a stern, upright collection-plate passer and forecloser. The kid was a boy of ten, with bas-relief freckles, and hair the colour of the cover of the magazine you buy at the news-stand when you want to catch a train. Bill and me figured that Ebenezer would melt down for a ransom of two thousand dollars to a cent. But wait till I tell you.

About two miles from Summit was a little mountain, covered with a dense cedar brake. On the rear elevation of this mountain was a cave. There we stored provisions.

One evening after sundown, we drove in a buggy past old Dorset's house. The kid was in the street, throwing rocks at a kitten on the opposite fence.

'Hey, little boy!' says Bill, 'would you like to have a bag of candy and a nice ride?'

The boy catches Bill neatly in the eye with a piece of brick.

'That will cost the old man an extra five hundred dollars,' says Bill, climbing over the wheel.

That boy put up a fight like a welter-weight cinnamon bear; but at last, we got him down in the bottom of the buggy and drove away. We took him up to the cave, and I hitched the horse in the cedar brake. After dark I drove the buggy to the little village, three miles away, where we had hired it, and walked back to the mountain.

Bill was pasting court-plaster over the scratches and bruises on his features. There was a fire burning behind the big rock at the entrance of the cave, and the boy was watching a pot of boiling coffee, with two buzzard tailfeathers stuck in his red hair. He points a stick at me when I come up, and says:

'Ha! cursed paleface, do you dare to enter the camp of Red Chief, the terror of the plains?'

'He's all right now,' says Bill, rolling up his trousers and examining some bruises on his shins. 'We're playing Indian. We're making Buffalo Bill's show look like magic-lantern views of Palestine in the town hall. I'm Old Hank, the Trapper, Red Chief's captive, and I'm to be scalped at daybreak. By Geronimo! that kid can kick hard.'

Yes, sir, that boy seemed to be having the time of his life. The fun of camping out in a cave had made him forget that he was a captive himself. He immediately christened me Snake-eye, the Spy, and announced that, when his braves returned from the warpath, I was to be broiled at the stake at the rising of the sun.

Then we had supper; and he filled his mouth full of bacon and bread and gravy, and began to talk. He made a during-dinner speech something like this;

'I like this fine. I never camped out before; but I had a pet 'possum once, and I was nine last birthday. I hate to go to school. Rats ate up sixteen of Jimmy Talbot's aunt's speckled hen's eggs. Are there any real Indians in these woods? I want some more gravy. Does the trees moving make the wind blow? We had five puppies. What makes your nose so red, Hank? My father has lots of money. Are the stars hot? I whipped Ed Walker twice, Saturday. I don't like girls. You dassent catch toads unless with a string. Do oxen make any noise? Why are oranges round? Have you got beds to sleep on in this cave? Amos Murray has got six toes. A parrot can talk but a monkey or a fish can't. How many does it take to make twelve?'

Every few minutes he would remember that he was a pesky redskin, and pick up his stick rifle and tiptoe to the mouth of the cave to rubber for the scouts of the hated paleface. Now and then he would let out a war-whoop that made Old Hank the Trapper shiver. That boy had Bill terrorized from the start.

'Red Chief,' says I to the kid, 'would you like to go home?'

'Aw, what for?' says he. 'I don't have any fun at home. I hate to go to school. I like to camp out. You won't take me back home again, Snake-eye, will you?'

'Not right away,' says I. 'We'll stay here in the cave a while.'

'All right!' says he. 'That'll be fine. I never had such fun in all my life.'

We went to bed about eleven o'clock. We spread down some wide blankets and quilts and put Red Chief between us. We weren't afraid he'd run away. He kept us awake for three hours, jumping up and reaching for his rifle and screeching, 'Hist! pard,' in mine and Bill's ears, as the fancied crackle of a twig or the rustle of a leaf revealed to his young imagination the stealthy approach of the outlaw band. At last, I fell into a troubled sleep, and dreamed that I had been kidnapped and chained to a tree by a ferocious pirate with red hair.

Just at daybreak, I was awakened by a series of awful screams from Bill. They weren't yells, or howls, or shouts, or whoops, or yawps, such as you'd expect from a manly set of vocal organs – they were simply indecent, terrifying, humiliating screams, such as women emit when they see ghosts or caterpillars. It's an awful thing to hear a strong, desperate, fat man scream incontinently in a cave at daybreak.

I jumped up to see what the matter was. Red Chief was sitting on Bill's chest, with one hand twined in Bill's hair. In the other he had the sharp case-knife we used for slicing bacon; and he was industriously and realistically trying to take Bill's scalp, according to the sentence that had been pronounced upon him the evening before.

I got the knife away from the kid and made him lie down again. But, from that moment, Bill's spirit was broken. He laid down on his side of the bed, but he never closed an eye again in sleep as long as that boy was with us. I dozed off for a while, but along toward sun-up I remembered that Red Chief had said I was to be burned at the stake at the rising of the sun. I wasn't nervous or afraid; but I sat up and lit my pipe and leaned against a rock.

'What you getting up so soon for, Sam?' asked Bill.

'Me?' says I. 'Oh, I got a kind of pain in my shoulder. I thought sitting up would rest it.'

'You're a liar!' says Bill. 'You're afraid. You was to be burned at sunrise, and you was afraid he'd do it. And he would, too, if he could find a match. Ain't it awful, Sam? Do you think anybody will pay out money to get a little imp like that back home?'

'Sure,' said I. 'A rowdy kid like that is just the kind that parents dote on. Now, you and the Chief get up and cook breakfast, while I go up on the top of this mountain and reconnoitre.'

I went up on the peak of the little mountain and ran my eye over the contiguous vicinity. Over toward Summit I expected to see the sturdy yeomanry of the village armed with scythes and pitchforks beating the country-side for the dastardly kidnappers. But what I saw was a peaceful landscape dotted with one man ploughing with a dun mule. Nobody was dragging the creek; no couriers dashed hither and yon, bringing tidings of no news to the distracted parents. There was a sylvan attitude of somnolent sleepiness pervading that section of the external outward surface of Alabama that lay exposed to my view. 'Perhaps,' says I to myself, 'it has not yet been discovered that the wolves have borne away the tender lambkin from the fold. Heaven help the wolves!' says I, and I went down the mountain to breakfast.

When I got to the cave I found Bill backed up against the side of it, breathing hard, and the boy threatening to smash him with a rock half as big as a coconut.

'He put a red-hot boiled potato down my back,' explained Bill, 'and then mashed it with his foot; and I boxed his ears. Have you got a gun about you, Sam?'

I took the rock away from the boy and kind of patched up the argument. 'I'll fix you,' says the kid to Bill. 'No man ever yet struck the Red Chief but what he got paid for it. You better beware!'

After breakfast the kid takes a piece of leather with strings wrapped around it out of his pocket and goes outside the cave unwinding it.

'What's he up to now?' says Bill anxiously. 'You don't think he'll run away, do you Sam?'

'No fear of it,' says I. 'He don't seem to be much of a home body. But we've got to fix up some plan about the ransom. There don't seem to be much excitement around Summit on account of his disappearance; but maybe they haven't realized yet that he's gone. His folks may think he's spending the night with Aunt Jane or one of the neighbours. Anyhow, he'll be missed to-day. To-night we must get a message to his father demanding the two thousand dollars for his return.'

Just then we heard a kind of war-whoop, such as David might have emitted when he knocked out the champion Goliath. It was a sling that Red Chief had pulled out of his pocket, and he was whirling it around his head.

I dodged, and heard a heavy thud and a kind of a sigh from Bill, like a horse gives out when you take his saddle off. A niggerhead rock the size of an egg had caught Bill just behind his left ear. He loosened himself all over and fell in the fire across the frying-pan of hot water for washing the dishes. I dragged him out and poured cold water on his head for half an hour.

By and by, Bill sits up and feels behind his ear and says: 'Sam, do you know who my favourite Biblical character is?'

'Take it easy,' says I. 'You'll come to your senses presently.'

'King Herod,' says he. 'You won't go away and leave me here alone, will you, Sam?'

I went out and caught that boy and shook him until his freckles rattled.

'If you don't behave,' says I, 'I'll take you straight home. Now, are you going to be good, or not?'

'I was only funning,' says he sullenly, 'I didn't mean to hurt Old Hank. But what did he hit me for? I'll behave, Snake-eye, if you won't send me home, and if you'll let me play the Black Scout to-day.'

'I don't know the game,' says I. 'That's for you and Mr Bill to decide. He's your playmate for the day. I'm going away for a while, on business. Now, you come in and make friends with him, and say you are sorry for hurting him, or home you go, at once.'

I made him and Bill shake hands, and then I took Bill aside and told him I was going to Poplar Cove, a little village three miles from the cave, and find out what I could about how the kidnapping had been regarded in Summit. Also, I thought it best to send a peremptory letter to old man Dorset that day, demanding the ransom and dictating how it should be paid.

'You know, Sam,' says Bill, 'I've stood by you without batting an eye in earthquakes, fire and flood – in poker games, dynamite outrages, police raids, train robberies and cyclones. I never lost my nerve yet till we kidnapped that two-legged skyrocket of a kid. He's got me going. You won't leave me long with him, will you, Sam?'

'I'll be back some time this afternoon,' says I. 'You must keep the boy amused and quiet till I return. And now we'll write the letter to old Dorset.'

Bill and I got paper and pencil and worked on the letter while Red Chief, with a blanket wrapped around him, strutted up and down, guarding the mouth of the cave. Bill begged me tearfully to make the ransom fifteen hundred dollars instead of two thousand. 'I ain't attempting,' says he, 'to decry the celebrated moral aspect of parental affection, but we're dealing with humans, and it ain't human for anybody to give up two thousand dollars for that forty-pound chunk of freckled wildcat. I'm willing to take a chance at fifteen hundred dollars. You can charge the difference up to me.'

So, to relieve Bill, I acceded, and we collaborated a letter that ran this way:

EBENEZER DORSET, ESQ.:

*We have your boy concealed in a place far from Summit. It is useless for you or the most skilful detectives to attempt to find him. Absolutely the only terms on which you can have him restored to you are these: We demand fifteen-hundred dollars in large bills for his return; the money to be left at midnight to-night at the same spot and in the same box as your reply – as hereinafter described. If you agree to these terms, send your answer in writing by a solitary messenger to-night at half-past eight o'clock. After crossing Owl Creek, on the road to Poplar Cove, there are three large trees about a hundred yards apart, close to the fence of the wheat-field on the right-hand side. At the bottom of the fence-post, opposite the third tree, will be found a small pasteboard box.*

*The messenger will place the answer in this box and return immediately to Summit.*

*If you attempt any treachery or fail to comply with our demand as stated,*
*you will never see your boy again.*

*If you pay the money as demanded, he will be returned to you safe and well*
*within three hours. These terms are final, and if you do not accede to them no*
*further communication will be attempted.*

TWO DESPERATE MEN.

I addressed this letter to Dorset, and put it in my pocket. As I was
about to start, the kid comes up to me and says: 'Aw, Snake-eye, you
said I could play the Black Scout while you was gone.'

'Play it, of course,' says I. 'Mr Bill will play with you. What kind of
game is it?'

'I'm the Black Scout,' says Red Chief, 'and I have to ride to the
stockade to warn the settlers that the Indians are coming. I'm tired of
playing Indian myself. I want to be the Black Scout.'

'All right,' says I. 'It sounds harmless to me. I guess Mr Bill will help
you foil the pesky savages.'

'What am I to do?' asks Bill, looking at the kid suspiciously.

'You are the hoss,' says Black Scout. 'Get down on your hands and
knees. How can I ride to the stockade without a hoss?'

'You'd better keep him interested,' said I, 'till we get the scheme
going. Loosen up.'

Bill gets down on his all fours, and a look comes in his eye like a
rabbit's when you catch it in a trap.

'How far is it to the stockade, kid?' he asks in a husky manner of
voice.

'Ninety miles,' says the Black Scout. 'And you have to hump yourself
to get there on time. Whoa, now!'

The Black Scout jumps on Bill's back and digs his heels in his side.

'For Heaven's sake,' says Bill, 'hurry back, Sam, as soon as you can. I
wish we hadn't made the ransom more than a thousand. Say, you quit
kicking me or I'll get up and warm you good.'

I walked over to Poplar Cove and sat around the post office and store,
talking with the chaw-bacons that came in to trade. One whiskerando
says that he fears Summit is all upset on account of Elder Ebenezer
Dorset's boy having been lost or stolen. That was all I wanted to know.
I bought some smoking tobacco, referred casually to the price of black-
eyed peas, posted my letter surreptitiously and came away. The

postmaster said the mail-carrier would come by in an hour to take the mail on to Summit.

When I got back to the cave Bill and the boy were not to be found. I explored the vicinity of the cave, and risked a yodel or two, but there was no response.

So I lighted my pipe and sat down on a mossy bank to await developments.

In about half an hour I heard the bushes rustle, and Bill wabbled out into the little glade in front of the cave. Behind him was the kid stepping softly like a scout, with a broad grin on his face. Bill stopped, took off his hat and wiped his face with a red handkerchief. The kid stopped about eight feet behind him.

'Sam,' says Bill, 'I suppose you'll think I'm a renegade, but I couldn't help it. I'm a grown person with masculine proclivities and habits of self-defence, but there is a time when all systems of egotism and predominance fail. The boy is gone. I have sent him home. All is off. There was martyrs in old times,' goes on Bill, 'that suffered death rather than give up the particular graft they enjoyed. None of 'em ever was subjugated to such supernatural tortures as I have been. I tried to be faithful to our articles of depredation; but there came a limit.'

'What's the trouble, Bill?' I asks him.

'I was rode,' says Bill, 'the ninety miles to the stockade, not barring an inch. Then, when the settler was rescued, I was given oats. Sand ain't a palatable substitute. And then, for an hour I had to try to explain to him why there was nothin' in holes, how a road can run both ways and what makes the grass green. I tell you, Sam, a human can only stand so much. I takes him by the neck of his clothes and drags him down the mountain. On the way he kicks my legs black-and-blue from the knees down; and I've got to have two or three bites on my thumb and hand cauterized.

'But he's gone' – continues Bill – 'gone home. I showed him the road to Summit and kicked him about eight feet nearer there at one kick. I'm sorry we lose the ransom; but it was either that or Bill Driscoll to the madhouse.'

Bill is puffing and blowing, but there is a look of ineffable peace and growing content on his rose-pink features.

'Bill,' says I, 'there isn't any heart disease in your family, is there?'

'No,' says Bill, 'nothing chronic except malaria and accidents. Why?'

'Then you might turn around,' says I, 'and have a look behind you.'

Bill turns and sees the boy and loses his complexion and sits down plump on the ground and begins to pluck aimlessly at grass and little sticks. For an hour I was afraid of his mind. And then I told him that my scheme was to put the whole job through immediately and that we would get the ransom and be off with it by midnight if old Dorset fell in with our proposition. So Bill braced up enough to give the kid a weak sort of a smile and a promise to play the Russian in a Japanese war with him as soon as he felt a little better.

I had a scheme for collecting that ransom without danger of being caught by counterplots that ought to commend itself to professional kidnappers. The tree under which the answer was to be left – and the money later on – was close to the road fence with big, bare fields on all sides. If a gang of constables should be watching for anyone to come for the note they could see him a long way off crossing the fields or in the road. But no, siree! At half-past eight I was up in that tree as well hidden as a tree toad, waiting for the messenger to arrive.

Exactly on time, a half-grown boy rides up the road on a bicycle, locates the pasteboard box at the foot of the fencepost, slips a folded piece of paper into it and pedals away again back toward Summit.

I waited an hour and then concluded the thing was square. I slid down the tree, got the note, slipped along the fence till I struck the woods, and was back at the cave in another half an hour. I opened the note, got near the lantern and read it to Bill. It was written with a pen in a crabbed hand, and the sum and substance of it was this:

TWO DESPERATE MEN.

GENTLEMEN – *I received your letter to-day by post, in regard to the ransom you ask for the return of my son. I think you are a little high in your demands, and I hereby make you a counter-proposition, which I am inclined to believe you will accept. You bring Johnny home and pay me two hundred and fifty dollars in cash, and I agree to take him off your hands. You had better come at night, for the neighbours believe he is lost, and I couldn't be responsible for what they would do to anybody they saw bringing him back.*

*Very respectfully,*

EBENEZER DORSET.

'Great pirates of Penzance!' says I; 'of all the impudent—'

But I glanced at Bill, and hesitated. He had the most appealing look in his eyes I ever saw on the face of a dumb or a talking brute.

'Sam,' says he, 'what's two hundred and fifty dollars, after all? We've got the money. One more night of this kid will send me to a bed in Bedlam. Besides being a thorough gentleman, I think Mr. Dorset is a spendthrift for making us such a liberal offer. You ain't going to let the chance go, are you?'

'Tell you the truth, Bill,' says I, 'this little ewe lamb has somewhat got on my nerves to. We'll take him home, pay the ransom and make our get-away.'

We took him home that night. We got him to go by telling him that his father had bought a silver-mounted rifle and a pair of moccasins for him, and we were going to hunt bears the next day.

It was just twelve o'clock when we knocked at Ebenezer's front door. Just at the moment when I should have been abstracting the fifteen hundred dollars from the box under the tree, according to the original proposition, Bill was counting out two hundred and fifty dollars into Dorset's hand.

When the kid found out we were going to leave him at home he started up a howl like a calliope and fastened himself as tight as a leech to Bill's leg. His father peeled him away gradually, like a porous plaster.

'How long can you hold him?' asks Bill.

'I'm not as strong as I used to be,' says old Dorset, 'but I think I can promise you ten minutes.'

'Enough,' says Bill. 'In ten minutes I shall cross the Central, Southern and Middle Western States, and be legging it trippingly for the Canadian border.'

And, as dark as it was, and as fat as Bill was, and as good a runner as I am, he was a good mile and a half out of Summit before I could catch up with him.

# William is Hypnotised

## Richmal Crompton

It seemed to William and his friends the Outlaws as if school had been comparatively peaceful till Bertie appeared upon the scene. Bertie was the headmaster's nephew who had come to the school for a term only (which to some of his associates seemed long enough – if not too long) and stayed with his uncle. Unfortunately he was in William's form. Everybody except William and his form agreed that Bertie was charming. He had a beautiful smile and beautiful manners. Old ladies were often heard to declare that he must have a beautiful soul. He would recite beautiful poetry for hours on end without stopping. He had a beautiful conscience. It was 'his beautiful conscience that annoyed the Outlaws most. His beautiful conscience was always making him tell his uncle anything that he thought his uncle ought to know. And the things which he thought his uncle ought to know were just the things which the Outlaws thought his uncle ought not to know. For instance, Bertie thought that his uncle ought to know that the Outlaws were keeping white mice in their desks, while the Outlaws on the other hand did not consider it at all necessary for his uncle to know this. Again, Bertie's beautiful conscience forced him to tell his uncle that it was the Outlaws who had stitched up the sleeves of his gown so securely that he had to go about for a whole morning without it, and this again the Outlaws did not consider it necessary for his uncle to know. Bertie thought that his uncle ought to know that it was the Outlaws who, when a committee meeting was being held at the school, had changed the position of all the neatly printed little notices, 'To the Committee room,' so that the committee, after wandering desolately round and round the corridor, found themselves ultimately in the bootroom in the basement. All these things Bertie conscientiously reported to his uncle, and his uncle visited the full force of his wrath upon the Outlaws. The uncle, as a matter of fact, did not quite approve of Bertie's beautiful conscience, but he could not resist the temptation to get a bit of his own back on the Outlaws. He'd suffered in (comparative) silence from the Outlaws for so long. He'd always found it so difficult ever to lay the crimes of which he was certain that the Outlaws were responsible at the Outlaws' door, that it was impossible to resist the circumstantial evidence laid ready to his hand day by day by the conscientious Bertie. The result of all this was that the advent of Bertie coincided with a period of what the Outlaws regarded as unmerited persecution for the Outlaws themselves. Sometimes idly on the way home from school the Outlaws laid tentative plans of vengeance upon Bertie, but they never came to anything because the Outlaws tempered boldness with discretion. A mass attack upon the unctuous Bertie would be highly enjoyable, but the resultant interview with Bertie's uncle would be less so. The Outlaws cherished a deep respect for Bertie's uncle's right arm. They had come into pretty frequent contact with it, they were good judges of its strength and they knew that it was not to be unduly provoked.

'What it comes to,' said William indignantly as they walked home discussing the situation, 'what it comes to is that we simply can't do *anythin'* excitin', not while he's about, simply can't do *anythin'* . . .'

'There was yesterday,' agreed Ginger disconsolately, 'when he went an' told old Markie that it was *me* what had put the hedgehog into Mr Hopkins' desk.'

A blissful smile dawned upon William's freckled countenance. 'It was funny, wasn't it?' he said simply, 'watchin' him put his hand into the desk without lookin' to get his ruler out an' then seein' his face . . .'

Ginger gave a constrained smile. 'Yes,' he said, 'I daresay it seems funny to you. It seemed funny to me yesterday but you din't have to go up to *him* about it this mornin'. An' that old Bertie grinnin' at me all over the place afterwards . . .'

'Never mind,' said Henry consolingly, 'it's only for a few weeks now. He's goin' at the end of the term.'

'What worries me,' said William slowly, 'what worries me is lettin' him go at the end an' nothin' happenin' to him. I mean him goin' round makin' trouble all over the place like this an' then jus' goin' off at the end of the term an' *nothin'* happenin' to him.'

'Let's jus' be glad he's going off at all,' said Douglas philosophically, 'an' never mind nothin' happenin' to him. Let's jus' be glad that things 'll stop happenin' to *us*.'

"Sides,' said Henry, 'if we *did* do anythin' to him . . . you know what he is . . . he'd tell *him* an' then jus' go about grinnin' at us. You know what he is.'

'Yes,' said William sadly and thoughtfully, 'we know what he *is*, but – it jus' seems a pity, that's all.'

It was the Vicar's wife who first suggested the pageant, but once suggested the idea took root firmly in the village. Mrs Bott of the Hall took it up and so did Mrs Lane and Mrs Franks and Mrs Robinson and all the rest of them.

Arrangements went on apace. The junior inhabitants of the village looked on with apathy. 'No children to be in it' had been pronounced very early on in the proceedings. The activities of the Outlaws may have had something to do with the distrust with which the senior element of the village regarded the junior.

William and the Outlaws treated the whole affair with superior contempt.

'A pageant!' said William scornfully, 'Huh! An ole *pageant*. Jus' dressin' up in silly clothes an' having a procession. Jus' a lot of silly ole grown-ups. Huh! Well, I bet I could make a better pageant than that ole thing, if I tried. I *bet* I could. Well, *I* wun't be in it not if they asked me. I'm *glad* they've not asked me 'cause I wun't be in it not if they did.'

He was none the less disconcerted and secretly much annoyed to hear that despite the ban on children Bertie was to be in it. Bertie was to be Queen Elizabeth's page.

Queen Elizabeth was Mrs Bertram of The Limes. She was a newcomer to the village and her most striking characteristic was a likeness to the Virgin Queen as represented in her more famous portraits. She considered it a great social asset and was never tired of drawing attention to it. It was, as a matter of fact, Mrs Bertram who had first suggested the pageant to the Vicar's wife. And despite the reluctance of the committee and the ban they had placed on the younger generation, Mrs Bertram had insisted on having a boy page.

'We've – er – never found it wise,' objected the Vicar's wife mysteriously.

'But where I used to live,' said Mrs Bertram indignantly, 'we always had children in the pageants. Without exception. There's something so

romantic and beautiful about children.' Mrs Bertram, it is perhaps
unnecessary to add, had no children of her own.

The Vicar's wife cleared her throat and spoke again still
mysteriously.

'Perhaps,' she said. 'Quite. But one or two occasions in this village
have been spoilt – *wrecked* by the presence of certain children.'

'The children of this village,' said Mrs Franks still with something of
the Vicar's wife's mysteriousness in her tone, 'seem, I don't know why,
to bring bad luck to anything they take part in—'

Someone seemed to murmur the two words 'William Brown' in the
background and then they all changed the subject.

But the next day Mrs Bertram met Bertie and fell in love with him at
once. She found him 'adorable' and at the next pageant committee
meeting she announced her firm intention of having him for her page.

'I *must*,' she said, 'I *must* have a page and he's a perfectly adorable
boy. He'll look sweet in white satin.'

'Oh, *he's* all right,' said the Vicar's wife with relief, 'there couldn't be
any harm in having *him*. It's—' again she dropped her voice and spoke
darkly, mysteriously, 'it's some of the others.'

So it was decided that Bertie was to be Queen Elizabeth's page.


Bertie received the honour complacently. He, like Mrs Bertram,
thought that he was eminently suitable for a page. Moreover, his
position as the only boy in the village admitted to the pageant delighted
him. While still retaining his charming manners towards the grown-
ups he began to put on more and more side when with his con-
temporaries. He was enjoying his position of supremacy over the
Outlaws. He had a pretty well-founded idea that William, despite his
professed scorn, would have loved to be in the pageant. He smiled
sweetly and meaningly at William in public and in private informed his
uncle that it was William who had introduced the mouse into the
drawing class and the handful of squibs into the anthracite stove . . .


Bertie joined William in the playground where William and the
Outlaws were playing leap frog during 'break.'

'Hello, William,' he said pleasantly.

He always affected great friendliness of manner towards William and
the Outlaws.

William, gathering together all his forces, took a mighty leap over both Ginger's and Douglas' back, landed on his nose, picked himself up, said 'Crumbs!' in a tone that expressed mingled pride in his exploit and concern for his nose and ignored equally Bertie's presence and greeting.

'You've heard about the pageant they're going to have in the village, haven't you?' went on Bertie, still with his most engaging smile.

William addressed his Outlaws still as though not seeing Bertie. 'Bet I can do three of you,' he said vaingloriously. 'Come on, Henry . . . you stand with Ginger and Douglas and I bet I'll do all three of you.'

'They decided not to have any children in at first,' went on Bertie suavely, 'but in the end they're to have just one for Queen Elizabeth's page. Me.'

Ginger, Douglas and Henry crouched down. William went back, took a mighty run, a mighty leap and – landed on the top of Douglas and Henry. The wriggling mass of Outlaws disentangled themselves. William's nose, brought a second time in violent contact with the asphalt playground, began to bleed copiously. William held to it a grimy handkerchief already saturated in ink and mud and watched with interest the effect of the introduction of the fresh colour.

Douglas was persisting with great indignation that William had broken his neck and Henry was accusing Ginger of having completely altered the shape of his head by sitting on it violently on the asphalt. They abused each other with gusto and great impartiality.

'Sayin' you could jump three an' then bangin' down upon us like that . . . I tell you my neck's completely broke. I can feel it.'

'You couldn't go on livin' if your neck was broke.'

'Well, I prob'ly won't go on livin'. I feel almost as if I was dyin' now.'

'Well, you must've stretched out after I started – all of you. You didn't look as stretched out as all that before I started . . . and look at my nose . . . your neck can't be so bad 'cause it's not even bleedin'.'

'You don't know what it *feels* like havin' someone *sittin'* on your head. It's absolutely squashed up my ears somethin' terrible.'

'Jolly good thing. They stuck out enough before.'

Above the fracas came again Bertie's sweet and patient and gentlemanly little voice.

'I'm going to be Queen Elizabeth's page. I'm going to be the only boy in the pageant.'

'I'll try again,' said William, still holding his handkerchief to his bleeding nose. 'I bet I do it this time. I din' go back far enough that time before I started an' I bet if I go far enough back and you keep more squashed up together I can do all three of you.'

'No, thanks,' said Ginger holding his neck in both hands. 'I'm not goin' to be jumped on again with a broken neck.'

'Nor me,' said Henry tenderly caressing his ears, 'with squashed ears.'

A crowd of boys had gathered round.

Bertie again upraised his clear young voice.

'Don't you wish it was you going to be in the pageant instead of me, William?' he said.

William, his hair dishevelled, his collar burst open, his nose still bleeding, turned and surveyed him with slow scorn.

'Huh!' he said, 'you think you're goin' to be in the pageant, do you? Huh! Well, let *me* tell *you*, you're *not*. An' you think I'm not goin' to be, do you? Well, let *me* tell *you*, I *am*.'

It was a momentous announcement. There was a dead silence. Everybody gazed at William with surprise. Then Bertie giggled.

'You needn't be so mad at me, William,' he said. '*I* didn't tell uncle that you put the mouse in the drawing class.'

At that moment the bell rang.

No one had been more surprised by William's announcement than William himself. He had as a matter of fact felt a certain secret soreness at Bertie's inclusion in the pageant. Had William been asked to be a page in the pageant in the first instance his indignation and scorn would have known no bounds. But the fact that children were expressly excluded had filled him with as great an indignation as the enforced inclusion of him in any capacity would have caused him. And the further news that the ban had been raised in favour of Bertie – and Bertie alone – was regarded by William as an insult.

But until William saw the faces of his schoolmates, impressed despite themselves by his solemn prophecy, he had hardly realised what he had said. He had meant merely to reply crushingly to the obnoxious Bertie. He found that he had issued a challenge which he must justify or lose his prestige for ever. He spent the next two lessons (Geography and History) biting his pencil frowningly and wondering how on earth he could eject Bertie from the pageant and insert himself. He had a dark suspicion that even were he successful in ejecting Bertie he would be the last boy in the village to be chosen as page in his stead. He was so quiet during those lessons that the Geography and History masters, comparing notes afterwards, thought (without any great regret) that perhaps he was sickening for something.

On the way home with Ginger, Douglas and Henry he was still thoughtful. After a desultory conversation on the state of William's nose and Ginger's neck and Henry's ears and the question whether William could or could not have cleared them if he'd had a longer run and they'd been closer together, and a brief commentation on the dulness of the Geography and History lessons (William's failure to provide the usual diversions had been much resented by his classmates), Henry suddenly said:

'I say, William, what you said, 'bout him not bein' in the pageant, you din' *mean* it, did you?'

Nothing on earth would ever induce William to retire from a position he had once taken up.

''Course I did!' said William.

'Well, how c'n you make him not be in it an' you in it?' challenged Douglas incredulously.

William took refuge in a 'Huh!' dark with meaning and hidden triumph, and added, yet more darkly and mysteriously, 'Jus' you wait an' see.'

Rather to William's consternation his prophecy spread round the school and opinion on the subject became sharply divided. William's followers supported William and Bertie's followers supported Bertie. For Bertie had a following and quite a large one. Any boy who lived as Bertie lived in close proximity to the head master and suffered from such a beautiful conscience as Bertie's would have had a large following among a certain kind of boy. Though only, as I said, boys of a certain kind, they were very enthusiastic and admiring followers. They delighted in jeering at William from behind hedges and from the safe protection of their garden walls.

'Yah! Who thinks he's going' to be in the pageant? *Yah!* Who thinks he's goin' to be a page? YAH!'

On these occasions William, passing below, assumed his famous

expressionless expression and was apparently deaf, dumb and blind so
that the pleasure of jeering at him was small indeed. William possessed
the art of retaining an utterly impassive, almost imbecile, cast of
features in face of all provocation. It had always been one of his most
potent weapons. Whenever the jeerers ventured into open country it
was quite different. William then allowed his natural expressions and
actions free play. William's followers supported him loyally. Their faith
in him was unbounded.

''Course he's goin' to be in the pageant,' they said. 'Jus' you wait an'
see.'

It was a common sight during that time to see a follower of William's
engaged in personal combat with a follower of Bertie as the only means
in their power of deciding whether or no William would be in the
pageant in Bertie's place.

William's immediate circle – the Outlaws – though their official
attitude was that there was no doubt at all that William would be in the
pageant, and that Bertie would not, were in private apprehensive.

'I don' see how you're goin' to get into the ole pageant,' said Ginger
despondently.

William, even before his Outlaws, preserved the attitude of the hero
who trusts in his star.

''*Course* I am,' he said with his inimitable swagger, 'jus' you wait an'
see.'

But in his heart William too felt apprehensive. The day of the pageant
grew nearer. Bertie was attending rehearsals and behaving as beautifully as ever and there seemed no likelihood at all of his being ejected.
For a few days William made frenzied efforts to establish himself in
general public opinion as the sort of boy who would make a suitable
page, but he soon gave them up. He himself found the process too
wearing and no one else seemed to notice it. Wild plans of imprisoning
Bertie and stealing his costume were dismissed as impossible. The day
of the pageant drew nearer and nearer. William looked forward to it
now solely as a day of humiliation. He regretted bitterly his rash
prophecy, though in public he continued doggedly to support it with
innumerable 'Huhs' and ''*course* I ams.' The personal humiliation
William minded less than the humiliation to his loyal followers who
were fighting so many battles on his behalf.

*　　*　　*　　*　　*　　*

The day of the pageant had arrived. The pageant was to pass along the village street and the boys of William's school, including William, were to be massed outside the school to cheer it on its way. The only member of the school who would not be present was Bertie who would be in the pageant as Queen Elizabeth's page. Bertie had gone home for the weekend to visit his parents and to fetch the page's suit which his mother had made for him. Bertie was enjoying his triumph over William. To make it yet more enjoyable he had told his uncle just before he went away that it was William who had uprooted the daffodils in his garden bed by night and planted rows of brussel sprouts in their stead, and William had had a painful interview with the Head on the subject that very morning. As it happens to be one of the few crimes committed in the neighbourhood for which in reality William was not responsible, he felt perhaps unduly bitter about it, forgetting, as one is apt to do on such occasions, how many crimes he had perpetrated successfully and without retribution.

He walked slowly along the road with Ginger and Henry and Douglas.

'*Well*,' commented Ginger with a deep sigh. There was no need to ask what he meant. The day had come and William's public downfall seemed imminent and inevitable.

'Yes,' said Douglas bitterly. 'I dunno why you kept sayin' all the time that you *was* goin' to be in it.'

'Yes,' said Henry with spirit, 'why ever did you go an' *say* a silly thing like that for?'

'Oh, shut up!' groaned William, relinquishing his heroic pose and abandoning himself to his depression.

And just then they saw the figure of Bertie coming jauntily down the road towards them with a suitcase in one hand. He approached them with his beautiful smile.

'Hello!' he said. 'I've been home for the weekend. Got my page's clothes with me in the case. I'll have to be quick and change or I shan't be ready on time. You goin' to watch, I suppose!'

His meaning smile flickered at William as he spoke. William had assumed again his expressionless expression.

'S'pose we'll have to,' said Ginger with an air of boredom.

'I've had a jolly good time at home for the week end,' went on Bertie who was evidently longing to confide in someone.

'An uncle took me to a sort of show,' he went on excitedly, 'an' I saw a hypnotiser – you know, a man what hypnotised people an' they did whatever he told them.'

'How'd he do it?' said William.

'He jus' looked at 'em an' moved his hands about an' then told them they were cats or dogs or rabbits till he told em' to stop an' when they came to they didn't remember anythin' about it.'

William was silent for a minute the he said slowly: 'Bet you couldn' do it on me.'

'I bet I could if I tried,' said Bertie.

'All right,' said William. 'Go on, try.'

Bertie, after a moment's hesitation, put down his suit-case and made several passes with his hands before William's face.

'Now you're a cat,' he said without much conviction.

To the surprise of both Bertie and the watching Outlaws William promptly dropped on hands and knees and began to miaow loudly. Bertie's face beamed with pleasure.

'Now you're a dog,' he said.

William began to bark.

'Now you're a rabbit,' said Bertie almost drunk with delight and pride. William, not quite knowing what else to do, wrinkled his nose up and down.

'Now you can come unhypnotised.'

William stood up slowly and blinked. 'I don't remember doin' anythin',' he said. 'I bet I din' do anythin'.'

'But you *did*,' squeaked Bertie excitedly, 'you *did*. You acted like a cat and a dog and a rabbit.' He appealed to Henry, Douglas and Ginger, 'didn't he?'

Henry and Douglas and Ginger, who were not quite sure yet what William wanted of them but were prepared blindly to support him in anything, merely nodded.

'*There!*' said Bertie triumphantly.

'I don't believe you,' said William, 'anyway, try again . . . try something harder – cats and dogs and rabbits are easy, I expect – trying making me do somethin' I can't do ordin'ry. I can't turn cart wheels ordin'ry.'

The Outlaws gasped at this amazing untruth. But Bertie believed it. He was ready to believe anything. He was drunk with his success as a hypnotist. Again he made passes before William's face and again William assumed the languishing expression which he believed suitable to one hypnotised. 'Turn cart wheels,' ordered Bertie. William turned six perfect cart wheels one after the other.

'Now come unhypnotised,' said Bertie quickly, anxious to prove his success.

'You did turn cart wheels, didn't he?' to Douglas, Ginger and Henry.

Again Douglas, Ginger and Henry nodded non-commitally.

''*Course* I didn't,' said William aggressively. 'I don' believe you. I *can*'t turn cart wheels.'

'But you can when you're hypnotised,' said Bertie, 'you can do things when you're hypnotised that you can't do when you're not hypnotised. You can do anything you're told to when you're hypnotised. I'm a hypnotiser, I am,' he swaggered about, 'I can make anyone do anythin' I like, I can.'

'I remember readin' about hypnotism in a book once,' said William slowly, 'it said that anyone could hypnotise people standin' jus' near them, but that only a very good hypnotiser could make someone do somethin' where he couldn't see them.'

'I could,' boasted Bertie, 'I bet I could. I'm a good hypnotiser, I am.'

'I don't b'lieve you did me at all,' said William calmly. 'I don't remember anythin'.'

'But you *don't* remember when you're hypnotised,' explained Bertie impatiently, 'that's all the point of it . . . you don't remember.'

'Then how'm I to know you *did* hypnotise me?' said William simply.

'*They* saw,' said Bertie pointing to his witnesses. 'I *did* hypnotise him, didn't I?'

The witnesses, still not quite sure what their leader's tactics were, again nodded non-committally.

'I don't b'lieve you, any of you,' said William defiantly, 'you're pullin' my leg – all of you. He didn't hypnotise me. I *didn't* carry on like a rabbit, or any of those things he said.'

Bertie stamped, almost in tears.

'You did . . . you *did*.'

It was evident that more than anything in the world at that moment he longed to convince William of his hypnotic powers.

'In this book I read,' went on William, 'it said that only very good hypnotisers could make anyone do anything with a suitcase. It said that those two were the hardest things that only very good hypnotisers could do – makin' anyone do something when they can't see 'em doin', an' makin' anyone do somethin' with a suitcase . . . But we've not got a suitcase here,' he glanced contemptuously at the case that contained Bertie's page's costume. 'That's too small to be a suitcase. It wun't do.'

'It *is* a suitcase and it would do,' said Bertie, 'it *would* do and I bet I could make you do something with it.'

'I bet you couldn't,' said William. 'I don't believe you're a hypnotiser at all. Tell you what,' slowly, 'I'll believe you if—'

'Yes?' said Bertie eagerly.

'If you c'n make me do the two hardest things – make me do somethin' with this suitcase an' make me do somethin' where you can't see me doin' it . . . Tell you what—' as though a sudden idea had just struck him.

'Yes?'

'I'll b'lieve you if you can make me take this suitcase down the road, an' in at our gate an' round to the back of our house an' back again here – an' tell me to do somethin' – anythin' – to prove to me that I've done it.'

''Course I can do that,' said Bertie boastingly. 'I can do that easy 's easy.'

'Well, do it then,' challenged William.

Bertie again made passes before his face and William composed his features again to that utter imbecility that was meant to imply the hypnotised state.

'Take the suitcase,' ordered Bertie, 'and take it down the road and round your house an' back again here an' do somethin' – anything – to show yourself that you've been hypnotised.'

Still wearing his expression of imbecility, William picked up the suitcase and walked down the road. The watchers saw him go down his drive and disappear behind his house. After a short interval he reappeared, still with the suitcase and still with his imbecile expression, though, a close observer might have noticed, rather breathless, came again along the drive up the road and joined the four watchers. He held something in his clasped hand. Bertie's face was a proud beam of triumph.

'There, you've *done* it,' he shouted gleefully. 'Now, come unhypnotised.'

William assumed his normal expression and blinked.

'I didn't do it,' he said. 'I told you, you couldn't make me do it.'

'But you *did* it,' screamed Bertie.

William slowly unclasped his hand and looked down at something he held in his palm.

'Crumbs!' he ejaculated as though deeply impressed, 'here's Jumble's ball what he was playing with this mornin' in the garden. I *knew* it was in the garden. So I *must*'ve jus' been there.'

'So you *know* I'm a hypnotiser now,' said Bertie with a swagger.

'Yes, I do,' said William, 'I know that you're a hypnotiser now.'

But at that moment the church clock struck two and Bertie suddenly remembered that as well as being a hypnotiser he was Queen Elizabeth's page.

'Crumbs!' he said seizing his suitcase, 'I must go and change or I'll be late.' He smiled maliciously at William. 'Hope you'll enjoy watchin' the procession,' he said as he ran off.

William, Ginger and Douglas and Henry stood and watched him.

Then William turned and, followed by the others, went quickly homewards.

Bertie stood in his bedroom surveying the contents of his suitcase. He found them amazing. They seemed to comprise not a page's costume but a much worn and tattered Red Indian costume. Still – he knew that his mother had made the costume in accordance with Mrs Bertram's directions. Perhaps Elizabeth's page wore this curious costume. Perhaps he didn't dress like other pages. Anyway his mother and Mrs Bertram ought to know. They'd arranged it between them. And there didn't seem to be anything else in the case. He turned it upside down. No . . . only this. This must be right. Anyway, the only thing to do was to put it on. It must be all right really. He put it on . . . fringed trousers and coat of a sort of khaki and a feathered head dress. He looked at it doubtfully in the mirror. Yes, it did look funny, but he supposed it must be all right . . . really he supposed that they must have made it from pictures of the real thing . . . it must be the sort of dress that Elizabeth's page really wore. . . . Funny . . . very funny . . . he'd never looked at it before and his mother had made it without trying it on, but if he hadn't *known* that it was a page's costume made by his mother according to directions sent to her by Mrs Bertram, he'd have thought that it was a Red Indian costume. It was just like a Red Indian costume. But he was late already. He hurried down to the Vicarage where the actors in the pageant were to assemble.

Mrs Bertram had been having hysterics on and off ever since she got up. Mrs Bertram was 'highly strung.' (Other people sometimes found a less flattering name for it.) Mrs Bertram often hinted to her friends that the very fact of her likeness to Queen Elizabeth was a strain on the nervous system which less heroic natures would have found unendurable. Everything seemed to have gone wrong with her since she began to dress for the pageant. Her dress was wrong, for one thing. She was sure that it was fuller than it ought to be. It took six or seven people to calm her about her dress. Then her hair was wrong. It wouldn't go right. The hairdresser came to do it and she tore it down again and had another fit of hysterics. The six or seven people managed with great difficulty to calm her again and get her hair up though she said that there was a fate against her and that she was going to sue the hairdresser for damages and that she'd never looked so hideous before in her life. The Vicar's wife with the kindest intention and merely in order to calm her, assured her that she had, and this brought on yet another attack. Then, fearing that the six or seven comforters were going to desert her, she said that her shoes were wrong. She said that they were the wrong shape and that they were too big. When her six or seven comforters had proved that they were not too big she had another fit of hysterics and said that they were too small. The whole cast was needed to calm her over the shoes and she said finally that she supposed she'd have to wear them and that she hoped she'd never again be called upon to suffer as she'd suffered that day and that people who weren't highly strung had no idea how terribly she suffered and that she got no sympathy and she knew she looked a sight and that if this was how she was going to be treated she'd never be in another pageant as long as she lived. Then she suddenly began to suffer about her page. She'd told him to be here an hour before time and he wasn't and she wouldn't act without a page. She didn't care what anyone said. She *wouldn't* act without a page. It was an insult to expect her to. Her comforters assured her that Bertie would be in time. Bertie had never been known to be late for anything. Then she began to suffer about Bertie's stockings. She'd said particularly to his mother that he must have good white silk stockings to go with his white satin suit and shoes and she was sure that he'd have common ones. If he came in common white silk stockings she wouldn't act in the pageant. She *wouldn't* act with a page with common white silk stockings. It would be an insult to expect her to. . . .

It was just a quarter past two and he hadn't come and she'd *told* him to be there by half-past one, and if he didn't come she wouldn't be in the pageant at all. She wouldn't stir a foot, and she'd sue them all for damages. She sat down on a chair with her back to the door and had another fit of hysterics. The whole cast had gathered round her. They were looking rather anxious. It was time to start on the procession and her page had not turned up and they saw that nothing on earth would persuade Gloriana to set off without him. She was still suffering terribly.

'I – I'll just send up to his uncle's, shall I?' Sir Walter Raleigh was suggesting when the door opened and Bertie stood upon the threshold dressed in the full panoply of a Red Indian. He smiled very sweetly at them all.

'I'm so sorry I'm so late,' he said. 'Am I all right?'

'Is that you, child?' said the Virgin Queen in a hoarse, suffering voice without turning her head.

'Yes,' said Bertie. 'I'm so sorry I'm late.'

The others were watching him, paralysed with horror.

'Have you got on *common* silk stockings?' said Elizabeth wearily, still without turning her head. 'I'm *worn* out body and soul by all this worry and anxiety and responsibility . . . have you got on *common* silk stockings, boy?'

Bertie looked down at his khaki frilled trousers.

'No,' he said brightly. 'No, I haven't got on common silk stockings at all.'

Elizabeth was evidently still too worn out in body and soul to turn her head. She appealed to the others. 'Has he got on common silk stockings?' she asked.

She was met by silence. The others were still gazing at Bertie in paralysed horror.

Slowly Mrs Bertram turned round. She saw Bertie dressed as a Red Indian. Her face changed to a mask of fury. She uttered a piercing scream.

'You wretch!' she said, 'you hateful, *hateful* boy!'

Then with a spirit worthy of the virgin queen herself she flung herself upon the unfortunate Bertie and boxed his ears. . . .

The cast of the pageant was in despair. Bertie, battered and bewildered, had fled howling homewards and Mrs Bertram was suffering more terribly even than she had suffered before. She was engaged in gliding from one fit of hysterics into another. In the intervals she informed them that nothing would induce her to take her part in the pageant without a page and that it was an insult to ask her to and that they couldn't get a page now and that she'd sue the boy's mother for damages and that she'd sue them all for damages and that she'd never get over this as long as she lived. They stood around her offering *sal-volatile* and smelling salts and *eau-de-Cologne* and sympathy and consolation. They coaxed and soothed and pleaded all to no avail. Mrs Bertram continued to suffer. A mild and well-meaning suggestion from Sir Walter Raleigh that she should lend her clothes to someone else who didn't mind going without a page threw her into such a state that Sir Walter Raleigh crept into the next room so that the sight of him might not continue to increase her sufferings.

'All right,' he remarked despondently to the Vicar's favourite aspidistra, 'she *can* sue me for damages and write to the papers about me' (these had been two of her milder threats). '*I* don't care.'

Then when the chaos and despair and suffering were at their height there came a loud knock at the door. The Vicar's wife went to open it. In the doorway stood a boy with a bullet head, fair bristly hair and very plain features. It was Ginger. His expression was a good imitation of William's most expressionless one.

'Please do you want a page?' he said stolidly, ''cause I know a boy what's got a page's suit what wun't mind comin' an' bein' a page for you.'

There was a moment's tense silence, then someone said eagerly:

'Where is he? Would it take long to fetch him? Could he put it on quickly?'

'He's here,' said Ginger, 'an' he's got it on.'

He put both his fingers into his mouth and emitted an ear-splitting whistle.

Another boy, wearing a white satin suit, emerged from the shadow of the doorway and entered the room. It was William. He wore his imbecile expression as a protection against awkward questions. They gazed at him open-mouthed. Mrs Bertram abruptly ceased suffering. In the background the Vicar's wife was heard to groan: 'It's that boy . . . it's that awful William Brown.'

But there was no time for asking questions. Already the procession would be late. Mrs Bertram cast one piercing glance at him from head to foot. The others watched her breathlessly. His stockings were of quite good silk and his suit was perfect.

'I don't like his face,' she pronounced finally, 'but the suit's all right. Let him come.'

The route of the procession of the pageant was thickly lined. Near the school was a massed crowd of boys among which stood Bertie looking bewildered and infuriated. Next to him stood Ginger who was explaining the situation to him patiently for the twentieth time.

'You see, Bertie, you're such a good hypnotist . . . you hypnotised him so that he didn't know what he was doin'. You told him to go round with that case an' do somethin' to show himself that he'd been round . . . well, you'd hypnotised him so well that he did two things 'stead of only one. He got the ball *an'* he changed the things in the case. He ran upstairs an' changed them for something of his own . . . while he was hypnotised an' din't know what he was doin'. He was only doin' somethin' to show that he'd taken it round same as you said, but he din' know what he was doin' 'cause he was hypnotised. Well, when he came to himself an' found that white satin suit where his Red Indian things used to be (Douglas's fetchin' that Red Indian suit back from your house now) he din't know what to do. He din't know where it'd come from 'cause he'd been hypnotised when he put it there an' heard that the pageant wanted a page he thought he'd try'n help them by puttin' on the white satin suit that he didn't know where it had come from 'cause of bein' hypnotised an' go over jus' to see if he could help them 'cause he'd heard that they wanted a page an' he din't know where the white suit had come from 'cause of bein' hypnotised when he put it there . . .'

But a sudden hush fell. The procession was approaching. The central figure of the procession was Mrs. Bertram as Queen Elizabeth. Behind

her walked William as the page. Behind William walked his dog
Jumble – as unpolished-looking a dog as was William a boy. Jumble
had joined the procession as it passed William's gate and had firmly
resisted all attempts at ejection. William's appearance had been the
subject of many unfavourable comments as he passed along the route
behind Mrs Bertram.

'*Most* unsuitable . . .' had been the kindest.

'To think of choosing *that* boy when they must have had the choice of
all the boys in the village.'

'I'd heard that they were going to have Bertie. . . . I must say I think
they'd have been wiser to have a boy of that type.'

'There's nothing in the least – *romantic* or mediaeval about his face.'

'When I think of him chasing my cat yesterday . . .'

'He's so *plain*.'

'And that *awful* dog.'

But when he reached the place where the school was massed a
mighty roar of applause burst forth. The air rang with cheers and with
'Good ole Williams.'

William was not quite proof against it. The expressionlessness of his
expression flickered and broke up for just a second. He grinned and
blushed like any *jeune première*.

Then, hastily composing his features again to imbecility, he passed
on. . . .

# Me Da Went Off the Bottle!

*Paul Vincent Carroll*

It all began on the day me da took the pledge. I was just a nipper at the time, chasing A, B and C down the algebraic labyrinths, and calculating how long it took to fill a cistern by the senseless method of leaving an ingoing and an outgoing tap open simultaneously. My elder brother, Paddy, did all the milking and manuring and general slave work of the farm for little or no wages according to the mood of me da. My goodlooking sister, Kay, was mooneyed about Jerry Doyle who was just back from Dublin with a veterinary diploma. My father, Peter, in his sober senses was a martinet, strict to the point of tyranny and given to nagging and girning if everything wasn't just plumb right. But when he was reasonably lit up with a few balls of Jamieson's Three Star, he was as decent and generous a spud as you could get, and it was a delight to hear him singing 'Lord Clare's Dragoons', even if he was wholly incapable of singing in time or in tune. On such happy occasions, the family rejoiced and was glad.

I was always the first, little ferret that I was, to announce the glad tidings that me da was on the bottle. 'Me da's after comin' out of Mike Regan's pub and he's singin',' I would exclaim hilariously and chuck my Algebra and Professor Meiklejohn's Latin roots into the clothes basket.

'He has a drop in him, praises to God,' my harassed mother would say, and put on a kettle of water in readiness for the punch. And mind you, she liked her ball o' malt as well as any woman, only when me da went on the wagon she, poor thing, had to follow suit.

But as ill-luck would have it, a young pioneering priest with a pale tubercular face and the eyes of a zealot came to the parish to assist the old Canon who was a charming old chap who read Bernard Shaw and tolerated everything with the single exception of sexual promiscuity. It was the only sin in the calendar he outlawed, and as he was touching seventy he could never understand what mossy banks and dew-wet meadows were made for. This young priest's father had been a publican, and although the profits from good porter and bad whiskey had paid for his long training in Maynooth Seminary, he had for the drink a hatred that seemed to consume his unhealthy being.

In his all-embracing campaign against it, he selected twelve elderly men, good men and true, to be the spearhead of his open war on Bacchus, and believe it or not he christened them his twelve apostles. They were intended to be a living and eloquent example to the young men of the parish. The old Canon suffered this pioneering activity with a patient shrug and merely removed his bottle of Jamieson from the communal cupboard to a small wall cabinet in his bedroom.

You can imagine our consternation when on one dreary Sunday morning me da put on his swallow-tail suit, with his black Parnell tie and his half-gallon hat and gravely announced to the assembled family that he was St. Peter.

From that moment on, our lives jointly and severally became a living hell. The good old glass of hot malt that submerged the prim Christian in me da and made him charitable and kindly was gone forever, and on his ponderous watch-chain he wore a total abstinence medal the size of a five shilling piece. He became the most cantankerous little spitfire imaginable, totting up poor mother's account books, grudgingly giving poor Paddy a miserable half-crown on Saturday nights, instead of the habitual ten shilling note and a bottle of Guinness, and warning Kay that if she as much as looked the same side of the road as young Doyle was on, he'd hang her off one of the bacon hooks in the kitchen ceiling as a deterrent to fleshly and unmaidenly thoughts and desires. As for me, if he caught me knocking jam jars off the pier of the gate with my catapult instead of finding the cubical content of a pyramid standing on its end, he promised me four of the best on the bottom and a double ration of the same at bedtime.

Of course we all went to mother with our woes and worries.

'Mother, what sort of a man is that you married at all, at all? Were you out of your senses or what? If we slipped out to the dance tonight, mother, could you possibly square it with your conscience to swear that we were over at the Church instead?'

And she, poor thing, would soothe us and beg us to have patience. But me da's zeal got worse instead of better as the days lengthened into weeks, and the drier his stomach got for want of a rozener the sourer he got in the tongue. But each of the Apostles watched their colleagues with the eye of a hawk and me poor da daren't give in. Mother, cute old thing that she was, used to put a bottle of stout here and there about the house where his roving eye would catch it, but he invariably hopped it venomously off the pier of the gate outside much to mother's chagrin. So logical and sensibly moral was my mother that she even went the length of saying a secret Novena that me da would go back on the bottle; but her prayers weren't heard.

Then one evening, to our horror, he marched us all to church – mother in her sable bonnet, Paddy in his shiny bowler, Kay in her little blue cape and I in one of those infernal skull-caps that were a target for the unprintable eloquence of the less respectable boyos of the parish. And there in the presence of this ecstatic and tubercular-ridden cleric, with me da as St Peter pompously erect, we raised our lighted candles and renounced forever the works and pomps of the fiend that Satan posted in every beer bottle.

The first casualty under this iron regime was Kay. It came from a kiss stolen by Jerry Doyle behind a cowshed door while Kay was milking our black cow, Roisin Dubh. I was keeping watch for them in fair return for a bar of chocolate, two bulls-eyes, a bar of a sticky sweet called 'Peggy's Leg', and a mug of warm milk straight from the generous udder of the said Roisin Dubh. But St Peter must have been peering through a chink in the delapidated woodwork of the shed, for he was upon us like a lightning flash.

Kay was seventeen, but seventeen or not, in the presence of us all with her gym skirt drawn up she got six whizzers of an ashplant across her pink bloomers. I remember that evening creeping up to her bedroom with a chunk of bread and cheese and how, shaking with sobs, she put her head into me for sympathy, her big luminous eyes swimming with tears and the long sheeny mane of her hair round her white shoulders. How I hated religion and temperance and all the things that hadn't a little human weakness in them to make them pliable and lovable. I swore to Kay that, if she'd stop sobbing, I'd carry notes between her and Jerry and do it for nothing, and I'd bear twelve of the best from him before I'd give them away.

'And anyway,' I added with a wave, 'won't you and Jerry be married when they're all in hell!'

This made Kay suddenly laugh and the laughing became so contagious that we had to bury our heads under the bedclothes in case such an incongruous noise should be heard in the sober house of me da.

But it was the quiet sombre Paddy, the inscrutable man of the fields who rebelled. It happened one day when we were all expecting me da home from the fair whither he had gone to sell a fine milking cow and a few yearlings. We were as usual all round mother begging her to ask him to make this concession or that, but of course she could only give us sympathy without promises. It was then that Paddy lifted me da's framed photograph from the mantlepiece – the one he got taken as St Peter, with the temperance badge prominently displayed on his watch-chain – and in a moment of terrific tension smashed it into smithereens on the floor and then venomously danced on it.

It was a moment I have never forgotten, with poor Kay in the shakers with fear, me mother grovelling on the floor stupidly trying to reassemble the broken fragments and I hopping around like a wasp in a jam jar. To me it was the unfurling of the rebel flag. I looked up at the fine defiant face of my brother. He was Robert Emmet, Wolfe Tone and Parnell all rolled into one. I wanted madly to be ordered to charge!

'Bravo, Paddy!' I burst out involuntarily, and immediately stopped a corrective left swing from mother than left me sitting half-dazed among the milk churns with about as much fight in me as a doctored tom-cat.

'I'll say I knocked it off the shelf myself when I was cleaning,' said my mother.

'Lies!' yelled Paddy.

'And how else can we live but by lies?' cried mother, 'and the sour puss on your da for want of a drop.'

Then Paddy petrified us in earnest. He lifted the heavy poker purposefully and brandished it.

'There will be no lies told tonight,' announced Paddy with strange quiet. 'I smashed his damned photo and I trampled on it. That's what he'll be told!'

Kay burst into tears.

'Take that poker from Paddy, mother,' she cried, 'and hide it.'

'If you'd touch your da with that, you'd wither,' cried mother. 'Even Hell wouldn't have you!'

'One solitary word out of him,' said Paddy tensely, 'and I'll split him open!'

In the petrified silence that followed, Paddy deliberately went to me da's special armchair – dare any one sit in it but him! – and drawing it roughly in front of the fire, seated himself in it complete with the poker, and began to whistle.

By this time mother and Kay were so nerve-ridden that they both had to run to the old toilet in the garden. I went cautiously to Paddy, eager to get rid of this new and dreadful menace. I clapped him approvingly on the shoulder as man to man. 'No one thinks more of you than meself, Paddy,' says I, 'but as man to man and for the sake of the women . . .'

It was like as if a wind suddenly caught me up in an idle frolic. I landed head first in a large barrel of flour and emerged from it gasping for breath and wildly trying to sweep the flour out of my eyes, ears and mouth. Paddy's maniacal he-haw-haws made me even worse, and the return of Kay and me mother didn't improve the situation. You could have cut the tension with a butter knife, and it became evident to all of us that serious and indeed even tragic happenings were not only possible but probable. Whatever the blazes got hold of Paddy, he seemed determined to pile on the agony, for when poor Kay meekly handed him half-a-crown she had saved up to buy a blue ribbon to freshen up her washed-out blouse, he sent it whizzing viciously through the window. Then with a deliberate and ominous calmness he went to the vegetable barrel, selected a large turnip and ceremoniously placed it before him on the top of the oven. With evident relish, he wielded the heavy poker and cleft it in halves.

'What on earth are you at, Paddy?' cried my mother.

'That was just me da's head, Mother,' he answered emotionlessly. 'It'll be just like that.'

I had had enough. I could feel the blood in me congealing horribly. I ran from the house. But I was no sooner outside than I heard in the lane a step there was no mistaking. I dashed back into the house, deftly seized the poker, and flung it through the window.

'Me da's comin',' I cried. 'He's in the lane.'

Determined to please me da and to be on the right side in the imminent fury, I seized my Algebra study-book and began hysterically ejaculating about two crazy trains, A and B, departing at amazing speeds from two stations, X and Y, on the stroke of midnight. At what exact second would they meet? And how far from station X? . . . Ah, sure, what the hell did it matter where they met and when! Wouldn't they be better to collide decently and be done with it, for wasn't Paddy goin' to kill me da anyway?

Me mother craved and Kay sobbed and entreated but it was of no avail. Paddy sat on in me da's chair, swinging his lanky legs and whistling furiously. Then as the calm of impending tragedy descended on us like a funeral shroud, we heard the familiar step, then another and another till our hearts thumped like hammers. The knob turned awkwardly, there was a little stagger, a slight snort of glee and a sudden miraculous burst of highly-unmelodious song:

> *'For never when our swords were set,*
> *And never when the sabres met,*
> *Could we the Saxon soldiers get*
> *To stand the shock of Clare's Dragoons . . . '*

I leaped from my seat at the table and threw the algebraic book of tortures into the flour barrel.

'Me da's on the bottle,' I roared.

Me mother raised her eyes meekly to heaven and crossed her hands.

'Praises be to the high God for His mercies,' she whispered devoutly.

The next minute me da was amongst us, clapping us all on the shoulders and greeting us like loved ones back from the strangers.

'Yerra, sit down, da, you'll be dead beat,' said Paddy, jumping up from the forbidden chair. But me da gave him a friendly push and landed him back into it.

'Sit where you are, Paddy, boy,' he exclaimed. 'And there's a fiver for you.'

'It's too much altogether, da. I won't take it,' protested Paddy.

'There's more where it came from,' answered me da, planking a bottle of stout in Paddy's lap. 'What did I get, Paddy, for the red cow with the white star?'

'You got seventy pounds for her,' said Paddy, with one eye closed.

'Guineas,' said me da triumphantly.

'Begosh, da, you were always a powerful man at a fair!' ejaculated Paddy.

'Praises be to God,' interposed me mother, who praised God for a most incongruous variety of things.

Then with a twinkle in his eye he looked at Kay who blushed furiously and didn't know whether she was going to be kissed or caned. But in a second he had an arm about her and the big tears were coming unbidden. Then opening a parcel he handed her a lovely summer dress with an alluring green sash on it.

'Mother,' said me da, 'put this dress on Kay tomorrow because that pup, Jerry Doyle, is comin' here to ask for her. I'm afraid you're goin' to lose your daughter.'

And with that Kay ran embarrassed to mother and buried her face in her breast.

'And pup's the word, mind you,' continued me da, 'comin' up to me at the fair, with a stiff jaw. "You're not good enough for her," says I. But he took the wind out of me sails right away. "Indeed, I'm not *half* good enough for her," he answered looking me straight in the eye. Now, what can you do with a cute pup like that?'

It was at this precise moment that his roving eye lit on *me* as I stood, robinishly, with my ear cocked for every word. Then suddenly he rapped out at me:

'What's the factors of X cubed minus Y cubed?'

'X minus Y into X squared plus XY plus Y squared,' I rapped back at him.

'Good man,' he exclaimed, throwing at me a poke of black balls that I caught neatly on the wing. 'You'll be a scholar yet. I'll either make a priest or a stockbroker out of you accordin' as God directs me.'

He then handed mother a bottle of Irish, winked knowingly at her and went singing into the little parlour.

'Hot water and cut a lemon and hurry,' ordered me mother breathlessly. And we all busied ourselves around her in an atmosphere of happiness and relief. It was at this moment that Mrs Mullen, our nearest neighbour, came in surreptitiously and caught my mother excitedly by the arm.

'I have a terrible bit o' news for you, Mrs Grady,' she moaned. 'St Bartholomew is after landin' in to me, and he's as full as a piper.'

'Bless your innocence,' ejaculated me mother. 'Go and have a peep at St Peter singin' Clare's Dragoons in the parlour. And she poured out two stiff drams which they took with delicious relish.

It was the beginning of normal humanity again. The land became sweeter from the human foibles of the people who toiled it, and the harvest was golden with rustic feasts and weddings. The delicate little priest whose name I forget, having worn himself out advocating a Puritanism that is foreign to the men of the fields, was quietly transferred to be chaplain to a small Convent, and the old Canon stoically rescued his bottle from his bedroom and having restored it to its rightful cupboard, settled down comfortably in his old armchair to chortle over Shaw's strange 'Gospel of the Brothers Barnabas!'

# Gilray's Flower-pot

*J. M. Barrie*

I charge Gilray's unreasonableness to his ignoble passion for cigarettes; and the story of his flower-pot has therefore an obvious moral. The want of dignity he displayed about that flower-pot, on his return to London, would have made any one sorry for him. I had my own work to look after, and really could not be tending his chrysanthemum all day. After he came back, however, there was no reasoning with him, and I admit that I never did water his plant, though always intending to do so.

The great mistake was in not leaving the flower-pot in charge of William John. No doubt I readily promised to attend to it, but Gilray deceived me by speaking as if the watering of a plant was the merest pastime. He had to leave London for a short provincial tour, and, as I see now, took advantage of my good nature.

As Gilray had owned his flower-pot for several months, during which time (I take him at his word) he had watered it daily, he must have known he was misleading me. He said that you got into the way of watering a flower-pot regularly just as you wind up your watch. That certainly is not the case. I always wind up my watch, and I never watered the flower-pot. Of course, if I had been living in Gilray's rooms with the thing always before my eyes I might have done so. I proposed to take it into my chambers at the time; but he would not hear of that. Why? How Gilray came by his chrysanthemum I do not inquire; but whether, in the circumstances, he should not have made a clean breast of it to me is another matter. Undoubtedly it was an unusual thing to put a man to the trouble of watering a chrysanthemum daily without giving him its history. My own belief has always been that he got it in exchange for a pair of boots and his old dressing-gown. He hints that it was a present; but, as one who knows him well, I may say that he is the last person a lady would be likely to give a chrysanthemum to. Besides, if he was so proud of the plant he should have stayed at home and watered it himself.

He says that I never meant to water it, which is not only a mistake but unkind. My plan was to run downstairs immediately after dinner every evening and give it a thorough watering. One thing or another, however, came in the way. I often remembered about the chrysanthemum while I was in the office; but even Gilray could hardly have expected me to ask leave of absence merely to run home and water his plant. You must draw the line somewhere, even in a Government office. When I reached home I was tired, inclined to take things easily, and not at all in a proper condition for watering flower-pots. Then Arcadians would drop in. I put it to any sensible man or woman, could I have been expected to give up my friends for the sake of a chrysanthemum? Again, it was my custom of an evening, if not disturbed, to retire with my pipe into my cane-chair, and there pass the hours communing with great minds, or when the mood was on me, trifling with a novel. Often when I was in the middle of a chapter Gilray's flower-pot stood up before my eyes crying for water. He does not believe this, but it is the solemn truth. At those moments it was touch-and-go whether I watered his chrysanthemum or not. Where I lost myself was in not hurrying to his rooms at once with a tumbler. I said to myself that I would go when I had finished my pipe; but by that time the flower-pot had escaped my memory. This may have been weakness; all I know is that I should have saved myself much annoyance if I had risen and watered the chrysanthemum there and then. But would it not have been rather hard on me to have had to forsake my books for the sake of Gilray's flowers and flower-pots and plants and things? What right has a man to go and make a garden of his chambers?

All the three weeks he was away, Gilray kept pestering me with letters about his chrysanthemum. He seemed to have no faith in me – a detestable thing in a man who calls himself your friend. I had promised to water his flower-pot; and between friends a promise is surely sufficient. It is not so, however, when Gilray is one of them. I soon hated the sight of my name in his handwriting. It was not as if he had said outright that he wrote entirely to know whether I was watering his plant. His references to it were introduced with all the appearance of afterthoughts. Often they took the form of postscripts: 'By the way, are you watering my chrysanthemum?' or, 'The chrysanthemum ought to be a beauty by this time;' or, 'You must be quite an adept now at watering plants.' Gilray declares now that, in answer to one of these ingenious epistles, I wrote to him saying that I 'had just been watering his chrysanthemum'. My belief is that I did no such thing; or, if I did, I meant to water it as soon as I had finished my letter. (He has never been able to bring this home to me, he says, because he burned my correspondence. As if a business man would destroy such a letter.) It was yet more annoying when Gilray took to post-cards. To hear the postman's knock and then discover, when you are expecting an important communication, that it is only a post-card about a flower-pot – that is really too bad. And then I consider that some of the post-cards bordered upon insult. One of them said, 'What about chrysanthemum? – reply at once'. This was just like Gilray's overbearing way; but I answered politely and (so far as I knew) truthfully, 'Chrysanthemum all right'.

Knowing that there was no explaining things to Gilray, I redoubled my exertions to water his flower-pot as the day for his return drew near. Once, indeed, when I rang for water, I could not for the life of me remember what I wanted it for when it was brought. Had I had any forethought I should have let the tumbler stand just as it was to show it to Gilray on his return. But, unfortunately, William John had misunderstood what I wanted the water for, and put a decanter down beside it. Another time I was actually on the stair rushing to Gilray's door, when I met the housekeeper and, stopping to talk to her, lost my opportunity again. To show how honestly anxious I was to fulfil my promise, I need only add that I was several times awakened in the watches of the night by a haunting consciousness that I had forgotten to water Gilray's flower-pot. On these occasions I spared no trouble to remember again in the morning. I reached out of bed to a chair and turned it upside down, so that the sight of it when I rose might remind me that I had something to do. With the same object I crossed the tongs and poker on the floor. Gilray maintains that instead of playing 'fool's tricks' like these ('fool's tricks!') I should have got up and gone at once to his rooms with my water-bottle. What? and disturb my neighbours? Besides, could I reasonably be expected to risk catching my death of cold for the sake of a wretched chrysanthemum? One reads of men doing such things for young ladies who seek lilies in dangerous ponds or edelweiss on overhanging cliffs. But Gilray was not my sweetheart, nor,

I feel certain, any other person's.

I come now to the day prior to Gilray's return. I had just reached the office when I remembered about the chrysanthemum. It was my last chance. If I watered it once I should be in a position to state that, whatever condition it might be in, I had certainly been watering it. I jumped into a hansom, told the cabby to drive to the Inn, and twenty minutes afterwards had one hand on Gilray's door, while the other held the largest water-can in the house. Opening the door I rushed in. The can nearly fell from my hand. There was no flower-pot. I rang the bell. 'Mr. Gilray's chrysanthemum!' I cried. What do you think William John said? He coolly told me that the plant was dead and had been flung out days ago. I went to the theatre that night to keep myself from thinking. All next day I contrived to remain out of Gilray's sight. When we met he was stiff and polite. He did not say a word about the chrysanthemum for a week, and then it all came out in a rush. I let him talk. With the servants flinging out the flower-pots faster than I could water them, what more could I have done? A coolness between us was inevitable. This I regretted, but my mind was made up on one point: I would never do Gilray a favour again.

# Narapoia

## Alan Nelson

I don't know exactly how to explain it to you, Doctor,' the young man began. He smoothed back his slick black hair that shone like a phonograph record and blinked his baby blue eyes. 'It seems to be the opposite of a persecution complex.'

Dr Manly J. Departure was a short severe man who made a point of never exhibiting surprise. 'The opposite of a persecution complex?' he said, permitting one eyebrow to elevate. 'How do you mean – the opposite of a persecution complex, Mr McFarlane?'

'Well, for one thing, I keep thinking that I'm following someone.' McFarlane sat placidly in the big easy chair, hands folded, pink cheeks glowing, the picture of health and tranquility. Dr Departure stirred uneasily.

'You mean you think someone is following *you*, don't you?' the doctor corrected.

'No. No, I don't! I mean that while I'm walking along the street, suddenly I have this feeling there is somebody just ahead of me. Somebody I'm after. Someone I'm following. Sometimes I even begin to run to catch up with him! Of course – there's no one there. It's inconvenient. Damned inconvenient. And I hate to run.'

Dr Departure fiddled with a pencil. 'I see. Is there anything else?'

'Well, yes. I keep having this feeling that people . . . that people . . . well, it's really very silly . . .'

'It's quite all right,' Dr Departure purred. 'Feel free to tell me anything.'

'Well, I keep having this strange feeling that people are plotting to do me good. That they're trying to be benevolent and kind toward me. I don't know exactly who they are, or why they wish me all this kindness, but . . . it's all very fantastic, isn't it?'

It had been a long hard day for Dr Departure. Somehow he did not feel up to any more symptoms. He busied himself for the rest of the hour obtaining factual background. McFarlane was 32; happily married; healthy, normal childhood; satisfactory employment as a radio repairman; no physical complaints; no bad dreams; no drinking; no history of parental discord; no financial worries. Nothing.

'Shall we say Thursday at ten, then?' he smiled, ushering McFarlane out.

At ten minutes to ten on Thursday, Dr Departure looked at his appointment book and frowned. Well, maybe he wouldn't show up. Very often that happened. He certainly hoped that this would be one of the occasions. Opposite of a persecution complex! Delusions of beneficence! Indeed! The man must be . . . he checked himself hastily. He'd almost said 'mad'. At that moment the door buzzer sounded and McFarlane was grinning and shaking his hand.

'Well, well.' Dr Departure's affability seemed somewhat hollow. 'Any new developments?'

'Seems to me I'm getting worse,' McFarlane beamed. 'This business of following someone, I mean. Yes sir. Yesterday, I must have walked five miles!'

Dr. Departure relaxed into his chair across the desk.

'Well, now, suppose you tell me more about it. *All* about it. Just *anything* that comes to mind.'

McFarlane frowned.

'What do you mean, Doctor, just anything that comes to mind?'

'Just ramble on – about anything – whatever comes into your head.'

'I'm not sure I understand. Could you show me what you mean, Doctor? Just by way of illustration?'

The doctor permitted himself a little chuckle.

'Why, it's very simple . . . Well . . . like right now I'm thinking how one time I stole some money out of Mother's purse . . . and now I'm thinking about my wife, wondering what to get her for our wedding anniversary . . .' The doctor looked up hopefully. 'See? Just anything like that.'

'Anything like what? I still don't quite understand.' But McFarlane's face was not puzzled; it was eager. 'Could you give me just a couple more illustrations? They're very interesting.'

The doctor found himself relating disconnected, half-forgotten images. McFarlane sat back with a strangely contented expression.

At the end of the hour, Dr Departure was quite exhausted. His voice was hoarse; his collar and tie askew. ' . . . and well, my wife – she completely dominates me . . . I always was very sensitive that my eyes are slightly crossed . . . I never will forget – that time in the attic, with the little girl across the street . . . I was only eleven I guess . . .' Reluctantly, he broke off, wiped his eyes and glanced at his watch.

'I feel much better,' he heard McFarlane say. 'Shall we say Tuesday at ten?'

Next Tuesday at ten, Dr Departure inwardly braced himself.

'There'll be no more nonsense like last Thursday's session,' he assured himself, but he had no cause for concern. McFarlane was strangely silent and preoccupied. He carried a large cardboard box, which he carefully set upon the floor before seating himself in the leather chair. The doctor prodded him with a few preliminary questions.

'I'm afraid I'm beginning to be troubled with hallucinations, Doctor,' McFarlane finally volunteered.

Dr Departure mentally rubbed his hands. He was back on old familiar territory now. He felt more comfortable.

'Ah, hallucinations!'

'Rather, they're not really hallucinations, Doctor. You might say they were the *opposite* of hallucinations.'

Dr Departure rested his eyes a moment. The smile disappeared from his face. McFarlane continued:

'Last night, for instance, Doctor, I had a nightmare. Dreamed there was a bit ugly bird perched on my short-wave set waiting for me to wake up. It was a hideous thing – a fat bulbous body and a huge beak that turned upward like a sickle. Blood-shot eyes with pouches under them. And ears, Doctor. Ears! Did you ever hear of a bird with ears? Little tiny, floppy ears, something like a cocker spaniel's. Well, I woke up, my heart was pounding, and what do you think? There actually *was* an ugly fat bird with ears sitting on the short-wave set.'

Dr Departure perked up again. A very simple case of confusing the real with the unreal. Traditional. Almost classical.

'A real bird on the short-wave set?' he asked gently. 'With blood-shot eyes?'

'Yes,' McFarlane replied. 'I know it sounds silly. I know it's hard to believe.'

'Oh, not at all. Not at all. That type of visual aberration is a common enough phenomenon.' The doctor smiled soothingly. 'Nothing to . . .'

McFarlane interrupted him by reaching down and hoisting the carton onto the desk. 'You don't understand, Doctor,' he said. 'Go ahead. Open it.'

The doctor looked at McFarlane a moment, then at the brown box which was punctured with air holes and tied with heavy twine. Disconcertedly, the doctor cut the string and folded back the top flaps. He leaned over and peered in – then sucked in his breath. Pouchy, blood-shot eyes leered up at him. Floppy ears. The up-side-down beak. An obscene-looking bird.

'His name is Lafayette,' McFarlane said, tossing a few bread crumbs into the carton which were quickly devoured with a noisy, repulsive gulp. 'He rather grows on you after a while, don't you think?'

After McFarlane left with his hallucination, the doctor sat a few moments meditating. He felt a little dizzy and lightheaded as though he had just emerged from a ride through the Tunnel of Horrors at the beach.

Maybe I *am* witnessing an entirely new psychosis, he told himself. Funny things are happening in the world today. He saw himself before the American Psychiatric Congress delivering a monograph: 'The Emergence of a New Psychosis.' This new disorder apparently had symptoms opposite from Paranoia – he could call it Narapoia. Hopefully, Dr Departure foresaw the possibility that some of his colleagues would insist on naming it after its discoverer: 'Departureomania.' He would be famous; his name linked with Freud. A sickening thought struck him. Supposing this man McFarlane was a malingerer! A fake! By God, he'd find out! Quickly, he buzzed his secretary, Miss Armstrong, and instructed her to cancel all appointments for the rest of the day. Then he reached for his hat and fled from the building.

Three days later the telephone in Dr Departure's office rang. Miss Armstrong answered it. It was Mrs Departure.

'No, he isn't here,' Miss Armstrong said. 'As a matter of fact he hasn't been here for three days except to bounce in and out for his mail.'

'I don't know what's the matter with that man.' Mrs Departure's exasperated voice rattled the receiver. 'He's gone half the night, too. Comes home utterly exhausted. What do you suppose he's writing in that little notebook?'

'Frankly, I'm worried about him,' Miss Armstrong replied. 'He's so irritable. And in such a frightful rush all the time.'

'You're looking peaked, Doc,' McFarlane said, at his next meeting a week later. It was the first time the doctor had sat behind the desk for many days. His legs ached. Stealthily, beneath the desk, he slipped off both scuffed shoes to relieve the pressure from his blistered feet.

'Never mind about me,' the doctor snapped. 'How are *you*?' The doctor's fingers twitched. He was much thinner and his face was pale and drawn.

'I think I must be getting better,' McFarlane announced. 'I have the feeling lately that someone is following *me*.'

'Nonsense!' Dr Departure snapped at him irritably. 'It's just your imagination.' He squinted his eyes and gazed at McFarlane. If only he could be sure this McFarlane was not faking. So far there was nothing to indicate he was. After all, his sudden urge on the streets to overtake someone seemed perfectly genuine. McFarlane would raise his head, his pace would quicken, and away he would go. 'Well, I'll just have to watch him a little while longer,' the doctor told himself. He closed his eyes a moment, reviewing his activities for the previous week: the long cross-city jaunts in which he had almost lost McFarlane a dozen times; the long, long waits outside restaurants and bars waiting for McFarlane to emerge. 'I'll just have to keep going until I get all the facts,' he thought. But he was a little concerned with the weight he'd lost, and with the strange ringing noises in his head which had recently developed. . . .

At the end of the hour, McFarlane tiptoed out of the office. Dr Departure was snoring fuzzily.

On the day of McFarlane's next appointment with the doctor, he was met at the door by Miss Armstrong. 'Doctor isn't here,' she informed him. 'He's taken a leave of absence for three months – possibly a year.'

'Oh, I'm sorry to hear it,' McFarlane said. 'He *was* looking done in, though. Where is he, on vacation?'

'As a matter of fact, he's at Marwood Sanitarium.'

A strange puzzled look suddenly settled over McFarlane's face and he gazed into space a moment. Presently, he smiled at the secretary.

'I just had the funniest feeling,' he said. 'Suddenly I feel like I'm completely cured. All of a sudden. Just when you told me about Dr Departure.'

The doctors had quite a time with Dr Departure at the sanitarium.

'Just tell us anything that comes into your mind,' they urged. Departure's eyes were glazed and he was very excited.

'I've got to follow him, I tell you! I can't let him get out of sight. Not for an instant. He's got a bird with baggy eyes and floppy ears.'

'Very interesting. *All* very interesting!' The doctors gloomed among themselves, shaking their heads scientifically:

'Something entirely new!'

'It's rather like a persecution complex – isn't it – only the opposite!'

'He seems to have the delusion he is following someone. Amazing, isn't it?'

'Probably the emergence of a brand new psychosis. I suggest that we observe him very closely.'

And here one of the doctors went so far as to suggest further that they allow Dr Departure to move about the city at will – closely watched, of course, by alternately selected members of their staff – so that all his actions could be carefully noted . . .

# Confessions of A Failed Southern Lady
## Kindergarten

*Florence King*

When we got home from the beach it was time for me to start school. I was enrolled in Kindergarten B, or beginning kindergarten, which met from one to three.

Mama and I walked down a crooked little street called Rock Creek Church Road to Raymond Elementary. The kindergarten classroom was on the ground floor. It had its own toilet, a piano, a bird in a gilded cage, and bulletin boards full of cheery paper cut-outs. Glassfront cabinets containing building blocks, pots of paste, and stacks of construction paper lined the walls.

At one o'clock the teacher clapped her hands, announced that school was in session, and dismissed the mothers with a gracious but pointed nod. They gathered themselves up reluctantly and moved toward the door. That's when it started. A little boy near me opened his mouth and bawled, and it traveled around the room like a virus. Each time another child broke down, its mother came catapulting through the door with arms outstretched and features shattered. It was a mass engulfment. One child threw up, another held his breath, another hurled himself on the floor and kicked, and one little girl simply collapsed and curled up like a bean. Her mother knelt beside her and burst into tears.

Mine was standing in the doorway looking disgusted. She caught my eye and mouthed *Are you all right?* I nodded. It was a lie, I was miserable: I wasn't used to children and they were getting on my nerves. Worse, it appeared that I was a child, too. I hadn't known that before; I thought I was just short. Who were these watery moles anyhow? Were they always this noisy? I waved to Mama and she left.

The janitor came in and mopped up the vomit and the bean was carried out in maternal arms. The rest of the mothers stood outside the door pressing their faces into distorted shapes against the glass and making mist with their heated breaths. I felt proud of Mama for being such a brick. The teacher, less tactful now, shooed them away with a desperate two-handed gesture like someone flapping a towel at a clutch of rioting hens, and they departed at last.

Once they were gone, the class calmed down and grew quiet except for the sounds made by a vigorous thumbsucker. I was dying for a cup of coffee. The teacher seated us at long worktables, passed out drawing paper and crayons, and told us to draw a picture of anything we liked. I picked the *Titanic* because Herb had just told me about it and shown me photographs from his ship book. I drew an ocean liner and colored it in . Depicting an iceberg on white paper stumped me until I remembered Herb saying that icebergs look blue. When I finished, I printed *R.M.S. Titanic* on the bow and signed my name in script in the lower right-hand corner, pulling the tail of the *g* around to underline the whole business the way ancestors did in documents.

When I handed the drawing to the teacher, she stared at it for a very long time.

'*R.M.S. Titanic*,' she said at last. 'Do you know what that means?'

'Yes, ma'am. Royal Mail Steamer.'

'Why did you make the smokestacks yellow? They're supposed to be red.'

'No, ma'am, the *Titanic* was White Star Line. They had yellow ones. Red is for Cunard.'

'I see.'

She reached for a sheet of paper and began writing. A misunderstood feeling stirred in me, destined to be the first of many in a lifetime dappled with this sort of thing. I throbbed with alarm when she folded the note and pinned it to the shoulder of my dress with one of the emergency safety pins she kept on the lapel of her suit.

'When your mother comes to get you, make sure she reads that.'

'What did I do?'

'Nothing. Just tell your mother to read the note.'

I don't know why she didn't wait and tell Mama herself. Maybe her teachers' college had taught her never to discuss a child with a parent when the child is present. More likely, she simply couldn't take any more mothers that day.

The note said: *Florence is too advanced for Kindergarten B. Please bring her to Kindergarten A beginning tomorrow at nine o'clock.*

Translated into Mama it said: 'She was the only one that didn't cry! You should have heard all those goddamn sissies! I swear, they reminded me of Preston Hunt and his "daddy," except they were carrying on over their mothers.'

'It was the picture, Louise, and the fact that she signed her name to it,' Herb argued, gazing proudly at my artwork. 'That's what "advanced" means. It was knowledge, not behavior.'

'No, it was because she was brave!'

'She's in school, not the Coldstream Guards.'

'Be that as it may, she got promoted the first day. That's what worries me,' Granny said darkly. 'It doesn't do for a girl to be too bright. She might never come unwell – all her blood will go to her brain. She reads too much now. There's something unrefined about a reading woman, they always reek of the lamp. How can she grow up to be a lady if she's always got her nose in a book?'

Herb winced. As much of an anglophile as Granny was, she did not appreciate certain finer points of usage as practiced on the other side of the Big Water.

'Mrs. Ruding,' he chided, 'I am not a duke, a marquess, or an earl. Therefore, Florence can't be a lady. What you mean is "gentlewoman." '

'Oh, I don't like that,' Granny said, wrinkling her nose in distaste. 'It sounds masculine.'

'Oh, shit.'

Granny took my kindergarten coup as a personal challenge to her ladysmithery. Casting around for an antidote to my burgeoning intellectualism, she forced me to submit to knitting lessons. Under her tutelage I grasped the basic knit-and-purl easy enough, but my needles refused to click or flash or lend themselves to any of the verbs associated with dexterous womanhood. They scraped.

'You will make your father a scarf for his birthday,' Granny ordered.

Herb liked conservative colors so I began with slate gray, but I soon tired of looking at it and switched to dark blue. The blue bored me after a few rows so I chose a ball of light gray and knitted on. Pleased by my show of industry, Granny left me to my own devices and went off to Richmond to visit her sister. I had to have the scarf finished by the time she got back. To make the task more bearable I changed colors every day, using maroon, royal blue, magenta, vermilion, yellow, orange, red, and purple. By the time Granny came home, the scarf was four feet long and contained every shade in her knitting basket. She and Jensy were horrified when they saw it.

'It look lak Joseph's coat.'

'It'll go with anything.' Mama chuckled.

I had knitted in the privacy of the room Granny and I now shared, so Herb had not seen the insane rainbow that would soon be his. Granny took it off the needle and blocked it, and I wrapped it in conservative dark green paper.

Granny gave him the usual pajamas and socks. Mama's gift was even less of a surprise: she took five dollars out of the housekeeping money he had just given her, stuck it in an envelope, and handed it back to him, saying, 'Happy birthday, buy yourself a book.'

He opened my gift last. Only an English face could have resisted a double take on seeing what was inside, but fortunately he had one. Holding up my garish handiwork, he wrapped it around his hand the way a man fashions a mock knot in a tie to see how it will look on.

'I say, that's a handsome scarf. I'll be proud to wear this. Thank you, little one.'

And he did wear it. That night he stood before the mirror in his tuxedo and wrapped my lumpy gift around his neck as though it were the finest evening silk. When he put on his overcoat, the wool puffed out around his collar like a goiter but the master mold of fashion did not seem to notice. When he came home, he wrapped it carefully in tissue paper and put it away in his bureau with the same care he gave to all his possessions. He wore the scarf all that winter; never in the history of haberdashery was anything so awful so cherished.

# The Prisoner of Zenda

## *David Niven*

*The Prisoner of Zenda*, the classic story of intrigue and high adventure in Ruritania, was an ideal film subject. Donald Ogden Stewart and John Balderston turned out a masterful screenplay full of duels, chases, coronations and ballroom spectacles.

Selznick assembled the cast he had hoped for and for four months a great time was had by all. Usually when one makes a film, it is a little like being too long on an ocean voyage. At the end of the trip, total strangers who have been thrown together for several weeks part, swearing eternal allegiance to each other, but never do much about it. *Zenda* was different. Everyone became friends and remained so.

Colman was the leader and very much the star – a most serious and dedicated performer who was never his easygoing self until the end of the day when Tommy would come and lead me to the star bungalow to join him in his ritual six o'clock 'beaker'.

Madeleine Carroll was a porcelain beauty of great sweetness and fun and Mary Astor, who looked like a beautiful and highly shockable nun, had a sweet expression, a little tiny turned-up nose and made everyone feel she was in desperate need of protection. In point of fact, she was by her own admission happiest and at her best in bed. She was also, it turned out, highly indiscreet and confided all in her private journal, starting each revealing daily entry . . . 'Dear Diary . . .'

'Dear Diary' right in the middle of the picture caused a major reshuffling of the shooting schedule because it was stolen and turned up as prime evidence in a highly publicised divorce case in which Mary had to give evidence.

If 'Dear Diary' caused a stir among the *Zenda* company, it was nothing to the upheavals and near heart attacks it perpetrated throughout the upper echelons of the film colony. Mary, it appeared, had been a very busy girl indeed and her partners had gleefully been awarded marks in 'Dear Diary' for performance, stamina, etc., etc.

After being absent for days in a blaze of scandal, and being laid bare (to coin a phrase) for all to see, Mary returned to the set of *Zenda*, looking just as sweet and demure as ever and everyone, as usual, desperately wanted to protect her.

C. Aubrey Smith was over seventy when *Zenda* was made. Six feet four, ramrod straight, alert and vigorous, never did he forget a line or misunderstand a piece of direction: unfailingly courteous, kind and helpful, he was beloved by all.

Every Sunday, he ordered me to turn out for the Hollywood Cricket Club; I always called him 'Sir', and, though dreading long hot afternoons in the field – I obeyed.

His great craggy face was frequently creased by worry because he loved England very deeply and as it was early in 1937, he had little faith in the way Neville Chamberlain was coping with the Rome-Berlin Axis and Germany's anti-Comintern Pact with Japan. Refusing to read the 'local rags', the *Los Angeles Times* or the *Examiner* trusting only *The Times* of London to keep him up to date, and with air mail across the Atlantic almost non-existent, Aubrey was usually eight to ten days behind a crisis. Nobody spoiled his fun by telling him the news so it was almost two weeks after it had happened that the old man flung down his morning paper and boomed across the set:

'The blood feller's done it!'

'Who, Sir? . . . What, Sir?' we chorused.

'That whippersnapper Hitler! . . . he's marched into Austria!'


John Cromwell, the director, was highly respected and highly efficient but he was a little low on humour, which created certain hazards for Raymond Massey and Doug Jr., two of the most inveterate gigglers in the business.

The scene at the State Ball was most important: Colman, masquerading as the King, was proposing to Princess Flavia in a small ante-room. Outside a courtier was eavesdropping. At the end of the long intimate love scene, this courtier, a large fat man with a mauve face, had to hurry to Fairbanks, Massey and myself waiting in our resplendent uniforms at the bottom of a long flight of steps at the entrance to the castle. On arrival he had to say two words – 'Good news!'

It was what is known as a 'production shot' . . . designed to give richness, size and colour to the film by showing the maximum number of people in their magnificent costumes and the most advantageous views of the extravagant sets.

The famous Chinese cameraman, James Wong Howe, had excelled himself. By a 'marshalling yards' arrangement of tracks and overhead trolleys, his cameras were able, all in one flowing movement, to witness the love scene, then follow the mauve-faced courtier through several ante-rooms filled with beautifully gowned ladies and bemedalled gentlemen across a giant white marble multi-pillared patio, round a lily pond upon which cruised haughty black swans, thence up a flight of ornate stairs into the candle-lit main ballroom where three hundred couples of the handsomest and most glamorous extras were executing a carefully rehearsed waltz.

Past the minstrels' gallery the mauve courtier hurried, on through the kitchens and vestibules, followed everywhere by a battery of wondering eyes . . . what would his message be?

Finally, the big moment came – satin-breeched flunkeys flung open the huge main doors and as the tension mounted, he ponderously descended one hundred and twenty steps to our little group waiting at the bottom.

'Good news!' he said loudly, and we reeled back. It was bad news for us . . . he had breath like a buzzard.

When the courtier tramped back to his starting position for the next run-through, we dared not look at each other. Fairbanks, I sensed, was beginning to vibrate and out of the corner of my eye, I could see that Ray Massey was making a great production of polishing his monocle.

We suffered through half a dozen more rehearsals and six more broadsides from 'Halitosis Harry'. By the time John Cromwell was satisfied and ordered the first 'take' we realised we were doomed, a sort of schoolboy hysteria had gripped us and although we still avoided each other's eyes, we knew we could never get through the scene.

'Let's pretend it's drains,' I whispered.

We could hear the love scene being played in the distance and with dread we followed the sounds of the courtier's slow progress towards us. The orchestra, in the ballroom, fell silent as he approached the end of his journey so that his two golden words could be recorded for posterity.

The doors above us were flung open and our tormentor, relieved to be at the end of his complicated trip, descended smugly towards us.

'Good news!' he said.

We greeted his announcement with gales of pent-up laughter.

'Cut!! . . . What the hell's going on?' demanded a furious Cromwell, rushing up, but the angrier he became, the more uncontrollable became our mirth.

Fairbanks behaved in a most craven manner.

'Ask Mr Massey what's wrong,' he blurted out with tears streaming down his face . . . 'He's the oldest.'

Ray's suggestion didn't help at all.

'Gee, Mr Cromwell, perhaps it would give us a kind of springboard if the gentleman *whispered* the line.'

The whisper brought us a whiff of pure phosgene.

In the end Cromwell rearranged his shooting schedule so that our reactions to the fateful 'news' could be photographed the following day when, as he succinctly put it, 'You bastards will have had a whole night to calm down.'

Hollywood always felt that the leading characters of costume pictures should be seen riding prancing, frothing and often unmanageable steeds, so when we came to the shooting of the coronation procession, I had a few words with the Senior Wrangler, some currency changed hands and I was mounted on a nice quiet old mare. Unfortunately, she was on heat. Trotting through the cheering citizens beside the golden coach bearing Ronnie and Madeleine, resplendent in cuirasse and silver helmet topped by a golden eagle, I was blissfully unaware of danger gathering like a storm astern of me. Ray was riding a large black stallion.

A high-pitched whinnying rose above the screams of hurriedly departing townsfolk and about six feet of easily identifiable stallion equipment passed me like a torpedo. I turned in my saddle to find thrashing hooves and gnashing teeth all around me. Far above, I saw Ray's horrified face. Not wanting to go down with the ship, I hurriedly disembarked by flinging myself to the ground, leaving my mare to her happy fate and Ray to a ringside seat. For a while it looked as though he was riding a rocking horse.

David Selznick's *Prisoner of Zenda* was a triumphant success, critically and financially, and a testament to what happens when a producer infuses all those around him with loyalty, enthusiasm and a real joy in their work.

Fifteen years later, L. B. Mayer decided to make some easy money and ordered a remake of *The Prisoner of Zenda*. Feeling that he could not improve upon the way his son-in-law had captured the Anthony Hope classic, he insisted that the new version be made with identical sets, word for word, shot for shot, and close-up for close-up: it had to be exactly the same as the old one, but with new faces. He cast Stewart Granger in the Colman role and James Mason misguidedly attempted to follow Doug Junior. To David Oliver Selznick's great amusement the result was a critical and financial disaster.

# The Man in the Brown Paper Bag

*Clive James*

In Trevor's living-room, my suitcase against the wall served as a headboard. Folded clothes made a pillow. Beyond, into the centre of the room, stretched the brown paper bag, forming my bed. Wriggling into it took some time, but once inserted I could settle down in comparative warmth for a long night of turning from one side to the other. It was the hardness of the floor which compelled frequent movement. A lot of this I could do in my sleep, because my body, albeit much abused, was still young and supple, and I have always had Napoleon's gift of falling asleep at will, although unfortunately it has not always been accompanied by his gift of waking up again. The problem resided not in how the hardness of the floor affected my sleep, but in how the noise the paper bag made affected Trevor.

As he lay there in the darkness on his enviably luxurious convertible divan, it was as if, somewhere nearby, a giant packet of crisps was being eaten by one of those cinema patrons who think that they are being unobtrusive if they take only a few crisps at a time and chew them very slowly. When Trevor could bear no more he would switch on his modernistic tubular bedside light, wake me up and tell me to be quiet. Invariably I would discover, upon waking, that my bladder, which was already showing signs of being weakened by the steady inundation of cider, demanded emptying. So I had to get out of the paper bag, go away, pee, come back and get back in, thus creating a double uproar. When Trevor switched his light off again I would lie there trying not to move. Only a dead man or a yoga adept can keep that up for more than twenty minutes. Judging that Trevor was asleep again, I would essay a surreptitious turn to one side, making no more noise than a shy prospective bride unwrapping a lace-trimmed silk nightgown from its tissues. This movement completed, for a long time I would lie there, inhaling and exhaling as shallowly as possible and waiting until the sound of Trevor's steady breathing deepened into the second level of sleep. Only then would I make the necessary full turn on to the other side. A man tearing up a thin telephone directory while wading through dead leaves would have been hard put to be so silent. But if, after these manoeuvres, I dropped off to sleep, it was inevitable that an involuntary shift of weight would sooner or later produce the full effect of a large, empty cardboard box being attacked by a flock of woodpeckers. I can be sure of this because sometimes the noise woke me up as well.

Even after the student-codifying catastrophe and the subsequent agonising reappraisal, my powers of self-deception were still in healthy shape, but it was not easy to convince myself that mere lack of sleep lowered my performance at the library. I preferred to think that it was the frustration caused by not sleeping with Lilith. Having convinced myself of this, I did my best to make her see reason. In no sense of the phrase was she having any. Probably she had already guessed that I was an irredeemable incompetent. Certainly Mr Volumes had rumbled me early on. The evidence was hard to miss. I always arrived late. Oliver Goldsmith, accused of the same thing, pointed out that he always left early. Lacking his self-confidence, I merely looked sheepish. 'YOU MUST KEEP TIME, YOU KNOW,' Mr Volumes told me and the rest of the borough. Lilith had been transferred to another branch so there was nothing exciting to look at except the tramps who came in to get out of the cold. They would sit at the big leather-topped table pretending to read *Country Life* but it was obvious that the blood-bag eyes couldn't focus on anything except a bottle of methylated spirits or a tin of boot polish. You could make bets with yourself about which disease they would succumb to first, cirrhosis or gangrene. Once a month they were rounded up and hospitalised so that their socks could be removed surgically. Skin ingrained with dirt has the anomalous effect, in the right light, of looking expensively tanned, as if by the Riviera sun: an observation which, once I had made it, depressed me deeply. But the real killer was boredom. Stamping the cards of borrowers, I ran out of answers for the little old ladies who wanted to know if they had already read the book they were thinking about taking out. The smart ones used a personalised coding system. One of them would put a small inked cross on page 81 of every book before bringing it back, so that later on in the library she could turn to that page and, if she saw her mark, be reminded not to take the book out again. Another would draw a circle in red pencil around the last word on page 64. There were hundreds of them at it all the time. If you picked up a book by Dorothy L. Sayers or Margery Allingham and flicked through it, you would see a kaleidoscope of dots, crosses, blobs, circles, swastikas, etc. It was interesting but not interesting enough. When I met Lilith in the evening, I complained about having trouble concentrating. She advanced the theory that for someone whose destiny was to read and write books there could be no profit in being obliged all day to do nothing except pick them up and put them down. I took some comfort from this advice, although the historic evidence should have suggested that it was fallacious. Jorge Luis Borges and Archibald MacLeish had each pursued a successful literary career while working as a librarian. Philip Larkin was currently doing the same, although I didn't know that. Admittedly Proust had been a disaster as a librarian but that was mainly because, instead of turning up late, he never turned up at all. When Mr Volumes began hinting, in his subtle way, that I might think of pursuing a similar course, I did my long perfected number of resigning one step ahead of the boot.

Jobless in winter in a paper bag. My discomfiture had a Miltonic ring to it. But now that I was merely working through a sentence towards the day of release, defeat was easier to shrug off, or even to cherish as a token of my rebellious nature. There is also the possibility that I was clinically certifiable at the time. Sex starvation was in its downhill phase and something had gone seriously wrong with my teeth. The half-dozen of them that I had already lost didn't hurt, but those remaining in my head rarely did less than give a sharp twinge when I sucked anything – air, for example. Under Lilith's influence I was now attempting to vary my egg, bacon and sausage diet with the occasional helping of steamed greens, but the treatment was a holding operation at best. The connection between the teeth and the brain is intimate and potentially devastating: that much I knew. But you wouldn't catch me going to a dentist. I was too smart for that.

Breathing carefully through the nose – never an easy trick for a chronic sinus sufferer – I auditioned for a new job at a light metal-work factory off the Holloway Road. The supervisor wore a grey lab coat, had a short back and sides haircut polished with a buffing wheel, and favoured blunt speech. 'I'll speak bluntly,' he rapped. 'Don't like your general appearance. Don't like the beard. Don't like the fingernails.

Should have worn a suit, not that jacket. Shouldn't wear a jacket like that unless you're in the army. If you have to wear a jacket like that, should wear it tomorrow, not to your interview. Interview, you should be standing up straight, not slouching like that. Shouldn't be smoking. I'm not smoking. Why are you? Hope we won't be seeing those shoes again `. . .' The roar, clank, thump and *chong chong* of the stamping machines out on the factory floor drowned some of this out but not enough. I listened stunned, which was obviously the desired reaction, because I was taken on, as a general workman, at nine pounds a week before stoppages. Young British-born readers with qualifications but no job will doubtless wince to read of an immigrant with a job but no qualifications. All I can say is that things were different then. The economy was already collapsing but everybody thought the noise was bustle.

With proof of my employed status I found new digs around the corner from Trevor's, in Tufnell Park Road proper. Since it was by now clear that Tufnell Park was my Berlin and my Paris, it was only fitting that I should become resident in its Kurfürstendamm or Champs-Elysées. From the awe-inspiring single-story edifice of Tufnell Park tube station, Tufnell Park Road swept down majestically for half a mile until it met Holloway Road in a *carrefour* blazing with the glamorous white light of the launderette. At No. 114 I was exactly half-way down the road, and thus equidistant from the only two points of interest. My room was in the basement, with a window opening not so much on the back garden as under it, so that I looked out into a cross section of the earth. But the rent was a more than reasonable thirty shillings a week. In fact it was a snip. Mrs Bennett had not kept up with the times. She was eighty plus and walked with a stoop, which meant, since she was not very tall in the first place, that I often didn't see her before falling over her.

Not seeing her was made easier by the darkness. Her connections with the outside world had been broken on the day when her fiancé sailed away to the Middle East on the same ship as Rupert Brooke. Out there he had suffered the same fate, but without writing any poems. Understandably the modern world had ceased to interest her from that moment, and she had declined to keep up with its inventions, including any light-bulb more powerful than forty watts. The chintz furniture was well dusted but so faded that it was virtually monochrome. No doubt it was all still a riot of colour to her eyes. In the corridors and on the staircase it would have been easier to find one's way by the weak light of the frosted bulbs if only the wallpaper had been a brighter colour. But it was all brown: brown on brown with dark brown wooden trimmings. Sometimes through the layers of varnish you could see the ghost of a William Morris print, like jungle under a flooded river full of mud. Once, while she was waiting, it must have been a bright little house he would have been glad to come home to. Then she went on waiting without an object and it all turned dark. I could sympathise, but things got very tricky on the stairs, which I had to spend a certain amount of time groping up and down because the toilet was on the floor above. If you ran into her in the dark, no matter how slowly you were going, it usually meant a tumble. For her a fall would probably have entailed multiple fractures, but she was so low down that she acted as a fulcrum. It was always the rest of us – everyone in the house at some time or other – who took the dive. This wasn't so bad if you were going upstairs at the time, but if you were heading in the opposite direction it could involve a sudden plunge into the brown void, with a good chance of cracking your head against a skirting-board the colour and consistency of petrified gravy.

With its narrow bed, single-bar radiator and burnt umber decor, my little room was an unlikely setting for happiness, yet Lilith took one look at me in my new context and immediately granted the favours so long withheld. Perhaps she had been touched by the spirit of Christmas. The snow began early that year and a good deal of it had already occupied the top half of the vista through my window, above the half filled with dark earth. She had come a long way by bus to cook me my weekly lifesaving meal of liver and greens. I was knackered from a hard day in the factory. Also, chary of the effect that the cold air had on my bared teeth, I wasn't doing much talking. This was probably the key factor. Eloquence might get you started with a woman but it is often taciturnity which seals the bargain. Shakespeare has a line about it – in *Henry IV, Part I*, I think. Those who can rhyme their way into a lady's favour do always reason themselves out again. Not being able to say anything, I couldn't say the wrong thing, which left Lilith, undistracted by importunities, free to decide that in such a depth of winter there was no further point in leaving her beautiful body lonely. There is also a slim chance that I was an irresistible object of pathos, but experience suggests that even the warmest and most generous woman can be moved to tears of compassion without feeling impelled to take off her clothes.

The only real explanation, however, is that I got lucky, not only then but for the rest of my life. Right through that epic of a winter she came to me several times a week. The first love affair I had had which lasted long enough for me to get used to it, it did wonders for my confidence. It probably did wonders for my arrogance, too: her queenly bearing could not, as I recall, prevent my taking her for granted unless she issued the occasional verbal reproof. Innate tolerance – plus, no doubt, vivid memories of Emu Coogan's impecuniosity – made her slow to remonstrate, so I got away with what seemed a lot even at the time, and strikes me in retrospect as something close to white slavery. When I packed her off home on the last bus it was only common sense to give her the poems I was sending out, each batch of them accompanied by a folded self-addressed envelope and placed inside another envelope addressed to an editor. To expect her not only to post the letters but to buy the stamps for each envelope was possibly a bit much. She did it without complaining. Hearing no protest, I took everything and gave nothing.

Some stupidities only time can cure. What could be gained by experience I gained then; or the essentials of it anyway, and the deep self-doubt that inhibits and cripples was obviated at an early stage. Which is not to say that I was permanently immunised against all anxiety. In future liaisons, that particularly humiliating version of impotence known as first night failure was always to be a hazard. But when it struck, it did so in perspective, as an embarrassment rather than an affliction. All it means, if you wilt that way with a lady, is that you haven't yet really met her. You're not trying to make love to a woman, you're trying not to miss an opportunity. I have heard men say that such a thing has never happened to them. The claim, I think, speaks as much against their imaginations as for their virility, but no doubt they are telling the truth. The truth might even redound to their credit; never to be unmanned could be a sign of manhood. Those of us who can't plausibly make the same boast have at least some comfort. We find out the hard way, if that's the appropriate phrase, whether the lady has a forgiving soul. Since no other kind of woman is worth getting mixed up with, the man who crumples at the first sign of impatience should be glad to consider himself forewarned, if not forearmed.

In this case the question became academic after the first evening, and for a long winter that should have been a disaster I put on satisfaction like a weightlifter putting on muscle. Without Lilith I might have been not just unhappy, but dead. The winter deepened into the worst since 1947, then the worst since the year after the Great Fire, then the worst since the last Ice Age. The cleared snow formed long ridges at the sides of the roads. These ice ridges turned dark with dirt: burial mounds for long ships, they were pitted like breeze blocks. With thousands of tons of water lying around in frozen form, the anomalous consequence was a water shortage. So many pipes burst that the system just packed up. You had to draw your household water from a stand-pipe in the street. The residents of 114 Tufnell Park Road took turns to do this on behalf of Mrs Bennett, whose only recorded journey outside the front gate was instantly defeated by the frozen snow-ridge at the road's edge. It was taller than she was. After gazing for a while into that threatening escarpment of refrigerated lucent suet, she turned back bewildered.

Bewildered and coughing. Many old people died younger than they should have, that winter. If they were poor they died of hypothermia. If they were well enough off to keep their radiators going full-time, it was the acid fogs that got them. The fogs, the last great fogs that London was ever to see, were Dickensian epics through which I groped home from work each evening, lucky to be young and mobile. The bus that brought Lilith to me would arrive an hour late, its headlights diffused by the fog into opalescent radiance. Mrs Bennett was always glad to see Lilith and usually arranged to be on the stairs so that we could both fall over her. But soon her cough confined her to her room. For a while I was mildly afraid that she had withdrawn because of the shock induced by my poems, which she had asked to see – or had at any rate agreed to be shown – yet had obviously found to be not quite the sort of thing she had grown used to at the time when dear Rupert was into cleanness leaping. Eventually her cough became audible even through the ceiling and thus disabused me of my typically solipsistic notion. You had to be above a certain age to cough like that but anyone who qualified could be sure that there would be nothing temporary about the affliction. Once it started there was only one way of stopping it. Each droplet of fog had a molecule of sulphuric acid attached. The fog looked romantic if your beautiful girl-friend had stepped off a bus and was materialising out of it towards you with the dark outline of her duffle-coat taking shape against the nacreous cloud. To the old people it was breathtaking in a different way. Mrs Bennett was only one of the many who tried to hide from it in the bedroom. But the mist with the sharp taste got in through the old warped door jambs and the place where the window sash would no longer sit square.

Even had she been in sight she would probably still have been out of mind. Her star lodger was too busy being the horny-handed proletarian and tireless young lover. Actually the demands of the first component of this dual role often threatened to inhibit my achievements in the second. After a night spent shivering – if Lilith had been there, my room seemed colder than ever after she was gone – I arrived already tired at the machine shop, where the warm air that would otherwise have been welcome was offset by the continual uproar. The machines were devoted to taking $6' \times 4'$ sheets of metal and punching or drilling various patterns of holes in them. Punches went CHUNK CHUNK and drills went YERK YERK. An acre of machines doing both these things produced a clamour which one's ringing ears might have analysed as CHUNK YERK CHUNK YERK if one's body had not been vibrating. Physically walking on air from the interminably reiterated percussion, I heard the sound as CHU-CHU-CHUNK (CHERK YUNK!) YER-YER-YERK (UNK UNK!) ERK ERK, or sounds to that effect. The machine operators, who had been doing the same sort of work since the Second World War or even earlier, watched the flow of cutting oil and the glittering spillage of metal waste with understandable indifference. Once upon a time the perforated plates had been going into Lancaster bombers and there was point to the work. A team from *Picture Post* had come to take photographs of them cheerfully doing their bit. Now the perforated plates were going into the backs of slot machines that sold Kit-Kats and packets of Smiths Crisps. Alienation, as defined by the young Marx but better described by the older William Morris, was a palpable presence. Where Marx and Morris had both been wrong, however, was in the assumption that men alienated from their labour must necessarily be denatured. The machine-operators all drove second-hand but immaculately kept Rovers or Riley Pathfinders and had enough spare cigarettes to 'lend' me about a packet a day between them. I was the alienated one and opium was my religion.

My job was to help a man called Fred load as-yet-unperforated metal plates of specified gauge on to a trolley, wheel them to the machines, unload them in sequence, load the finished plates and wheel them back to the racks in which they were stored vertically until shipment. At the beginning and end of this chain of events there was a mildly thrilling moment when Fred picked up and put down the heavier plates by means of a Ferris hoist which ran on a rail in the roof. It was controlled electrically from a hand-set. Fred pressed the buttons on the hand-set and I steadied the plates so that they didn't swing around and swipe anybody. You couldn't call Fred's job skilled labour, so as his assistant I scarcely rated as a dogsbody. This situation was made no easier by Fred's personality. A dedicated racist, he lurked outside the machine-shop door at lunchtime so that he could shout 'ANY COCONUTS?' to the West Indian girls in transit between the steam laundry and the greasy spoon. Even worse, from my angle, he liked to shout racist jokes to me while we were working. He had a theory that all Australians were descended from Aborigines, and that any Australian immigrant into Britain was therefore part of the universal black conspiracy to deprive the British working class of employment. Compounded by the Wagnerian banging and jangling, his sentiments had the same effect on me as the iron band tightening around Cavaradossi's head. Fred's first word was always 'EAR!', by which he meant 'Here!' He kept yelling that until I paid attention. 'EAR! (CHU-CHU-CHUNK) THIS JEW (CHERK YUNK!) ANNA NIG-NOG (YUNK CHERK!) SO EASE ALL BLACK FROM A BOO POLISH (YER-YER-YERK) . . .' Fred didn't put me off the cockney accent, which had already influenced my own, no doubt with ludicrous results. But he would have gone a fair way towards putting me off the proletariat, if I had really believed that it existed. In fact my belief in such things was only theoretical, and even the theory was a fag-end. It had always been transparently obvious to me that there could be no such thing as the masses. There were only people. Even Fred was unique. That was the awful thing about him.

Thus the little factory chuntered on, with Fred and me pushing and pulling our trolley endlessly around its inner perimeter. Meanwhile the rest of the country was gradually coming to a standstill. For some reason which nobody has ever been able to figure out, the British consider themselves to be living in a tropical climate into which any intrusion of snow, no matter how brief, is always regarded as Freak

Weather Conditions. The railways, for example, are invariably brought to a halt by any snowfall heavy enough to make the rails show white instead of silver. The drivers in their Hawaiian shirts and dark glasses climb down from their cabins and quit. The trains are not allowed to move again until the commuters have had a day's rest and the tabloid newspapers – even more cretinous than the Australian equivalents – have had a chance to run headlines about the Freak Weather Conditions. (BRR! SAYS BR: IT'S SNOW-GO!) It will be understood, then, that in the winter under discussion the trains vanished for weeks on end. So did most of the livestock. The sheep were so far down that the army was using echo-sounders to find them. Then somebody had to look for the army. It would have been a good story if it had ended at the proper time. But it all went on and on. History, however, has to be truly disastrous before it impinges on your personal odyssey. For me, with my new assurance, the snow was just a backdrop. Secure within, I was looking outwards for the first time.

The owner of the business arrived in a Bentley to tour the shop-floor, his blazered school-age son in attendance. They paraded like royalty, with their hands behind their backs. Only the blunt-spoken supervisor got his hand shaken. It was because his hand was clean. In Australia the air would have been thick with first names. I really was in another country, an observer as flabbergasted by exotic ritual as those first Portuguese in China whose astonished narrative stands out even in Hakluyt's vast codex of the strange. Fascinated, I neglected to steady a batch of steel plates which Fred had just picked up with the hoist. The swinging load knocked him backwards off his feet and on to the trolley, where he lay pondering the implications while the plates shook themselves out of the grip of the hoist, crashed to the concrete on their edges a few inches from his head, and, considerably tilting away from him – instead of, as they might equally well have done, towards – accumulated thunderously on the floor like playing cards in Valhalla. At this point, but for an entirely unconnected reason, the supervisor cut the power in the machines. The owner wished to address his work-force. The clangour stopped with a reverse shock, an inburst of sound, a downroar. Fred, never quick at adjusting to circumstances, was still yelling. '. . . UCKING NIG-NOG GIT, YOU'RE AFTER MY JOB!' The owner and his son left hurriedly, even as the blunt-spoken supervisor headed towards me, his eyes narrowed with purpose.

# The Reunion

## *Charles Dickens*

Flora, always tall, had grown to be very broad too, and short of breath; but that was not much. Flora, whom he had left a lily, had become a peony; but that was not much. Flora, who had seemed enchanting in all she said and thought, was diffuse and silly. That was much. Flora, who had been spoiled and artless long ago, was determined to be spoiled and artless now. That was a fatal blow.

This is Flora!

'I am sure,' giggled Flora, tossing her head with a caricature of her girlish manner, such as a mummer might have presented at her own funeral, if she had lived and died in classical antiquity, 'I am ashamed to see Mr Clennam, I am a mere fright, I know he'll find me fearfully changed, I am actually an old woman, it's shocking to be found out, it's really shocking!'

He assured her that she was just what he had expected and that time had not stood still with himself.

'Oh! But with a gentleman it's so different and really you look so amazingly well that you have no right to say anything of the kind, while, as to me, you know – oh!' cried Flora with a little scream, 'I am dreadful!'

The Patriarch, apparently not yet understanding his own part in the drama under representation, glowed with vacant serenity.

'But if we talk of not having changed,' said Flora, who, whatever she said, never once came to a full stop, 'look at Papa, is not Papa precisely what he was when you went away, isn't it cruel and unnatural of Papa to be such a reproach to his own child, if we go on in this way much longer people who don't know us will begin to suppose that I am Papa's Mama!'

That must be a long time hence, Arthur considered.

'Oh Mr. Clennam you insincerest of creatures,' said Flora, 'I perceive already you have not lost your old way of paying compliments, your old way when you used to pretend to be so sentimentally struck you know – at least I don't mean that, I – oh I don't know what I mean!' Here Flora tittered confusedly, and gave him one of her old glances.

The Patriarch, as if he now began to perceive that his part in the piece was to get off the stage as soon as might be, rose, and went to the door by which Pancks had worked out, hailing that Tug by name. He received an answer from some little Dock beyond, and was towed out of sight directly.

'You mustn't think of going yet,' said Flora – Arthur had looked at his hat, being in a ludicrous dismay, and not knowing what to do: 'you could never be so unkind as to think of going, Arthur – I mean Mr Arthur – or I suppose Mr Clennam would be far more proper – but I am sure I don't know what I am saying – without a word about the dear old days gone for ever, when I come to think of it I dare say it would be much better not to speak of them and it's highly probable that you have some much more agreeable engagement and pray let Me be the last person in the world to interfere with it though there *was* a time, but I am running into nonsense again.'

Was it possible that Flora could have been such a chatterer in the days she referred to? Could there have been anything like her present disjointed volubility in the fascinations that had captivated him?

'Indeed I have little doubt,' said Flora, running on with astonishing speed, and pointing her conversation with nothing but commas, and very few of them, 'that you are married to some Chinese lady, being in China so long and being in business and naturally desirous to settle and extend your connection nothing was more likely than that you should propose to a Chinese lady and nothing was more natural I am sure than that the Chinese lady should accept you and think herself very well off too, I only hope she's not a Pagodian dissenter.'

'I am not,' returned Arthur, smiling in spite of himself, 'married to any lady, Flora.'

'Oh good gracious me I hope you never kept yourself a bachelor so long on my account!' tittered Flora; 'but of course you never did why should you, pray don't answer, I don't know where I'm running to, oh do tell me something about the Chinese ladies whether their eyes are really so long and narrow always putting me in mind of mother-of-pearl fish at cards and do they really wear tails down their back and plaited too or is it only the men, and when they pull their hair so very tight off their foreheads don't they hurt themselves, and why do they stick little bells all over their bridges and temples and hats and things or don't they really do it?' Flora gave him another of her old glances. Instantly she went on again, as if he had spoken in reply for some time.

'Then it's all true and they really do! good gracious Arthur! – pray excuse me – old habit – Mr Clennam far more proper – what a country to live in for so long a time, and with so many lanterns and umbrellas too how very dark and wet the climate ought to be and no doubt actually is, and the sums of money that must be made by those two trades where everybody carries them and hangs them everywhere, the little shoes too and the feet screwed back in infancy is quite surprising, what a traveller you are!'

In his ridiculous distress, Clennam received another of the old glances without in the least knowing what to do with it.

'Dear dear,' said Flora, 'only to think of the changes at home Arthur – cannot overcome it, and seems so natural, Mr Clennam far more proper – since you became familiar with the Chinese customs and language which I am persuaded you speak like a Native if not better for you were always quick and clever though immensely difficult no doubt, I am sure the tea chests alone would kill *me* if I tried, such changes Arthur – I am doing it again, seems so natural, most improper – as no one could have believed, who could have ever imagined Mrs Finching when I can't imagine it myself!'

'Is that your married name?' asked Arthur, struck, in the midst of all this, by a certain warmth of heart that expressed itself in her tone when she referred, however oddly, to the youthful relation in which they had stood to one another. 'Finching?'

'Finching oh yes isn't it a dreadful name, but as Mr F. said when he proposed to me which he did seven times and handsomely consented I must say to be what he used to call on liking twelve months, after all, he wasn't answerable for it and couldn't help it could he, Excellent man, not at all like you but excellent man!'

Flora had at last talked herself out of breath for one moment. One moment; for she recovered breath in the act of raising a minute corner of her pocket-handkerchief to her eye, as a tribute to the ghost of the departed Mr F., and began again.

'No one could dispute, Arthur – Mr Clennam – that it's quite right you should be formally friendly to me under the altered circumstances and indeed you couldn't be anything else, at least I suppose not you ought to know, but I can't help recalling that there *was* a time when things were very different.'

'My dear Mrs Finching,' Arthur began, struck by the good tone again.

'Oh not that nasty ugly name, say Flora!'

'Flora. I assure you, Flora, I am happy in seeing you once more, and in finding that, like me, you have not forgotten the old foolish dreams, when we saw all before us in the light of our youth and hope.'

'You don't seem so,' pouted Flora, 'you take it very coolly, but however I know you are disappointed in me, I suppose the Chinese ladies – Mandarinesses if you call them so – are the cause or perhaps I am the cause myself, it's just as likely.'

'No, no,' Clennam entreated, 'don't say that.'

'Oh I must you know,' said Flora, in a positive tone 'what nonsense not to, I know I am not what you expected, I know that very well.'

In the midst of her rapidity, she had found that out with the quick perception of a cleverer woman. The inconsistent and profoundly unreasonable way in which she instantly went on, nevertheless, to interweave their long-abandoned boy and girl relations with their present interview, made Clennam feel as if he were light-headed.

'One remark,' said Flora, giving their conversation, without the slightest notice and to the great terror of Clennam, the tone of a love-quarrel, 'I wish to make, one explanation I wish to offer, when your Mama came and made a scene of it with my Papa and when I was called down into the little breakfast-room where they were looking at one another with your Mama's parasol between them seated on two chairs like mad bulls what was I to do?'

'My dear Mrs Finching,' urged Clennam – 'all so long ago and so long concluded, is it worth while seriously to –'

'I can't Arthur,' returned Flora, 'be denounced as heartless by the whole society of China without setting myself right when I have the opportunity of doing so, and you must be very well aware that there was Paul and Virginia which had to be returned and which was returned without note or comment, not that I mean to say you could have written to me watched as I was but if it had only come back with a red wafer on the cover I should have known that it meant Come to Pekin Nankeen and What's the third place, barefoot.'

'My dear Mrs Finching, you were not to blame, and I never blamed you. We were both too young, too dependent and helpless, to do anything but accept our separation – Pray think how long ago,' gently remonstrated Arthur.

'One more remark,' proceeded Flora with unslackened volubility, 'I wish to make, one more explanation I wish to offer, for five days I had a cold in the head from crying which I passed entirely in the back drawing-room – there is the back drawing-room still on the first floor and still at the back of the house to confirm my words – when that dreary period had passed a lull succeeded years rolled on and Mr F. became acquainted with us at a mutual friend's, he was all attention he called next day he soon began to call three evenings a week and to send in little things for supper it was not love on Mr F.'s part it was adoration, Mr F. proposed with the full approval of Papa and what could I do?'

'Nothing whatever,' said Arthur, with the cheerfulest readiness, 'but what you did. Let an old friend assure you of his full conviction that you did quite right.'

'One last remark,' proceeded Flora, rejecting commonplace life with a wave of her hand, 'I wish to make, one last explanation I wish to offer, there *was* a time ere Mr F. first paid attentions incapable of being mistaken, but that is past and was not to be, dear Mr Clennam you no longer wear a golden chain you are free I trust you may be happy, here is Papa who is always tiresome and putting in his nose everywhere where he is not wanted.'

With these words, and with a hasty gesture fraught with timid caution – such a gesture had Clennam's eyes been familiar with in the old time – poor Flora left herself at eighteen years of age, a long long way behind again; and came to a full stop at last.

Or rather, she left about half of herself at eighteen years of age behind, and grafted the rest on to the relict of the late Mr F.; thus making a moral mermaid of herself, which her once boy-lover contemplated with feelings wherein his sense of the sorrowful and his sense of the comical were curiously blended.

For example. As if there were a secret understanding between herself and Clennam of the most thrilling nature; as if the first of a train of post-chaises and four, extending all the way to Scotland, were at that moment round the corner; and as if she couldn't (and wouldn't) have walked into the Parish Church with him, under the shade of the family umbrella, with the Patriarchal blessing on her head, and the perfect concurrence of all mankind; Flora comforted her soul with agonies of mysterious signalling, expressing dread of discovery. With the sensation of becoming more and more light-headed every minute, Clennam saw the relict of the late Mr F. enjoying herself in the most wonderful manner, by putting herself and him in their old places, and going through all the old performances – now, when the stage was dusty, when the scenery was faded, when the youthful actors were dead, when the orchestra was empty, when the lights were out. And still, through all this grotesque revival of what he remembered as having once been prettily natural to her, he could not but feel that it revived at sight of him, and that there was a tender memory in it.

The Patriarch insisted on his staying to dinner, and Flora signalled 'Yes!' Clennam so wished he could have done more than stay to dinner – so heartily wished he could have found the Flora that had been, or that never had been – that he thought the least atonement he could make for the disappointment he almost felt ashamed of, was to give himself up to the family desire. Therefore, he stayed to dinner.

Pancks dined with them. Pancks steamed out of his little dock at a quarter before six, and bore straight down for the Patriarch, who happened to be then driving, in an inane manner, through a stagnant account of Bleeding Heart Yard. Pancks instantly made fast to him and hauled him out.

'Bleeding Heart Yard?' said Pancks, with a puff and a snort. 'It's a troublesome property. Don't pay you badly, but rents are very hard to get there. You have more trouble with that one place than with all the places belonging to you.'

Just as the big ship in tow gets the credit, with most spectators, of being the powerful object, so the Patriarch usually seemed to have said himself whatever Pancks said for him.

'Indeed?' returned Clennam, upon whom this impression was so efficiently made by a mere gleam of the polished head that he spoke the ship instead of the Tug. 'The people are so poor there?'

'*You* can't say, you know,' snorted Pancks, taking one of his dirty hands out of his rusty iron-grey pockets to bite his nails, if he could find any, and turning his beads of eyes upon his employer, 'whether they're poor or not. They say they are, but they all say that. When a man says he's rich, you're generally sure he isn't. Besides, if they *are* poor, you can't help it. You'd be poor yourself if you didn't get your rents.'

'True enough,' said Arthur.

'You're not going to keep open house for all the poor of London,' pursued Pancks. 'You're not going to lodge 'em for nothing. You're not going to open your gates wide and let 'em come free. Not if you know it, you ain't.'

Mr Casby shook his head, in placid and benignant generality.

'If a man takes a room off you at half-a-crown a week, and when the week comes round hasn't got the half-crown, you say to that man, Why have you got the room, then? If you haven't got the one thing, why have you got the other? What have you been and done with your money? What do you mean by it? What are you up to? That's what *you* say to a man of that sort; and if you didn't say it, more shame for you!' Mr Pancks here made a singular and startling noise, produced by a strong blowing effort in the region of the nose, unattended by any result but that acoustic one.

'You have some extent of such property about the east and north-east here, I believe?' said Clennam, doubtful which of the two to address.

'Oh, pretty well,' said Pancks. 'You're not particular to east or north-east, any point of the compass will do for you. What you want is a good investment and a quick return. You take it where you can find it. You ain't nice as to situation – not you.'

There was a fourth and most original figure in the Patriarchal tent, who also appeared before dinner. This was an amazing little old woman, with a face like a staring wooden doll too cheap for expression, and a stiff yellow wig perched unevenly on the top of her head, as if the child who owned the doll had driven a tack through it anywhere, so that it only got fastened on. Another remarkable thing in this little old woman was, that the same child seemed to have damaged her face in two or three places with some blunt instrument in the nature of a spoon; her countenance, and particularly the tip of her nose, presenting the phenomena of several dints, generally answering to the bowl of that article. A further remarkable thing in this little old woman was, that she had no name but Mr F.'s Aunt.

She broke upon the visitor's view under the following circumstances: Flora said when the first dish was being put on the table, perhaps Mr

Clennam might not have heard that Mr F. had left her a legacy?
Clennam in return implied his hope that Mr F. had endowed the wife
whom he adored, with the greater part of his worldly substance, if not
with all. Flora said, oh yes, she didn't mean that, Mr F. had made a
beautiful will, but he had left her as a separate legacy, his Aunt. She
then went out of the room to fetch the legacy, and, on her return, rather
triumphantly presented 'Mr F.'s Aunt.'

The major characteristics discoverable by the stranger in Mr F.'s
Aunt, were extreme severity and grim taciturnity; sometimes interrupted by a propensity to offer remarks in a deep warning voice, which,
being totally uncalled for by anything said by anybody, and traceable
to no association of ideas, confounded and terrified the mind. Mr F.'s
Aunt may have thrown in these observations on some system of her
own, and it may have been ingenious, or even subtle: but the key to it
was wanted.

The neatly-served and well-cooked dinner (for everything about the
Patriarchal household promoted quiet digestion) began with some
soup, some fried soles, a butter-boat of shrimp sauce, and a dish of
potatoes. The conversation still turned on the receipt of rents. Mr F.'s
Aunt, after regarding the company for ten minutes with a malevolent
gaze, delivered the following fearful remark:

'When we lived at Henley, Barnes's gander was stole by tinkers.'

Mr Pancks courageously nodded his head and said, 'All right,
ma'am.' But the effect of this mysterious communication upon Clennam was absolutely to frighten him. And another circumstance
invested this old lady with peculiar terrors. Though she was always
staring, she never acknowledged that she saw any individual. The
polite and attentive stranger would desire, say, to consult her inclina-
tions on the subject of potatoes. His expressive action would be
hopelessly lost upon her, and what could he do? No man could say, 'Mr
F.'s Aunt, will you permit me?' Every man retired from the spoon, as
Clennam did, cowed and baffled.

There was mutton, a steak, and an apple-pie – nothing in the
remotest way connected with ganders – and the dinner went on like a
disenchanted feast, as it truly was. Once upon a time Clennam had sat
at that table taking no heed of anything but Flora; now the principal
heed he took of Flora was to observe, against his will, that she was very
fond of porter, that she combined a great deal of sherry with sentiment,

and that if she were a little overgrown, it was upon substantial grounds. The last of the Patriarchs had always been a mighty eater, and he disposed of an immense quantity of solid food with the benignity of a good soul who was feeding some one else. Mr Pancks, who was always in a hurry, and who referred at intervals to a little dirty notebook which he kept beside him (perhaps containing the names of the defaulters he meant to look up by way of dessert), took in his victuals much as if he were coaling; with a good deal of noise, a good deal of dropping about, and a puff and a snort occasionally, as if he were nearly ready to steam away.

All through dinner, Flora combined her present appetite for eating and drinking with her past appetite for romantic love, in a way that made Clennam afraid to lift his eyes from his plate; since he could not look towards her without receiving some glance of mysterious meaning or warning, as if they were engaged in a plot. Mr F.'s Aunt sat silently defying him with an aspect of the greatest bitterness, until the removal of the cloth and the appearance of the decanters, when she originated another observation – struck into the conversation like a clock, without consulting anybody.

Flora had just said, 'Mr Clennam, will you give me a glass of port for Mr F.'s Aunt.'

'The Monument near London Bridge,' that lady instantly proclaimed, 'was put up arter the Great Fire of London; and the Great Fire of London was not the fire in which your uncle George's workshops was burned down.'

Mr Pancks, with his former courage, said, 'Indeed, ma'am? All right!' But appearing to be incensed by imaginary contradiction, or other ill-usage, Mr F.'s Aunt, instead of relapsing into silence, made the following additional proclamation:

'I hate a fool!'

She imparted to this sentiment, in itself almost Solomonic, so extremely injurious and personal a character by levelling it straight at the visitor's head, that it became necessary to lead Mr F.'s Aunt from the room. This was quietly done by Flora; Mr F.'s Aunt offering no resistance, but inquiring on her way out, 'What he come there for, then?' with implacable animosity.

When Flora returned, she explained that her legacy was a clever old lady, but was sometimes a little singular, and 'took dislikes' – peculiarities of which Flora seemed to be proud rather than otherwise. As Flora's good nature shone in the case, Clennam had no fault to find with the old lady for eliciting it, now that he was relieved from the terrors of her presence; and they took a glass or two of wine in peace. Foreseeing then that the Pancks would shortly get under weigh, and that the Patriarch would go to sleep, he pleaded the necessity of visiting his mother, and asked Mr Pancks in which direction he was going?

'Citywards, sir,' said Pancks.

'Shall we walk together?' said Arthur.

'Quite agreeable,' said Pancks.

Meanwhile Flora was murmuring in rapid snatches for his ear, that there *was* a time and that the past was a yawning gulf however and that a golden chain no longer bound him and that she revered the memory of the late Mr F. and that she should be at home tomorrow at half-past one and that the decrees of Fate were beyond recall and that she considered nothing so improbable as that he ever walked on the north-west side of Gray's-Inn Gardens at exactly four o'clock in the afternoon. He tried at parting to give his hand in frankness to the existing Flora – not the vanished Flora, or the mermaid – but Flora wouldn't have it, couldn't have it, was wholly destitute of the power of separating herself and him from their bygone characters. He left the house miserably enough; and so much more light-headed than ever, that if it had not been his good fortune to be towed away, he might, for the first quarter of an hour, have drifted anywhere.

# My Day: An Introduction of Sorts

*Fran Lebowitz*

12:35 p.m. – The phone rings. I am not amused. This is not my favorite way to wake up. My favorite way to wake up is to have a certain French movie star whisper to me softly at two-thirty in the afternoon that if I want to get to Sweden in time to pick up my Nobel Prize for Literature I had better ring for breakfast. This occurs rather less often than one might wish.

Today is a perfect example, for my caller is an agent from Los Angeles who informs me that I don't know him. True, and not without reason. He is audibly tan. He is interested in my work. His interest has led him to the conclusion that it would be a good idea for me to write a movie comedy. I would, of course, have total artistic freedom, for evidently comic writers have taken over the movie business. I look around my apartment (a feat readily accomplished by simply glancing up) and remark that Dino De Laurentiis would be surprised to hear that. He chuckles tanly and suggests that we talk. I suggest that we *are* talking. He, however, means *there* and at my own expense. I reply that the only way I could get to Los Angeles at my own expense is if I were to go by postcard. He chuckles again and suggests that we talk. I agree to talk just as soon as I have won the Nobel Prize – for outstanding achievement in physics.

12:55 p.m. – I try to get back to sleep. Although sleeping is an area in which I have manifested an almost Algeresque grit and persistence, I fail to attain my goal.

1:20 p.m. – I go downstairs to get the mail. I get back into bed. Nine press releases, four screening notices, two bills, an invitation to a party in honor of a celebrated heroin addict, a final disconnect notice from New York Telephone, and three hate letters from *Mademoiselle* readers demanding to know just what it is that makes me think that I have the right to regard houseplants – *green, living* things – with such marked distaste. I call the phone company and try to make a deal, as actual payment is not a possibility. Would they like to go to a screening? Would they care to attend a party for a heroin addict? Are they interested in knowing just what it is that makes me think that I have the right to regard houseplants with such marked distaste? It seems they would not. They would like $148.10. I agree that this is, indeed, an understandable preference, but caution them against the bloodless quality of a life devoted to the blind pursuit of money. We are unable to reach a settlement. I pull up the covers and the phone rings. I spend the next few hours fending off editors, chatting amiably, and plotting revenge. I read. I smoke. The clock, unfortunately, catches my eye.

3.40 p.m. – I consider getting out of bed. I reject the notion as being unduly vigorous. I read and smoke a bit more.

4:15 p.m. – I get up feeling curiously unrefreshed. I open the refrigerator. I decide against the half a lemon and jar of Gulden's mustard and on the spur of the moment choose instead to have breakfast out. I guess that's just the kind of girl I am – whimsical.

5:10 p.m. – I return to my apartment laden with magazines and spend the remainder of the afternoon reading articles by writers who, regrettably, met their deadlines.

6:55 p.m. – A romantic interlude. The object of my affections arrives bearing a houseplant.

9:30 p.m. – I go to dinner with a group of people that includes two fashion models, a fashion photographer, a fashion photographer's representative, and an art director. I occupy myself almost entirely with the art director – drawn to him largely because he knows the most words.

2:05 p.m. – I enter my apartment and prepare to work. In deference to the slight chill I don two sweaters and an extra pair of socks. I pour myself a club soda and move the lamp next to the desk. I reread several old issues of *Rona Barrett's Hollywood* and a fair piece of *The Letters of Oscar Wilde*. I pick up my pen and stare at the paper. I light a cigarette. I stare at the paper. I write, 'My Day: An Intro- duction of Sorts.' Good. Lean yet cadenced. I consider my day. I become unaccountably depressed. I doodle in the margin. I jot down an idea I have for an all-black version of a Shakespearean comedy to be called *As You Likes It*. I look longingly at my sofa, not unmindful of the fact that it converts cleverly into a bed. I light a cigarette. I stare at the paper.

4:50 a.m. – The sofa wins. Another victory for furniture.

# A Fight With A Trout

*Charles Dudley Warner*

Trout-fishing in the Adirondacks would be a more attractive pastime than it is, but for the popular notion of its danger. The trout is a retiring and harmless animal, except when he is aroused and forced into a combat; and then his agility, fierceness and vindictiveness become apparent. No one who has studied the excellent pictures representing men in an open boat, exposed to the assaults of long-enraged trout flying at them through the open air with open mouth, ever ventures with his rod upon the lonely lakes of the forest without a certain terror, or ever reads of the exploits of daring fishermen without a feeling of admiration for their heroism. Most of their adventures are thrilling, and all of them are, in narration, more or less unjust to the trout: in fact, the object of them seems to be to exhibit, at the expense of the trout, the shrewdness, the skill, and the muscular power of the sportsman. My own simple story has few of these recommendations.

We had built our bark camp one summer, and were staying on one of the popular lakes of the Saranac region. It would be a very pretty region if it were not so flat; if the margins of the lakes had not been flooded by dams at the outlets – which have killed the trees, and left a rim of ghastly dead-wood like the swamps of the under-world pictured by Doré's bizarre pencil – and if the pianos at the hotels were in tune. It would be an excellent sporting-region also (for there is water enough) if the fish commissioners would stock the waters, and if previous hunters had not pulled all the hair and skin off from the deers' tails. Formerly sportsmen had a habit of catching the deer by the tails, and of being dragged in mere wantonness round and round the shores. It is well known that, if you seize a deer by this 'holt', the skin will slip off like the peel from a banana. This reprehensible practice was carried so far, that the traveler is now hourly pained by the sight of peeled-tail deer mournfully sneaking about the wood.

We had been hearing, for weeks, of a small lake in the heart of the virgin forest, some ten miles from our camp, which was alive with trout, unsophisticated, hungry trout: the inlet to it was described as *stiff* with them. In my imagination I saw them lying there in ranks and rows, each a foot long, three tiers deep, a solid mass. The lake had never been visited, except by stray sable-hunters in the winter, and was known as the Unknown Pond. I determined to explore it; fully expecting, however, that it would prove to be a delusion, as such mysterious haunts of the trout usually are. Confiding my purpose to Luke, we secretly made our preparations, and stole away from the shanty one morning at daybreak. Each of us carried a boat, a pair of blankets, a sack of bread, pork, and maple-sugar; while I had my case of rods, creel, and book of flies, and Luke had an axe and the kitchen utensils. We think nothing of loads of this sort in the woods.

Five miles through a tamarack-swamp brought us to the inlet of Unknown Pond, upon which we embarked our fleet, and paddled down its vagrant waters. They were at first sluggish, winding among *triste* fir-trees, but gradually developed a strong current. At the end of three miles a loud roar ahead warned us that we were approaching rapids, falls and cascades. We paused. The danger was unknown. We had our choice of shouldering our loads and making a *détour* through the woods, or of 'shooting the rapids'. Naturally we chose the more dangerous course. Shooting the rapids has often been described, and I will not repeat the description here. It is needless to say that I drove my frail bark through the boiling rapids, over the successive waterfalls, amid rocks and vicious eddies, and landed, half a mile below, with whitened hair and a boat half full of water; and that the guide was upset, and boat, contents and man were strewn along the shore.

After this common experience we went quickly on our journey, and, a couple of hours before sundown, reached the lake. If I live to my dying-day, I never shall forget its appearance. The lake is almost an exact circle, about a quarter of a mile in diameter. The forest about it was untouched by axe, and unkilled by artificial flooding. The azure water had a perfect setting of evergreens, in which all the shades of the fir, the balsam, the pine, and the spruce were perfectly blended; and at intervals on the shore in the emerald rim blazed the ruby of the cardinal-flower. It was at once evident that the unruffled waters had never been vexed by the keel of a boat. But what chiefly attracted my attention, and amused me, was the boiling of the water, the bubbling and breaking, as if the lake were a vast kettle, with a fire underneath. A tyro would have been astonished at this common phenomenon; but sportsmen will at once understand me when I say that the water *boiled* with the breaking trout. I studied the surface for some time to see upon what sort of flies they were feeding, in order to suit my cast to their appetites; but they seemed to be at play rather than feeding, leaping high in the air in graceful curves, and tumbling about each other as we see them in Adirondack pictures.

It is well known that no person who regards his reputation will ever kill a trout with anything but a fly. It requires some training on the part of the trout to take to this method. The uncultivated, unsophisticated trout in unfrequented waters prefers the bait; and the rural people, whose sole object in going a-fishing appears to be to catch fish, indulge them in their primitive taste for the worm. No sportsman, however, will use anything but a fly, except he happens to be alone.

While Luke launched my boat, and arranged his seat in the stern, I prepared my rod and line. The rod is a bamboo, weighing seven ounces, which has to be spliced with a winding of silk thread every time it is used. This is a tedious process; but, by fastening the joints in this way, a uniform spring is secured in the rod. No one devoted to high art would think of using a socket joint. My line was forty yards of untwisted silk upon a multiplying reel. The 'leader' (I am very particular about my leaders) had been made to order from a domestic animal with which I had been acquainted. The fisherman requires as good a catgut as the violinist. The interior of the house-cat, it is well known, is exceedingly sensitive; but it may not be so well known that the reason why some cats leave the room in distress when a piano-forte is played is because the two instruments are not in the same key, and the vibrations of the chords of the one are in discord with the catgut of the other. On six feet of this superior article I fixed three artificial flies – a simple brown hackle, a gray body with scarlet wings, and one of my own invention, which I thought would be new to the most experienced fly-catcher. The trout-fly does not resemble any known species of insect. It is a 'conventionalized' creation, as we say of ornamentation. The theory is, that, fly-fishing being a high art, the fly must not be a tame imitation of nature, but an artistic suggestion of it. It requires an artist to construct one; and not every bungler can take a bit of red flannel, a peacock's feather, a flash of tinsel thread, a cock's plume, a section of a hen's wing, and fabricate a tiny object that will not look like any fly, but still will suggest the universal conventional fly.

I took my stand in the centre of the tipsy boat; and Luke shoved off, and slowly paddled towards some lily-pads, while I began casting – unlimbering my tools, as it were. The fish had all disappeared. I got out, perhaps, fifty feet of line, with no response, and gradually increased it to one hundred. It is not difficult to learn to cast; but it is difficult to learn not to snap off the flies at every throw. Of this, however, we will not speak. I continued casting for some moments, until I became satisfied that there had been a miscalculation. Either the trout were too green to know what I was at, or they were dissatisfied with my offers. I reeled in, and changed the flies (that is, the fly that was not snapped off). After studying the color of the sky, of the water, and of the foliage, and the moderated light of the afternoon, I put on a series of beguilers, all of a subdued brilliancy, in harmony with the approach of evening. At the second cast, which was a short one, I saw a splash where the leader fell, and gave an excited jerk. The next instant I perceived the game, and did not need the unfeigned 'dam' of Luke to convince me that I had snatched his felt hat from his head, and deposited it among the lilies. Discouraged by this, we whirled about, and paddled over to the inlet, where a little ripple was visible in the tinted light. At the very first cast I saw that the hour had come. Three trout leaped into the air. The danger of this manoeuvre all fishermen understand. It is one of the commonest in the woods: three heavy trout taking hold at once, rushing in different directions, smash the tackle into flinders. I evaded this catch, and threw again. I recall the moment. A hermit thrush, on the tip of a balsam, uttered his long, liquid, evening note. Happening to look over my shoulder, I saw the peak of Marcy gleam rosy in the sky (I can't help it that Marcy is fifty miles off, and cannot be seen from this region: these incidental touches are always used). The hundred feet of silk swished through the air, and the tail-fly fell as lightly on the water as a three-cent-piece (which no slamming will give the weight of a ten) drops upon the contribution-plate. Instantly there was a rush, a swirl. I struck, and 'Got him, by –!' Never mind what Luke said I got him by. 'Out on a fly!' continued that irreverent guide; but I told him to back water and make for the centre of the lake. The trout, as soon as he felt the prick of the hook, was off like a

shot, and took out the whole of the line with a rapidity that made it
smoke. 'Give him the butt!' shouted Luke. It is the usual remark in such
an emergency. I gave him the butt; and, recognizing the fact and my
spirit, the trout at once sank to the bottom, and sulked. It is the most
dangerous mood of a trout; for you cannot tell what he will do next. We
reeled up a little, and waited five minutes for him to reflect. A
tightening of the line enraged him, and he soon developed his tactics.
Coming to the surface, he made straight for the boat faster than I could
reel in, and evidently with hostile intentions. 'Look out for him!' cried
Luke as he came flying in the air. I evaded him by dropping flat in the
bottom of the boat; and when I picked my traps up, he was spinning
across the lake as if he had a new idea: but the line was still fast. He did
not run far. I gave him the butt again; a thing he seemed to hate, even as
a gift. In a moment the evil-minded fish, lashing the water in his rage
was coming back again, making straight for the boat, as before. Luke,
who was used to these encounters, having read of them in the writings
of travelers he had accompanied, raised his paddle in self-defense. The
trout left the water about ten feet from the boat, and came directly at me
with fiery eyes, his speckled sides flashing like a meteor. I dodged as he
whisked by with a vicious slap of his bifurcated tail, and nearly upset
the boat. The line was of course slack; and the danger was that he would
entangle it about me, and carry away a leg. This was evidently his
game; but I untangled it, and only lost a breast-button or two by the
swiftly moving string. The trout plunged into the water with a hissing
sound, and went away again with all the line on the reel. More butt;
more indignation on the part of the captive. The contest had now been
going on for half an hour, and I was getting exhausted. We had been
back and forth across the lake, and round and round the lake. What I
feared was, that the trout would start up the inlet, and wreck us in the
bushes. But he had a new fancy, and began the execution of a
manoeuvre which I had never read of. Instead of coming straight
towards me, he took a large circle, swimming rapidly, and *gradually
contracting his orbit*. I reeled in, and kept my eye on him. Round and
round he went, narrowing his circle. I began to suspect the game; which
was, to twist my head off. When he had reduced the radius of his circle
to about twenty-five feet, he struck a tremendous pace through the
water. It would be false modesty in a sportsman to say that I was not
equal to the occasion. Instead of turning round with him, as he

expected, I stepped to the bow, braced myself, and let the boat swing. Round went the fish, and round we went like a top. I saw a line of Mount Marcys all round the horizon; the rosy tint in the west made a broad band of pink along the sky above the tree-tops; the evening star was a perfect circle of light, a hoop of gold in the heavens. We whirled and reeled, and reeled and whirled. I was willing to give the malicious beast butt and line and all, if he would only go the other way for a change.

When I came to myself, Luke was gaffing the trout at the boat-side. After we had got him in, and dressed him, he weighed three-quarters of a pound. Fish always lose by being 'got in and dressed.' It is best to weigh them while they are in the water. The only really large one I ever caught got away with my leader when I first struck him. He weighed ten pounds.

# Home Cooking

## *Leslie Thomas*

'Would you like some coffee, sir?' asked Schorner. 'We make great coffee.' He glanced at Bryant. The general said: 'No thanks. I'd really like to take a looksee around the evacuation region. Is it under way now? Are they being moved out?'

'It started today, sir,' said Bryant. Schorner had nodded at him. 'We hope that everybody will be out, with all the belongings they can take with them, within two weeks.'

Georgeton had turned back towards his car. 'The civilian population can't be very pleased about things,' he suggested, ' . . . about us.'

Bryant was careful. 'Nobody's happy about it, sir. Obviously. But they're getting on with it. It's all part of the war, most of them understand that.'

'Right, let's go,' said the general. 'Maybe we can get a bite to eat on the route. I figure we'll learn more like that than sitting with our own army.'

Bryant swallowed. 'Well, yes . . . I suppose that could be arranged, sir. I could phone the hotel at Wilcoombe. But . . . it won't be very special, I'm afraid. Not what you would get in America.'

'That's okay, son,' said Georgeton easily. 'I didn't come across the ocean to eat.'

At first Bryant conducted them along the coast road, along the elongated landing beach. They stood in a tight group, Bryant a short distance away, collars up against the rattling wind, looking out to the Channel through binoculars, as if by some chance they would be able to see their enemy a hundred and more miles away. Bryant had stood separately, out of deference, in case they should be discussing things not meant for his subaltern's ears. The general pointed out to sea and Schorner and Scarlett gazed dutifully in that direction. Bryant had a faint reminder of one of the pictures of childhood, 'The Boyhood of Raleigh'. Georgeton's voice was carried back to him by the wind. 'Start Bay, Start Point. A good place to begin.'

He heard Schorner approve and smiled to himself because Schorner had said the same thing earlier. They turned back from the beach. 'Where are the lakes?' asked Georgeton. 'The lakes are important.'

Schorner glanced towards Bryant, as if wondering how much he knew. The senior officer trudged back to the exposed road and the staff car. 'The lakes are just along behind the road, just a few hundred yards,' said Bryant. 'They're known as the leys.'

'If the GI hears that he'll think we've set up a whole load of easy women for him,' joked the general as they climbed into the warmth of the car. 'Boy, will he be disappointed.' He shook his head and laughed: 'Wow, the leys,' he repeated.

They drove for a minute with the gushing sea on one side and dark high reeds, swaying as though threatening them on the other. Soon the car cleared the banks and the small lakes came into view. 'Hold it,' instructed Georgeton. 'Let's take a look from here.'

They left the car and leaned against it, sheltering, looking out over the ribbed and ruffled water of the modest lakes. Some geese took concern and flapped away from their habitation with a startling honking. There was a narrow bridge going across from the coast road to the further bank of the lakes, a distance of a hundred yards. It was supported on wooden piles. The wind seemed to move it.

The general studied the riffled water with care, raising his field glasses like a bird watcher, searching the reeded banks on the far side. Scarlett and Schorner both followed his gaze through their field glasses. Bryant felt a little foolish standing there with only his eyes. He put his hand up like a shield and followed the direction of their watching. All he could see was cold, trapped water and grey-green winter rushes.

Georgeton took a long time examining the water and its fringes. Then he raised his glasses to the hinterland, rising, but not steeply, up through the wooded Devon coombes. Some fields were pale, January green, others vivid ploughed red. A few cattle dawdled on a meadow across the water. The general examined each of the rifts, the coombes, that sliced steeply into the quiet landscape. 'Good,' he said: 'That's real good.'

He turned a quarter turn and took in the roofs and walls of

Wilcoombe, climbing the hill to the west. The church pointed like an admonishment into the dun sky. 'That town would be outside the area,' said Georgeton.

'Yes, sir,' replied Schorner. 'Just. The boundary will be at the western edge of the lakes. That's where the wire will be.'

'I hope the gunners can shoot straight,' muttered Georgeton. 'I don't care for the idea of them massacring the English before they've accounted for any Germans.

He turned quickly on Bryant. It was as if he had suddenly made an important military decision. 'Lieutenant,' he said, using the English pronunciation, 'I'm hungry.'

'Yes, sir,' said Bryant. He ventured, 'I was afraid you might say that.'

The Americans laughed together. Scarlett winked at him, his first sign of friendliness. The general said: 'Like I said, son, I didn't come all this way to eat well. Maybe it will give us some idea of how you British have suffered.'

Bryant thought it might. He said: 'I tried the hotel in Wilcoombe, but they didn't advise it themselves, not their lunch. The Telcoombe Beach Hotel sounded more promising, so I've asked them to keep a table for four. I had to take it. It's necessary to make a booking.'

'They get short of tables?' asked Scarlett.

'No, food,' replied Bryant.

They laughed again and Georgeton patted the English officer on the back. 'Okay,' he said as they climbed once more into the car. 'Let them do their worst.'

'That's what I'm afraid of,' said Bryant.

The Telcoombe Beach Hotel was a raddled, once-white building, set immediately against the short sand and reed bluffs that divided the shore from the straight road. On one side it put a brave but ageing face to the sea and on the other looked over the more placid water of the leys and the elevated countryside behind them. Bryant was conscious of moving lace curtains and faces flitting against the windows as they left the car. It had begun to rain, immediately heavy, and it splattered against them as they ran to the hotel's porch entrance.

Inside they were greeted by a distraught elderly woman in the tired black and white fatigues of an English waitress. 'Mr Bonner's away,' she apologized immediately. She saw Bryant's uniform and turned to him as a compatriot. 'Would you tell them that he's had to go to Plymouth,' she pleaded as if the Americans understood only a foreign tongue. 'He couldn't put it off,' she continued. 'Even for the military.' She began to take their coats, almost staggering under the weight. Georgeton kindly told her not to concern herself and they put the greatcoats on the hooks of a fine brass hall-stand.

'Don't worry about Mr Bonner,' Bryant assured her. The Americans looked amused. 'We don't want any fuss. Just whatever you happen to have for lunch.'

There was a glass door immediately behind him. A small, crooked, black painted door, the panes half muffled with a faded flower curtain. First the curtain moved, then the door opened and an old face appeared. A nervously smiling elderly lady emerged.

'King George the Fifth once stayed here,' she announced. 'He said he enjoyed it. He wrote it down in the visitors' book.'

The officers turned and examined the shrivelled and stooped figure. 'Yes, Mrs Katlin,' said the waitress with subdued impatience. 'But I don't suppose these gentlemen would be very interested in that. They're Americans.'

'They ought to be,' said the old lady stoutly. 'If they intend to blow the place up . . . Our late gracious King laid his head here. Nothing seems to matter any more.'

She closed the door with a finality which suggested she could not bear to discuss the story further. The waitress frowned apologetically. 'Mrs Katlin is our oldest resident,' she explained, indicating that said everything. 'She was actually here when the late King stayed. She's never forgotten.' The woman led them into a low dining-room. It was tatty but clean. A table with a white cloth had been set near the window. The cloth was so starched it looked like cardboard. A glass jug of water stood among the shining cutlery. 'She's our only resident now,' went on the waitress as she led them to the corner. 'And of course she will be having to move on.' She had been holding back a sniff which now escaped. 'Or be killed,' she sobbed dramatically. She turned away still sniffing.

The men grimaced at each other. 'I'm beginning to feel suspiciously like a louse already,' muttered Georgeton. He glanced at Bryant. 'Do all the folk react like that?'

'A great many,' nodded Bryant. 'But they'll get over it. Some of them may even enjoy it. Particularly the younger people. They won't feel so trapped. It's the most exciting thing that's happened around here since Drake played bowls.'

'Sure,' said Georgeton as if he personally recalled the incident. 'On Plymouth Hoe. That can't be too far.'

'About eighteen miles,' said Bryant.

'And the Pilgrim Fathers, they sailed from Plymouth, right?' put in Scarlett.

'I think they cheated,' smiled Bryant. 'Or somebody has. The truth is they sailed from Southampton. They only put into Plymouth because of a storm.'

'I wonder how they felt,' ruminated Schorner. 'They set off for the New World and they land in their own country. I bet some of them felt like walking straight back home.'

Bryant thought a quick look went between them. He coughed and passed the menu, pounded out on a near-blind typewriter, around the table. A second waitress, a fair representation of the menu smudged on her apron, appeared and stood with apprehensive obedience at the table. 'Sprouts?' asked General Georgeton. 'I am about to display my ignorance. What is a sprout?'

Scarlett and Schorner looked towards Bryant. The young Englishman said: 'Sprouts, sir? They're green and sort of oval.'

'Like small cabbages,' put in the waitress quite briskly. 'Boiled.'

'Gee, I must taste them. And what's this "meat of the day"?'

'Spam,' she replied defiantly. She gave a huffy little glance at Bryant now, her former nervousness gone, as if to ask how these men thought they were going to beat the Third Reich if they were not even aware of the existence of sprouts and Spam.

'It's American, I believe,' put in Bryant tentatively.

The first waitress, the woman who had been at the front door, sidled towards the table. 'It's Tang today,' she informed Bryant from the corner of her mouth.

He looked up, embarrassed, and said to the Americans: 'Sorry, it's Tang.'

'What's Tang?' inquired Schorner after a look at the general.

'Same as Spam,' said the woman firmly.

The second waitress nodded like someone whose language was being interpreted. 'It's the same,' she said.

The general said: 'There's no point in coming from America to eat American Spam or Tang. I guess I'll take the sausages.'

Bryant shot a warning glance towards Scarlett. But it was too late. The first waitress said: 'That's all there is. Apart from Tang.'

The second waitress wrote the order laboriously on her pad. 'Everybody?' she said briskly.

The three Americans nodded. Bryant attempted to say something but the woman darted to him challengingly and he miserably acquiesced. 'Four sausages,' she enunciated triumphantly. 'Sprouts and boiled.' Nobody argued. She looked up from her pad brightly. 'Egg?' she suggested. 'We do have egg today.'

'It's dried egg,' said Bryant, desperately shaking his head at the Americans. 'It's not like real egg.'

The waitress regarded him as she might regard a traitor. 'Nothing's like the real thing these days is it, sir,' she puffed. She violently crossed out the word Egg from her pad. 'Dessert?' she said. She paused. 'I suppose nobody wanted the soup, did they?' she said. Even she was against them having the soup. Her unhappy eyes turned down to Bryant, now seeking him as an ally. 'Brown Windsor,' she whispered. She shook her head in warning.

Bryant's eyes went around the puzzled Amercian faces. 'The soup is Brown Windsor,' he announced.

'Sounds like a horse,' said Scarlett jocularly.

'It probably is,' muttered Bryant.

The waitress sniffed fiercely. 'No soup then,' she said. 'Now, dessert.'

'I want Yorkshire pudding,' said General Georgeton decisively. 'I heard all about Yorkshire pudding. Is it on the menu?'

The waitress returned her face to Bryant. 'You tell him,' she suggested.

He nodded. 'Well, sir, Yorkshire pudding is not actually pudding. You eat it with meat.'

'We've got some,' the waitress put in stoutly. 'From yesterday. But we've got no meat to go with it.' She brightened. 'You can still have it, though.'

Bryant rolled his eyes, but the general was pleased with his own show of initiative. 'Okay, okay,' he said enthusiastically. 'I'll take it.' The others nodded. They would too.

'Good,' said the waitress like a schoolteacher getting through at last to a class of backward pupils. 'Now, dessert. How about gooseberries?'

'How about them?' said Schorner. He leaned towards Bryant. 'For Christ's sake, what are gooseberries?'

'They're green,' replied the waitress before Bryant could speak. 'Sometimes a bit hairy. You have them with custard.' She paused and leaned forward confidingly. 'That's yellow.'

'I guess we'll stick with the Yorkshire pudding,' decided the general.

'But . . . ' began the waitress.

Bryant leaned heavily towards her. 'Yorkshire pudding,' he said.

'For pudding?'

'For pudding,' he confirmed.

She slapped her notepad shut, sniffed and turned. 'As you wish,' she said. 'It's your funeral.'

When she had disappeared through yet another lace-curtained door, this one apparently to the kitchen, for the lace was adhering to the steamed panes of glass, Bryant spread his hands apologetically. 'It's the war . . . ' he began.

'I didn't know it was that serious,' mentioned Scarlett. 'Can you get a drink in this hotel?'

'Oh, I should think so.' The first waitress was hovering near the back wall of the dining-room. He motioned her to the table. 'Could we have something to drink,' he asked. Her eyes went to the table but he forestalled her. 'Apart from the water,' he said.

'There's wine,' she said confidingly. 'Norwegian.'

'Norwegian? I didn't know . . .'

'Well, *we* don't know for sure. There was some Norwegians here and they *said* it came from Norway, but I thought it was odd myself. It didn't have a label on it, so I don't know what it is. They were nice boys though, pilots. Two of them got killed over Salcombe . . . ' she hesitated guiltily. 'Though we're not supposed to say that, are we.'

'Do you have anything else?'

'Beer,' she said. 'And scrumpy.'

The general, using his initiative again, asked: 'Scrumpy?'

'Cider, sir. Local brew,' said Bryant quickly.

'Okay, let's try that. When in Rome . . .'

'Four half-pints then,' ordered Bryant cautiously. 'Not the rough stuff.'

'It's getting near the bottom of the barrel,' muttered the waitress. 'There's all sorts of muck down there. At the bottom.'

'Four halves,' repeated Bryant firmly.

He was beginning to feel like someone besieged, repelling relays of attacks. No sooner had the first waitress retreated than the second reappeared, new stains on her pinafore, bearing a tray which, from a distance, appeared to be on fire.

'Red hot,' she called cheerfully as she advanced on them. 'Sausages, sprouts and boiled.'

The first waitress brought the four half-pints of cider and put them on the table as the food was being passed around. She stood, with a sort of perverse proprietorial attitude, while the wood-like sausages, the steaming green sprouts and the weeping potatoes were placed in front of the strangers.

'Thank you,' they chorused. 'Thank you.' Bryant looked down through the steam rising to his face from the plate and covered his eyes. Jesus, what a mess.

General Georgeton nodded cheerfully at him through the steam. It had begun to make his eyes water. Scarlett and Schorner examined the food with their forks.

The waitress produced a gravy boat and poured a libation over Scarlett's plate. Schorner watched with silent concern and then raised his hand. 'No soup, thank you,' he said.

The General followed quickly. 'No soup, thanks. I don't want to ruin it.'

Bryant thought it was best to be silent. Resolutely, he kept his eyes down while he began to eat. The wordlessness from the Americans, however, eventually forced him to look up. Schorner had opened a sausage and tasted the sawdust-like filling. He quickly picked up his cider and drank just as suddenly, swallowing the sausage debris and the cider together, a combination that set him coughing. Scarlett was eating something and patently not enjoying it. The general said quietly: 'When we start to bomb this area, let's make sure we hit the sprout fields, okay?'

# Confessions of A Failed Southern Lady
## Junior High

*Florence King*

I graduated from elementary school that spring. Near the end of the sixth grade we were given an IQ test without being told what it was. The teacher, a huggybear, became so unhinged by the mere thought of a sabot being tossed into her leveling machine that she spent most of the morning praising the forthcoming test in an Aeschylean speech that sounded like Clytemnestra compulsively telling everyone who would listen that she had never, no never, committed adultery.

'I have some good news! You're going to take the most wonderful test tomorrow. It's going to be *fun*! I'll bet you think that's too good to be true, don't you? Well, it *is* true – how about that? Now, it's a *leetle* bit different from what you're used to. You have to use a special pencil, and you'll be timed. But it has lots of pictures of things like, oh, slices of pie and circles and squares and such. And best of all – oh, I know you'll be happy to hear this – you won't get a grade on it!'

'Then why are we taking it?' I asked.

I got the look all Cassandras get. 'To help you get used to grownup tests,' the huggybear replied, forcing a laugh. 'You're growing up and going to junior high.'

After the test, Peg and I compared notes. Considering our long-standing mutual aid pact wherein I copied her math and she copied my spelling, our reactions were not surprising.

'I finished the pies way ahead of time,' she said, 'but I only got halfway through the part with the story and the list of words.'

'I was the other way around. The story and words were easy but the pies got on my nerves.'

'You were supposed to figure out which pieces made a whole circle and which were the extra ones that didn't fit.'

'I know. That's why they got on my nerves.'

'I bet they're trying to find out what we're good at.'

'But they already know.'

A voice behind us spoke.

'They're trying to find out who's smart and who's dumb so they'll know what track to put us in when we get to junior high.'

It was Ann Hopkins, the only girl in the sixth grade able to wear a skirt without suspenders to hold it up. She was what Granny called 'overdeveloped.'

'What's a track?' I asked.

'There's 7A1, 7A2, 7A3, and 7A4. Four is smartest, three is next-to-smartest, two is average, and one is dumb. I want to be in 7A2 so I can be popular. Average kids are always the most popular.' Her eyes widened. 'It's even more important for girls to be average. Boys don't like smart girls but you have to be smart enough to ask the right questions when a boy is explaining something to you, so that's why I want to be average. You get the most dates.'

On a hot rainy September morning, Peg, Helen, and I walked to Powell Junior High just above 14th and Park Road. My New Look transparent plastic raincoat, the last word in postwar fashion, was so long that water dripped off the hem directly into the top of my socks. We squished into the building and followed the signs to the auditorium and took seats. At nine the principal entered, followed by four women teachers. He mounted the podium and unfolded some papers.

'I will call the names of those of you assigned to 7A4. When you hear your name, rise and stand by the wall until the group is complete.'

Our three names were not among the ones he called. When the intellectual plutocrats had left with their new homeroom teacher, the principal began on the 7A3s. We were in it, and so was Ann Hopkins. As we made our way to the wall, Peg and I exchanged a resigned glance.

'Words,' she said.

'Pies,' I replied.

Ann groaned at the thought of being next-to-smartest instead of average.

A pretty blond teacher named Miss Ogilvy beckoned us to follow her. As I squished moistly behind her I admired the way her New Look skirt swirled glamourously in undulating waves near her ankles. It also stayed up on her hips, while mine was pinned to my undershirt. To complete the contrast, she looked as fresh as a daisy and I was beginning to smell. It was the plastic raincoat. Some amazing new synthetic chemical, as yet unperfected, was wafting from it like vapor from a cesspool. I sniffed at my forearm and nearly gagged. Whatever it was, it had clung tenaciously to me.

In homeroom, Miss Ogilvy arranged us alphabetically, made a seating chart, assigned lockers, gave us our class schedules, and asked for someone to act as class chaplain for the daily Bible reading. I scrunched down and concealed my face in my stinking arms, terrified that she would pick me because I looked – yes, *looked* – like a class chaplain. Ann Hopkins volunteered for the job and I breathed again.

When the first period bell rang we remained seated because our first class was English and Miss Ogilvy was also our English teacher. After issuing us our books, she passed out composition paper and told us to write a theme on one of the topics she listed on the blackboard. They were: 'What I Did This Summer,' 'What I Want To Be When I Grow Up,' and 'My Family.'

I had no idea what I wanted to be when I grew up. Ann Hopkins did. I glanced over and saw her scrawling 'Wife and mother' in her purple ink and circling the dot over the *i* in her customary way. She and I had already clashed over her ambitions. For all I had heard about ancestors, I had no wish to be one. The idea of having children so they could have children so *they* could have children frightened me. It seemed so pointless, like that blissful measure of time in Heaven that so comforted the devout: 'If a bird transferred every grain of sand on every beach, grain by grain, and dropped them in the ocean, that is the beginning of eternity.'

I derived comfort from what I called 'overness,' possibly because Herb's Socratic dialogues always ended in such neat, inescapable conclusions. Thinking of him, I decided to write on 'My Family.'

My grandmother lives with us. She is my mother's mother, but new people moving into our building always guess it wrong. They think my father is her son instead of her son-in-law because he's so polite to her. When I didn't catch a mother-in-law joke on the radio, Aunt Charlotte said it was because I never saw the kind of stuff that usually goes on between a man and his mother-in-law.

Granny's friends like my father, too. They are all Daughters. When they come to see her, he always tells them little things about history that they like. Tessie Satterfield, who brought me into this world, calls my father a prince among men. Jensy, the colored woman who works for us, says they broke the mold when they made my father. The librarians at Mount Pleasant all like him, too. All women like my father but he doesn't have any men friends. I guess that's because he's so nice.


I felt I could have done better if only I had not smelled. My arms had absorbed most of the chemical and reeked at the slightest movement; trying to contain it had affected my penmanship as well as my thoughts. When the bell rang I rushed into the girls' room and washed myself wherever the raincoat had touched me, but the smell remained, at least in my imagination.

I could not afford a lapse like this. I was used to being a pariah for flattering reasons, but now I was a real pariah and it made me feel vulnerable. Dimly I sensed that a female with a personality like mine has to make sure that she looks and smells good at all times, or as Henry Adams put it: 'Those who study Greek must take pains with their dress.' So far I had kept the watery moles in a state of resentful awe, but if I stank, their mood would change to scorn and I would be powerless. Nobody cared how a loner boy smelled, but a girl who is a misanthrope must be nice to be near.

The raincoat fiasco traumatized me so much that I did something completely out of character: I took Granny's long-ignored advice on ladylike graciousness and tried to be friendly.

The object of my sudden warmth was a late enrollee named Harriet Mudd, who stalked into homeroom the next morning and thrust her card at Miss Ogilvy. She had muscular shoulders, thick glasses, and tiny black eyes with an odd bright shine. Her complexion was taupe and her demeanour grim.

'I'm afraid all the lockers have been assigned, Harriet,' said Miss Ogilvy, 'but I'm sure one of the girls would be happy to share hers with you.' She turned to us. 'Do I have a volunteer?'

Every female hand in the room shot up. All the Virginless American dynamos were eager to practice goodness without clout. It felt strange not being the only one with my hand down, but this sort of thing happens to the best of us. Ann Hopkins was waving her arm frantically and I nearly tore mine out of its socket as I hacked desperately at the air near Miss Ogilvy's face.

'All right, Florence, thank you. Please take Harriet out in the hall and show her your combination.'

I rose triumphantly and gave Harriet a bright smile. Her face remained immobile. I told myself she was just shy. As I worked the combination lock, she seemed to be listening for a click like safecrackers in the movies; her eyes, miniscule to begin with, turned into mere pinpoints. She reached into her sacklike purse for a small black notebook, wrote down the combination, then replaced the notebook with a swift, secretive gesture. She uttered not a word the whole time but I looked on her silence as a challenge to my newly acquired charm. I would soon have those taupe toes curling.

She spoke her first sentence to me at three-fifteen that afternoon when I tried to put a book on the locker shelf.

'You touch this locker again and I'll kill you.'

I looked around; she couldn't possibly be talking to me – this sort of thing never happened to gracious ladies who made everybody happy. But there was no one else in the hall; I was alone with my new friend. She grabbed my books off the shelf and threw them at me.

'My Pop was a war hero,' she growled. 'He drove a tank for Patton. He killed lots of people and he showed me and my brother how to do it. You smear axle grease on an icepick and stick it straight in their heart. When you pull it back out, the grease seals the hole so it don't show and the doctor thinks you died of something natural.'

She dipped into her haversack and pulled out an evil-looking pointed instrument and a can stamped WESTERN AUTO STORES.

'That's for you if you don't stay away from this locker.'

She slammed the door shut and jerked her head toward the stairs, taking no chances that I would sneak back and open it after she was gone. I decided not to argue with her. A girl who called her father Pop was capable of anything. I descended the stairs, my spine crawling at the sound of her ponderous tread behind me.

Peg and Helen were waiting for me outside.

'Why are you taking all those books home?'

'Er, I have a lot of homework.'

'Already? It's only the second day of school.'

I almost told them about the death threat but I hated to publicize my defeats, especially one I had volunteered for. How would it look if I admitted to a falling out with my new lockermate after only five hours? Even the chronically unpopular took longer than that to get a feud going, and this was more than a feud. Needing time to think, I brushed off their questions and changed the subject to one guaranteed to absorb us all the way home: pubic hair.

I spent the evening with the story on the tip of my tongue. Each time I almost told it, I considered the consequences and stopped. I could not tell Granny. An uncomprehending veteran of my social wars, she would only say, 'What did you *do* to the poor child to upset her so?' I could not tell Herb. He was for good news, like report cards. There was something almost sacrilegious about the idea of going to Herb for help in this sort of crisis; it would have been a travesty, like using a fine linen napkin to wash a car. Herb was a luxury, like Ashley, and the situation clearly called for a necessity.

That meant Mama, but I did not see how she could rescue me this time. Harriet was not a teacher or a tombstone but a girl my age, and Mama could not move in on a kid, even a monster kid. Besides, in a funny way I was afraid that if she met Harriet they would take a liking to each other. After all, they were both loaded for bear; I had a fleeting fantasy of the two of them going out on a rampage together and having a grand old time. The knowledge that they were sisters under the skin was painful, like having a brother whom Mama loved better than me. While Harriet was not a boy, she was much closer to being one than I was, so she loomed in my mind as the son Mama had wanted.

That night I lay in bed reviewing my options. The most direct solution, guaranteed to please Mama, was to beat Harriet up. There were two holes in this approach that no amount of axle grease could close. First, although I was taller, Harriet was much stronger; it would be no exaggeration to describe her figure as burly. Second, how could I, with my long history of peer problems, walk into junior high on the third day of school and start slamming the new girl around for no apparent reason? When the dust settled I would, of course, reveal my reason, but how would it sound? 'She threatened to stick an icepick in my heart.' Who would believe it? Harriet would only deny it. A search of her haversack would bear me out, but that solution was flawed, too. Violent people invariably have an animal shrewdness that I knew I lacked. Somewhere between the fray and the principal's office Harriet, like Lizzie Borden, would find some way to get rid of her incriminating weapon, leaving me holding the icepickless and greaseless bag.

A quieter solution was to tell Miss Ogilvy in private, but that would bring me up against the same credibility problem. Teachers are old hands at childish hyperbole. 'She threatened to stick an *icepick* in your *heart?*' 'Yes, ma'am.' If I had known Miss Ogilvy better she might – I say *might* – have believed me, but after only three days? No. Not in 1947. Schools were peaceful places in those days.

My third option was to call Harriet's bluff, but having looked into those glittering peppercorns that passed for eyes, I didn't dare risk it. She *might* stab me. I was afraid of her but more afraid of what she represented. Like all embers of the shabby genteel class, I hated low-class people. Being a shabby genteel Southerner only intensified this prejudice; we are bottomless wells of aristocratic disdain and empty thimbles of aristocratic power. All we can do is badmouth poor white trash.

For the remaining days of that week I carried my books everywhere. Nobody paid any attention; I was always carrying books. As long as the weather stayed warm I could count on not being noticed, but what would happen if I started carrying a coat around I did not know.

By happy chance I never found out. My problem was solved suddenly and permanently on Saturday morning when Granny opened the newspaper and uttered a cry of despair.

'Oh, the poor little soul! Did you know a girl named Harriet Mudd? It says she went to your school.'

Her past tenses were music to my ears. I jumped up and read over her shoulder.

BRONZE STAR WINNER AND FAMILY
KILLED IN COLLISION WITH TRAIN:
SUICIDE RULED

*Cumberland, Md. – A speeding B&O freight train took the lives of Albert J. Mudd, his wife, and their two children Friday night when the decorated 3rd Army veteran drove onto the tracks here. Witnesses said Mudd, who had been under psychiatric care at Walter Reed Hospital, shouted 'Here I come,*

*Georgie!' and crashed through a lowered signal bar in an apparently
deliberate attempt to end his life.*

The story went on to list the names and schools of Harriet and her
brother. It was true. Somebody Up There liked me.

'Did you know her?' Granny asked sorrowfully.

'Just a little,' I said, struggling to keep a grievous expression on my
face.

'Mudd . . .' she said pensively. 'That's an old Maryland name. Was
she descended from that doctor who was involved in the Lincoln
assassination?'

'She could have been.'

In homeroom on Monday morning, Ann Hopkins, who had already
lectured me on the need to show boys how deep the waters of womanly
emotion ran, burst into tears and simulated a fainting spell. That the
boys looked distinctly uncomfortable escaped her notice. Miss Ogilvy,
no believer in letting students verbalize their finer feelings, insisted on
an immediate end to the display and called for a constructive response.

'Flowers!' Ann sobbed. 'We have to send flowers!'

'That would be appropriate,' said Miss Ogilvy. She looked around in
that way teachers have when they are getting ready to appoint a
volunteer. My hand was down but now there was a clear logic to her
choice.

'Florence, since you were Harriet's lockermate, would you take up a
collection and stop by the florist's this afternoon?'

I went up and down the aisles gathering nickels and dimes, my smile
muscles aching from suppression. When I had all the money together,
we voted on what kind of flowers to send. It should have been over then,
but Ann Hopkins still had some more womanly feeling to let out.

'Miss Ogilvy, I think Florence should lead us in prayer.'

Miss Ogilvy handed me the Bible and I read the Twenty-third
Psalm, all the while thinking that the death of the Mudd family was the
greatest event in the history of genetics since Mendel crossed his peas. I
was in a state of delirious joy the whole day, but I had to hide it. All the
girls went round with dolorous faces and spent lunch hour talking in
hushed tones about what a wonderful person Harriet had been. None of
them chose to remember that they had known her for only four days,
and that during this time she had not even said hello to them. They

competed with each other to deliver the most moving testimonial to her basic sweetness; what she was *really* like, 'deep down' and 'inside' and 'in her heart.' Each girl *knew* how warm and friendly Harriet had been, and I, who did know, had to keep quiet.

By lunch hour the next day, the Legend of Harriet Mudd had sprung up like a Nashville hit. It was the human comedy, female version; being unable to find the essential goodness in Harriet was an admission that there was no goodness in oneself, so all the girls in our homeroom related tender little stories about her: some thoughtful favor she had done them, something sweet she had said to them, a cute joke she had told. And I, to whom she had spoken as Cato to Carthage, had to keep quiet.

Do you think that's all I had to endure? Read on with me, the best is yet to be. When I got home that afternoon, Granny was wearing her good black hat.

'Change into your church dress, we're going to pay a call at the funeral parlor. I've invited Mrs Bell to go with us.'

The caskets were closed, of course, so Mrs Bell did not have a very good time. It was a shame, because she would have been the ideal person to help me realize my fantasy of folding Harriet's taupe fingers around an icepick. Picturing the scene in my mind, I doubled over and Granny patted my shaking shoulders, so I had to pretend I was crying.

The other mourners were extremely fat women with mean mouths and red-faced men with little pieces of toilet paper stuck on razor nicks. Granny gave them a dubious glance.

'These people look right trashy to me but we must pay our respects.'

'We're all equal in death,' said Mrs Bell.

Granny was so pleased by my show of womanly grief that she added an extra dollar to her share of my allowance that week. Of far greater value was the lesson I learned from the whole ungodly mess: I never again tried to make myself liked.

# Bicycle Fever

## E. F. Benson

The bicycles arrived a week later, nickel-plated and belled and braked; Lucia's had the Borough Arms of Tilling brilliantly painted on the tool-bag behind her saddle. They were brought up to Mallards after dark; and next morning, before breakfast, the two rode about the garden paths, easily passing up the narrow path into the kitchen garden, and making circles round the mulberry tree on the lawn ('Here we go round the mulberry tree' light-heartedly warbled Lucia) and proving themselves adepts. Lucia could not eat much breakfast with the first public appearance so close, and Georgie vainly hoped that tropical rain would begin. But the sun continued to shine, and at the shopping hour they mounted and bumped slowly down the cobbles of the steep street into the High Street, ready to ring their bells. Irene was the first to see them, and she ran by Lucia's side.

'Marvellous, perfect person,' she cried, putting out her hand as if to lay it on Lucia's. 'What is there you can't do?'

'Yes, dear, but don't touch me,' screamed Lucia in panic. 'So rough just here.' Then they turned to the smooth tarmac of the High Street.

Eve saw them next.

'Dear, oh, dear, you'll both be killed!' she squealed. 'There's a motor coming at such a pace. Kenneth, they're riding bicycles!'

They passed superbly on. Lucia dismounted at the post-office; Georgie, applying his brake with exquisite delicacy, halted at the poulterer's with one foot on the pavement. Elizabeth was in the shop and Diva came out of the post-office.

'Good gracious me,' she cried. 'Never knew you could. And all this traffic!'

'Quite easy, dear,' said Lucia. 'Order a chicken, Georgie, while I get some stamps.'

She propped her bicycle against the kerb; Georgie remained sitting till Mr Rice came out of the poulterer's with Elizabeth.

'What a pretty bicycle!' she said, green with jealousy. 'Oh, there's Worship, too. Well, this is a surprise! So accomplished!'

They sailed on again. Georgie went to the lending library, and found that the book Lucia wanted had come, but he preferred to have it sent to Mallards: hands, after all, were meant to take hold of handles. Lucia went on to the grocer's, and by the time he joined her there, the world of Tilling had collected: the Padre and Evie, Elizabeth and Benjy and Mr Wyse, while Susan looked on from the Royce.

'Such a saving of time,' said Lucia casually to the admiring assembly. 'A little spin in the country, Georgie, for half an hour?'

They went unerringly down the High Street, leaving an amazed group behind.

'Well, there's a leddy of pluck,' said the padre. 'See, how she glides along. A mistress of a' she touches.'

Elizabeth was unable to bear it, and gave an acid laugh.

'Dear Padre!' she said. 'What a fuss about nothing! When I was a girl I learned to ride a bicycle in ten minutes. The easiest thing in the world.'

'Did ye, indeed, me'm,' said the Padre, 'and that was very remarkable, for in those days, sure, there was only those great high machines, which you rode straddle.'

'Years and years after that,' said Elizabeth, moving away.

He turned to Evie.

'A bicycle would be a grand thing for me in getting about the parish,' he said. 'I'll step into the bicycleshop, and see if they've got one on hire for to learn on.'

'Oh, Kenneth, I should like to learn, too,' said Evie. 'Such fun!'

Meantime the pioneers, rosy with success, had come to the end of the High Street. From there the road sloped rapidly downhill. 'Now we can put on the pace a little, Georgie,' said Lucia, and she shot ahead. All her practisings had been on the level roads of the marsh or on the sea-shore, and at once she was travelling much faster than she had intended, and with eyes glued on the curving road, she fumbled for her brake. She completely lost her head. All she could find in her agitation was her bell, and, incessantly ringing it, she sped with ever increasing velocity down the short steep road towards the bridge over the railway. A policeman on point duty stepped forward, with the arresting arm of the law held out to stop her, but as she took no notice he stepped very hastily back again, for to commit suicide and possibly manslaughter, was a more serious crime than dangerous riding. Lucia's face was contorted with agonised apprehension, her eyes stared, her mouth was wide open, and all the young constable could do by way of identification was to notice, when the unknown female had whisked by him, that the bicycle was new and that there was the Borough coat of arms on the tool-bag. Lucia passed between a pedestrian and a van, just avoiding both: she switch-backed up and down the railway-bridge, still ringing her bell . . . Then in front of her lay the long climb of the Tilling hill, and as the pace diminished she found her brake. She dismounted, and waited for Georgie. He had lost sight of her in the traffic, and followed her cautiously in icy expectation of finding her and that beautiful new bicycle flung shattered on the road. Then he had one glimpse of her swift swallow-flight up the steep incline of the railway-bridge. Thank God she was safe so far! He traversed it himself and then saw her a hundred yards ahead up the hill. Long before he reached her his impetus was exhausted, and he got off.

'Don't hurry, dear,' she called to him in a trembling voice. 'You were right, quite right to ride cautiously. Safety first *always*.'

'I felt very anxious about you,' said Georgie, panting as he joined her. 'You oughtn't to have gone so fast. You deserve to be summoned for dangerous riding.'

A vision, vague and bright, shot through Lucia's brain. She could not conceive a more enviable piece of publicity than, at her age, to be summoned for so athletic a feat. It was punishable, no doubt, by law, but like a *crime passionel*, what universal admiration it would excite! What a dashing Mayor!

'I confess I was going very fast,' she said, 'but I felt I had such complete control of my machine. And so exhilarating. I don't suppose anybody has ever ridden so fast down Landgate Street. Now, if you're rested, shall we go on?'

They had a long but eminently prudent ride, and after lunch a well-earned siesta. Lucia, reposing on the sofa in the garden-room, was awakened by Grosvenor's entry from a frightful nightmare that she was pedalling for all she was worth down Beachy Head into the arms of a policeman on the shore.

'Inspector Morrison, ma'am,' said Grosvenor. 'He'll call again if not convenient.'

Nightmare vanished: the vague vision grew brighter. Was it possible? . . .

'Certainly, at once,' she said springing up and Inspector Morrison entered.

'Sorry to disturb your Worship,' he said, 'but one of my men has reported that about eleven a.m. to-day a new bicycle with the arms of Tilling on the tool-bag was ridden at a dangerous speed by a female down Landgate Street. He made inquiries at the bicycle shop and found that a similar machine was sent to your house yesterday. I therefore ask your permission to question your domestics—'

'Quite right to apply to me, Inspector,' said Lucia. 'You did your duty. Certainly I will sign the summons.'

'But we don't know who it was yet, ma'am. I should like to ask your servants to account for their whereabouts at eleven a.m.'

'No need to ask them, Inspector,' said Lucia. 'I was the culprit. Please send the summons round here and I will sign it.'

'But, your Worship—'

Lucia was desperately afraid that the Inspector might wriggle out of summoning the Mayor and that the case would never come into Court. She turned a magisterial eye on him.

'I will not have one law for the rich and another for the poor in Tilling,' she said. 'I was riding at a dangerous speed. It was very thoughtless of me, and I must suffer for it. I ask you to proceed with the case in the ordinary course.'

This one appearance of Lucia and Georgie doing their shopping on bicycles had been enough to kindle the spark of emulation in the breasts of the more mature ladies of Tilling. It looked so lissom, so gaily adolescent to weave your way in and out of traffic and go for a spin in the country, and surely if Lucia could, they could also. Her very casualness made it essential to show her that there was nothing remarkable about her unexpected feat. The bicycle shop was besieged with inquiries for machines on hire and instructors. The Padre and Evie were the first in the field, and he put off his weekly visit to the workhouse that afternoon from half-past two till half-past three, and they hired the two bicycles which Lucia and George no longer needed.

Diva popped in next, and was chagrined to find that the only lady's bicycle was already bespoken, so she engaged it for an hour on the following morning. Georgie that day did quite complicated shopping alone, for Lucia was at a committee meeting at the Town Hall. She rode there – a distance of a hundred and fifty yards – to save time, but the gain was not very great, for she had to dismount twice owing to the narrow passage between posts for the prevention of vehicular traffic. Georgie, having returned from his shopping, joined her at the Town Hall when her meeting was over, and, with brakes fully applied, they rode down into the High Street, *en route* for another dash into the country. Susan's Royce was drawn up at the bicycle-shop.

'Georgie, I shan't have a moment's peace,' said Lucia, 'until I know whether Susan has ambitions too. I must just pop in.'

Both the Wyses were there. Algernon was leaning over Susan's shoulder as she studied a catalogue of the newest types of tricycles . . .

The Mayoress alone remained scornful and aloof. Looking out from her window one morning, she observed Diva approaching very slowly up the trafficless road that ran past Grebe buttressed up by Georgie's late instructor, who seemed to have some difficulty in keeping her perpendicular. She hurried to the garden-gate, reaching it just as Diva came opposite.

'Good morning, dear,' she said. 'Sorry to see that you're down with it, too.'

'Good morning, dear,' echoed Diva, with her eyes glued to the road in front of her. 'I haven't the slightest idea what you mean.'

'But is it wise to take such strenuous exercise?' asked Elizabeth. 'A great strain surely on both of you.'

'Not a bit of a strain,' called Diva over her shoulder. 'And my instructor says I shall soon get on ever so quick.'

The bicycle gave a violent swerve.

'Oh, take care,' cried Elizabeth in an anxious voice, 'or you'll get off ever so quick.'

'We'll rest a bit,' said Diva to her instructor, and she stepped from her machine and went back to the gate to have it out with her friend. 'What's the matter with you,' she said to Elizabeth, 'is that you can't bear us following Lucia's lead. Don't deny it. Look in your own heart, and you'll find it's true, Elizabeth. Get over it, dear. Make an effort. Far more Christian!'

'Thank you for your kind interest in my character, Diva,' retorted Elizabeth. 'I shall know now where to come when in spiritual perplexity.'

'Always pleased to advise you,' said Diva. 'And now give me a treat. You told us all you learned to ride in ten minutes when you were a girl. I'll give you my machine for ten minutes. See if you can ride at the end of it! A bit coy, dear? Not surprised. And rapid motion might be risky for your relaxed throat.'

There was a moment's pause. Then both ladies were so pleased at their own brilliant dialectic that Elizabeth said she would pop in to Diva's establishment for tea, and Diva said that would be charming.

In spite of Elizabeth (or perhaps even because of her) this revival of the bicycling nineties grew most fashionable. Major Benjy turned traitor and was detected by his wife surreptitiously practising with the gardener's bicycle on the cinder path in the kitchen garden. Mr Wyse suddenly appeared on the wheel riding in the most elegant manner. Figgis, his butler, he said, happened to remember that he had a bicycle put away in the garage and had furbished it up. Mr Wyse introduced a new style: he was already an adept and instead of wearing a preoccupied expression, made no more of it than if he was strolling about on foot. He could take a hand off his handle-bar, to raise his hat to the Mayor, as if one hand was all he needed. When questioned about this feat, he said that it was not really difficult to take both hands off without instantly crashing, but Lucia, after several experiments in the garden, concluded that Mr Wyse, though certainly a very skilful performer, was wrong about that. To crown all, Susan, after a long wait at the corner of Porpoise Street, where a standing motor left only eight or nine feet of the roadway clear, emerged majestically into the High Street on a brand new tricycle. 'Those large motors,' she complained to the Mayor, 'ought not to be allowed in our narrow streets.'

The Town Hall was crowded to its utmost capacity on the morning that Lucia was summoned to appear before her own Court for dangerous riding. She had bicycled there, now negotiating the anti-vehicular posts with the utmost precision, and, wearing her semi-official hat, presided on the Borough Bench. She and her brother magistrates had two cases to try before hers came on, of which one was that of a motor-cyclist whose brakes were out of order. The Bench, consulting together, took a grave view of the offence, and imposed a penalty of twenty shillings. Lucia in pronouncing sentence, addressed some severe remarks to him: he would have been unable to pull up, she told him, in case of an emergency, and was endangering the safety of his fellow citizens. The magistrates gave him seven days in which to pay. Then came the great moment. The Mayor rose, and in a clear unfaltering voice, said:

'Your Worships, I am personally concerned in the next case, and will therefore quit my seat on the Bench. Would the senior of Your Worships kindly preside in my temporary absence?'

She descended into the body of the Town Hall.

'The next case before your Worships,' said the Town Clerk, 'is one of dangerous riding of a push-bicycle on the part of Mrs Lucia Pillson. Mrs Lucia Pillson.'

She pleaded guilty in a voice of calm triumph, and the Bench heard the evidence. The first witness was a constable, who swore that he would speak the truth, the whole truth and nothing but the truth. He was on point duty by the railway-bridge at 11 a.m. on Tuesday the twelfth instant. He observed a female bicyclist approaching at a dangerous speed down Landgate Street, when there was a lot of traffic about. He put out his arm to stop her, but she dashed by him. He estimated her speed at twenty miles an hour, and she seemed to have no control over her machine. After she had passed, he observed a tool-bag on the back of the saddle emblazoned with the Borough coat-of-arms. He made enquiries at the bicycle-shop and ascertained that a machine of this description had been supplied the day before to Mrs Pillson of Mallards House. He reported to his superior.

'Have you any questions, your Worsh – to ask the witness?' asked the Town Clerk.

'None,' said Lucia eagerly. 'Not one.'

The next witness was the pedestrian she had so nearly annihilated. Lucia was dismayed to see that he was the operator with the fire-pot. He began to talk about his experiences when tarring telegraph-posts some while ago, but, to her intense relief, was promptly checked and told he must confine himself to what occurred at 11 a.m. on Tuesday. He deposed that at that precise hour, as he was crossing the road by the railway-bridge, a female bicyclist dashed by him at a speed which he estimated at over twenty miles an hour. A gratified smile illuminated the Mayor's face, and she had no questions to ask him.

That concluded the evidence, and the Inspector of Police said there were no previous convictions against the accused.

The Bench consulted together: there seemed to be some difference of opinion as to the amount of the fine. After a little discussion the temporary Chairman told Lucia that she also would be fined twenty shillings. She borrowed it from Georgie, who was sitting near, and so did not ask for time in which to pay. With a superb air she took her place again on the Bench.

Georgie waited for her till the end of the sitting, and stood a little in the background, but well in focus, while Lucia posed on the steps of the Town Hall, in the act of mounting her bicycle, for the photographer of the *Hampshire Argus*. His colleague on the reporting staff had taken down every word uttered in this *cause célèbre* and Lucia asked him to send proofs to her, before it went to press. It was a slight disappointment that no reporters or photographers had come down from London, for Mrs Simpson had been instructed to inform the Central News Agency of the day and hour of the trial . . . But the Mayor was well satisfied with the local prestige which her reckless athleticism had earned for her. Elizabeth, indeed, had attempted to make her friends view the incident in a different light, and she had a rather painful scene on the subject with the Padre and Evie.

'All too terrible,' she said. 'I feel that poor Worship has utterly disgraced herself, and brought contempt on the dignified office she holds. Those centuries of honourable men who have been Mayors here must turn in their graves. I've been wondering whether I ought not, in mere self-respect, to resign from being Mayoress. It associates me with her.'

'That's not such a bad notion,' said the Padre, and Evie gave several shrill squeaks. 'On the other hand, I should hate to desert her in her trouble,' continued the Mayoress. 'So true what you said in your sermon last Sunday, Padre, that it's our duty as Christians always to stand by our friends, whenever they are in trouble and need us.'

'So because she needs you, which she doesn't an atom,' burst out Evie, 'you come and tell us that she's disgraced herself, and made everybody turn in their graves. Most friendly, Elizabeth.'

'And I'm of wee Wifie's opinion, mem,' said the Padre, with the brilliant thought of Evie becoming Mayoress in his mind, 'and if you feel you canna' preserve your self-respect unless you resign, why, it's your Christian duty to do so, and I warrant that won't incommode her, so don't let the standing by your friends deter you. And if you ask me what I think of Mistress Lucia's adventure, 'twas a fine spunky thing to have gone flying down the Landgate Street at thirty miles an hour. You and I daurna do it, and peradventure we'd be finer folk if we daur. And she stood and said she was guilty like a God-fearing upstanding body and she deserves a medal, she does. Come awa', wifie: we'll get to our bicycle-lesson.'

The Padre's view was reflected in the town generally, and his new figure of thirty miles an hour accepted. Though it was a very lawless and dangerous feat, Tilling felt proud of having so spirited a Mayor. Diva indulged in secret visions of record-breaking when she had learned to balance herself, and Susan developed such a turn of speed on her tricycle that Algernon called anxiously after her 'Not so fast, Susan, I beg you. Supposing you met something.' The Padre scudded about his parish on the wheel, and, as the movement grew, Lucia offered to coach anybody in her garden. It became fashionable to career up and down the High Street after dark, when traffic was diminished, and the whole length of it resounded with tinkling bells and twinkled with bicycle lamps. There were no collisions, for everyone was properly cautious, but on one chilly evening the flapping skirt of Susan's fur coat got so inextricably entangled in the chain of her tricycle that she had to shed it, and Figgis trundled coat and tricycle back to Porpoise Street in the manner of a wheel-barrow.

As the days grew longer and the weather warmer, picnic-parties were arranged to points of interest within easy distance, a castle, a church or a Martello tower, and they ate sandwiches and drank from their thermos flasks in ruined dungeons or on tombstones or by the edge of a moat. The party, by reason of the various rates of progress which each found comfortable, could not start together, if they were to arrive fairly simultaneously, and Susan on her tricycle was always the first to leave Tilling, and Diva followed. There was some competition for the honour of being the last to leave: Lucia, with the cachet of furious riding to her credit, waited till she thought the Padre must have started, while he was sure that his normal pace was faster than hers. In consequence, they usually both arrived very late and very hot. They all wondered how they could ever have confined physical exercise within the radius of pedestrianism, and pitied Elizabeth for the pride that debarred her from joining in these pleasant excursions.

# Lord Emsworth and the Girl Friend

## *P. G. Wodehouse*

The day was so warm, so fair, so magically a thing of sunshine and blue skies and bird-song that anyone acquainted with Clarence, ninth Earl of Emsworth, and aware of his liking for fine weather, would have pictured him going about the place on this summer morning with a beaming smile and an uplifted heart. Instead of which, humped over the breakfast table, he was directing at a blameless kippered herring a look of such intense bitterness that the fish seemed to sizzle beneath it. For it was August Bank Holiday, and Blandings Castle on August Bank Holiday became in his lordship's opinion, a miniature Inferno.

This was the day when his park and grounds broke out into a noisome rash of swings, roundabouts, marquees, toy balloons and paper bags; when a tidal wave of the peasantry and its squealing young engulfed those haunts of immemorial peace. On August Bank Holiday he was not allowed to potter pleasantly about his gardens in an old coat: forces beyond his control shoved him into a stiff collar and a top hat and told him to go out and be genial. And in the cool of the quiet evenfall they put him on a platform and made him make a speech. To a man with a day like that in front of him fine weather was a mockery.

His sister, Lady Constance Keeble, looked brightly at him over the coffee-pot.

'What a lovely morning!' she said.

Lord Emsworth's gloom deepened. He chafed at being called upon – by this woman of all others – to behave as if everything was for the jolliest in the jolliest of all possible worlds. But for his sister Constance and her hawk-like vigilance, he might, he thought, have been able at least to dodge the top hat.

'Have you got your speech ready?'

'Yes.'

'Well, mind you learn it by heart this time and don't stammer and dodder as you did last year.'

Lord Emsworth pushed plate and kipper away. He had lost his desire for food.

'And don't forget you have to go to the village this morning to judge the cottage gardens.'

'All right, all right, all right,' said his lordship testily. 'I've not forgotten.'

'I think I will come to the village with you. There are a number of those Fresh Air London children staying there now, and I must warn them to behave properly when they come to the Fete this afternoon. You know what London children are. McAllister says he found one of them in the gardens the other day, picking his flowers.'

At any other time the news of this outrage would, no doubt, have affected Lord Emsworth profoundly. But now, so intense was his self-pity, he did not even shudder. He drank coffee with the air of a man who regretted that it was not hemlock.

'By the way, McAllister was speaking to me again last night about that gravel path through the yew alley. He seems very keen on it.'

'Glug!' said Lord Emsworth – which, as any philologist will tell you, is the sound which peers of the realm make when stricken to the soul while drinking coffee.

Concerning Glasgow, that great commercial and manufacturing city in the county of Lanarkshire in Scotland, much has been written. So lyrically does the Encyclopaedia Britannica deal with the place that it covers twenty-seven pages before it can tear itself away and go on to Glass, Glastonbury, Glatz and Glauber. The only aspect of it, however, which immediately concerns the present historian is the fact that the citizens it breeds are apt to be grim, dour, persevering, tenacious men; men with red whiskers who know what they want and mean to get it. Such a one was Angus McAllister, head-gardener at Blandings Castle.

For years Angus McAllister had set before himself as his earthly goal the construction of a gravel path through the Castle's famous yew alley. For years he had been bringing the project to the notice of his employer, though in anyone less whiskered the latter's unconcealed loathing would have caused embarrassment. And now, it seemed, he was at it again.

'Gravel path!' Lord Emsworth stiffened through the whole length of his stringy body. Nature, he had always maintained, intended a yew alley to be carpeted with a mossy growth. And, whatever Nature felt about it, he personally was dashed if he was going to have men with Clydeside accents and faces like dissipated potatoes coming along and mutilating that lovely expanse of green velvet. 'Gravel path, indeed! Why not asphalt? Why not a few hoardings with advertisements of liver pills and a filling-station? That's what the man would really like.'

Lord Emsworth felt bitter, and when he felt bitter he could be terribly sarcastic.

'Well, I think it is a very good idea,' said his sister. 'One could walk there in wet weather then. Damp moss is ruinous to shoes.'

Lord Emsworth rose. He could bear no more of this. He left the table, the room and the house and, reaching the yew alley some minutes later, was revolted to find it infested by Angus McAllister in person. The head-gardener was standing gazing at the moss like a high priest of some ancient religion about to stick the gaff into the human sacrifice.

'Morning, McAllister,' said Lord Emsworth coldly.

'Good morrrrning, your lorrudsheep.'

There was a pause. Angus McAllister, extending a foot that looked like a violin-case, pressed it on the moss. The meaning of the gesture was plain. It expressed contempt, dislike, a generally anti-moss spirit: and Lord Emsworth, wincing, surveyed the man unpleasantly through his pince-nez. Though not often given to theological speculation, he was wondering why Providence, if obliged to make head-gardeners, had found it necessary to make them so Scotch. In the case of Angus McAllister, why, going a step further, have made him a human being at all? All the ingredients of a first-class mule simply thrown away. He felt that he might have liked Angus McAllister if he had been a mule.

'I was speaking to her leddyship yesterday.'

'Oh?'

'About the gravel path I was speaking to her leddyship.'

'Oh?'

'Her leddyship likes the notion fine.'

'Indeed! Well . . .'

Lord Emsworth's face had turned a lively pink, and he was about to release the blistering words which were forming themselves in his mind when suddenly he caught the head-gardener's eye, and paused. Angus McAllister was looking at him in a peculiar manner, and he knew what that look meant. Just one crack, his eye was saying – in Scotch, of course

– just one crack out of you and I tender my resignation. And with a sickening shock it came home to Lord Emsworth how completely he was in this man's clutches.

He shuffled miserably. Yes, he was helpless. Except for that kink about gravel paths, Angus McAllister was a head-gardener in a thousand, and he needed him. He could not do without him. That, unfortunately, had been proved by experiment. Once before, at the time when they were grooming for the Agricultural Show that pumpkin which had subsequently romped home so gallant a winner, he had dared to flout Angus McAllister. And Angus had resigned, and he had been forced to plead – yes, plead – with him to come back. An employer cannot hope to do this sort of thing and still rule with an iron hand. Filled with the coward rage that dares to burn but does not dare to blaze, Lord Emsworth coughed a cough that was undisguisedly a bronchial white flag.

'I'll – er – I'll think it over, McAllister.'

'Mphm.'

'I have to go to the village now. I will see you later.'

'Mphm.'

'Meanwhile, I will – er – think it over.'

'Mphm.'

The task of judging the floral displays in the cottage gardens of the little village of Blandings Parva was one to which Lord Emsworth had looked forward with pleasurable anticipation. It was the sort of job he liked. But now, even though he had managed to give his sister Constance the slip and was free from her threatened society, he approached the task with downcast spirit. It is always unpleasant for a proud man to realize that he is no longer captain of his soul; that he is to all intents and purposes ground beneath the number twelve heel of a Glaswegian head-gardener; and, brooding on this, he judged the cottage gardens with a distrait eye. It was only when he came to the last on his list that anything like animation crept into his demeanour.

This, he perceived, peering over its rickety fence, was not at all a bad little garden. It demanded closer inspection. He unlatched the gate and pottered in. And a dog, dozing behind a water-butt, opened one eye and looked at him. It was one of those hairy, nondescript dogs, and its gaze was cold, wary and suspicious, like that of a stockbroker who thinks someone is going to play the confidence trick on him.

Lord Emsworth did not observe the animal. He had pottered to a bed of wallflowers and now, stooping, he took a sniff at them.

As sniffs go, it was an innocent sniff, but the dog for some reason appeared to read into it criminality of a high order. All the indignant householder in him woke in a flash. The next moment the world had become full of hideous noises, and Lord Emsworth's preoccupation was swept away in a passionate desire to save his ankles from harm.

As these chronicles of Blandings Castle have already shown, he was not at his best with strange dogs. Beyond saying 'Go away, sir!' and leaping to and fro with an agility surprising for one of his years, he had accomplished little in the direction of a reasoned plan of defence when the cottage door opened and a girl came out.

'Hoy!' cried the girl.

And on the instant, at the mere sound of her voice, the mongrel, suspending hostilities, bounded at the new-comer and writhed on his back at her feet with all four legs in the air. The spectacle reminded Lord Emsworth irresistibly of his own behaviour in the presence of Angus McAllister.

He blinked at his preserver. She was a small girl, of uncertain age – possibly twelve or thirteen, though a combination of London fogs and early cares had given her face a sort of wizened motherliness which in some odd way caused his lordship from the first to look on her as belonging to his own generation. She was the type of girl you see in back streets carrying a baby nearly as large as herself and still retaining sufficient energy to lead one little brother by the hand and shout recrimination at another in the distance. Her cheeks shone from recent soaping, and she was dressed in a velveteen frock which was obviously the pick of her wardrobe. Her hair, in defiance of the prevailing mode, she wore drawn tightly back into a short pigtail.

'Er – thank you,' said Lord Emsworth.

'Thank you, sir,' said the girl.

For what she was thanking him, his lordship was not able to gather. Later, as their acquaintance ripened, he was to discover that this strange gratitude was a habit with his new friend. She thanked everybody for everything. At the moment, the mannerism surprised him. He continued to blink at her through his pince-nez.

Lack of practice had rendered Lord Emsworth a little rusty in the art of making conversation to members of the other sex. He sought in his mind for topics.

'Fine day.'

'Yes sir. Thank you, sir.'

'Are you' – Lord Emsworth furtively consulted his list – 'are you the daughter of – ah – Ebenezer Sprockett?' he asked, thinking, as he had often thought before, what ghastly names some of his tenantry possessed.

'No, sir. I'm from London, sir.'

'Ah? London, eh? Pretty warm it must be there.' He paused. Then, remembering a formula of his youth: 'Er – been out much this Season?'

'No, sir.'

'Everybody out of town now, I suppose? What part of London?'

'Drury Lane, sir.'

'What's your name? Eh, what?'

'Gladys, sir. Thank you, sir. This is Ern.'

A small boy had wandered out of the cottage, a rather hard-boiled specimen with freckles, bearing surprisingly in his hand a large and beautiful bunch of flowers. Lord Emsworth bowed courteously and with the addition of this third party to the *tête-à-tête* felt more at his ease.

'How do you do,' he said. 'What pretty flowers.'

With her brother's advent, Gladys, also, had lost diffidence and gained conversational aplomb.

'A treat, ain't they?' she agreed eagerly. 'I got 'em for 'im up at the big 'ahse. Coo! The old josser the plice belongs to didn't arf chase me. 'E found me picking 'em and 'e sharted somefin' at me and come runnin' after me, but I copped 'im on the shin wiv a stone and 'e stopped to rub it and I come away.'

Lord Emsworth might have corrected her impression that Blandings Castle and its gardens belonged to Angus McAllister, but his mind was so filled with admiration and gratitude that he refrained from doing so. He looked at the girl almost reverently. Not content with controlling savage dogs with a mere word, this superwoman actually threw stones at Angus McAllister – a thing which he had never been able to nerve himself to do in an association which had lasted nine years – and, what was more, copped him on the shin with them. What nonsense, Lord Emsworth felt, the papers talked about the Modern Girl. If this was a specimen, the Modern Girl was the highest point the sex had yet reached.

'Ern,' said Gladys, changing the subject, 'is wearin' 'air-oil todiy.'

Lord Emsworth had already observed this and had, indeed, been moving to windward as she spoke.

'For the Feet,' explained Gladys.

'For the feet?' It seemed unusual.

'For the Feet in the pork this afternoon.'

'Oh, you are going to the Fete?'

'Yes, sir, thank you, sir.'

For the first time, Lord Emsworth found himself regarding that grisly social event with something approaching favour.

'We must look out for one another there,' he said cordially. 'You will remember me again? I shall be wearing' – he gulped – 'a top hat.'

'Ern's going to wear a stror penamaw that's been give 'im.'

Lord Emsworth regarded the lucky young devil with frank envy. He rather fancied he knew that panama. It had been his constant companion for some six years and then had been torn from him by his sister Constance and handed over to the vicar's wife for her rummage sale.

He sighed.

'Well, good-bye.'

'Good-bye, sir. Thank you, sir.'

Lord Emsworth walked pensively out of the garden and, turning into the little street, encountered Lady Constance.

'Oh, there you are, Clarence.'

'Yes,' said Lord Emsworth, for such was the case.

'Have you finished judging the gardens?'

'Yes.'

'I am just going into the end cottage here. The vicar tells me there is a little girl from London staying there. I want to warn her to behave this afternoon. I have spoken to the others.'

Lord Emsworth drew himself up. His pince-nez were slightly askew, but despite this his gaze was commanding and impressive.

'Well, mind what you say,' he said authoritatively. 'None of your district-visiting stuff, Constance.'

'What do you mean?'

'You know what I mean. I have the greatest respect for the young lady to whom you refer. She behaved on a certain recent occasion – on two recent occasions – with notable gallantry and resource, and I won't have her ballyragged. Understand that!'

*   *   *

The technical title of the orgy which broke out annually on the first
Monday in August in the park of Blandings Castle was The Blandings
Parva School Treat, and it seemed to Lord Emsworth, wanly watching
the proceedings from under the shadow of his top hat, that if this was
the sort of thing schools looked on as pleasure he and they were
mentally poles apart. A function like the Blandings Parva School Treat
blurred his conception of Man as Nature's Final Word.

The decent sheep and cattle to whom this park normally belonged
had been hustled away into regions unknown, leaving the smooth
expanse of turf to children whose vivacity scared Lord Emsworth and
adults who appeared to him to have cast aside all dignity and every
other noble quality which goes to make a one hundred per cent British
citizen. Look at Mrs Rossiter over there, for instance, the wife of Jno.
Rossiter, Provisions, Groceries and Home-Made Jams. On any other
day of the year, when you met her, Mrs Rossiter was a nice, quiet,
docile woman who gave at the knees respectfully as you passed. Today,
flushed in the face and with her bonnet on one side, she seemed to have
gone completely native. She was wandering to and fro drinking
lemonade out of a bottle and employing her mouth, when not so
occupied, to make a devastating noise with what he believed was
termed a squeaker.

The injustice of the thing stung Lord Emsworth. This park was his
own private park. What right had people to come and blow squeakers
in it? How would Mrs Rossiter like it if one afternoon he suddenly
invaded her neat little garden in the High Street and rushed about over
her lawn, blowing a squeaker.

And it was always on these occasions so infernally hot. July might
have ended in a flurry of snow, but directly the first Monday in August
arrived and he had to put on a stiff collar out came the sun, blazing with
tropic fury. Of course, admitted Lord Emsworth, for he was a fair-
minded man, this cut both ways. The hotter the day, the more quickly
his collar lost its starch and ceased to spike him like a javelin. This
afternoon, for instance, it had resolved itself almost immediately into
something which felt like a wet compress. Severe as were his sufferings,
he was compelled to recognize that he was that much ahead of the
game.

A masterful figure loomed at his side.

'Clarence!'

Lord Emsworth's mental and spiritual state was now such that not even the advent of his sister Constance could add noticeably to his discomfort.

'Clarence, you look a perfect sight.'

'I know I do. Who wouldn't in a rig-out like this? Why in the name of goodness you always insist . . .'

'Please don't be childish, Clarence. I cannot understand the fuss you make about dressing for once in your life like a reasonable English gentleman and not like a tramp.'

'It's this top hat. It's exciting the children.'

'What on earth do you mean, exciting the children?'

'Well, all I can tell you is that just now, as I was passing the place where they're playing football – Football! In weather like this! – a small boy called out something derogatory and threw a portion of a coconut at it.'

'If you will identify the child,' said Lady Constance warmly, 'I will have him severely punished.'

'How the dickens,' replied his lordship with equal warmth, 'can I identify the child? They all look alike to me. And if I did identify him, I would shake him by the hand. A boy who throws coconuts at top hats is fundamentally sound in his views. And stiff collars . . .'

'Stiff! That's what I came to speak to you about. Are you aware that your collar looks like a rag? Go in and change it at once.'

'But, my dear Constance . . .'

'At once, Clarence. I simply cannot understand a man having so little pride in his appearance. But all your life you have been like that. I remember when we were children . . .'

Lord Emsworth's past was not of such purity that he was prepared to stand and listen to it being lectured on by a sister with a good memory.

'Oh, all right, all right, all right,' he said. 'I'll change it, I'll change it.'

'Well, hurry. They are just starting tea.'

Lord Emsworth quivered.

'Have I got to go into that tea-tent?'

'Of course you have. Don't be so ridiculous. I do wish you would realize your position. As master of Blandings Castle . . .'

A bitter, mirthless laugh from the poor peon thus ludicrously described drowned the rest of the sentence.

It always seemed to Lord Emsworth, in analysing these entertainments, that the August Bank Holiday Saturnalia at Blandings Castle
reached a peak of repulsiveness when tea was served in the big
marquee. Tea over, the agony abated, to become acute once more at the
moment when he stepped to the edge of the platform and cleared his
throat and tried to recollect what the deuce he had planned to say to the
goggling audience beneath him. After that, it subsided again and
passed until the following August.

Conditions during the tea hour, the marquee having stood all day
under a blazing sun, were generally such that Shadrack, Meshach and
Abednego, had they been there, could have learned something new
about burning fiery furnaces. Lord Emsworth, delayed by the revision
of his toilet, made his entry when the meal was half over and was
pleased to find that his second collar almost instantaneously began to
relax its iron grip. That, however, was the only gleam of happiness
which was to be vouchsafed him. Once in the tent, it took his
experienced self but a moment to discern that the present feast was
eclipsing the frightfulness all its predecessors.

Young Blandings Parva, in its normal form, tended rather to the
stolidly bovine than the riotous. In all villages, of course, there must of
necessity be an occasional tough egg – in the case of Blandings Parva
the names of Willie Drake and Thomas (Rat-Face) Blenkiron spring to
the mind – but it was seldom that the local infants offered anything
beyond the power of a curate to control. What was giving the present
gathering its striking resemblance to a reunion of *sans-culottes* at the
height of the French Revolution was the admixture of the Fresh Air
London visitors.

About the London child, reared among the tin cans and cabbage
stalks of Drury Lane and Clare Market, there is a breezy insouciance
which his country cousin lacks. Years of back-chat with annoyed
parents and relatives have cured him of any tendency he may have had
towards shyness, with the result that when he requires anything he
grabs for it, and when he is amused by any slight peculiarity in the
personal appearance of members of the governing class he finds no
difficulty in translating his thoughts into speech. Already, up and down
the long tables, the curate's unfortunate squint was coming in for
hearty comment, and the front teeth of one of the school-teachers ran it

a close second for popularity. Lord Emsworth was not, as a rule, a man of swift inspiration, but it occurred to him at this juncture that it would be a prudent move to take off his top hat before his little guests observed it and appreciated its humorous possibilities.

The action was not, however, necessary. As he raised his hand a rock cake, singing through the air like a shell, took it off for him.

Lord Emsworth had had sufficient. Even Constance, unreasonable woman though she was, could hardly expect him to stay and beam genially under conditions like this. All civilized laws had obviously gone by the board and Anarchy reigned in the marquee. The curate was doing his best to form a provisional government consisting of himself and the two school-teachers, but there was only one man who could have coped adequately with the situation and that was King Herod, who – regrettably – was not among those present. Feeling like some aristocrat of the old *régime* sneaking away from the tumbril, Lord Emsworth edged to the exit and withdrew.

Outside the marquee the world was quieter, but only comparatively so. What Lord Emsworth craved was solitude, and in all the broad park there seemed to be but one spot where it was to be had. This was a red-tiled shed, standing beside a small pond, used at happier times as a lounge or retiring-room for cattle. Hurrying thither, his lordship had just begun to revel in the cool, cow-scented dimness of its interior when from one of the dark corners, causing him to start and bite his tongue, there came the sound of a subdued sniff.

He turned. This was persecution. With the whole park to mess about in, why should an infernal child invade this one sanctuary of his? He spoke with angry sharpness. He came of a line of warrior ancestors and his fighting blood was up.

'Who's that?'

'Me, sir. Thank you, sir.'

Only one person of Lord Emsworth's acquaintance was capable of expressing gratitude for having been barked at in such a tone. His wrath died away and remorse took its place. He felt like a man who in error has kicked a favourite dog.

'God bless my soul!' he exclaimed. 'What in the world are you doing in a cowshed?'

'Please, sir, I was put.'

'Put? How do you mean, put? Why?'

'For pinching things, sir.'

'Eh? What? Pinching things? Most extraordinary. What did you – er – pinch?'

'Two buns, two jem-sengwiches, two apples and a slicer cake.'

The girl had come out of her corner and was standing correctly at attention. Force of habit had caused her to intone the list of purloined articles in the sing-song voice in which she was wont to recite the multiplication-table at school, but Lord Emsworth could see that she was deeply moved. Tear-stains glistened on her face, and no Emsworth had ever been able to watch unstirred a woman's tears. The ninth Earl was visibly affected.

'Blow your nose,' he said, extending his handkerchief.

'Yes, sir. Thank you, sir.'

'What did you say you had pinched? Two buns . . .'

'. . . Two jem-sengwiches, two apples and a slicer cake.'

'Did you eat them?'

'No, sir. They wasn't for me. They was for Ern.'

'Ern? Oh, ah, yes. Yes, to be sure. For Ern, eh?'

'Yes, sir.'

'But why the dooce couldn't Ern have – er – pinched them for himself? Strong, able-bodied young feller, I mean.'

Lord Emsworth, a member of the old school, did not like this disposition on the part of the modern young man to shirk the dirty work and let the woman pay.

'Ern wasn't allowed to come to the treat, sir.'

'What! Not allowed? Who said he mustn't?'

'The lidy, sir.'

'What lidy?'

'The one that come in just after you'd gorn this morning.'

A fierce snort escaped Lord Emsworth. Constance! What the devil did Constance mean by taking it upon herself to revise his list of guests without so much as a . . . Constance, eh? He snorted again. One of these days Constance would go too far.

'Monstrous!' he cried.

'Yes, sir.'

'High-handed tyranny, by Gad. Did she give any reason?'

'The lidy didn't like Ern biting 'er in the leg, sir.'

'Ern bit her in the leg?'

'Yes, sir. Pliying 'e was a dorg. And the lidy was cross and Ern wasn't allowed to come to the treat, and I told 'im I'd bring 'im back something nice.'

Lord Emsworth breathed heavily. He had not supposed that in these degenerate days a family like this existed. The sister copped Angus McAllister on the shin with stones, the brother bit Constance in the leg . . . It was like listening to some grand old saga of the exploits of heroes and demigods.

'I thought if I didn't 'ave nothing myself it would make it all right.'

'Nothing?' Lord Emsworth started. 'Do you mean to tell me you have not had tea?'

'No, sir. Thank you, sir. I thought if I didn't 'ave none, then it would be all right Ern 'aving what I would 'ave 'ad if I 'ad 'ave 'ad.'

His lordship's head, never strong, swam a little. Then it resumed its equilibrium. He caught her drift.

'God bless my soul!' said Lord Emsworth. 'I never heard anything so monstrous and appalling in my life. Come with me immediately.'

'The lidy said I was to stop 'ere, sir.'

Lord Emsworth gave vent to his loudest snort of the afternoon.

'Confound the lidy!'

'Yes, sir. Thank you, sir.'

Five minutes later Beach, the butler, enjoying a siesta in the housekeeper's room, was roused from his slumbers by the unexpected ringing of a bell. Answering its summons, he found his employer in the library, and with him a surprising young person in a velveteen frock, at the sight of whom his eyebrows quivered and, but for his iron self-restraint, would have risen.

'Beach!'

'Your lordship?'

'This young lady would like some tea.'

'Very good, your lordship.'

'Buns, you know. And apples, and jem – I mean jam-sandwiches, and cake, and that sort of thing.'

'Very good, your lordship.'

'And she has a brother, Beach.'

'Indeed, your lordship?'

'She will want to take some stuff away for him.' Lord Emsworth turned to his guest. 'Ernest would like a little chicken, perhaps?'

'Coo!'

'I beg your pardon?'

'Yes, sir. Thank you, sir.'

'And a slice or two of ham?'

'Yes, sir. Thank you, sir.'

'And – he has no gouty tendency?'

'No, sir. Thank you, sir.'

'Capital! Then a bottle of that new lot of port, Beach. It's some stuff they've sent me down to try,' explained his lordship. 'Nothing special, you understand,' he added apologetically, 'but quite drinkable. I should like your brother's opinion of it. See that all that is put together in a parcel, Beach, and leave it on the table in the hall. We will pick it up as we go out.'

A welcome coolness had crept into the evening air by the time Lord Emsworth and his guest came out of the great door of the castle. Gladys, holding her host's hand and clutching the parcel, sighed contentedly. She had done herself well at the tea-table. Life seemed to have nothing more to offer.

Lord Emsworth did not share this view. His spacious mood had not yet exhausted itself.

'Now, is there anything else you can think of that Ernest would like?' he asked. 'If so, do not hesitate to mention it. Beach, can you think of anything?'

The butler, hovering respectfully, was unable to do so.

'No, your lordship. I ventured to add – on my own responsibility, your lordship – some hard-boiled eggs and a pot of jam to the parcel.'

'Excellent! You are sure there is nothing else?'

A wistful look came into Gladys's eyes.

'Could he 'ave some flarze?'

'Certainly,' said Lord Emsworth. 'Certainly, certainly, certainly. By all means. Just what I was about to suggest my – er – what is flarze?'

Beach, the linguist, interpreted.

'I think the young lady means flowers, your lordship.'

'Yes, sir. Thank you sir. Flarze.'

'Oh?' said Lord Emsworth. 'Oh? Flarze?' he said slowly. 'Oh, ah, yes. I see. H'm!'

He removed his pince-nez, wiped them thoughtfully, replaced them, and gazed with wrinkling forehead at the gardens that stretched gaily out before him. Flarze! It would be idle to deny that those gardens contained flarze in full measure. They were bright with Achillea, Bignonia Radicans, Campanula, Digitalis, Euphorbia, Funkia, Gypsophila, Helianthus, Iris, Liatris, Monarda, Phlox Drummondi, Salvia, Thalictrum, Vinca and Yucca. But the devil of it was that Angus McAllister would have a fit if they were picked. Across the threshold of this Eden the ginger whiskers of Angus McAllister lay like a flaming sword.

As a general rule, the procedure for getting flowers out of Angus McAllister was as follows. You waited till he was in one of his rare moods of complaisance, then you led the conversation gently round to the subject of interior decoration, and then, choosing your moment, you asked if he could possibly spare a few to be put in vases. The last thing you thought of doing was to charge in and start helping yourself.

'I – er – . . .' said Lord Emsworth.

He stopped. In a sudden blinding flash of clear vision he had seen himself for what he was – the spineless, unspeakably unworthy descendant of ancestors who, though they may have had their faults, had certainly known how to handle employees. It was 'How now, varlet!' and 'Marry come up, thou malapert knave!' in the days of previous Earls of Emsworth. Of course, they had possessed certain advantages which he lacked. It undoubtedly helped a man in his dealings with the domestic staff to have, as they had had, the rights of the high, the middle and the low justice – which meant, broadly, that if you got annoyed with your head-gardener you could immediately divide him into four head-gardeners with a battle-axe and no questions asked – but even so, he realized that they were better men than he was and that, if he allowed craven fear of Angus McAllister to stand in the way of this delightful girl and her charming brother getting all the flowers they required, he was not worthy to be the last of their line.

Lord Emsworth wrestled with his tremors.

'Certainly, certainly, certainly,' he said, though not without a qualm. 'Take as many as you want.'

And so it came about that Angus McAllister, crouched in his potting-shed like some dangerous beast in its den, beheld a sight which first froze his blood and then sent it boiling through his veins. Flitting to and fro through his sacred gardens, picking his sacred flowers, was a small girl in a velveteen frock. And – which brought apoplexy a step closer – it was the same small girl who two days before had copped him on the shin with a stone. The stillness of the summer evening was shattered by a roar that sounded like boilers exploding, and Angus McAllister came out of the potting-shed at forty-five miles per hour.

Gladys did not linger. She was a London child, trained from infancy to bear herself gallantly in the presence of alarms and excursions, but this excursion had been so sudden that it momentarily broke her nerve. With a horrified yelp she scuttled to where Lord Emsworth stood and, hiding behind him, clutched the tails of his morning-coat.

'Oo-er!' said Gladys.

Lord Emsworth was not feeling so frightfully good himself. We have pictured him a few moments back drawing inspiration from the nobility of his ancestors and saying, in effect, 'That for McAllister!' but truth now compels us to admit that this hardy attitude was largely due to the fact that he believed the head-gardener to be a safe quarter of a mile away among the swings and roundabouts of the Fete.

The spectacle of the man charging vengefully down on him with gleaming eyes and bristling whiskers made him feel like a nervous English infantryman at the Battle of Bannockburn. His knees shook and the soul within him quivered.

And then something happened, and the whole aspect of the situation changed.

It was, in itself, quite a trivial thing, but it had an astoundingly stimulating effect on Lord Emsworth's morale. What happened was that Gladys, seeking further protection, slipped at this moment a small, hot hand into his.

It was a mute vote of confidence, and Lord Emsworth intended to be worthy of it.

'He's coming,' whispered his lordship's Inferiority Complex agitatedly.

'What of it?' replied Lord Emsworth stoutly.

'Tick him off,' breathed his lordship's ancestors in his other ear.

'Leave it to me,' replied Lord Emsworth.

He drew himself up and adjusted his pince-nez. He felt filled with a cool masterfulness. If the man tendered his resignation, let him tender his damned resignation.

'Well, McAllister?' said Lord Emsworth coldly.

He removed his top hat and brushed it against his sleeve.

'What is the matter, McAllister?'

He replaced his top hat.

'You appear agitated, McAllister.'

He jerked his head militantly. The hat fell off. He let it lie. Freed from its loathsome weight he felt more masterful than ever. It had just needed that to bring him to the top of his form.

'This young lady,' said Lord Emsworth, 'has my full permission to pick all the flowers she wants, McAllister. If you do not see eye to eye with me in this matter, McAllister, say so and we will discuss what you are going to do about it, McAllister. These gardens, McAllister, belong to me, and if you do not – er – appreciate that fact you will, no doubt, be able to find another employer – ah – more in tune with your views. I value your services highly, McAllister, but I will not be dictated to in my own garden, McAllister. Er – dash it,' added his lordship, spoiling the whole effect.

A long moment followed in which Nature stood still, breathless. The Achillea stood still. So did the Bignonia Radicans. So did the Campanula, the Digitalis, the Euphorbia, the Funkia, the Gypsophila, the Helianthus, the Iris, the Liatris, the Monarda, the Phlox Drummondi, the Salvia, the Thalictrum, the Vinca and the Yucca. From far off in the direction of the park there sounded the happy howls of children who were probably breaking things, but even these seemed hushed. The evening breeze had died away.

Angus McAllister stood glowering. His attitude was that of one sorely perplexed. So might the early bird have looked if the worm earmarked for its breakfast had suddenly turned and snapped at it. It had never occurred to him that his employer would voluntarily suggest that he sought another position, and now that he had suggested it Angus McAllister disliked the idea very much. Blandings Castle was in his bones. Elsewhere, he would feel an exile. He fingered his whiskers, but they gave him no comfort.

He made his decision. Better to cease to be a Napoleon than be a Napoleon in exile.

'Mphm,' said Angus McAllister.

'Oh, and by the way, McAllister,' said Lord Emsworth, 'that matter of the gravel path through the yew alley. I've been thinking it over, and I won't have it. Not on any account. Mutilate my beautiful moss with a beastly gravel path? Make an eyesore of the loveliest spot in one of the finest and oldest gardens in the United Kingdom? Certainly not. Most decidedly not. Try to remember, McAllister, as you work in the gardens of Blandings Castle, that you are not back in Glasgow, laying out recreation grounds. That is all, McAllister. Er – dash it – that is all.'

'Mphm,' said Angus McAllister.

He turned. He walked away. The potting-shed swallowed him up. Nature resumed its breathing. The breeze began to blow again. And all over the gardens birds who had stopped on their high note carried on according to plan.

Lord Emsworth took out his handkerchief and dabbed with it at his forehead. He was shaken, but a novel sense of being a man among men thrilled him. It might seem bravado, but he almost wished – yes, dash it, he almost wished – that his sister Constance would come along and start something while he felt like this.

He had his wish.

'Clarence!'

Yes, there she was, hurrying towards him up the garden path. She, like McAllister, seemed agitated. Something was on her mind.

'Clarence!'

'Don't keep saying "Clarence!" as if you were a dashed parrot,' said Lord Emsworth haughtily. 'What the dickens is the matter, Constance?'

'Matter? Do you know what the time is? Do you know that everybody is waiting down there for you to make your speech?'

Lord Emsworth met her eye sternly.

'I do not,' he said. 'And I don't care. I'm not going to make any dashed speech. If you want a speech, let the vicar make it. Or make it yourself. Speech! I never heard such dashed nonsense in my life.' He turned to Gladys. 'Now, my dear,' he said, 'if you will just give me time to get out of these infernal clothes and this ghastly collar and put on something human, we'll go down to the village and have a chat with Ern.'

# 'We Have with Us Tonight'

## (HOW IT FEELS TO BE A LECTURER)

### *Stephen Leacock*

Not only during my tour in England, but for many years past it has been my lot to speak and to lecture in all sorts of places, under all sorts of circumstances, and before all sorts of audiences. I say this, not in boastfulness, but in sorrow. Indeed, I only mention it to establish the fact that when I talk of lecturers and speakers I talk of what I know.

Few people realize how arduous and how disagreeable public lecturing is. The public sees the lecturer step out on to the platform in his little white waistcoat and his long-tailed coat and with a false air of a conjurer about him, and they think him happy. After about ten minutes of his talk they are tired of him. Most people tire of a lecture in ten minutes; clever people can do it in five. Sensible people never go to lectures at all. But the people who do go to a lecture and who get tired of it presently hold it as a sort of a grudge against the lecturer personally. In reality his sufferings are worse than theirs.

For my own part, I always try to appear as happy as possible while I am lecturing. I take this to be part of the trade of anybody labelled a humorist and paid as such. I have no sympathy whatever with the idea that a humorist ought to be a lugubrious person with a face stamped with melancholy. This is a cheap and elementary effect belonging to the level of a circus clown. The image of 'laughter shaking both his sides' is the truer picture of comedy. Therefore I say that I always try to appear cheerful at my lectures and even to laugh at my own jokes. But even this arouses a kind of resentment in some of the audience. 'Well, I will say,' said a stern-looking woman who spoke to me after one of my lectures, 'you certainly do seem to enjoy your own fun.' 'Madam,' I answered, 'if I didn't, who would?' But in reality the whole business of being a public lecturer is one long variation of boredom and fatigue. So I propose to set down here some of the many trials which the lecturer has to bear.

The first of the troubles which anyone who begins giving public lectures meets at the very outset is the fact that the audience won't come to hear him. This happens invariably and constantly, and not through any fault or shortcoming of the speaker.

I don't say that this happened very often to me in my tour in England. In nearly all cases I had crowded audiences: by dividing up the money that I received by the average number of people present to hear me I have calculated that they paid thirteen cents each. And my lectures are evidently worth thirteen cents. But at home in Canada I have very often tried the fatal experiment of lecturing for nothing, and in that case the audience simply won't come. A man will turn out at night when he knows he is going to hear a first-class thirteen-cent lecture; but when the thing is given for nothing, why go to it?

The city in which I live is overrun with little societies, clubs, and associations always wanting to be addressed. So at least it is in appearance. In reality the societies are composed of presidents, secretaries, and officials who want the conspicuousness of office, and a large list of other members who won't come to the meetings. For such an association the invited speaker who is to lecture for nothing prepares his lecture on 'Indo-Germanic Factors in the Current of History.' If he is a professor, he takes all the winter at it. You may drop in at his house at any time, and his wife will tell you that he is 'upstairs working on his lecture.' If he comes down at all, it is in carpet slippers and dressing-gown. His mental vision of his meeting is that of a huge gathering of keen people with Indo-Germanic faces, hanging upon every word.

Then comes the fated night. There are seventeen people present. The lecturer refuses to count them. He refers to them afterwards as 'about a hundred'. To this group he reads his paper on the Indo-Germanic Factor. It takes him two hours. When it is over the chairman invites discussion. There is *no* discussion. The audience is willing to let the Indo-Germanic factors go unchallenged. Then the chairman makes this speech. He says:

'I am very sorry indeed that we should have had such a very poor turn-out to-night. I am sure that the members who were not here have missed a real treat in the delightful paper that we have listened to. I want to assure the lecturer that if he comes to the Owls' Club again we can guarantee him next time a capacity audience. And will any

members, please, who haven't paid their dollar this winter pay it either
to me or to Mr Sibley as they pass out?'

I have heard this speech (in the years when I have had to listen to it)
so many times that I know it by heart. I have made the acquaintance of
the Owls' Club under so many names that I recognize it at once. I am
aware that its members refuse to turn out in cold weather; that they do
not turn out in wet weather; that when the weather is really fine it is
impossible to get them together; that the slightest counter-attraction –
a hockey match, a sacred concert – goes to their heads at once.

There was a time when I was the newly appointed occupant of a
college chair and had to address the Owls' Club. It is a penalty that all
new professors pay, and the Owls batten upon them like bats. It is one
of the compensations of age that I am free of the Owls' Club for ever.
But in the days when I still had to address them I used to take it out of
the Owls in a speech delivered, in imagination only and not out loud, to
the assembled meeting of the seventeen Owls, after the chairman had
made his concluding remarks. It ran as follows:

'Gentlemen – if you are such, which I doubt. I realize that the paper
which I have read on 'Was Hegel a deist?' has been an error. I spent all
the winter on it, and now I realize that not one of you pups know who
Hegel was or what a deist is. Never mind. It is over now, and I am glad.
But just let me say this, only this, which won't keep you a minute. Your
chairman has been good enough to say that if I come again you will get
together a capacity audience to hear me. Let me tell you that if your
society waits for its next meeting till I come to address you again, you
will wait indeed. In fact, gentlemen – I say it frankly – it will be in
another world.'

But I pass over the audience. Suppose there is a real audience, and
suppose them all duly gathered together. Then it becomes the business
of that gloomy gentleman – facetiously referred to in the newspaper
reports as the genial chairman – to put the lecturer to the bad. In nine
cases out of ten he can do so. Some chairmen, indeed, develop a great
gift for it. Here are one or two examples from my own experience:

'Gentlemen,' said the chairman of a society in a little village town in
Western Ontario to which I had come as a paid (a very humbly paid)
lecturer, 'we have with us tonight a gentleman' (here he made an
attempt to read my name on a card, failed to read it, and put the card
back in his pocket) 'a gentleman who is to lecture to us on' (here he

looked at his card again), 'on Ancient – Ancient – I don't very well see
what it is – Ancient – Britain? Thank you, on Ancient Britain. Now, this
is the first of our series of lectures for this winter. The last series, as you
all know, was not a success. In fact, we came out at the end of the year
with a deficit. So this year we are starting a new line and trying the
experiment of cheaper talent.'

Here the chairman gracefully waved his hand toward me, and there
was a certain amount of applause. 'Before I sit down,' the chairman
added, 'I'd like to say that I am sorry to see such a poor turn-out-tonight and to ask any of the members who haven't paid their dollar to
pay it either to me or to Mr Sibley as they pass out.'

Let anybody who knows the discomfiture of coming out before an
audience on any terms judge how it feels to crawl out in front of them
labelled 'cheaper talent.'

Another charming way in which the chairman endeavours to put
both the speaker for the evening and the audience into an entirely good
humour is by reading out letters of regret from persons unable to be
present. This, of course, is only for grand occasions when the speaker
has been invited to come under very special auspices. It was my fate,
not long ago, to 'appear' (this is the correct word to use in this
connection) in this capacity when I was going about Canada trying to
raise some money for the relief of the Belgians. I travelled in great glory
with a pass on the Canadian Pacific Railway (not since extended:
officials of the road, kindly note this) and was most kindly entertained
wherever I went.

It was, therefore, the business of the chairman at such meetings as
these to try and put a special distinction or *cachet* on the gathering. This
is how it was done:

'Ladies and gentlemen,' said the chairman, rising from his seat on
the platform with a little bundle of papers in his hand, 'before I
introduce the speaker of the evening I have one or two items that I want
to read to you.' Here he rustled his papers, and there was a deep hush in
the hall while he selected one. 'We had hoped to have with us tonight
Sir Robert Borden, the Prime Minister of this Dominion. I have just
received a telegram from Sir Robert in which he says that he will not be
able to be here.' (*Great applause.*) The chairman put up his hand for
silence, picked up another telegram, and continued: 'Our committee,
ladies and gentlemen, telegraphed an invitation to Sir Wilfrid Laurier

very cordially inviting him to be here tonight. I have here Sir Wilfrid's answer in which he says that he will not be able to be with us.' (*Renewed applause.*) The chairman again put up his hand for silence and went on, picking up one paper after another: 'The Minister of Finance regrets that he will be unable to come. (*Applause.*) 'Mr. Rodolphe Lemieux' (*applause*) 'will not be here.' (*Great applause.*) 'The Mayor of Toronto' (*applause*) 'is detained on business.' (*Wild applause.*) 'The Anglican Bishop of the Diocese' (*applause*), 'the Principal of the University College, Toronto' (*great applause*) 'the Minister of Education' (*applause*) – 'none of these are coming.' There was a great clapping of hands and enthusiasm, after which the meeting was called to order with a very distinct and palpable feeling that it is one of the most distinguished audiences ever gathered in the hall.

Here is another experience of the same period while I was pursuing the same exalted purpose. I arrived in a little town in Eastern Ontario, and found to my horror that I was billed to 'appear' *in a church.* I was supposed to give readings from my works, and my books are supposed to be of a humorous character. A church hardly seemed the right place to get funny in. I explained my difficulty to the pastor of the church, a very solemn-looking man. He nodded his head, slowly and gravely, as he grasped my difficulty. 'I see,' he said, 'I see, but I think that I can introduce you to our people in such a way as to make that right.'

When the time came, he led me up on to the pulpit platform of the church, just beside and below the pulpit itself with a reading desk and a big Bible and a shaded light beside it. It was a big church, and the audience, sitting in half darkness, as is customary during a sermon, reached away back into the gloom. The place was packed full and absolutely quiet. Then the chairman spoke.

'Dear friends,' he said, 'I want you to understand that it will be all right to laugh tonight. Let me hear you laugh heartily, laugh right out, just as much as ever you want to, because' (and here his voice assumed the deep, sepulchral tones of the preacher) 'when we think of the noble object for which the professor appears tonight we may be assured that the Lord will forgive anyone who will laugh at the professor.'

I am sorry to say, however, that none of the audience, even with the plenary absolution in advance, were inclined to take a chance on it.

I recall in this same connection the chairman of a meeting at a certain town in Vermont. He represents the type of chairman who turns up so late at the meeting that the committee have no time to explain to him properly what the meeting is about or who the speaker is. I noticed on this occasion that he introduced me very guardedly by name (from a little card) and said nothing about the Belgians, and nothing about my being (supposed to be) a humorist. This last was a great error. The audience, for want of guidance, remained very silent and decorous and well-behaved during my talk. Then, somehow, at the end, while someone was moving a vote of thanks the chairman discovered his error. So he tried to make it good. Just as the audience were getting up to put on their wraps he rose, knocked on his desk, and said:

'Just a minute, please, ladies and gentlemen, just a minute. I have just found out – I should have known it sooner, but I was late in coming to this meeting – that the speaker who has just addressed you has done so in behalf of the Belgian Relief Fund. I understand that he is a well-known Canadian humorist (ha ha!), and I am sure that we have all been immensely amused (ha ha!). He is giving his delightful talks (ha ha!), though I didn't know this till just this minute – for the Belgian Relief Fund, and he is giving his services for nothing. I am sure, when we realize this, we shall all feel that it has been well worth while to come. I am only sorry that we didn't have a better turn-out-tonight. But I can assure the speaker that if he will come again we shall guarantee him a capacity audience. And I may say that if there are any members of this association who have not paid their dollar this season, they can give it either to myself or to Mr Sibley as they pass out.'

With the amount of accumulated experience that I had behind me I was naturally interested during my lectures in England in the chairmen who were to introduce me. I cannot help but feel that I have acquired a fine taste in chairmen. I know them just as other experts know old furniture and Pekingese dogs. The Witty Chairman, the Prosy Chairman, the Solemn Chairman – I know them all. As soon as I shake hands with the chairman in the committee room I can tell exactly how he will act.

There are certain types of chairmen who have so often been described and are so familiar that it is not worth while to linger on them. Everybody knows the chairman who says, 'Now, ladies and gentlemen, you have not come here to listen to *me*. So I will be very brief – in fact, I will confine my remarks to just one or two very short observations.' He then proceeds to make observations for twenty-five minutes. At the end of it he remarks, with charming simplicity, 'Now I know that you are all impatient to hear the lecturer—.'

And everybody knows also the chairman who comes to the meeting with a very imperfect knowledge as to who or what the lecturer is, and is driven to introduce him by saying:

'Our lecturer of the evening is widely recognized as one of the greatest authorites on – on – on his subject in the world today. He comes to us from – from a great distance, and I can assure him that it is a great pleasure to this audience to welcome a man who has done so much to – to – to advance the interests of – of – everything as he has.'

But this man, bad as he is, is not so bad as the chairman whose preparation for introducing the lecturer has obviously been made at the eleventh hour. Just such a chairman it was my fate to strike in the form of a local alderman, built like an ox, in one of those small manufacturing places in the north of England where they grow men of this type and elect them to office.

'I never saw the lecturer before,' he said, 'but I've read his book' (I have written nineteen books). 'The committee was good enough to send me over his book last night. I didn't read it all, but I took a look at the preface, and I can assure him he is very welcome. I understand he comes from a college—' Then he turned directly towards me and said in a loud voice, 'What was the name of that college over there you said you came from?'

'McGill,' I answered equally loudly.

'He comes from McGill,' the chairman boomed out. 'I never heard of McGill myself, but I can assure him he's welcome. He's going to lecture to us on – what did you say it was to be about?'

'It's a humorous lecture,' I said.

'Ay, it's to be a humorous lecture, ladies and gentlemen, and I'll venture to say it will be a rare treat. I'm only sorry I can't stay for it myself, as I have to get back to the Town Hall for a meeting. So without more ado I'll get off the platform and let the lecturer go on with his humour.'

A still more terrible type of chairman is the one whose mind is evidently preoccupied and disturbed with some local happening and who comes on to the platform with a face imprinted with distress. Before introducing the lecturer he refers in moving tones to the local sorrow, whatever it is. As a prelude to a humorous lecture this is not gay.

Such a chairman fell to my lot one night before a gloomy audience in a London suburb.

'As I look about this hall tonight,' he began in a doleful whine, 'I see many empty seats.' Here he stifled a sob. 'Nor am I surprised that a great many of our people should prefer tonight to stay quietly at home.'

I had no clue to what he meant. I merely gathered that some peculiar sorrow must have overwhelmed the town that day.

'To many it may seen hardly fitting that after the loss our town has sustained we should come out here to listen to a humorous lecture.'

'What's the trouble?' I whispered to a citizen sitting beside me on the platform.

'Our oldest resident,' he whispered back, 'he died this morning.'

'How old?'

'Ninety-four,' he whispered.

Meantime the chairman, with deep sobs in his voice, continued:

'We debated in our committee whether or not we should have the lecture. Had it been a lecture of another character our position would have been less difficult—'

By this time I began to feel like a criminal.

'The case would have been different had the lecture been one that contained information, or that was inspired by some serious purpose, or that could have been of any benefit. But this is not so. We understand that this lecture which Mr Leacock has already given, I believe, twenty or thirty times in England—'

Here he turned to me with a look of mild reproval while the silent audience, deeply moved, all looked at me as at a man who went round the country insulting the memory of the dead by giving a lecture thirty times.

'We understand, though this we shall have an opportunity of testing for ourselves presently, that Mr Leacock's lecture is not of a character which – has not, so to speak, the kind of value – in short, is not a lecture of that class.'

Here he paused and choked back a sob.

'Had our poor friend been spared to us for another six years he would have rounded out the century. But it was not to be. For two or three years past he has noted that somehow his strength was failing, that, for some reason or other, he was no longer what he had been. Last month he began to droop. Last week he began to sink. Speech left him last Tuesday. This morning he passed away, and he has gone now, we trust, in safety to where there are no lectures.'

The audience were now nearly in tears.

The chairman made a visible effort towards firmness and control.

'But yet,' he continued, 'our committee felt that, in another sense, it was our duty to go on with our arrangements. I think, ladies and gentlemen, that the war has taught us all that it is always our duty to "carry on," no matter how hard it may be, no matter with what reluctance we do it, and, whatever be the difficulties and the dangers, we must carry on to the end; for, after all, there is an end, and by resolution and patience we can reach it.'

'I will, therefore, invite Mr Leacock to deliver to us his humorous lecture, the title of which I have forgotten, but I understand it to be the same lecture which he has already given thirty or forty times in England.'

But contrast with this melancholy man the pleasing and genial person who introduced me, all upside-down, to a metropolitan audience.

He was so brisk, so neat, so sure of himself that it didn't seem possible that he could make any kind of mistake. I thought it unnecessary to coach him. He seemed absolutely all right.

'It is a great pleasure,' he said, with a charming easy appearance of being entirely at home on the platform, 'to welcome here tonight our distinguished Canadian fellow-citizen, Mr Learoyd.' He turned half-way towards me as he spoke with a sort of gesture of welcome, admirably executed. If only my name had been Learoyd instead of Leacock it would have been excellent.

'There are many of us,' he continued, 'who have awaited Mr Learoyd's coming with the most pleasant anticipations. We seemed from his books to know him already as an old friend. In fact, I think I do not exaggerate when I tell Mr Learoyd that his name in our city has long been a household word. I have very, very great pleasure, ladies and gentlemen, in introducing to you Mr Learoyd.'

As far as I know, the chairman never knew his error. At the close of my lecture he said that he was sure that the audience were 'deeply indebted to Mr Learoyd,' and then, with a few words of rapid, genial apology, buzzed off, like a humming bird, to other avocations. But I have amply forgiven him. Anything for kindness and geniality; it makes the whole of life smooth. If that chairman ever comes to my home town he is hereby invited to lunch or dine with me, as Mr Learoyd or under any name that he selects.

Such a man is, after all, in strong contrast to the kind of chairman who has no native sense of the geniality that ought to accompany his office. There is, for example, a type of man who thinks that the fitting way to introduce a lecturer is to say a few words about the finances of the society to which he is to lecture (for money) and about the difficulty in getting members to turn out to hear lectures.

Everybody has heard such a speech a dozen times. But it is the paid lecturer sitting on the platform who best appreciates it. It runs like this:

'Now, ladies and gentlemen, before I invite the lecturer of the evening to address us there are a few words I would like to say. There are a good many of the members who are in arrears with their fees. I am aware that these are hard times and it is difficult to collect money, but at the same time the members ought to remember that the expenses of the society are very heavy. The fees that are asked by the lecturers, as I suppose you know, have advanced very greatly in the last few years. In fact, I may say that they are becoming almost prohibitive.'

This discourse is pleasant hearing for the lecturer. He can see the members who have not yet paid their annual dues eyeing him with hatred. The chairman goes on:

'Our finance committee were afraid at first that we could not afford to bring Mr Leacock to our society. But fortunately, through the personal generosity of two of our members, who subscribed ten pounds each out of their own pockets, we were able to raise the required sum.'

Applause: during which the lecturer sits looking and feeling like the embodiment of 'the required sum.'

'Now, ladies and gentlemen,' continues the chairman, 'what I feel is that when we have members in the society who are willing to make this sacrifice – because it is a sacrifice, ladies and gentlemen – we ought to support them in every way. The members ought to think it their duty to turn out to the lectures. I know that it is not an easy thing to do. On a cold night, like this evening, it is hard – I admit it is hard – to turn out from the comfort of one's own fireside and come and listen to a lecture.

But I think that the members should look at it not as a matter of personal comfort, but as a matter of duty towards this society. We have managed to keep this society alive for fifteen years, and, though I don't say it in any spirit of boasting, it has not been an easy thing to do. It has required a good deal of pretty hard spadework by the committee. Well, ladies and gentlemen, I suppose you didn't come here to listen to me, and perhaps I have said enough about our difficulties and troubles. So without more ado (this is always a favourite phrase with chairmen) 'I'll invite Mr Leacock to address the society – oh! just one word before I sit down: will all those who are leaving before the end of the lecture kindly go out through the side door and step as quietly as possible? Mr Leacock.'

Anybody who is in the lecture business knows that that introduction is far worse than being called Mr Learoyd.

When any lecturer goes across to England from this side of the water there is naturally a tendency upon the part of the chairman to play upon this fact. This is especially true in the case of a Canadian like myself. The chairman feels that the moment is fitting for one of those great imperial thoughts that bind the British Empire together. But sometimes the expression of the thought falls short of the full glory of the conception.

Witness this (word for word) introduction that was used against me by a clerical chairman in a quiet spot in the south of England.

'Not so long ago, ladies and gentlemen,' said the vicar, 'we used to send out to Canada various classes of our community to help build up that country. We sent out our labourers, we sent out scholars and professors. Indeed, we even sent out our criminals. And now,' with a wave of his hand towards me, 'they are coming back.'

There was no laughter. An English audience is nothing if not literal; and they are as polite as they are literal. They understood that I was a reformed criminal, and as such they gave me a hearty burst of applause.

But there is just one thing that I would like to chronicle here in favour of the chairman and in gratitude for his existence. Even at his worst he is far better than having no chairman at all. Over in England a great many societies and public bodies have adopted the plan of 'cutting out the chairman.' Wearying of his faults, they have forgotten the reasons for his existence and undertake to do without him.

The result is ghastly. The lecturer steps on to the platform alone and unaccompanied. There is a feeble ripple of applause; he makes his miserable bow and explains with as much enthusiasm as he can who he is. The atmosphere of the thing is so cold that an arctic expedition isn't in it with it. I found also the further difficulty that in the absence of the chairman very often the audience, or a large part of it, doesn't know who the lecturer is. On many occasions I received on appearing a wild burst of applause under the impression that I was somebody else. I have been mistaken in this way for M. Briand, then Prime Minister of France, for Charlie Chaplin, for Mrs Asquith – but stop, I may get into a libel suit. All I mean is that without a chairman 'we celebrities' get terribly mixed up together.

To one experience of my tour as a lecturer I shall always be able to look back with satisfaction. I nearly had the pleasure of killing a man with laughing. American lecturers have often dreamed of doing this. I nearly did it. The man in question was a comfortable, apoplectic-looking man with the kind of merry, rubicund face that is seen in countries where they don't have prohibition. He was seated near the back of the hall and was laughing uproariously. All of a sudden I realised that something was happening. The man had collapsed sideways on to the floor. A little group of men gathered about him: they lifted him up, and I could see them carrying him out a silent and inert mass. As in duty bound, I went right on with my lecture. But my heart beat high with satisfaction. I was sure that I had killed him. The reader may judge how high these hopes rose when, a moment or two later, a note was handed to the chairman, who then asked me to pause for a moment in my lecture and stood up and asked, 'Is there a doctor in the audience?' A doctor rose and silently went out. The lecture continued, but there was no more laughter: my aim had now become to kill another of them and they knew it. They were aware that if they started laughing they might die. In a few minutes a second note was handed to the chairman. He announced very gravely, 'A second doctor is wanted.' The lecture went on in deeper silence than ever. All the audience were waiting for a third announcement. It came. A new message was handed to the chairman. He rose and said, 'If Mr Murchison, the undertaker is in the audience, will he kindly step outside?'

That man, I regret to say, got well. Disappointing though it is to read it, he recovered. I sent back next morning from London a telegram of inquiry (I did it, in reality, so as to have a proper proof of his death), and received the answer, 'Patient doing well; is sitting up in bed and reading Lord Haldane's *Relativity*: no danger of relapse.'

# The Ball at the Mansion House

*George and Weedon Grossmith*

APRIL 30.

Perfectly astounded at receiving an invitation for Carrie and myself from the Lord and Lady Mayoress to the Mansion House, to 'meet the Representatives of Trades and Commerce'. My heart beat like that of a schoolboy. Carrie and I read the invitation over two or three times. I could scarcely eat my breakfast. I said – and I felt it from the bottom of my heart – 'Carrie darling, I was a proud man when I led you down the aisle of the church on our wedding day; that pride will be equalled, if not surpassed, when I lead my dear, pretty wife up to the Lord and Lady Mayoress at the Mansion House.' I saw the tears in Carrie's eyes, and she said: 'Charlie dear, it is *I* who have to be proud of you. And I am very, very proud of you. You have called me pretty; and as long as I am pretty in your eyes, I am happy. You, dear old Charlie, are *not* handsome, but you are *good*, which is far more noble.' I gave her a kiss, and she said: 'I wonder if there will be any dancing? I have not danced with you for years.'

I cannot tell what induced me to do it, but I seized her round the waist, and we were silly enough to be executing a wild kind of polka when Sarah entered, grinning, and said: 'There is a man, mum, at the door who wants to know if you want any good coals.' Most annoyed at this. Spent the evening in answering, and tearing up again, the reply to the Mansion House, having left word with Sarah if Gowing or Cummings called we were not at home. Must consult Mr Perkupp how to answer the Lord Mayor's invitation.

MAY 1.

Carrie said: 'I should like to send mother the invitation to look at.' I consented, as soon as I had answered it. I told Mr Perkupp, at the office, with a feeling of pride, that we had received an invitation to the

Mansion House; and he said, to my astonishment, that he himself gave in my name to the Lord Mayor's secretary. I felt this rather discounted the value of the invitation, but I thanked him; and in reply to me, he described how I was to answer it. I felt the reply was too simple; but of course Mr Perkupp knows best.

MAY 2.
Send my dress-coat and trousers to the little tailor's round the corner, to have the creases taken out. Told Gowing not to call next Monday, as we were going to the Mansion House. Send similar note to Cummings.

MAY 3.
Carrie went to Mrs James, at Sutton, to consult about her dress for next Monday. While speaking incidentally to Spotch, one of our head clerks, about the Mansion House, he said: 'Oh, I'm asked, but don't think I shall go.' When a vulgar man like Spotch is asked I feel my invitation is considerably discounted. In the evening, while I was out, the little tailor brought round my coat and trousers, and because Sarah had not a shilling to pay for the pressing, he took them away again.

MAY 4.
Carrie's mother returned the Lord Mayor's invitation, which was sent to her to look at, with apologies for having upset a glass of port over it. I was too angry to say anything.

MAY 5.
Bought a pair of lavender kid-gloves for next Monday, and two white ties, in case one got spoiled in the tying.

MAY 6, SUNDAY.
A very dull sermon, during which, I regret to say, I twice thought of the Mansion House reception tomorrow.

MAY 7.
A big red-letter day; viz., the Lord Mayor's reception. The whole house upset. I had to get dressed at half-past six, as Carrie wanted the room to herself. Mrs James had come up from Sutton to help Carrie; so I could not help thinking it unreasonable that she should require the entire

attention of Sarah, the servant, as well. Sarah kept running out of the house to fetch 'something for missis,' and several times I had, in my full evening-dress, to answer the back-door.

The last time it was the greengrocer's boy, who, not seeing it was me, for Sarah had not lighted the gas, pushed into my hands two cabbages and half-a-dozen coal-blocks. I indignantly threw them on the ground, and felt so annoyed that I so far forgot myself as to box the boy's ears. He went away crying, and said he should summons me, a thing I would not have happen for the world. In the dark, I stepped on a piece of the cabbage, which brought me down on the flags all of a heap. For a moment I was stunned, but when I recovered I crawled upstairs into the drawing-room and on looking into the chimney-glass discovered that my chin was bleeding, my shirt smeared with the coal-blocks, and my left trouser torn at the knee.

However, Mrs James brought me down another shirt, which I changed in the drawing-room. I put a piece of court-plaster on my chin, and Sarah very neatly sewed up the tear at the knee. At nine o'clock Carrie swept into the room, looking like a queen. Never have I seen her look so lovely, or so distinguished. She was wearing a satin dress of sky-blue – my favourite colour – and a piece of lace, which Mrs James lent her, round the shoulders, to give a finish. I thought perhaps the dress was a little too long behind, and decidly too short in front, but Mrs James said it was *à la mode*. Mrs James was most kind, and lent Carrie a fan of ivory with red feathers, the value of which, she said, was priceless, as the feathers belonged to the Kachu eagle – a bird now extinct. I preferred the little white fan which Carrie bought for three-and-six at Shoolbred's, but both ladies sat on me at once.

We arrived at the Mansion House too early, which was rather fortunate, for I had an opportunity of speaking to his lordship, who graciously condescended to talk with me some minutes; but I must say I was disappointed to find he did not even know Mr Perkupp, the principal.

I felt as if we had been invited to the Mansion House by one who did not know the Lord Mayor himself. Crowds arrived, and I shall never forget the grand sight. My humble pen can never describe it. I was a little annoyed with Carrie, who kept saying: 'Isn't it a pity we don't know anybody?'

Once she quite lost her head. I saw someone who looked like

Franching, from Peckham, and was moving towards him when she seized me by the coat-tails, and said quite loudly: 'Don't leave me,' which caused an elderly gentleman, in a court-suit, and a chain round him, and two ladies, to burst out laughing. There was an immense crowd in the supper-room, and, my stars! it was a splendid supper – any amount of champagne.

Carrie made a most hearty supper, for which I was pleased; for I sometimes think she is not strong. There was scarcely a dish she did not taste. I was so thirsty, I could not eat much. Receiving a sharp slap on the shoulder, I turned, and, to my amazement, saw Farmerson, our ironmonger. He said, in the most familiar way: 'This is better than Brickfield Terrace, eh?' I simply looked at him, and said coolly: 'I never expected to see you here.' He said, with a loud coarse laugh: 'I like that – if *you*, why not *me*?' I replied: 'Certainly.' I wish I could have thought of something better to say. He said: 'Can I get your good lady anything?' Carrie said: 'No, I thank you,' for which I was pleased. I said, by way of reproof to him: 'You never sent today to paint the bath, as I requested.' Farmerson said: 'Pardon me, Mr Pooter, no shop when we're in company, please.'

Before I could think of a reply, one of the sheriffs, in full Court costume, slapped Farmerson on the back and hailed him as an old friend, and asked him to dine with him at his lodge. I was astonished. For full five minutes they stood roaring with laughter, and stood digging each other in the ribs. They kept telling each other they didn't look a day older. They began embracing each other and drinking champagne.

To think that a man who mends our scraper should know any member of our aristocracy! I was just moving with Carrie, when Farmerson seized me rather roughly by the collar, and addressing the sheriff, said: 'Let me introduce my neighbour, Pooter.' He did not even say 'Mister'. The sheriff handed me a glass of champagne. I felt, after all, it was a great honour to drink a glass of wine with him, and I told him so. We stood chatting for some time, and at last I said: 'You must excuse me now if I join Mrs. Pooter.' When I approached her, she said: 'Don't let me take you away from your friends. I am quite happy standing here alone in a crowd, knowing nobody!'

As it takes two to make a quarrel, and as it was neither the time nor the place for it, I gave my arm to Carrie, and said: 'I hope my darling little wife will dance with me, if only for the sake of saying we had danced at the Mansion House as guests of the Lord Mayor.' Finding the dancing after supper was less formal, and knowing how much Carrie used to admire my dancing in the days gone by I put my arm round her waist and we commenced a waltz.

A most unfortunate accident occurred. I had got on a new pair of boots. Foolishly, I had omitted to take Carrie's advice; namely, to scratch the soles of them with the points of the scissors or to put a little wet on them. I had scarcely started when, like lightning, my left foot slipped away and I came down, the side of my head striking the floor with such violence that for a second or two I did not know what had happened. I need hardly say that Carrie fell with me with equal violence, breaking the comb in her hair and grazing her elbow.

There was a roar of laughter, which was immediately checked when people found that we had really hurt ourselves. A gentleman assisted Carrie to a seat, and I expressed myself pretty strongly on the danger of having a plain polished floor with no carpet or drugget to prevent people slipping. The gentleman, who said his name was Darwitts, insisted on escorting Carrie to have a glass of wine, an invitation which I was pleased to allow Carrie to accept.

I followed, and met Farmerson, who immediately said, in his loud voice: 'Oh, are you the one who went down?'

I answered with an indignant look.

With execrable taste, he said: 'Look here, old man, we are too old for this game. We must leave these capers to the youngsters. Come and have another glass, that is more in our line.'

Although I felt I was buying his silence by accepting, we followed the others into the supper-room.

Neither Carrie nor I, after our unfortunate mishap, felt inclined to stay longer. As we were departing, Farmerson said: 'Are you going? if so, you might give me a lift.'

I thought it better to consent, but wish I had first consulted Carrie.

*After the Mansion House Ball.*
*Carrie offended. Gowing also offended.*
*A pleasant party at the Cummings'.*
*Mr Franching, of Peckham,*
*visits us.*

MAY 8.

I woke up with a most terrible headache. I could scarcely see, and the back of my neck was as if I had given it a crick. I thought first of sending for a doctor; but I did not think it necessary. When up, I felt faint, and went to Brownish's, the chemist, who gave me a draught. So bad at the office, had to get leave to come home. Went to another chemist in the City, and I got a draught. Brownish's dose seems to have made me worse; have eaten nothing all day. To make matters worse, Carrie, every time I spoke to her, answered me sharply – that is, when she answered at all.

In the evening I felt very much worse again and said to her: 'I do believe I've been poisoned by the lobster mayonnaise at the Mansion House last night'; she simply replied, without taking her eyes from her sewing: 'Champagne never did agree with you.' I felt irritated, and said: 'What nonsense you talk; I only had a glass and a half, and you know as well as I do—' Before I could complete the sentence she bounced out of the room. I sat over an hour waiting for her to return; but as she did not, I determined I would go to bed. I discovered Carrie had gone to bed without even saying 'good night'; leaving me to bar the scullery door and feed the cat. I shall certainly speak to her about this in the morning.

MAY 9.

Still a little shaky, with black specks. The *Blackfriars Bi-weekly News* contains a long list of the guests at the Mansion House Ball. Disappointed to find our names omitted, though Farmerson's is in plainly enough with MLL after it, whatever that may mean. More than vexed, because we had ordered a dozen copies to send to our friends. Wrote to the *Blackfriars Bi-weekly News*, pointing out their omission.

Carrie had commenced her breakfast when I entered the parlour. I helped myself to a cup of tea, and I said, perfectly calmly and quietly: 'Carrie, I wish a little explanation of your conduct last night.'

She replied, 'Indeed! and I desire something more than a *little* explanation of your conduct the night before.'

I said, coolly: 'Really, I don't understand you.'

Carrie said sneeringly: 'Probably not; you were scarcely in a condition to understand anything.'

'I was astonished at this insinuation and simply ejaculated:

'Caroline!'

She said: 'Don't be theatrical, it has no effect on me. Reserve that tone for your new friend. *Mister* Farmerson, the ironmonger.'

I was about to speak, when Carrie, in a temper such as I have never seen her in before, told me to hold my tongue. She said: 'Now *I'm* going to say something! After professing to snub Mr Farmerson, you permit him to snub *you*, in my presence, and then accept his invitation to take a glass of champagne with you, and you don't limit yourself to one glass. You then offer this vulgar man, who made a bungle of repairing our scraper, a seat in our cab on the way home. I say nothing about his tearing my dress in getting in the cab, nor of treading on Mrs James's expensive fan, which you knocked out of my hand, and for which he never even apologized; but you smoked all the way home without having the decency to ask my permission. That is not all! At the end of the journey, although he did not offer you a farthing towards his share of the cab, you asked him in. Fortunately, he was sober enough to detect, from my manner, that his company was not desirable.'

Goodness knows I felt humiliated enough at this; but, to make matters worse, Gowing entered the room, without knocking, with two hats on his head and holding the garden-rake in his hand, with Carrie's fur tippet (which he had taken off the downstairs hall-peg) round his neck, and announced himself in a loud, coarse voice: 'His Royal Highness, the Lord Mayor!' He marched twice round the room like a buffoon, and finding we took no notice, said: 'Hulloh! what's up? Lovers' quarrel, eh?'

There was a silence for a moment, so I said quietly: 'My dear Gowing, I'm not very well, and not quite in the humour for joking; especially when you enter the room without knocking, an act which I fail to see the fun of.'

Gowing said: 'I'm very sorry, but I called for my stick, which I thought you would have sent round.' I handed him his stick, which I remembered I had painted black with the enamel paint, thinking to improve it. He looked at it for a minute with a dazed expression and said: 'Who did this!'

I said: 'Eh, did what?'

He said: 'Did what? Why, destroyed my stick! It belonged to my poor uncle, and I value it more than anything I have in the world! I'll know who did it.'

I said: 'I'm very sorry. I dare say it will come off. I did it for the best.'

Gowing said: 'Then all I can say is, it's a confounded liberty; and I *would* add, you're a bigger fool than you look, only *that's* absolutely impossible.'

MAY 12.
Got a single copy of the *Blackfriars Bi-weekly News*. There was a short list of several names they had omitted; but the stupid people had mentioned our names as 'Mr and Mrs C. Porter'. Most annoying! Wrote again and I took particular care to write our name in capital letters, POOTER, so that there should be no possible mistake this time.

MAY 16.
Absolutely disgusted on opening the *Blackfriars Bi-weekly News* of today, to find the following paragraph: 'We have received two letters from Mr and Mrs Charles Pewter, requesting us to announce the important fact that they were at the Mansion House Ball.' I tore up the paper and threw it in the waste-paper basket. My time is far too valuable to bother about such trifles.

MAY 21.
The last week or ten days terribly dull, Carrie being away at Mrs James's, at Sutton. Cummings also away. Gowing, I presume, is still offended with me for black-enamelling his stick without asking him.

MAY 22.
Purchased a new stick mounted with silver, which cost seven-and-sixpence (shall tell Carrie five shillings), and sent it round with nice note to Gowing.

MAY 23.
Received strange note from Gowing; he said: 'Offended? not a bit, my boy. I thought you were offended with me for losing my temper. Besides, I found after all it was not my poor uncle's stick you painted. It was only a shilling thing I bought at a tobacconist's. However, I am much obliged to you for your handsome present all the same.'

MAY 24.
Carrie back. Hoorah! She looks wonderfully well, except that the sun
has caught her nose.

MAY 25.
Carrie brought down some of my shirts and advised me to take them to
Trillip's round the corner. She said: 'The fronts and cuffs are much
frayed.' I said without a moment's hesitation; 'I'm *frayed* they are.' Lor!
how we roared. I thought we should never stop laughing. As I
happened to be sitting next the driver going to town on the 'bus, I told
him my joke about the 'frayed' shirts. I thought he would have rolled off
his seat. They laughed at the office a good bit too over it.

MAY 26.
Left the shirts to be repaired at Trillip's I said to him: 'I'm *'fraid* they
are *frayed*.' He said, without a smile: 'They're bound to do that, sir.'
Some people seem to be quite destitute of a sense of humour.

JUNE 1.
The last week has been like old times, Carrie being back, and Gowing
and Cummings called every evening nearly. Twice we sat out in the
garden quite late. This evening we were like a pack of children, and
played 'consequences'. It is a good game.

JUNE 2.
'Consequences' again this evening. Not quite so successful as last night;
Gowing having several times overstepped the limits of good taste.

JUNE 4.
In the evening Carrie and I went round to Mr and Mrs Cummings' to
spend a quiet evening with them. Gowing was there, also Mr Stillbrook. It was quiet but pleasant. Mrs Cummings sang five or six songs,
'No, Sir', and 'The Garden of Sleep', being best in my humble
judgement; but what pleased me most was the duet she sang with
Carrie – classical duet, too. I think it is called, 'I would that my love!' It
was beautiful. If Carrie had been in better voice, I don't think
professionals could have sung it better. After supper we made them sing
it again. I never liked Mr Stillbrook since the walk that Sunday to the

'Cow and Hedge', but I must say he sings comic-songs well. His song: 'We don't want the old men now', made us shriek with laughter, especially the verse referring to Mr Gladstone; but there was one verse I think he might have omitted, and I said so, but Gowing thought it was the best of the lot.

JUNE 6.

Trillip brought round the shirts and, to my disgust, his charge for repairing was more than I gave for them when new. I told him so, and he impertinently replied: 'Well, they are better now than when they were new.' I paid him, and said it was a robbery. He said: 'If you wanted your shirt-fronts made out of pauper-linen, such as is used for packing and book-binding, why didn't you say so?'

JUNE 7.

A dreadful annoyance. Met Mr Franching, who lives at Peckham, and who is a great swell in his way. I ventured to ask him to come home to meat-tea, and take pot-luck. I did not think he would accept such a humble invitation; but he did, saying in a most friendly way, he would rather 'peck' with us than by himself. I said: 'We had better get into this blue 'bus.' He replied: 'No blue-bussing for me. I have had enough of the blues lately. I lost a cool "thou" over the Copper Scare. Step in here.'

We drove up home in style, in a hansom-cab, and I knocked three times at the front door without getting an answer. I saw Carrie, through the panels of ground-glass (with stars), rushing upstairs. I told Mr Franching to wait at the door while I went round to the side. There I saw the grocer's boy actually picking off the paint on the door, which had formed into blisters. No time to reprove him; so went round and effected an entrance through the kitchen window. I let in Mr Franching, and showed him into the drawing-room. I went upstairs to Carrie, who was changing her dress, and told her I had persuaded Mr Franching to come home. She replied: 'How can you do such a thing? You know it's Sarah's holiday, and there's not a thing in the house, the cold mutton having turned with the hot weather.'

Eventually Carrie, like a good creature as she is, slipped down, washed up the teacups, and laid the cloth, and I gave Franching our views of Japan to look at while I ran round to the butcher's to get three chops.

JULY 30.

The miserable cold weather is either upsetting me or Carrie or both.
We seem to break out into an argument about absolutely nothing, and
this unpleasant state of things usually occurs at meal-times.

This morning, for some unaccountable reason, we were talking
about balloons, and we were as merry as possible; but the conversation
drifted into family matters, during which Carrie, without the slightest
reason, referred in the most uncomplimentary manner to my poor
father's pecuniary trouble. I retorted by saying that 'Pa, at all events,
was a gentleman,' whereupon Carrie burst out crying. I positively
could not eat any breakfast.

At the office I was sent for by Mr Perkupp, who said he was very
sorry, but I should have to take my annual holidays from next
Saturday. Franching called at office and asked me to dine at his club,
'The Constitutional'. Fearing disagreeables at home after the 'tiff' this
morning, I sent a telegram to Carrie, telling her I was going out to dine
and she was not to sit up. Bought a little silver bangle for Carrie.

JULY 31.

Carrie was very pleased with the bangle, which I left with an affection-
ate note on her dressing-table last night before going to bed. I told
Carrie we should have to start for our holiday next Saturday. She
replied quite happily that she did not mind, except that the weather
was so bad, and she feared that Miss Jibbons would not be able to get
her a seaside dress in time. I told Carrie that I thought the drab one
with pink bows looked quite good enough; and Carrie said she should
not think of wearing it. I was about to discuss the matter, when,
remembering the argument yesterday, resolved to hold my tongue.

I said to Carrie: 'I don't think we can do better than "Good old
Broadstairs".' Carrie not only, to my astonishment, raised an objection
to Broadstairs, for the first time, but begged me not to use the
expression, 'Good old', but to leave it to Mr Stillbrook and other
*gentlemen* of his type. Hearing my 'bus pass the window, I was obliged to
rush out of the house without kissing Carrie as usual; and I shouted to
her: 'I leave it to you to decide.' On returning in the evening, Carrie
said she thought as the time was so short she had decided on Broadstairs, and had written to Mrs Beck, Harbour View Terrace, for
apartments.

AUGUST 1.

Ordered a new pair of trousers at Edwards's, and told them not to cut them so loose over the boot; the last pair being so loose and also tight at the knee, looked like a sailor's, and I heard Pitt, that objectionable youth at the office, call out 'Hornpipe' as I passed his desk. Carrie has ordered of Miss Jibbons a pink Garibaldi and blue-serge skirt, which I always think looks so pretty at the seaside. In the evening she trimmed herself a little sailor-hat, while I read to her the *Exchange and Mart*. We had a good laugh over my trying on the hat when she had finished it; Carrie saying it looked so funny with my beard, and how the people would have roared if I went on the stage like it.

AUGUST 2.

Mrs Beck wrote to say we could have our usual rooms at Broadstairs. That's off our mind. Bought a coloured shirt and a pair of tan-coloured boots, which I see many of the swell clerks wearing in the City, and hear are all the 'go'.

AUGUST 3.

A beautiful day. Looking forward to tomorrow. Carrie bought a parasol about five feet long. I told her it was ridiculous. She said: 'Mrs James, of Sutton, has one twice as long'; so the matter dropped. I bought a capital hat for hot weather at the seaside. I don't know what it is called, but it is the shape of the helmet worn in India, only made of straw. Got three new ties, two coloured handkerchiefs, and a pair of navy-blue socks at Pope Brothers. Spent the evening packing. Carrie told me not to forget to borrow Mr Higgsworth's telescope, which he always lends me, knowing I know how to take care of it. Sent Sarah out for it. While everything was seeming so bright, the last post brought us a letter from Mrs Beck, saying: 'I have let all my house to one party, and am sorry I must take back my words, and am sorry you must find other apartments; but Mrs Womming, next door, will be pleased to accommodate you, but she cannot take you before Monday, as her rooms are engaged Bank Holiday week.'

# Ho for the Hols

## Goodby to Skool
## (for a bit)

### *Geoffrey Willans*

'Boys,' sa headmaster GRIMES, smiling horibly, 'st. custad's hav come
to the end of another term.'

Can there be a note of relief in his craked voice? There can be no
doubt of the feelings of the little pupils. CHEERS! HURRAH!
WHIZZ-O! CHARGE! TA-RAN-TA-RA! The little chaps raise the
roof of big skool, which do not take much doing as most of it is coming
off already.

'Ah, molesworth,' bellow GRIMES to molesworth 2, who is dancing a
hornpipe on a desk, 'not *too* much excitement. We hav not broken up
yet, dere boy.'

'Wot, sir?'

'Not too much excite—'

'Speak up, sir.'

'GET DOWN OFF THAT FLIPPING DESK OR YOU WILL
GET 6!'

At last, order is restored and end of term marks are read chiz chiz
chiz. Another loud cheer greet the fakt that i am botom in eng. fr. geom.
geog. div. algy and hist. When grabber get his ushaul prize i.e. the mrs
joyful prize for rafia work there are boos and catcalls nothing can stop
the mitey upsurge of popular feeling.

'SILENCE!' below GRIMES. 'You are unfare. You kno how he won
this prize.'

'Sure!' we roar, '£5 to you, £1 all round to the staff and a botle of beer
for the olde matronne. The same story.'

'SILENCE OR I WILL KANE THE LOT!'

Methinks his unatural benevolence is waring as thin as peason's second-best pare of trousis. The mob is hushed by this thort.

'Now see here,' sa GRIMES, 'see here, scum. We gives you edducation here, see? We gives you maners and disscipline, don't we? Don't forget them when you gets 'ome. Do not forget to sa "pardon" at some breach of etikette and tuck the old serviet into the colar firmly. Should egg be droped upon the tie remove same quietly with the thumb as you 'av seen me do. Be a credit to St. custards! DISMISS!'

With one mad yell the mob, armed with stumps and bits torn from desks, surge away down the pasage, trampling the masters under foot. A buket of water fall on GRIMES and the term end in a series of wizard rags and japes. Cars arive, driven by parents with drawn, white faces. The rolls for grabber, a bentley for peason and a cranky old grid for fotherington-tomas. For the rest it is the old skool bus for the station.

'Six quid,' hiss the driver to GRIMES, 'and i'll put the lot over a cliff.'

'And deprive me of my living?'

'You hav yore jellied eels and the whelk stall in the new cross road, not to mention other enterprises.'

'Begone, tempter!'

With a roar the skool bus drive off. Goodby, sir, goodby, skool, goodby, matronne, goodby, skool dog ect. No more lat. no more french. Wave wave and we are free.

Cheers for home and the maison molesworth! All are pleased to see us, dogs charge, cats miaouw and parot whistle poly wolly doodle. Wipe mud on carpet, change clothes, eat super cream buns and relax. So far only 62 people hav said we are taller, 96 that we are like mum, 107 that we are like pater and all hav asked if we had a good term. It is the same old story. Soon we are lying back in pater's chair, eating bullseyes.

'Wot is on the t.v. we hav nothing to do,' we sa.

'Nothing,' sa the parot, 'the programmes are lousy' he is browned off becos since we have a t.v. he hav not been able to get a word in edgeways.

Mum seme to hav run out of conversation.

'Tell us about skool,' she sa, at last.

'Skool? The masters are all teddy boys and would slit you with a broken botle for 2 pins. The food is uneatable and conditions are vile.'

'You poor darlings!'

'It is horible,' blub molesworth 2.

'My poor little lambs ect' hem-hem rather embarassing mum look as
if she will burst into tears, good old mum. All mums are the same and
luv there wee ones somebody hav got to, after all. I send her for my mail
and litely thumb over the leters i.e. 16 football pools, 1 bill from the
bookmaker, a badge from the golly club, an invitation to a dance chiz
and HO! wot is this, eh?

DERE FREND,

    Welcome! in sending for details of the Goliath, the Strong Man
course you are opening a new life. If you are a pigmy i can make a
giant of you with bulging mussles and HERCULEAN strength in
6 weeks. Write at once with P.O. for 2/6.

                                   (signed) G. GOLIATH.

Gosh! This is something! A new future open up by the time we return
to skool i can hav giant strength. How wizard that will be next term.

*Scene: big skool at st. custard's. Goliath molesworth is unpacking his tuck box.*

PEASON: Hullo, o weedy wet, you hav a face like a squished tomato.
MOLESWORTH: (*thinks*) Poor fule, he do not kno
                    (*enter sigismund the mad maths master*)
SIGISMUND: Come on get cracking no talking no smoking, no entrance
you are in my clutches agane.
                    (*He striketh peason.*)
MOLESWORTH: Stop! Enuff!
(*sigismund aim a wicked blow with the protractors. molesworth catch them, bust
them, brake an iron bar with his teeth, lift a statue of j. caesar, leap 82 feet, beat is
chest, crunch a skool cake, do 2 back somersaults and aim a rabit punch at
sigismund.*)
MOLESWORTH: Take that.
SIGISMUND: Wow!
MOLESWORTH: And that and that and that and that—
SIGISMUND: Do not repeat yoreself.
(*M. toss him over his shoulder and the bout is over. Sigismund is down for the count
the crowd roars.*)
At this point the dreme is interrupted.

'Would you like another cake, nigel?'
'No, thanks, mum. I hav some correspondence.'
'To whom are you writing?'
'Just to the golly club, mum. Just to the golly club.'
i write to the golly club thanking them for their good wishes. Also to Goliath for the strong man course. We shall see.

And so the hols proceed. I quarrel with molesworth 2 and he do not seme to see my point of view. Let him wate. Ocasionally there are treats e.g. gran come to see us in her 90 m.p.h. sports car and zoom about the roads which is more dangerous than the skool bus. Boys come in to pla and depart in tears. The parot see sooty on the t.v. and sa a rude word. He want to get an audition and kepe saing 'Cock-a-doodle-doo' and swank he is a cock he will not get to first base. Then come the FELL DAY i.e.

*dere nigel and molesworth 2*

GLORIA AND HYACINTH

## AT HOME

dancing 8–10.30. Cakes, creme buns, trifle, jelly, chocs, crackers, whisky for paters and gin for maters. Do not miss this unique ocasion.
A snip!!!!!

CURSES! me dancing with gurlies? gosh. i ring the bell for mater and issue stern protest but in vane. It will be good for me to go, she sa. Also gloria and hyacinth are such nice little gurls and i must learn to dance early before it is too late chiz chiz chiz.

Another weedy party and lots of weedy little gurls with pig tales and also some joly big ones. a nice lady come up with a knuckle duster and ask me to dance with tough baby called honoria. Cornered, i bow, take gurl by my gloved hand and draw her litely on the floor. After a few turns she speke shyly:

'This is a waltz, you big lout. You hav kicked me 5 times.'
'And, fare made, i will kick thee agane.'
'Sez you? I will do yu if you do.'

'I shall do thee first, see if i do not.'

And so to the lite strains the young couples in the first flush of their youth whirl round and round to the strains of the craked gramophone. Wot young hopes and ideals are confined in these innocent breasts, wot – SPLOSH! Wot can that be? It is hyacinth who hav thrown a jelly at gloria she have been sipping mater's gin. Gloria respond with the trifle cheers cheers cheers. 'Go it, gloria,' shout honoria, 'tear out her hare' and molesworth 2 zoom by dive bombing with eclares. A wizard confusion ranes.

'Did you enjoy the party, nigel?' sa mum when we get home.

'Oh yes,' i reply, tired but hapy. 'Altho next time you mite send us to the moulin rouge or an apache's dance hall.'

The weeks and days pass on winged feet. Soon we shall hav to think of getting our things together for the new term. Ah-me! All those pants and vests and shirts got out for another tour of duty. The happy relationship between me and molesworth 2 hav broken up in cries of 'Shall', 'Shan't'. 'You are.' 'You aren't' ect.

'Wot did you sa about the masters at yore skool, nigel?' ask mum. 'The ones who are teddy boys?'

'They would rip you with a botle for 2 pins, mater.'

'So would i,' she sa. 'So would i.'

As for Goliath i never hear from him agane. The golly club thank me for my contribution to party funds. They hav made me a golly Captain now. i must hav put the P.O. in the wrong envelope. I would rather be Goliath than a Golly Captain any day but that is life.

## HEE-HEE FOR TEE-VEE

Gosh super! we hav something to contend with which no other generation hav ever had before i.e. the television cheers cheers cheers. Everbody kno wot a t.v. is it is a square box with a screen. You switch on and o hapen, then just when you hav given up hope and are going off to buzz conkers a great booming voice sa, 'That's an interesting point, postlethwaite. Wot does higginbottom feel? Higginbottom? ect ect.' It may be an interesting point but i could not care less and just go away agane when a ghastly face suddenly appere. It is worse than a squished tomato but it hold me in hypnotic trance and it is the same with molesworth 2, tho he always look dopey like that. We sit and watch more and more ghastley faces with our mouths open and even forget to chew the buble gum we are slaves of the machine.

Of course all boys and gurls hav to go through a time when there is no t.v. xcept at the postman's down the road. Yore mater and pater then sa weedy things.

i will not hav one in the house.

the programmes are simply terible, my dear.

it is bad for children.

it destroy the simple pursuits of leisure.

Hem-hem if they only knew what the simple pursuits of leisure were like potting stones at vilage oiks or teaching parot rude words they would not hesitate for a moment. Anyway they get one in the end and sa 'Children can only look for 1 hour at suitable programmes' then they forget all about it until we are halfway through '1984' and molesworth 2 sa 'if that is the best a rat can do i do not think much of it.' 'The rat,' i sa, 'is exactly like thou, o clot-faced wet.' Then mater become aware of our presence and hury the dreamy-eyed little felows up wood hill to blanket fair, as dear nana sa.

When you setle down to it this is wot hapens in your dulce domum (lat.)

*Scene: A darkened room with glowing fire. Mum, Nana, me and molesworth 2 are goggling at the screen. So are the cats, dogs, rats, mice and various bugs about the place.*

T.V. Are you a clump-press minder? (Grate cheers)
MATER: I thort he was an aero-dynamicist or a moulding-clamp turner . . . I really think. . . .
ALL: Sshh!
              (*Enter pater, tired from the office.*)
PATER: Are you looking at that friteful thing agane?
     Programmes are terible. Nothing to look at.
              (*With a roar and a ratle he put coal on the fire*).
ALL: Sshh!
     (Pater setle down. molesworth 2 aim his gat at very fat gentleman in specs. It is the same gun with which he shot mufin the mule, mcdonald hobley, a ping-pong champion, three midgets, a great-

crested grebe, a persian student and lady Boyle and a budgerigar.)

MOLESWORTH 2. Ah-ah-ah-ah-ah. Got you.

ALL: Ssh!

MATER: Do you not think it would be better if their heads were not three feet away from their shoulders?

(Pater go and twiddle knobs. First of all there is a snowstorm then what seem like the batle of jutland, then an electronic bombardment. Finaly a vast explosion.)

MATER: You hav ruined it, clot.

NANA: Boost the contrast.

MOLESWORTH 2: Adjust the definition.

ME: O gosh, hurry up.

(Now picture is upside down, then leaning drunkenly, then it disappear altogether amid boos and catcalls. Finaly Nana do it.)

T.V. Are you conected with seaweed? (Huge cheer)

MATER: look at tibby the cat he canot stand this man. . . .

ALL: Sssh.

PATER: He's a guggle-gouger. . . .

(And so it go on. Supper is not cooked, fires go out, kettles boil their heads off, slates fall off the roof and house burn down, but we are all still looking at a nature film in w. africa chiz in fact we hav seen more monkeys since we got the t.v. than ever before xcept at st. custard's where peason hav the face of a wild baboon.)

Aktually t.v. is v. cultural for boys and improving to the mind. You learn so many things that when you go back to skool all are quite surprised.

MOLESWORTH 1: To the q. whether the hydrogen bomb should be banned i give a categorical 'no'. unless there can be international agreement to co-exist in disarmament.

MOLESWORTH 2: That is a valid point, o weedy wet. Do you kno the population of chile?

MOLESWORTH 1: No. But everyone should look both ways before crossing the road and wot can be more dramatic than man's fight against the locust, eh?

MOLESWORTH 2: The problem of asia is the problem of over-population and now i will pla brahams etude number 765000 in F flat. . . .

You kno wot this mean he is going to zoom to the piano and pla fairy bells nothing can stop him the whole skool will rock and plaster drop from the ceiling, chandeliers will shake and light bulbs burst. Hav to take cover until it is all over when the head of an elk, dislodged by the blast, fall on my head chiz chiz that is life.

So you will see that t.v. is a joly good thing and very restful to the nerves, my dear. You can talk about it next day, particularly to those who hav no sets and hav not seen the programmes. This make you very popular socially, with the smart set of 3B, and take your mind off the lessons. It also gives rise to several wizard wheezes. For instance, why not start a maths lesson with a ghastley face smiling at you?

'And now, 3B, we are going to show you the elementary principles of vulgar fractions so we hope simper simper you will be able simper to get the things into yore thick heads without carving the desk or sticking compasses into fotherington-Tomas. Simper. May we also remind you that there is cocoa and buns at break and from 10.30 to 11.15 there is a gorgeous lesson in which Cotta will be beaten for the umpteenth time by the Belgians with darts and arows?'

With a huge SIMPER the picture fade. Which only leave time to prepare placard for the final wizard wheeze.

molesworth, next sentence. Marcus and Balbus, my dearest friends, are walking out of the city. Come along, boy.

You do not need to sa er-er and scratch yore head or even ask what the blazes the two cissies are doing walking out of the city for. You just hoist your placard for a technical hitch:

NORMAL SERVICE
WILL BE RESTORED
AS SOON AS POSS.

# The Root of All Evil

*Graham Greene*

This story was told me by my father who heard it directly from his father, the brother of one of the participants; otherwise I doubt whether I would have credited it. But my father was a man of absolute rectitude, and I have no reason to believe that this virtue did not then run in the family.

The events happened in 189–, as they say in old Russian novels, in the small market town of B——. My father was German, and when he settled in England he was the first of the family to go further than a few kilometres from the home commune, province, canton or whatever it was called in those parts. He was a Protestant who believed in his faith, and no one has a greater ability to believe, without doubt or scruple, than a Protestant of that type. He would not even allow my mother to read us fairy-stories, and he walked three miles to church rather than go to one with pews. 'We've nothing to hide,' he said. 'If I sleep I sleep, and let the world know the weakness of my flesh. Why,' he added, and the thought touched my imagination strongly and perhaps had some influence on my future, 'they could play cards in those pews and no one the wiser.'

That phrase is linked in my mind with the fashion in which he would begin this story. 'Original sin gave man a tilt towards secrecy,' he would say. 'An open sin is only half a sin, and a secret innocence is only half innocent. When you have secrets, there, sooner or later, you'll have sin. I wouldn't let a Freemason cross my threshold. Where I come from secret societies were illegal, and the government had reason. Innocent though they might be at the start, like that club of Schmidt's.'

It appears that among the old people of the town where my father lived were a couple whom I shall continue to call Schmidt, being a little uncertain of the nature of the laws of libel and how limitations and the like affect the dead. Herr Schmidt was a big man and a heavy drinker, but most of his drinking he preferred to do at his own board to the discomfort of his wife, who never touched a drop of alcohol herself. Not that she wished to interfere with her husband's potations; she had a proper idea of a wife's duty, but she had reached an age (she was over sixty and he well past seventy) when she had a great yearning to sit quietly with another woman knitting something or other for her grandchildren and talking about their latest maladies. You can't do that at ease with a man continually on the go to the cellar for another litre. There is a man's atmosphere and a woman's atmosphere, and they don't mix except in the proper place, under the sheets. Many a time Frau Schmidt in her gentle way had tried to persuade him to go out of an evening to the inn. 'What and pay more for every glass?' he would say. Then she tried to persuade him that he had need of men's company and men's conversation. 'Not when I'm tasting a good wine,' he said.

So last of all she took her trouble to Frau Muller who suffered in just the same manner as herself. Frau Muller was a stronger type of woman and she set out to build an organization. She found four other women starved of female company and female interests, and they arranged to forgather once a week with their sewing and take their evening coffee together. Between them they could summon up more than two dozen grandchildren, so you can imagine they were never short of subjects to talk about. When one child had finished with the chicken-pox, at least two would have started the measles. There were all the varying treatments to compare, and there was one school of thought which took the motto 'starve a cold' to mean 'if you starve a cold you will feed a fever' and another school which took the more traditional view. But their debates were never heated like those they had with their husbands, and they took it in turn to act hostess and make the cakes.

But what was happening all this time to the husbands? You might think they would be content to go on drinking alone, but not a bit of it. Drinking's like reading a 'romance' (my father used the term with contempt, he had never turned the pages of a novel in his life); you don't need talk, but you need company, otherwise it begins to feel like work. Frau Muller had thought of that and she suggested to her husband – very gently, so that he hardly noticed – that, when the women were meeting elsewhere, he should ask the other husbands in with their own drinks (no need to spend extra money at the bar) and they could sit as silent as they wished with their glasses till bedtime. Now and then no doubt one of them would remark on the wet or the fine day, and another would mention the prospects for the harvest, and a third would say that they'd never had so warm a summer as the summer of 188–. Men's talk, which, in the absence of women, would never become heated.

But there was one snag in this arrangement and it was the one which caused the disaster. Frau Muller roped in a seventh woman, who had been widowed by something other than drink, by her husband's curiosity. Frau Puckler had a husband whom none of them could abide, and, before they could settle down to their friendly evenings, they had to decide what to do about him. He was a little vinegary man with a squint and a completely bald head who would empty any bar when he came into it. His eyes, coming together like that, had the effect of a gimlet, and he would stay in conversation with one man for ten minutes on end with his eyes fixed on the other's forehead until you expected sawdust to come out. Unfortunately Frau Puckler was highly respec- ted. It was essential to keep from her any idea that her husband was unwelcome, so for some weeks they had to reject Frau Muller's proposal. They were quite happy, they said, sitting alone at home with a glass when what they really meant was that even loneliness was preferable to the company of Herr Puckler. But they got so miserable all this time that often, when their wives returned home, they would find their husbands tucked up in bed and asleep.

It was then Herr Schmidt broke his customary silence. He called round at Herr Muller's door, one evening when the wives were away, with a four-litre jug of wine, and he hadn't got through more than two litres when he broke silence. This lonely drinking, he said, must come to an end – he had had more sleep the last few weeks than he had had in six months and it was sapping his strength. 'The grave yawns for us,' he said, yawning himself from habit.

'But Puckler?' Herr Muller objected. 'He's worse than the grave.'

'We shall have to meet in secret,' Herr Schmidt said. 'Braun has a fine big cellar,' and that was how the secret began; and from secrecy, my father would moralize, you can grow every sin in the calendar. I pictured secrecy like the dark mould in the cellar where we cultivated our mushrooms, but the mushrooms were good to eat, so that their secret growth . . . I always found an ambivalence in my father's moral teaching.

It appears that for a time all went well. The men were happy drinking together – in the absence, of course, of Herr Puckler, and so were the women, even Frau Puckler, for she always found her husband in bed at night ready for domesticities. He was far too proud to tell her of his ramblings in search of company between the strokes of the town-clock. Every night he would try a different house and every night he found only the closed door and the darkened window. Once in Herr Braun's cellar the husbands heard the knocker hammering overhead. At the Gasthof too he would look regularly in – and sometimes irregularly, as though he hoped that he might catch them off their guard. The street-lamp shone on his bald head, and often some late drinker going home would be confronted by those gimlet-eyes which believed nothing you said. 'Have you seen Herr Muller tonight?' or 'Herr Schmidt, is he at home?' he would demand of another reveller. He sought them here, he sought them there – he had been content enough aforetime drinking in his own home and sending his wife down to the cellar for a refill, but he knew only too well, now he was alone, that there was no pleasure possible for a solitary drinker. If Herr Schmidt and Herr Muller were not at home, where were they? And the other four with whom he had never been well acquainted, where were they? Frau Puckler was the very reverse of her husband, she had no curiosity, and Frau Muller and Frau Schmidt had mouths which clicked shut like the clasp of a well-made handbag.

Inevitably after a certain time Herr Puckler went to the police. He refused to speak to anyone lower than the Superintendent. His gimlet-eyes bored like a migraine into the Superintendent's forehead. While the eyes rested on the one spot, his words wandered ambiguously. There had been an anarchist outrage at Schloss – I can't remember the name; there were rumours of an attempt on a Grand Duke. The Superintendent shifted a little this way and a little that way on his seat, for these were big affairs which did not concern him, while the squinting eyes bored continuously at the sensitive spot above his nose where his migraine always began. Then the Superintendent blew loudly and said, 'The times are evil,' a phrase which he had remembered from the service on Sunday.

'You know the law about secret societies,' Herr Puckler said.

'Naturally.'

'And yet here, under the nose of the police,' and the squint-eyes bored deeper, 'there exists just such a society.'

'If you would be a little more explicit . . .'

So Herr Puckler gave him the whole row of names, beginning with Herr Schmidt. 'They meet in secret,' he said. 'None of them stays at home.'

'They are not the kind of men I would suspect of plotting.'

'All the more dangerous for that.'

'Perhaps they are just friends.'

'Then why don't they meet in public?'

'I'll put a policeman on the case,' the Superintendent said half-heartedly, so now at night there were two men looking around to find where the six had their meeting-place. The policeman was a simple man who began by asking direct questions, but he had been seen several times in the company of Puckler, so the six assumed quickly enough that he was trying to track them down on Puckler's behalf and they became more careful than ever to avoid discovery. They stocked up Herr Braun's cellar with wine, and they took elaborate precautions not to be seen entering – each one sacrificed a night's drinking in order to lead Herr Puckler and the policeman astray. Nor could they confide in their wives for fear that it might come to the ears of Frau Puckler, so they pretended the scheme had not worked and it was every man for himself again now in drinking. That meant they had to tell a lot of lies if they failed to be the first home – and so, my father said, sin began to enter in.

One night too, Herr Schmidt, who happened to be the decoy, led Herr Puckler a long walk into the suburbs, and then seeing an open door and a light burning in the window with a comforting red glow and being by that time very dry in the mouth, he mistook the house in his distress for a quiet inn and walked inside. He was warmly welcomed by a stout lady and shown into a parlour, where he expected to be served with wine. Three young ladies sat on a sofa in various stages of undress and greeted Herr Schmidt with giggles and warm words. Herr Schmidt was afraid to leave the house at once, in case Puckler was lurking outside, and while he hesitated the stout lady entered with a bottle of champagne on ice and a number of glasses. So for the sake of the drink (though champagne was not his preference – he would have liked the local wine) he stayed, and thus out of secrecy, my father said, came the second sin. But it didn't end there with lies and fornication.

When the time came to go, if he were not to overstay his welcome, Herr Schmidt took a look out of the window, and there, in place of Puckler, was the policeman walking up and down the pavement. He must have followed Puckler at a distance, and then taken on his watch while Puckler went rabbiting after the others. What to do? It was growing late; soon the wives would be drinking their last cup and closing the file on the last grandchild. Herr Schmidt appealed to the kind stout lady; he asked her whether she hadn't a back-door so that he might avoid the man he knew in the street outside. She had no back-door, but she was a woman of great resource, and in no time she had decked Herr Schmidt out in a great cartwheel of a skirt, like peasant-women in those days wore at market, a pair of white stockings, a blouse ample enough and a floppy hat. The girls hadn't enjoyed themselves so much for a long time, and they amused themselves decking his face with rouge, eye-shadow and lipstick. When he came out of the door, the policeman was so astonished by the sight that he stood rooted to the spot long enough for Herr Schmidt to billow round the corner, take to his heels down a side-street and arrive safely home in time to scour his face before his wife came in.

If it had stopped there all might have been well, but the policeman had not been deceived, and now he reported to the Superintendent that members of the secret society dressed themselves as women and in that guise frequented the gay houses of the town. 'But why dress as women to do that?' the Superintendent asked, and Puckler hinted at orgies which went beyong the natural order of things. 'Anarchy,' he said, 'is out to upset everything, even the proper relationship of man and woman.'

'Can't you be more explicit?' the Superintendent asked him for the second time; it was a phrase of which he was pathetically fond, but Puckler left the details shrouded in mystery.

It was then that Puckler's fanaticism took a morbid turn; he suspected every large woman he saw in the street at night of being a man in disguise. Once he actually pulled the wig off a certain Frau Hackenfurth (no one till that day, not even her husband, knew that she wore a wig), and presently he sallied out into the streets himself dressed as a woman with the belief that one transvestite would recognize another and that sooner or later he would find himself enlisted in the secret orgies. He was a small man and he played the part better than

Herr Schmidt had done – only his gimlet-eyes would have betrayed him
to an acquaintance in daylight.

The men had been meeting happily enough now for two weeks in
Herr Braun's cellar, the policeman had tired of his search, the Superintendent was in hopes that all had blown over, when a disastrous
decision was taken. Frau Schmidt and Frau Muller in the old days had
the habit of cooking pasties for their husbands to go with the wine, and
the two men began to miss this treat which they described to their
fellow drinkers, their mouths wet with the relish of the memory. Herr
Braun suggested that they should bring in a woman to cook for them – it
would mean only a small contribution from each, for no one would
charge very much for a few hours' work at the end of the evening. Her
duty would be to bring in fresh warm pasties every half an hour or so as
long as their wine-session lasted. He advertised the position openly
enough in the local paper, and Puckler, taking a long chance – applied,
dressed up in his wife's best Sunday blacks. He was accepted by Herr
Braun, who was the only one who did not know herr Puckler except by
repute, and so Puckler found himself installed at the very heart of the
mystery, with a grand opportunity to hear all their talk. The only
trouble was that he had little skill at cooking and often with his ears to
the cellar-door he allowed the pasties to burn. On the second evening
Herr Braun told him that, unless the pasties improved, he would find
another woman.

However Puckler was not worried by that because he had all the
information he required for the Superintendent, and it was a real
pleasure to make his report in the presence of the policeman, who
contributed nothing at all to the inquiry.

Puckler had written down the dialogue as he had heard it, leaving out
only the long pauses, the gurgle of the wine-jugs, and the occasional
rude tribute that wind makes to the virtue of young wine. His report
read as follows:

Inquiry into the Secret Meetings held in the Cellar of Herr Braun's
House at 27 – strasse. The following dialogue was overheard by the
investigator.
*Muller:* If the rain keeps off another month, the wine harvest will be
better than last year.
*Unidentified voice:* Ugh.

*Schmidt:* They say the postman nearly broke his ankle last week. Slipped on a step.

*Braun:* I remember sixty-one vintages.

*Dobel:* Time for a pasty.

*Unidentified voice:* Ugh.

*Muller:* Call in that cow.

The investigator was summoned and left a tray of pasties.

*Braun:* Careful. They are hot.

*Schmidt:* This one's burnt to a cinder.

*Dobel:* Uneatable.

*Kastner:* Better sack her before worse happens.

*Braun:* She's paid till the end of the week. We'll give her till then.

*Muller:* It was fourteen degrees midday.

*Dobel:* The town-hall clock's fast.

*Schmidt:* Do you remember that dog the major had with black spots?

*Unidentified voice:* Ugh.

*Kastner:* No, why?

*Schmidt:* I can't remember.

*Muller:* When I was a boy we had plum-duff they never make now.

*Dobel:* It was the summer of '87.

*Unidentified voice:* What was?

*Muller:* The year Mayor Kalnitz died.

*Schmidt:* '88.

*Muller:* There was a hard frost.

*Dobel:* Not as hard as '86.

*Braun:* That was a shocking year for wine.

So it went on for twelve pages. 'What's it all about?' the Superintendent asked.

'If we knew that, we'd know all.'

'It sounds harmless.'

'Then why do they meet in secret?'

The policeman said 'Ugh' like the unidentified voice.

'My feeling is,' Puckler said, 'a pattern will emerge. Look at all those dates. They need to be checked.'

'There was a bomb thrown in '86,' the Superintendent said doubtfully. 'It killed the Grand Duke's best grey.'

'A shocking year for wine,' Puckler said. 'They missed. No wine. No royal blood.'

'The attempt was mistimed,' the Superintendent remembered.

'The town-hall clock's fast,' Puckler quoted.

'I can't believe it all the same.'

'A code. To break a code we have need of more material.'

The Superintendent agreed with some reluctance that the report should continue, but then there was the difficulty of the pasties. 'We need a good assistant-cook for the pasties,' Puckler said, 'and then I can listen without interruption. They won't object if I tell them that it will cost no more.'

The Superintendent said to the policeman, 'Those were good pasties I had in your house.'

'I cooked them myself,' the policeman said gloomily.

'Then that's no help.'

'Why no help?' Puckler demanded. 'If I can dress up as a woman, so can he.'

'His moustache?'

'A good blade and a good lather will see to that.'

'It's an unusual thing to demand of a man.'

'In the service of the law.'

So it was decided, though the policeman was not at all happy about the affair. Puckler, being a small man, was able to dress in his wife's clothes, but the policeman had no wife. In the end Puckler was forced to agree to buy the clothes himself; he did it late in the evening, when the assistants were in a hurry to leave and were unlikely to recognize his gimlet-eyes, as they judged the size of the skirt, blouse, knickers. There had been lies, fornication: I don't know in what further category my father placed the strange shopping expedition, which didn't, as it happened, go entirely unnoticed. Scandal – perhaps that was the third offence which secrecy produced, for a late customer coming into the shop did in fact recognize Puckler, just as he was holding up the bloomers to see if the seat seemed large enough. You can imagine how quickly that story got around, to every woman except Frau Puckler, and she felt at the next sewing-party an odd – well, it might have been deference or it might have been compassion. Everyone stopped to listen when she spoke; no one contradicted or argued with her, and she was not allowed to carry a tray or pour a cup. She began to feel so like an invalid that she developed a headache and decided to go home early.

She could see them all nodding at each other as though they knew what was the matter better than she did, and Frau Muller volunteered to see her home.

Of course she hurried straight back to tell them about it. 'When we arrived,' she said, 'Herr Puckler was not at home. Of course the poor woman pretended not to know where he could be. She got in quite a state about it. She said he was always there to welcome her when she came in. She had half a mind to go round to the police-station and report him missing, but I dissuaded her. I almost began to believe that she didn't know what he was up to. She muttered about the strange goings-on in town, anarchists and the like, and would you believe it, she said that Herr Puckler told her a policeman had seen Herr Schmidt dressed up in women's clothes.'

'The little swine,' Frau Schmidt said, naturally referring to Puckler, for Herr Schmidt had the figure of one of his own wine-barrels. 'Can you imagine such a thing?'

'Distracting attention,' Frau Muller said, 'from his own vices. For look what happened next. We come to the bedroom, and Frau Puckler finds her wardrobe door wide open, and she looks inside, and what does she find – her black Sunday dress missing. "There's truth in the story after all," she said, "and I'm going to look for Herr Schmidt," but I pointed out to her that it would have to be a very small man indeed to wear her dress.'

'Did she blush?'

'I really believe she knows nothing about it.'

'Poor, poor woman,' Frau Dobel said. 'And what do you think he does when he's all dressed up?' and they began to speculate. So thus it was, my father would say, that foul talk was added to the other sins of lies, fornication, scandal. Yet there still remained the most serious sin of all.

That night Puckler and the policeman turned up at Herr Braun's door, but little did they know that the story of Puckler had already reached the ears of the drinkers, for Frau Muller had reported the strange events to Herr Muller, and at once he remembered the gimlet-eyes of the cook Anna peering at him out of the shadows. When the men met, Herr Braun reported that the cook was to bring an assistant to help her with the pasties and as she had asked for no extra money he had consented. You can imagine the babble of voices that broke out

from these silent men when Herr Muller told his story. What was
Puckler's motive? It was a bad one or it would not have been Puckler.
One theory was that he was planning with the help of an assistant to
poison them with the pasties in revenge for being excluded. 'It's not
beyond Puckler,' Herr Dobel said. They had good reason to be
suspicious, so my father, who was a just man, did not include unworthy
suspicion among the sins of which the secret society was the cause.
They began to prepare a reception for Puckler.

Puckler knocked on the door and the policeman stood just behind
him, enormous in his great black skirt with his white stockings crinkling
over his boots because Puckler had forgotten to buy him suspenders.
After the second knock the bombardment began from the upper
windows. Puckler and the policeman were drenched with unmention-
able liquids, they were struck with logs of wood. Their eyes were
endangered from falling forks. The policeman was the first to take to his
heels, and it was a strange sight to see so huge a woman go beating
down the street. The blouse had come out of the waistband and flapped
like a sail as its owner tacked to avoid the flying objects – which now
included a toilet-roll, a broken teapot and a portrait of the Grand Duke.

Puckler, who had been hit on the shoulder with a rolling-pin, did not
at first run away. He had his moment of courage or bewilderment. But
when the frying-pan he had used for pasties struck him, he turned too
late to follow the policeman. It was then that he was struck on the head
with a chamber-pot and lay in the street with the pot fitting over his
head like a vizor. They had to break it with a hammer to get it off, and
by that time he was dead, whether from the blow on the head or the fall
or from fear or from being stifled by the chamber-pot nobody knew,
though suffocation was the general opinion. Of course there was an
inquiry which went on for many months into the existence of an
anarchist plot, and before the end of it the Superintendent had become
secretly affianced to Frau Puckler, for which nobody blamed her, for
she was a popular woman – except my father who resented the secrecy
of it all. (He suspected that the Superintendent's love for Frau Puckler
had extended the inquiry, since he pretended to believe her husband's
accusations.)

Technically, of course, it was murder – death arising from an illegal
assault – but the courts after about six months absolved the six men.
'But there's a greater court,' my father would always end his story, 'and

in that court the sin of murder never goes unrequited. You begin with a secret,' and he would look at me as though he knew my pockets were stuffed with them, as indeed they were, including the note I intended to pass the next day at school to the yellow-haired girl in the second row, 'and you end with every sin in the calendar.' He began to recount them over again for my benefit. 'Lies, drunkenness, fornication, scandal-bearing, murder, the subornation of authority.'

'Subornation of authority?'

'Yes,' he said and fixed me with his glittering eye. I think he had Frau Puckler and the Superintendent in mind. He rose towards his climax. 'Men in women's clothes – the terrible sin of Sodom.'

'And what's that?' I asked with excited expectation.

'At your age,' my father said, 'some things must remain secret.'

# The Sticky Wicket

## *James Herriot*

I wondered how long this feeling of novelty at being a married man would last. Maybe it went on for years and years. At any rate I did feel an entirely different person from the old Herriot as I paced with my wife among the stalls at the garden fête.

It was an annual affair in aid of the Society for the Prevention of Cruelty to Children and it was held on the big lawn behind the Darrowby vicarage with the weathered brick of the old house showing mellow red beyond the trees. The hot June sunshine bathed the typically English scene; the women in their flowered dresses, the men perspiring in their best suits, laughing children running from the tombola to the coconut shy or the ice-cream kiosk. In a little tent at one end, Mrs Newbould, the butcher's wife, thinly disguised as Madame Claire the fortune teller, was doing a brisk trade. It all seemed a long way from Glasgow.

And the solid citizen feeling was heightened by the pressure of Helen's hand on my arm and the friendly nods of the passers-by. One of these was the curate Mr Blenkinsopp. He came up to us, exuding, as always, a charm that was completely unworldly.

'Ah, James,' he murmured. 'And Helen!' He beamed on us with the benevolence he felt for the entire human race. 'How nice to see you here!'

He walked along with us as the scent from the flower beds and the trodden grass rose in the warm air.

'You know, James, I was just thinking about you the other day. I was in Rainby – you know I take the service there every second week – and they were telling me they were having great difficulty in finding young men for the cricket team. I wondered if you would care to turn out for them.'

'Me? Play cricket?'

'Yes, of course.'

I laughed. 'I'm afraid I'm no cricketer. I'm interested in the game and I like to watch it, but where I come from they don't play it very much.'

'Oh, but surely you must have played at some time or other.'

'A bit at school, but they go more for tennis in Scotland. And anyway it was a long time ago.'

'Oh well, there you are.' Mr Blenkinsopp spread his hands. 'It will come back to you easily.'

'I don't know about that,' I said. 'But another thing, I don't live in Rainby, doesn't that matter?'

'Not really,' the curate replied. 'It is such a problem finding eleven players in these tiny villages that they often call on outsiders. Nobody minds.'

I stopped my stroll over the grass and turned to Helen. She was giving me an encouraging smile and I began to think, well . . . why not? It looked as though I had settled in Yorkshire. I had married a Yorkshire girl. I might as well start doing the Yorkshire things, like playing cricket – there wasn't anything more Yorkshire than that.

'All right then, Mr Blenkinsopp,' I said. 'You're not getting any bargain but I don't mind having a go.'

'Splendid! The next match is on Tuesday evening – against Hedwick. I am playing so I'll pick you up at six o'clock.' His face radiated happiness as though I had done him the greatest favour.

'Well, thanks,' I replied. 'I'll have to fix it with my partner to be off that night, but I'm sure it will be OK'

The weather was still fine on Tuesday and, going round my visits, I found it difficult to assimilate the fact that for the first time in my life I was going to perform in a real genuine cricket match.

It was funny the way I felt about cricket. All my experience of the game was based on the long-range impressions I had gained during my Glasgow boyhood. Gleaned from newspapers, from boys' magazines, from occasional glimpses of Hobbs and Sutcliffe and Woolley on the cinema newsreels, they had built up a strangely glamorous picture in my mind. The whole thing, it seemed to me, was so deeply and completely English; the gentle clunk of bat on ball, the white-clad figures on the wide sweep of smooth turf; there was a softness, a graciousness about cricket which you found nowhere else; nobody ever got excited or upset at this leisurely pursuit. There was no doubt at all that I looked on cricket with a romanticism and nostalgia which would have been incomprehensible to people who had played the game all their lives.

Promptly at six Mr Blenkinsopp tooted the horn of his little car outside the surgery. Helen had advised me to dress ready for action and she had clearly been right because the curate, too, was resplendent in white flannels and blazer. The three young farmers crammed in the back were, however, wearing open-necked shirts with their ordinary clothes.

'Hello, James!' said Mr Blenkinsopp.

'Now then, Jim,' said two of the young men in the back. But 'Good afternoon, Mr Herriot,' said the one in the middle.

He was Tom Willis, the captain of the Rainby team and in my opinion, one of nature's gentlemen. He was about my own age and he and his father ran the kind of impoverished small-holding which just about kept them alive. But there was a sensitivity and refinement about him and a courtesy which never varied. I never cared how people addressed me and a lot of the farmers used my first name, but to Tom and his father I was always Mr Herriot. They considered it was the correct way to address the vet and that was that.

Tom leaned from the back seat now, his lean face set in its usual serious expression.

'It's good of you to give up your time, Mr Herriot. I know you're a busy man but we're allus short o' players at Rainby.'

'I'm looking forward to it, Tom, but I'm no cricketer, I'll tell you now.'

He gazed at me with gentle disbelief and I had an uncomfortable feeling that everybody had the impression that because I had been to college I was bound to have a blue.

Hedwick was at the top end of Allerdale, a smaller offshoot of the main Dale, and as we drove up the deep ever-narrowing cleft in the moorland I wound down the window. It was the sort of country I saw every day but I wasn't used to being a passenger and there was no doubt you could see more this way. From the overlapping fringe of heather far above, the walls ran in spidery lines down the bare green flanks to the softness of the valley floor where grey farmhouses crouched; and the heavy scent of the new cut hay lying in golden swathes in the meadows drifted deliciously into the car. There were trees, too, down here, not the stunted dwarfs of the high country above us, but giants in the exultant foliage of high summer.

We stopped at Hedwick because we could go no further. This was the head of the Dale, a cluster of cottages, a farm and a pub. Where the road curved a few cars were drawn up by the side of a solid-looking wall on which leaned a long row of cloth-capped men, a few women and chattering groups of children.

'Ah,' said Mr Blenkinsopp. 'A good turn-out of spectators. Hedwick always support their team well. They must have come from all over the Dale.'

I looked around in surprise. 'Spectators?'

'Yes, of course. They've come to see the match.'

Again I gazed about me. 'But I can't see the pitch.'

'It's there,' Tom said. 'Just over t'wall.'

I leaned across the rough stones and stared in some bewilderment at a wildly undulating field almost knee deep in rough grass among which a cow, some sheep and a few hens wandered contentedly. 'Is this it?'

'Aye, that's it. If you stand on t'wall you can see the square.'

I did as he said and could just discern a five foot wide strip of bright green cut from the crowding herbage. The stumps stood expectantly at either end. A massive oak tree sprouted from somewhere around mid-on.

The strip stood on the only level part of the field, and that was a small part. Within twenty yards it swept up steeply to a thick wood which climbed up the lower slopes of the fell. On the other side it fell away to a sort of ravine where the rank grass ended only in a rocky stream. The wall bordering the near side ran up to a group of farm buildings.

There was no clubhouse but the visiting team were seated on a form on the grass while nearby, a little metal score board about four feet high stood near its pile of hooked number plates.

The rest of our team had arrived, too, and with a pang of alarm I noticed that there was not a single pair of white flannels among them. Only the curate and I were properly attired and the immediate and obvious snag was that he could play and I couldn't.

Tom and the home captain tossed a coin. Hedwick won and elected to bat. The umpires, two tousled-haired, sunburnt young fellows in grubby white coats strolled to the wicket, our team followed and the Hedwick batsmen appeared. Under their pads they both wore navy blue serge trousers (a popular colour among both teams) and one of them sported a bright yellow sweater.

Tom Willis with the air of authority and responsibility which was natural to him began to dispose the field. No doubt convinced that I was a lynx-eyed catcher he stationed me quite close to the bat on the off side then after a grave consultation with Mr Blenkinsopp he gave him the ball and the game was on.

And Mr Blenkinsopp was a revelation. In his university sweater, gleaming flannels and brightly coloured cap he really looked good. And indeed it was soon very clear that he was good. He handed his cap to the umpire, retreated about twenty yards into the undergrowth, then turned and, ploughing his way back at ever increasing speed, delivered the ball with remarkable velocity bang on the wicket. The chap in yellow met it respectfully with a dead bat and did the same with the next but then he uncoiled himself and belted the third one high over the fielders on to the slope beneath the wood. As one of our men galloped after it the row of heads above the wall broke into a babel of noise.

They cheered every hit, not with the decorous ripple of applause I had always imagined, but with raucous yells. And they had plenty to shout about. The Hedwick lads, obviously accustomed to the peculiarities of their pitch wasted no time on classical strokes; they just gave a great hoick at the ball and when they connected it travelled immense distances. Occasionally they missed and Mr Blenkinsopp or one of our other bowlers shattered their stumps but the next man started cheerfully where they left off.

It was exhilarating stuff but I was unable to enjoy it. Everything I did, in fact my every movement proclaimed my ignorance to the knowledgeable people around me. I threw the ball in to the wrong end, I left the ball when I should have chased it and sped after it when I should have stayed in my place. I couldn't understand half the jargon which was being bandied about. No, there was not a shadow of a doubt about it; here in this cricket mad corner of a cricket mad county I was a foreigner.

Five wickets had gone down when a very fat lad came out to bat. His appearance of almost perfect rotundity was accentuated by the Fair Isle sweater stretched tightly over his bulging abdomen and judging by

the barrage of witticisms which came from the heads along the wall it
seemed he was a local character. He made a violent cross-batted swish
at the first delivery, missed, and the ball sank with a thud into his
midriff. Howls of laughter arose from players, spectators and umpires
alike as he collapsed slowly at the crease and massaged himself ruefully.
He slashed at the next one and it flew off the edge of his bat like a bullet,
struck my shinbone a fearful crack and dropped into the grass.
Resisting the impulse to scream and hop around in my agony I gritted
my teeth, grabbed the ball and threw it in.

'Oh well stopped, Mr Herriot,' Tom Willis called from his position at
mid on. He clapped his hands a few times in encouragement.

Despite his girth the fat lad smote lustily and was finally caught in
the outfield for fifteen.

The next batsman seemed to be taking a long time to reach the
wicket. He was shuffling, bent-kneed, through the clover like a very old
man, trailing his bat wearily behind him, and when he finally arrived at
the crease I saw that he was indeed fairly advanced in years. He wore
only one pad, strapped over baggy grey trousers which came almost up
to his armpits and were suspended by braces. A cloth cap surmounted a
face shrunken like a sour apple. From one corner of the downturned
mouth a cigarette dangled.

He took guard and looked at the umpire.

'Middle and leg,' he grunted.

'Aye, that's about it, Len,' the umpire replied.

Len pursed his little mouth.

'About it . . . about it . . .? Well is it or bloody isn't it?' he inquired
peevishly.

The young man in white grinned indulgently. 'Aye it is, Len, that's
it.'

The old man removed his cigarette, flicked it on to the grass and took
up his guard again. His appearance suggested that he might be out first
ball or in fact that he had no right to be there at all, but as the delivery
came down he stepped forward and with a scything sweep thumped the
ball past the bowler and just a few inches above the rear end of the cow
which had wandered into the line of fire. The animal looked round in
some surprise as the ball whizzed along its backbone and the old man's
crabbed features relaxed into the semblance of a smile.

'By gaw, vitnery,' he said, looking over at me, 'ah damn near made a bit of work for tha there.' He eyed me impassively for a moment. 'Ah reckon tha's never took a cricket ball out of a cow's arse afore, eh?'

Len returned to the job in hand and proved a difficult man to dislodge. But it was the batsman at the other end who was worrying Tom Willis. He had come in first wicket down, a ruddy faced lad of about nineteen wearing a blue shirt and he was still there piling on the runs.

At the end of the over, Tom came up to me. 'Fancy turning your arm over, Mr Herriot?' he inquired gravely.

'Huh?'

'Would you like a bowl? A fresh man might just unsettle this feller.'

'Well . . . er . . . ' I didn't know what to say. The idea of me bowling in a real match was unthinkable. Tom made up my mind by throwing me the ball.

Clasping it in a clammy hand I trotted up to the wicket while the lad in the blue shirt crouched intently over his bat. All the other bowlers had hurled their missiles down at top speed but as I ambled forward it burst on me that if I tried that I would be miles off my target. Accuracy, I decided, must be my watch word and I sent a gentle lob in the direction of the wicket. The batsman, obviously convinced that such a slow ball must be laden with hidden malice followed its course with deep suspicion and smothered it as soon as it arrived. He did the same with the second but that was enough for him to divine that I wasn't bowling off breaks, leg breaks or googlies but simply little dollies and he struck the third ball smartly into the ravine.

There was a universal cry of '*Maurice!*' from our team because Maurice Briggs, the Rainby blacksmith was fielding down there and since he couldn't see the wicket he had to be warned. In due course the ball soared back from the depths, propelled no doubt by Maurice's strong right arm, and I recommenced my attack. The lad in blue thumped my remaining three deliveries effortlessly for six. The first flew straight over the wall and the row of cars into the adjoining field, the next landed in the farmyard and the third climbed in a tremendous arc away above the ravine and I heard it splash into the beck whence it was retrieved with a certain amount of profanity by the invisible Maurice.

An old farm man once said to me when describing a moment of embarrasment. 'Ah could've got down a mouse'ole.' And as I returned to my place in the field I knew just what he meant. In fact the bowler at the other end got through his over almost without my noticing it and I was still shrunk in my cocoon of shame when I saw Tom Willis signalling to me.

I couldn't believe it. He was throwing me the ball again. It was a typically magnanimous gesture, a generous attempt to assure me that I had done well enough to have another go.

Again I shambled forward and the blue-shirted lad awaited me, almost licking his lips. He had never come across anyone like me before and it seemed too good to be true that I should be given another over; but there I was, and he climbed gratefully into each ball I sent down and laid into it in a kind of ecstasy with the full meat of the bat.

I would rather not go into details. Sufficient to say that I have a vivid memory of his red face and blue shirt and of the ball whistling back over my head after each delivery and of the almost berserk yells of the spectators. But he didn't hit every ball for six. In fact there were two moments of light relief in my torment; one when the ball smashed into the oak tree, ricocheted and almost decapitated old Len at the other end; the other when a ball snicked off the edge of the bat and ploughed through a very large cow pat, sending up a noisome spray along its course. It finished at the feet of Mr Blenkinsopp and the poor man was clearly in a dilemma. For the last hour he had been swooping on everything that came near him with the grace of the born cricketer.

But now he hovered over the unclean object, gingerly extending a hand then withdrawing it as his earthier colleagues in the team watched in wonder. The batsmen were galloping up and down, the crowd was roaring but the curate made no move. Finally he picked the thing up with the utmost daintness in two fingers, regarded it distastefully for a few moments and carried it to the wicketkeeper who was ready with a handful of grass in his big gloves.

At the end of the over Tom came up to me. 'Thank ye, Mr Herriot, but I'm afraid I'll have to take you off now. This wicket's not suited to your type of bowling – not takin' spin at all.' He shook his head in his solemn way.

I nodded thankfully and Tom went on. 'Tell ye what, go down and relieve that man in the outfield. We could do wi' a safe pair of hands down there.'

\*    \*    \*

I obeyed my skipper's orders and descended to the ravine and when
Maurice had clambered up the small grassy cliff which separated me
from the rest of the field I felt strangely alone. It was a dank, garlic-
smelling region, perceptively colder than the land above and silent
except for the gurgle of the beck behind me. There was a little hen house
down here with several hens pecking around and some sheep who
obviously felt it was safer than the higher ground.

I could see nothing of the pitch, only occasional glimpses of the heads
of players so I had no idea of what was going on. In fact it was difficult
to believe I was still taking part in a cricket match but for the
spectators. From their position along the wall they had a grandstand
view of everything and in fact were looking down at me from short
range. They appeared to find me quite interesting, too, because a lot of
them kept their eyes on me, pulling their pipes and making remarks
which I couldn't hear but which caused considerable hilarity.

It was a pity about the spectators because it was rather peaceful in
the ravine. It took a very big hit to get down there and I was more or less
left to ruminate. Occasionally the warning cries would ring out from
above and a ball would come bounding over the top. Once a skied drive
landed with a thud in a patch of deep grass and with an enraged
squawking a Rhode Island cockerel emerged at top speed and legged it
irascibly to a safer haven.

Now and then I clawed my way up the bank and had a look at the
progress of the game. Len had gone but the lad in blue was still there.
After another dismissal I was surprised to see one of the umpires give
his coat to the outgoing batsman, seize the bat and start laying about
him. Both umpires were in fact members of the team.

It was after a long spell of inaction and when I was admiring the long
splash of gold which the declining sun was throwing down the side of
the fell when I heard the frantic yells. '*Jim! James! Mr Herriot!*' The
whole team was giving tongue and, as I learned later, the lad in the blue
shirt had made a catchable shot.

But I knew anyway. Nobody but he could have struck the blow
which sent that little speck climbing higher and higher into the pale
evening sky above me; and as it began with terrifying slowness to fall in
my direction time came to a halt. I was aware of several of my team
mates breasting the cliff and watching me breathlessly, of the long row
of heads above the wall, and suddenly I was gripped by a cold resolve. I

was going to catch this fellow out. He had humiliated me up there but it was my turn now.

The speck was coming down faster now as I stumbled about in the tangled vegetation trying to get into position. I nearly fell over a ewe with two big fat lambs sucking at her then I was right under the ball, hands cupped, waiting.

It fell, at the end, like a cannon ball, heavy and unyielding, on the end of my right thumb, bounded over my shoulder and thumped mournfully on the turf.

A storm of derision broke from the heads, peals of delighted laughter, volleys of candid comment.

'Get a basket!' advised one worthy.

'Fetch 'im a bucket!' suggested another.

As I scrabbled for the ball among the herbage I didn't know which was worse – the physical pain which was excruciating, or the mental anguish. After I had finally hurled the thing up the cliff I cradled the throbbing thumb in my other hand and rocked back and forth on my heels, moaning softly.

My team mates returned sadly to their tasks but Tom Willis, I noticed, lingered on, looking down at me.

'Hard luck, Mr Herriot. Very easy to lose t'ball against them trees.' He nodded encouragingly then was gone.

I was not troubled further in the innings. We never did get blueshirt out and he had an unbeaten sixty-two at the close. The Hedwick score was a hundred and fifty-four, a very useful total in village cricket.

There was a ten minute interval while two of our players donned the umpires' coats and our openers strapped on their pads. Tom Willis showed me the batting list he had drawn up and I saw without surprise that I was last man in.

'Our team's packed with batting, Mr Herriot,' he said seriously. 'I couldn't find a place for you higher up the order.'

Mr Blenkinsopp, preparing to receive the first ball, really looked the part, gay cap pulled well down, college colours bright on the broad V of his sweater. But in this particular situation he had one big disadvantage; he was too good.

All the coaching he had received had been aimed at keeping the ball down. An 'uppish' stroke was to be deplored. But everything had to be uppish on this pitch.

As I watched from my place on the form he stepped out and executed a flawless cover drive. At Headingley the ball would have rattled against the boards for four but here it travelled approximately two and a half feet and the fat lad stooped carelessly, lifted it from the dense vegetation and threw it back to the bowler. The next one the curate picked beautifully off his toes and flicked it to square leg for what would certainly have been another four anywhere else. This one went for about a yard before the jungle claimed it.

It saddened me to watch him having to resort to swiping tactics which were clearly foreign to him. He did manage to get in a few telling blows but was caught on the boundary for twelve.

It was a bad start for Rainby with that large total facing them and the two Hedwick fast bowlers looked very formidable. One of them in particular, a gangling youth with great long arms and a shock of red hair seemed to fire his missiles with the speed of light, making the batsmen duck and dodge as the ball flew around their ears.

'That's Tagger Hird,' explained my nearest team mate on the bench. 'By gaw 'e does chuck 'em down. It's a bugger facin' him when the light's getting bad.'

I nodded in silence. I wasn't looking forward to facing him at all, in any kind of light. In fact I was dreading any further display of my shortcomings and I had the feeling that walking out there to the middle was going to be the worst part of all.

But meanwhile I couldn't help responding to the gallant fight Rainby were putting up. As the match went on I found we had some stalwarts in our ranks. Bert Chapman the council roadman and an old acquaintance of mine strode out with his ever present wide grin splitting his brick-red face and began to hoist the ball all over the field. At the other end Maurice Briggs the blacksmith, sleeves rolled high over his mighty biceps and the bat looking like a Woolworths toy in his huge hands, clouted six after six, showing a marked preference for the ravine where there now lurked some hapless member of the other team. I felt for him, whoever it was down there; the sun had gone behind the hills and the light was fading and it must have been desperately gloomy in those humid depths.

And then when Tom came in he showed the true strategical sense of a captain. When Hedwick were batting it had not escaped his notice that they aimed a lot of their shots at a broad patch of particularly impenetrable vegetation, a mato grosso of rank verdure containing not only tangled grasses but nettles, thistles and an abundance of nameless flora. The memory of the Hedwick batsmen running up and down while his fielders thrashed about in there was fresh in his mind as he batted, and at every opportunity he popped one with the greatest accuracy into the jungle himself.

It was the kind of innings you would expect from him; not spectacular, but thoughtful and methodical. After one well-placed drive he ran seventeen while the fielders clawed at the undergrowth and the yells from the wall took on a frantic note.

And all the time we were creeping nearer to the total. When eight wickets had fallen we had reached a hundred and forty and our batsmen were running whether they hit the ball or not. It was too dark by now, to see, in any case, with great black banks of cloud driving over the fell top and the beginnings of a faint drizzle in the air.

In the gathering gloom I watched as the batsman swung, but only managed to push the ball a few yards up the pitch. Nevertheless he broke into a full gallop and collided with his partner who was roaring up from the other end. They fell in a heap with the ball underneath and the wicketkeeper, in an attempt at a run-out, dived among the bodies and scrabbled desperately for the ball. Animal cries broke out from the heads on the wall, the players were all bellowing at each other and at that moment I think the last of my romantic illusions about cricket slipped quietly away.

But soon I had no more time to think about such things. There was an eldritch scream from the bowler and our man was out LBW It was my turn to bat.

Our score was a hundred and forty-five and as, dry-mouthed, I buckled on my pads, the lines of the poem came back to me. 'Ten to win and the last man in.' But I had never dreamed that my first innings in a cricket match would be like this, with the rain pattering steadily on the grass and the oil lamps on the farm winking through the darkness.

Pacing my way to the wicket I passed close by Tagger Hird who eyed me expressionlessly, tossing the ball from one meaty hand to another and whistling softly to himself. As I took guard he began his pounding run up and I braced myself. He had already dropped two of our batsmen in groaning heaps and I realised I had small hope of even seeing the ball.

But I had decided on one thing! I wasn't going to just stand there and take it. I wasn't a cricketer but I was going to try to hit the ball. And as Tagger arrived at full gallop and brought his arm over I stepped out and aimed a violent lunge at where I thought the thing might be. Nothing happened. I heard the smack on the sodden turf and the thud into the wicketkeeper's gloves, that was all.

The same thing happened with the next two deliveries. Great flailing blows which nearly swung me off my feet but nothing besides the smack and the thud. As Tagger ran up the fourth time I was breathless and my heart was thumping. I was playing a whirlwind innings except that I hadn't managed to make contact so far.

Again the arm came over and again I leapt out. And this time there was a sharp crack. I had got a touch but I had no idea where the ball had gone. I was standing gazing stupidly around me when I heard a bellowed '*Come on!*' and saw my partner thundering towards me. At the same time I spotted a couple of fielders running after something away down on my left and then the umpire made a signal. I had scored a four.

With the fifth ball I did the same thing and heard another crack, but this time, as I glared wildly about me I saw there was activity somewhere behind me on my right. We ran three and I had made seven.

There had been a no-ball somewhere and with the extra delivery Tagger scattered my partner's stumps and the match was over. We had lost by two runs.

'A merry knock, Mr Herriot,' Tom said, as I marched from the arena. 'Just for a minute I was beginnin' to think you were goin' to pull it off for us there.'

There was a pie and pea supper for both teams in the pub and as I settled down with a frothing pint of beer the thought kept coming back to me. Seven not out! After the humiliations of the evening it was an ultimate respectability. I had not at any time seen the ball during my innings and I had no idea how it had arrived in those two places but I had made seven not out. And as the meal arrived in front of me – delicious home-made steak and kidney pie with mounds of mushy peas – and I looked around at the roomful of laughing sunburnt men I began to feel good.

Tom sat on one side of me and Mr Blenkinsopp on the other. I had been interested to see that the curate could sink a pint with the best of them and he smiled as he put down his glass.

'Well done indeed, James. Nearly a story book ending. And you know, I'm quite sure you'd have clinched it if your partner had been able to keep going.'

I felt myself blushing. 'Well it's very kind of you, but I was a bit lucky.'

'Lucky? Not a bit of it!' said Mr Blenkinsopp. 'You played two beautiful strokes – I don't know how you did it in the conditions.'

'Beautiful strokes?'

'Most certainly. A delightful leg glance followed by a late cut of the greatest delicacy. Don't you agree, Tom?'

Tom sprinkled a little salt on his peas and turned to me. 'Ah do agree. And the best bit was how you got 'em up in the air to clear t'long grass. That was clever that was.' He conveyed a forkful of pie to his mouth and began to munch stolidly.

I looked at him narrowly. Tom was always serious so there was nothing to be learned from his expression. He was always kind, too, he had been kind all evening.

But I really think he meant it this time.

# Supermarket Checkout

*Victoria Wood*

*An impatient woman customer is having her groceries checked out by a slow girl on the till. She looks at a packet of bacon.*

**Till girl**    It's got no price on. Did you notice how much they were?
**Customer**    No, I didn't.

*She looks around and holds up the bacon.*

**Till girl**    Won't be long.
**Customer**    Good

*Long pause.*

**Till girl**    We're a bit short-handed today. Us that works here gets the old food cheap, and if it's something like a pork pie, you can actually die, apparently. So the girl that checks the prices, she's probably, you know, passed on.

**Customer**    Honestly, I thought you girls on the tills knew all the prices.

**Till girl**    I've only come on the till today. I was in meat packing before, then an overall came free so I come here.

**Customer**    But surely you wear an overall when you're packing meat?

**Till girl**    No, you must bring something from home. I had our dog's blanket.

**Customer**    You can't have dogs in a place where food is prepared.

**Till girl**    I didn't. It's dead. It were called Whiskey. It ate one of the pork pies from here.

**Customer**    But you do wear gloves, don't you, when you're wrapping meat?

| | |
|---|---|
| **Till girl** | I did, woolly ones. I get a lot of colds, I like to have something to wipe my nose on. I liked it in the meat-packing department, it were dead near the toilet. |
| **Customer** | Well it sounds disgusting. Who's in charge of that department? |
| **Till girl** | Mr Waterhouse. He's not here. He goes to some sort of a special clinic on Thursdays. I'll do your veg, anyway. |

*She coughs and splutters all over it.*

| | |
|---|---|
| | Sorry. I've caught this cold off Susan on smoked meats. They're not smoked when they come, but she's on sixty a day. |
| **Customer** | It's all over the cauliflower. |
| **Till girl** | Sorry. |

*She wipes it on her overall.*

| | |
|---|---|
| | Corned beef, ninety-eight. It's funny how much tins can actually blow out without bursting, isn't it? |
| **Customer** | You can't sell a blown tin. |
| **Till girl** | We can, they're dead popular. |
| **Customer** | Oh look, how much longer is this going to take? |
| **Till girl** | Do you want me to ask the supervisor? |
| **Customer** | Yes, thank you. |

*The till girl speaks into intercom.*

| | |
|---|---|
| **Till girl** | Hello? |
| **Intercom** | Hello? |
| **Till girl** | Hello, Mrs Brinsley, it's Gemma here. |
| **Intercom** | Hello Gemma, nice to talk to you. |
| **Till girl** | Nice to talk to you, Mrs Brinsley. How's your boils? |
| **Intercom** | Worse. |
| **Till girl** | So putting you on the cheese counter hasn't helped? Well, what I'm calling about, I've a lady here, and she's brought me a packet of bacon with no price. |
| **Intercom** | Is it streaky? |

**Till girl**     Well, it is a bit but it'll probably wash off.

                  *She wipes it with filthy dishcloth.*

                  The sell-by-date is 5 August 1984. No, hang on.

                  *She scrapes something off.*

                  1964.

**Intercom**      Three and nine.
**Till girl**     Three and nine, thank you.
**Customer**      You mean that bacon's twenty years old?
**Till girl**     I don't know. I was away when we did addings. *(She finishes checking out the rest of the stuff.)*
**Customer**      This place is a disgrace – filthy, unhygienic, the food's not safe to eat, the staff are all positively diseased.
**Till girl**     That's two pounds seventy-one pence, please.
**Customer**      On the other hand, it's very cheap and easy to park. Bye.

# Gilbreths and Company

## *Frank B. Gilbreth*

Dad's theories ranged from Esperanto, which he made us study because he thought it was the answer to half the world's problems, to immaculate conception, which he said wasn't supported by available biological evidence. His theories on social poise, although requiring some minor revision as the family grew larger, were constant to the extent that they hinged on unaffectation.

A poised, unaffected person was never ridiculous, at least in his own mind, Dad told us. And a man who didn't feel ridiculous could never lose his dignity. Dad seldom felt ridiculous, and never admitted losing his dignity.

The part of the theory requiring some revision was that guests would feel at home if they were treated like one of our family. As Mother pointed out, and Dad finally admitted, the only guest who could possibly feel like a member of our family was a guest who, himself, came from a family of a dozen, headed by a motion study man.

When guests weren't present, Dad worked at improving our table manners. Whenever a child within his reach took too large a mouthful of food, Dad's knuckles would descend sharply on the top of the offender's head, with a thud that made Mother wince.

'Not on the head, Frank,' she protested in shocked tones. 'For mercy sakes, not on the head!'

Dad paid no attention except when the blow had been unusually hard. In such cases he rubbed his knuckles ruefully and replied:

'Maybe you're right. There must be softer places.'

If the offender was at Mother's end of the table, out of Dad's reach, he'd signal her to administer the skull punishment. Mother, who never disciplined any of us, or even threatened discipline, ignored the signals. Dad would then catch the eye of a child sitting near the offender and, by signals, would deputize him to carry out the punishment.

'With my compliments,' Dad would say, when the child with the full mouth turned furiously on the one who had knuckled him. 'If I've told you once, I've told you a hundred times to cut your food up into little pieces. How am I going to drive that into your skull?'

'Not on the head,' Mother repeated. 'Mercy, Maud, not on the head!'

Anyone with an elbow on the table might suddenly feel his wrist seized, raised and jerked downward so that his elbow hit the table hard enough to make the dishes dance.

'Not on the elbow, Frank. That's the most sensitive part of the body. Any place but the elbow.'

Mother disapproved of all forms of corporal punishment. She felt, though, that she could achieve better results in the long run by objecting to the part of the anatomy selected for the punishment, rather than the punishment itself. Even when Dad administered vitally needed punishment on the conventional area, the area where it is supposed to do the most good, Mother tried to intervene.

'Not on the end of the spine,' she'd say in a voice indicating her belief that Dad was running the risk of crippling us for life. 'For goodness' sake, not on the end of the spine!'

'Where, then?' Dad shouted furiously in the middle of one spanking. 'Not on the top of the head, not on the side of the ear, not on the back of the neck, not on the elbow, not across the legs, and not on the seat of the pants. Where did your father spank you? Across the soles of the by-jingoed feet like the heathen Chinese?'

'Well, not on the end of the spine,' Mother said. 'You can be sure of that.'

Skull-rapping and elbow-thumping became a practice in which everybody in the family, except Mother, participated until Dad deemed our table manners satisfactory. Even the youngest child could mete out the punishment without fear of reprisal. All during meals, we watched each other, and particularly Dad, for an opportunity. Sometimes the one who spotted a perched elbow would sneak out of his chair and walk all the way around the table, so that he could catch the offender.

Dad was quite careful about his elbows, but every so often would forget. It was considered a feather in one's cap to thump any elbow. But the ultimate achievement was to thump Dad's. This was considered not just a feather in the cap, but the entire head-dress of a full Indian chief.

When Dad was caught and his elbow thumped, he made a great to-do over it. He grimaced as if in excruciating pain, sucked in air through his teeth, rubbed the elbow, and claimed he couldn't use his arm for the remainder of the meal.

Occasionally he would rest an elbow purposely on the edge of the table, and make believe he didn't notice some child who had slipped out of a chair and was tip-toeing towards him. Just as the child was about to reach out and grab the elbow, Dad would slide it into his lap.

'I've got eyes in the back of my head,' Dad would announce.

The would-be thumper, walking disappointedly back to his chair, wondered if it wasn't just possible that Dad really did.

Both Dad and Mother tried to impress us that it was our responsibility to make guests feel at home. There were guests for meals almost as often as not, particularly business friends of Dad's, since his office was in the house. There was no formality and no special preparations except a clean napkin and an extra place at the table.

'If a guest is sitting next to you, it's your job to keep him happy, to see that things are passed to him,' Dad kept telling us.

George Isles, a Canadian author, seemed to Lillian to be an unhappy guest. Mr Isles was old, and told sad but fascinating stories.

'Once upon a time there was an ancient, poor man whose joints hurt when he moved them, whose doctor wouldn't let him smoke cigars, and who had no little children to love him,' Mr Isles said. He continued with what seemed to us a tale of overwhelming loneliness, and then concluded:

'And do you know who that old man was?'

We had an idea who it was, but we shook our heads and said we didn't. Mr Isles looked sadder than ever. He slowly raised his forearm and tapped his chest with his forefinger.

'Me,' he said.

Lillian, who was six, was sitting next to Mr Isles. It was her responsibility to see that he was happy, and she felt somehow that she had failed on the job. She threw her arms around his neck and kissed his dry, old man's cheek.

'You do too have little children who love you,' she said, on the brink of tears. 'You do too!'

Whenever Mr Isles came to call after that, he always brought one

box of candy for Mother and us, and a separate box for Lillian.
Ernestine used to remark, in a tone tinged with envy, that Lill was
probably New Jersey's youngest gold-digger, and that few adult gold-
diggers ever had received more, in return for less.

Dad was an easy-going host, informal and gracious, and we tried to
pattern ourselves after him.

'Any more vegetables, boss?' he'd ask Mother. 'No? Well, how about
mashed potatoes? Lots of them. And plenty of lamb. Fine. Well, sir, I
can't offer you any vegetables, but how about . . .'

'Oh, come on, have some more beef,' Frank urged a visiting German
engineer. 'After all, you've only had three helpings.'

'There's no need to gobble your grapefruit like a pig,' Fred told a
woman professor from Columbia University, who had arrived late and
was trying to catch up with the rest of us. 'If we finish ahead of you,
we'll wait until you're through.'

'I'm sorry, but I'm afraid I can't pass your dessert until you finish
your lima beans,' Dan told a guest on another occasion. 'Daddy won't
allow it, and you're my responsibility. Daddy says a Belgian family
could live a week on what's thrown away in this house every day.'

'Daddy, do you think that what Mr Fremonville is saying is of
general interest?' Lill interrupted a long discourse to ask.

Dad and Mother, and most of the guests, laughed away remarks like
these without too much embarrassment. Dad would apologize and
explain the family rule involved, and the reason for it. After the guests
had gone, Mother would get us together and tell us that while family
rules were important, it was even more important to see that guests
weren't made uncomfortable.

Sometimes after a meal, Dad's stomach would rumble and, when
there weren't any guests, we'd tease him about it. The next time it
rumbled, he'd look shocked and single out one of us.

'Billy,' he said. 'Please! I'm not in the mood for an organ recital.'

'That was your stomach, not mine, Daddy. You can't fool me.'

'You children have the noisiest stomachs I've ever heard. Don't you
think so, Lillie?'

Mother looked disapprovingly over her mending.

'I think,' she said, 'there are Eskimos in the house.'

One night, Mr. Russell Allen, a young engineer, was a guest for
supper. Jack, in a high chair across the table from him, accidentally

swallowed some air and let out a belch that resounded through the dining-room and, as we found out later, was heard even in the kitchen by Mrs Cunningham. It was such a thorough burp, and had emerged from such a small subject, that all conversation was momentarily suspended in amazement. Jack, more surprised than anybody, looked shocked. He reached out his arm and pointed a chubby and accusing forefinger at the guest.

'Mr Allen,' he said in offended dignity. 'Please! I'm not in the mood for an organ recital.'

'Why, Jackie!' said Mother, almost in tears. 'Why, Jackie. How could you?'

'Out,' roared Dad. 'Skiddoo. Tell Mrs Cunningham to give you the rest of your supper in the kitchen. And I'll see you about this later.'

'Well, you say it,' Jack sobbed as he disappeared towards the kitchen, 'You say it when your stomach rumbles.'

Dad was blushing. The poise which he told us he valued so highly had disappeared. He shifted uneasily in his seat and fumbled with his napkin. Nobody could think of a way to break the uneasy silence.

Dad cleared his throat, with efficient thoroughness. But the silence persisted, and it hung heavily over the table.

'Lackaday,' Dad finally said. The situation was getting desperate, and he tried again. 'Lack a couple of days,' Dad said with a weak, artificial laugh. We felt sorry for him and for Mother and Mr Allen, who were just as crimson as Dad. The silence persisted.

Dad suddenly flung his napkin on the table, and walked out into the kitchen. He returned holding Jack by the hand. Jack was still crying.

'All right, Jackie,' Dad said. 'Come back and sit down. You're right, you learned it from me. First you apologise to Mr Allen. Then we'll tell him the whole story. And then none of us will ever say it again. As your Mother told us, it all comes from having Eskimos in the house.'

Dad's sister, Aunt Anne, was an ample Victorian who wore full, sweeping skirts and high ground-gripper shoes. She was older than Dad, and they were much alike and devoted to each other. She was kindly but stern, big-bosomed, and every inch a lady. Like Dad, she had reddish brown hair and a reddish brown temper. She, her husband, and their grown children, whom we worshipped, lived a few blocks from us in Providence. Aunt Anne was an accomplished pianist and gave music lessons at her house at 26 Cabot Street. Dad thought it would be nice if all of us learned to play something. Dad admitted he was as green as any valley when it came to music, but he had a good ear and he liked symphonies.

Aunt Anne must have sensed almost immediately that we had no talent. She knew, though, that any such admission would have a depressing effect on Dad, who took it for granted that his children had talent for everything. Consequently, Aunt Anne stuck courageously to a losing cause for six years, in an unusual display of devotion and fortitude above and beyond the regular call of family duty.

When she finally became convinced of the hopelessness of teaching us the piano, she shifted us to other instruments. Although we had no better success, the other instruments at least were quieter than the piano and, more important, only one person could play them at a time.

Our Anne was shifted to the violin, Ernestine to the mandolin, and Martha and Frank to the 'cello. It was awful at home when we practised, and Dad would walk smirking through the house with wads of cotton sticking prominently from his ears.

'Never mind,' he said, when we told him we didn't seem to be making any progress. 'You stick with it. You'll thank me when you're my age.'

Unselfishly jeopardizing her professional reputation as a teacher, Aunt Anne always allowed each of us to play in the annual recitals at her music school. Usually we broke down in the middle, and always had a demoralizing effect on the more talented children, and on their parents in the audience.

To salvage what she could of her standing as a teacher, Aunt Anne used to tell the audience before we went on stage that we had only recently shifted from the piano to stringed instruments. The implication, although not expressed in so many words, was that we had already mastered the piano and were now branching out along other musical avenues.

Just before we started to play, she affixed mutes to our strings and whispered:

'Remember, your number should be played softly, softly as a little brook tinkling through a still forest.'

The way we played it, it didn't tinkle. As Dad whispered to Mother at one recital: 'If I heard that coming from the back fence at night, I'd either report it to the police or heave shoes at it.'

* * *

Aunt Anne was good to us and we loved her and her family, but like Dad she insisted on having her own way. While we reluctantly accepted Dad's bossing as one of the privileges of his rank as head of the family, we had no intention of accepting it from anybody else, including his eldest sister.

After we moved to Montclair, Aunt Anne came to stay with us for several days while Mother and Dad were away on a lecture tour. She made it plain from the start that she was not a guest, but the temporary commander-in-chief. She even used the front stairs, leading from the front hall to the second floor, instead of the back stairs, which led from the kitchen to a hallway near the girls' bathroom. None of us was allowed to use the front stairs because Dad wanted to keep the varnish on them looking nice.

'Daddy will be furious if he comes home and finds you've been using his front stairs,' we told Aunt Anne.

'Nonsense,' she cut us off. 'The back stairs are narrow and steep, and I for one don't propose to use them. As long as I'm here, I'll use any stairs I have a mind to. Now rest your features and mind your business.'

She sat at Dad's place at the foot of the table, and we resented this, too. Ordinarily, Frank, as the oldest boy, sat in Dad's place, and Anne, as the oldest girl, sat at Mother's. We also disapproved of Aunt Anne's blunt criticism of how we kept our bedrooms, and some of the changes she made in the family routine.

'What do you do, keep pigeons in here?' she'd say when she walked into the bedroom shared by Frank and Bill. 'I'm coming back in fifteen minutes, and I want to find this room in apple-pie order.'

And: 'I don't care what time your regular bedtime is. As long as I'm in charge, we'll do things my way. Off with you now.'

Like Grandma and Dad, Aunt Anne thought that all Irishmen were shiftless, and that Tom Grieves was the most shiftless of all Irishmen. She told him so at least once a day, and Tom was scared to death of her.

Experience has established the fact that a person cannot move from a small, peaceful home into a family of a dozen without having something finally snap. We saw this happen time after time with Dad's stenographers and with the cooks who followed Mrs Cunningham. In order to reside with a family of a dozen it is necessary either (1) to be brought up from birth in such a family, as we were; or (2) to become accustomed to it as it grew, as Dad, Mother, and Tom Grieves did.

It was at the dinner table that something finally snapped in Aunt Anne.

We had spent the entire meal purposely making things miserable for her. Bill had hidden under the table, and we had removed his place and chair so she wouldn't realise he was missing. While we ate, Billy thumped Aunt Anne's legs with the side of his hand.

'Who's kicking me?' she complained. 'Saints alive!'

We said no one.

'Well, you don't have a dog, do you?'

We didn't, and we told her so. Our collie had died some time before this.

'Well, somebody's certainly kicking me. Hard.'

She insisted that the child sitting on each side of her slide his chair towards the head of the table, so that no legs could possibly reach her. Bill thumped again.

'Somebody *is* kicking me,' Aunt Anne said, 'and I intend to get to the bottom of it. Literally.'

Bill thumped again. Aunt Anne picked up the table-cloth and looked under the table, but Bill had anticipated her and retreated to the other end. The table was so long you couldn't see that far underneath without getting down on your hands and knees, and Aunt Anne was much too dignified to stoop to any such level. When she put the table-cloth down again, Bill crawled forward and licked her hand.

'You do too have a dog,' Aunt Anne said accusingly, while she dried her hand on a napkin. 'Speak up now! Who brought that miserable cur into the house?'

Bill thumped her again and retreated. She picked up the table-cloth and looked. She put it down again, and he licked her hand. She looked again, and then dangled her hand temptingly between her knees. Bill couldn't resist this trap, and this time Aunt Anne was ready for him. When he started to lick, she snapped her knees together like a vice, trapped his head in the folds of her skirt, and reached down and grabbed him by the hair.

'Come out of there, you scamp you,' she shouted. 'I've got you. You can't get away this time. Come out, I say.'

She didn't give Bill a chance to come out under his own power. She yanked, and he came out by the hair of his head, screaming and kicking.

In those days, Bill was no snappy dresser. He liked old clothes, preferably held together with safety-pins, and held up by old neck-ties. When he wore a neck-tie around his neck, which was as seldom as possible, he sometimes evened up the ends by trimming the longer with a pair of scissors. His knickers usually were partially unbuttoned in the front – what the Navy calls the commodore's privilege. They were completely unfastened at the legs and hung down to his ankles. During the course of a day, his stockings rode gradually down his legs and, by dinner, had partially disappeared into his sneakers. When Mother was at home, she made him wear such appurtenances as a coat and a belt. In her absence, he had grown slack.

When Aunt Anne jerked him out, a piece of string connecting a button-hole in his shirt with a button-hole in the front of his trousers suddenly broke. Bill grabbed for his pants, but it was too late.

'Go to your room, you scamp you,' Aunt Anne said, shaking him. 'Just wait till your father comes home. He'll know how to take care of you.'

Bill picked up his knickers and did as he was told. He had a new respect for Aunt Anne, and the whole top of his head was smarting from the hair-pulling.

Aunt Anne sat down with deceptive calm, and gave us a disarming smile.

'I want you children to listen carefully to me,' she almost whispered. 'There's not a living soul here, including the baby, who is cooperative. I've never seen a more spoiled crowd of children.'

As she went on, her voice grew louder. Much louder. Tom Grieves opened the pantry door a crack and peeked in.

'For those of you who like to believe that an only child is a selfish child, let me say you are one hundred per cent wrong. From what I have seen, this is the most completely selfish household in the entire world.'

She was roaring now, wide open, and it was the first time we had ever seen her that way. Except that her voice was an octave higher, it might have been Dad, sitting there in his own chair.

'From this minute on, pipe down every last one of you, or I'll lambaste the hides off you. I'll fix you so you can't sit down for a month. Do you understand? Does everybody understand? In case you don't realise it, *I've had enough!*'

With that, determined to show us she wasn't going to let us spoil her

meal, she put a piece of pie in her mouth. But she was so upset that she
choked, and slowly turned a deep purple. She clutched at her throat.
We were afraid she was dying, and were ashamed of ourselves.

Tom, watching at the door, saw his duty. Putting aside his fear of her,
he ran into the dining-room and slapped her on the back. Then he
grabbed her arms and held them high over her head.

'You'll be all right in a minute, Aunt Anne,' he said.

His system worked. She gurgled and finally caught her breath. Then,
remembering her dignity, she jerked her arms out of his hands and
drew herself up to her full height.

'Keep your hands to yourself, Grieves,' she said in a tone that
indicated her belief that his next step would be to loosen her corset.
'Don't ever let me hear you make the fatal mistake of calling me "Aunt
Anne" again. And after this, mind your own' – she looked slowly
around the table and then decided to say it anyway – '*damned* business.'

There was no doubt after that about who was boss, and Aunt Anne
had no further trouble with us. When Dad and Mother returned home,
all of us expected to be disciplined. But we had misjudged Aunt Anne.

'You look like you've lost weight,' Dad said to her. 'The children
didn't give you any trouble, did they?'

'Not a bit,' said Aunt Anne. 'They behaved beautifully, once we got
to understand each other. We got along just fine, didn't we, children?'

She reached out fondly and rumpled Billy's hair, which didn't need
rumpling.

'Ouch,' Billy whispered to her, grinning in relief. 'It still hurts. Have
a heart.'

We had better success with another guest whom we set out deliberately
to discourage. She was a woman psychologist who came to Montclair
every fortnight from New York to give us intelligence tests. It was her
own idea, not Dad's or Mother's, but they welcomed her. She was
planning to publish a paper about the effects of Dad's teaching methods
on our intelligence quotients.

She was thin and sallow, with angular features and a black
moustache, not quite droopy enough to hide a horsey set of upper teeth.
We hated her and suspected that the feeling was mutual.

At first her questions were legitimate enough: Arithmetic, spelling,
languages, geography, and the sort of purposeful confusion – about

ringing numbers and underlining words – in which some psychologists place particular store.

After we had completed the initial series of tests, she took us one by one into the parlour for personal interviews. Even Mother and Dad weren't allowed to be present.

The interviews were embarrassing and insulting.

'Does it hurt when your mother spanks you?' she asked each of us, peering searchingly into our eyes and breathing into our faces. 'You mean your mother never spanks you?' She seemed disappointed. 'Well, how about your father? Oh, he does?' That appeared to be more heartening news. 'Does your mother pay more attention to the other children than she does to you? How many baths do you take a week? Are you sure? Do you think it would be nice to have another baby brother? You do? Goodness!'

We decided that if Dad and Mother knew the kinds of questions we were being asked, they wouldn't like them any better than we did. Anne and Ernestine had made up their minds to explain the situation to them, when destiny delivered the psychologist into our hands, lock, stock and moustache.

Mother had been devising a series of job aptitude tests, and the desk by her bed was piled with pamphlets and magazines on psychology. Ernestine was running idly through them one night, while Mother was reading aloud to us from *The Five Little Peppers and How they Grew*, when she came across a batch of intelligence tests. One of them was the test which the New York woman was in the process of giving us – not the embarrassing personal questions, but the business of circling numbers, spelling, and filling in blanks. The correct answers were in the back.

'Snake's hips,' Ernestine crowed. 'Got it!'

Mother looked up absently from her book. 'Don't mix up my work, Ernie,' she said. 'What are you after?'

'Just want to borrow something,' Ern told her.

'Well, don't forget to put it back when you're through with it, will you? Where was I? Oh, I remember. Joel had just said that if necessary he could help support the family by selling papers and shining shoes down at the depot.'

She resumed her reading.

The psychologist had already given us the first third of the test. Now Anne and Ernestine tutored us on the second third, until we could run right down a page and fill in the answers without even reading the questions. The last third was an oral word-association test, and they coached us on that, too.

'We're going to be the smartest people she ever gave a test to,' Ern told us. 'And the queerest, too. Make her think we're smart, but uncivilized because we haven't had enough individual attention. That's what she wants to think, anyway.'

'Act nervous and queer,' Anne said. 'While she's talking to you, fidget and scratch yourself. Be as nasty as you can. That won't require much effort from most of you; there's no need our tutoring you on that.'

The next time the psychologist came out from New York, she sat us at intervals around the walls of the parlour, with books on our laps to write on. She passed each of us a copy of the second third of the test.

'When I say commence, work as quickly as you can,' she told us. 'You have half an hour, and I want you to get as far along in the tests as you can. If any of you should happen to finish before the time is up, bring your papers to me.' She looked at her watch. 'Ready? Now turn your test-papers over and start. Remember, I'm watching you, so don't try to look at your neighbour's paper.'

We ran down the pages, filling in the blanks. The older children turned in their papers within ten minutes. Lillian, the youngest being examined, finally turned hers in within twenty.

The psychologist looked at Lillian's paper, and her mouth dropped open.

'How old are you, dearie?' she asked.

'Six,' said Lill. 'I'll be seven in June.'

'There's something radically wrong here,' the visitor said. 'I haven't had a chance to grade all of your paper, but do you know you have a higher I.Q. than Nicholas Murray Butler?'

'I read a lot,' Lill said.

The psychologist glanced at the other tests and shook her head.

'I don't know what to think,' she sighed. 'You've certainly shown remarkable improvement in the last two weeks. Maybe we'd better get on to the last third of the test. I'm going to go around the room and say a word to each of you. I want you to answer instantly the first word that comes into your mind. Now won't that be a nice little game?'

Anne twitched. Ernestine scratched. Martha bit her nails.

'We'll go by ages,' the visitor continued. 'Anne first.'

She pointed to Anne. 'Knife,' said the psychologist.

'Stab, wound, bleed, slit-throat, murder, disembowel, scream, shriek,' replied Anne, without taking a breath and so fast that the words flowed together.

'Jesus,' said the psychologist. 'Let me get that down. You're just supposed to answer one word, but let me get it all down anyway.' She panted in excitement as she scribbled in her pad.

'All right, Ernestine. Your turn. Just one word. "Black".'

'Jack,' said Ernestine.

The visitor looked at Martha. 'Foot.'

'Kick,' said Martha.

'Hair.'

'Louse,' said Frank.

'Flower.'

'Stink,' said Bill.

The psychologist was becoming more and more excited. She looked at Lill.

'Droppings,' said Lill, upsetting the apple-cart.

'But I haven't even asked you your word yet,' the visitor exclaimed. 'So that's it. Let me see what your word was going to be. I thought so. Your word was "bird". And they told you to say "droppings", didn't they?'

Lill nodded sheepishly.

'And they told you just how to fill out the rest of the test, didn't they? I suppose the answers were given to you by your mother, so you would impress me with how smart you are.'

We started to snicker and then to roar. But the psychologist didn't think it was funny.

'You're all nasty little cheats,' she said. 'Don't think for a minute you pulled the wool over my eyes. I saw through you from the start.'

She picked up her wraps and started for the front door. Dad had heard us laughing, and came out of his office to see what was going on. If there was any excitement, he wanted to be in on it.

'Well,' he beamed, 'it sounds as if it's been a jolly test. Running along so soon? Tell me, frankly, what do you think of my family?'

She looked at us and there was an evil glint in her eye.

'I'm glad you asked me that,' she whinnied. 'Unquestionably, they are smart. Too damned smart for their breeches. Does that answer your question? As to whether they were aided and abetted in an attempted fraud, I cannot say. But my professional advice is to bear down on them. A good thrashing right now, from the oldest to the youngest, might be just the thing.'

She slammed the front door, and Dad looked glumly at us.

'All right,' he sighed. 'What have you been up to? That woman's going to write a paper on the family. What did you do to her?'

Anne twitched. Ernestine scratched. Martha bit her nails. Dad was getting angry.

'Hold still and speak up. No nonsense!'

'Do you want another baby brother?' Anne asked.

'Does it hurt when your mother spanks you?' said Ernestine.

'When did you have your last bath?' Martha inquired. 'Are you sure? Hmmm?'

Dad raised his hands in surrender and shook his head. He looked old and tired now.

'Sometimes I don't know if it's worth it,' he said. 'Why didn't you come and tell your mother and me about it, if she was asking questions like that? Oh well . . . On the other hand . . . Why, the bearded old goat!'

Dad started to smile.

'If she writes a paper about any of that I'll sue her for everything she owns, including her birth certificate. If she has one.'

He opened the door into his office.

'Come in and give me all the frightful details.'

'After you, Dr Butler,' Ernestine told Lill.

A few minutes later, Mother came into the office, where we were perched on the edges of her and Dad's desks. The stenographers had abandoned their typewriters and were crowded around us.

'What's the commotion, Frank?' she asked Dad. 'I could hear you bellowing all the way up in the attic.'

'Oh, Lord,' Dad wheezed. 'Start at the beginning, kids. I want your mother to hear this, too. The bearded old goat – not you, Lillie.'

# The Commandant's Goat

## *A. G. Cummins*

When Martin Kirkpatrick first arrived in Odonga he brought with him a salmon rod, a spinning reel and a box full of assorted lures. During the twelve months of his first tour of duty he fished industriously in the muddy and crocodile-infested waters of the Bonga River, which flowed below the fort. Then he went on leave. He spent his leave on his father's property in County Mayo, and when he came back he brought a box of gelignite instead of the fishing tackle. He said that an engineer who was building a pier for the Congested Districts Board had given him the gelignite, and told him that it was the best bait he had ever used.

The box was labelled 'CONDENSED MILK – STOW AWAY FROM BOILERS,' and he said he had had the devil of a time bringing it out, for the package had fallen off the top of a barrow-load of luggage on the pier at Kingstown, and given him such a fright that he had always carried it himself after that. Martin does not look a bit the sort of fellow to be carrying a box of condensed milk, and I am not surprised that the Customs people were suspicious; but he has a most persuasive tongue and a smile no one can resist, so in the end he got through all right.

As soon as he arrived in Egypt, where he was known, he changed the label to 'MEDICAL COMFORTS – URGENT,' and added 'GLASS – WITH CARE'. He knew everyone would understand that; but he got a bad scare when he found his cook just beginning to break open the box with a hammer when some brandy was wanted in a hurry. He reached Taufikia safely, and when he found that the launch from Odonga was waiting for him he thought his troubles were over, but, all the same, he had the box stowed aft with his personal kit, for he did not dare to risk it forward with his servants after the incident of the cook and the hammer.

The launch is very small, and takes four days, with luck, to reach the fort, and by the afternoon of the second day it was so hot under the awning that Martin said the infernal box might just as well have been stowed inside the boiler. He got his boys to sprinkle water all over the top and sides of the awning, and in doing so they managed to soak his bedding and tear a hole in his mosquito curtain, so he had a rotten night; but he felt safer all the same, and loaded himself up with quinine as a precaution against the mosquitoes.

When he arrived at Odonga, Angus Buchanan and I were the only British officers in the station, and Angus, as acting Commandant, when he heard how temperamental gelignite could be, would not allow the box to be stored in the fort. We were all agreed that it would be safer outside the perimeter, but it was hard to know just where to put it. There was a little straw hut not far from the ramparts which no one ever entered except the three of us, and at length we decided to store it there. The rest of Martin's fishing equipment, consisting of an iron punt and a small portable motor to clamp on to her stern, were to come up from Khartoum as soon as the river was open for the transport of stores; but it was several weeks before these accessories arrived, and during the interval we got quite used to the little box of gelignite in the corner of the hut.

We were all pretty busy at the time, superintending the repair of the hutments in the fort and *harimat* before the rains, and we had not much time to think of fishing. We did, indeed, discuss the morality of the wholesale and unsportsmanlike slaughter which Martin proposed, but we came to the conclusion that he had had sufficient provocation in the past to justify any measures of retaliation.

The Bonga River is alive with fish. At certain seasons the whole surface boils with rises, or what pass for rises with the great brutes that show themselves. What they rise at no one knows. Perhaps they are just sunning themselves. You can throw the most tempting things at them – from 'Devons' to chicken guts – but they never pay any attention. The natives seem to have no difficulty in killing them, for they have long since abandoned the gentle art of seduction in favour of more primitive methods involving the use of a spear.

They have numerous ways of going about the job, from the least sporting method of simply jabbing a long spear into the muddy water until it sticks in something, to the exceptionally elegant practice of marking a rising fish and pinking him with a harpoon as he goes down.

This last, a combination of shooting and dry-fly fishing, is, I presume, only practised successfully by the high priests of the art. The performer sits on his hunkers in the bow of a dug-out canoe, which is propelled by a companion kneeling in the stern. As these dug-outs capsize if you stick out your tongue crooked, and as the river is full of man-eating crocodiles, it will be seen that the element of danger, which some idiots consider essential in sport, is by no means lacking.

I have seen many a good fish killed by this method at ranges up to thirty feet. When the shot is successful the haft of the harpoon comes off, and, being attached to the line, acts as a buoy by which the fish can be traced if he proves too big to be played from the canoe. All these methods, except the last, and that only because he was not intended by nature for squatting on his hunkers, had been tried by Martin during his first tour of duty. Only a few whiskered, eel-shaped and leathery-looking brutes rewarded his perseverance, and it was annoying to have an Egyptian, armed with a throwing-net, wade in beside him and, at the first cast, produce six silvery beauties weighing from two to three pounds apiece. It did not comfort Martin at all to hear that this particular kind of fish was not to be taken with a hook. He examined their mouths and decided that they ought to be trained differently. But he bought a throwing-net all the same and tried to use it. He got so wet practising that he fished one afternoon without his shirt, and as a result lost all the skin of his back from sunburn. He learnt to throw it quite decently in the end, but by that time all the silvery fish had gone up-stream or down-stream or something, and the others just burrowed into the mud and stayed there when the net was thrown over them.

The harpoon method, practised from the bank, was the most fun, and we all tried it with a weapon which Angus borrowed from one of the men. The trouble was that the fish never rose in quite the spot we were looking at, and we were always late. Another thing that made it hard was that the line attached to the harpoon used to get tangled as one held it coiled loosely in the left hand while waiting for a rise. The only time any of us hit anything was when Angus threw at one fish and pinked another, which rose about three yards away from the first, and on that occasion he was so excited that he dropped the end of the line. The harpoon and the fish were recovered next day by a native, but it was not quite the same thing as if Angus had completed the evolution himself.

I think that anyone who has fished in the Bonga will be inclined to agree with Martin that 'it's all right to be a sportsman and all that sort of thing, old boy, but it's no good being a damn fool.'

The rains had started, and the river was rising by the time the punt and the motor attachment arrived. This was the first small boat to reach the station, and it opened up great possibilities. Martin said the motor made no more noise than the ticking of a clock, and would drive her at about ten miles an hour, so we decided to run up-stream that afternoon to a big bend in the river to look for a herd of elephants which had been reported a few days before. Angus and I got our kit and guns ready, while Martin busied himself unpacking the motor. It looked very simple, and the instructions on the card that came with it were short and concise. It seemed to me that they took a good deal of knowledge for granted, but Martin was confident that he remembered all about the one he had tried on Lough-Mask, and so, as soon as he had got the thing clamped on to the stern of the punt, we carried down our rifles and kit and deposited them in the bows. I wanted to put in the oars in case the motor failed us, but Martin said that it really was not necessary, and that, if I would just step on board and be prepared to cast off when he told me to, he would get the motor started.

It appeared that all you had to do was to turn a little handle a few times, and then the clock would start ticking. Martin turned it at intervals for about half an hour while we sat in the sun and gave advice, and then he asked Angus to have a try. Angus worked for nearly five minutes, and then turned her over to me. He said he was sure Martin had been wrong in mixing the oil and petrol before putting them in the tank. I, frankly, did not know, but I wanted to have a try for the elephants, so I took the wheel. It was a small horizontal thing with a vertical handle, and was very awkward to turn. I worked at it hard for ten minutes, and was on the point of giving up when there was a sort of explosion in the motor, and the handle spun round in the reverse direction, nearly knocking me overboard.

Martin jumped up excitedly. 'That's it,' he exclaimed. 'Now we've got it. Let me take her.'

I was not sorry to hand over, for it was extraordinarily hot work. Martin worked hopefully for a few minutes; with gradually fading interest for an hour, and then, as the sun was declining, he gave it up, and we carried our kit back to the fort.

That night the conversation turned to gelignite. Martin, though temporarily defeated by the motor, was not downhearted, and was determined that his new method of fishing should be a success. He enlarged on the probability of monstrous fish lying in the deep pool below the fort, and speculated on the number of crocodiles that would be dislodged by the explosion. Two of the company mules had been seized, while drinking, during the past month, and a sentry with a rifle had been posted beside the pool ever since. But the big crocodiles were too wary to show themselves. The gelignite was just the thing to blow them out of their lairs, Martin said.

It must be understood that this happened before the war made us all familiar with high explosives. Hand grenades and bombs were out of date, and the use of cordite and its powerful brethren was left with gratitude in the capable hands of the Royal Engineers. We had an exaggerated respect for the little box of gelignite. The name was new to us, and its properties, as described to Martin by the Congested Districts Engineer, were terrifying enough. Apparently the slightest friction was sufficient to set it off. It was much more dangerous than cordite, and twice as powerful. It came, Martin said, in sticks about six inches long, and you had to make a hole in the stick and insert a detonator and a fuse. The engineer had supplied the detonators, and Martin had bought the fuse in Dublin. Three or four inches of fuse was the length recommended, and it would burn all right under water.

Martin suggested that we should try the pool below the fort on the next afternoon, and Angus and I had not the courage to refuse. I did not sleep at all well that night – it was hot and airless – and my temper was none too good in consequence when I went to see Angus next morning in his office. Angus was due to go on leave by the next boat bound north, and I must say he looked that morning as if he needed a change of air. I had some important papers for signature, and sat down to wait until the Egyptian Officer-in-Charge-of-Supplies had finished, and it was while I was waiting that the Commandant's goat walked into the office.

I have not mentioned the Commandant or his goat before: the former because he was on leave and does not come into the story, and the goat because he was a thoroughly bad animal and I did not want to bring him in until I had to. As a matter of fact, my papers, though important enough, could easily have waited until the next day, but I really wanted to see Angus about this matter of the gelignite. It did not seem quite right to me that the only three British officers in the station should embark together on such a risky business, and I was going to suggest to Angus that, as acting Commandant, he ought not to do it. I knew it would be hard to talk him round, but I thought that, putting it officially in the office, I had a chance of success. Even if he felt he could not back out himself, he might possibly order me not to go.

The infernal goat ruined my plans. I have said he was a bad animal. He was more than that – he was a bad goat. The Commandant had found him, a little weak-kneed kid, in an abandoned village up the river, and adopted him. Fed at first by a finger dipped in condensed milk, he was weaned on straw bottle-covers and cigarettes. Such a diet must have an evil effect, even on a goat. He never developed any horns, but he grew to a most amazing size and fatness, with a short sleek coat and a stumpy tail, which we used as a handle. He used to put his forefeet up on the mess table, knock off the cigarette-box, and then, bolting as many cigarettes as he could, would bound away from his pursuers *maaing* defiance. But his favourite food, his caviare, as one might say, was the tissue-paper on which copies of official correspondence were made. Chased by the whole company he would dodge round the inside of the fort with his mouth full of 'flimsies', snatched from the table of some unwary clerk. There was no way of punishing him short of death, for you cannot beat a goat, and if he was banished from the fort he always came back over the ramparts. He was a bad animal, but we were very fond of him all the same.

Well, as I have said, I was sitting in the Commandant's office in no very amiable frame of mind when the goat came in. He often showed up there on hot mornings, and lay down in the cool darkness of the corner where the porous water-jar stood. He was all right if you kept an eye on him. On this occasion, before going to his corner, he ambled over to me to have his head scratched. I scratched it mechanically, for my mind was fully occupied with other matters. The Supplies Officer had finished his business, and was just gathering up his papers, when suddenly a little gust of wind came eddying in through the doorway, picked up one of the 'flimsies' and deposited it playfully on the sandy floor. With an explosive '*Maa*' of delight, the goat bounded from under my hand, seized the paper in his mouth and was out of the door like a flash.

In a moment all was confusion. 'Stop him, sare,' yelled the Supplies Officer; 'it is the monthly return – I have no copy.'

Angus jumped up from behind his table, yelling to the orderly to catch the goat. Together we sprang for the doorway. Together we reached it. It was narrow, but it was only made of sticks and grass, and we crashed through. The goat was in full career across the parade ground, but from every side men were running to intercept him. The emergency was one which recurred at frequent intervals, and everyone knew what to do. If the beast was allowed to stop for a second he would swallow the paper – the only chance was to keep him on the move. It was hot out there in the glare of the morning sun, and the infernal goat, for all his bulk, twisted and doubled like a polo pony; but in the end one of the buglers got him by the tail, and though the youngster only acted as a feeble brake, it was enough, and the paper was recovered, damaged but still legible.

Martin had taken part in the chase, and when it was over he suggested that we had better adjourn to the mess for a 'cooler' before beginning work again. We did, and over the 'cooler' arranged the details of our afternoon's fishing. Angus made no objection, and I had not the courage to say anything in front of Martin. Looking back on it one can see that the confounded goat sealed his own fate.

In the afternoon Martin brought the box round to the mess, and we opened it. Angus made a feeble protest about doing it inside the fort, but Martin said it would be all right if we opened it gently. He got a chisel from the mess sergeant, and, working with great care, prised the lid off. One of the nails gave a screech as it came out, and we all jumped – even Martin. There was a good deal of tissue-paper inside and a packet of detonators in one corner, and when these were removed we came on the gelignite. It looked harmless enough, but I noticed that Martin handled it pretty gingerly. He picked out the smallest stick he could find, put one of the detonators in his pocket, and asked me to take the box back to the little hut. I stumbled as I was going through the gate, and nearly fainted with terror, but I replaced the box in the hut. There was some tissue-paper sticking out from under the lid, but I did not dare to stuff it back. It was hinted pretty freely, later, that I forgot to shut the door behind me when I went out. I do not know. I was not quite myself.

Angus got the boat out while Martin was cutting off a piece of fuse, and finally we all set out for the big pool down-stream from the fort. Angus took his seat in the bow, and Martin had, of course, to sit in the stern, so I rowed. We were all silent for a bit. Then Angus spoke, and his voice sounded strange.

'How are you going to make the hole in the gelignite for the detonator?' he asked.

'I sharpened up a pencil,' answered Martin. 'It's just about the right size, I think.'

'Is it smooth?' asked Angus, thinking evidently of the possibility of friction.

'As smooth as I could get it,' said Martin, 'but I couldn't find any sandpaper.'

'Good Heavens!' I groaned, and rowed as slowly as I could.

Presently we reached the pool and stopped in mid-stream. Martin was fumbling in his pocket when Angus spoke again.

'I don't know what you fellows feel about it,' he said, 'but I hate it. Have you ever done this sort of thing before, Martin?'

'Never,' replied Martin, and produced the stick of gelignite and the pencil.

'It's all right for you, of course,' went on Angus gloomily. 'You've *been* on leave, but I'm going next week.'

'By Jove, it's quite soft!' cried Martin, pressing the pencil into the gelignite. 'This is easy.' He fitted the detonator into the hole.

'Don't twist it, you ass,' I whispered tensely. 'Remember the friction.'

'Now for the fuse,' said Martin, disregarding me. 'I've brought along about a foot, so as to give us plenty of time to get clear before the explosion.'

This was unexpectedly thoughtful of Martin, and we registered relief. But the worst was to come. He worked silently for a bit, and then a puzzled expression came over his face. 'Dash it,' he muttered, 'this fuse is too small. It'll never stay in the detonator when I heave it overboard.'

It seemed as if our experiment would not take place after all, and, faced with this possibility, I had a strange revulsion of feeling. Instead of being relieved, I was genuinely disappointed. When you have screwed yourself up to a thing, however unwillingly, it is most annoying when it does not come off. But Martin was not to be so easily defeated. He took out the detonator and looked at it.

'I believe I could bite this thing on to the fuse,' he said.

'For Heaven's sake look out, man,' I urged him. 'Those detonators are infernally dangerous things in themselves. They're enough to blow your hand off.'

'I know,' he said, and put it in his mouth.

I could not stand it, and turned away my head. 'Oh, my rotten tooth,' I heard him mutter as he bit on the metal. His voice expressed intense relief when he spoke again. 'There, that's fixed it,' he said. 'And now for a match.'

'Are you sure it's the right kind of fuse?' asked Angus anxiously from the bow.

'I think so,' answered Martin. 'The man who sold it to me said it would burn all right under water.'

'I mean, is it a slow fuse?' continued Angus.

'He said it was slow; but I tried a bit this morning, and it didn't seem particularly slow to me. That's why I brought a long piece. Are you all ready?' Martin took up his matchbox.

'Go ahead!' said I, and turned the punt's nose towards the bank.

You could not see the flame of the match in the bright sunlight, and it seemed as if Martin had been holding it to the fuse for nearly a minute before there was a sudden jet of sparks from the end. 'Holy Smoke!' he yelled, and chucked the gelignite into the water.

I pulled with all my might, but the punt seemed to travel with nightmare slowness. All eyes were fixed upon the curl of smoke rising from the oily patch where the infernal machine had sunk.

'Pull!' yelled Angus, and smote me on the back. I gave a mighty heave. The punt surged forwards and stopped abruptly. I shot back from my seat on top of Angus' legs, pinning him down in the bows. Martin lurched, tripped over the thwart and fell upon my stomach. We struggled, cursing, in the bottom of the boat.

I suppose it must have been ten seconds before Martin and I managed to scramble over Angus into the long grass on the bank. We lay flat on our stomachs, and in a moment Angus joined us, looking, as Martin expressed it afterwards, 'bloody murder'. It seemed about half an hour since the thing had been thrown overboard, but still the spiral of smoke curled upwards from the water. Then suddenly there was a faint *pop*: an insignificant pimple rose gently on the calm bosom of the stream, and our experiment was over.

'That was only the detonator,' whispered Angus. 'It must have fallen out of the gelignite.'

'An inch of fuse would have been enough,' murmured Martin. 'We'll do better next time.'

We were all feeling, I think, a little ashamed of ourselves as we boarded the punt again and rowed out to look for stunned fish. There were no stunned fish, so we landed Martin on the point below the fort, and smoked our pipes in temporary security while he went up to fetch more gelignite and detonators. Apparently it was company washing-day, and most of the men were down beside the water in various stages of undress, while the bank was covered with white garments spread out to dry in the afternoon sunshine. It was a peaceful scene: women drawing water, children playing and men sitting or standing in groups under the scanty shade of the thorn-trees.

Martin had not been gone more than a few minutes when we heard him shouting from the direction of the fort. His voice was plain, but we could not catch what he was saying. At any rate he was in great excitement, and we pulled the punt on to the bank and started up the slope to see what it was all about. A silence had fallen on the busy scene.

And then, round the corner of the ramparts, came a stream of runners. Well out in front bounded the Commandant's goat. *Maaing* furiously and bounding about in the most extraordinary way, he sped towards us. Wondering what new crime he had committed, we assumed the usual formation, crouching in readiness to spring and catch him by the tail. Martin was close behind, and shouted as he ran. And now his words were audible.

'Look out! Look out!' he shouted. 'Don't touch him! Let him pass! He's mad! He has bolted all the gelignite! If he falls he'll explode!'

Hardly had Martin yelled the last words when he put his foot in a hole and came the most unholy cropper on his head. But his message had been given, and the crowd understood – understood, at least, that the goat must be given free passage. We all turned and fled for our lives.

The last act of the drama was tragic. Poor old goat! There was no doubt as to the stimulating action of the gelignite. It made him mad all right, or perhaps only drunk. I have seen men 'drunk' from eating cordite. Perhaps gelignite is even more powerful. His caperings were fantastic, his *maaings* continuous. I wonder what he thought of us all! The rôles were reversed. Instead of being the pursed, he was the pursuer. Finally, he seemed to get exhausted and tottered back towards the bank of the river. He waded in – for a drink, I suppose. We watched in silence. Would the water calm him?

The 'curtain' took us by surprise. A ripple moved swiftly across the stream. A long ugly snout broke the surface for a moment. There was a rush, a mighty splashing, a last frenzied *maa*, and the Commandant's goat vanished beneath the water.

'It was all your fault,' said Martin to me when we reached the mess. 'You must have left the door of the hut open.'

'Confound you and your beastly gelignite,' was all that I could reply. I was fond of that goat.

# Oh My Word!

## Frank Muir and Denis Norden

*It is a riddle wrapped in a mystery inside an enigma*

*Winston Churchill*
*Description of Russian foreign policy*

Knowing that my old friend Sherlock Holmes was partial to a newly-baked loaf, I stopped off at his bakers in Chamber Street before going on to his chambers in Baker Street.

But Holmes was not there.

This hardly surprised me. One day he might be in Marrakech removing secret papers from the safe of the Bosnian consulate in the guise of a Japanese wrestler, the next foiling an attempt to sabotage an assault on the Matterhorn in the guise of an Egyptian channel swimmer. There was no telling.

I settled myself in a comfortable old leather chair to await his return. The loaf looked delicious. I took a bite of the crust. It splintered with the noise of a small-calibre pistol shot and I was deluged with crumbs.

Quite a large part of my time was spent waiting for Holmes but this was no matter. I had no dependants to consider: I just sat there, a crusty old bachelor.

He, on the other hand, was the world's greatest criminologist; the ideal man to call upon when the Empire stood in jeopardy. I mused upon an idea I had had for some time of mounting an exhibition of relics of some of his greater triumphs: the odd hat-band, spy, dead dog and so forth. I would call it the Ideal Holmes Exhibition.

It was a quarter to five the following afternoon that I was interrupted from my reverie by a distant but unmistakable sound: the oath of a cabby who has been under-tipped. Moments later I heard footsteps on the stairs and Holmes appeared in the doorway. He flung his deerstalker hat away from him distractedly. It circled the room twice, clearly seeking a suitable landing site, before settling gently upon the beak of a stuffed ptarmigan. And then he saw me and his eyes lit up.

'Lily Langtry!' he cried, taking my hand. 'By all that's delightful!'

'It's me – Watson!' I said.

'Then what are you doing there in a dress covered with beige spots?' he demanded fiercely.

'They are breadcrumbs, old friend,' I said, brushing them off. I could see that he had something on his mind.

After a moment of restless pacing he suddenly said, 'I have just been given tea by Her Majesty's Foreign Secretary – '

'Earl Grey?'

'No,' he said. 'A fairly ordinary Darjeeling. Grown, I rather fancy, on that south-facing hill just above the handbag factory. He gave me very worrying news.'

Holmes paced the room again. The cat was sitting asleep on his chair and Holmes bent to tickle it behind an ear.

'Watson, my violin if you please.'

I handed it to him and with a forehand drive worthy of the great Dr Grace himself, he batted the cat out of the chair and on to the floor. He settled himself comfortably into the chair.

'I am informed, Watson, that there is in this country an important Balkan princeling, here under the protection of Her Britannic Majesty. He has travelled from his own squalid little country to Britain in order to undergo an operation at which our British surgeons lead the world. The removal of an in-growing toe-nail.'

'Just so. What we medical men call a "piggyectomy".'

'Would you mind shutting up while I'm talking?'

I nodded assent.

'The Foreign Office believe that an attempt is going to be made on the prince's life. Tonight.'

'But by whom? Holmes. By whom? – if you will pardon the understandable interruption.'

'There is a secret sect in Russia whose members are trained in all techniques of assassination. Their job is to spread out over Europe and foment revolution. They are fanatics and will stop at nothing – not even road signs saying "Major Road Ahead".'

'Good grief,' I whispered.

'When a member is fully trained there is a strange Russian indoctrination ceremony. Their leader, a mysterious lady known as Sister Anna, kisses him on both cheeks twice and he is then known by a special name.'

'What name?'

'He is thereafter known as an – Anarchist.'

My blood went cold.

'Our information is that they are in London and have their orders to poison the prince tonight, thus provoking a diplomatic incident which might lead to a major conflagration among the leading nations of Europe.'

Holmes had already taken every precaution. A police constable was on duty by the side of every bed in the Charing Cross Hospital where the prince lay. Eight men were on permanent duty round the prince's bed. No visitors were to be allowed in. The prince was to eat nothing and drink nothing until it was all over.

'Wait a minute, Holmes. The prince will be under an anaesthetic. Can they not get him *then* and make him swallow something?'

'He will not lose consciousness at any time. A local anaesthetic will be applied to his foot, which will go to sleep.'

'Ah yes. A condition we doctors call comatose.'

'What is worrying me, Watson, is that these fiends are masters of disguise. I am sure that they are already within the hospital disguised as porters, or matrons or bunches of grapes. But how – how, man – will they strike? How will they force the poison *down* him? They must force the poison *down* him in some manner or . . .'

'But, Holmes, you have nothing to go on!'

'Then I will borrow your bike.'

I waited for two hours, fortifying myself with eating the remains of the loaf, which I found lodged within my waistcoat.

He strode into the room with a look of quiet triumph on his hawk-like face.

'The assassination will not take place,' he said. 'I found the murder device and the fiends have been apprehended, lurking within the hospital walls disguised as light diets. This is what they proposed to use to introduce the poison into the prince!'

He flung on to the table an object I knew well from my medical practice. It was a long rubber tube with a bulb at one end. Near the end of the tube was an odd bulge.

'There is the proof that the villains were Russian anarchists,' he cried.

'But how did they suppose to use this to poison the prince?' I faltered. 'By what system?'

'Alimentary, my dear Watson. If you will do me the goodness to take the device apart I will deduce what you will find therein.'

I did so.

'I think you will find,' said Holmes, 'that you have in your hand a wee doll, made of wood, with "Made in the Ukraine" stamped on its base.'

'Correct, Holmes.'

'It is, of course, the smallest of a nest of eight, which are popular with Russian children. Be careful how you handle it, Watson. Inside the doll will be a poison which is tasteless, odourless, colourless and for which even our music-halls have no known anecdote.'

'There seems to be a piece of paper wrapped around the doll, Holmes.'

'I think you will find that it is a page ripped at random from some cheap edition of a mystery novel. It is there to hold the doll firmly within the tube.'

'Correct. It is a page from Wilkie Collins's famous mystery, *The Woman in White*. Amazing, Holmes! But how did you deduce from this device that it spelled Russia?'

Holmes lit his pipe, injected himself with a snort of cocaine and played a swift chorus of Monti's *Czardas* on the violin before saying, quietly: 'See what it is, man – ?

'It is a wee doll wrapped in a mystery inside an enema.'

# Getting Married

## *A. A. Milne*

### I. THE DAY

Probably you thought that getting married was quite a simple business. So did I. We were both wrong; it is the very dickens. Of course, I am not going to draw back now. As I keep telling Celia, her Ronald is a man of powerful fibre, and when he says he will do a thing he does it – eventually. She shall have her wedding all right; I have sworn it. But I do wish that there weren't so many things to be arranged first.

The fact that we had to fix a day was broken to me one afternoon when Celia was showing me to some relatives of hers in the Addison Road. I got entangled with an elderly cousin on the hearth-rug; and though I know nothing about motor-bicycles I talked about them for several hours under the impression that they were his subject. It turned out afterwards that he was equally ignorant of them, but thought they were mine. Perhaps we shall get on better at a second meeting. However, just when we were both thoroughly sick of each other, Celia broke off her gay chat with an aunt to say to me:

'By the way, Ronald, we did settle on the eleventh, didn't we?'

I looked at her blankly, my mind naturally full of motor-bicycles.

'The wedding,' smiled Celia.

'Right-o,' I said with enthusiasm. I was glad to be assured that I should not go on talking about motor-bicycles for ever, and that on the eleventh, anyhow, there would be a short interruption for the ceremony. Feeling almost friendly to the cousin, I plunged into his favourite subject again.

On the way home Celia returned to the matter.

'Or you would rather it was the twelfth?' she asked.

'I've never heard a word about this before,' I said. 'It all comes as a surprise to me.'

'Why, I'm *always* asking you.'

'Well, it's very forward of you, and I don't know what young people are coming to nowadays. Celia, what's the *good* of my talking to your cousin for three hours about motor-bicycling? Surely one can get married just as well without that?'

'One can't get married without settling the day,' said Celia, coming cleverly back to the point.

Well, I suppose one can't. But somehow I had expected to be spared all this bother. I think my idea was that Celia would say to me suddenly one evening, 'By the way, Ronald, don't forget we're being married to-morrow,' and I should have said 'Where?' And on being told the time and place I should have turned up pretty punctually; and after my best man had told me where to stand, and the clergyman had told me what to say, and my solicitor had told me where to sign my name, we should have driven from the church a happy married couple . . . and in the carriage Celia would have told me where we were spending the honeymoon.

However, it was not to be so.

'All right, the eleventh,' I said. 'Any particular month?'

'No,' smiled Celia, 'just any month. Or, if you like, every month.'

'The eleventh of June,' I surmised. 'It is probably the one day in the year on which my uncle Thomas cannot come. But no matter. The eleventh let it be.'

'Then that's settled. And at St Miriam's?'

For some reason Celia has set her heart on St Miriam's. Personally I have no feeling about it. St Andrew's-by-the-Wardrobe or St Bartholomew's-Without would suit me equally well.

'All right,' I said, 'St Miriam's.'

There, you might suppose, the matter would have ended; but no.

'Then you will see about it to-morrow?' said Celia persuasively.

I was appalled at the idea.

'Surely,' I said, 'this is for you, or your father, or – or somebody to arrange.'

'Of *course* it's for the bridegroom,' protested Celia.

'In theory, perhaps. But anyhow not the bridegroom personally. His best man . . . or his solicitor . . . or . . . I mean, you're not suggesting that I myself – Oh, well, if you insist. Still, I must say I don't see what's the good of having a best man *and* a solicitor if – Oh, all right, Celia, I'll go tomorrow.'

So I went. For half an hour I padded round St Miriam's nervously, and then summoning up all my courage, I knocked my pipe out and entered.

'I want,' I said jauntily to a sexton or a sacristan or something – 'I want – er – a wedding.' And I added, 'For two.'

He didn't seem as nervous as I was. He inquired quite calmly when I wanted it.

'The eleventh of June,' I said. 'It's probably the one day in the year on which my Uncle Thomas – However, that wouldn't interest you. The point is that it's the eleventh.'

The clerk consulted his wedding-book. Then he made the surprising announcement that the only day he could offer me in June was the seventeenth. I was amazed.

'I am a very old customer,' I said reproachfully. 'I mean, I have often been to your church in my time. Surely – '

'We've weddings fixed on all the other days.'

'Yes, yes, but you could persuade somebody to change his day, couldn't you? Or if he is very much set on being married on the eleventh you might recommend some other church to him. I dare say you know of some good ones. You see, Celia – my – that is, we're particularly keen for some reason, on St Miriam's.'

The clerk didn't appreciate my suggestion. He insisted that the seventeenth was the only day.

'Then will you have the seventeenth?' he asked.

'My dear fellow, I can't possibly say off-hand,' I protested. 'I am not alone in this. I have a friend with me. I will go back and tell her what you say. She may decide to withdraw her offer altogether.'

I went back and told Celia.

'Bother,' she said. 'What shall we do?'

'There are other churches. There's your own, for example.'

'Yes, but you know I don't like that. Why *shouldn't* we be married on the seventeenth?'

'I don't know at all. It seems an excellent day; it lets in my Uncle Thomas. Of course, it may exclude my Uncle William, but one can't have everything.'

'Then will you go and fix it for the seventeenth tomorrow?'

'Can't I send my solicitor this time?' I asked. 'Of course, if you particularly want me to go myself, I will. But really, dear, I seem to be living at St Miriam's nowadays.'

And even that wasn't the end of the business. For, just as I was leaving her, Celia broke it to me that St. Miriam's was neither in her parish nor in mine, and that, in order to qualify as a bridegroom, I should have to hire a room somewhere near.

'But I am very comfortable where I am,' I assured her.

'You needn't live there, Ronald. You only want to leave a hat there, you know.'

'Oh, very well,' I sighed.

She came to the hall with me; and, having said good-bye to her, I repeated my lesson.

'The seventeenth, fix it up tomorrow, take a room near St Miriam's, and leave a hat there. Good-bye.'

'Good-bye. . . And oh, Ronald!' She looked at me critically as I stood in the doorway. 'You might leave *that* one,' she said.


## II. FURNISHING

'By the way,' said Celia suddenly, 'what have you done about the fixtures?'

'Nothing,' I replied truthfully.

'Well, we must do *something* about them.'

'Yes. My solicitor – he shall do something about them. Don't let's talk about them now. I've only got three hours more with you, and then I must dash back to my work.'

I must say that any mention of fixtures has always bored me intensely. When it was a matter of getting a house to live in I was all energy. As soon as Celia had found it, I put my solicitor on to it; and within a month I had signed my name in two places, and was the owner of a highly residential flat in the best part of the neighbourhood. But my effort so exhausted me that I have felt utterly unable since to cope with the question of the curtain-rod in the bathroom or whatever it is that Celia means by fixtures. These things will arrange themselves somehow, I feel confident.

Meanwhile the decorators are hard at work. A thrill of pride inflates me when I think of the decorators at work. I don't know how they got there; I suppose I must have ordered them. Celia says that *she* ordered them and chose all the papers herself, and that all I did was to say that the papers she had chosen were very pretty; but this doesn't sound like me in the least. I am convinced that I was the man of action when it came to ordering decorators.

'And now,' said Celia one day, 'we can go and choose the electric-light fittings.'

'Celia,' I said in admiration, 'you're a wonderful person. I should have forgotten all about them.'

'Why, they're about the most important thing in the flat.'

'Somehow I never regarded anybody as choosing them. I thought they just grew in the wall. From bulbs.'

When we got into the shop Celia became business-like at once.

'We'd better start with the hall,' she told the man.

'Everybody else will have to,' I said, 'so we may as well.'

'What sort of a light did you want there?' he asked.

'A strong one,' I said; 'so as to be able to watch our guests carefully when they pass the umbrella-stand.'

Celia waved me away and explained that we wanted a hanging lantern. It appeared that this shop made a speciality not so much of the voltage as of the lamps enclosing it.

'How do you like that?' asked the man, pointing to a magnificent affair in brass. He wandered off to a switch, and turned it on.

'Dare you ask him the price?' I asked Celia. 'It looks to me about a thousand pounds. If it is, say that you don't like the style. Don't let him think we can't afford it.'

'Yes,' said Celia, in a careless sort of way. 'I'm not sure that I care about that. How much is it?'

'Two pounds.'

I was not going to show my relief. 'Without the light, of course?' I said disparagingly.

'How do you think it would look in the hall?' said Celia to me.

'I think our guests would be encouraged to proceed. They'd see that we were pretty good people.'

'I don't like it. It's too ornate.'

'Then show us something less ornate,' I told the man sternly.

He showed us things less ornate. At the end of an hour Celia said she thought we'd better get on to another room, and come back to the hall afterwards. We decided to proceed to the drawing-room.

'We must go all out over these,' said Celia; 'I want these to be really beautiful.'

At the end of another hour Celia said she thought we'd better get on to my workroom. My workroom, as the name implies, is the room to which I am to retire when I want complete quiet. Sometimes I shall go there after lunch . . . and have it.

'We can come back to the drawing-room afterwards,' she said. 'It's really very important that we should get the right ones for that. Your room won't be so difficult, but, of course, you must have awfully nice ones.'

I looked at my watch.

'It's a quarter to one,' I said. 'At 2.15 on the seventeenth of June we are due at St Miriam's. If you think we shall have bought anything by then, let's go on. If, as seems to me, there is no hope at all, then let's have lunch today anyhow. After lunch we may be able to find some way out of the impasse.'

After lunch I had an idea.

'This afternoon,' I said, 'we will begin to get some furniture together.'

'But what about the electric fittings? We must finish off those.'

'This is an experiment. I want to see if we can buy a chest of drawers. It may just be our day for it.'

'And we settle the fittings to-morrow. Yes?'

'I don't know. We may not want them. It all depends on whether we can buy a chest of drawers this afternoon. If we can't, then I don't see how we can ever be married on the seventeenth of June. Somebody's got to be, because I've engaged the church. The question is whether it's going to be us. Let's go and buy a chest of drawers this afternoon, and see.'

The old gentleman in the little shop Celia knew of was delighted to see us.

'Chestesses? Ah, you 'ave come to the right place.' He led the way into the depths. 'There now. There's a chest – real old, that is.' He gave it a hearty smack. 'You don't see a chest like that nowadays. They can't *make* 'em. Three pound ten. You couldn't have got that tomorrer. I'd have sold it for four pound to-morrer.'

'I knew it was our day,' I said.

'Real old, that is. Spanish me'ogany, all oak lined. That's right, sir, pull the drawers out and see for yourself. Let the lady see. There's no imitation there, lady. A real old chest, that is. Come in 'ere in a week and you'd have to pay five pounds for it. Me'ogany's going up, you see, that's how.'

'Well?' I said to Celia.

'It's perfectly sweet. Hadn't we better see some more?'

We saw two more. Both of them Spanish me'ogany, oak lined, pull-the-drawers-out-and-see-for-yourself-lady. Half an hour passed rapidly.

'Well?' I said.

'I really don't know which I like best. Which do you?'

'The first; it's nearer the door.'

'There's another shop just over the way. We'd better just look there too, and then we can come back to decide tomorrow.'

We went out. I glanced at my watch. It was 3.30, and we were being married at 2.15 on the seventeenth of June.

'Wait a moment,' I said, 'I've forgotten my gloves.'

I may be a slow starter, but I am very firm when roused. I went into the shop, wrote a cheque for the three chests of drawers, and told the man where to send them. When I returned, Celia was at the shop opposite, pulling the drawers out of a real old mahogany chest which was standing on the pavement outside.

'This is even better,' she said. 'It's perfectly adorable. I wonder if it's more expensive.'

'I'll just ask,' I said.

I went in and, without an unnecessary word, bought that chest too. Then I came back to Celia. It was 3.45, and on the seventeenth of June at 2.15 – Well, we had four chests of drawers towards it.

'Celia,' I said, 'we may just do it yet.'

### III. THE HONEYMOON

'I know I oughtn't to be dallying here,' I said; 'I ought to be doing something strenuous in preparation for the wedding. Counting the bells at St Miriam's, or varnishing the floors in the flat, or – Tell me what I ought to be doing, Celia, and I'll go on not doing it for a bit.'

'There's the honeymoon,' said Celia.

'I knew there was something.'

'Do tell me what you're doing about it?'

'Thinking about it.'

'You haven't written to anyone about rooms yet.'

'Celia,' I said reproachfully, 'you seem to have forgotten why I am marrying you.'

When Celia was browbeaten into her present engagement, she said frankly that she was only consenting to marry me because of my pianola, which she had always coveted. In return I pointed out that I was only asking her to marry me because I wanted somebody to write my letters. There opened before me, in that glad moment, a vista of invitations and accounts-rendered all answered promptly by Celia, instead of put off till next month by me. It was a wonderful vision to one who (very properly) detests letter-writing. And yet, here she was, even before the ceremony, expecting me to enter into a deliberate correspondence with all sorts of strange people who as yet had not come into my life at all. It was too much.

'We will get,' I said, 'your father to write some letters for us.'

'But what's he got to do with it?'

'I don't want to complain of your father, Celia, but it seems to me that he is not doing his fair share. There ought to be a certain give-and-take in the matter. *I* find you a nice church to be married in – good. *He* finds you a nice place to honeymoon in – excellent. After all, you are still his daughter.'

'All right,' said Celia, 'I'll ask father to do it "Dear Mrs Bunn, my little boy wants to spend his holidays with you in June. I am writing to ask you if you will take care of him and see that he doesn't do anything dangerous. He has a nice disposition, but wants watching." ' She patted my head gently. 'Something like that.'

I got up and went to the writing-desk.

'I can see I shall have to do it myself,' I sighed. 'Give me the address and I'll begin.'

'But we haven't quite settled where we're going yet, have we?'

I put the pen down thankfully and went back to the sofa.

'Good! Then I needn't write today, anyhow. It is wonderful, dear, how difficulties roll away when you face them. Almost at once we arrive at the conclusion that I needn't write today. Splendid! Well, where

shall we go? This will want a lot of thought. Perhaps,' I added, 'I
needn't write tomorrow.'

'We had almost fixed on England, hadn't we?'

'Somebody was telling me that Lynton was very beautiful. I should
like to go to Lynton.'

'But *every one* goes to Lynton for their honeymoon.'

'Then let's be original and go to Birmingham. "The happy couple
left for Birmingham, where the honeymoon will be spent." Sensation.'

' "The bride left the train at Ealing." More sensation.'

'I think the great thing,' I said, trying to be business-like, 'is to fix the
county first. If we fixed on Rutland, then the rest would probably be
easy.'

'The great thing,' said Celia, 'is to decide what we want. Sea, or river,
or mountains, or – or golf.'

At the word golf I coughed and looked out of the window.

Now I am very fond of Celia – I mean of golf, and – what I really
mean, of course, is that I am very fond of both of them. But I do think
that on a honeymoon Celia should come first. After all, I shall have
plenty of other holidays for golf . . . although, of course, three weeks in
the summer without any golf at all – Still, I think Celia should come
first.

'Our trouble,' I said to her, 'is that neither of us has ever been on a
honeymoon before, and so we've no idea what it will be like. After all,
why should we get bored with each other? Surely we don't depend on
golf to amuse us?'

'All the same, I think your golf *would* amuse me,' said Celia. 'Besides,
I want you to be as happy as you possibly can be.'

'Yes, but supposing I was slicing my drives all the time, I should be
miserable. I should be torn between the desire to go back to London
and have a lesson with the professional and the desire to stay on
honeymooning with you. One can't be happy in a quandary like that.'

'Very well then, no golf. Settled?'

'Quite. Now then, let's decide about the scenery. What sort of soil do
you prefer?'

When I left Celia that day we had agreed on this much: that we
wouldn't bother about golf, and that the mountains, rivers, valleys, and
so on should be left entirely to Nature. All we were to inquire for was (in
the words of an advertisement Celia had seen) 'a perfect spot for a

honeymoon.'

In the course of the next day I heard of seven spots; varying from a spot in Surrey 'dotted with firs,' to a dot in the Pacific spotted with – I forget what, natives probably. Taken together they were the seven only possible spots for a honeymoon.

'We shall have to have seven honeymoons,' I said to Celia when I had told her my news. 'One honeymoon, one spot.'

'Wait,' she said. 'I have heard of an ideal spot.'

'Speaking as a spot expert, I don't think that's necessarily better than an only possible spot,' I objected. 'Still, tell me about it.'

'Well, to begin with, it's close to the sea.'

'So we can bathe when we're bored. Good.'

'And it's got a river, if you want to fish – '

'I don't. I should hate to catch a fish who was perhaps on his honeymoon too. Still, I like the idea of a river.'

'And quite a good mountain, and lovely walks, and, in fact, everything. Except a picture-palace, luckily.'

'It sounds all right,' I said doubtfully. 'We might just spend the next day or two thinking about my seven spots, and then I might . . . possibly . . . feel strong enough to write.'

'Oh, I nearly forgot. I *have* written, Ronald.'

'You have?' I cried. 'Then, my dear, what else matters? It's a perfect spot.' I lay back in relief. 'And there, thank 'Evings, is another thing settled. Bless you!'

'Yes. And, by the way, there *is* golf quite close too. But that,' she smiled, 'needn't prevent us going there.'

'Of course not. We shall just ignore the course.'

'Perhaps, so as to be on the safe side, you'd better leave your clubs behind.'

'Perhaps I'd better,' I said carelessly.

All the same I don't think I will. One never knows what may happen . . . and at the outset of one's matrimonial career to have to go to the expense of an entirely new set of clubs would be a most regrettable business.

'I suppose,' I said, 'it's too late to cancel this wedding now?'

'Well,' said Celia, 'the invitations are out, and the presents are pouring in, and mother's just ordered the most melting dress for herself that you ever saw. Besides, who's to live in the flat if we don't?'

'There's a good deal in what you say. Still, I am alarmed, seriously alarmed. Look here.' I drew out a printed slip and flourished it before her.

'Not a writ? My poor Ronald!'

'Worse than that. This is the St Miriam's bill of fare for weddings. Celia, I had no idea marriage was so expensive. I thought one rolled-gold ring would practically see it.'

It was a formidable document. Starting with 'full choir and organ' which came to a million pounds, and working down through 'boys' voices only,' and 'red carpet' to 'policemen for controlling traffic – per policeman, 5s.,' it included altogether some two dozen ways of disposing of my savings.

'If we have the whole menu,' I said, 'I shall be ruined. You wouldn't like to have a ruined husband.'

Celia took the list and went through it carefully.

'I might say "Season," ' I suggested, 'or "Press." '

'Well, to begin with,' said Celia, 'we needn't have a full choir.'

'Need we have an organ or a choir at all? In thanking people for their kind presents you might add, "By the way, do you sing?" Then we could arrange to have all the warblers in the front. My best man or my solicitor could give the note.'

'Boys' voices only,' decided Celia. 'Then what about bells?'

'I should like some nice bells. If the price is "per bell" we might give an order for five good ones.'

'Let's do without bells. You see, they don't begin to ring till we've left the church, so they won't be any good to *us*.'

This seemed to me an extraordinary line to take.

'My dear child,' I remonstrated, 'the whole thing is being got up not for ourselves, but for our guests. We shall be much too preoccupied to appreciate any of the good things we provide – the texture of the red carpet or the quality of the singing. I dreamt last night that I quite forgot about the wedding-ring till 1.30 on the actual day, and the only cab I could find to take me to a jeweller's was drawn by a camel. Of course, it may not turn out to be as bad as that, but it will certainly be an anxious afternoon for both of us. And so we must consider the entertainment entirely from the point of view of our guests. Whether their craving is for champagne or bells, it must be satisfied.'

'I'm sure they'll be better without bells. Because when the policemen call out "Mr Spifkins' carrriage," Mr Spifkins mightn't hear if there were a lot of bells clashing about.'

'Very well, no bells. But, mind you,' I said sternly, 'I shall insist on a clergyman.'

We went through the rest of the menu, course by course.

'I know what I shall do,' I said at last. 'I shall call on my friend the Clerk again, and I shall speak to him quite frankly. I shall say, "Here is a cheque for a thousand pounds. It is all I can afford – and, by the way, you'd better pay it in quickly or it will be dishonoured. Can you do us up a nice wedding for a thousand inclusive?" '

'Like the Christmas hampers at the stores.'

'Exactly. A dozen boys' voices, a half dozen of bells, ten yards of awning, and twenty-four oranges, or vergers, or whatever it is. We ought to get a nice parcel for a thousand pounds.'

'Or,' said Celia, 'we might send the list round to our friends as suggestions for wedding presents. I'm sure Jane would love to give us a couple of policemen.'

'We'd much better leave the whole thing to your father. I incline more and more to the opinion that it is *his* business to provide the wedding. I must ask my solicitor about it.'

'He's providing the bride.'

'Yes, but I think he might go further. I can't help feeling that the bells would come very well from him. "Bride's father to bridegroom – A peal of bells." People would think it was something in silver for the hall. It would do him a lot of good in business circles.'

'And that reminds me,' smiled Celia, 'there's been some talk about a present from Miss Popley.'

I have come to the conclusion that it is impossible to get married decently unless one's life is ordered on some sort of system. Mine never has been; and the result is that I make terrible mistakes – particularly in the case of Miss Popley. At the beginning of the business, when the news got round to Miss Popley, I received from her a sweet letter of congratulation. Knowing that she was rather particular in these matters I braced myself up and thanked her heartily by return of post. Three days later, when looking for a cheque I had lost, I accidentally came across her letter. 'Help, help!' I cried. 'This came days ago, and I haven't answered yet.' I sat down at once and thanked her enthusiastically. Another week passed and I began to feel that I must really make an effort to catch my correspondence up; so I got out all my letters of congratulation of the last ten days and devoted an afternoon to answering them. I used much the same form of thanks in all of them . . . with the exception of Miss Popley's, which was phrased particularly warmly.

So much for that. But Miss Popley is Celia's dear friend also. When I made out my list of guests I included Miss Popley; so, in her list, did Celia. The result was that Miss Popley received two invitations to the wedding . . . Sometimes I fear she must think we are pursuing her.

'What does she say about a present?' I asked.

'She wants us to tell her what we want.'

'What *are* we to say? If we said an elephant – '

'With a small card tied on to his ear, and "Best wishes from Miss Popley" on it. It would look heavenly among the other presents.'

'You see what I mean, Celia. Are we to suggest something worth a thousand pounds, or something worth ninepence? It's awfully kind of her, but it makes it jolly difficult for us.'

'Something that might cost anything from ninepence to a thousand pounds,' suggested Celia.

'Then that washes out the elephant.'

'Can't you get the ninepenny ones now?'

'I suppose,' I said, reverting to the subject which most weighed on me, 'she wouldn't like to give the men's voices for the choir?'

'No, I think a clock,' said Celia. 'A clock can cost anything you like – or don't like.'

'Right-o. And perhaps we'd better settle now. When it comes, how many times shall we write and thank her fot it?'

Celia considered 'Four times, I think,' she said.

Well, as Celia says, it's too late to draw back now. But I shall be glad when it's all over. As I began by saying, there's too much 'arranging' and 'settling' and 'fixing' about the thing for me. In the necessary negotiations and preparations I fear I have not shone. And so I shall be truly glad when we have settled down in our flat . . . and Celia can restore my confidence in myself once more by talking loudly to her domestic staff about 'The Master'.

# Memoirs of a Drudge

## *James Thurber*

Mr Thurber . . . went to Ohio State University for his formal education. His informal education included . . . drudgery on several newspapers – in Columbus, in New York, and in Paris. – From *Horse Sense in American Humor*, by Walter Blair.

I don't know about that. There is, of course, a certain amount of drudgery in newspaper work, just as there is in teaching classes, tunnelling into a bank, or being President of the United States. I suppose that even the most pleasurable of imaginable occupations, that of batting baseballs through the windows of the R.C.A. Building, would pall a little as the days ran on. Seldom, it is true, do I gather my grandchildren about my knees and tell them tall tales out of my colourful years as a leg man, but I often sit in the cane-seated rocker on the back porch, thinking of the old days and cackling with that glee known only to ageing journalists. Just the other evening, when the womenfolks were washing up the supper dishes and setting them to dreen, they could hear me rocking back and forth and laughing to myself. I was thinking about the Riviera edition of the *Chicago Tribune* in southern France during the winter of 1925–6.

Seven or eight of us had been assigned to the task of getting out a little six-page newspaper, whose stories were set up in 10-point type, instead of the customary 8-point, to make life easier for everybody, including the readers. Most of our news came by wire from the Paris edition, and all we had to do was write headlines for it, a pleasurable occupation if you are not rushed, and we were never rushed. For the rest, we copied from the *Éclaireur de Nice et du Sud-Est*, a journal filled with droll and mystical stories, whose translation, far from being drudgery, was pure joy. Nice, in that indolent winter, was full of knaves and rascals, adventurers and impostors, *pochards* and *indiscrets*, whose ingenious exploits, sometimes in full masquerade costume, sometimes in the nude, were easy and pleasant to record.

We went to work after dinner and usually had the last chronicle of the diverting day written and ready for the linotypers well before midnight. It was then our custom to sit around for half an hour, making up items for the society editor's column. She was too pretty, we thought, to waste the soft southern days tracking down the arrival of prominent persons on the Azure Coast. So all she had to do was stop in at the Ruhl and the Negresco each day and pick up the list of guests who had just registered. The rest of us invented enough items to fill up the last half of her column, and a gay and romantic cavalcade, indeed, infested the littoral of our imagination. 'Lieutenant General and Mrs Pendleton Gray Winslow,' we would write, 'have arrived at their villa, Heart's Desire, on Cap d'Antibes, bringing with them their prize Burmese monkey, Thibault.' Or 'The Hon. Mr Stephen H. L. Atterbury, Chargé-d'Affaires of the American Legation in Peru, and Mrs Atterbury, the former Princess Ti Ling of Thibet are motoring to Monte Carlo from Aix-en-Provence, where they have been visiting Mr Atterbury's father, Rear Admiral A. Watson Atterbury, U.S.N., retired. Mr Stephen Atterbury is the breeder of the famous Schnauzer-Pincer, Champion Adelbert von Weigengrosse of Tamerlane, said to be valued at $15,000.' In this manner we turned out, in no time at all, and with the expenditure of very little mental energy, the most glittering column of social notes in the history of the American newspaper, either here or abroad.

As the hour of midnight struck twice, in accordance with the dreamy custom of town and church clocks in southern France, and our four or five hours of drudgery were ending, the late Frank Harris would often drop in at the *Tribune* office, and we would listen to stories of Oscar Wilde, Walt Whitman, Bernard Shaw, Emma Goldman and Frank Harris. Thus ran the harsh and exacting tenor of those days of slavery.

It is true that the languorous somnolence of our life was occasionally broken up. This would happen about one night a week, around ten o'clock, when our French composing room went on strike. The printers and their foreman, a handsome, black-bearded giant of a man, whose rages resembled the mistral, wanted to set up headlines in their own easygoing way, using whatever size type was handiest and whatever space it would fit into most easily. That is the effortless hit-or-miss

system which has made a crazy quilt of French newspaper headlines for
two hundred years, and André and his men could not understand why
we stubbornly refused to adopt so sane and simple a method. So now
and then, when he couldn't stand our stupid and inviolable headline
schedules any longer, André would roar into our little city room like a
storm from the Alps. Behind him in the doorway stood his linotypers,
with their hats and coats on. Since the Frenchmen could comprehend
no English and spoke only *Niçois*, an argot entirely meaningless to us,
our arguments were carried on in shouting and gesticulating and a
great deal of waving of French and American newspapers in each
other's faces. After a while all the combatants on both sides would
adjourn to the bar next door, still yelling and gesturing, but after four or
five rounds of beer we would fall to singing old Provençal songs and new
American ones, and there would be a truce for another six or seven
days, everybody going back to work, still singing.

On one of those nights of battle, song and compromise, several of us
defenders of the immutable American headline went back to the bar
after we had got the *Tribune* to press and sat up till dawn, drinking *grog
américain.* Just as the sun came up, we got on a train for Cannes, where
the most talked-about international struggle of the year was to take
place that afternoon, the tennis match between Suzanne Lenglen and
Helen Wills. As we climbed aboard, one of my colleagues, spoiling for
an argument, declared that a French translation he had read of Edgar
Allen Poe's 'The Raven' was infinitely superior to the poem in the
original English. How we had got around to this curious subject I have
no idea, but it seemed natural enough at the time. I remember that a
young reporter named Middleton visited all the compartments on the
train, demanding of their sleepy and startled French occupants if they
did not believe that a raven was more likely to say '*Jamais plus*' than
'Nevermore'. He returned with the claim that our fellow-passengers to
a man were passionately on the side of '*Jamais plus*'. So passed a night of
drudgery in the fond, far-away days of the Third Republic and the
Riviera edition of the *Chicago Tribune*.

We had the long days of warm blue weather for our own, to climb the
Corniche roads or wind up the mountain in a *char à bancs* examining the
little miracles and grotesqueries of the time.

I wrote only one story a day, usually consisting of fewer than a
thousand words. Most of the reporters, when they went out on

assignments, first had to get their foot in the door, but the portals of the fantastic and the unique are always left open. If an astonished botanist produced a black evening primrose, or thought he had produced one, I spent the morning prowling his gardens. When a lady in the West Seventies sent in word that she was getting messages from the late Walter Savage Landor in heaven, I was sent up to see what the importunate poet had on his mind. On the occasion of the arrival in town of Major Monroe of Jacksonville, Florida, who claimed to be a hundred and seventeen years old, I walked up Broadway with him while he roundly cursed the Northern dogs who jostled him, bewailing the while the passing of Bob Lee and Tom Jackson and Joe Johnston. I studied gypsies in Canarsie and generals in the Waldorf, listened to a man talk backward, and watched a blindfolded boy play ping-pong. Put it all together and I don't know what it comes to, but it wasn't drudgery.

It was not often, in the *Post* or no *Sturn-und-Drang* phase, that I wandered farther afield than the confines of Greater New York. On the occasion of the hundred-and-fiftieth anniversary of Washington's crossing the Delaware, however, I was sent over to Trenton to report the daylong celebration. (Once in a long while I got a spot news assignment like that.) At a little past ten in the morning I discovered the hotel room which a group of the more convivial newspapermen had set up as their headquarters, and at a little past twelve I was asleep in a chair there. When I woke up it was dark, and the celebration was over. I hadn't sent anything to my paper, and by that time it was too late. I went home. The *Post*, I found out, had used the Associated Press account of what went on in Trenton.

When I got to work the next morning, the city editor came over to my desk. 'Let's see,' he said, 'what did I send you out on yesterday?' 'It didn't pan out,' I told him. 'No story.' 'The hell with it, then,' he said. 'Here, get on this – lady says there are violets growing in the snow over in Red Bank.' 'Violets don't grow in the snow,' I reminded him. 'They might in Red Bank,' he said. 'Slide on over there.' I slid instead to a bar and put in a phone call to the Chief of Police in Red Bank. A desk sergeant answered and I asked him about the violets. 'Ain't no violence over here,' he told me, and hung up. It wasn't much to hang a story on, as we say, but I hung one on it. But first I had a few more drinks with a man I had met at the bar, very pleasant fellow, captain of a barge or

something. Shortly after the strange case of the violets in the snow, I left
the newspaper game and drifted into the magazine game.

And now, in closing, I wish to leave with my little readers, both boys
and girls, this parting bit of advice: Stay out of the magazine game.

# The Glacier

## *W. E. Bowman*

Two days later we reached the snout of the glacier and commenced the long haul to Base Camp. Here we roped up for the first time. Jungle went first as route-finder, with Shute, who was to take films of us at some convenient point. With them were ten porters carrying camera and accessories. Burley and Wish followed. The former was suffering from glacier lassitude but was expected to acclimatize shortly. Then came Constant and Prone. The latter had developed German measles but was receiving the best of treatment at his own capable hands. The porters were distributed between the various parties. I stayed behind to meditate for a while on the responsibilities of leadership, and so brought up the rear.

The glacier was over a mile wide, deeply crevassed and littered with innumerable blocks of ice, most of them twenty to thirty feet high. The place was a veritable maze. Even the highest peaks were hidden from sight.

After some hours' march I was gratified to see in front of me the film gear, fully operational, with Shute at the handle. I left him to pack up his things with the help of his porters and carried on. An hour later I was surprised to see him once more, again turning the camera. I concluded that he had passed me without my noticing – as might easily happen – and was glad to congratulate him on his energy. He looked at me in surprise and swore that he had not moved from that spot since setting up his camera over an hour ago. I was about to remind him that this was neither the time nor the place for such witticisms when I was astounded to hear a call from behind. Imagine my amazement when I found that it was Jungle, who, instead of being out in front, had evidently dropped behind and been passed by the rest of us. Following him were a number of porters, in a long straggling line, and then, to our mutual bewilderment, came Burley and Wish.

I must admit that I was completely baffled. It was one of those moments when one doubts one's own sanity. I had, with my own eyes, seen the four people who were now with me set out ahead of me. Of these, I had passed Shute, who had nevertheless appeared ahead of me, while the others, whom I had not passed at all, were now behind me. It was too much to believe that we had passed each other in this complicated way without noticing it.

The question was: where were Constant and Prone?

It was Shute who supplied the answer.

'Jungle, you fool!' he cried. 'You've been and gone round in a circle!'

At once it came clear to me. We were stretched out along the circumference of a circle, everybody following everybody else. Shute had gone on filming us without bothering to identify us as we passed, and we had all gone round twice. If it hadn't been for him, who was the only easily recognisable feature of our route, we might have gone on all day.

Confirmation came shortly afterwards with the arrival of Constant and Prone. I think they must have been suffering from altitude deafness, for they were shouting at each other as though they were half a mile apart instead of only a rope's length. I congratulated myself on my arrangement of the party; two men who could carry on a spirited conversation after several hours' hard marching at 15,000 feet were obviously kindred spirits. It is one of the deeper rewards of leadership to find that one's manipulation of the human element has been successful.

I decided that the occasion was suitable for a halt, and over a glass of champagne we discussed the reasons for the mistake. I asked all to give their opinion candidly, without regard to susceptibilities. It is my belief that men are better friends for facing the truth together, and that evasion of any kind leads to distrust in the long run.

It was encouraging to hear how they responded to the appeal. Shute was particularly outspoken, and this, I thought, was a good sign in one who was to be Jungle's constant companion.

What none of us could understand was how Jungle, using his compass, as he assured us he had done, could have turned through a circle. The problem was solved by Shute, who made Jungle demonstrate his method. They wandered off together, and soon they, too, were discussing the matter at the top of their voices. Altitude deafness was, I thought, unusually prevalent that day.

When they returned Shute gave us the answer. 'The silly fool forgot to release the catch on his compass,' he told us. 'Naturally, it pointed north whatever direction he took.'

'It might happen to anyone,' I said. It is my experience that a man supplies his best when he is trusted. Nothing saps a man's confidence in himself so much as mistrust from those over him. It would have been fatal to the expedition to allow Jungle to doubt himself – to say nothing of the effect upon him in later life. I take no credit for my forbearance; such things are the essence of leadership; either one has them or one has not.

For this reason I sent Jungle off again after the break, confident that he would not make the same mistake twice.

Nor did he. After we had been on the go for about four hours I found the party at the edge of a vast crevasse – all except Jungle, who was in it. His compass had directed him to it, and rather than make a long detour in a doubtful direction he had insisted on being lowered into the crevasse, intending to climb up the other side by cutting steps. He had been down there for two hours and nobody knew whether he was making progress for his voice was multiplied by echoes and reached the surface as an undecipherable chorus. For all they knew he might be completely stuck.

It is in such moments of crisis that a man's real character is revealed. The veneer of manners and sophistication which enabled him to bluff his way in the civilized world is of no avail to him now. Unless he is heart of oak he will show some crack or blemish, some weakness which will betray him and his comrades. I am glad to be able to record that in this emergency each and all of the party emerged with flying colours. It is perhaps not too much to say that during the final stages of the assault, when things were as black as they could be and only character stood between us and destruction, the confidence engendered by that early incident provided the last ounce of effort which enabled us to win through.

Each, of course, met the crisis in his own way. Burley, with the *sang-froid* of a Napoleon, took the opportunity to recuperate his strength – sapped by glacier lassitude – by taking a nap. Wish was boiling a piece of ice over a primus stove in order to determine the boiling point of ice. Shute had detached the lens of his camera and was correcting it for the

reduced refractive index of the rarefied atmosphere. Constant was
improving his knowledge of the language by a shouting contest with the
Bang. And Prone was treating himself for swollen glands, which he
suspected to be incipient.

The behaviour of my companions on this occasion has been, I freely
admit it, an example and inspiration to me on more than one occasion
when panic threatened. I was both humbled by their calmness and
warmed by the confidence which they evidently placed in me, upon
whom the responsibility rested. They knew I would not fail them.

But time was pressing. If Jungle was to be rescued from his
predicament before nightfall, something had to be done, and done
quickly. Obviously, someone must go down after him; but who should
it be? Thanks to the morning's incident I had the answer. To Shute
alone should go the privilege of risking his life for his friend.

It speaks volumes for Shute's modesty that he did his best to concede
the honour to someone else. But I could not allow him to forgo his real
desire, and we soon had him dangling on a rope.

After he had descended some distance he disappeared from sight,
and his voice became as incoherent as Jungle's. We lowered away until
the rope hung slack, then awaited developments.

After some minutes it dawned on me that we now had two men down
the crevasse without being a step further forward. Neither could
communicate with us, and we dared not haul on the ropes for fear of
injuring them.

The situation was desperate.

It was Burley who, waking up at this juncture, supplied the solution.
'Send down a walkie-talkie,' he said. 'We've carried the blasted things
all this way; let's get some good out of them.'

It was a brilliant suggestion. Burley, I decided, must have the
honour of descending with a radio set. Like Shute, he modestly declined
the privilege, but I insisted. Soon he, too, disappeared from sight. I
could have sworn that his last words were something about 'keep my
ruddy mouth shut in future'; but this could not have been the case –
unless, of course, it was another of Burley's incomprehensible
witticisms.

Wish switched on another radio, and we waited breathlessly.
Nothing happened. A horrible suspicion came over me.

'Is the set in order?' I asked.

'How the devil do I know?' said Wish. 'Jungle's the expert.'

It was true. None of us knew how to use the radio. Jungle was to have instructed us at the meeting in London, but he had been unavoidably absent.

There was nothing else for it; Wish must go down. He would get Jungle to write down instructions, which would be pulled up by me on a line, one end of which Wish would take down with him.

Down he went; and up, in due course, came the message: 'Batteries not yet installed. Are packed in one of the loads, but Burley does not know which one. Send down champagne.'

This, I decided, would never do. Some channel of communication had to be opened. I scribbled the message: 'Please tell me what to do.' I wrapped this around the neck of a champagne bottle, tied the line round it and lowered it into the crevasse. I gave them five minutes to write a reply and hauled up the line. The message read: 'Send down another bottle.'

I hope I am not unduly harsh in thinking this an inconsiderate reply; certainly I might be forgiven for thinking so at the time. But, not wishing to appear dictatorial, I did as they requested, sending with the bottle another message: 'I earnestly beg of you to consider my position. All means must be used to extricate you from your predicament. Please advise at earliest convenience.'

Back came the following: 'Yours of even date to hand. Jungle overcome by vertigo. Absolutely imperative you send four bottles of champagne immediately, otherwise cannot answer for consequences.'

This, of course, put the matter in a different light, and I repented my quick judgment. I have since talked the affair over with Totter, who confirms my original opinion that the first message was not quite in the best tradition; but at the time I was anxious to make amends for my unfounded and ungallant suspicion that the request for the second bottle was without justification, and I thereby erred into leniency. That the message was justified must certainly be conceded; we – that is, Totter and I – question only the manner in which it was delivered which made no acknowledgement of my own difficult position. But it is hard for me, who was at least on *terra firma*, to judge the feelings of those below. Perhaps I have, after all, been unfair to them; if so, I tender sincere apology.

I naturally lost no time in fulfilling the last urgent request, sending with the champagne another appeal for instructions.

The next message read: 'Jungle seized with convulsions. Send down Prone with five bottles.'

This worried me more than I care to say. It seemed to me that champagne was the last thing one would prescribe for convulsions. But Prone, who, sick as he was, pulled himself together manfully when I read the message to him and seemed almost lively for the first time in weeks, assured me that it was just the thing. So we sent him down too.

I gave them time to talk over the situation, then pulled up the cord. Up came an empty bottle, with this message round its neck: 'Bung Ho!'

At the same moment strange sounds began to issue from the crevasse. At first I could not believe my ears, but at last I was forced to the conclusion that my comrades were *singing*. Having some knowledge of British folk-tunes I was able, with some degree of certainty, to identify the music as 'Oh, My Darling Clementine', although, multiplied by echoes, it sounded rather like a full-size choir singing a kind of fugal Clementine. The result was not unpleasing, and I rejoiced that my friends had not lost heart; but unless they intended the song as a code message it was no help to me in my dilemma. I feared that although they were putting up a brave front my companions were in a situation of great peril.

This seemed also to be the opinion of Constant. 'They need me down there!' he said, and before I quite realised what he was about the brave fellow had pushed several bottles into his pockets, belayed the rope to an icicle, and was sliding out of sight.

Time went by, and the singing continued. I raised and lowered the line several times, but no message appeared. I was well-nigh desperate. Six human lives depended on my clear thinking and decisive action; but I was completely at a loss. My impulse was to descend the crevasse myself, even if it were to perish with my colleagues; but this would leave us with no means of communication with the surface.

The porters had long since settled themselves comfortably on their loads and were smoking the inevitable pipe of *stunk*. I could expect no help from that quarter.

Or so I thought. But I was to receive a lesson on the invaluable qualities of the Yogistani porter, without whom the expedition could not have been successful. The Bang, whose name, by the way, was Bing, suddenly rose to his feet and came across to the crevasse, bringing with him a small but immensely broad and powerful porter, Bung by name. Without a word being spoken, Bung took hold of one end of a rope and was lowered by Bing into the crevasse. Hardly had the rope gone slack when a piercing whistle sounded from below. Bing at once began to haul in again, and you can imagine my astonishment and relief when Bung came safely to the surface holding Burley by his jacket with a mighty fist. Burley, dangling like a puppet, was happily singing 'Yo, Heave-Ho!' – as well he might.

It was too simple. One by one my companions were hauled to the surface, and a cordial reunion took place. I am not ashamed to admit that I shed a quiet tear. Jungle, carried away no doubt by relief at his narrow escape – although I like to think that some small part of his feeling was genuine affection – thumped me so hard on the back that I fell down; and Wish, who seemed a little light-headed after his ordeal, apparently thought it of the greatest urgency that he should inform me that he had measured the depth of the crevasse, which was exactly 153 feet. This seemed to him, for some reason, excruciatingly funny.

When all but Constant had been safely restored to *terra firma* Bing and Bung went back to their comrades. They had evidently forgotten Constant, or were, perhaps, unable to count up to seven. I went over to them and endeavoured to indicate by signs what I wished them to do. I was met by blank scowls. Their meagre intelligence was evidently incapable of grasping my meaning. I lined the rest of the team up, leaving a gap in the middle, and pointed to this gap and to the crevasse, then went through the motions of lowering and raising a rope and greeting a companion saved from the abyss. All nodded encouragingly – a few even applauded – but no one made a move. I went through the whole performance again; this time they took not the slightest notice, but puffed away at their *stunk* as if everything were normal.

The team had clasped each other around the shoulders and, still in line, capered sideways on the ice like a row of chorus girls, singing 'Don't Put Your Daughter On The Stage, Mrs Worthington'. Poor fellows, they were still slightly hysterical from the effects of their ordeal.

I was on the point of unmanly panic when Bing got to his feet, came over to me, leered in a most objectionable fashion into my face and scratched the palm of one hand with the forefinger of the other. He did it in a most deliberate and odious way, as though the act had some esoteric significance.

It was horrible. I honestly thought for a moment that he was trying to bewitch me. One never knows what goes on in the heads of such primitive people. After all, this was the Mysterious East; who knew what might not happen?

The others stopped dancing and gathered round. I appealed to them for advice. What should I do?

It was Burley who told me, although how he came to know about it I cannot imagine.

'Grease it, old boy,' he said; 'grease it.'

I looked at him in astonishment. What was I to grease, and why?

Luckily, Burley took charge. To my amazement he produced a *bohee* ($\frac{3}{4}$d.) and offered it to Bing. The latter shook his head and scratched harder at his palm. Burley added another *bohee*, with the same result.

It seemed to me exactly as if they were bargaining over the price of something. Constant has since explained the matter to me. It appears that the number six is sacred to the Yogistani. Every sixth occurrence of a thing is treated in a special way. The sixth day is a day of rest. The sixth son is put to the priesthood. The sixth pipeful of *stunk* is smoked in honour of one's grandfather; and so on. The prescribed ritual may, however, be waived provided that a suitable offering is made to the gods. In this particular case, five lives had been saved; the gods had been deprived of the presence of five Europeans. To deprive them of a sixth would be the grossest sacrilege, and only a heavy monetary offering could adjust the matter.

The bargaining went on for some time. The Bang was evidently a devout person, for he upheld staunchly the rights of his gods. The final figure was *bohees* a thousand (£3.2s.6d.). Payment was made, and the Bang went to the crevasse, taking Bung with him. But this move did not appear to be popular with the rest of the porters, who had been gesticulating and shouting during the bargaining. They now rushed after Bing and Bung and surrounded them; and everybody began to yell at the top of his voice.

The argument went on for some minutes. Evidently, the porters were against the rescue, their superstitious minds were no doubt still uneasy, in spite of the handsome offering.

At last, to our great relief, the Bang appeared to be getting the upper hand. Soon the hubbub was quietened to a mild uproar and the two rescuers forced their way through the mob. In no time at all Constant was restored to us, none the worse for his adventure except for a distressing attack of hiccups. I now realised that it was past time to halt for the night, and gave the order to make camp. We turned in a happy and united party.

Some time in the small hours I awoke with a faint suspicion that there were undercurrents to this episode. Why, for instance, had the dramatic rescue taken place only when it was too late for further marching? I put away such ignoble thoughts at once, and mention them only as evidence of the deterioration which sets in at high altitudes due to the rarefied atmosphere.

Next morning no one was fit to travel. Burley, in reaction from his magnificent effort of the day before, had gone down again with glacier lassitude, and Prone was prostrate with a sharp attack of pins and needles. The others complained of glacier depression and pressed Prone to prescribe champagne. But the latter was, unfortunately, too ill to attend to them, and I dared not on my own initiative take the responsibility of administering so potent a medicine.

I need hardly say that champagne was carried for medicinal purposes only.

I was anxious to push on to Base Camp. We were already behind in our programme. Moreover, we were still on the glacier, and at any moment a crevasse might open beneath our feet, precipitating us into the abyss. I therefore gave the order to strike camp.

My companions were hoisted on to the backs of stalwart porters, and even I, feeling somewhat overcome by recent emotional experiences, allowed myself to be transported in the same way. Bing, the Bang, who had shown initiative in the crevasse incident, was sent ahead as route-finder. The day passed without incident. I awoke at noon to find the vast precipice of the North Wall towering above us. We were at Base Camp.

# Digital Clocks and Pocket Calculators: Spoilers of Youth

*Fran Lebowitz*

I was in certain respects a rather precocious youngster. My glance, right from the start, was fraught with significance and I was unquestionably the first child on my block to use the word *indisposed* in a sentence. My childhood was not, however, quite the gay whirl that one might imagine from the above statements. As a whistler I was only fair and I am to this very day unable to assume even a humane attitude in regard to gerbils. But then as now, I was always capable of dealing with the larger issues – it was, and is, the little things that get me down.

I did not learn how to tell time until I was nine years old. This is an unusually advanced age at which to master the art, except perhaps in Southern California.

My parents were understandably upset about my inability to tell time, for they possessed the foresight to realize that any child who talked back with such verve and snap would one day need a lawyer who charged by the hour. Furthermore, their infinite wisdom told them that it was exceedingly unlikely that the bill would arrive reading: Consultation on contract with agent, $150.00. One and one-half hours. From big hand on twelve, little hand on three, to little hand on four, big hand on six.

Their concern for my future well-being drove them to frantic efforts in an attempt to instill in me the knowledge that so painfully eluded my grasp. Night after night I sat at the kitchen table and surveyed a bewildering array of clocks made from oatmeal cookies, peanut butter lids, and crayoned circles of colored paper. They spelled each other – first one parent and then the other – taking turns on watch, so to speak. They were diligent, patient, and kind and I nodded my head and looked alert, all the while seething with fury at the injustices of a world in which we didn't have Christmas but we did have Time. As the days wore on and my ignorance persisted, my parents toyed with the idea of renting me out as a parlor game or at least trading me in for a child who couldn't learn something else – so weary were they of round, flattish objects.

Outside invervention came in the form of an offer of help from my aunt to take me on for the week of my winter vacation. I was duly dispatched to Poughkeepsie, where I was alternately bribed with banana milk shakes and tortured with clocks devised from paper plates, circular throw pillows, and overturned frying pans. At the end of the week I was returned to my parents a thing that was once a child – as ever unable to tell time and newly addicted to banana milk shakes in a household that considered blenders frivolous.

Some months later I was taking a bath when I suddenly shouted 'Eureka!' and at long last such concepts as twenty of eight and ten after twelve were touched with meaning.

It should be readily apparent to all that under no circumstances will I ever consider yielding the need for such hard-won knowledge. That there does indeed exist the very real danger of such a possibility is entirely due to the invention of the digital clock. I spent the best years of my life learning to tell time and I'm not stopping now. Neither should you. Here's why:

1. Regular clocks tell real time. Real time is time such as half-past seven.
2. Digital clocks tell fake time. Fake time is time such as nine-seventeen.
3. Nine-seventeen is fake time because the only people who ever have to know that it's nine-seventeen are men who drive subway trains.
4. I am not a man who drives a subway train.
5. You are not a man who drives a subway train.
6. I can tell this without even seeing you because anyone who has to know that it's nine-seventeen cannot possibly risk looking away.
7. Real watch faces are in the shape of watch faces because they must accommodate all of the things that make up a real watch, such as numbers, hands, and little minute lines.

8. Digital watch faces are in the shape of watch faces for no apparent reason. This cannot help but have an unsettling effect upon the young.

Now that I have set the record straight on the matter of Time I should like to direct your attention briefly to another unacceptable invention:

Pocket Calculators: It Took Me Three Years to Learn How to Do Long Division and So Should They

1. The rigors of learning how to do long division have been a traditional part of childhood, just like learning to smoke. In fact, as far as I am concerned, the two go hand in hand. Any child who cannot do long division by himself does not deserve to smoke. I am really quite a nice girl and very fond of children but I do have my standards. I have never taught a child to smoke before he has first taken a piece of paper and a pencil and demonstrated to my satisfaction that he can correctly divide 163 by 12.

2. Pocket calculators are not inexpensive and, generally speaking, parents would be better off spending the money on themselves. If they *must* throw it away on their offspring they would do well to keep in mind that a pack of cigarettes rarely costs more than seventy-five cents.

3. It is unnatural for *anyone*, let alone a *child*, to be able under any circumstances whatsoever to divide 17.3 by 945.8.

4. Pocket calculators encourage children to think that they have all the answers. If this belief were actually to take hold they might well seize power, which would undoubtedly result in all of the furniture being much too small.

## A Final Word

I am not personally a parent. But I do have two godchildren and am expecting a third. I am naturally concerned for their future. If I ruled the world you could bet your boots that none of them would ever set their eyes on any such contraptions as digital clocks and pocket calculators. But alas, I do not rule the world and that, I am afraid, is the story of my life – always a godmother, never a God.

# No Sale

*Walter R. Brooks*

Once upon a time there was a broker named George Plaskett. He had a nice house and a wife named Ethel and a seat on the Stock Exchange and a man to drive his car. He lived in Great Neck. He went into the city every day except Sunday when he stayed home and looked at his stamp collection which was in two big books on top of the piano. Every evening when they did not go out to a party the Plasketts turned on all the lights and had a party of their own.

Mr Plaskett was very popular at parties because he could mix a great many different drinks without even looking them up in the book and because he always told the ladies the funny jokes the other brokers had told him during the day and the ladies told them to their husbands and everybody had a good laugh. All the people in Great Neck said What a lucky man Mr Plaskett is to be sure.

Well, by and by hard times came along and Mr Plaskett got worried. Nobody wanted any brokering done. He kept on going to the city every day but there wasn't anything to do and he spent his time looking at his stamp collection which he had taken in with him. The brokers didn't tell each other funny jokes any more and when he wanted some to tell at parties he had to look them up in old magazines and nobody laughed at them very much.

He didn't say anything to Mrs Plaskett about the hard times but she guessed it one day when he told her she couldn't have the mink coat she said she wanted for Christmas. She got sort of mad. She said Why George Plaskett how can you sit there and say I can't have that coat when you promised it to me and I can prove you promised it by Mother because she was here and she heard you say it. And Mr Plaskett said Your mother never stops talking long enough to hear anything. And Mrs Plaskett began to cry and went into her bedroom.

Now Mr Plaskett needed ten thousand dollars very badly that day to save his business. So he sat down on a chair and said hell twice and then he got up and went into the bedroom and said Ethel I guess you don't know how bad things are brokers would all be committing suicide but they can't make enough to pay funeral expenses and I may even lose my stamp collection. I sent it over to Beebe and Beebe to-day to see if they would make me an offer for it. Oh what a pity said Mrs Plaskett and she smiled in a funny way that Mr Plaskett didn't like so he said oh dear helplessly and looked unhappy. But Mrs Plaskett wouldn't look at him so he sighed very loud and went out in the other room and sat down and thought.

Well after about five minutes he had thought all the thoughts he could think of and Mrs Plaskett hadn't come out to see him thinking and his stamp collection was at Beebe and Beebe's so he picked up a book. It was an old book on magic. It opened first at a page that had recipes on it with notes in Mrs Plaskett's handwriting and he thought it was a cook book.

Then he read Take the juice of two spiders and a pinch of powdered thighbone of a parricide and he said That's funny and looked at the top of the page and read Love philtres and potions. He wasn't interested in that so he began looking at pictures of famous magicians mostly old men with beards and then he came to a chapter How to sell your soul to the devil. And he read There are many instances on record of great wealth having been attained by those who have made compacts with the evil one, and there were a number of pictures of the devil some with horns and a tail and others very ordinary looking so that you wouldn't have guessed they were anybody special.

Well Mr Plaskett went on reading and by and by Mrs Plaskett stuck her head out and said George what are you doing? And Mr Plaskett said I am going to sell my soul to the devil. And Mrs Plaskett said You'd better sell some stocks to your customers. Then Mr Plaskett got mad and he said I've told you fifty times that they won't buy anything now and I don't know how to make money any other way and I don't want to lose my stamp collection. So Mrs Plaskett said Well go ahead and sell your old soul then such as it is you might as well get something out of it but for goodness' sake try to drive a decent bargain you know you're a fool at business. And she sniffed and shut the door.

Well Mr. Plaskett hadn't really been serious when he said he was going to sell his soul because he didn't know much about it or have any idea what it was worth. But Mrs Plaskett made him mad and anyway maybe he could save his stamp collection. So he read over the directions and then he got some gin and put it in four saucers in the corners of the room and tried to light it. But it was the gin he used for company and wouldn't burn so he had to get a new bottle that had just come.

That burned nicely and then he drew pentacles and inter-twining circles on the floor like the book said and then he stood in the middle with a lighted candle in his hand and read out loud from the book the magic words. He read them very loud so the devil would be sure to hear and just in the middle of it Mrs Plaskett opened the door again and said George what on earth.

Oh said Mr Plaskett please let me alone I told you what I was doing. And Mrs Plaskett said I smelt gin, and Mr Plaskett said Of course you did I have to use it in raising the devil. And Mrs Plaskett said Well if you're going to raise the devil you might at least not do it in my living-room when I'm trying to sleep why don't you go out to the garage? And she sniffed and shut the door again. So Mr Plaskett began all over again.

And when he got through nothing happened. There wasn't any clap of thunder and there wasn't any smell of brimstone only burned gin. Mr Plaskett stood still for a minute with the candle in his hand looking foolish and then be began tidying up the room so Mrs Plaskett wouldn't be cross at breakfast.

And just then the telephone-bell rang. He went to it and said Yes crossly and a far-off voice said Hello Plaskett this is the devil and I got your call but I had a lot of business in Washington and couldn't get there would it be all right if I dropped in to-morrow? And Mr Plaskett said Sure come to lunch, and the voice said OK about one? and Mr Plaskett said Swell I'll expect you and hung up and went to bed.

Well, Mr Plaskett's mind was so full of the devil that he didn't sleep very well and he was late at the office next morning. His secretary said Good morning dear there are three men waiting to see you, and Mr Plaskett said What do they look like? and the secretary said Oh just like three men – nobody I know, and Mr Plaskett said Well I don't suppose the devil would send in his own name anyway, and the secretary laughed because she thought it was one of Mr Plaskett's little jokes.

So the first man that came in was tall and dark and had a hooked nose and a little read feather in his hatband and Mr Plaskett felt sure he was the devil. So he bowed and the man bowed and said speaking very quick Well Mr Plaskett I assume you are still of the same mind about selling, and Mr Plaskett said yes. And the man said Of course you understand that a lot of these things are being thrown on the market nowadays and I can't buy everything that is offered to me but I have looked yours over and I will offer you two thousand dollars. What said Mr Plaskett tut tut that is no offer at all I imagine I know values better than that.

For he had thought that even if his soul wasn't worth 10,000 dollars he would try to get that for it because it was the exact sum he needed to save his business. Then the tall man talked a lot about how the market had sunk and about how even missionaries were almost a drug on the market and he said he knew it was hard to give up one's most cherished possessions but after all they didn't pay any interest and in these times an increase in value was doubtful.

That may be true said Mr Plaskett but if you get it you'll pay me 10,000 dollars not a penny less. Three thousand said the man Not a cent more. Nine thousand said Mr Plaskett. Take it or leave it. Four thousand said the man And that's my last word.

And so they agreed on seven thousand and the man wrote out a check and then he said You understand I am paying that much for only one reason because I want all those Hawaiian missionary stamps. What said Mr Plaskett You are not the devil? And the man laughed and said No I am Mr Beebe of Beebe and Beebe the stamp merchants you will have your joke Mr Plaskett good morning.

Well well said Mr Plaskett to himself That was pretty nice and I am glad he wasn't the devil because I only need three thousand more and I ought to be able to get that much for my soul. Then the next man came in and he was a Mr Peabody a fat man in a velour hat and Mr Plaskett said to himself He doesn't look like the pictures in the book but it would be just like the devil to wear a velour hat and maybe he's him and he bowed politely.

Now Mr Peabody was not the devil at all but an insurance man, and Mr Plaskett's politeness was so unusual in his experience that he began to cry. Come come old chap said Mr Plaskett and Mr Peabody said, Oh dear please excuse me I'm really very happy my old aunt in Lansing died last week and left me 200,000 dollars and this is my last day selling insurance.

What you are an insurance salesman said Mr Plaskett Out of my
sight. No no shouted Mr Peabody falling on his knees. Don't say it don't
say it you are the first man who has been polite to me in forty years and
long ago I made a vow that the first man who was really nice to me I
would give half my fortune to if I ever had one and now I have one and
half of it is yours. What said Mr Plaskett You mean you will give me one
hundred thousand dollars? Yes said Mr Peabody and he took the
fountain-pen he always had ready in his hand and made out a paper
that said Mr Plaskett was to have half his aunt's estate and shook hands
and said good-bye.

Aha said Mr Plaskett Now I have one hundred and seven thousand
dollars and my soul is going up I shall not sell it for less than five
hundred thousand dollars and a steam yacht. He looked at his watch
and it was half past one and he said Well that last man out there must
certainly be the devil because Satan always keeps his appointments. So
the third man came in and he was a tough little man with a squint and
no hair and Mr Plaskett thought Well I suppose this is just one of the
devil's disguises but where can we go to lunch so we won't be seen
together? And he said Are you the devil? You said it said the little man
Well maybe I ain't the head devil but the boss sent me around to sell
you some protection Just sign this and everything will be OK.

And he handed Mr Plaskett a paper which would bind him to pay the
Brokers' Protective Association ten dollars monthly for life. But Mr
Plaskett laid the paper down without looking at it and said Well you go
pretty fast but understand now I am to have five hundred thousand
dollars and a steam yacht in good order or there's no deal. And the little
man said Geest you're nuts come on buddy sign the paper. How'd you
like to come home some night and find your house all blown to hell?

And Mr Plaskett said It has its points but how about that half million
have you got it with you? Then the little man got down off the desk
where he had been sitting and put his hand in his pocket and edged
toward the door and growled Geest what the boss mean sending me to
shake down a looney? And Mr Plaskett said Are you really the devil?
The little man said Sure don't kid yourself. All right said Mr Plaskett,
Then vanish. And as the little man didn't say anything Mr Plaskett said
Come on do some tricks.

Well the little man didn't do any tricks just stood and showed his
teeth so Mr Plaskett said Well I guess you aren't him after all but I can

prove it. And he began to say in a loud voice the formula he had read in the book which would make the devil disappear. And when the little man heard the Latin words he turned pale and ran out of the office screaming I can't do business with no looney and I won't what's more.

Well Mr Plaskett waited a while longer but nobody else called and he said to himself Well I guess the devil changed his mind but it's all right with me I have enough money anyway. So he went out to lunch.

A little while after lunch he started home because it was pretty slow in the office without his stamp collection to look at. When he got there the cook came in and said What'll I do about dinner? And Mr Plaskett said What do you mean do about dinner? And the cook said Well there was a dark complected gentleman called this noon he said he was to have lunch with you and you weren't here so Mrs Plaskett invited him to stay.

My goodness said Mr Plaskett, where did he go? He thought I meant the house and not the office. And the cook said I don't know Him and the missis went away about three and said to tell you they wouldn't be back and so what shall I do about dinner? And Mr Plaskett said Serve it serve it he's got her and maybe I'm . . . sorry . . . and maybe I'm not and he went into the living-room. There was a strong smell of brimstone in the living-room and chairs and tables were knocked every which way. I'm glad she put up a good fight said Mr Plaskett and lit a cigar.

Well that was the last he ever heard of either Mrs Plaskett or the devil and he still had his soul and didn't have to buy a mink coat. And he took some of the money from Mr Peabody's aunt's estate to start a new stamp collection.

# Eliza's Husband

## Barry Pain

### Bridge Abandoned

It is my opinion that there is not very much in this game of bridge about which we hear so much talk. It is not an intellectual game, and for that reason alone, quite apart from what took place at the Epsteins', I shall not go on with it. In two evenings I practically made myself master of the whole thing. I do not mean that I can always say off-hand what I should score at the end of a game, or what the precise value of a trick in any suit is. But as that information is given in a very clear and concise form on the back of every bridge marker, it is hardly worth the while of a busy man to burden his mind with it.

I was introduced to the game by a Mr Spratt, who was staying with Mr Timson, the curate at St Augustine's. Though intended for the Church, Mr Spratt seemed rather bent on seeing life. He was always getting up tea-parties, going to bazaars, singing at concerts, and so on.

We did not, on the two occasions to which I have referred, play for points. Mr Timson only consented to learn on this condition, which I think is to his credit. I may add that I am myself opposed to gambling, and consider that any game which is not worth playing for its own sake is not worth playing at all.

One evening, on my return from the City, Eliza said to me that she would not mind betting that the Epsteins had got somebody coming to dinner that night.

'What makes you think so?' I asked.

'Mrs Epstein was buying tinned mulligatawny at the grocer's yesterday afternoon, and I saw the asparagus going in myself this morning. That speaks for itself.'

Eliza was perfectly correct. A little later, happening to be at one of our upstairs windows, I cast an eye into the Epsteins' garden. Mr

Epstein had two strangers with him – both elderly men – and he was pointing out to them the place where the sweet-peas would be when they came up. I dismissed the subject from my mind. It was nothing to do with me, and I took no interest in it. All I said to Eliza was that if the Epsteins were going to give a dinner-party they might have remembered us, considering all the trouble we had had with their cat.

About nine o'clock that night Mrs Epstein's little boy brought a verbal message that Mr Epstein would be very glad if I would come in to make a four at bridge. My first impulse was to refuse. As I said to Eliza, if I am not good enough to be asked to dinner I am not good enough to be asked to anything. Eliza said that if she were me she would not be so silly.

The remark was as absurd as it was ungrammatical.

'If you were I,' I said to Eliza, 'you would be I. That is to say, you would be neither more silly nor less silly than I am. If you would only train yourself to look at things in a logical way, you would –'

'Are you going to keep that boy of the Epsteins' waiting all night while you make up your mind?'

If I must err, I would sooner err on the side of good nature. I sent word by the boy that I should be happy to oblige.

My observations from the window had shown me it would not be necessary to assume evening dress. I changed my coat for something rather more recent, and went round.

Mr Epstein introduced me to Mr Horrocks and Mr Bird. We four were to play bridge while Mrs Epstein read the evening paper. Mr and Mrs Epstein, Mr Horrocks, and Mr Bird were all of them slightly flushed in the face, and there was more laughter than I could find any sufficient reason for.

We cut for partners, and I found I had to play with Mr Epstein. He asked me what kind of a game I played. I said that my game was average.

I then understood him to say, 'I am hearty and strong. What are you?' I replied politely that I was well myself. This perfectly inoffensive remark was the signal for a burst of laughter. Mr Horrocks said it was capital. Mr Bird said it was very good.

Then Mr Horrocks said 'Weak-and-weak' to Mr Bird, and Mr Bird nodded. I looked at the back of my marker, but I could find no reference to weak-and-weak. This evidently was not the game as I understood it.

Mr Epstein left the declaration to me, and although I had a very curious hand I was not in the least doubtful as to what I should do. I held ten clubs headed by the ace, king, queen, and my other three cards were the ace of the other suits. The preponderance of clubs was beyond any possibility of a mistake, and I declared clubs accordingly.

When I put down my hand Mr Horrocks and Mr Bird were once more convulsed with laughter, but Mr Epstein seemed far from pleased. He said he could appreciate a joke as much as any man, but that he thought I was really going too far.

'I do not see what you have to grumble at,' I said. 'It looks to me perfectly sound. Unless the other side have some remarkably good cards we must make nearly every trick.'

'We must make absolutely every trick. It scores twenty-eight. We should also have made every trick at no trumps, which would have scored eighty-four below the line and a hundred and forty above it.'

This particular hand was never played. They simply wrote down a score and the cards were dealt again. That is not bridge as I understand it. Even if you think that you can win, you should play the thing out. You never know what the other side may have.

Mr Bird then went hearts and made game. I followed with a no-trump declaration, and only succeeded in getting two tricks. I had imagined from the weakness of my own hand that my partner must be strong, but with the exception of two aces and two kings he had no cards of any value.

We lost the rubber, and Mr Epstein produced his purse. Fivepence a hundred had been suggested, and I had consented to this. But both Mr Horrocks and Mr Bird positively refused to receive money. They said that if they did they would be unable to sleep that night. It appeared that they both had trains to catch, and that they could not play another rubber. Both of them told me that it had been a most interesting and amusing game, and that they were delighted to have met me.

As we were leaving I overheard Mr Horrocks saying in a low voice to Mr Epstein, 'This will be a lesson to you, Epstein.' So quite evidently Epstein was not justified in trying to teach me how the game of bridge should be played. However, he received the reproof quite meekly, and merely said, 'You bet!'

At the moment of writing the Epsteins have not sent round again to ask me to make a four at bridge. But when they do I have made up my mind to refuse. I shall say that I am very sorry to seem disobliging, but that I have abandoned bridge. I prefer a game which gives a little more exercise to my mental faculties.


## An Extraordinary Occurrence

Some days ago, as I was walking down Chancery Lane on my way back from seeing our firm's solicitors, I was the actual eye-witness of a most extraordinary occurrence. The road was very slippery at the time, and a taxi-cab skidded, and ran with its front wheels right up on the kerb. I need hardly point out that this might have resulted in the loss of one or more human lives. As a matter of fact, no one was even hurt, and the cab itself was not damaged. The man inside the cab did not get out; the driver simply backed it away from the kerb and went straight on. This sensational incident made a great impression upon me.

On returning to the office I went into Mr Bagshawe's room to tell him what our solicitors had said. As a rule, I confine my conversation with him to business subjects. He prefers it and has said so. But I could not but suppose that he would be interested in the narrow escape which I had just witnessed. I described it to him in detail. When I had finished he asked me my age. The question surprised me, but I was able to answer it with complete accuracy, giving not only the year but the odd number of days. When I had finished, he said: 'Then don't talk like an infant of six. It wastes time and I don't like it.'

Mr Bagshawe rather prides himself on taking everything very calmly and quietly, and I always make an allowance for his manner. I dare say dyspepsia has something to do with it. As I was going out to lunch I remarked to young Gillivant:

'I witnessed this morning a most extraordinary occurrence.'

Gillivant looked at me rather suspiciously.

'Well?' he said.

I told him what I had seen in Chancery Lane. I pointed out that the front wheels of the cab were right upon the kerb, and that if a child had been standing there it would probably have been knocked down and killed. I also observed what a remarkable thing it was that the cab itself did not overturn. When I had finished he winked his eye and said: 'No good, old man.'

I inquired what he meant.

'I mean you can't catch me with that silly old sell. You want me to ask what there was wonderful in it. Try it on the office-boy, I'm too old for it.'

I assured him that nothing was further from my mind than any attempt to deceive or to play a joke upon him. What I had narrated was a simple fact. He again told me that it was no good, and quite evidently did not believe me.

Later in the day I said to old Pridgeon: 'I saw something today which seems almost incredible. In fact I told it to young Gillivant and he flatly refused to believe it. It happened in Chancery Lane. I was walking down the Lane when a taxi-cab passed me. I noticed that the surface of the road was greasy, but did not give it a second thought. No idea of an accident was in my mind. Suddenly the cab swerved round – skidded, I suppose.'

I continued the story to the end. Old Pridgeon then said rather gruffly that I ought to be ashamed of myself and walked away. It was a perfectly senseless comment. I had no reason whatever to be ashamed of myself. In telling him of the occurrence I had made use of no blasphemous or improper expression.

It is not every day that I have an item of exceptional interest to take home from the City, but this was an occasion, and I took advantage of it at dinner-time.

'Strange things happen in London,' I said to Eliza.

She said, 'Well?'

'I was walking down Chancery Lane this morning when I witnessed what might have been a most terrible disaster. One of those red taxi-cabs happened to pass me. The surface of the road at the time was extremely slippery, and I have no doubt that the man had to apply his brakes suddenly owing to some exigency of the traffic. Be that as it may, I can assure you –'

And I continued the story as before. 'I venture to say,' I added, 'that that is the most extraordinary occurrence.'

'I saw another extraordinary occurrence this morning,' said Eliza, 'when I was out with baby.'

'Ah,' I said, 'what was that?'

'I saw a man and he's got two legs.'

'There's nothing extraordinary in that.'

'Oh, don't you see what a marvellous escape it was. If he'd had a hundred he'd have been a centipede.'

It was evidently of no use to discuss the matter with Eliza while she was in this frame of mind. I have, however, narrated the scene that I witnessed in Chancery Lane at length here, because I feel sure that it must interest my readers. I may add that the front wheels of that taxi-cab were at the very least half a foot upon the kerb.

## The Garden Fête

Eliza, who is far too much inclined to do things on her own responsibility, told me she had taken two tickets for a garden fête at Mr Buddilow's ('The Chestnuts') in aid of the new mission-room in Buxton Street. The tickets were a shilling each, but I am always willing to put my hand in my pocket for a good cause. I thought I should have been consulted – that was all – and said so.

'Besides,' I added, 'I am not personally acquainted with Mr Buddilow, and the whole thing is not in our parish.'

'No,' said Eliza. 'And I thought we might take baby. There is no charge for babies in arms. I could carry him some of the time, and you could – '

'If you knew anything whatever about garden fêtes, Eliza, you would know that they constitute a class of entertainment which is utterly and completely over the baby's head.'

As Eliza gave way on this point I raised no further objections. I understood from Eliza that there would be a band provided, and a *café chantant* in the Parisian manner, and various other attractions.

As it happened the weather was fine. I was a little in doubt as to the correct costume for the occasion. Eliza said I could go in anything and everybody else would. This was no help. Having regard to the fact that this was an entertainment or a religious object I went in a silk hat and frock-coat. Almost every man there was in a straw hat and flannels. If I had gone in a straw hat and flannels nobody else would have worn them. It seems to me sometimes as if everything

I do is fated to be wrong.

Mr Buddilow is a Justice of the Peace, and a man of very considerable wealth. His garden is beautiful and extends, I should say, to upwards of three acres. Some of the paths were marked 'Private', with a rope stretched across them. It was a small matter, but it annoyed me. I had paid my money on the understanding that the grounds were thrown open to the public. Only part of them was thrown open. Several entertainments were provided, but one had to pay extra for all of them, with the exception of the band. In that case, I asked myself, what was the admission money paid for in the original instance? It looked to me like sharp practice, and I do not like sharp practice, even for a religious object. There was a coconut-shy, with which I definitely refused to have anything to do. It is not an amusement for a man of my age, intelligence, and position. Eliza, I am sorry to say, so far forgot herself as to have a shy, and I regret to add that she got a coconut. I had to carry it all the rest of the afternoon, and most inconvenient it was. The band on the lawn wanted a man over them who knew what work was. Their intervals were from ten minutes to a quarter of an hour by my watch between the pieces. And even so, before I left they had begun to play some of the old selections again. Tea was provided in a refreshment tent, and we were told we could pay ninepence each, and I hope Eliza had anything she liked. Personally, I did not. If there is one thing I dislike more than stewed tea it is a cake which has been made with bad eggs. If I had not constantly reminded myself of the real necessity for a mission-room in Buxton Street, a very low neighbourhood, I might have got rather irritable about it.

The *café chantant* (pronounced 'caffy shongtong') was also on the fraudulent side. Admission was threepence and the entertainment only lasted a quarter of an hour. After that you were turned out and a fresh batch came in. It was far less gay than I had expected. Somebody sang 'The Holy City', there was a performance on the pianola, and the choir boys sang 'Oh! who will 'er the downs so free?' It was the tenth time they had sung it that afternoon, and they appeared to be justifiably sick of it. It is almost impossible for me to avoid taking a businesslike view of a business transaction. The entertainment was not worth threepence. Eliza had refused to enter, on the ground that by standing outside the tent she could hear it all just as well as if she was inside. As I told her, that was a matter entirely for her own conscience, and I did not wish to dictate. Soon afterwards Eliza said she had got tired of it and she should go home. I am glad to say that she took the coconut with her. I remained to see if there was any chance of my getting something approximating to my money's worth.

I was tired of walking about, and patent leather, though it gives a dressy appearance, has a tendency to draw the feet. Finding an unoccupied chair, I sat down. Almost immediately a cheerful old gentleman with a brown leather satchel stepped up to me and said: 'Twopence for the chair, please.' It was just a little beyond the limit. I asked bitterly how much I had to pay to be allowed to breathe. The satire was lost on him. He only laughed and said it was a jolly good idea; he would think about it.

I now come to the one thing in the afternoon that gave me any real satisfaction. I was passing a very small tent on which was a notice:

PROFESSOR RIENZI
*Phrenologist*
LEARN YOUR TRUE CHARACTER BY HIS INFALLIBLE METHOD

As nothing was said about the price I should not have dreamed of entering. I had been caught out often enough and did not propose to be caught again that afternoon. But at the door of the tent a remarkably pretty girl, fashionably dressed, was standing, and she ran up to me in the friendliest way and caught me by the arm.

'Do come and see the phrenologist, sir,' she said. 'Most interesting. He tells you all about your gifts and abilities by the bumps on your head, and the charge is only a shilling.'

I have often wished to have an independent and impartial view of my character, and it was for that reason – and not in the least because the girl was pretty – that I parted with my shilling. Inside the tent was a man in a dressing-gown with a very long white beard and thick white hair. He made me sit down and passed his hand over my head. His description of my character, to my mind, showed extraordinary insight. He told me many things about myself which, so far as I know, are not generally suspected.

As I left I thanked him, and I said to the girl that it was a wonderful performance and well worth the money. She said: 'Then you might run about and get some more to come. We did awfully well the first part of the afternoon, but now things are getting slack again.'

I did not run about. I left at once because I did not wish to be involved in any further expenditure. I also wished on my return to 'Meadowsweet' to make a note of all the phrenologist had said about me. He had said nothing which was not in the highest degree gratifying.

After dinner, while Eliza was knitting wool socks for the baby, I said: 'I want a serious answer to a serious question, Eliza.'

'A funny thing you always want that when I'm counting stitches. What is it?'

'Would you say, Eliza, that I was a man of an iron will?'

'No,' said Eliza.

'Yet I have been assured to-day by an absolute stranger that such is the case.'

'Of course, if he did not know you, he might make the mistake.'

'I do not know that it was a mistake. The man was a professor of phrenology, which is a wonderful science. He had his own special means of finding out what my gifts and abilities might be.'

'What else did he say?'

'He said that I had the artistic temperament but kept within proper bounds. Many years ago I was told by a man who had no interest in making the remark that I ought to have gone on the stage. The phrenologist practically repeated that. He said I had the dramatic instinct.'

'What did you pay him?' asked Eliza.

'One shilling.'

'He earned his money,' said Eliza thoughtfully. 'That was at the fête this afternoon, wasn't it?'

'It was: after you had left. It is in my nature to tire quickly of gaiety and excitement. I was pleased to find one small tent devoted to the serious study of one's inner nature.'

'You knew it was all spoof, of course. Miss Sakers told me all about it. Professor Rienzi is just young Buddilow dressed up, and the girl outside the tent is the girl he is going to marry. She had a bet with another girl that they'd take two pounds before six o'clock, and I expect she's won it. Pretty girls can always do what they like, can't they?'

As I pointed out to Eliza, all her statements proved, even if they were correct, was that young Mr Buddilow happens to be a man with a most extraordinary insight into character.

## The Letter to 'The Times'

I was talking over the subject the other day with one or two friends of mine, and we all agreed that dreams are very curious things. We cannot account for them.

My friends all had instances which happened within their own experience of dreams that had come true. These seem to be quite common, but they have never come my way.

'Why,' I said to Eliza that night, 'have I never had a dream that has come true? Men whom I cannot possibly think to be my superiors or even my equals seem to have dreams of this kind, or if they don't their wives do.'

'Don't seem to me the kind of thing I should worry about,' said Eliza.

'Look, for instance, at the dream that I had last night or early this morning. I was adding up an immensely long column of figures. The trouble was that I myself was one of the figures, so that when I got down to the bottom of the column to add them up, that put the addition all wrong. Mr Bagshawe came in at the moment, and I asked him what I should do about it, and he said the only thing to do was to wear larger boots in future. That is the kind of dream I get. It not only does not come true, but it cannot come true.'

'Last night,' said Eliza, 'I dreamt that some money came to me.'

'Seems to be much the same sort of dream as mine.'

'I don't know. We were sitting in this room together, and the girl knocked at the door, and brought in a letter, and the money was in the letter. That might happen.'

'I think not. Who's going to send you any money?'

At this moment a most singular and dramatic thing happened. Parker knocked at the door and brought in a letter for Eliza.

'Open it at once,' I said.

She did so. It contained a postal order for eighteenpence from the people at Grimsby who supply us with fish, and was accompanied by a letter apologizing for the mistake in the account which Eliza had pointed out to them.

'The first thing to do,' I said, 'is to make a note of the exact time at which the letter arrived.'

'Why?' said Eliza.

On second thoughts I could not exactly say why. All I could tell her was that it was usual. Whenever a dream comes true, people always make a note of the exact time. It seems to be one of the rules.

Eliza did not seem to attach much importance to the incident. She said that after all it was only eighteenpence, and it hardly seemed worth getting a supernatural warning about. At the same time, if those people at Grimsby tried anything of the kind on with her again, she would get her fish elsewhere. She then went up to see the baby, and I sat down at my bureau to prepare a careful and temperate statement of what had occurred for publication in the form of a letter in *The Times* newspaper.

I began as follows:

'Dear Sir, – It has been well observed by Shakespeare that there are more things in heaven and earth than are dreamed of –'

I stopped here, because I could not for the life of me remember the rest of the quotation. The memory is a very curious thing. You cannot explain it. That quotation is rather a favourite of mine. I use it constantly. And now it was gone.

However, I began again:

'Dear Sir, – It is a question whether a supernatural premonition is required with reference to a small consideration which in this case was precisely the sum of eighteenpence, but may be conditioned by a further question of commercial morality, or, at any rate, accuracy, on which it may be fairly said that the fortunes of this empire do under Providence to some considerable extent –'

I read this over again. It was all right, and I could see the meaning precisely. But perhaps it was better after all to shut out abstract considerations for which *The Times* newspaper, in the event of any unusual pressure of news, might not be able to find space. I therefore began again:

'Dear Sir, – A dream that came absolutely and literally true,' I wrote, 'although it merely involved the correction of a small sum in a tradesman's account, may perhaps be of some interest to those of your readers who are interested in such interesting subjects –'

The last phrase clearly needed to be recast. I was just going to recast it, when Eliza came in, and asked me what I was doing.

'I am preparing,' I said, 'a statement with reference to your dream and its fulfilment for publication in *The Times*. Our name, of course will not be given, nor the address. It is customary to enclose these as evidence of one's bona fides, but they form no part of the matter to be published.'

'Well,' said Eliza. 'I'm blest if it doesn't beat me altogether.'

'The problem,' I said, 'is one upon which I myself would be glad to hear –'

'Oh, I'm not talking about that,' said Eliza. 'You go to business in the City. You've got on pretty well. You've had your salary raised. And yet when you're at home you act just like a child. Do you mean to say you didn't know that I had never had any dream at all, and was just having a little game with you? I had written to complain about that account, and told them to put it right by return of post, or I should deal elsewhere. So of course I knew the money was coming.'

'In that case, Eliza, you made a statement to me which you must have known to be untrue. Conduct of that kind does not tend to increase my confidence in your character.'

'Oh, cheer up,' said Eliza. 'Everything's got to have a start. Even if the dream didn't come true, it would have come true if it had ever been a dream.'

'I want you to see the principle involved.'

'Yes,' said Eliza. 'And I want you to come and have a look at the waste pipe of the bath. I don't know what that girl's been doing to it, but the water won't run off. You had better bring a bit of cane with you or something of that kind.'

It seemed idle to pursue the subject further.

## The Cockroach

The other day, as I was leaving the office, old Pridgeon came up to me in a very free and easy way and said, 'What do you do about cockroaches?'

Now, I like Pridgeon very well, and in the matter of the greenhouse he certainly gave me some useful hints. But I should like to see him show a proper sense of difference which has occurred in our relations.

We are no longer on terms of equality. If I am not actually Pridgeon's master, I am at any rate approximate to that.

So I was rather stand-offish in my manner. I said, 'What do I do about cockroaches? I simply fail to understand you, Pridgeon.'

'Why,' said Pridgeon, 'what is the difficulty? What I mean is what do you do to get rid of cockroaches? It's simple enough, isn't it?'

'I do nothing to get rid of cockroaches, and have no need to do anything. In a house which is properly kept and looked after there are no cockroaches. We have none, and I cannot advise you.'

'Oh,' said Pridgeon, 'we've got them, and they're getting a bit too thick.'

I dismissed the subject from my mind at the moment, but when I got back, on my way up the High Street, I saw in an ironmonger's window a remarkably ingenious trap for cockroaches, acting electrically. The price, tenpence, was perhaps rather high for a thing of the kind, but scientific apparatus, as I found when I purchased the garden thermometer, nearly always runs into money. I determined that I would mention it to Pridgeon next day. The man himself is all right. It is merely that he has not the tact to adapt his manner to changed circumstances.

A few minutes later, in the course of casual conversation, Eliza said to me that Gladys rather believed that she had seen a black-beetle in the kitchen the night before. This naturally came to me as a bit of a shock.

'By black-beetle she means cockroach. They are an extremely annoying and disgusting thing to have in the house. May I inquire what she did about it?'

'Didn't do anything about it. Said it was too quick for her.'

'Well,' I said, 'after all, the very important thing is what you personally have done about it.'

'Nothing – same as Gladys. Have I got to pull my hair out every time the girl thinks she sees a black-beetle?'

'I never suggested that you should pull your hair out by the roots. I do suggest that in a house of this class, for which I pay forty sovereigns in rent every year, cockroaches should not be allowed to exist. However, it is the same old story. If anything has to be done, I must do it myself. Kindly give me my hat, please.'

I went out and purchased the cockroach trap which I had seen in the ironmonger's shop. Mr Pawling himself served me, and said that it was quite a new thing, for which he anticipated a great sale. I went over the directions with him and found the trap simple in construction and yet remarkably ingenious. The fact that the cockroach infallibly perished before it had ever reached the bait made it singularly economical in working. Also, as the trap reset itself automatically, it would destroy a million cockroaches with the same ease that it would destroy one. Science has always had a fascination for me, and I was really almost glad that we had a cockroach on which to experiment.

I showed Eliza the paper of directions and then explained the trap to her. As I had expected, she quite failed to appreciate the ingenuity of the mechanism.

'Unfortunately,' I said, 'I can only give you an explanation. I cannot provide you with the intelligence to understand it. I shall now take the trap into the kitchen and set it myself, placing it, as directed, near the range.'

'While you are there,' said Eliza, 'you had better catch that cockroach and read the paper of directions to it. Otherwise it won't know which way it has got to go into the trap, and it may miss the second turning on the right, and nothing happen at all.'

I told her that intentional silliness did not appeal to me, and went into the kitchen. I examined the trap at 9.30, at 10, at 10.30 and at 10.45. The cockroach was not yet caught, but I believe it is a well-known fact in natural history that these insects are nocturnal in their habits. I examined the trap again at eight o'clock next morning, and the cockroach was still not to be found. As I said to Eliza, in things of this kind all that one wants is a little patience.

On the following morning and the day after the cockroach remained at large, I tried changing the position of the trap, I also altered the character of the bait provided. But I did not get the result I anticipated. Eliza, of course, had to regard it as rather a joke.

'On the contrary,' I said, 'it is a very serious matter. The cockroach lays a great number of eggs, and lays them continuously.'

'Pity it isn't a hen,' said Eliza.

'You will adopt a different tone,' I said, 'when you find the house swarming with cockroaches from cellar to roof.'

'Well,' she said, 'what did you want to buy that rotten old trap for? That will never catch anything except the mug who bought it. Tenpence for a thing like that! A penny-worth of beetle poison from the chemist was what you wanted.'

'I think not. We have a child in this house. It would be highly dangerous.'

'So it would, if I kept the child in the kitchen all night. But then I don't.'

'The poison might contaminate the milk.'

'So it would, if I put it in it. But I shouldn't.'

It was useless to continue the subject with her. Rather reluctantly I had recourse to Pridgeon. Unfortunately he was in a rather bad temper with me.

'Did you get rid of those cockroaches, Pridgeon?' I said, quite pleasantly.

'I thought we were not interested in cockroaches, not since we got our rise and took a larger size in hats.'

I passed this over. 'On the contrary,' I said, 'I should be interested to know how you got rid of them. I might find occasion to use the same method one day. We are only human, even the best of us.'

'Well,' said Pridgeon, 'I will tell you what I did. I got a paving-stone measuring six feet by three, and laid it down in the garden. I then placed the cockroaches on the paving-stone and passed the garden roller over it two or three times. After that they gave me no more trouble. You try it yourself.'

It ended, as it always does, in Eliza having her own way. She put down the poison and it killed nothing. Of course, however, it would be too much to expect her to confess that she was in the wrong. What she says now is that the cockroach was never seen before or since, and that it is her belief that Gladys imagined it.

If that is the case, all I have to say is that there is tenpence thrown in the gutter because Eliza chooses to employ hysterical servants.


## The Duke of Coverdale

Young Gillivant accompanied me to the station – not by my invitation, but with some idea of making himself agreeable. The reason for this subsequently transpired. I did not dream of lending him half a sovereign, and I told him so. I quoted him that excellent proverb which says that those who borrow come to sorrow. He said he was ready to take his chance. It was just then that he pointed out to me on the platform a tall gentleman of distinguished appearance with a grey beard.

'Know who that is?' said Gillivant.

I admitted that I did not.

'That's the Duke of Coverdale. Frightfully wealthy bug.'

I think I have already mentioned that Gillivant is extremely well connected and has a wide knowledge of society. His Grace entered a first-class smoking compartment in the train which I myself was about to patronize. I got rid of Gillivant by letting him have eighteenpence to be going on with, and I then entered the same compartment as the Duke. No man is less a snob that I am, but it struck me it would be interesting to say that night to Eliza: 'Whom do you think I travelled down with this evening? No less a person than the Duke of Coverdale, one of the wealthiest of our English aristocracy.'

I had hardly entered the carriage before the Duke bent forward towards me with a delightful old-world courtesy, and asked me if I could oblige him with a light.

I said, 'With pleasure, sir.' I did not say 'your Grace', because I thought it quite possible that he did not wish for public recognition. At my suggestion he was condescending enough to put a few of my matches in his waistcoat for purposes of reference.

The train was just starting when a ticket inspector entered the compartment. I said 'Season', and he nodded. The Duke produced a ticket which was not of the right colour. The inspector glanced at it and said, 'Ninepence excess, please.'

'The firsts on this rotten line are so like the thirds that anyone may make a mistake,' said the Duke.

'Ninepence excess, please.'

'Besides, there's no room in the thirds. Never is at this time of day.'

'Ninepence excess, please,' said the inspector.

The Duke then handed him a threepenny piece, a stamp, and fivepence in coppers, and told him to go to the devil.

'Thank you, sir,' said the inspector and got out.

I could not help smiling to myself, as I reflected how very different the manner of this underling would have been if he had had any idea of the rank of the person whom he was addressing. I was not in the least surprised that the Duke had a third-class ticket. Men of great wealth can afford to indulge in their little eccentricities.

A little later I ventured to call his Grace's attention to the fact that the sky now presented a threatening aspect. He said he believed the country wanted rain, and as he then resumed his evening paper I did not press the matter further. However, as I got out at my station I said, 'Good evening,' and he very graciously returned the salutation.

When I reached home I called Eliza's attention to my matchbox.

'That's the ordinary twopence-a-dozen sort you always have, isn't it?'

'It is. What is rather interesting is that at this present moment some of the matches which were originally in that box are in the waistcoat pocket of one of our greatest land-owners, the Duke of Coverdale.'

'I wouldn't have stuck it, if I'd been you,' said Eliza. 'A man may borrow a match from you, but he has no business to pocket any.'

'He pocketed them by my express invitation. An extremely pleasant fellow. I had rather an interesting chat with him in the train coming down.'

'Duke of Coverdale,' said Eliza thoughtfully. 'I've come upon that name somewhere recently.'

'Nothing is more probable. His Grace is very much in the public eye. You have probably seen some reference to him in the newspaper.'

'May have done,' said Eliza. 'How do you know it was the Duke?'

'Gillivant pointed him out. He knows all those people.'

At dinner that night Eliza suddenly exclaimed, 'I've got it!'

'Got what?'

'I know where I came across the name of the Duke of Coverdale. His picture is in the fashionable weddings in this week's *Home Happiness*.'

'I'll trouble you for it.'

The picture was of a quite young man with an appearance of pimples on the face. The accompanying letterpress told me that he had been married a week previously, and was spending the honeymoon in the South of France.

'Is the picture like him?' asked Eliza.

'Not very,' I said. 'Photographs are so seldom satisfactory.'

I took that page of *Home Happiness* up to the office next morning, and confronted Gillivant with it.

'Ah,' he said. 'Somebody will get the sack over that. That's a bad blunder.'

I felt, and still feel, more inclined to believe the statements of *Home Happiness* than those of young Gillivant. However, I did not pursue the subject. I merely asked him if he had received the remittance that he expected, and if in that case he would kindly return me the small advance which I had made him.

It would certainly be a curious coincidence – and also highly unsatisfactory – if it turned out that the only time I ever had any conversation with a Duke, it was not a Duke at all.

## A Failure in Economy

I had been struck – as I suppose almost every thinking man must at some time have been struck – by the vast amount of rhubarb which is every year allowed to go to waste. Many of us grow far more than we can use, and only a greengrocer can ever hope to sell it.

It is not even easy to give it away. I remember that once, when Eliza's mother had obliged with the water rate and last quarter's rent until better times, I twice sent her a bundle of our own home-grown rhubarb as a token of gratitude. The poor old lady asked me as tactfully as possible through Eliza to send no more, as she found it produced acidity, and her servant had now turned against it. Some men would dismiss such a subject from their minds at once as a mere trifle, but I am not of that type. It is not to me a trifle that the beautiful gifts of Nature should be squandered. It was, moreover, a question which was being peculiarly brought home to me. At my new house, 'Meadowsweet', the rhubarb bed is simply out of all proportion. It occupies space of which I could make better use, if the landlord were less difficult about it. He is one of these men who have to be humoured. Rhubarb jam was attempted on a small scale, but as Eliza dislikes it, and I cannot say that I am fond of it myself, and they refuse to touch it in the kitchen, it hardly seemed worth the trouble and expense. Consequently I was rather impressed when old Pridgeon – a practical man in his way, though he could never rise to my position in the office – happened to say that rhubarb wine, after two or three years in bottle, was indistinguishable even by experts from the finest Chablis.

Here I seemed to see a way out of my difficulty. It would be a pleasure to me naturally to place a bottle of good wine on my table which was of my growing and manufacture. It was a still greater pleasure to feel that my rhubarb would not be wasted. The only trouble was that I was not acquainted with the standard process of the manufacture of rhubarb wine.

I first consulted the encyclopædia. Under the word 'rhubarb' I found that wine was one of the uses to which it might be put. I then turned up 'wine' and found that rhubarb was one of the substances from which wine might be made. Other information, of course, was given. I learned, for instance, that medicinal rhubarb is grown principally in Mongolia, and I picked up a thing or two about carbon dioxide. But not one word was said as to the process of manufacturing rhubarb wine. These encyclopædias need a deal of revision. I then wrote to the editor of *Home Happiness*, which we have every week, and asked him if he would kindly oblige me with a recipe for rhubarb wine in his 'Answers to Correspondents'. He kept me waiting for six weeks, and I then received this reply: 'The recipe for which "Constant Reader" asks is so well known that we do not think space could advantageously be given to it here.'

And then, as so often happens, a mere chance came to my assistance. It turned out that Parker's mother had made rhubarb wine, and that Parker thought she could remember how it was done. We got on to it at once. The process was much longer than I had expected, and Parker was far less certain about it than I could have wished. She was, for instance, not quite sure whether the bung should be put in the barrel or not.

However, one night the work was completed, and we went to bed at our usual hour. At about two in the morning we were awakened by a loud crash of glass. Eliza said there were burglars in the house. I was by no means sure of this myself, or I should probably have gone down, but I thought it best to take precautions. I keep a police whistle in our bedroom at night – a practice which I should recommend to every householder. I leaned out of the window and blew it sharply. Presently a policeman came along at a walking pace. A little more hurry would have shown a keener sense of duty.

'What's up?' he said.

'I have some reason to believe that this house has been broken into.

We have just heard a crash of glass. It sounded as if it might be the scullery window.

'I'll go round and have a look,' said the policeman.

He was back in a minute and said it was the window of the scullery, and that I had better come down and let him in. There was no necessity for that at the moment, as he could easily put his arm through the broken pane and push the fastening back, and then get in at the scullery window.

This was what he did at my suggestion. We heard him moving about heavily downstairs, and then he called up that he could find nobody. I could not be quite sure that was right, so I went down.

'No sign of any burglar,' said the policeman cheerily, 'but you've got a rare old mess in your scullery.'

I looked in to see what had happened. It was a great pity that I ever allowed myself to be guided by Parker at all.

The bung had been blown out of the cask and had broken the window, and the whole place was swimming in rhubarb wine. When I mentioned it to Pridgeon some days afterwards he said that it was secondary fermentation, and all my foolishness in trying to do a thing without learning the way first.

At this moment a second policeman appeared, and he also got in at the scullery window. They inspected the coal-cellar with great care, and still seemed to linger. They were pleasant-spoken men, and said that these accidents would happen. I suggested a glass of beer, and they fell in with it at once. They finished the last two bottles in the house, and then decided that they must be getting on.

Of course, if there was any right or justice in the world, the price of that broken window, and of the materials used for the rhubarb wine, and of those two bottles of beer, would all be stopped out of Parker's salary. But under the present conditions of domestic service such a thing is not feasible.

However, an incident of this kind often gets one's blood up, and next morning I went round to the landlord's agent and practically held a pistol to his head.

'Either that rhubarb goes or I go,' I said. He took a note of what I proposed to put there in its place, and said that he would communicate with the landlord. Negotiations are still pending, but my position is a strong one, last quarter's rent having been paid down on the actual day, and I have reason to hope that my determined stand will meet with success.

In any case, there will be no more rhubarb wine in my house. Eliza is quite definite about it. I need hardly add that the noise of the explosion and the breaking glass woke everybody in the house except Parker. That is the way these things happen.

# A Visit to the Barber

*Tom Sharpe*

At nine-fifteen Zipser took his seat in the barber's chair.

'Just a trim,' he told the barber.

The man looked at his head doubtfully.

'Wouldn't like a nice short back and sides, I don't suppose?' he asked mournfully.

'Just a trim, thank you,' Zipser told him.

The barber tucked the sheet into his collar. 'Don't know why some of you young fellows bother to have your hair cut at all,' he said. 'Seem determined to put us out of business.'

'I'm sure you still get lots of work,' Zipser said.

The barber's scissor clicked busily round his ears. Zipser stared at himself in the mirror and wondered once again at the disparity between his innocent appearance and the terrible passion which surged inside him. His eyes moved sideways to the rows of bottles, Eau de Portugal, Dr Linthrop's Dandruff Mixture, Vitalis, a jar of Pomade. Who on earth used Pomade? Behind him the barber was chattering on about football but Zipser wasn't listening. He was eyeing the glass case to his left where a box in one corner suggested the reason for his haircut. He couldn't move his head so that he wasn't sure what the box contained but it looked the right sort of box. Finally when the man moved forward to pick up the clippers Zipser turned his head and saw that he had been eyeing with quite pointless interest a box of razor blades. He turned his head further and scanned the shelves. Shaving creams, razors, lotions, combs, all were there in abundance but not a single carton of contraceptives.

Zipser sat on in a trance while the clippers buzzed on his neck. They must keep the damned things somewhere. Every hairdresser had them. His face in the mirror assumed a new uncertainty. By the time the barber had finished and was powdering his neck and waving a

Humorous Stories

handmirror behind him, Zipser was in no mood to be critical of the result. He got out of the chair and waved the barber's brush away impatiently.

'That'll be thirty pence, sir,' the barber said, and made out a ticket. Zipser dug into his pocket for the money. 'Is there anything else?' Now was the moment he had been waiting for. The open invitation. That 'anything else' of the barber had covered only too literally a multitude of sins. In Zipser's case it was hopelessly inadequate not to say misleading.

'I'll have five packets of Durex,' Zipser said with a strangled bellow.

'Afraid we can't help you,' said the man. 'Landlord's a Catholic. It's in the lease we're not allowed to stock them.'

Zipser paid and went out into the street, cursing himself for not having looked in the window to see if there were any contraceptives on display. He walked into Rose Crescent and stared into a chemist's shop but the place was full of women. He tried three more shops only to find that they were all either full of housewives or that the shop assistants were young females. Finally he went into a barber's shop in Sidney Street where the window display was sufficiently broad-minded.

Two chairs were occupied and Zipser stood uncertainly just inside the door waiting for the barber to attend to him. As he stood there the door behind him opened and someone came in. Zipser stepped to one side and found himself looking into the face of Mr Turton, his supervisor.

'Ah, Zipser, getting your hair cut?' It seemed an unnecessarily inquisitive remark to Zipser. He felt inclined to tell the wretched man to mind his own business. Instead he nodded dumbly and sat down.

'Next one,' said the barber. Zipser feigned politeness.

'Won't you . . . ?' he said to Mr Turton.

'Your need is greater than mine, my dear fellow,' the supervisor said and sat down and picked up a copy of *Titbits*. For the second time that morning Zipser found himself in a barber's chair.

'Any particular way?' the barber asked.

'Just a trim,' said Zipser.

The barber bellied the sheet out over his knees and tucked it into his collar.

'If you don't mind my saying so, sir,' he said, 'but I'd say you'd already had your hair cut this morning.'

Zipser, staring into the mirror, saw Mr Turton look up and his own face turn bright red.

'Certainly not,' he muttered. 'What on earth makes you thing that?' It was not a wise remark and Zipser regretted it before he had finished mumbling.

'Well, for one thing,' the barber went on, responding to this challenge to his powers of observation, 'you've still got powder on your neck.' Zipser said shortly that he'd had a bath and used talcum powder.

'Oh quite,' said the barber sarcastically, 'and I suppose all these clipper shavings . . .'

'Listen,' said Zipser conscious that Mr Turton has still not turned back to *Titbits* and was listening with interest, 'if you don't want to cut my hair . . .' The buzz of the clippers interrupted his protest. Zipser stared angrily at his reflection in the mirror and wondered why he was being dogged by embarrassing situations. Mr Turton was eyeing the back of his head with a new interest.

'I mean,' said the barber putting his clippers away, 'some people like having their hair cut.' He winked at Mr Turton and in the mirror Zipser saw that wink. The scissors clicked round his ears and Zipser shut his eyes to escape the reproach he saw in them in the mirror. Everything he did now seemed tinged with catastrophe. Why in God's name should he fall in love with an enormous bedder? Why couldn't he just get on with his work, read in the library, write his thesis and go to meetings of CUNA?

'Had a customer once,' continued the barber remorselessly, 'who used to have his hair cut three times a week. Mondays, Wednesdays and Fridays. Regular as clockwork. I asked him once, when he'd been coming for a couple of years mind you, I said to him, "Tell me, Mr Hattersley, why do you come and have your hair cut so often?" Know what he said? Said it was the one place he could think. Said he got all his best ideas in the barber's chair. Weird when you think about it. Here I stand all day clipping and cutting and right in front of me, under my hand you might say, there's all those thoughts going on unbeknown to me. I mean I must have cut the hair on over a hundred thousand heads in my time. I've been cutting hair for twenty-five years now and that's a lot of customers. Stands to reason some of them must have been having some pretty peculiar thoughts at the time. Murderers and sex maniacs I daresay. I mean there would be, wouldn't there in all that number?

Stands to reason.'

Zipser shrank in the chair. Mr. Turton had lost all interest in *Titbits* now.

'Interesting theory,' he said encouragingly. 'I suppose statistically you're right. I've never thought of it that way before.'

Zipser said it took all sorts to make a world. It seemed the sort of trite remark the occasion demanded. By the time the barber had finished, he had given up all thought of asking for contraceptives. He paid the thirty pence and staggered out of the shop. Mr. Turton smiled and took his place in the chair.

It was almost lunchtime.

# The Idyll of Miss Sarah Brown

*Damon Runyon*

Of all the high players this country ever sees, there is no doubt but that the guy they call The Sky is the highest. In fact, the reason he is called The Sky is because he goes so high when it comes to betting on any proposition whatever. He will bet all he has, and nobody can bet any more than this.

His right name is Obadiah Masterson, and he is originally out of a little town in southern Colorado where he learns to shoot craps, and play cards, and one thing and another, and where his old man is a very well-known citizen, and something of a sport himself. In fact, The Sky tells me that when he finally cleans up all the loose scratch around his home town and decides he needs more room, his old man has a little private talk with him and says to him like this:

'Son,' the old guy says, 'you are now going out into the wide, wide world to make your own way, and it is a very good thing to do, as there are no more opportunities for you in this burg. I am only sorry,' he says, 'that I am not able to bank-roll you to a very large start, but,' he says, 'not having any potatoes to give you, I am now going to stake you to some very valuable advice, which I personally collect in my years of experience around and about, and I hope and trust you will always bear this advice in mind.

'Son,' the old guy says, 'no matter how far you travel, or how smart you get, always remember this: Some day, somewhere,' he says, 'a guy is going to come to you and show you a nice brand-new deck of cards on which the seal is never broken, and this guy is going to offer to bet you that the jack of spades will jump out of this deck and squirt cider in your ear. But, son,' the old guy says, 'do not bet him, for as sure as you do you are going to get an ear full of cider.'

Well, The Sky remembers what his old man says, and he is always very cautious about betting on such propositions as the jack of spades jumping out of a sealed deck of cards and squirting cider in his ear, and so he makes few mistakes as he goes along. In fact, the only real mistake The Sky makes is when he hits St Louis after leaving his old home town, and loses all his potatoes betting a guy St Louis is the biggest town in the world.

Now of course this is before The Sky ever sees any bigger towns, and he is never much of a hand for reading up on matters such as this. In fact, the only reading The Sky ever does as he goes along through life is in these Gideon Bibles such as he finds in the hotel rooms where he lives, for The Sky never lives anywhere else but in hotel rooms for years.

He tells me that he reads many items of interest in these Gideon Bibles, and furthermore The Sky says that several times these Gideon Bibles keep him from getting out of line, such as the time he finds himself pretty much frozen-in over in Cincinnati, what with owing everybody in town except maybe the mayor from playing games of chance of one kind and another.

Well, The Sky says he sees no way of meeting these obligations and he is figuring the only thing he can do is to take a run-out powder, when he happens to read in one of these Gideon Bibles where it says like this:

'Better is it,' the Gideon Bible says, 'that thou shouldest not vow, than that thou shouldest vow and not pay.'

Well, The Sky says he can see that there is no doubt whatever but that this means a guy shall not welsh, so he remains in Cincinnati until he manages to wiggle himself out of the situation, and from that day to this, The Sky never thinks of welshing.

He is maybe thirty years old, and is a tall guy with a round kisser, and big blue eyes, and he always looks as innocent as a little baby. But The Sky is by no means as innocent as he looks. In fact, The Sky is smarter than three Philadelphia lawyers, which makes him very smart, indeed, and he is well established as a high player in New Orleans, and Chicago, and Los Angeles, and wherever else there is any action in the way of card-playing, or crap-shooting, or horse-racing, or betting on the baseball games, for The Sky is always moving around the country following the action.

But while The Sky will bet on anything whatever, he is more of a short-card player and a crap-shooter than anything else, and furthermore he is a great hand for propositions, such as are always coming up among citizens who follow games of chance for a living. Many citizens prefer betting on propositions to anything you can think of, because they figure a proposition gives them a chance to out-smart somebody, and in fact I know citizens who will sit up all night making up propositions to offer other citizens the next day.

A proposition may be only a problem in cards, such as what is the price against a guy getting aces back-to-back, or how often a pair of deuces will win a hand in stud, and then again it may be some very daffy proposition, indeed, although the daffier any proposition seems to be, the more some citizens like it. And no one ever sees The Sky when he does not have some proposition of his own.

The first time he ever shows up around this town, he goes to a baseball game at the Polo Grounds with several prominent citizens, and while he is at the ball game, he buys himself a sack of Harry Stevens' peanuts, which he dumps in a side pocket of his coat. He is eating these peanuts all through the game, and after the game is over and he is walking across the field with the citizens, he says to them like this:

'What price,' The Sky says, 'I cannot throw a peanut from second base to the home plate?'

Well, everybody knows that a peanut is too light for anybody to throw it this far, so Big Nig, the crap shooter, who always likes to have a little the best of it running for him, speaks as follows:

'You can have 3 to 1 from me, stranger,' Big Nig says.

'Two C's against six,' The Sky says, and then he stands on second base, and takes a peanut out of his pocket, and not only whips it to the home plate, but on into the lap of a fat guy who is still sitting in the grand stand putting the zing on Bill Terry for not taking Walker out of the box when Walker is getting a pasting from the other club.

Well, naturally, this is a most astonishing throw, indeed, but afterwards it comes out that The Sky throws a peanut loaded with lead, and of course it is not one of Harry Stevens' peanuts, either, as Harry is not selling peanuts full of lead at a dime a bag, with the price of lead what it is.

It is only a few nights after this that The Sky states another most unusual proposition to a group of citizens sitting in Mindy's restaurant when he offers to bet a C note that he can go down into Mindy's cellar and catch a live rat with his bare hands and everybody is greatly astonished when Mindy himself steps up and and takes the bet, for ordinarily Mindy will not bet you a nickel he is alive.

But it seems that Mindy knows that The Sky plants a tame rat in the cellar, and this rat knows The Sky and loves him dearly, and will let him catch it any time he wishes, and it also seems that Mindy knows that one of his dish washers happens upon this rat, and not knowing it is tame, knocks it flatter than a pancake. So when The Sky goes down into the cellar and starts trying to catch a rat with his bare hands he is greatly surprised how inhospitable the rat turns out to be, because it is one of Mindy's personal rats, and Mindy is around afterwards saying he will lay plenty of 7 to 5 against even Strangler Lewis being able to catch one of his rats with his bare hands, or with boxing gloves on.

I am only telling you all this to show you what a smart guy The Sky is, and I am only sorry I do not have time to tell you about many other very remarkable propositions that he thinks up outside of his regular business.

It is well-known to one and all that he is very honest in every respect, and that he hates and despises cheaters at cards, or dice, and furthermore The Sky never wishes to play with any the best of it himself, or anyway not much. He will never take the inside of any situation, as many gamblers love to do, such as owning a gambling house, and having the percentage run for him instead of against him, for always The Sky is strictly a player, because he says he will never care to settle down in one spot long enough to become the owner of anything.

In fact, in all the years The Sky is drifting around the country, nobody ever knows him to own anything except maybe a bank roll, and when he comes to Broadway the last time, which is the time I am now speaking of, he has a hundred G's in cash money, and an extra suit of clothes, and this is all he has in the world. He never owns such a thing as a house, or an automobile, or a piece of jewellery. He never owns a watch, because The Sky says time means nothing to him.

Of course some guys will figure a hundred G's comes under the head of owning something, but as far as The Sky is concerned, money is nothing but just something for him to play with and the dollars may as well be doughnuts as far as value goes with him. The only time The Sky ever thinks of money as money is when he is broke, and the only way he can tell he is broke is when he reaches into his pocket and finds nothing there but his fingers.

Then it is necessary for The Sky to go out and dig up some fresh scratch somewhere, and when it comes to digging up scratch, The Sky is practically supernatural. He can get more potatoes on the strength of a telegram to some place or other than John D. Rockefeller can get on collateral, for everybody knows The Sky's word is as good as wheat in the bin.

Now one Sunday evening The Sky is walking along Broadway, and at the corner of Forty-ninth Street he comes upon a little bunch of mission workers who are holding a religious meeting, such as mission workers love to do of a Sunday evening, the idea being that they may round up a few sinners here and there, although personally I always claim the mission workers come out too early to catch any sinners on this part of Broadway. At such an hour the sinners are still in bed resting up from their sinning of the night before, so they will be in good shape for more sinning a little later on.

There are only four of these mission workers, and two of them are old guys, and one is an old doll, while the other is a young doll who is tootling on a cornet. And after a couple of ganders at this young doll, The Sky is a goner, for this is one of the most beautiful young dolls anybody ever sees on Broadway, and especially as a mission worker. Her name is Miss Sarah Brown.

She is tall, and thin, and has a first-class shape, and her hair is a light brown, going on blonde, and her eyes are like I do not know what, except that they are one-hundred-per-cent eyes in every respect. Furthermore, she is not a bad cornet player, if you like cornet players, although at this spot on Broadway she has to play against a scat band in a chop-suey joint near by, and this is tough competition, although at that many citizens believe Miss Sarah Brown will win by a large score if she only gets a little more support from one of the old guys with her who has a big bass drum, but does not pound it hearty enough.

Well, The Sky stands there listening to Miss Sarah Brown tootling on the cornet for quite a spell, and then he hears her make a speech in which she puts the blast on sin very good, and boosts religion quite some, and says if there are any souls around that need saving the owners of same may step forward at once. But no one steps forward, so The Sky comes over to Mindy's restaurant where many citizens are congregated, and starts telling us about Miss Sarah Brown. But of course we already know about Miss Sarah Brown, because she is so beautiful, and so good.

Furthermore, everybody feels somewhat sorry for Miss Sarah Brown, for while she is always tootling the cornet, and making speeches, and looking to save any souls that need saving, she never seems to find any souls to save, or at least her bunch of mission workers never gets any bigger. In fact, it gets smaller, as she starts out with a guy who plays a very fair sort of trombone, but this guy takes it on the lam one night with the trombone, which one and all consider a dirty trick.

Now from this time on, The Sky does not take any interest in anything but Miss Sarah Brown, and any night she is out on the corner with the other mission workers, you will see The Sky standing around looking at her, and naturally after a few weeks of this, Miss Sarah Brown must know The Sky is looking at her, or she is dumber than seems possible. And nobody ever figures Miss Sarah Brown dumb, as she is always on her toes, and seems plenty able to take care of herself, even on Broadway.

Sometimes after the street meeting is over, The Sky follows the mission workers to their headquarters in an old storeroom around in Forty-eighth Street where they generally hold an indoor session, and I hear The Sky drops many a large coarse note in the collection box while looking at Miss Sarah Brown, and there is no doubt these notes come in handy around the mission, as I hear business is by no means so good there.

It is called the Save-a-Soul Mission, and it is run mainly by Miss Sarah Brown's grandfather, an old guy with whiskers, by the name of Arvide Abernathy, but Miss Sarah Brown seems to do most of the work, including tootling the corner, and visiting the poor people around and about, and all this and that, and many citizens claim it is a great shame that such a beautiful doll is wasting her time being good.

How The Sky ever becomes acquainted with Miss Sarah Brown is a very great mystery, but the next thing anybody knows, he is saying hello to her, and she is smiling at him out of her one-hundred-per-cent eyes, and one evening when I happen to be with The Sky we run into her walking along Forty-ninth Street, and The Sky hauls off and stops her, and says it is a nice evening, which it is, at that. Then The Sky says to Miss Sarah Brown like this:

'Well,' The Sky says, 'how is the mission dodge going these days? Are you saving any souls?' he says.

Well, it seems from what Miss Sarah Brown says the soul-saving is very slow, indeed, these days.

'In fact,' Miss Sarah Brown says, 'I worry greatly about how few souls we seem to save. Sometimes I wonder if we are lacking in grace.'

She goes on up the street, and The Sky stands looking after her, and he says to me like this:

'I wish I can think of some way to help this little doll,' he says, 'especially,' he says, 'in saving a few souls to build up her mob at the mission. I must speak to her again, and see if I can figure something out.'

But The Sky does not get to speak to Miss Sarah Brown again, because somebody weighs in the sacks on him by telling her he is nothing but a professional gambler, and that he is a very undesirable character, and that his only interest in hanging around the mission is because she is a good-looking doll. So all of a sudden Miss Sarah Brown plays a plenty of chill for The Sky. Furthermore, she sends him word that she does not care to accept any more of his potatoes in the collection box, because his potatoes are nothing but ill-gotten gains.

Well, naturally, this hurts The Sky's feelings no little, so he quits standing around looking at Miss Sarah Brown, and going to the mission, and takes to mingling again with the citizens in Mindy's, and showing some interest in the affairs of the community, especially the crap games.

Of course the crap games that are going on at this time are nothing much, because practically everybody in the world is broke, but there is a head-and-head game run by Nathan Detroit over a garage in Fifty-second Street where there is occasionally some action, and who shows up at this crap game early one evening but The Sky, although it seems he shows up there more to find company than anything else.

In fact, he only stands around watching the play, and talking with other guys who are also standing around and watching, and many of these guys are very high shots during the gold rush, although most of them are now as clean as a jaybird, and maybe cleaner. One of these guys is a guy by the name of Brandy Bottle Bates, who is known from coast to coast as a high player when he has anything to play with, and who is called Brandy Bottle Bates because it seems that years ago he is a great hand for belting a brandy bottle around.

This Brandy Bottle Bates is a big, black-looking guy, with a large beezer, and a head shaped like a pear, and he is considered a very immoral and wicked character, but he is a pretty slick gambler, and a fast man with a dollar when he is in the money.

Well, finally The Sky asks Brandy Bottle why he is not playing and Brandy laughs, and states as follows:

'Why,' he says, 'in the first place I have no potatoes, and in the second place I doubt if it will do me much good if I do have any potatoes the way I am going the past year. Why,' Brandy Bottle says, 'I cannot win a bet to save my soul.'

Now this crack seems to give The Sky an idea, as he stands looking at Brandy Bottle very strangely, and while he is looking, Big Nig, the crap shooter, picks up the dice and hits three times hand-running, bing, bing, bing. Then Big Nig comes out on a six and Brandy Bottle Bates speaks as follows:

'You see how my luck is,' he says. 'Here is Big Nig hotter than a stove, and here I am without a bob to follow him with, especially,' Brandy says, 'when he is looking for nothing but a six. Why,' he says, 'Nig can make sixes all night when he is hot. If he does not make this six, the way he is, I will be willing to turn square and quit gambling forever.'

'Well, Brandy,' The Sky says, 'I will make you a proposition. I will lay you a G note Big Nig does not get his six. I will lay you a G note against nothing but your soul,' he says. 'I mean if Big Nig does not get his six, you are to turn square and join Miss Sarah Brown's mission for six months.'

'Bet!' Brandy Bottle Bates says right away, meaning the proposition is on, although the chances are he does not quite understand the proposition. All Brandy understands is The Sky wishes to wager that Big Nig does not make his six, and Brandy Bottle Bates will be willing to bet his soul a couple of times over on Big Nig making his six, and figure he is getting the best of it, at that, as Brandy has great confidence in Nig.

Well, sure enough, Big Nig makes the six, so The Sky weeds Brandy Bottle Bates a G note, although everybody around is saying The Sky makes a terrible over-lay of the natural price in giving Brandy Bottle a G against his soul. Furthermore, everybody around figures the chances are The Sky only wishes to give Brandy an opportunity to get in action, and nobody figures The Sky is on the level about trying to win Brandy Bottle Bates' soul, especially as The Sky does not seem to wish to go any further after paying the bet.

He only stands there looking on and seeming somewhat depressed as Brandy Bottle goes into action on his own account with the G note, fading other guys around the table with cash money. But Brandy Bottle Bates seems to figure what is in The Sky's mind pretty well, because Brandy Bottle is a crafty old guy.

It finally comes his turn to handle the dice, and he hits a couple of times, and then he comes out on a four, and anybody will tell you that a four is a very tough point to make, even with a lead pencil. Then Brandy Bottle turns to The Sky and speaks to him as follows:

'Well, Sky,' he says, 'I will take the odds off you on this one. I know you do not want my dough,' he says. 'I know you only want my soul for Miss Sarah Brown, and,' he says, 'without wishing to be fresh about it, I know why you want it for her. I am young once myself,' Brandy Bottle says. 'And you know if I lose to you, I will be over there in Forty-eighth Street in an hour pounding on the door, for Brandy always settles.

'But, Sky,' he says, 'now I am in the money, and my price goes up. Will you lay me ten G's against my soul I do not make this four?'

'Bet!' The Sky says, and right away Brandy Bottle hits with a four.

Well, when word goes around that The Sky is up at Nathan Detroit's crap game trying to win Brandy Bottle Bates' soul for Miss Sarah Brown, the excitement is practically intense. Somebody telephones Mindy's, where a large number of citizens are sitting around arguing about this and that, and telling one another how much they will bet in support of their arguments, if only they have something to bet, and Mindy himself is almost killed in the rush for the door.

One of the first guys out of Mindy's and up to the crap game is Regret, the horse player, and as he comes in Brandy Bottle is looking for a nine, and The Sky is laying him twelve G's against his soul that he does not make this nine, for it seems Brandy Bottle's soul keeps getting more and more expensive.

Well, Regret wishes to bet his soul against a G that Brandy Bottle get his nine, and is greatly insulted when The Sky cannot figure his price any better than a double saw, but finally Regret accepts this price, and Brandy Bottle hits again.

Now many other citizens request a little action from The Sky, and if there is one thing The Sky cannot deny a citizen it is action, so he says he will lay them according to how he figures their word to join Miss

Sarah Brown's mission if Brandy Bottle misses out, but about this time The Sky finds he has no more potatoes on him, being now around thirty-five G's loser, and he wishes to give markers.

But Brandy Bottle says that while ordinarily he will be pleased to extend The Sky this accommodation, he does not care to accept markers against his soul, so then The Sky has to leave the joint and go over to his hotel two or three blocks away, and get the night clerk to open his damper so The Sky can get the rest of his bank roll. In the meantime the crap game continues at Nathan Detroit's among the small operators, while the other citizens stand around and say that while they hear of many a daffy proposition in their time, this is the daffiest that ever comes to their attention, although Big Nig claims he hears of a daffier one, but cannot think what it is.

Big Nig claims that all gamblers are daffy anyway, and in fact he says if they are not daffy they will not be gamblers, and while he is arguing this matter back comes The Sky with fresh scratch and Brandy Bottle Bates takes up where he leaves off, although Brandy says he is accepting the worst of it, as the dice have a chance to cool off.

Now the upshot of the whole business is that Brandy Bottle hits thirteen licks in a row, and the last lick he makes is on a ten, and it is for twenty G's against his soul, with about a dozen other citizens getting anywhere from one to five C's against their souls, and complaining bitterly of the price.

And as Brandy Bottle makes his ten, I happen to look at The Sky and I see him watching Brandy with a very peculiar expression on his face, and furthermore I see The Sky's right hand creeping inside his coat where I know he always packs a Betsy in a shoulder holster, so I can see something is wrong somewhere.

But before I can figure out what it is, there is quite a fuss at the door, and loud talking, and a doll's voice, and all of a sudden in bobs nobody else but Miss Sarah Brown. It is plain to be seen that she is all steamed up about something.

She marches right up to the crap table where Brandy Bottle Bates and The Sky and the other citizens are standing, and one and all are feeling sorry for Dobber, the doorman, thinking of what Nathan Detroit is bound to say to him for letting her in. The dice are still lying on the table showing Brandy Bottle Bates' last throw, which cleans The Sky and gives many citizens the first means they enjoy in several months.

Well, Miss Sarah Brown looks at The Sky, and The Sky looks at Miss Sarah Brown, and Miss Sarah Brown looks at the citizens around and about, and one and all are somewhat dumbfounded, and nobody seems to be able to think of much to say, although The Sky finally speaks up as follows:

'Good evening,' The Sky says. 'It is a nice evening,' he says. 'I am trying to win a few souls for you around here, but,' he says, 'I seem to be about half out of luck.'

'Well,' Miss Sarah Brown says, looking at The Sky most severely out of her hundred-per-cent eyes, 'you are taking too much upon yourself. I can win any souls I need myself. You better be thinking of your own soul. By the way,' she says, 'are you risking your own soul, or just your money?'

Well, of course up to this time The Sky is not risking anything but his potatoes, so he only shakes his head to Miss Sarah Brown's question, and looks somewhat disorganised.

'I know something about gambling,' Miss Sarah Brown says, 'especially about crap games. I ought to,' she says. 'It ruins my poor papa and my brother Joe. If you wish to gamble for souls, Mister Sky, gamble for your own soul.'

Now Miss Sarah Brown opens a small black leather pocketbook she is carrying in one hand, and pulls out a two-dollar bill, and it is such a two-dollar bill as seems to have seen much service in its time, and holding up this deuce, Miss Sarah Brown speaks as follows:

'I will gamble with you, Mister Sky,' she says. 'I will gamble with you,' she says, 'on the same terms you gamble with these parties here. This two dollars against your soul, Mister Sky. It is all I have, but,' she says, 'it is more than your soul is worth.'

Well, of course anybody can see that Miss Sarah Brown is doing this because she is very angry, and wishes to make The Sky look small, but right away The Sky's duke comes from inside his coat, and he picks up the dice and hands them to her and speaks as follows:

'Roll them,' The Sky says, and Miss Sarah Brown snatches the dice out of his hand and gives them a quick sling on the table in such a way that anybody can see she is not a professional crap shooter, and not even an amateur crap shooter, for all amateur crap shooters first breathe on the dice, and rattle them good, and make remarks to them, such as 'Come on, baby!'

In fact, there is some criticism of Miss Sarah Brown afterwards on account of her haste, as many citizens are eager to string with her to hit, while others are just as anxious to bet she misses, and she does not give them a chance to get down.

Well, Scranton Slim is the stick guy, and he takes a gander at the dice as they hit up against the side of the table and bounce back, and then Slim hollers, 'Winner, winner, winner,' as stick guys love to do, and what is showing on the dice as big as life, but a six and a five, which makes eleven, no matter how you figure, so The Sky's soul belongs to Miss Sarah Brown.

She turns at once and pushes through the citizens around the table without even waiting to pick up the deuce she lays down when she grabs the dice. Afterwards a most obnoxious character by the name of Red Nose Regan tries to claim the deuce as a sleeper and gets the heave-o from Nathan Detroit, who becomes very indignant about this, stating that Red Nose is trying to give his joint a wrong rap.

Naturally, The Sky follows Miss Brown, and Dobber, the doorman, tells me that as they are waiting for him to unlock the door and let them out, Miss Sarah Brown turns on The Sky and speaks to him as follows:

'You are a fool,' Miss Sarah Brown says.

Well, at this Dobber figures The Sky is bound to let one go, as this seems to be most insulting language, but instead of letting one go, The Sky only smiles at Miss Sarah Brown and says to her like this:

'Why,' The Sky says, 'Paul says "If any man among you seemeth to be wise in this world, let him become a fool, that he may be wise." I love you, Miss Sarah Brown,' The Sky says.

Well, now, Dobber has a pretty fair sort of memory, and he says that Miss Sarah Brown tells The Sky that since he seems to know so much about the Bible, maybe he remembers the second verse of the Song of Solomon, but the chances are Dobber muffs the number of the verse, because I look the matter up in one of these Gideon Bibles, and the verse seems a little too much for Miss Sarah Brown, although of course you never can tell.

Anyway, this is about all there is to the story, except that Brandy Bottle Bates slides out during the confusion so quietly even Dobber scarcely remembers letting him out, and he takes most of The Sky's potatoes with him, but he soon gets batted in against the faro bank out in Chicago, and the last anybody hears of him he gets religion all over again, and is preaching out in San Jose, so The Sky always claims he beats Brandy for his soul, at that.

I see The Sky the other night at Forty-ninth Street and Broadway, and he is with quite a raft of mission workers, including Mrs Sky, for it seems that the soul-saving business picks up wonderfully, and The Sky is giving a big bass drum such a first-class whacking that the scat band in the chop-suey joint can scarcely be heard. Furthermore, The Sky is hollering between whacks, and I never see a guy look happier, especially when Mrs Sky smiles at him out of her hundred-per-cent eyes. But I do not linger long, because The Sky gets a gander at me, and right away he begins hollering:

'I see before me a sinner of the deepest dye,' he hollers. 'Oh, sinner, repent before it is too late. Join with us, sinner,' he hollers, 'and let us save your soul.'

Naturally, this crack about me being a sinner embarrasses me no little, as it is by no means true, and it is a good thing for The Sky there is no copper in me, or I will go to Mrs Sky, who is always bragging about how she wins The Sky's soul by outplaying him at his own game, and tell her the truth.

And the truth is that the dice with which she wins The Sky's soul, and which are the same dice with which Brandy Bottle Bates wins all his potatoes, are strictly phony, and that she gets into Nathan Detroit's just in time to keep The Sky from killing old Brandy Bottle.

# Stone Walls do not a Prison Make

*Evelyn Waugh*

Paul's trial, which took place some weeks later at the Old Bailey, was a bitter disappointment to the public, the news editors and the jury and counsel concerned. The arrest at the Ritz, the announcement at St Margaret's that the wedding was postponed, Margot's flight to Corfu, the refusal of bail, the meals sent in to Paul on covered dishes from Boulestin's, had been 'front-page stories' every day. After all this, Paul's conviction and sentence were a lame conclusion. At first he pleaded guilty on all charges, despite the entreaties of his counsel, but eventually he was galvanised into some show of defence by the warning of the presiding judge that the law allowed punishment with the cat-o'-nine-tails for offences of this sort. Even then things were very flat. Potts as chief witness for the prosecution was unshakable, and was later warmly commended by the court; no evidence, except of previous good conduct, was offered by the defence; Margot Beste-Chetwynde's name was not mentioned, though the judge in passing sentence remarked that 'no one could be ignorant of the callous insolence with which, on the very eve of arrest for this most infamous of crimes, the accused had been preparing to join his name with one honoured in his country's history, and to drag down to his own pitiable depths of depravity a lady of beauty, rank and stainless reputation. The just censure of society,' remarked the judge, 'is accorded to those so inconstant and intemperate that they must take their pleasures in the unholy market of humanity that still sullies the fame of our civilisation; but for the traders themselves, these human vampires who prey upon the degradation of their species, society had reserved the right of ruthless suppression.' So Paul was sent off to prison, and the papers headed the column they reserve for home events of minor importance with PRISON FOR EX-SOCIETY BRIDEGROOM. JUDGE ON HUMAN VAMPIRES, and there, as far as the public were concerned, the matter ended.

Before this happened, however, a conversation took place which deserves the attention of all interested in the confused series of events of which Paul had become a part. One day, while he was waiting for trial, he was visited in his cell by Peter Beste-Chetwynde.

'Hullo!' he said.

'Hullo, Paul!' said Peter. 'Mamma asked me to come in to see you. She wants to know if you are getting the food all right she's ordered for you. I hope you like it, because I chose most of it myself. I thought you wouldn't want anything very heavy.'

'It's splendid,' said Paul. 'How's Margot?'

'Well, that's rather what I've come to tell you, Paul. Margot's gone away.'

'Where to?'

'She's gone off alone to Corfu. I made her, though she wanted to stay and see your trial. You can imagine what a time we've had with reporters and people. You don't think it awful of her, do you? And listen, there's something else. Can that policeman hear? It's this. You remember that awful old man Maltravers. Well, you've probably seen he's Home Secretary now. He's been round to Mamma in the most impossible Oppenheim kind of way, and said that if she'd marry him he could get you out. Of course he's obviously been reading books. But Mamma thinks it's probably true, and she wants to know how you feel about it. She rather feels the whole thing's her fault, really, and, short of going to prison herself, she'll do anything to help. You can't imagine Mamma in prison, can you? Well, would you rather get out now and her marry Maltravers, or wait until you do get out and marry her yourself? She was rather definite about it.'

Paul thought of Professor Silenus' 'In ten years she will be worn out', but he said:

'I'd rather she waited if you think she possibly can.'

'I thought you'd say that, Paul. I'm so glad. Mamma said: "I won't say I don't know how I shall ever be able to make up to him for all this, because I think he knows I can." Those were her words. I don't suppose you'll get more than a year or so, will you?'

'Good Lord, I hope not,' said Paul.

His sentence of seven years' penal servitude was rather a blow. 'In ten years she will be worn out,' he thought as he drove in the prison-van to Blackstone Gaol.

On his first day there Paul met quite a number of people, some of whom he knew already. The first person was a warder with a low brow and distinctly menacing manner. He wrote Paul's name in the 'Body Receipt Book' with some difficulty and then conducted him to a cell. He had evidently been reading the papers.

'Rather different from the Ritz Hotel, eh?' he said. 'We don't like your kind 'ere, see? And we knows 'ow to treat 'em. You won't find nothing like the Ritz 'ere, you dirty White Slaver.'

But there he was wrong, because the next person Paul met was Philbrick. His prison clothes were ill-fitting, and his chin was unshaven, but he still bore an indefinable air of the grand manner.

'Thought I'd be seeing you soon,' he said. 'They've put me on to reception bath cleaner, me being an old hand. I've been saving the best suit I can find for you. Not a louse on it, hardly.' He threw a little pile of clothes, stamped with the broad arrow, on to the bench.

The warder returned with another, apparently his superior officer. Together they made a careful inventory of all Paul's possessions.

'Shoes, brown, one pair; socks, fancy, one pair; suspenders, black silk, one pair,' read out the warder in a sing-song voice. 'Never saw a bloke with so much clothes.'

There were several checks due to difficulties of spelling, and it was some time before the list was finished.

'Cigarette case, white metal, containing two cigarettes; watch, white metal; tie-pin, fancy' – it had cost Margot considerably more than the warder earned in a year, had he only known – 'studs, bone, one pair; cuff links, fancy, one pair.' The officers looked doubtfully at Paul's gold cigar piercer, the gift of the best man. 'What's this 'ere?'

'It's for cigars,' said Paul.

'Not so much lip!' said the warder, banging him on the top of his head with the pair of shoes he happened to be holding. 'Put it down as "instrument". That's the lot,' he said, 'unless you've got false teeth. You're allowed to keep them, only we must make a note of it.'

'No,' said Paul.

'Truss or other surgical appliance?'

'No,' said Paul.

'All right! You can go to the bath.'

Paul sat for the regulation ten minutes in the regulation nine inches of warm water – which smelt reassuringly of disinfectant – and then put on his prison-clothes. The loss of his personal possessions gave him a curiously agreeable sense of irresponsibility.

'You look a treat,' said Philbrick.

Next he saw the Medical Officer, who sat at a table covered with official forms.

'Name?' said the Doctor.

'Pennyfeather.'

'Have you at any time been detained in a mental home or similar institution? If so, give particulars.'

'I was at Scone College, Oxford,' said Paul.

The Doctor looked up for the first time. 'Don't you dare to make jokes here, my man,' he said, 'or I'll soon have you in the straight-jacket in less than no time.'

'Sorry,' said Paul.

'Don't speak to the Medical Officer unless to answer a question,' said the warder at his elbow.

'Sorry,' said Paul unconsciously, and was banged on the head.

'Suffering from consumption, VD, or any contagious disease?' asked the MO.

'Not that I know of,' said Paul.

'That's all,' said the Doctor. 'I have certified you as capable of undergoing the usual descriptions of punishment as specified below, to wit, restraint of handcuffs, leg-chains, cross-irons, body-belt, canvas dress, close confinement, No. 1 diet, No. 2 diet, birch-rod and cat-o'-nine-tails. Any complaints?'

'But must I have all these at once?' asked Paul, rather dismayed.

'You will if you ask impertinent questions. Look after that man, officer; he's obviously a troublesome character.'

'Come 'ere, you,' said the warder. They went up a passage and down two flights of iron steps. Long galleries with iron railings stretched out in each direction, giving access to innumerable doors. Wire netting was stretched between the landings. 'So don't you try no monkey-tricks. Suicide isn't allowed in this prison. See?' said the warder. 'This is your cell. Keep it clean, or you'll know the reason why, and this is your number.' He buttoned a yellow badge on to Paul's coat.

'Like a flag-day,' said Paul.

'Shut up, you – ,' remarked the warder, and locked the door.

'I suppose I shall learn to respect these people in time,' thought Paul. 'They all seem so much less awe-inspiring then anyone I ever met.'

His next visit was from the Schoolmaster. The door was unlocked, and a seedy-looking young man in a tweed suit came into the cell.

'Can you read and write, D.4.12?' asked the newcomer.

'Yes,' said Paul.

'Public or secondary education?'

'Public,' said Paul. His school had been rather sensitive on this subject.

'What was your standard when you left school?'

'Well, I don't quite know. I don't think we had standards.'

The Schoolmaster marked him down as 'Memory defective' on a form, and went out. Presently he returned with a book.

'You must do your best with that for the next four weeks,' he said. 'I'll try and get you into one of the morning classes. You won't find it difficult, if you can read fairly easily. You see, it begins there,' he said helpfully, showing Paul the first page.

It was an English Grammar published in 1872.

'*A syllable is a single sound made by one simple effort of the voice,*' Paul read.

'Thank you,' he said; 'I'm sure I shall find it useful.'

'You can change it after four weeks if you can't get on with it,' said the Schoolmaster. 'But I should stick to it, if you can.'

Again the door was locked.

Next came the Chaplain. 'Here is your Bible and a book of devotion. The Bible stays in the cell always. You can change the book of devotion any week if you wish to. Are you Church of England? Services are voluntary – that is to say, you must either attend all or none.' The Chaplain spoke in a nervous and hurried manner. He was new to his job, and he had already visited fifty prisoners that day, one of whom had delayed him for a long time with descriptions of a vision he had seen the night before.

'Hallo, Prendy!' said Paul.

Mr. Prendergast looked at him anxiously. 'I didn't recognise you,' he said. 'People look so much alike in those clothes. This is most disturbing, Pennyfeather. As soon as I saw that you'd been convicted I was afraid they might send you here. Oh dear! oh dear! It makes everything still more difficult.'

'What's the matter, Prendy? Doubts again?'

'No, no, discipline, my old trouble. I've only been at the job a week. I was very lucky to get it. My bishop said that he thought there was more opening for a Modern Churchman in this kind of work than in the parishes. The Governor is very modern too. But criminals are just as bad as boys, I find. They pretend to make confessions and tell me the most dreadful things just to see what I'll say, and in chapel they laugh so much that the warders spend all their time correcting them. It makes the services seem so irreverent. Several of them got put on No. 1 diet this morning for singing the wrong words to one of the hymns, and of course that only makes me more unpopular. Please, Pennyfeather, if you don't mind, you mustn't call me Prendy, and if anyone passes the cell will you stand up when you're talking to me. You're supposed to, you see, and the Chief Warder has said some very severe things to me about maintaining discipline.'

At this moment the face of the warder appeared at the peep-hole in the door.

'I trust you realise the enormity of your offence and the justice of your punishment?' said Mr Prendergast in a loud voice. 'Pray for penitence.'

A warder came into the cell.

'Sorry to disturb you, sir, but I've got to take this one to see the Governor. There's D.4.18 down the way been asking for you for days. I said I'd tell you, only, if you'll forgive my saying so, I shouldn't be too soft with 'im sir. We know 'im of old. 'E's a sly old devil, begging your pardon, sir, and 'e's only religious when 'e thinks it'll pay.'

'I think that I am the person to decide that, officer,' said Mr Prendergast with some dignity. 'You may take D.4.12 to the Governor.'

Sir Wilfred Lucas-Dockery had not been intended by nature or education for the Governor of a prison; his appointment was the idea of a Labour Home Secretary who had been impressed by an appendix on the theory of penology which he had contributed to a report on the treatment of 'Conscientious Objectors'. Up to that time Sir Wilfred had held the Chair of Sociology at a Midland university; only his intimate friends and a few specially favoured pupils knew that behind his mild and professional exterior he concealed an ardent ambition to serve in the public life of his generation. He stood twice for Parliament, but so diffidently that his candidature passed almost unnoticed. Colonel MacAdder, his predecessor in office, a veteran of numberless unrecorded campaigns on the Afghan frontier, had said to him on his retirement: 'Good luck, Sir Wilfred! If I may give you a piece of advice, it's this. Don't bother about the lower warders or the prisoners. Give hell to the man immediately below you, and you can rely on him to pass it on with interest. If you make prison bad enough, people'll take jolly good care to keep out of it. That's been my policy all through, and I'm proud of it' (a policy which soon became quite famous in the society of Cheltenham Spa).

Sir Wilfred, however, had his own ideas. 'You must understand,' he said to Paul, 'that it is my aim to establish personal contact with each of the men under my care. I want you to take a pride in your prison and in your work here. So far as possible, I like the prisoners to carry on with their avocations in civilized life. What was this man's profession, officer?'

'White Slave traffic, sir.'

'Ah, yes. Well, I'm afraid you won't have much opportunity for that here. What else have you done?'

'I was nearly a clergyman once,' said Paul.

'Indeed? Well, I hope in time, if I find enough men with the same intention, to get together a theological class. You've no doubt met the Chaplain, a very broad-minded man. Still, for the present we are only at the beginning. The Government regulations are rather uncompromising. For the first four weeks you will have to observe the solitary confinement ordained by law. After that we will find you something more creative. We don't want you to feel that your personality is being stamped out. Have you any experience of art leather work?'

'No, sir.'

'Well, I might put you into the Arts and Crafts Workshop. I came to the conclusion many years ago that almost all crime is due to the repressed desire for aesthetic expression. At last we have the opportunity for testing it. Are you an extravert or an introvert?'

'I'm afraid I'm not sure, sir.'

'So few people are. I'm trying to induce the Home Office to instal an official psycho-analyst. Do you read the *New Nation*, I wonder? There is rather a flattering article this week about our prison called *The Lucas-Dockery Experiments*. I like the prisoners to know these things. It gives them corporate pride. I may give you one small example of the work we are doing that affects your own case. Up till now all offences connected with prostitution have been put into the sexual category. Now I hold that an offence of your kind is essentially acquisitive and shall grade it accordingly. It does not, of course, make any difference as far as your conditions of imprisonment are concerned – the routine of penal servitude is prescribed by Standing Orders – but you see what a difference it makes to the annual statistics.'

'The human touch,' said Sir Wilfred after Paul had been led from the room, 'I'm sure it makes all the difference. You could see with that unfortunate man just now what a difference it made to him to think that, far from being a mere nameless slave, he has now become part of a great revolution in statistics.'

'Yes, sir,' said the Chief Warder; 'and, by the way, there are two more attempted suicides being brought up tomorrow. You must really be more strict with them, sir. Those sharp tools you've issued to the Arts and Crafts School is just putting temptation in the men's way.'

Paul was once more locked in, and for the first time had the opportunity of examining his cell. There was little to interest him. Besides his Bible, his book of devotion – *Prayers on Various Occasions of Illness, Uncertainty and Loss, by the Rev. Septimus Bead, M.A., Edinburgh, 1863* – and his English Grammar, there were a little glazed pint pot, a knife and spoon, a slate and slate pencil, a salt-jar, a metal water-can, two earthenware vessels, some cleaning materials, a plank bed upright against the wall, a roll of bedding, a stool and a table. A printed notice informed him that he was not permitted to look out of the window. Three printed cards on the wall contained a list of other punishable offences, which seemed to include every human activity, some Church of England prayers, and an explanation of the 'system of progressive stages'. There was also a typewritten 'Thought for the Day', one of Sir Wilfred Lucas-Dockery's little innovations. The message for the first day of Paul's imprisonment WAS: SENSE OF SIN IS SENSE OF WASTE, *the Editor of the 'Sunday Express'*. Paul studied the system of progressive stages with interest. After four weeks, he read, he would be allowed to join in associated labour, to take half an hour's exercise on Sundays, to wear a stripe on his arm, if illiterate to have school instruction, to take one work of fiction from the library weekly, and, if special application were made to the Governor, to exhibit four photographs of his relatives or of approved friends; after eight weeks, provided that his conduct was perfectly satisfactory, he might receive a visit of twenty minutes' duration and write and receive a letter. Six weeks later he might receive another visit and another letter and another library book weekly.

Would Davy Lennox's picture of the back of Margot's head be accepted as the photograph of an approved friend, he wondered?

After a time his door was unlocked again and opened a few inches. A hand thrust in a tin, and a voice said: 'Pint pot quick!' Paul's mug was filled with cocoa, and the door again was locked. The tin contained bread, bacon and beans. That was the last interruption for fourteen hours. Paul fell into a reverie. It was the first time he had been really alone for months. How very refreshing it was, he reflected.

The next four weeks of solitary confinement were among the happiest of Paul's life. The physical comforts were certainly meagre, but at the Ritz Paul had learned to appreciate the inadequacy of purely physical comfort. It was so exhilarating, he found, never to have to make any decision on any subject, to be wholly relieved from the smallest consideration of time, meals or clothes, to have no anxiety ever about what kind of impression he was making; in fact, to be free. At some rather chilly time in the early morning a bell would ring, and the water would say: 'Slops outside!'; he would rise, roll up his bedding, and dress; there was no need to shave, no hesitation about what tie he should wear, none of the fidgeting with studs and collars and links that so distracts the waking moments of civilized man. He felt like the happy people in the advertisements for shaving soap who seem to have achieved very simply that peace of mind so distant and so desirable in the early morning. For about an hour he stitched away at a mail-bag, until his door was again unlocked to admit a hand with a lump of bread and a large ladle of porridge. After breakfast he gave a cursory polish to the furniture and crockery of his cell and did some more sewing until the bell rang for chapel. For a quarter of an hour or twenty minutes he heard Mr. Prendergast blaspheming against the beauties of sixteenth-century diction. This was certainly a bore, and so was the next hour, during which he had to march round the prison square, where between concentric paths of worn asphalt a few melancholy cabbages showed their heads. Some of the men during this period used to fall out under the pretence of tying a shoelace and take furtive bites at the leaves of the vegetables. If observed they were severely punished. Paul never felt any temptation to do this. After that the day was unbroken save for luncheon, supper and the Governor's inspection. The heap of sacking which every day he was to turn into mail-bags was supposed by law to keep him busy for nine hours. The prisoners in the cells on either side of him, who were not quite in their right minds, the warder told Paul, found some difficulty in finishing their task before lights out. Paul found that with the least exertion he had finished long before supper, and spent the evenings in meditation and in writing up on his slate the thoughts which had occurred to him during the day.

# Little Mother up the Mörderberg

## *H. G. Wells*

I think I mentioned when I was telling how I sailed my first aeroplane
that I made a kind of record at Arosa by falling down three separate
crevasses on three successive days. That was before little mother
followed me out there. When she came, I could see at a glance she was
tired and jaded and worried, and so, instead of letting her fret about in
the hotel and get into a wearing tangle of gossip, I packed her and two
knapsacks up, and started off on a long, refreshing, easy-going walk
northward, until a blister on her foot stranded us at the Magenruhe
Hotel on the Sneejoch. She was for going on, blister or no blister – I
never met pluck like mother's in all my life – but I said 'No. This is a
mountaineering inn, and it suits me down to the ground – or if you
prefer it, up to the sky. You shall sit in the veranda by the telescope, and
I'll prance about among the peaks for a bit.'

'Don't have accidents,' she said.

'Can't promise that, little mother,' I said; 'but I'll always remember
I'm your only son.'

So I pranced . . .

I need hardly say that in a couple of days I was at loggerheads with
all the mountaineers in that inn. They couldn't stand me. They didn't
like my neck with its strong, fine Adam's apple – being mostly men with
their heads *jammed* on – and they didn't like the way I bore myself and
lifted my aviator's nose to the peaks. They didn't like my being a
vegetarian and the way I evidently enjoyed it, and they didn't like the
touch of colour, orange and green, in my rough serge suit. They were all
of the dingy school – the sort of men I call gentlemanly owls – shy,
correct-minded creatures, mostly from Oxford, and as solemn over
their climbing as a cat frying eggs. Sage they were, great headnodders,
and 'I-wouldn't-venture-to-do-a-thing-like-that' – ers. They always
did what the books and guides advised, and they classed themselves by

their seasons; one was in his ninth season, and another in his tenth, and so on. I was a novice and had to sit with my mouth open for bits of humble-pie.

My style that! Rather!

I would sit in the smoking-room sucking away at a pipeful of hygienic herb tobacco – they said it smelt like burning garden rubbish – and waiting to put my spoke in and let a little light into their minds. They set aside their natural reticence altogether in their efforts to show how much they didn't like me.

'You chaps take these blessed mountains too seriously,' I said. 'They're larks, and you've got to lark with them.'

They just slued their eyes round at me.

'I don't find the solemn joy in fussing you do. The old-style mountaineers went up with alpenstocks and ladders and light hearts. That's my idea of mountaineering.'

'It isn't ours,' said one red-boiled hero of the peaks, all blisters and peeling skin, and he said it with an air of crushing me.

'It's the right idea,' I said serenely, and puffed at my herb tobacco.

'When you've had a bit of experience you'll know better,' said another, an oldish young man with a small grey beard.

'Experience never taught *me* anything,' I said.

'Apparently not,' said someone, and left me one down and me to play. I kept perfectly tranquil.

'I mean to do the Mörderberg before I go down,' I said quietly, and produced a sensation.

'When are you going down?'

'Week or so,' I answered, unperturbed.

'It's not the climb a man ought to attempt in his first year,' said the peeling gentleman.

'*You* particularly ought not to try it,' said another.

'No guide will go with you.'

'Foolhardy idea.'

'Mere brag.'

'Like to see him do it.'

I just let them boil for a bit, and when they were back to the simmer I dropped in, pensively, with, 'Very likely I'll take that little mother of mine. She's small, bless her, and she's as hard as nails.'

But they saw they were being drawn by my ill-concealed smile; and this time they contented themselves with a few grunts and grunt-like remarks, and then broke up into little conversations in undertones that pointedly excluded me. It had the effect of hardening my purpose. I'm a stiff man when I'm put on my mettle, and I determined that the little mother *should* go up the Mörderberg, where half these solemn experts hadn't been, even if I had to be killed or orphaned in the attempt. So I spoke to her about it the next day. She was in a deck-chair on the veranda, wrapped up in rugs and looking at the peaks.

'Comfy?' I said.

'Very,' she said.

'Getting rested?'

'It's so nice.'

I strolled to the rail of the veranda. 'See that peak there, mummy?' She nodded happily, with eyes half shut.

'That's the Mörderberg. You and me have got to be up there the day after to-morrow.'

Her eyes opened a bit. 'Wouldn't it be rather a climb, dearest?' she said.

'I'll manage that all right,' I said, and she smiled consentingly and closed her eyes.

'So long as you manage it,' she said.

I went down the valley that afternoon to Daxdam to get gear and guides and porters, and I spent the next day in glacier and rock practice above the hotel. That didn't add to my popularity. I made two little slips. One took me down a crevasse – I've an extraordinary knack of going down crevasses – and a party of three which was starting for the Kinderspitz spent an hour and a half fishing me out; and the other led to my dropping my ice-axe on a little string of people going for the Humpi glacier. It didn't go within thirty inches of anyone, but you might have thought from the row they made that I had knocked out the collective brains of the party. Quite frightful language they used, and three ladies with them, too!

The next day there was something very like an organized attempt to prevent our start. They brought out the landlord, they remonstrated with mother, they did their best to blacken the character of my two guides. The landlord's brother had a first-class row with them.

'Two years ago,' he said, 'they lost their Herr!'

'No particular reason,' I said, 'why you shouldn't keep yours on, is it?'

That settled him. He wasn't up to a polyglot pun, and it stuck in his mind like a fishbone in the throat.

Then the peeling gentleman came along and tried to overhaul our equipment. 'Have you got this?' it was, and 'Have you got that?'

'Two things,' I said, looking at his nose pretty hard, 'we haven't forgotten. One's blue veils and the other vaseline.'

I've still a bright little memory of the start. There was the pass a couple of hundred feet or so below the hotel, and the hotel – all name and windows – standing out in a great, desolate, rocky place against lumpy masses of streaky green rock, flecked here and there with patches of snow and dark shelves of rhododendron, and rising perhaps a thousand feet towards the western spur of the massif. Our path ran before us, meandering among the boulders down to stepping-stones over a rivulet, and then upward on the other side of the stream towards the Magenruhe glacier, where we had to go up the rocks to the left and then across the icefall to shelves on the precipitous face on the west side. It was dawn, the sun had still to rise, and everything looked very cold and blue and vast about us. Everyone in the hotel had turned out to bear a hand in the row – some of the *deshabilles* were disgraceful – and now they stood in a silent group watching us recede. The last word I caught was, 'They'll have to come back.'

'We'll come back all right,' I answered. 'Never fear.'

And so we went our way, cool and deliberate, over the stream and up and up towards the steep snowfields and icy shoulder of the Mörderberg. I remember that we went in absolute silence for a time, and then how suddenly the landscape gladdened with sunrise, and in an instant, as if speech had thawed, all our tongues were babbling.

I had one or two things in the baggage that I hadn't cared for the people at the inn to see, and I had made no effort to explain why I had five porters with the load of two and a half. But when we came to the icefall I showed my hand a little, and unslung a stout twine hammock for the mater. We put her in this with a rug round her, and sewed her in with a few stitches; then we roped off in line, with me last but one and a guide front and rear, and mummy in the middle carried by two of the porters. I stuck my alpenstock through two holes I had made in the shoulders of my jacket under my rucksack, T-shape to my body, so that when I went down a crevasse, as I did ever and again, I just stuck in its jaws and came up easy as the rope grew taut. And so, except for one or two bumps that made the mater chuckle, we got over without misadventure.

Then came the rock climb on the other side, requiring much judgment. We had to get from ledge to ledge as opportunity offered, and here the little mother was a perfect godsend. We unpacked her after we had slung her over the big fissure – I forget what you call it – that always comes between glacier and rock – and whenever we came to a bit of ledge within eight feet of the one we were working along, the two guides took her and slung her up, she being so light, and then she was able to give a foot for the next man to hold by and hoist himself. She said we were all pulling her leg, and that made her and me laugh so much that the whole party had to wait for us.

It was pretty tiring altogether doing that bit of the climb – two hours we had of it before we got to the loose masses of rock on the top of the arete. 'It's worse going down,' said the elder guide.

I looked back for the first time, and I confess it did make me feel a bit giddy. There was the glacier looking quite pretty, and with a black gash between itself and the rocks.

For a time it was pretty fair going up the rocky edge of the arete, and nothing happened of any importance, except that one of the porters took to grousing because he was hit on the shin by a stone I dislodged. 'Fortunes of war,' I said, but he didn't seem to see it, and when I just missed him with a second he broke out into a long, whining discourse in what I suppose he thought was German – *I* couldn't make head or tail of it.

'He says you might have killed him,' said the little mother.

'They say,' I quoted, 'What say they? *Let* them say.'

I was for stopping and filling him up with a feed, but the elder guide wouldn't have it. We had already lost time, he said, and the traverse round the other face of the mountain would be more and more subject to avalanches as the sun got up. So we went on. As we went round the corner to the other face I turned towards the hotel – it was the meanest little oblong spot by now – and made a derisive gesture or so for the benefit of anyone at the telescope.

We did get one rock avalanche that reduced the hindmost guide to audible prayer, but nothing hit us except a few bits of snow. The rest of the fall was a couple of yards and more out from us. We were on rock just then and overhung; before and afterwards we were edging along steps in an ice-slope cut by the foremost guide, and touched up by the porters. The avalanche was much more impressive before it came in sight, banging and thundering overhead, and it made a tremendous uproar in the blue deeps beneath, but in actual transit it seemed a mean show – mostly of stones smaller than I am.

'All right?' said the guide.

'Toned up,' I answered.

'I suppose it *is* safe, dear?' asked the little mother.

'Safe as Trafalgar Square,' I said. 'Hop along, mummykins.'

Which she did with remarkable agility.

The traverse took us on to old snow at last, and here we could rest for lunch – and pretty glad we were both of lunch and rest. But here the trouble with the guides and porters thickened. They were already a little ruffled about my animating way with loose rocks, and now they kicked up a tremendous shindy because instead of the customary brandy we had brought non-alcoholic ginger cordial. Would they even try it? Not a bit of it! It was a queer little dispute, high up in that rarefied air about food values and the advantages of making sandwiches with nuttar. They were an odd lot of men, invincibly set upon a vitiated and vitiating dietary. They wanted meat, they wanted alcohol, they wanted narcotics to smoke. You might have thought that men like these, living in almost direct contact with Nature, would have liked 'Nature' foods, such as plasmon, protose, plobose, digestine, and so forth. Not them! They just craved for corruption. When I spoke of drinking pure water one of the porters spat in a marked, symbolic manner over the precipice. From that point onward discontent prevailed.

We started again about half-past eleven, after a vain attempt on the part of the head guide to induce us to turn back. We had now come to what is generally the most difficult part of the Mörderberg ascent, the edge that leads up to the snowfield below the crest. But here we came suddenly into a draught of warm air blowing from the south-west, and everything, the guide said, was unusual. Usually the edge is a sheet of ice over rock. To-day it was wet and soft, and one could kick steps in it and get one's toes into rock with the utmost ease.

'This is where Herr Tomlinson's party fell,' said one of the porters, after we'd committed ourselves to the edge for ten minutes or so.

'Some people could fall out of a four-post bed,' I said.

'It'll freeze hard again before we come back,' said the second guide, 'and us with nothing but *verdammt* ginger inside of us.'

'You keep your rope taut,' said I.

A friendly ledge came to the help of mother in the nick of time, just as she was beginning to tire, and we sewed her up all but the feet in her hammock again, and roped her carefully. She bumped a bit, and at times she was just hanging over immensity and rotating slowly, with everybody else holding like grim death.

'My dear,' she said, the first time this happened, 'is it *right* for me to be doing this?'

'Quite right,' I said, 'but if you can get a foothold presently again – it's rather better style.'

'You're sure there's no danger, dear?'

'Not a scrap.'

'And I don't fatigue you?'

'You're a stimulant.'

'The view,' she said, 'is certainly becoming very beautiful.'

But presently the view blotted itself out, and we were in clouds and thin drift of almost thawing snowflakes.

We reached the upper snowfield about half-past one, and the snow was extraordinarily soft. The elder guide went in up to his armpits.

'Frog it,' I said, and spread myself out flat, in a sort of swimming attitude. So we bored our way up to the crest and along it. We went in little spurts and then stopped for breath, and we dragged the little mother after us in her hammock-bag. Sometimes the snow was so good we fairly skimmed the surface; sometimes it was so rotten we plunged right into it and splashed about. I went too near the snow cornice once and it broke under me, but the rope saved me, and we reached the summit about three o'clock without further misadventure. The summit was just bare rock with the usual cairn and pole. Nothing to make a fuss about. The drift of snow and cloudwisp had passed, the sun was blazing hot overhead, and we seemed to be surveying all Switzerland. The Magenruhe Hotel was at our toes, hidden, so to speak, by our chins. We squatted about the cairn, and the guides and porters were reduced to ginger and vegetarian ham-sandwiches. I cut and scratched an inscription, saying I had climbed on simple food, and claiming a record.

Seen from the summit the snowfields on the north-east side of the mountain looked extremely attractive, and I asked the head guide why that way up wasn't used. He said something in his peculiar German about precipices.

So far our ascent had been a fairly correct ascent in rather slow time. It was in the descent that that strain in me of almost unpremeditated originality had play. I wouldn't have the rope returning across the upper snowfield, because mother's feet and hands were cold, and I wanted her to jump about a bit. And before I could do anything to prevent it she had slipped, tried to get up by rolling over *down* the slope instead of up, as she ought to have done, and was leading the way, rolling over and over and over, down towards the guide's blessed precipices above the lower snowfield.

I didn't lose an instant in flinging myself after her, axe up, in glissading attitude. I'm not clear what I meant to do, but I fancy the idea was to get in front of her and put on the brake. I did not succeed, anyhow. In twenty seconds I had slipped, and was sitting down and going down out of my own control altogether.

Now, most discoveries are the result of accident, and I maintain that in that instant mother and I discovered two distinct and novel ways of coming down a mountain.

It is necessary that there should be first a snow slope above with a layer of softish, rotten snow on the top of ice, then a precipice, with a snow-covered talus sloping steeply at first and then less steeply, then more snow slopes and precipices according to taste, ending in a snowfield or a not-too-greatly-fissured glacier, or a reasonable, not-too-rocky slope. Then it all becomes as easy as chuting the chutes.

Mother hit on the sideways method. She rolled. With the snow in the adhesive state it had got into she had made the jolliest little snowball of herself in half a minute, and the nucleus of as clean and abundant a snow avalanche as anyone could wish. There was plenty of snow going in front of her, and that's the very essence of both our methods. You must fall on your snow, not your snow on you, or it smashes you. And you mustn't mix yourself up with loose stones.

I, on the other hand, went down feet first, and rather like a snow-plough; slower than she did, and if, perhaps, with less charm, with more dignity. Also I saw more. But it was certainly a tremendous rush. And I gave a sort of gulp when mummy bumped over the edge into the empty air and vanished.

It was like a toboggan ride gone mad down the slope until I took off from the edge of the precipice, and then it was like a dream.

I'd always thought falling must be horrible. It wasn't in the slightest degree. I might have hung with my clouds and lumps of snow about me for weeks, so great was my serenity. I had an impression then that I was as good as killed – and that it didn't matter. I wasn't afraid – that's nothing! – but I wasn't a bit uncomfortable. Whack! We'd hit something, and I expected to be flying to bits right and left. But we'd only got on to the snow-slope below, at so steep an angle that it was merely breaking the fall. Down we went again. I didn't see much of the view after that because the snow was all round and over my head, but I kept feet foremost and in a kind of sitting posture, and then I slowed and then I quickened again and bumped rather, and then harder, and bumped and then bumped again and came to rest. This time I was altogether buried in snow, and twisted sideways with a lot of heavy snow on my right shoulder.

I sat for a bit enjoying the stillness – and then I wondered what had become of mother, and set myself to get out of the snow about me. It wasn't so easy as you might think; the stuff was all in lumps and spaces like a gigantic sponge, and I lost my temper and struggled and swore a good deal, but at last I managed it. I crawled out and found myself on the edge of heaped masses of snow quite close to the upper part of the Magenruhe glacier. And far away, right up the glacier and near the other side, was a little thing like a black-beetle struggling in the heart of an immense split ball of snow.

I put my hands to my mouth and let out with my version of the yodel, and presently I saw her waving her hand.

It took me nearly twenty minutes to get to her. I knew my weakness, and I was very careful of every crevasse I came near. When I got up to her her face was anxious.

'What have you done with the guides?' she asked.

'They've got too much to carry,' I said. 'They're coming down another way. Did you like it?'

'Not very much, dear,' she said; 'but I dare say I shall get used to these things. Which way do we go now?'

I decided we'd find a snow-bridge across the *bergschrund* – that's the word I forgot just now – and so get on to the rocks on the east side of the glacier, and after that we had uneventful going right down to the hotel . . .

Our return evoked such a strain of hostility and envy as I have never met before or since. First they tried to make out we'd never been to the top at all, but mother's little proud voice settled that sort of insult. And, besides, there was the evidence of the guides and porters following us down. When they asked about the guides, 'They're following *your* methods,' I said, 'and I suppose they'll get back here to-morrow morning somewhere.'

That didn't please them.

I claimed a record. They said my methods were illegitimate.

'If I see fit,' I said, 'to use an avalanche to get back by, what's that to you? You tell me me and mother can't do the confounded mountain anyhow, and when we do you want to invent a lot of rules to disqualify us. You'll say next one mustn't glissade. I've made a record, and you know I've made a record, and you're about as sour as you can be. The fact of it is, you chaps don't know your own silly business. Here's a good, quick way of coming down a mountain, and you ought to know about it – '

'The chance that both of you are not killed was one in a thousand.'

'Nonsense! It's the proper way to come down for anyone who hasn't a hide-bound mind. You chaps ought to practise falling great heights in snow. It's perfectly easy and perfectly safe, if only you know how to set about it.'

'Look here, young man,' said the oldish young man with the little grey beard, 'you don't seem to understand that you and that lady have been saved by a kind of miracle – '

'Theory!' I interrupted. 'I'm surprised you fellows ever come to Switzerland. If I were your kind I'd just invent theoretical mountains and play for points. However, you're tired, little mummy. It's time you had some nice warm soup and tucked yourself up in bed. I shan't let you get up for six-and-thirty hours.'

But it's queer how people detest a little originality.

# The Mystery of the Hibernia

## *Anon*

The homeward voyage of that popular single-class ship the *Hibernia* was enlivened and the curiosity of her passengers strongly tickled by an incident. A young lady fell overboard. There was no mystery about that. And the usual routine followed. A number of people shouted 'Man overboard!' others swooned away, others threw over life-buoys. One rather bright but futile bird, anxious to help, discharged a deck-chair into the Red Sea. Several others followed suit. And a moiety ran about calling for hen-coops and hatch-covers, but modern ships do not seem to carry any. The sea-boat was immediately called away, and as soon as way was somewhat off the *Hibernia*, she hit the water with such a thump that the false teeth of the mate (or as we call him now, the First Officer), who was in command of her, came unshipped. This however, passed unnoticed, and the boat disappeared into the darkness of a very dark night. In about half an hour she returned bringing the lady, insensible.

Now this was all straightforward and above-board. There was nothing remarkable or mysterious in it. It had often happened before, and will happen again.

But the boat's crew reported finding a male passenger clinging to the same buoy with the young lady. Now this was surprising, because rescuers are usually seen departing over the bulwarks on their errands of mercy, and no one had seen this one go. Still the night was very dark, and it was just possible for a modest sort of fellow to do good by stealth, if really set on it, in this way.

Where the mystery came in was in this.

The man must, of course, have arrived back at the ship in the rescuing boat. There was ample evidence from her crew, but more especially from a quartermaster who had helped him into the boat, administered brandy to him, conversed with him and finally seen him leave the boat, climb the ladder and disappear into the ship through a brilliantly lighted entry-port. At this entry-port were gathered several persons, the captain being one of them, and both he and they stoutly denied having seen the man pass them. His identity was therefore a mystery, as well as his method of passing into a well-lighted crowded ship, not only unrecognised but unnoticed. The fact that the boat – an open one, of course – passed along more than half the length of the ship before reaching the ladder, and was under the eager gaze of many scores of passengers clustered along the bulwarks, only added to the puzzlement of all on board. The only person who could have solved the matter chose to remain silent. And a secret it remains to this day for all on board the *Hibernia*, with the exception of two fellow-passengers who were let into it later during the voyage, and a third – myself – who shared it some months afterwards.

I have often resented never being told how rabbits are produced from top-hats, or packs of cards dwindle before my very eyes to nothing, or billiard balls are exuded from the conjurer's anatomy. I think it very mean and petty on the conjurer's part. I shall not follow his example, but set forth here in the words of the mystery man just exactly what happened and how it happened. He desires his identity to remain undiscovered, so I will call him William; and the following are *ipsissima verba* of William on the matter.

'We were coming up the Red Sea,' continued William, 'on a fearfully hot night, following breeze, not a breath stirring on board and all that. A regular bender of a night. I had never spoken to her, but I had noticed her at meal-times and sometimes on deck. Well, it was nearing bed-time, about half-past nine, the time they let one on deck in pyjamas. I had found a nice place by the rail for my mattress, where there was a little draught of air, and I was longing for the bell to strike so as to go below and get out of my clothes. On the deck above me they were dancing in spite of the heat. I wondered how they managed to do it. I was leaning over the rail, looking down at the water sliding past and longing to jump in and get cool.

'Just at that moment there came a hail from above me – the bridge, I thought. I wasn't very interested in it, and yet listened again for it. It came again, much louder and clearer this time. "Man overboard!" The cry came so pat upon my longing for a plunge, it might have been an answer to a prayer, or a direct incitement by Providence to do the very thing I wanted to.

'A life-buoy hung at my knee. I lifted it from its hooks, clasped it tight and went over the top. I had jumped and was half-way there when I thought of sharks. I was still thinking of them when I hit the Red Sea. I didn't go far under, owing to the buoy. I came to the surface within a few feet of the great wall of sliding hull. Sharks vanished from my mind: another subject took their place – propeller blades. In the docks at the port of embarkation I had noticed a large board hanging to the ship's quarter. On it ran the legend, 'Beware of the twin-screws'. At the time this did not seem to concern me. It did so now, however. All this in a flash. I kicked out lustily with my legs, so as to get a little away from the ship. The roar of waters, mightily threshed, grew momentarily fiercer. It had in it the boom of a great mill-wheel, but a hundred times its fierceness. Now for it! I clutched and twined round my buoy; and then a cleaving, smashing rush – no words can describe the awful sound a propeller blade makes so near one's ear – and that danger was over. I was now in the maelstrom. A 15,000-ton ship driven at speed through water leaves a considerable pother behind her. I was drawn into this. The fun was sharp, but luckily short. I was buffeted, sucked down, thrown up, boxed this way and that. My breath held. I still clutched my buoy, and at length once more floated clear on smooth but still hissing water, very phosphorescent. Then the hiss died down, the sparks died out and I looked my last at the *Hibernia*, for the darkness just then swallowed her at one gulp. Darkness hid the sky, the horizon, the water about me, I might have been floating in space, and there was nothing even to feel, for the sea was just about the temperature of my body, and I didn't even feel wet. It did seem a little odd to be watching a departing ship from the Red Sea instead of *vice versa*. There was a long oily swell: I could feel the slow and gentle rhythm of it.

'Remembering, however, what I was there for, I let out a yell as soon as I had breath to do so. It seemed a foolish futile thing to expect to find anyone in that thick darkness, and I was the more surprised when I was answered and from quite close by a feeble but unmistakably human pipe. Towards it I urged my life buoy, and presently felt it tilt and dip as an unseen hand laid hold of it. I told the hand to get its owner inside the buoy as soon as possible. To this came a snuffling response, but no action. I had made up my mind that I was dealing with one of the Lascar crew. I was unwilling to be grappled by him, so, keeping the buoy between us, I slid my hand round its circumference, felt another hand, passed on warily up an arm, meeting two or three bangles and a wrist-watch *en route*, felt a neck and a necklace and wandered farther into hair and several combs. Seizing the hair, I dipped the head under water, brought it up inside the buoy, pulled the arms up, hung them outside and made all snug. There was no opposition. But when the spluttering was done, a woman's voice said, "Oh, you did hurt my head." I apologised and explained. There was no rejoinder. We were both rather full of Red Sea and short of breath.

Presently a drowsy voice said—

"'I suppose there are no watchmakers actually near here, are there?'"

"'Not in the immediate neighbourhood, so far as I know,' I replied.

"'That's a pity. My watch'll want looking to after all this. Aunt Amy's things are always good.'"

"'She gave it you in a present?,' I hazarded. I felt that chattiness was the line.

"'As a present – yes,' came the voice – that of rather an acid sleep-talker.

'Sharks – I had forgotten about them. They recurred again. I wished they hadn't. I felt that my legs dangled a great deal more than desirable. I wished I could curl them up out of harm's way round my neck. Did they – sharks, not legs – always follow ships continuously in the Red Sea? Or did they just give them a look-in occasionally? I recollected seeing a dead horse dropped overboard in these waters. The sharks had him before we had left him a hundred yards astern. A nasty sight, all dorsal fins and foam and blood. True, there had been none visible about us as we lay in Aden harbour two days ago, and lots of little boys were diving for pennies. Someone had said that one of them had been taken not long before, leg bitten clean off, and in Suez sharks were always to be seen cruising round every ship, and were caught sometimes. No – on the whole these reflections were not comfortable. Again, could one hear a shark coming, or did he just take your leg off without any warning? Better, anyway, to be taken kicking than passive, so I pulled up my legs and kicked. But that's tiring work.

'The sleep-talker resumed—

"'You're making a lot of noise. D'you want a crowd to collect?'"

"'I was rather trying to keep the crowd away,' I replied.

"'I can't see anyone about,' she continued rather testily. 'I can't see anything. Not even you. Who are you?'"

"'From the *Hibernia*. Who are you?" I said.

"'I'm not anybody. Nor are you. We died a short time ago. I don't know exactly how long ago – and I don't know how I died."

"'People don't,' I replied. "The survivors know, of course. But who *were* you then?"

"'I was Mary Seton. I sat next my aunt, Aunt Amy, you know, and she sat next the captain. Perhaps you noticed us?"

'Now how had Mary Seton come to tumble overboard? Most certainly I had noticed her – everyone did – and a less headlong type of beauty I could not have conceived. And her aunt was noticeable too – a Madonna-like person, very composed. Poor aunt – how was her composure standing it now?

"'Also of Mary Monica,' burbled on the quiet sleepy voice at my elbow, 'only daughter of the above, who died at sea, aged 19 years and 10 months – that's how Aunt Amy will have it put up."

'I left her spinning epitaphs and resumed kicking. When I had finished, I asked her whether she was feeling sleepy, and advised her to try and keep awake.

"'Look out for the boat," I said. "They'll be sending one back for us soon."

"'I'm not feeling exactly sleepy," she replied. "Only all muzzy in my head, and it hurts so. Would you mind passing your hand over it ever so gently just to feel if there's anything wrong there?"

"'Yes," I said. "I'll feel my way up your arm if you don't mind. I'll feel ever so gently."

'Poor Mary Seton! No wonder she was muzzy. My fingers traced a long jagged scalp wound, and gently as I did so, I felt the head wince and heard a sharp in-drawing of her breath. The warm blood was still oozing from it on to my fingers. The cause was obvious. On such a hot night as this, every porthole would have out its windscoop, and anyone falling from deck would be almost certain to hit one. She had been lucky not to have hit hers harder. I explained this.

"'I think you must have hit your head very slightly when you fell – painful, but nothing to worry about – nothing that the doctor, or your aunt for that matter, can't put right. It's the salt water that makes it so painful."

'For the first time during our desultory conversation she woke up and spoke eagerly.

'"Will it show when it's healed? I mean will there be any scar?"

'Ah, woman! I touched you there. Vanity! vanity! dead or alive, all is vanity! On receiving my assurances, she resumed her drowsy chat.

'"I suppose that's what killed me, then. I'm certain I didn't just die in the ordinary way, and I know I wasn't drowned, because I've never been in the water, although my mouth seems full of salt."

'I let her maunder on. With one hand on the life-line of the buoy and a very little treading water, I found myself well able to keep afloat. I took a good look round. Hours seemed to have passed since we had seen the last of *Hibernia*. By now, of course, any search must have been given up. The boat would have returned to the ship long ago, and she would have proceeded on her voyage. It wasn't for a boat that I looked, but I had an idea that ships always carried a patent buoy on the bridge, which could be dropped at once, and which on striking the water showed a light. It was this that I had looked for, and was still looking for. But the *Hibernia* either didn't carry one of these buoys, or they had forgotten to drop it, and therefore the possible chance of its guiding a boat to somewhere near us was quite absolutely nil. One could rule it clean out of one's thoughts and abandon any foolish hope of being found. But showing and disappearing as we rose on the crest or sunk into the trough of the silent invisible swell, was one very faint star. I judged it to be well down almost on the horizon, and sometimes it looked to be on the sea. It was the sole visible feature, and therefore comforting; it relieved the void. But as stars went, it was a poor enough affair.

'"But they don't send boats for souls, do they?" My companion had resumed her talk.

'"Of course they do," I said. "How could souls get anywhere?"

'"Why," she objected, "they just float about in space like us till they grow wings and become angels, but that might take ages."

'We were apparently entering the Realm Psychological, when an interruption occurred. Without sound or other warning, and not growing gradually on our vision, but bursting on our eyeballs with an intolerable glare, a boat! Its oars moving up and down, up and down, like the legs of some great black beetle, a man sharply silhouetted standing in the bows, a flare in his raised hand and flakes of fire dropping from it into the sea. She was not heading towards us: she would miss us by hundreds of yards, and we were hundreds of yards beyond the radius of light. The flare was already dying out. But on that totally silent night one good shout and salvation! What easier? I gathered my breath, put all my strength behind the effort and let fly. A feeble croak not ranging half the boat's distance from us was all the result! Treading water, kicking for sharks and small talk had done me in.

'"Scream!" I croaked at my companion. "Scream!" I shook her by the elbow.

'"I can't," came the drowsy reply. "I'm dead."

'"You jade!" I gasped out.

'Then the light went out, the boat with it and my hopes with both.

'"Was that heaven?" came in an awe-struck murmur.

'"Yes," I said. "And we might have got in if you had screamed."

'"No one screams to get into heaven."

'Honestly, I could have struck her. If the boat appeared again I resolved to pinch her till, dead or alive, she howled again.

'A fairly miserable silence followed. Argument with deceased would, I felt, be a waste of breath, and of that I hadn't overmuch to spare. I was beginning to expect dawn, and a day afloat in the Red Sea – no hats, nothing to drink (I was already parched) and the slow consequences. Sharks might appear as friends then.

'Then as suddenly as before the boat burst upon us, heading our way, but a long way off, now seen, now in the trough, and much too far off to try pinching yet. I watched her slow approach. Vertically up and down went the oars, a poor half-hearted stroke. Lascars only, of course. Heavy oars and a heavy sea-boat – still, coming ever so slowly our way. The light dwindled. The figure holding it stooped, dropped the old flare and erected himself, holding a new one. So soon as I could hear the thump of oars, I'd try the pinch.

'Then the oars stopped. Someone in the stern stood up, hand shading eyes, and looked – every way but our way! Oars again started their deliberate and deadalive movements. The boat veered from us. At this my hand crept along the buoy, found a hand, felt up to the fleshiest part of the forearm, gathered a finger and thumbful of it and pinched the wet flesh for all I was worth. But all the pinch had gone out of me. The girl never winced.

'Again the boat stopped. I could hear voices. They were scarcely one hundred yards distant. But I had shot my last bolt. I lay silent and helpless. The light went out, oars thumped again.

'But I hadn't shot my last bolt. Fate, that sorry impish jade, who loves a joke but carries it too far sometimes, supplied me with another noise. I remembered that once I could cat-call. Instantly I sucked two fingers dry, and, wondering whether I could recall my boyhood's proudest achievement and my brothers' envy, I inserted them and breathed what breath I still had in me through them. Result amazing! I cleft the thick darkness once. The rowing ceased, another flare was burnt. I could see them looking towards us, but we lay just beyond the circle of light. I spurred myself to one more effort, and it produced an answering hail. On the tail of it crept the boat, and with it the light, till it touched us, lit up our wet white faces (that's how they first saw us, they said later), and then, "There she is," and then again, "Why, there are two of 'em." Of course. I hadn't thought of it before. No one had seen me go overboard.

'Our troubles were ended. We were bundled aboard. The girl was passed aft to the doctor. I relapsed happily on to the bottom boards, where five minutes' rest and a brandy flask made me as good as new.

'On the way back to the ship we picked up my star. It was the patent buoy after all, and had been floating not a couple of hundred yards from us all the time. I asked the quartermaster when it would be dawning. He said, "Why, bless you, sir, it ain't gone four bells yet. You haven't been gone not much more than half an hour."

'The red and green lights of the *Hibernia* looked vastly pleasant as we neared her. To make sure we found her, she let out a short bellow now and then from her syren. Then as we opened her, there came into view the rows and rows of cheerful lighted scuttles and the glimmer of her many lighted decks, and heads clustered like bees along her rail. Like bees they buzzed and like human beings they cheered as we passed along to the companion-ladder. This had been rigged during our absence. At the lighted entry-port at the top stood a waiting group, the skipper, a lady, some stewardesses. But that deck had been cleared. As we hooked on, the doctor called out from the boat, "All right, sir! all right, Mrs Seton." And the clustered heads along the rails above broke out afresh.

'I effected my return on board by great luck and without the smallest trouble or notice. In the hurry of the event, they had not lighted up the companion-way. The entry-port at the top was brightly illuminated, but the stairway up to it was in total darkness, as was the boat. Up we all went in a bunch, closely following the doctor and his blanketed burden. The waiting group at the top had eyes for none but these two, and none of them knew then that Miss Seton was not the only one picked up. At the top, all turned to the left, I to the right. Before me lay the long empty perspective of white enamelled steel walls, with the red curtains from open cabin doors swinging out and back with the ship's motion. I had a clear run to my cabin and reached it without meeting a soul. In ten minutes I had changed and stowed my wet duds in my soiled linen bag. Then I hurried upstairs to hear all about it.

'I did hear all about it. I had an hour of real undiluted joy before turning in. The decks were still humming with excitement. An event had occurred, not a meal, which is the usual sort of event on board ship, and which, through over-frequency, loses its eventhood, but something that set rumour flying, liars lying and everyone talking. I circulated from group to group, discreetly merging myself with each in turn, a wide-eyed seeker after the authentic, an eager gobbler-up of the last detail. Before turning in an hour later, I confess to have experienced joys that I can only describe as poignant.

'Thus (overheard at the first group): "I give you my word she *would* sit on the rail, just here where my hand is now. We begged her not to, but she would: sort of bravado. She hooked her toes under the third rail and said she'd do well enough. Then, by Dam – you see the double awning here, just above where her head was? – well, hang me, if a blinkin' rat didn't fall out from between the two awnings and slap into her lap. A real old buck bilge rat; and after him the ship's cat. Well – I ask you – who wouldn't? She – I mean Miss Seton – came unstuck, and over she went into the soup – biff!"

'"And you after her, Charlie, my lad!" from a scoffer.

'I passed to the next group, edged in and merged—

'"And there she was as cool as a cucumber, surrounded by sharks."

'I got no forrader here, for they kept on harping on sharks and cucumbers, and I felt that more succulent stuff awaited me elsewhere. It did. I inoculated myself unobtrusively into a very promising group, its members' eyes all on stalks, the jaws of some of the more emotional slightly slaverous. A lady was holding forth, a born narrator, recklessly lavish of grace-notes and embroidery. She was giving a recitation rather than telling them all about it. I missed just a few of the opening bars and came in at—

"'. . . a real British sailor sort of man, such *true* blue eyes, bluff and hearty, with a sort of Berserk beard – *you* know – *honey*-coloured." (No – I didn't know. Bluff and hearty eyes I could allow – but not eyes with a honey-coloured beard). She continued, emphasising nearly every third word: "This is what he told me, and he was obviously speaking the truth: 'Lady,' he said, 'we'd bin nosin' around for the matter of a hower or two in that frail little craf', looking for that pore young lady. Ah! it was dark and the seas breaking terrible. But we didn't care, yooman life hung at the stake. Presently I sez to my mate, 'Alf,' sez I, 'd'y 'ear anything?' 'No,' sez Alf. 'Listen,' sez I. Well, we stops lab'rin' at the oar and listens. 'There 'tis again,' sez I. 'Where?' sez Alf. 'Out there,' sez I. After a bit Alf sez eagerlike, 'I 'ear – a yim!' And so 'twas, lady– Greenland's Hicy Mountains aringin' like church bells acrost them watery wastes. Didn't 'arf make me want to cry. But I masters it and sings out, 'Give way, my hearties! lay down to it!' Ay – didn't we make her travel! Straight toward Greenland's Hicy we heads, quite disre-gardless of sharks and that. But 'twas thirsty work, what with the dangers we run and the 'eat and the anxiety and all. Presently we sights her, calm as calm a-settin' in her life-buoy singing among the sharks – stacks of 'em, lady, if you'll believe me. If I may say so, lady, that pore girl – young lady, I *should* say – is a 'oly one, settin' there and yim-singing among all them perils. Well, I lifts her up in m'yarms – as light as a feather she was – and she looks up in my face so trustful-like and she sez, 'Thank you, quartermaster.' Just that. I broke down arter that, ay, I did – growed man and all – and so did Alf, wors'n me. We sets there crying like babies.'"

'The actual recitation ended here – that is to say, *oratio recta* ended and *obliqua* set in, with a spot or two of recta thrown in for effect. "If I may say so," continued the lady, "that simple sailor is a religious man – deeply religious. He was so touched by what he, poor fellow, called the yim. And he *did* look so *parched*, quite husky. He had that *thirsty* look in his eye – *you* know. I called to a passing steward and ordered him to bring a lemon squash *at once*, with lots of ice in it. But the sailor, poor man, looked quite put out. He said how grateful he was, but added, 'Not that, lady – not that. I never takes nothin', only stout in the Red Sea, lady, and ice sits cold to the stomach, pard'ning your presence, lady.' I asked the *dear* fellow whether he was *quite* sure that fermented liquor was good for him during such a heat-wave as we were having. He said he was perfectly certain that it was, even in the 'hottest latitoods.' So I ordered him a *small* bottle of stout. I really didn't dare to let him have a big one. And he went away, that *true* heart, quite silent, without *another* word. Such a *dear* man, what I call a *true* British tar."

'Oh, but this was rich! This was rare! Well did I know that hearty honey-bearded tar – the ship's butcher, no less – almost as much a fixture, almost as familiar to her passengers as *Hibernia*'s buff-and-blue funnels. I warrant he had never pulled an oar in his life, or been afloat probably in any craft less frail than an ocean-going ship. A man of strength, our butcher, a mingler of strong drink, mighty to drink it and quite unashamed in asking for it. A small bottle of stout to the likes of him! Oh, the glorious irony of it! Oh, the insult! I was now so full of hiccoughy pains owing to suppressed mirth that I had to mount to the deserted boat-deck and let it gush from me into the night.'

'I drifted to yet another group. Here they had got hold of me at last. I had been thinking it was about time. Someone was saying, "Oh, I believe it's all nonsense. Two people could never have happened to fall overboard at the same time." "Yes, but," said another, 'one of them might have jumped in after the other, mightn't he?" "I'll give you two reasons why not," said the first. "First, he couldn't have gone overboard without *someone* seeing him, could he? And next, still less could have come alongside in an open boat under the eyes of hundreds of us without being noticed."

' "And yet, he was in that open boat."

'This from me in the measured grave tones of one who knew. At once I became the focal point. "No," I said, "don't ask me. I know nothing." This touched that chord of receptivity which in the right atmosphere twangs so readily in the average human breast and ensures unquestioning belief in the most palpable guff. My audience were all certain now that I knew something, if not everything, and they were ready to gorge it. "No," I said, waving them off, yet luring them on. "Don't ask me. All I say is that we shall never know who the man was and (I added) reason too!" I had hit on the exact wave-length, tuned in, my three-valve set had attained perfect receptivity and, I felt sure, would reproduce as perfectly. I paused here. Then, "Mind you, what I say is only my belief, my private personal belief, but I can add two and two as well as another, and this is what it seems to me to come to. The man picked up with Miss Seton was one of the ship's people. He was found safe and snug inside the buoy, she, outside – among the sharks. Naturally, the ship has her good name to keep up. Naturally, it'll be all hushed up. You wait and see. No – I don't know who he was. I told you I knew nothing."

'No one among my audience thought of asking how I had come by the figures which had made up my simple sum. No one found anything odd in my inference that a life-buoy was a sort of water-tight-shark-proof buoy in which a man might sit immune from danger. But one of the brighter lads asked, "But how about his coming alongside in that open boat and us all looking down into it and not spotting him?" I crushed this worm that had ventured to turn and query my statements. "Consider a moment," I said. "You looked down into an open boat certainly. But what could you see? Whom could you recognize? Nobody. It was pitch dark down there. Now what about it, eh?" I strode away with the superior air of one who can add up two and two, but finds that others can't.

'I had sown my libellous seed. I felt that during the night it would germinate, that next day it would have "taken hold," as gardeners say. I laid me down in my chosen airy spot on deck and fell asleep to the thud of the propellers which had swished so close past my head such a short while ago.

'I was right. Next day the seed had taken hold, firm hold, of the minds of all. It was an established fact now that the boat had picked up a man with Miss Seton. But it was a mystery as to who that man was. Clearly the ship was making a hush-hush matter of it. No one else would – and why? Because there was something discreditable to hide. And why should the ship want to hide it? Because one of her own people had not come out of it too well. That was the simple logic of it. No getting out of that. And so all the world wondered. It was a very idle world, glad to have something to wonder at. It walked the deck or lay in its chair and wondered and cogitated.

'At dinner that night the Skipper made an effort to dispel the mystery. He may have succeeded, but my seed had taken a good hold. And it didn't much matter, for with our arrival in the Canal and the departure of prickly heat, we had other things to think about. But that night the Old Man rose from his chair and addressed us as fellows:—

'"With reference to last night's happenings, I'm glad to tell you all that Miss Seton is going on as well as can be expected. She hasn't, of course, been worried with questions, but she says that she remembers nothing of what happened. That being so, we are left in the dark as to who the man was who went overboad after her, gave her a life-buoy and, in short, saved her life. I can, however, assure you that the rumour which has come to my ears as to that man being one of the ship's company is untrue. I have made the most careful inquiries, and I can assure everyone that there's nothing in it. No, the man who went overboard is here in this saloon. He hears my words and I see him, though I don't know which of you he is. He did a manly thing. He'd do a manlier, if I may say so, if he'd own up to it. Mrs Seton is very anxious to thank him, and so are we all. Now!" He looked round, did the old noodle, as if he really expected someone to be still manlier and get up and say, "I'm the man." There was a dead silence. Then someone jumped up and began "For he's a jolly good fellow." Then everyone else jumped up and joined in. And there was I roaring louder than anyone that I was a jolly good fellow! After that a would-be horsey man, who had probably attended a selling lottery once, sang out, "Fifty pounds in the lottery. Great Unknown for sale! Any offers, gentlemen? No advance? Well, then, going, going, gone! Great Unknown goes for £50. Owner taking nothing." That finished it.

'We reached Marseilles. Most of the passengers cleared off here. The Setons were to have gone, but Miss Seton, though up and about, was not fit for the railway journey. I was also to have gone, but changed my mind at the last moment. I usually hate the Bay and the up-Channel voyage, but I seemed to fancy both this time.

'We were quite a reduced crowd on board now, and I saw a good deal of the Setons. One day Miss Seton recurred to that night in the Red Sea. She told me that it was all a closed book to her still, and that she was like a person who had had a dream and couldn't remember what it was about. But she rather thought it might come back to her, as such dreams did sometimes. I felt pretty safe, however.

'The Bay was topping, like a mill-pond. The decks were no longer crowded; one could pick and choose one's place. One day Miss Seton and I had tucked ourselves up in deck-chairs in a sheltered spot, for it was turning colder now. She wasn't very talkative that day, but suddenly she said—

'"Were you the man who went overboard after me?"'

"I asked her whatever made her ask a question like that.

"'I don't quite know,'" she said. "Several things perhaps. Intuition perhaps, or curiosity, or perhaps because you might be the sort of man to do that sort of thing. But, anyway, I think you've given yourself away."

"'How so?'"

"'Why, because if it hadn't been you, you'd have said no and not answered my question with another. See? Besides, my dream's coming back to me – in spots, you know – just here and there something's filling in the picture of that night. I remember, for instance, the rat quite plainly. And was it you who called me a jade? Someone did, and the voice seems rather familiar."

'Well, the cat came out of the bag. It had to. It's no good trying to win out in a cross-examination by a woman. I swore her to secrecy, of course, except her aunt, who at that moment came blowing along as she was always doing now. It had become a joke between Miss Seton and me; we called her the *mauvais courant d'air*. So I cleared out. But, my eye! wasn't she snotty with me later on! Not much Madonna-like calm about her when roused, I can tell you. "Aggravating" and "making silly mysteries" were some of the things she said. She did sting, especially when she said she hated "mock heroics." Miss Seton only made it worse with, "But, Aunt Amy, he *is* a hero," and I worse again – I was quite nettled now and forgot myself – by saying, "I'm damned if I am." But things blew over in time, and aunt and I got quite nice to one another.

'I was sorry when the voyage ended. I'm not usually. Miss Seton was rather extra cheerful when she said goodbye – more than I was. And the aunt gave me their London address and said, "Come and look us up one of these days, won't you?"

'I did look them up. They were awfully hospitable folk, and I went pretty often. Of course, I had long been over head and ears with Miss Seton, but I had kept it to myself, and I don't think she had any inkling of it. But one day I went there meaning to propose. What worried me was this. Miss Seton might conceivably think herself, quite wrongly, under some sort of obligation to me for having let me share her buoy. I felt that on that account she might say yes, while on every other account she would say no. You see my point? Well, I decided to have no nonsense of that sort, and to make it clear to her that I couldn't receive a yes on those terms. So when we were alone, I told her that I knew she was full of commonsense and wouldn't let me down in the matter I was about to speak of. She looked rather puzzled and said she hoped not. Then I said that great issues hung upon her answer to a question I was about to ask her. She looked less puzzled now, so I went on—

'"You mustn't let any imaginary sense of obligation to me influence your answer. You see that, of course?"

'She looked rather bored and said no. But she meant yes, really. The matter now seemed to me to have been made perfectly clear, but to make quite sure I said, "Word of honour now!"

'And she said, "Yes, but I don't know what you're driving at."

'"You will in a minute," I said.

'Then I proposed.

'She sat silent – I expect it was rather unexpected – for quite two minutes by the clock. She sniffed a little, but quite audibly. I thought she was about to cry.

'Well, I saw that she had forgotten her word of honour and wanted to say no, only the obligation wouldn't let her. That's how I figured it out. The best thing I could do was to make it easier for her by clearing out. So I said, "I shall leave you to think things over," and I went.

'Later on, after casting it up, I felt quite positive that her real feelings towards me were no, but that her unreal or obligation feelings would have forced her to say yes. You can't trust a woman's word in everything: she'd have let me down. I was glad I left her before that happened.

'To make things easier for her, I wrote and refused for her. I worded my letter very carefully, so that she could see that I wouldn't change my mind.

'She never answered it. Sensible of her, I thought.'

Had William been the *parfyte gentyle* knight, he should now have departed to some remote part of the earth, where in a temperature of 40° under zero or 120° above it he could have awaited an end to his miseries. He might have passed, perhaps lessened, the interim by attacking the larger carnivora with inadequate small-bore rifles or even the long-bow. But he did none of these things. Having fulfilled so excellently the rôle of blundering cockchafer, he had assumed that of the moth anxious to singe its wings: he remained in London. He was not in the least aware of the hash he had tried to make of things.

Mary Seton had been bewildered and baffled by William's method. But she possessed the grace of humour, and a woman will forgive more easily than any other the fault of quixotry in the man she loves. She wept all over her aunt, but the position was not hopeless.

Thus the moth was fluttering in melancholy-wise down Piccadilly some fortnight later when it sighted the approach of Mrs Seton. Desire for a singe overcame the fear of a snub, and it held on its course towards her and did not escape up Halfmoon Street.

Mrs Seton was a woman of the world, and received William kindly, but immediately took him into custody. She remarked that it was quite a long time since he had been to see them; what had he been doing with himself? Oh yes, thanks, Mary was quite well – at least, quite well in herself, but rather mopish, off her sleep. Quite unaccountable. Too much season, she supposed. 'We must do what we can to cheer her up.'

'So,' thought William, 'Mary had not confided in her.'

But William knew rather less than nothing of the sex.

It was borne in on him that his part in the cheering-up process was to come back to lunch – nor was he loth to fall in with this implication.

Mary came trilling and tripping down to that meal. There were no signs of mope. Her lover, who had expected a Niobe in half-mourning, if not a French widow under a cascade of crêpe, was again puzzled. During the meal she was bright, chatty and not the least constrained. After it, when her aunt and William were alone for a moment, the latter said—

'I'm glad your niece is so bright. I had rather gathered from what you said——'

It was then that the violet-ray burnt momentarily in aunt's eye and illuminated William's dull understanding as she hissed—

'Oh! you – you – *Man!*' adding at once in normal tones as Mary re-entered, 'I'm simply snowed under with letters to write. I'm going to leave you two to amuse one another.'

Some two hours later they were still amusing one another. An endless spoony wrangle was in process. They were seated in a chair capable of holding two in a vertical plane, and William was saying—

'But, my sweetheart, weren't you just a little in a hurry? And your meaning wasn't very clear, was it? I don't think it's usually done like that.'

'But, my ownest, you sniffed, you positively sniffed. You must allow that. And naturally I took it for granted that——'

'But, my sweet, mayn't I sniff when I'm too frightfully happy? Why, if I had been perfectly sure of your real meaning, I might have sobbed or even howled.'

'I didn't think sniffiness was usual under the circumstances,' said William.

'No; but then you have such a lot to learn about us, darling. And then came your dear horrid letter just as if I had proposed and you were refusing me. Aunt Amy and I cried all over each other about it.'

'But I thought you hadn't told your aunt anything about it?'

Mary screwed her neck round – their positions necessitated contortions. She eyed him like a dove and cooed like one—

'Oh, you – you – dearest and best, but *Man!*'

At that moment Mrs Seton gave evidences of being outside the door. William made efforts to rectify their postures.

'Not on your life,' said Mary. 'And if you don't mind, I'm now going to really cling. Aunt Amy will simply love it.'

'I suppose,' said Aunt Amy, after envisaging things, 'you've accepted my niece this time?'

'I have,' said William in a strangled voice, 'for the second time of asking.'

# A Chain of Circumstance

## W. A. Darlington

'How I hate lovers!' said Mary Nicholls suddenly, in a venomous tone.

Her husband, outstretched contentedly on the lawn beside her deck-chair, opened his eyes.

'Didn't know you had any,' he said.

'Well, of course, *if* I had any, you *wouldn't* know. But I didn't mean that, idiot. What I meant was, how I hate having engaged couples staying in the house.'

'Meaning George and Caroline?'

'Meaning, especially, George and Caroline.'

'Oh, I don't know.' Bob Nicholls rolled over on to his stomach – which, he felt suddenly, would look less conspicuous that way – and considered the point. 'It means they're practically potty for the time being, I admit. But they work their pottiness off on one another, and don't hurt anybody else.'

'That's all you know! D'you realize that I'm never sure from one meal-time to the next whether they're going to be on speaking terms or not? If they're not, they won't sit next to each other. If they are, they want to sit in each other's laps.'

'Not an easy position,' remarked Bob flippantly.

'Not half so difficult as mine, to have to cope with it. If they've quarrelled they glower at their plates and don't speak, and if they've made it up they hold hands under the table and don't speak either.'

'Well, a little silence never hurt anybody. We all talk too much.'

'I dare say. But there's silence *and* silence.'

Bob picked a blade of grass and chewed it ruminatively gazing out across the valley and thinking vaguely that the River Wandle looked very pretty when the sun caught it.

'What's the matter with George and Caro?' he asked at last. '*We* weren't so up-and-down when we were engaged, were we? I remember you made me feel I'd like to murder you once or twice, but I never let it appear in my manner.'

'They've been engaged too long, that's what it is. And I've quite decided not to have them here again together until they're married – or until they've come unstuck for good.'

'Jolly little week-enders they'd be then!'

'Jollier than at present, anyhow. Is that George coming this way?'

'It is. And looking like a hearse-horse.'

'Oh dear! I did hope they'd have made it up by now . . . Hullo, George.'

George Cardwell was one of those people who get christened 'George' almost automatically. He was big, solid and, at ordinary times, reliable. He was excellent at games, and pretty good at his work. He was twenty-six years of age.

'Hullo,' he returned grumpily.

'Prithee, why so pale, fond lover?' inquired Bob, who was a well read man in a quiet way and never let mere tact stand in the way of an apposite quotation.

'Oh, shut up!' growled George.

'You and Caro haven't been quarrelling *again*, have you?' Mary demanded in a stern voice. Really, she felt, this was beyond bearing. George and/or Caroline must be spoken to sharply. Preferably George.

'Yes, we have.'

'Well, really, George . . .'

'Don't bother to go on, Mary. I know what you're going to say. I know Caro and I have spoilt your party for you. Well, it won't happen again. It's over. She's chucked me.'

He slumped down on the grass and looked so miserable that Mary, in spite of her irritation, began to administer comfort.

'I shouldn't worry. She's done that several times before.'

'Yes, but she's never done this before!'

He brought a hand out of a pocket and displayed something which glittered in the sun.

'She's given you back the ring?' said Bob in a surprised tone. 'How very Victorian!'

George gave a wry smile.

'Not so very Victorian, as a matter of fact,' he said grimly. 'She plugged it at my head.'

'Did she hit you?' Bob asked with interest.

'I caught it,' said George simply. 'Force of habit,' he added, as if it had occurred to him that some explanation of so undignified a proceeding was necessary. 'Rather a good catch, as a matter of fact.'

Mary, still the ministering angel, brought the conversation back to the point.

'Never mind, George. She'll come round.'

'She won't. It's a real bust-up this time. And upon my word, it's almost a relief.'

He did not look relieved, however; and Mary, forgetting how ready she had been a few minutes ago to discuss the possibility of the engagement coming unstuck, broke into protest.

'But, George – it's madness. Look how you love each other!'

'Do we?' George's voice was bitter.

'Of course you do.'

'I couldn't face a lifetime of this sort of thing.'

'It wouldn't happen once you were married.'

'How can you know that?'

'Because neither of you is like that, really. What was it about, this time?'

'Oh, something I said to her about young Harrison.'

'Geoffrey? Why, he's only a boy. You don't mean to say you were jealous of *him*?'

'No, of course not. It was just – oh, just that I couldn't stand seeing Caro buttering him up when she hadn't a civil word to say to me. She was doing it to annoy me, of course, I dare say I've been a fool.'

'You certainly have – both of you!' said Mary's husband in heartfelt tones.

'Be quiet, Bob . . . George, you've simply got to get married.'

'Who to?'

'Don't be silly. Caro of course.'

'You should have seen the look in her eyes when she threw that ring. No, that's over. Anyhow, I don't want a wife who throws things.'

'She *isn't* that sort. You know it as well as I do.'

'Well, she never was before . . .'

'And she isn't now. It's this ridiculous long engagement that's getting on both your nerves. Why don't you get married at once?'

'Not enough money.'

Bob sat up straight.

'Why, good Lord, you've got heaps for a start. A steady job . . .'

'Five hundred a year,' put in George.

'And Caro's people will be good for . . .'

'Another hundred at the most.'

'Well, that's six hundred.'

'And how far will that go?'

'All the way, if you're careful,' said Mary.

George looked obstinate.

'Caro and I decided at the start,' he said, 'that we wouldn't get married till we could afford it comfortably. So many people' – his voice took on the slight sing-song of one repeating a formula he knows by heart – 'make a mess of things by having to start by saving and scrimping. We made up our minds to be sensible.'

'Sensible! My aunt!' commented Bob. He got up and marched away.

Mary gazed pensively at his retreating back.

'It doesn't seem to work, does it, George dear? Why not give up the idea of waiting? You can manage all right now in a quiet way, and you'll very soon have more. I shouldn't go on being sensible if I were you – it's so silly.'

'But . . .'

She faced him squarely.

'Tell me, George, honestly – would *you* mind making do on what you've got, till you get a rise?'

'No, of course not. But would it be fair to Caroline?'

'Who wants you to be fair to Caroline?'

George laughed ruefully.

'Caroline, I expect.'

'Not she. You go and knock her on the head with a spanner, and tell her she's got to marry you and make the best of it. You'll be surprised how meek she'll be, once she sees you mean business.'

George stared.

'But Caro isn't like that,' he said.

'All women are like that to some extent,' Mary replied with energy. 'Anyhow, try it. You can't make things worse than they are at present.'

'That's true.' George jumped to his feet. 'You're right, Mary. I'll see if I can find her now.'

He was off, before Mary could utter a word to restrain him, or point out that it would be wiser to let some interval elapse before putting her well-meant advice into execution. She lay back in her deck-chair and sighed. Bob was quite right. People in love were, practically speaking, potty. No good bothering about them. She picked up a book from beside her chair and began to read.

Her peace was not long unbroken, however. A voice behind her said 'Mary' in a tense stage whisper, and Caroline Coxhead poked her head out of some bushes like a supernatural character in a pastoral play – a wood-nymph, or something.

She might have made a very satisfactory wood-nymph, Mary thought, for she was fair, slight and extremely graceful. Ordinarily, too, she was a very pretty girl; but at the moment her features were distorted by love out of their normally pleasant expression into something more fitted to a satyr than a dryad.

'Hallo, Caro,' said Mary, resignedly shutting her book. 'Did he find you?'

'George? No.' Miss Coxhead emerged from concealment. 'I've managed to dodge him. Look here, Mary – I'm going. I know it's no way to behave, and I'm sorry if it spoils your party; but I can't stick it any longer. Anyhow, I'm not fit to associate with.'

'But – but when?'

'Now. Your maids packed my things. And I've just seen Bob, and he's promised to drive me to Halston to catch the 3.25.'

'But what about poor George?'

'Nothing. I'm not going to see him again. Heavens – he's coming! Good-bye, Mary. Forgive me sometime.'

'Caro . . .' Mary began. But Caroline had melted into the bushes again. A real dryad could not have done it more neatly.

George came up at a distracted gallop.

'I say, Mary – was that Caro with you?'

'Yes,' said Mary wearily. Really, she reflected, from the way people shot in and out, she might be a character in a French farce, instead of a lady enjoying the after-lunch peace of her own garden.

'Where's she gone?'

'I don't know. But I know where she's going.'

'Where?'

'Home.'

'When?'

'Bob's taking her to catch the 3.25.'

'Then I must get hold of her at once.'

'She won't see you.'

'I'll hide in the car, or something.'

'That'll be no good. It's simply silly to have a scene with her now. You must give her time to simmer down, and then get her by herself.'

'How can I if she's off practically at once? And when she's gone, I shan't be able to catch her. She'll hide from me, or get engaged to somebody else. I must do it now.'

'You can't,' said Mary calmly. 'There goes the car.'

It was true. Bob's big Sunbeam was clearly audible in the drive. George bounded up a bank to a spot which commanded a distant view of the lodge gates, and was just in time to see the car's long yellow body turning into the main road.

He turned on Mary furiously.

'Now look what you've done, keeping me here talking,' he shouted. 'Is this a conspiracy, or what?'

'Of course it's not a conspiracy. I'm on your side, George. Don't be so violent.'

'Dash it, you were telling me to *be* violent not half an hour ago.'

'Yes, but at the proper time, and with the right person. Now listen, George. I'll tell you what to do.'

'Do? It's too late to do anything!'

'Nonsense! Look at your watch.'

George obeyed, and his eyebrows went up.

'Why, it's barely a quarter to three! They'll be miles too early for the train.'

'Exactly. Caro wanted to get out of your way.'

'Well, what do I do? Follow, and have it out in Halston station? Rather public.'

'No, idiot. Get your car and catch the train at the station *before* Halston. That's Statham. It's only seven miles away, and a good road. You'll do it easily.'

'And then?'

'At Halston, you'll see Bob putting Caro into the train. He'll see that she gets a carriage to herself. It's not hard on that line. At the next stop – Dogferry – you join her just as the train's starting. And that'll give you fifteen miles of the slowest local service in England before you get to

Templeton Junction. Half an hour to knock her on the head in – and good luck to you!'

But her last words were wasted. George was half-way to the garage by the time they were uttered.

Fred Cropper, guard on the London and Home Counties Railway, blew his whistle, swung himself into his van as it lumbered past him, settled down in the little seat provided for him by his employers, and began to muse morosely on life. Being a guard on the little branch line which ran up the Wandle Valley from Templeton Junction to Barnstead was not an arduous occupation, and he found plenty of time for introspection.

Life, as Fred Cropper saw it, was a safe but dull affair. In the days when he first joined the L. and H.C. Railway Company as a very young porter, he had had a vast, vague ambition. He saw himself becoming, some day, general superintendent, or something of that kind.

Nothing of the sort had happened, however. He had gone from safe, dull jobs to safe, dull jobs. The big occasion, the chance to prove himself had never come his way.

Even in the War, owing to the flatness of his feet, Safety and Dullness had continued to mark Mr Cropper for their own. In fact, nothing had ever happened to him, and it seemed unlikely, now, that anything ever would.

The Wandle Valley Branch was no sphere of action for an adventurous spirit. It was a friendly little line, on which most of the passengers generally knew one another by sight, and nearly all were known by name to Mr Cropper. Even when strangers did appear, he could generally give a pretty accurate guess at their reason for visiting the Valley.

Such a life, thought Mr Cropper with an unwonted flash of imagery, was as sluggish as the Wandle itself, that torpid stream along which he was carried week in, week out, three times a day (except Sundays) on and on for ever.

The worst part of the whole thing, he mused grimly, was that his work was not even necessary.

Tom Taylor, the driver of the engine, a man of action rather than words, would be perfectly capable of working the Wandle Valley train by himself. All his, Cropper's, waving of his flag and blowing of his whistle was nothing more than a ridiculous formality. So was the word 'Guard' on his uniform. Whom, or what, was he ever called upon to guard, and from what danger?

The train here pulled up at Statham. The platform was almost deserted, as usual. Mr. Cropper watched a tousled and flustered young man get in at the back of the train. Then he waved his symbolical flag and blew his redundant whistle, and Tom Taylor moved on towards Halston.

Mr Cropper went back to his little seat, and let his thoughts play round the tousled young man. A stranger he was, and looked like a gentleman – though you couldn't always tell, nowadays. Probably staying with the Penfolds at Statham Manor; but why he should be hatless, tousled and flustered was not apparent.

Halston. Ah, here was Mr Nicholls of Burdsley Grange, seeing off a girl. A very pretty girl, too, whom Mr Cropper did not remember to have seen on the Wandle Valley Branch before. Perhaps the Nichollses had sent over to Templeton Junction to fetch her when she arrived. However that might be, Mr Cropper felt pleased that she had not gone back the same way. He was highly susceptible, in a quiet and respectful way, and a passionate devotee of the films. This girl, thought Mr Cropper, was as beautiful as any film-star.

It seemed to Mr Cropper that the tousled young man was also highly susceptible. Leaning half out of his carriage window and holding one hand before his face, he was watching the girl in a way which the guard could not help thinking was distinctly furtive.

The whistle blew, the flag waved, and the train proceeded. Dogferry was the next station – a lonely building, little better than a mere 'halt', which seldom consigned many passengers to Mr Cropper's charge.

There were none today. The platform was deserted. For form's sake, the guard alighted. But just as he was about to signal the train on again, the tousled young man left his carriage, and slunk swiftly towards the front of the train. Just before he got to the first-class compartment where the pretty girl was, he paused, and waited.

Mr Cropper saw his game. He was going to wait until the train started, and then he was going to get in beside the girl, scrape acquaintance with her, annoy her – perhaps worse!

The question was, what could be done about it? As guard, Mr Cropper felt himself to have duties as chaperone towards this very pretty girl. Yet what could he do? If the young man would only make his intentions clear by getting into the carriage now, it would be easy. Mr Cropper could then walk along the train and stare in at the carriage window in a repressive way, to let the young man see that Law and Order had an official eye upon him. He might even demand to see the young man's ticket, and order him back into the third class from which he had come.

But so long as the young man stayed on the platform Mr Cropper was helpless. Once the train started, and the young man was in the girl's carriage, she would be at his mercy for the long run across Templeton Marshes. Mr Cropper remembered a lurid crime-story he had once read, in which a homicidal lunatic dismembered a woman in a railway carriage in circumstances roughly similar to these. If this nice girl arrived at Templeton Junction in small pieces, would not he, Cropper, be morally responsible? What, oh what, was he to do?

The problem was solved by Tom Taylor who, having spent the past half-minute wondering exasperatedly what the 'ell ole Fred thought 'e was playin' at, took the law into his own hands and started the train. Mr Cropper gave a convulsive jerk with his flag, nearly swallowed his whistle, and leapt into his van, forgetting entirely in his perturbation to notice which carriage the young man entered. Ah well, he felt, perhaps it was as well. The responsibility was out of his hands now, anyway. And no doubt the girl was quite capable of looking after herself. These modern girls were equal to anything. Well, perhaps not homicidal lunatics and dismemberment; but almost anything else.

Meanwhile, in ignorance of the perturbation of soul and conscience she was causing to a responsible official, Caro sat hunched up in a corner of her carriage. She was thankful to be alone, and to be able to soak herself in misery away from the tactful sympathy of her late host.

Bob Nicholls had tried her patience very severely. In the car on the way to the station he had engaged her in earnestly cheerful conversation on a variety of impersonal topics, until Caro could cheerfully have brained him. But her only weapon was an umbrella, and there was no room to swing it properly in the Sunbeam.

On the platform, waiting for the train, things had grown worse and worse. Bob had found his stock of impersonal topics rapidly running low, and was obviously asking himself why this infernal girl had insisted on getting here so much too early. Caro, her fingers itching on her umbrella, had tried hard to persuade him to leave her. He would plainly have been thankful to do so, but that his code of hospitality forbade. So he had stayed, and kept up an increasingly laborious trickle of polite conversation, until Caro had had great trouble to restrain herself from loud yells.

She was in no mood for sympathy. Certain though she was that she had done the right thing in tearing George violently and finally from his place in her life, she was finding the operation exquisitely painful. But now that she was able to suffer in peace, she did feel, in a way, better.

She felt as a man might feel after having had a tooth out. He might value the tooth while it was in his head; but once it had been condemned by the dentist, he must make up his mind not only to its loss, but to the pain that its loss would cause. The pain would be sharp, but temporary; the ultimate benefit would be permanent.

Thinking of the future relief was a great help, she found. The knowledge that the intolerable ache must pass made it seem instantly less intolerable. Just so might the dentist's victim tell himself, in the midst of his sorrows, how wise he had been not to keep the tooth in his head, and how thankful he would soon be for his wisdom.

For the moment, however, Caro could not deny that she felt very unhappy indeed. She gazed resentfully out of the window. The tender green of the Wandle Valley was altogether out of keeping with her mood. She ought, she felt, to be gazing out upon a landscape riven by coal-mines and disfigured by slag heaps.

The train stopped at a station. Bathed in sunshine it looked horribly cheerful. Its platform was deserted, except for a small white dog which was scratching itself with a disgustingly contented smile. The spectacle revolted her, and she moved across to the far side of the compartment.

As the train started again – which it did with a jerk, as if it were annoyed about something – her carriage door was wrenched open, and somebody got in. This was the last straw! Now, she supposed, she would have to spend her time refusing the conversational gambits of some garrulous old spinster, or other pest! She gazed resolutely out of the window.

Then it occurred to her that garrulous old spinsters don't, as a rule, wrench open doors and enter moving trains. Also, the reflection in her window-pane showed her a figure in the opposite corner which, though dim, was obviously large and male.

Shifting her position, she let her eye drift casually round the compartment, to see if her companion was the kind of large male who could be quietly ignored, or the kind that might have to be coped with later.

She gave a violent start.

Decidedly he would have to be coped with, not later but here and now.

'George!' she said, and gasped. 'How on earth did you get here?'

She felt the kind of incredulous horror that a dentist's patient might experience on finding that a tooth which he had thought was safely out had returned to its post, prepared to go on giving trouble exactly as before.

'And what the devil,' returned George, 'do you mean by playing me such a trick?'

He glowered at her ferociously. During the last half-hour or so he had managed to lash himself into a very satisfactory passion. There was a quality in his glower which Caro did not remember to have encountered in any of the series of stand-up fights into which their engagement seemed to have degenerated. She felt a thrill – but whether of fear or of pleasure, or a queer combination of the two, she did not give herself time to inquire. She thrust the emotion back into her sub-consciousness, and turned at bay.

'That's *my* business!' she said defiantly.

'Is it indeed? I'll soon show you about that, my girl!'

George advanced toward her in an attitude of menace. Again Caro felt that untimely thrill. She had never realized that George was so large. But afraid? Of George! What an idea! She was furious, that was all. Still, this certainly was a new sidelight on George's character. She suddenly began to wonder if she knew him quite as well as she had thought.

All the same, fury came uppermost. What a rotten thing it was to do, to corner her like this and threaten her with his superior brute force. If this sort of thing could be allowed to happen, what, Caro demanded of herself, was civilization for?

She glanced about her, and her eye fell on a notice which the L. & H.C. Railway, in an unwonted fit of levity, had put into verse for her benefit.

To stop the train (said the L. & H.C.)

Pull down the chain.

It added, in prose, that if you took this advice for insufficient reason, the tariff charge was £5 a pull.

But Caro was in no mood to boggle about by-laws. At the moment her life had only one purpose – to teach George a lesson. Here was an implement handy to do it with. Very well then.

She reached up and caught hold of the chain.

'If you come one inch farther,' she said through her teeth, 'I'll pull!'

George laughed.

'Don't be a something fool,' he said. Trusting to the fact that in ordinary life nobody pulls down chains and stops trains except in cases of murder or severe illness, he stepped forward. And Caro pulled.

For a long, awful moment they stared at each other. Then the train began to slow down.

'Well,' said George. 'Now you *have* done it!'

Caro released the chain, which hung down in a slack loop where only a few moments ago it had been so beautifully taut. She made some futile effort to return it to its original position, but in vain. It continued to hang in a slack loop; and the train continued to slow down.

'Oh George!' said Caro, suddenly abandoning her high horse and becoming a damsel in distress appealing to her natural protector. 'What *shall* we do!'

George failed to adapt himself to the new attitude.

'What *can* we do?' he asked unhelpfully. 'You were going to give me in charge or something, weren't you? Better go on with it – unless you expect me to explain that I did it for a lark, and produce a fiver.'

'It'll have stopped in a second. *George!*'

There was a note of pleading in her voice which melted George to some extent.

'Oh, all right!' he said. He paused a moment to reconnoitre the situation. Then he lay down on the floor, with an air of distaste and ill-usage.

'I've fainted. Whatever happens, stick to that. I fainted, and you were frightened and called for help.'

'But your clothes – they'll be filthy.'

'You should have thought of that before you began pulling chains. And anyhow, why does it matter to you how filthy I get?'

He closed his eyes coldly, as the train stopped with a final jerk.

The consternation which the pulling down of the chain had caused in the carriage was as nothing to that which it engendered in the guard's van. Mr. Cropper was in a pitiful panic. He had never had his communication chain pulled before, and had almost forgotten that such things could happen. He applied his brake with the feeling that he was probably signing his own death-warrant. As the train slowed down, he remembered the hefty build of that tousled young man, glanced at his own inconsiderable frame, and shivered.

Nevertheless, duty called. And if it was fate's decree that he should suffer, at least he had the consolation that he would suffer in a worthy cause – for the girl was really a very pretty girl indeed.

As he trotted along beside the line, he hoped that Tom Taylor would have the impulse to come to his assistance. He needed a man of action. But Tom merely hung a surprised face out of his cab and did not move. As for the handful of passengers, not one of them even troubled to look out of the window. Stoppages on the Wandle Valley Branch were not infrequent, and the Wandle Valley intellect was slow to react even to an emotion so universal as curiosity. Fred Cropper felt very lonely as he arrived at the fatal compartment. Guards on American trains, he seemed to remember from the films, carried guns. He thought it an excellent idea.

He climbed up, peeped in – and nearly fell off the foot-board. The girl was standing up, with her back to him. The hefty young man lay at her feet. She had knocked him out! Heavens, what a girl!

Relief surged through Fred Cropper's soul. He suddenly found himself capable of dealing with the situation. He opened the carriage-door firmly.

The girl turned.

'Oh, Guard,' she said. 'I – I hope you don't mind, but I pulled the chain. You see, this gentleman fainted, and I didn't know quite what to do.'

('Fainted!' thought Mr Cropper sardonically. Evidently the girl was frightened of the effects of her deed. He must reassure her.)

He bent down and felt the young man's heart. It was beating. Indeed, it was pounding heavily.

'It's all right, miss. You haven't hurt him. He's alive all right. You're a brave young lady – what did you hit him with?'

'I *haven't* hit him.' Her astonishment, thought Mr Cropper, was very cleverly put on. 'He fainted, I tell you.'

'No need to say that, miss, really there isn't. Anything you done, you done in self-defence. Ugly looking customer, too.'

'But I didn't do anything. This gentleman's my – er – he's a – a friend of mine.'

Mr Cropper, noticing her hesitation over the word 'friend', drew his own conclusions. Now that the danger was past, she wanted to avoid getting mixed up in a nasty affair. He could appreciate that. But it was his duty to the company not to allow this miscreant to get off scot free; and it was his duty to himself to get any credit that might be going.

Tom Taylor's grimy and puzzled face appeared at this point outside the window.

'What's up, Fred?'

'Young lady been set on, Tom. She laid him out good and proper, an' now she wants to make out he's a friend of hers.'

'But he *is* a friend of mine,' Caro interrupted wildly. 'We were travelling together.'

Mr Cropper pounced like a cross-examining counsel.

'There you are, Tom. He *wasn't* travellin' with her. I seen him watching her out o' window at Halston, an' creepin' along the platform at Dogferry to get in beside her.'

'Ah,' said Tom. ''E looks that sort.'

This was acute of Mr Taylor, for he was not in a position to see more of George than his right boot. Caro turned on him indignantly.

'He isn't that sort, I tell you. He's my fiancé.'

Fred Cropper shook his head, as one who had come sorrowfully to the conclusion that he could not believe a single syllable that this girl said.

'You said friend just now,' he pointed out. 'No, miss, I'm sorry, but we got our dooty to do. Let's get him out of the carriage, Tom.'

Angry and bewildered, Caro sank down on to the seat. Horrid pictures of police-court proceedings began to pass through her mind.

What could she say or do, now that she was a discredited witness? George might have an idea; but George was committed to remaining an inert mass, and was now being lifted out of the carriage, none too gently, by the big engine-driver and the little guard. George evidently realized that it would be better for him to remain in his faint until she had succeeded, somehow or other, in making the atmosphere less hostile towards him. But how?

They laid George on the grass at the side of the line, and Caro heard the engine-driver say:

'What we got to do now, Fred, is bring 'im to an' then ask 'im what the 'ell 'e means by it. You stand by to bash 'im if 'e tries anything before I get back.'

He departed towards the engine on some mysterious errand.

Meanwhile, Wandle Valley had begun to realize that something unusual was up. The passengers were beginning to leave the train and gather round; and a low muttering showed that they were hearing with indignation the guard's highly-coloured version of what had happened.

The muttering grew louder, the indignation deeper. Caro remembering lurid tales she had heard of slow but fierce rustic passions, decided that the time had come for drastic, even dramatic, action.

She leapt from the carriage, and suddenly appeared, standing over the recumbent George and facing the citizenry as Mark Antony did over the body of Caesar.

'Listen!' she said imperiously. 'You must listen – all of you. You're making a horrible mistake. This gentleman was my fiancé. This morning we quarrelled, and I broke the engagement and ran away. He followed me, and when he got to my carriage, he fainted. And that's all that happened.'

She paused.

The urgency of her words had penetrated the Wandle Valley intellect. If the young chap really had behaved like this, pondered Wandle Valley, then perhaps young chap was not quite such a villain after all. Indeed, young chap was not so much a villain as one of these here great lovers you see on the pictures. Wandle Valley, its dramatic sense pleasantly titillated, waited for the next step.

Caro, who had done a good deal of amateur acting in her time, could feel that she was holding her audience. Suddenly she realized that what was now wanted was a stroke of pure theatre. Well, why not? Since her linen was being washed in public anyhow, let it be washed thoroughly, and with a flourish.

She crossed her hands on her breast and looked demurely down.

'You see,' she said, with an effective catch in her voice, 'I love him!'

An ill-timed smile appeared on George's face. Whether it signified gratification or derision Caro did not wait to consider. She delivered a powerful but surreptitious kick to George's short ribs, and the smile was obliterated.

Wandle Valley was impressed. It recognized the familiar signs. The downcast eyes, the blush of modesty (really of shame, but Wandle Valley was not to know that) – such were the known tokens of maidenly surrender. Mr Cropper's romantic soul was specially touched. His late monstrous suspicions of this admirable young man were now quite gone. He felt, dimly, that it would be a fit conclusion if the young man now came to himself in time for the final embrace and fade-out.

Caro, not at all dimly, felt the same. It was all very well for George to be careful, but she felt he was now carrying caution to a ridiculous extreme. She gave expression to this feeling with another surreptitious but well-aimed kick. George gave a convulsive movement and a realistic groan, and played up.

He opened his eyes.

'Where am I?' he asked, in the accepted form for these occasions.

Then he raised himself on his elbow.

'Caro darling!' he said, and flopped back on to the ground and closed his eyes once more.

Mr Cropper, and the rest, scarce forbore to cheer. The scene was going well. What is more, it would probably have continued to go well, but for Tom Taylor, who broke in upon it at this point.

That single-minded man of action, bent on his scheme for bringing George to and then asking what the 'ell 'e meant by it, had gone in search of water.

Such water as he had on his engine was hissing hot, and unsuitable as a cure for fainting fits. He had therefore taken an empty coal-bucket, and had filled it at a brackish marsh-pool which bordered on the railway embankment. The fluid thus obtained was muddy, and moreover had proved a fertile breeding-ground for duckweed and a nursery for myriads of tiny tadpoles. Also, the bucket had a rich deposit of coal-dust on its sides.

However, Mr Taylor was in no mood to consider the finer feelings of the kind of young man who annoyed beautiful girls in trains. He strode into the crowd and, before anybody had a chance to warn him of the change in popular opinion, discharged half of the dingy compound in his bucket into George's face.

It certainly brought the victim too. George sat up, gasping. Duckweed was in his hair, a mixture of mud and soot was running down his cheeks, tadpoles leapt uneasily in his lap. He was a pathetic sight, and all that was maternal in Caroline was roused by it. She forgot play-acting.

'George!' she cried. 'Oh, George, my poor sweet!' and she gathered him in her arms.

To Mr Taylor's intense indignation, it was he that was asked what the hell he meant by it. Wandle Valley turned on him as one man. Not only had he committed an unprovoked assault on an innocent man, but he had spoilt the only romantic close-up that Wandle Valley was ever likely to see in real life with a piece of vulgar slap-stick. Wandle Valley was annoyed with Mr Taylor, and said so.

Thereupon Mr Taylor lost his temper in his turn, issued an ultimatum that if Wandle Valley wasn't back in its places in two twos, he would take the train on to Templeton without it. He strode back to his engine, every inch the man of action, and Wandle Valley forgot righteous indignation in an undignified scramble for seats.

Of all this, Caro and George were beautifully unconscious. They had shared the mud, the soot, the duckweed and the tadpoles between them with such impartiality that it would have been difficult for an uninstructed observer to decide which had been Mr Taylor's original patient, and were now standing up hand in hand, bedraggled but blissful. Lost in a world of their own, they were busy planning a future which took no account of the immediate necessity of getting to Templeton Junction.

Mr Taylor gave a warning toot on his whistle. They did not hear it. Mr Cropper walked over to them, and gave a deferential cough. He might have been the Invisible Man for all the notice they took of him.

'Then you'll marry me at once, darling?'

'I'll marry you to-morrow, if we can get a special licence in the time.'

'Excuse me, miss . . .'

'And you won't mind being poor?'

'So long as I've got you, I don't mind anything. I knew it when I saw your poor face all covered with mud and stuff.'

'Excuse me, miss, but . . .'

'What fools we've been all this time!'

'What utter fools!'

'If you'll pardon me, sir . . .'

'But we've come to our senses at last!'

'Darling!'

'Sweetheart!'

'Please, miss . . .'

'I say,' said George, coming to earth suddenly. 'We'd better get back into the train, or it'll be going on without us!'

They scrambled to their feet and dashed for their carriage, leaving the Invisible Man following forlornly behind.

# The Butterfly Frolic

*Margaret Atwood*

If you let one worm out of a can of worms, all the other worms will follow. Aunt Lou used to say that; she had many useful maxims, some traditional, some invented by her. For instance, I've heard 'The tongue is the enemy of the neck' elsewhere, but never 'There's more than one cat in any bag' or 'Don't count on your rabbits before they're out of the hat'. Aunt Lou believed in discretion, though only in important matters.

That was one reason I never told Arthur much about my mother. If I'd started on her, he would've found out about me soon enough. I invented a mother for his benefit, a kind, placid woman who died of a rare disease – lupus, I think it was – shortly after I met him.

Luckily he was never curious about my past: he was too busy telling me about his. I heard all about his own mother: how she'd claimed to have known the very instant Arthur was conceived and dedicated him to the ministry (Anglican) right then and there in her womb, how she'd threatened to cut his thumbs off when she caught him playing with himself at the age of four. I knew about his contempt for her and for her belief in hard work and achievement, so curiously like his own, and about his fear of her orderliness, symbolized by her flower borders which he was forced to weed. I heard about her dislike of drinking and also about his father's bar in the recreation room in that Fredericton judge's mansion he claimed to have left so far behind, with the miniature gold Scotsmen's heads on the bottletops, perversely like nipples, or so I imagined them. I knew about the various hysterical letters his mother had written, disowning him for this or that, politics, religion, sex. One came when she learned we were living together, and she never did forgive me.

To all these monstrosities and injustices I listened faithfully, partly out of a hope that I would gradually come to understand him, but mostly from habit. At one stage of my life I was a good listener, I cultivated listening, I figured I'd better be good at it because I wasn't very good at anything else. I would listen to anyone about anything, murmuring at appropriate moments, reassuring, noncommittal, sympathetic as a pillow. I even took up eavesdropping behind doors and in buses and restaurants, but this was hardly the same, since it was unilateral. So it was easy to listen to Arthur, and I ended up knowing a lot more about his mother than he did about mine, not that it did me much good. Knowledge isn't necessarily power.

I did tell him one thing though, which should've made more of an impression on him than it did: my mother named me after Joan Crawford. This is one of the things that always puzzled me about her. Did she name me after Joan Crawford because she wanted me to be like the screen characters she played – beautiful, ambitious, ruthless, destructive to men – or because she wanted me to be successful? Joan Crawford worked hard, she had willpower, she built herself up from nothing, according to my mother. Did she give me someone else's name because she wanted me never to have a name of my own? Come to think of it, Joan Crawford didn't have a name of her own either. Her real name was Lucille LeSueur, which would have suited me much better. Lucy the Sweat. When I was eight or nine and my mother would look at me and say musingly, 'To think that I named you after Joan Crawford,' my stomach would contract and plummet and I would be overcome with shame; I knew I was being reproached, but I'm still not sure what for. There's more than one side to Joan Crawford, though. In fact there was something tragic about Joan Crawford, she had big serious eyes, an unhappy mouth and high cheekbones, unfortunate things happened to her. Perhaps that was it. Or, and this is important: Joan Crawford was thin.

I was not, and this is one of the many things for which my mother never quite forgave me. At first I was merely plump; in the earliest snapshots in my mother's album I was a healthy baby, not much heftier than most, and the only peculiar thing is that I was never looking at the camera; instead I was trying to get something into my mouth: a toy, a hand, a bottle. The photos went on in an orderly series, though I didn't exactly become rounder, I failed to lose what is usually referred to as baby fat. When I reached the age of six the pictures stopped abruptly. This must have been when my mother gave up on me, for it was she who used to take them; perhaps she no longer wanted my growth recorded. She had decided I would not do.

I became aware of this fairly soon. My mother enrolled me in a dancing school, where a woman called Miss Flegg, who was almost as slender and disapproving as my mother, taught tap dancing and ballet. The classes were held in a long room over a butcher shop, and I could always remember the way the smell of sawdust and raw meat gave way to the muggy scent of exhausted feet, mingled with Miss Flegg's Yardley cologne, as I trudged up the dusty stairs. My mother took this step partly because it was fashionable to enroll seven-year-old girls in dancing schools – Hollywood musicals were still popular – and partly because she hoped it would make me less chubby. She didn't say this to me, she said it to Miss Flegg; she was not yet calling me fat.

I loved dancing school. I was even quite good at the actual dancing, although Miss Flegg sometimes rapped her classroom pointer sharply on the floor and said, 'Joan dear, I wish you would stop thumping.' Like most little girls of that time I idealized ballet dancers, it was something girls could do, and I used to press my short piggy nose up against jewelry store windows and goggle at the china music-box figurines of shiny ladies in brittle pink skirts, with roses on their hard ceramic heads, and imagine myself leaping through the air, lifted by a thin man in black tights, light as a kite and wearing a modified doily, my hair full of rhinestones and glittering like hope. I worked hard at the classes, I concentrated, and I even used to practice at home, wrapping myself in a discarded lace bathroom curtain I had begged from my mother as she was about to stuff it into the garbage can. She washed it first though; she didn't like dirt. I longed for a pair of satin toe shoes, but we were too young, Miss Flegg explained, the bones in our feet had not hardened. So I had to settle for black slippers with an unromantic elastic over the instep.

Miss Flegg was an inventive woman; I suppose these days she would be called creative. She didn't have much scope for her inventiveness in the teaching of elementary steps to young children, which was largely a matter of drill, but she let herself go on the annual spring recital. The recital was mostly to impress the parents, but it was also to impress the little girls themselves so they would ask to be allowed to take lessons the next year.

Miss Flegg choreographed the entire program. She also constructed the sets and props, and she designed the costumes and handed out patterns and instructions to the mothers, who were supposed to sew them. My mother disliked sewing but for this event she buckled down and cut and pinned just like all the other mothers. Maybe she hadn't given up on me after all, maybe she was still making an effort.

Miss Flegg organized the recital into age groups, which corresponded to her dancing classes. There were five of them: Teenies, Tallers, Tensies, Tweeners and Teeners. Underneath her spiny exterior, the long bony hands, the hair wrenched into a bun, and the spidery eyebrows, done, I realized later, with a pencil, she had a layer of sentimentality, which set the tone for her inventions.

I was a Teenie, which was in itself a contradiction in terms, for as well as being heavier than everyone else in the class I had begun to be taller. But I didn't mind, I didn't even notice, for I was becoming more wildly excited about the recital every day. I practiced for hours in the basement, the only place I was allowed to do it after I had accidentally knocked over and broken my mother's white-and-gold living-room lamp in the shape of a pineapple, one of a set. I twirled beside the washing machine, humming the dance music in my head, I curtseyed to the furnace (which in those days still burned coal), I swayed in and out between the sheets drying double-folded on the line, and when I was exhausted I climbed the cellar stairs, out of breath and covered with coal dust, to be confronted by my mother with her mouth full of pins. After I'd been scrubbed I would be stood on a chair and told to turn around slowly. I could barely hold still even to have my costumes tried on.

My mother's impatience was almost equal to my own, though it was of another sort. She may have started to regret sending me to dancing school. For one thing, I wasn't getting any slimmer; for another, I now made twice as much noise as I had at first, especially when I rehearsed my tap number in my patent leather shoes with metal tips toe and heel, on the hardwood of the hall floor, which I had been ordered not to do; and for another, she was having trouble with the costumes. She'd follow the instructions, but she couldn't get them to look right.

There were three of them, for the Teenies were doing three numbers: 'Tulip Time,' a Dutch ballet routine for which we had to line up with partners and move our arms up and down to simulate windmills; 'Anchors Aweigh,' a tap dance with quick turns and salutes (this was soon after the end of the war and military motifs were still in vogue); and 'The Butterfly Frolic,' a graceful number whose delicate flittings were more like my idea of what dancing should be. It was my favorite, and it had my favorite costume too. This featured a gauzy skirt, short, like a real ballerina's, a tight bodice with shoulder straps, a headpiece with spangled insect antennae, and a pair of colored cellophane wings with coathanger frames, supplied by Miss Flegg. The wings were what I really longed for but we weren't allowed to put them on until the day itself, for fear of breakage.

But it was this costume that was bothering my mother. The others were easier: the Dutch outfit was a long full skirt with a black bodice and white sleeves, and I was the rear partner anyway. The 'Anchors Aweigh' number had middy dresses with naval braid trim, and this was all right too since they were high-necked, long-sleeved and loose around the waist. I was in the back row because of my height; I hadn't been picked as one of the three stars, all with Shirley Temple curls, who were doing solos on drums made out of cheese crates. But I didn't mind that much: I had my eye on the chief butterfly spot. There was a duet with the only boy in the class; his name was Roger. I was slightly in love with him. I hoped the girl who was supposed to do it would get sick and they would have to call me in. I'd memorized her part as well as my own, more or less.

I stood on the chair and my mother stuck pins into me and sighed; then she told me to turn slowly, and she frowned and stuck in some more pins. The problem was fairly simple: in the short pink skirt, with my waist, arms and legs exposed, I was grotesque. I am reconstructing this from the point of view of an adult, an anxious, prudish adult like my mother or Miss Flegg; but with my jiggly thighs and the bulges of fat where breasts would later be and my plump upper arms and floppy waist, I must have looked obscene, senile almost, indecent; it must have been like watching a decaying stripper. I was the kind of child, they would have thought back then in the early months of 1949, who should not be seen in public with so little clothing on. No wonder I fell in love with the nineteenth century: back then, according to the dirty post-cards of the time, flesh was a virtue.

My mother struggled with the costume, lengthening it, adding another layer of gauze to conceal the outlines, padding the bodice; but it was no use. Even I was a little taken aback when she finally allowed me to inspect myself in the three-sided mirror over her vanity table. Although I was too young to be much bothered by my size, it wasn't quite the effect I wanted. I did not look like a butterfly. But I knew the addition of the wings would make all the difference. I was hoping for magic transformations, even then.

The dress rehearsal was in the afternoon, the recital the same evening. They were so close together because the recital was to be held, not in the room over the butcher shop, which would have been too cramped, but in the public school auditorium, rented for a single Saturday. My mother went with me, carrying my costumes in a cardboard dress box. The stage was cramped and hollow-sounding but was redeemed by velvet curtains, soft purple ones; I felt them at the first opportunity. The space behind it was vibrating with excitement. A lot of the mothers were there. Some of them had volunteered to do makeup and were painting the faces of theirs and other people's daughters, the mouths with dark-red lipstick, the eyelashes with black mascara which stiffened them into spikes. The finished and costumed girls were standing against the wall so as not to damage themselves, inert as temple sacrifices. The bigger pupils were strolling about and chatting; it wasn't as important to them, they had done it before, and their numbers were to be rehearsed later.

'Tulip Time' and 'Anchors Aweigh' went off without a hitch. We changed costumes backstage, in a tangle of arms and legs, giggling nervously and doing up each other's hooks and zippers. There was a crowd around the single mirror. The Tallers, who were alternating with us, did their number, 'Kitty Kat Kapers,' while Miss Flegg stood in the wings, evaluating, waving time with her pointer, and occasionally shouting. She was wrought up. As I was putting on my butterfly costume, I saw my mother standing beside her.

She was supposed to be out in the front row where I'd left her, sitting on a folding chair, her gloves in her lap, smoking and jiggling one of her feet in its high-heeled open-toed shoe, but now she was talking with Miss Flegg. Miss Flegg looked over at me; then she walked over, followed by my mother. She stood gazing down at me, her lips pressed together.

'I see what you mean,' she said to my mother. When resenting this scene later on, I always felt that if my mother hadn't interfered Miss Flegg would have noticed nothing, but this is probably not true. What she was seeing, what they were both seeing, was her gay, her artistic, her *spiritual* 'Butterfly Frolic' being reduced to something laughable and unseemly by the presence of a fat little girl who was more like a giant caterpillar than a butterfly, more like a white grub if you were really going to be accurate.

Miss Flegg could not have stood this. For her, the final effect was everything. She wished to be complimented on it, and wholeheartedly, not with pity or suppressed smiles. I sympathize with her now, although I couldn't then. Anyway, her inventiveness didn't desert her. She leaned down, placed her hand on my round bare sholder, and drew me over to a corner. There she knelt down and gazed with her forceful black eyes into mine. Her blurred eyebrows rose and fell.

'Joan, dear,' she said, 'how would you like to be something special?'

I smiled at her uncertainly.

'Would you do something for me, dear?' she said, warmly.

I nodded. I liked to help.

'I've decided to change the dance a little,' she said. 'I've decided to add a new part to it; and because you're the brightest girl in the class, I've chosen you to be the special, new person. Do you think you can do that, dear?'

I had seen enough of her to know that this kindess was suspect, but I fell for it anyway. I nodded emphatically, thrilled to have been selected. Maybe I'd been picked to do the butterfly duet with Roger, maybe I would get bigger, more important wings. I was eager.

'Good,' said Miss Flegg, clamping her hand on my arm. 'Now come and hop into your new costume.'

'What am I going to be?' I asked as she led me away.

'A mothball, dear,' she answered serenely, as if this were the most natural thing in the world.

Her inventive mind, and possibly earlier experiences, had given her a fundamental rule for dealing with situations like this: if you're going to be made to look ridiculous and there's no way out of it, you may as well pretend you meant to. I didn't learn this rule till much later, not consciously. I was wounded, desolated in fact, when it turned out that Miss Flegg wanted me to remove my cloudy skirt and spangles and put on one of the white teddy-bear costumes the Tensies were using for their number, 'Teddy Bears' Picnic.' She also wanted me to hang around my neck a large sign that said MOTHBALL, 'So they'll all understand, dear, what you're supposed to be.' She herself would make the sign for me, in the interval between the rehearsal and the performance.

'Can I wear my wings?' I asked. It was beginning to seep through to me, the monstrousness of the renunciation she was asking me to make.

'Now, who ever heard of a mothball with wings?' she said in what was supposed to be a jocular but practical manner.

Her idea was that once the butterflies had finished their cavorting, I would lumber among them in the white suit and the sign, and the butterflies would be coached to scatter. It would be cute, she told me.

'I liked the dance the way it was,' I said tentatively. 'I want it to be the way it was.' I was on the verge of crying; probably I had already begun.

Miss Flegg's manner changed. She put her face down close to mine so I could see the wrinkles around her eyes up close and smell the sour toothpaste smell of her mouth, and said, slowly and distinctly, 'You'll do as I say or you won't be in the dance at all. Do you understand?'

Being left out altogether was too much for me. I capitulated, but I paid for it. I had to stand in the mothball suit with Miss Flegg's hand on my shoulder while she explained to the other Teenies, sylphlike in their wispy skirts and shining wings, about the change in plans and my new, starring role. They looked at me, scorn on their painted lips; they were not taken in.

I went home with my mother, refusing to speak to her because she had betrayed me. It was snowing lightly, though it was April, and I was glad because she had on her white open-toed shoes and her feet would get wet. I went into the bathroom and locked the door so she couldn't get at me; then I wept uncontrollably, lying on the floor with my face against the fluffy pink bath mat. Afterwards I pulled the laundry hamper over so I could stand on it and look into the bathroom mirror. My made-up face had run, there were black streaks down my cheeks like sooty tears and my purple mouth was smudged and swollen. What was the matter with me? It wasn't that I couldn't dance.

My mother pleaded briefly with me through the locked bathroom door, then she threatened. I came out, but I wouldn't eat any dinner: someone besides me would have to suffer. My mother wiped the makeup off my face with Pond's Cold Cream, scolding me because it would have to be done over, and we set out again for the auditorium.

(Where was my father? He wasn't there.)

I had to stand enviously in the wings, red-faced and steaming in the hated suit, listening to the preliminary coughs and the scraping of folding chairs, then watching while the butterflies tinkled through the movements I myself had memorized, I was sure, better than any of them. The worst thing was that I still didn't understand quite why this was being done to me, this humiliation disguised as a privilege.

At the right moment Miss Flegg gave me a shove and I lurched onto the stage, trying to look, as she had instructed me, as much like a mothball as possible. Then I danced. There were no steps to my dance, as I hadn't been taught any, so I made it up as I went along. I swung my arms, I bumped into the butterflies, I spun in circles and stamped my feet as hard as I could on the boards of the flimsy stage, until it shook. I threw myself into the part, it was a dance of rage and destruction, tears rolled down my cheeks behind the fur, the butterflies would die; my feet hurt for days afterwards. 'This isn't me,' I kept saying to myself, 'they're making me do it'; yet even though I was concealed in the teddy-bear suit, which flopped about me and made me sweat, I felt naked and exposed, as if this ridiculous dance was the truth about me and everyone could see it.

The butterflies scampered away on cue and much to my surprise I was left in the center of the stage, facing an audience that was not only laughing but applauding vigorously. Even when the beauties, the tiny thin ones, trooped back for their curtsey, the laughter and clapping went on, and several people, who must have been fathers rather than mothers, shouted 'Bravo mothball!' It puzzled me that some of them seemed to like my ugly, bulky suit better than the pretty ones of the others.

After the recital Miss Flegg was congratulated on her priceless touch with the mothball. Even my mother appeared pleased. 'You did fine,' she said, but I still cried that night over my thwarted wings. I would never get a chance to use them now, since I had decided already that much as I loved dancing school I was not going back to it in the fall. It's true I had received more individual attention than the others, but I wasn't sure it was a kind I liked. Besides, who would think of marrying a mothball? A question my mother put to me often, later, in other forms.

# Blackhead

*Anthony Powell*

Outside the Army Council Room, side by side on the passage wall, hung, so far as I knew, the only pictures in the building, a huge pair of subfusc massively framed oil-paintings, subject and technique of which I could rarely pass without re-examination. The murkily stiff treatment of these two unwontedly elongated canvases, although not in fact executed by Horace Isbister RA, recalled his brush work and treatment, a style that already germinated a kind of low-grade nostalgia on account of its naïve approach and total disregard for any 'modern' develoment in the painter's art. The merging harmonies – dark brown, dark red, dark blue – depicted incidents in the wartime life of King George V: *Where Belgium greeted Britain*, showing the bearded monarch welcoming Albert, King of the Belgians, on arrival in this country as an exile from his own: *Merville, December 1st, 1914*, in which King George was portrayed chatting with President Poincaré, this time both with beards, the President wearing a hat somewhat resembling the head-dress of an *avocat* in the French lawcourts. Perhaps it was fur, on account of the cold. This time too busy to make a fresh assessment, aesthetic or sartorial, I passed the pictures by. Finn's door was locked. He might still be with the General, more probably was himself making a round of branches concerned with the evacuation. There was nothing for it but Blackhead, and restrictions on straw for hospital palliasses.

The stairs above the second floor led up into a rookery of lesser activities, some fairly obscure of definition. On these higher storeys dwelt the Civil branches and their subsidiaries, Finance, Internal Administration, Passive Air Defence, all diminishing in official prestige as the altitude steepened. Finally the explorer converged on attics under the eaves, where crusty hermits lunched frugally from paper bags, amongst crumb-powdered files and documents ineradicably tattooed with the circular brand of the teacup. At these heights, vestiges of hastily snatched meals endured throughout all seasons, eternal as the unmelted upland snows. Here, under the leads, like some unjustly confined prisoner of the Council of Ten, lived Blackhead. It was a part of the building rarely penetrated, for even Blackhead himself preferred on the whole to make forays on others, rather than that his own fastness should be invaded.

'You'll never get that past Blackhead,' Pennistone had said, during my first week with the Section.

'Who's Blackhead?'

'Until you have dealings with Blackhead, the word "bureaucrat" will have conveyed no meaning to you. He is the super-*tchenovnik* of the classical Russian novel. Even this building can boast no one else quite like him. As a special treat you can negotiate with Blackhead this afternoon on the subject of the issue of screwdrivers and other tools to Polish civilian personnel temporarily employed at military technical establishments.'

This suggested caricature, Pennistone's taste for presenting individuals in dramatic form. On the contrary, the picture was, if anything, toned down from reality. At my former Divisional Head-quarters, the chief clerk, Warrant Officer Class I Mr Diplock had, in fact, often proved himself in evolving a really impregnable system of obstruction and preclusion; awareness of such falling short of perfection perhaps telling on his nerves and finally causing him to embezzle and desert.

'Blackhead is a man apart,' said Pennistone. 'Even his colleagues are aware of that. His minutes have the abstract quality of pure extension.'

It was true. Closely 'in touch' with the Finance branch, he was, for some reason, not precisely categorized as one of them. Indeed, all precision was lacking where the branch to which Blackhead belonged was in question, even the house telephone directory, usually unequivo-cal, becoming all at once vague, even shifty. The phrase 'inspection and collation of governmental civil and economic administration in relation to Allied military liaison' had once been used by a member of one of the Finance branches themselves, then hastily withdrawn as if too explicit, something dangerous for security reasons to express so openly. Such prevarication hinted at the possibility that even his fellows by now could not exactly determine – anyway define to a layman – exactly what Blackhead really did. His rank, too, usually so manifest in every civil servant, seemed in Blackhead's case to have become blurred by time and attrition. To whom was he responsible? Whom – if anyone – did he transcend? Obviously in the last resort he was subservient to the Permanent Under-Secretary of State for War, and Blackhead himself would speak of Assistant Under Secretaries – even of Principals – as if their ranks represented unthinkable heights of official attainment. On the other hand, none of these people seemed to have the will, even the power, to control him. It was as if Blackhead, relatively humble though his grading might be, had become an anonymous immanence of all their kind, a fetish, the Voodoo deity of the whole Civil Service to be venerated and placated, even if better – safer – hidden away out of sight: the mystic holy essence incarnate of arguing, encumbering, delaying, hair-splitting, all for the best of reasons.

Blackhead might be a lone wolf, a one-man band, but he was a force that had to be reckoned with, from whom there was no court of appeal, until once in a way Operations would cut the Gordian knot, brutally disregarding Blackhead himself, overriding his objections, as it were snapping asunder the skinny arm he had slipped through the boltsockets of whatever administrative door he was attempting to hold against all comers. Operations would, as I say, sometimes thrust Blackhead aside, and continue to wage war unimpeded by him against the Axis. However, such a confrontation took place only when delay had become desperate. There was no doubt he would make himself felt by delaying tactics when the evacuation got under way, until something of that drastic sort took place.

'Of course I'm not an officer,' he had once remarked bitterly to Pennistone when a humiliation of just that kind had been visited on him, 'I'm only Mr Blackhead.'

Some years after the war was over – by chance attending a gathering of semi-official character, possibly a *soirée* organized for a fund or charity – I inquired Blackhead's story from a former colleague of his who happened to be present. This personage (even in war days of distinguished rank, one of the *hauts fonctionnaires* on the second floor) would at first do no more than laugh, loudly though a shade uncomfortably. He seemed anxious to evade the question. In fact, all at length recoverable from his answers, such as they were, became reduced to the hypothesis that Blackhead had been deliberately relegated to an appointment peculiar to himself – that in which our Section had dealings with him – chiefly in order to keep him out of the way of more important people. As unique occupant of his individual branch, even if he did not promote the war effort, he did not greatly impede it – so, at least, my informant insisted – while duties almost anywhere else might prove less innocuous. This highly successful person nodded several times when he admitted that. Self-esteem made the reply a little unacceptable to me. Did we matter so little? I argued the point. Why could not Blackhead be eradicated entirely? No such machinery existed. That was definite. Blackhead's former colleague showed himself as nearly apologetic about the fact as anyone of his calling had it in him. He fiddled with the decoration round his neck.

'The process was known afterwards as doing a Blackhead,' he allowed. 'Alternatively, having a Blackhead done on you. The public may think we're a staid crowd, but we have our professional jokes like everyone else. I say, what are your views on liquid refreshment? Would it be acceptable? I wouldn't say no myself. Don't I see a buffet over there? Let's make tracks.'

This subsequent conversation explained why Pennistone and the rest of us, like Jacob and the Angel, had to wrestle with Blackhead until the coming of day, or nearly that. Such was the biblical comparison that came to mind as I climbed the stairs leading to Blackhead's room, the moral exile to which his own kind had banished him emphasized not only by its smallness, but also by the fact that he lived there alone, isolation rare for one of his putatively low degree – if, indeed, his degree was low. I opened the door a crack, but further enlargement of entry was blocked by sheer stowage of paper, the files thickly banked about the floor like wholesale goods awaiting allotment to retailers, or, more credibly, the residue of a totally unsaleable commodity stored up here out of everyone's way. Blackhead himself was writing. He jumped up for a second and fiercely kicked a great cliff of files aside so that I could squeeze into the room. Then he returned to whatever he was at, his right hand moving feverishly across the paper, while his left thumb and forefinger, both stained with ink, rested on the handle of a saucerless cup.

'I'll attend to you in a minute, Jenkins.'

Not only was Blackhead, so to speak, beyond rank, he was also beyond age; beyond or outside Time. He might have been a worn – terribly worn – thirty-five; on the other hand (had not superannuation regulations, no doubt as sacred to Blackhead as any other official ordinances, precluded any such thing), he could easily have achieved threescore years and ten, with a safe prospect for his century. Emaciated, though obviously immensely strong, he was probably in truth approaching fifty. His hair, which formed an irregular wiry fringe over a furrowed leathery brow, was of a metallic shade that could have been natural to him all his life.

'Glad you've come, Jenkins,' he said, putting his face still closer to the paper on which he was writing. 'Pennistone minuted me . . . Polish Women's Corps . . . terms I haven't been able fully to interpret . . . In short don't at all comprehend . . .'

His hand continued to move at immense speed, with a nervous shaky intensity, backwards and forwards across the page of the file, ending at last in a signature. He blotted the minute, read through what he had written, closed the covers. Then he placed the file on an already overhanging tower of similar dockets, a vast rickety skyscraper of official comment, based on the flimsy foundation of a wire tray. At this final burden, the pyramid began to tremble, at first seemed likely to topple over. Blackhead showed absolute command of the situation. He steadied the pile with scarcely a touch of his practised hand. Then, eyes glinting behind his spectacles, he rose jerkily and began rummaging about among similar foothills of files ranged on a side table.

'Belgian Women's Corps, bicycle for . . . Norwegian military attaché, office furniture . . . Royal Netherlands Artillery, second echelon lorries . . . Czechoslovak Field Security, appointment of cook . . . Distribution of Polish Global Sum in relation to other Allied commitments – now we're getting warm . . . Case of Corporal Altmann, legal costs in alleged rape – that's moving away . . . Luxembourg shoulder flashes – right out . . . Here we are . . . Polish Women's Corps, soap issue for – that's the one I wanted a word about.'

'I really came about the question of restrictions on straw for stuffing hospital palliasses in Scotland.'

Blackhead paused, on the defensive at once.

'You can't be expecting an answer on straw already?'

'We were hoping—'

'But look here . . .'

'It must be a week or ten days'

'Week or ten days? Cast your eyes over these, Jenkins.'

Blackhead made a gesture with his pen in the direction of the files stacked on the table amongst which he had been excavating.

'Barely had time to glance at the straw,' he said. 'Certainly not think it out properly. It's a tricky subject, straw.'

'Liaison HQ in Scotland hoped for a quick answer.'

'Liaison HQ in Scotland are going to be disappointed.'

'What's so difficult?'

'There's the Ministry of Supply angle.'

'Can't we ignore them for once?'

'Ministry of Agriculture may require notification. Straw interests them . . . We won't talk about that now. What I want you to tell me, Jenkins, is what Pennistone means by this . . .'

Blackhead held – thrust – the file forward in my direction.

'Couldn't we just cast an eye over the straw file too, if you could find it while I try to solve this one.'

Blackhead was unwilling, but in the end, after a certain amount of search, the file about hospital palliasses was found and also extracted.

'Now it's the Women's Corps I want to talk about,' he said. 'Issue of certain items – soap, to be exact, and regulations for same. There's a principle at stake. I pointed that out to Pennistone. Read this . . . where my minute begins . . .'

To define the length of a 'minute' – an official memorandum authorizing or recommending any given course – is, naturally, like trying to lay down the size of a piece of chalk. There can be short minutes or long minutes, as there might be a chalk down or a fragment of chalk scarcely perceptible to the eye. Thus a long minute might be divided into sections and sub-headings, running into pages and signed by an authority of the highest rank. On the other hand, just as a piece of chalk might reasonably be thought of as a length of that limestone convenient for writing on a blackboard, the ordinary run of minutes exchanged between such as Pennistone and Blackhead might be supposed, in general, to take a fairly brief form – say two or three, to perhaps ten or a dozen, lines. Blackhead pointed severely to what he had written. Then he turned the pages several times. It was a real Marathon of a minute, even for Blackhead. When it came to an end at last he tapped his finger sharply on a comment written below his own signature.

'Look at this,' he said.

He spoke indignantly. I leant forward to examine the exhibit, which was in Pennistone's handwriting. Blackhead had written, in all, three and a half pages on the theory and practice of soap issues for military personnel, with especial reference to the Polish Women's Corps. Turning from his spidery scrawl to Pennistone's neat hand, two words only were inscribed. They stood out on the file:

*Please amplify. D. Pennistone. Maj. GS.*

Blackhead stood back.

'What do you think of that?' he asked.

I could find no suitable answer, in fact had nearly laughed, which would have been fatal, an error from which no recovery would have been possible.

'He didn't mention the matter to me.'

'As if I hadn't gone into it carefully,' said Blackhead.

'You'd better have a word with Pennistone.'

'Word with him? Not before I've made sure about the point I've missed. He wouldn't have said that unless he knew. I thought you'd be able to explain, Jenkins. If he thinks I've omitted something, he'd hardly keep it from you.'

'I'm at a loss – but about the palliasse straw—'

'What else can he want to know?' said Blackhead. 'It's me that's asking the questions there, not him.'

'You'll have to speak together.'

'Amplify, indeed,' said Blackhead. 'I spent a couple of hours on that file.'

Blackhead stared down at what Pennistone had written. He was distraught; aghast. Pennistone had gone too far. We should be made to suffer for this frivolity of his. That was, if Blackhead retained his sanity.

'What would you like me to do about it?'

Blackhead took off his spectacles and pointed the shafts at me.

'I'll tell you what,' he said. 'I could send it to F 17 (b) for comments. They're the *only ones*, in my view, who might take exception to not being consulted. They're a touchy lot. Always have been. I may have slipped up in not asking them, but I'd have never guessed Pennistone would have spotted that.'

'The thing we want to get on with is the straw.'

'Get on with?' said Blackhead. 'Get on with? If Pennistone wants to get on with things, why does he minute me in the aforesaid terms?

That's what I can't understand.'

'Why not talk to him when he comes back. He's at Polish GHQ at the moment. Can't we just inspect the straw file?'

Blackhead had been put so far off his balance that his usual obstinacy must have become impaired. Quite unexpectedly, he gave way all at once about the straw. We discussed the subject of palliasses fully, Blackhead noting in the file that 'a measure of agreement had been reached'. It was a minor triumph. I also prepared the way for papers about the evacuation, but this Blackhead could hardly take in.

'I can't understand Pennistone writing that,' he said. 'I've never had it written before – *please amplify* – not in all my service, all the years I've worked in this blessed building. It's not right. It suggests a criticism of my method.'

I left him gulping the chill dregs of his tea. Finn would probably be back in his room now, ready to hear the substance of what Q (Ops.) Colonel had said.

# Motion Study Tonsils

## Frank B. Gilbreth

Dad thought the best way to deal with sickness in the family was simply to ignore it.

'We don't have time for such nonsense,' he said. 'There are too many of us. A sick person drags down the performance of the entire group. You children come from sound pioneer stock. You've been given health, and it's your job to keep it. I don't want any excuses. I want you to stay well.'

Except for measles and whooping cough, we obeyed orders. Doctors' visits were so infrequent we learned to identify them with Mother's having a baby.

Dad's mother, who lived with us for a while, had her own secret for warding off disease. Grandma Gilbreth was born in Maine, where she said the seasons were Winter, July and August. She claimed to be an expert in combating cold weather and in avoiding head colds.

Her secret prophylaxis was a white bag, filled and saturated with camphor, which she kept hidden in her bosom. Grandma's bosom offered ample hiding space not only for the camphor but for her eyeglasses, her handkerchief, and, if need be, for the bedspread she was crocheting.

Each year, as soon as the first frost appeared, she made twelve identical white, camphor-filled bags for each of us.

'Mind what Grandma says and wear these all the time,' she told us. 'Now if you bring home a cold it will be your own blessed fault, and I'll skin you alive.'

Grandma always was threatening to skin someone alive, or draw and quarter him, or scalp him like a Red Indian, or spank him till his bottom blistered.

Grandma averred she was a great believer in 'spare the rod and spoil the child'. Her own personal rod was a branch from a lilac bush, which grew in the side lawn. She always kept a twig from this bush on the top of her dresser.

'I declare, you're going to catch it now,' she would say. 'Your mother won't spank you and your father is too busy to spank you, but your grandma is going to spank you till your bottom blisters.'

Then she would swing the twig with a vigour which belied her years. Most of her swings were aimed so as merely to whistle harmlessly through the air. She'd land a few light licks on our legs, though, and since we didn't want to hurt her feelings we'd scream and holler as if we were receiving the twenty-one lashes from a Spanish inquisitor. Sometimes she'd switch so vigorously at nothing that the twig would break.

'Ah, you see? You were so bad that I had to break my whip on you. Now go right out in the yard and cut me another one for next time. A big, thick one that will hurt even more than this one. Go along now. March!'

On the infrequent occasions when one of us did become sick enough to stay in bed, Grandma and Dad thought the best treatment was the absent treatment.

'A child abed mends best if left to himself,' Grandma said, while Dad nodded approval. Mother said she agreed, too, but then she proceeded to wait on the sick child hand and foot.

'Here, darling, put my lovely bed jacket around your shoulders,' Mother would tell the ailing one. 'Here are some magazines, and scissors and paste. Now how's that? I'm going down to the kitchen and fix you a tray. Then I'll be up and read to you.'

A cousin brought measles into the house, and all of us except Martha, were stricken simultaneously. Two big adjoining bedrooms upstairs were converted into hospital wards – one for the boys and the other for the girls. We suffered together for two or three miserable, feverish, itchy days, while Mother applied cocoa butter and ice packs. Dr Burton, who had delivered most of us, said there was nothing to worry about. He was an outspoken man, and he and Dad understood each other.

'I'll admit, Gilbreth, that your children don't get sick very often,' Dr Burton said, 'but when they do it messes up the public health statistics for the entire state of New Jersey.'

'How come, Mr Bones?' Dad asked.

'I have to turn in a report every week on the number of contagious diseases I handle. Ordinarily, I handle a couple of cases of measles a week. When I report that I had eleven cases in a single day, they're liable to quarantine the whole town of Montclair and close up every school in Essex County.'

'Well, they're probably exceptionally light cases,' Dad said. 'Pioneer stock, you know.'

'As far as I'm concerned, measles is measles, and they've got the measles.'

'Probably even pioneers got the measles,' Dad said.

'Probably so. Pioneers had tonsils, too, and so do your kids. Really ugly tonsils. They ought to come out.'

'I never had mine out.'

'Let me see them,' Dr Burton ordered.

'There's nothing the matter with them.'

'For God's sake don't waste my time,' said Dr Burton. 'Open your mouth and say "Ah".'

Dad opened his mouth and said 'Ah.'

'I thought so,' Dr Burton nodded. 'Yours ought to come out too. Should have had them taken out years ago. I don't expect you to admit it, but you have sore throats, don't you? You have one right this minute, haven't you?'

'Nonsense,' said Dad. 'Never sick a day in my life.'

'Well, let yours stay in if you want. You're not hurting anybody but yourself. But you really should have the children's taken out.'

'I'll talk it over with Lillie,' Dad promised.

Once the fever from the measles had gone, we all felt fine, although we still had to stay in bed. We sang songs, told continued stories, played spelling games and riddles, and had pillow-fights. Dad spent considerable time with us, joining in the songs and all the games except pillow-fights, which were illegal. He still believed in letting sick children alone, but with all of us sick – or all but Martha, at any rate – he became so lonesome he couldn't stay away.

He came into the wards one night after supper, and took a chair over in a corner. We noticed that his face was covered with spots.

'Daddy,' asked Anne, 'what's the matter with you? You're all broken out in spots.'

'You're imagining things,' said Dad, smirking. 'I'm all right.'

'You've got the measles.'

'I'm all right,' said Dad. 'I can take it.'

'Daddy's got the measles, Daddy's got the measles.' Dad sat there grinning, but our shouts were enough to bring Grandma on the run.

'What's the matter here?' she asked. And then to Dad. 'Mercy sakes, Frank, you're covered with spots.'

'It's just a joke,' Dad told his mother, weakly.

'Get yourself to bed. A man your age ought to know better. Shame on you.'

Grandma fumbled down her dress and put on her glasses. She peered into Dad's face.

'I declare, Frank Gilbreth,' she told him, 'sometimes I think you're more trouble than all of your children. Red ink! And you think it's a joke to scare a body half to death. Red ink!'

'A joke,' Dad repeated.

'Very funny,' Grandma muttered as she stalked out of the room. 'I'm splitting my sides.'

Dad sat there glumly.

'Is it red ink, Daddy?' we asked, and we agreed with him that it was, indeed, a very good joke. 'Is it? You really had us fooled.'

'You'll have to ask your grandma,' Dad sulked. 'She's a very smart lady. She knows it all.'

Martha, who appeared immune to measles, nevertheless wasn't allowed to come into the wards. She couldn't go to school, since the house was quarantined, and the week or two of being an 'only child' made her so miserable that she lost her appetite. Finally, she couldn't stand it any more, and sneaked into the sick rooms to visit us.

'You know you're not allowed in here,' said Anne. 'Do you want to get sick?'

Martha burst into tears. 'Yes,' she sobbed. 'Oh, yes.'

'Don't tell us you miss us? Why, I should think it would be wonderful to have the whole downstairs to yourself, and be able to have Mother and Dad all by yourself at dinner.'

'Dad's no fun any more,' said Mart. 'He's nervous. He says the quiet at the table is driving him crazy.'

'Tell him that's not of general interest,' said Ern.

It was shortly after the measles epidemic that Dad started applying motion study to surgery to try to reduce the time required for certain operations.

'Surgeons really aren't much different from skilled mechanics,' Dad said, 'except that they're not so skilled. If I can get to study their motions, I can speed them up. The speed of an operation often means the difference between life and death.'

At first, the surgeons he approached weren't very cooperative.

'I don't think it will work,' one doctor told him. 'We aren't dealing with machines. We're dealing with human beings. No two human beings are alike, so no set of motions could be used over and over again.'

'I know it will work,' Dad insisted. 'Just let me take some moving pictures of operations and I'll show you.'

Finally he got permission to set up his movie equipment in an operating-room. After the film was developed he put it in the projector which he kept in the parlour and showed us what he had done.

In the background was a cross-section screen and a big clock with 'GILBRETH' written across its face and a hand which made a full revolution every second. Each doctor and nurse was dressed in white, and had a number on his cap to identify him. The patient was on an operating table in the foreground. Off to the left, clad in a white sheet, was something that resembled a snow-covered Alp. When the Alp turned around, it had a stop-watch in its hand. And when it smiled at the camera you could tell through the disguise that it was Dad.

It seemed to us, watching the moving pictures, that the doctors did a rapid, business-like job of a complicated abdominal operation. But Dad, cranking the projector behind us, kept hollering that it was 'stupidity incorporated.'

'Look at that boob – the doctor with No. 3 on his cap. Watch what he's going to do now. Walk all the way around the operating table. Now see him reach way over there for that instrument? And then he decides that he doesn't want that one after all. He wants this one. He should call the instrument's name, and that nurse – No. 6, she's his caddy – should hand it to him. That's what she's there for. And look at his left hand – dangling there at his side. Why doesn't he use it? He could work twice as fast.'

The result of the moving picture was that the surgeons involved managed to reduce their ether time by fifteen per cent. Dad was far from satisfied. He explained that he needed to take moving pictures of five or six operations, all the same type, so that he could sort out the good motions from the wasted motions. The trouble was that most patients refused to be photographed, and hospitals were afraid of law-suits.

'Never mind, dear,' Mother told him. 'I'm sure the opportunity will come along eventually for you to get all the pictures that you want.'

Dad said that he didn't like to wait; that when he started a project, he hated to put it aside and pick it up again piecemeal whenever he found a patient, hospital and doctor who didn't object to photographs. Then an idea hit him, and he snapped his fingers.

'I know,' he said. 'I've got it. Dr Burton has been after me to have the kids' tonsils out. He says they really have to come out. We'll rig up an operating-room in the laboratory here, and take pictures of Burton.'

'It seems sort of heartless to use the children as guinea-pigs,' Mother said doubtfully.

'It does for a fact. And I won't do it unless Burton says it's perfectly all right. If taking pictures is going to make him nervous or anything, we'll have the tonsils taken out without the motion study.'

'Somehow or other I can't imagine Dr Burton being nervous,' Mother said.

'Me either. I'm going to call him. And you know what? I feel a little guilty about this whole deal. So, as conscience balm, I'm going to let the old butcher take mine out, too.'

'I feel a little guilty about the whole deal, too,' said Mother. 'Only thank goodness I had mine taken out when I was a girl.'

Dr Burton agreed to do the job in front of a movie camera.

'I'll save you for the last, Old Pioneer,' he told Dad. 'The best for the last. Since the first day I laid eyes on your great, big, beautiful tonsils, I knew I wouldn't be content until I got my hands on them.'

'Stop drooling and put away your scalpel, you old flatterer you,' said Dad. 'I intend to be the last. I'll have mine out after the kids get better.'

Dr Burton said he would start with Anne and go right down the ladder, through Ernestine, Frank, Bill and Lillian.

Martha alone of the older children didn't need to have her tonsils out, the doctor said, and the children younger than Lillian could wait a while.

The night before the mass operation, Martha was told she would sleep at the house of Dad's oldest sister, Aunt Anne.

'I don't want you underfoot,' Dad informed her. 'The children who are going to have their tonsils out won't be able to have any supper tonight or breakfast in the morning. I don't want you around to lord it over them.'

Martha hadn't forgotten how we neglected her when she finally came down with the measles. She lorded it over us plenty before she finally departed.

'Aunt Anne always has apple pie for breakfast,' she said, which we all knew to be perfectly true, except that sometimes it was blueberry instead of apple. 'She keeps a jar of doughnuts in the pantry and she likes children to eat them.' This, too, was unfortunately no more than the simple truth. 'Tomorrow morning, when you are awaiting the knife, I will be thinking of you. I shall try, if I am not too full, to dedicate a doughnut to each of you.'

She rubbed her stomach with a circular motion, and puffed out her cheeks horribly as if she were chewing on a whole doughnut. She opened an imaginary doughnut jar and helped herself to another, which she rammed into her mouth.

'My goodness, Aunt Anne,' she said, pretending that the lady was in the room, 'those doughnuts are even more delicious than usual.' . . . 'Well why don't you have another, Martha?' . . . 'Thanks, Aunt Anne, I believe I will.' . . . 'Why don't you take two or three, Martha?' . . . 'I'm so full of apple pie I don't know whether I could eat two more, Aunt Anne. But since it makes you happy to have people eat your cooking, I will do my best.'

'Hope you choke, Martha, dear,' we told her.

The next morning, the five of us selected to give our tonsils for motion study assembled in the parlour. As Martha had predicted, our stomachs were empty. They growled and rumbled. We could hear beds being moved around upstairs, and we knew the wards were being set up again. In the laboratory, which adjoined the parlour, Dad, his movie camera-man, a nurse, and Dr Burton were converting a desk into an operating table, and setting up the cross-section background and lights.

Dad came into the parlour, dressed like an Alp again. 'All right Anne, come on.' He thumped her on the back and smiled at the rest of us. 'There's nothing to it. It will be over in just a few minutes. And think of the fun we'll have looking at the movies and seeing how each of you looks when he's asleep.'

As he and Anne went out, we could see that his hands were trembling. Sweat was beginning to pop through his white robe. Mother came in and sat with us. Dad had wanted her to watch the operations, but she said she couldn't. After a while we heard Dad and a nurse walking heavily up the front stairs, and we knew Anne's operation was over and she was being carried to bed.

'I know I'm next, and I won't say I'm not scared,' Ernestine confided. 'But I'm so hungry all I can think of is Martha and that pie. The lucky dog.'

'And doughnuts,' said Bill. 'The lucky dog.'

'Can we have pie and doughnuts after our operations?' Lill asked Mother.

'If you want them,' said Mother, who had had her tonsils out.

Dad came into the room. His robe was dripping sweat now. It looked as if the spring thaw had come to the Alps.

'Nothing to it,' he said. 'And I know we got some great movies. Anne slept just like a baby. All right, Ernestine, girl. You're next; let's go.'

'I'm not hungry any more,' she said. 'Now I'm just scared.'

A nurse put a napkin saturated with ether over Ern's nose. The last thing she remembered was Mr Coggin, Dad's photographer, grinding away at the camera. 'He should be cranking at two revolutions a second,' she thought. 'I'll count and see if he is. And one and two and three and four. That's the way Dad says to count seconds. You have to put the "and" in between the numbers to count at the right speed. And one and two and three . . .' She fell asleep.

Dr Burton peered into her mouth.

'My God, Gilbreth,' he said. 'I told you I didn't want Martha.'

'You haven't got Martha,' Dad said. 'That's Ernestine.'

'Are you sure?'

'Of course I'm sure, you jackass. Don't you think I know my own children?'

'You must be mistaken,' Dr Burton insisted. 'Look at her carefully. There, now, isn't that Martha?'

'You mean to say you think I can't tell one child from another?'

'I don't mean to say anything, except if that isn't Martha we've made a horrible mistake.'

'We?' Dad squealed. 'We? I've made no mistake. And I hope I'm wrong in imagining the sort of mistake you've made.'

'You see, all I know them by is their tonsils,' said Dr. Burton. 'I thought these tonsils were Martha. They were the only pair that didn't have to come out.'

'No,' roared Dad. 'Oh, no!' Then growing indignant: 'Do you mean to tell me you knocked my little girl unconscious for no reason at all?'

'It looks as if I did just that, Gilbreth. I'm sorry, but it's done. It was damned careless. But you do have an uncommon lot of them, and they all look just alike to me.'

'All right, Burton,' Dad said. 'Sorry I lost my temper. What do we do?'

'I'm going to take them out anyway. They'd have to come out eventually at any rate, and the worst part of an operation is dreading it beforehand. She's done her dreading, and there's no use to make her do it twice.'

As Dr Burton leaned over Ernestine, some reflex caused her to knee him in the mouth.

'Okay, Ernestine, if that's really your name,' he muttered. 'I guess I deserved that.'

As it turned out, Ernestine's tonsils were recessed and bigger than the doctor had expected. It was a little messy to get at them, and Mr Coggin, the movie camera-man, was sick in a waste-paper basket.

'Don't stop cranking,' Dad shouted at him, 'or your tonsils will be next. I'll pull them out by the roots, myself. Crank, by jingo, crank.'

Mr Coggin cranked. When the operation was over, Dad and the nurse carried Ernestine upstairs.

When Dad came into the parlour to get Frank, he told Mother to send someone over to Aunt Anne's for Martha.

'Apple pie, doughnuts or not, she's going to have her tonsils out,' he said. 'I'm not going through another day like this one again in a hurry.'

Frank, Bill, and Lillian had their tonsils out, in that order. Then Martha arrived, bawling, kicking, and full of pie and doughnuts.

'You said I didn't have to have my tonsils out, and I'm not going to have my tonsils out,' she screamed at the doctor. Before he could get her on the desk which served as the operating table, she kicked him in the stomach.

'The next time I come to your house,' he said to Dad as soon as he could get his breath, 'I'm going to wear a chest protector and a catcher's mask.' Then to the nurse: 'Give some ether to Martha, if that's really her name.'

'Yes, I'm Martha,' she yelled through the towel. 'You're making a mistake.'

'I told you she was Martha,' Dad said triumphantly.

'I know,' Dr Burton said. 'Let's not go into that again. She's Martha, but I've named her tonsils Ernestine. Open your mouth, Martha, you sweet child, and let me get Ernestine's tonsils. Crank on, Mr Coggin. Your film may be the first photographic record of a man slowly going berserk.'

All of us felt terribly sick that afternoon, but Martha was in agony.

'It's a shame,' Grandma kept telling Martha, who was named for her and was her especial pet. 'They shouldn't have let you eat all that stuff and then brought you back here for the butchering. I don't care whether it was the doctor's fault or your father's fault. I'd like to skin them both alive and then scalp them like Red Indians.'

While we were recuperating, Dad spent considerable time with us, minimized our discomforts, and kept telling us we were just looking for sympathy.

'Don't tell me,' he said. 'I saw the operations, didn't I? Why, there's only the little, tiniest cut at the back of your throat. I don't understand how you can do all that complaining. Don't you remember the story about the Spartan boy who kept his mouth shut while the fox was chewing on his vitals?'

It was partly because of our complaining, and the desire to show us how the Spartan boy would have had his tonsils out, that Dad decided to have only a local anaesthetic for his operation. Mother, Grandma, and Dr Burton all advised against it. But Dad wouldn't listen.

'Why does everyone want to make a mountain out of a molehill over such a minor operation?' he said. 'I want to keep an eye on Burton and see that he doesn't mess up the job.'

The first day that we children were well enough to get up, Dad and Mother set out in the car for Dr Burton's office. Mother had urged Dad to call a taxi. She didn't know how to drive, and she said Dad probably wouldn't feel like doing the driving on the way home. But Dad laughed at her qualms.

'We'll be back in about an hour,' Dad called to us as he tested his three horns to make sure he was prepared for any emergency. 'Wait lunch for us. I'm starving.'

'You've got to hand it to him,' Anne admitted as the Pierce Arrow bucked up Wayside Place. 'He's the bee's knees, all right. We were all scared to death before our operations. And look at him. He's looking forward to it.'

Two hours later, a taxicab stopped in front of the house, and the driver jumped out and opened the door for his passengers. Then Mother emerged, pale and red-eyed. She and the driver helped a crumpled mass of moaning blue serge to alight. Dad's hat was rumpled and on sideways. His face was grey and sagging. He wasn't crying, but his eyes were watering. He couldn't speak and he couldn't smile.

'He's sure got a load on all right, Mrs Gilbreth,' said the driver enviously. 'And still early afternoon, too. Didn't even know he touched the stuff, myself.'

We waited for the lightning to strike, but it didn't. The seriousness of Dad's condition may be adjudged by the fact that he contented himself with a withering look.

'Keep a civil tongue in your head,' said Mother in one of the sharpest speeches of her career. 'He's deathly ill.'

Mother and Grandma helped Dad up to his room. We could hear him moaning, all the way downstairs.

Mother told us all about it that night, while Dad was snoring under the effects of sleeping pills. Mother had waited in Dr Burton's ante-room while the tonsilectomy was being performed. Dad had felt wonderful while under the local anaesthetic. When the operation was half over, he had come out into the ante-room, grinning and waving one tonsil in a pair of forceps.

'One down and one to go, Lillie,' he had said. 'Completely painless. Just like rolling off a log.'

After what had seemed an interminable time, Dad had come out into the waiting-room again, and reached for his hat and coat. He was still grinning, only not so wide as before.

'That's that,' he said. Almost painless. All right, boss, let's go. I'm still hungry.'

Then, as Mother watched, his high spirits faded and he began to fall to pieces.

'I'm stabbed,' he moaned. 'I'm haemorrhaging. Burton, come here. Quick! What have you done to me?'

Dr Burton came out of his office. It must be said to his credit that he was sincerely sympathetic. Dr Burton had had his own tonsils out.

'You'll be all right, Old Pioneer,' he said. 'You just had to have it the hard way.'

Dad obviously couldn't drive, so Mother had called the taxi. A man from the garage towed Foolish Carriage home later that night.

'I tried to drive it home,' the garage man told Mother, 'but I couldn't budge it. I got the engine running all right, but it just spit and bucked every time I put it in gear. Durndest thing I ever saw.'

'I don't think anyone but Mr Gilbreth understands it,' Mother said.

Dad spent two weeks in bed, and it was the first time any of us remembered his being sick. He couldn't smoke, eat, or talk. But he could glare, and he glared at Bill for two full minutes when Bill asked him one afternoon if he had had his tonsils taken out like the Spartans used to have theirs removed.

Dad didn't get his voice back until the very day that he finally got out of bed. He was lying there, propped up on pillows, reading his office mail. There was a card from Mr Coggin, the photographer.

'Hate to tell you, Mr Gilbreth, but none of the moving pictures came out. I forgot to take off the inside lens-cap. I'm terribly sorry. Coggins. P.S. I quit.'

Dad threw off the covers and reached for his bath-robe. For the first time in two weeks, he spoke:

'I'll track him down to the ends of the earth,' he croaked. 'I'll take a blunt button-hook and pull his tonsils out by the by-jingoed roots, just like I promised him. He doesn't quit. He's fired.'

# The Elopement

## *Caryl Brahms and S. J. Simon*

Will the ice hold?

In nurseries all over England frilly knickers and sailors suits have stopped shaking snowstorms over alpine chalets in crystal globes to ask this all-important question.

The sturdy hedges of England are covered with frost. Small cottages are humped beneath their eiderdowns of snow. And punch is being brewed wherever the stage-coach stops to change its horses. If the Camberwell–Birmingham stage-coach[1] lurches up a little late to-day they will forgive it.

All through the country, ditches, ponds, lakes and fens are freezing fast. Will there be skating at Lengey? Will the ice hold?

At Regent's Park Gideon Gloom and Aubrey Brandibal are consuming their weekly witty breakfast unattended. They have sent Bumblebottom the butler to test the ice on the lake.

At Eton or possibly Harrow[2] the boys have been given a half-holiday to go skating. Soon their skates will be making a noise like a twig in the wheel of a pennyfarthing as they hopefully circle around the rather wobbly games master.

But at the moment they are having a roll-call.

'Ramsbottom,' chants the prefect sternly.

'Higginbottom?'

'Applebottom?'[3]

'Winterbottom?'

'Sidebottom?'

[1] By way of Hampstead Heath.
[2] No 'Who's Who' handy.
[3] Formerly Appfelbaum.

'Shufflebottom?'
He pauses:
'Sitwell.'

Bumblebottom the butler comes back from the ice. He is wringing wet.
'Fallen in?' asks Gideon Gloom.
Bumblebottom glares.
But Aubrey Brandibal chuckles contentedly. There is a providence
in the fall of a butler. He beats Gideon Gloom to it.
'Skating on thin ice,' he comments.

They are skating in Regent's Park. Top-hats, tight waists and plaid
trousers have replaced the ducks and the gulls. With them, mantled in
sapphire and green and purple and indeed every shade and colour you
can think of, the ladies glide less daringly. Snowflakes swim gently in
the bright air and a Military Band, not on skates, is playing 'Gold and
Silver' on the island.
   The lakeside is one mass of admiring relatives. The too old, the too
young, the too expectant, and the too timid – the latter with carefully
sprained ankles.
   The main object of their admiration is the flashing Beau Bugle, who
is arranging himself to look his best as he glides into a rocker.
   Henry James, who has reached a sticky passage in Daisy, has taken
the morning off to watch his friend skate. Beside him sits the young
woman the Beau has thoughtfully brought along to admire him.
   'Is he not graceful?' she cooes.
   'Graceful?' Henry James's face is pickered with thought. He weighs
the word. He tastes it. He nods.
   'Yes,' he agrees. 'It is, as it were, an admirable description.'
   On the ice a studious boy has notched two crosses a short distance
apart. Planting himself at the nearest notch he signals his father to
watch. The attention of his parent attracted he sets off and laboriously
completes half an oval to reach the notch opposite.
   'Look, father,' he cries exultantly, 'I've skated a straight line!'
   Old Mr Einstein inspects the oval. He frowns. He shakes his head.
The boy has been working too hard.
   'Albert,' he pleads. 'Come home and have a nice cup of tea.'

Something has gone wrong with Beau Bugle's rocker. Can it be that he has overbalanced? The young lady, brought to admire him, claps her hands in anguish.

'Dear me,' says Henry James. 'It would appear that your graceful young friend has fallen . . .' He pauses. The perfect word eludes him. His face works as he searches for it. Painfully he digs it up from the furthest reaches of his vocabulary. Ah – here it is. Clear, expressive and perfect in its description of the object, as it were, apprehended.

'Down,' he finishes triumphantly.

But who is this smoothly skating top-booted villain? It is Spencer Faggot, gracefully cracking his riding-whip with one hand and warding off evicted widows with the other. This leaves him no hand with which to twirl his moustachios. A pity, but it cannot be helped. Behind him stocky, wobbly, but still upright, skates our Uncle Clarence.

Uncle Clarence is getting very fond of Spencer. Has not the dear fellow paid his debt in full – more than in full – for those shares to the value of thirty thousand pounds in the Esquimo Trading Company our villain has given him will soon be worth double. He has Spencer's word for this. With a mighty effort our staggering Uncle catches up with our swaggering villain.

'I say,' he asks, 'could you tell me the time?'

At Claremont Crescent the Crossing Sweeper has abandoned his soap box. As a matter of fact he is in Regent's Park earning his twopences strapping on skates. At the moment he is looking with disappointment at his palm. Only a tanner from young Master Rudyard – And him due to earn five bob a word when he grows up! It fair made a radical of you!

But had he remained at Claremont Crescent he would have sworn that he had never seen it so animated, not since old Mr Purplehammer came home in a rickshaw!

All down the shade, heads were bobbing out of windows. In the sun the knife boy made excited signs to the little servant girl. He had the afternoon off. The little servant girl ran (without effort) up four flights of stairs and (without turning a hair) invented a grandmother at this very moment dying. But this only reminded Aunt Lobelia that it was time for another dose of medicine.

From the gate of Number 26 the amiable Belinda Clutterwick comes out laughing between Archie and his best friend Algy. They have only one pair of skates among them, but this will be plenty, as neither Archie nor Algy intend to do anything more strenuous than watch Belinda skate and to discuss their plans for visiting the Great Exhibition in Chapter 17, or possibly the chapter after.

From the side entrance of Number 27 the wretched Benjamin sneaks guiltily out. The top-hat he is carrying fails to conceal the pair of skates he has placed in it. Henrietta has forbidden him to go on the ice where a Clutterwick might laugh at him at any moment.

Down the path, his affianced on his arm, comes Pelham Clutterwick. Obviously he has inherited the earth. Neither of them are carrying skates. As for la Cabuchon, she cannot understand how the English can bear to disarrange themselves so vigorously . . .

On the ice Beau Bugle prepares to sail gracefully into the figure eight. The young woman he has brought along to admire him clasps her hands in rapture. But the clasp tightens and soon it has become a clutch of anguish.

'Dear me,' says Henry James. 'Our ambitious young friend seems to have fallen . . .' He pauses. The perfect word vanishes. His face works. Ah – he has caught up with it. Clear, eloquent, and perfect in its summing up of the state of affairs.

'Again,' he points out very pleased with himself.

. . . But for her part la Cabuchon is going to Regent's Park to keep Pelham happy. Besides, it gives her pleasure to collect pained bows from bourgeois matrons still *epatées*.

She bows politely to Honest Ernest, off to the lake on his pennyfarthing, stops for a word with old Mr Purplehammer, dragging his toboggan, and – triumph! – there is the wretched Benjamin.

With evident pleasure la Cabuchon arranges her features in the expression of future Clutterwick about to cut a Shuttleforth dead in her own right.

From a window of Number 27 Henrietta watches grimly. But she is not displeased with the new engagement. The enemy morale could do with a bit of stiffening.

'Julia,' she calls out. 'It is time you were on your way to the Park. Honest Mr Shillingsworth has just gone by on his pennyfarthing.'

'Just ready, Mama!' A flushed and sparkling vision throws her arms round dear Mama with unusual warmth and picks up her skates.

Henrietta looks at her suspiciously.

'You understand, child,' she says. 'You are to skate with Mr Shillingsworth whenever he asks you. And you, Mrs. Marble, see to it that she is free to accept.'

Mrs Marble looks black. She has not been on the ice for twenty years come Michaelmas.[1]

They depart.

As they round the corner Julian Clutterwick steps jauntily out of Number 26. He sounds exactly like John Gielgud humming Mendelssohn's 'Wedding March.'

In the music-room at Windsor Castle the Queen, in her clear young voice, has been singing to Mr Mendelssohn.

'I have been so nervous,' she tells the Maestro. 'Usually I have a lot of breath and can hold a note for a very long time.'

'Ah,' says Mr Mendelssohn.

Swinging his skates, Julian makes straight for Regent's Park. Behind him puffs the rebellious Pumbleberry, who has had about enough of this. If Master Julian does not elope soon, he will wash his hands of the whole affair.

*       *       *

In Regent's Park elegant couples are gliding through the bright air. Little boys and little girls, young ladies and young gentlemen, mamas and papas – everybody in short save the governesses. Cheeks are flushed, eyes are glowing and voices sound high and clear like the notes of a candelabra caught in a gust of wind. Tumblers are beginning to find their feet and the skilled are skimming over the ice as though they had invented the pastime.'

'Beau Bugle has just achieved a triple reverse boomerang and is still upright. Mr Henry James is a little upset about this. He has thought of the perfect word to express the thud of a body that has met the earth

[1] An English Michaelmas.

with, as it were, a hard impact. But no matter, he consoles himself.
Doubtless his rash young friend will afford him some other opportunity
to make use of the word 'bump'.

And over the duffer and dandy, the rogue and radical, the virtuous
and villainous, and the ought-to-be-soundly-spanked-and-sent-to-bed,
the snow falls softly down.

Powdered with snowflakes and glowing like anything, the board of
Directors of the London, Chatham and Dover and the London,
Brighton and South Coast Railway have a nonchalant air. They have
taken the afternoon off from finding a name for their nice new terminus.
But the thing has become a passion. As they whizz past each other they
shout impromptu suggestions over their shoulders.

'Oliver Cromwell,' halloos a skater in a snuff-coloured waistcoat.

'Pretentious,' they shout back.

'The Kohinoor!' cried the Secretary.

They brood on it as they circle. They circle each other again.

'Sounds like a pleasure steamer,' they lament.

'Mr Disraeli!'

'Don't!' they chorus.


Beneath its impromptu bower of paper roses now powdered with
snowflakes the military band breaks into a march. Our Uncle Clarence,
in a strong baritone, informs Mr Purplehammer that he is a soldier of
the Queen, m'lad. Mr Purplehammer takes no interest in this.
Someone has stolen his toboggan. There it had stood, bright and
spanking new, and then before he had time to say 'Kitchener of
Khartoum'—it had vanished. But he is not going to take this thing
lying down. He will find his toboggan if he has to search all afternoon.

He stares suspiciously at an animated group by the Bridge. They
seem very interested in something. Most suspicious! With something
less than his usual assured gait old Mr Purplehammer entrusts himself
to the ice.

But the animated group is not gazing at a toboggan. They are in fact
gazing at our heroine. And who can blame them as she stands there,
smiling and dimpling and as flushed as the young Queen Victoria when
she proposed to Prince Albert of Saxe-Coburg. Beside her Honest
Ernest is pleading for a dance. He has been taking lessons from Beau
Bugle, he tempts her, and is now confident that he can reverse on

skates. Julia looks round. But the cursing Julian has been collared by a Clutterwick so she deems she might as well glide away on Honest Ernest's arm.

Mr Purplehammer snorts. All that fuss about a young gal when a man has lost his toboggan! He trundles off to look for it.

With something less than his customary assurance Mr Pumbleberry entrusts himself to the ice. He is right to be cautious.

Not a hundred yards away, Mrs Marble, too, is setting out. She has strapped on a pair of skates and she looks like a battleship – a battleship on the slips. Very slowly, very carefully, she launches one foot on the ice. All right so far. Very slowly, very carefully, she launches the other. Disaster!

There is a hand outstretched. She clutches. She looks at it. It belongs to Mr Pumbleberry. But it is the only hand offered, so gritting her teeth she levers. But she levers too hard. Mr Pumbleberry comes tumbling down too.

Someone else is struggling to his feet. Can it be Beau Bugle? The young lady brought to admire him has burst into tears and gone home to Mama. But Mr Henry James is fascinated by the shades of meaning with which he has been able to surround and, as it were, delineate his friend's misfortunes.

'Am I to take it,' he inquires, 'that this is the correct position in which to terminate and, in fact, conclude the spread eagle?'

Beau Bugle blushes. 'Well, no,' he admits, 'but you ought to have seen me do it last Tuesday week.'

The face of Mr. Henry James puckers in anguish. It is indeed a task to find the comment that will imply the exact shade of meaning to answer his rash young friend's lament over his absence from the scene on that occasion. He concentrates. Somewhere the word exists. He gropes, he considers, he perseveres. Gradually it comes to him. A little polishing – and he has it!

'Ah!' says Mr Henry James.

Mrs Marble and Mr Pumblberry have struggled to their feet. To achieve this they have been forced to support each other. They unclutch. They bow coldly. Each waits for the other to start off.

There is a feminine shriek, the sound of skates at high speed. A terrified blonde does an orange and lemon between our two opposing forces, staggers wildly, regains her balance and rushes on. Behind her crouched low and sounding a coach-horn whizzes the harp-master. He makes straight for the space between Mrs Marble and Mr Pumbleberry, stretches out his coach-horn to trip them up, beams gummily and dashes on after the blonde.

From the ice Mrs. Marble looks after him.

'Sometimes,' she tells the prostrate Pumbleberry, 'I feel I could wring Mr. Marx's merry little neck.'

The snow is falling faster. All over the country stern fathers are gazing out of darkened doors. If only this keeps up, they tell themselves, it will be just the night to turn their erring daughters out.

At the Lyceum Theatre Henry Irving, in *The Bells*, is brushing the snow off his boots.

Regent's Park is fast beginning to look like the square in St Petersburgh when the Stravinski music grows cold and the bright colours of the Benois scene are spangled with paper flakes thrown with abandon from the flies.

Julian has managed to shake off his Clutterwick cousin and is now roaming the ice in search of Julia. Ah! There she is, skating with Honest Ernest.

He starts towards her. But suddenly he checks. A terrified blonde is whizzing round him. She is followed by the whooping harp-master. Faster and faster they circle round Julian as he stands, frustrated and aloof, and looking just like John Gielgud induced to play IT in a very fast game of kiss-in-the-ring. As he waits in vain for an opportunity to break through, Honest Ernest and Julia skate tantalisingly out of his vision to the strains of the 'Barcarolle' from the *Tales of Hoffmann*.

In Naples a religious procession which has been wending its way along the waterside, falters, halts and scatters in all directions. The peasants have just seen the devil himself playing a tune that was born in hell. And the Power of Darkness has brought a friend – doubtless Judas Iscariot. It can only mean the end of the world.

At the waterside the dark-cloaked Paganini makes a gesture of despair. Even the houses have turned their backs on him.

'Do I really look like Satan?' he asks his friend.

Tactfully his friend changes the subject. 'What do you think of this,' he says. He hums a bit.

Paganini listens intently. 'You'll have to be careful with the orchestration,' he comments.

'It is superb,' says his friend modestly. 'Especially the part where I bring in the 'cellos. I am calling it,' he announces, 'The Rhapsody in Blue.'

Paganini looks pained. 'I wouldn't do that if I were you,' he warns. 'Grand'mère Gershwin is hoarding it for the grandson due to be born in America next century.'

'Ah, well,' says Rossini, resigned, 'in that case I'd better call it the Overture to William Tell.'

The 'Barcarolle' is still rocking the canal. Like the loveliest, silliest symphony in the world, the skaters link, glide and turn, and even those who are here only to watch feel themselves suddenly a part of the Carnival.

All except old Mr Purplehammer. He is still looking for his toboggan.

'Your servant, m'am.' He bows stiffly to the Lady Caroline Lamb. 'And have you by chance seen a toboggan. A new toboggan?'

Poor little poppet! The warm-hearted Lady Caroline Lamb takes pity on him. 'Have you,' she asks, 'looked for it on the slope in that part of the Park where they are planning to have an Open-air theatre? They're tobogganing there.'

Mr Purplehammer brightens. It has not occurred to him to search that locality.

'Come,' says Lady Caroline Lamb. 'We will look for it together.'

She takes his hand and skims away like a very gay lark piloting a pelican.

But what is this lashing riding-whip, this twirled moustachio, travelling down the slope at high speed? Reader, you are right. It is our villain mounted on Mr Purplehammer's toboggan. He has had to get away from the evicted widows somehow.

'Jugglers and Jackals,' he curses, as halfway down the slope he spies our heroine on the arms of another. He thinks quickly. Action – or this Savoury Snack will be wafted away from him.

He pulls out his high-powered binoculars. Who is this rival who is threatening to carry his Vampsome Violet away from him? He focuses. 'Better – it is Honest Ernest – This should be easy!'

Pausing only to instruct Uncle Clarence to drag his toboggan to the top of the hill, Spencer Faggot makes for his prey.

A dear fellow, thinks Uncle Clarence, trudging up the slope. But just a little thoughtless. He has not once remembered that Uncles like tobogganing, too.

Spencer Faggot has decided to avoid violence. He will rely instead on the traditional phrase for striking terror into timorous souls.

'Fly at once,' he hisses. 'All is known.'

Honest Ernest's conscience is clear. He does not fly. He stands where he is and blinks.

But if Spencer were so easily daunted he would not be our villain. He looks at Julia, who is standing aloof and eyeing this obnoxious friend of Papa's with disdain. Why he must be thirty if he is a day!

Inflamed by her coldness Spencer twirls a moustachio. An Appetising Apricot! Worth fighting for! Ruthlessly he returns to the fray.

'Honest Ernest,' he says. 'I bring bad news. Your pennyfarthing is on fire.'

'Impossible,' says Honest Ernest. But doubt seizes him. He dashes off to look.

Spencer Faggot offers Julia his arm.

'Come, come, my pretty one,' he says. 'Let us toboggan together.'

'Oh, no, Mr. Faggot,' says Julia. 'I don't want to toboggan. Really I don't.'

But Spencer is a masterful man. In a masterful swoop he picks up our heroine and carries her up the slope. Her little hands beat frantically against that wicked breast. Her little skates try vainly to kick him under the chin. And her little voice cries havoc to the unheeding air. After the antics of merry little Mr Marx this is the merest badinarie to the skaters in Regent's Park.

But one heart is pierced by those little cries. Heedless of personal dignity Julian dives through the whooping circle made by the harp-master and the pursued blonde, and dashes to the rescue of his beloved. In full flight he skims past Lady Caroline Lamb still guiding the cautious Mr Purplehammer up the slope.

Mrs Marble and Mr Pumbleberry, too, have heard the cry of

distress. They have also seen Julian disappearing into the distance. Mrs Marble sticks a stiff foot on the ice.

'Better take these things off,' she says pointing grimly to her skates, 'and slide for it.'

But already our villain has carried our heroine to the top of the slope. He plucks Uncle Clarence from the toboggan and places Julia in his seat.

'Please, Mr Faggot,' says Julia. 'I don't like tobogganing.'

'Nonsence, my child,' says Uncle Clarence. 'There's nothing to be afraid of. See, I'll come with you.'

But as Uncle Clarence prepares with a certain dignity to climb on the back, a human catapult hurls itself on the toboggan and pushes him off.

'Hold tight, my darling,' says Julian.

And before our villain can think quickly enough to intercept them, our hero and our heroine, together and entranced, are speeding down the slope.

'Mr Julian,' beseeches Mr Pumbleberry. 'Wait. I cannot find a tea-tray.'

'Miss Julia,' cried Mrs Marble blackly. 'Come back. Come back – or I'll tell Mama!'

'Come back,' cried Mr Purplehammer, beside himself. 'It's my toboggan.'

But our pair wave happy hands and speed on their escape.

'Can't understand it,' says Uncle Clarence puzzled. 'She said she didn't like tobogganing.'


Down the well-proportioned terraces carved out of Regency butter, black bonneted, black mantled, and black elastic booted, comes an endless procession of governesses. They are on their way to present an Address of Farewell to the First Governess in the Land.

The Baroness Lehzen, her task magnificently accomplished, is leaving our shores for ever. It is many a year since her counsel has been sought or her views received with anything more than a gentle Royal indulgence.

Through the wintry scene they come, the little sisters of gentility, advancing with the timid steps of very determined mice. Their faces shine like polished loft-ripened apples, wrinkled but good, their hair is parted in the middle, their hands are clasping the potatoes too cooled-off to comfort the grasping paws of their charges. Each has her neatly folded serviceable umbrella. Each has a pocket in the hem of her topmost petticoat, a-bulge with sponges, permanently damp from wiping simple sums off innumerable blackboards, and packets of peppermints for surreptitious refreshment. And safe in some alien temporary home, each has her possessions stored away in a painted tin trunk.

Like a serpent in mourning the procession makes its way throught the Park gates in the direction of Kensington Palace.

The toboggan has come to rest. Julian is feverishly unstrapping Julia's skates.

There is not a moment to lose.

The whole world has joined in the pursuit of our lovers. Skaters, chaperones, onlookers and children stream across the Park like many coloured ribbons on the wind. Even the band looks restless and has quickened the tempo of the *gallop* into a *furiante*. At this rate they'll soon be able to join in the chase themselves.

The slope is crowded with shouting figures, tumbling over themselves and one another in their wild downward rush. It is like one of Mr Cruickshank's cartoons come streaming to life.

Only merry little Mr Marx has not realized that this pursuit differs in any way from his usual method of progress, and he is still whooping his way between the knocked over citizens while his terrified blonde knocks over a few more in her effort to elude him.

Our lovers look back. The landscape is full of angry marionettes. Clutterwicks are tumbling over Shuttleforths. Shuttleforths are clambering across Clutterwicks. The feud is in danger, but at the moment this does not matter.

Already our lovers can distinguish the figures of the leading pursuers. There is Mr Purplehammer shouting defiantly. There is black Mrs Marble like a battleship in action. There is Lady Caroline Lamb, skimming and tripping and picking herself up and urging our lovers to make haste. There is our villain belabouring a hobby-horse snatched from a blubbing child. There is Honest Ernest falling off his pennyfarthing again. There is Beau Bugle explaining how quickly he would overtake the fugitives if only he had a pair of skis with him. And there is, Mr Henry James utterly miserable. He can find no combination of words to capture and, as it were, purvey the finer shades of the scene.

'Run quickly,' urges Julian. 'Bestir yourself, my angel.'

They fly. But their lead is slender. Already they can hear the puffs of Mr Pumbleberry, the cracks of our villains whip, and the 'Pon my souls' of Uncle Clarence.

A refuge presents itself. It is the Coliseum. It contains the painted diorama of our great Metropolis.

'In here,' says Julian.

They hurry inside.


The Coliseum stands to the south of the Lake. For many months it has been astonishing London with its diorama. Thousands have flocked to see its pictures of the Metropolis, painted by Bouton and Daguerre, which were changed two or three times every year. And when fine art palled the Coliseum added to its grottoes, a Gothic aviary, a temple of Theseus, two large conservatories, a Swiss chalet (with mountain scenery and real water), and a zoo from Central Africa. To view our painted Metropolis the public is accommodated in a circular room and turned round, much like the eye in a socket.

But Messieurs Bouton and Daguerre will soon have to get busy again, for attendances have started to fall off. To finish the season the resourceful authorities have engaged Lord George Sanger to act as compère to the views, and the resourceful Lord Sanger has brought Mademoiselle Lala to lead the admiration. To disarm suspicion she has abandoned her waltzing horses and is dressed as a Continental tourist speaking no English. To aid her disguise she is carrying a tambourine and ejaculating 'Vesuvius.'

'Now this,' says Lord George Sanger, pointing with his wand, 'is Cremorne.'

Our lovers come panting to rest in front of the gardens. They look round. For the moment they are safe. Black Mrs Marble has only got as far as Pimlico while the Clutterwicks and Shuttleforths are sorting themselves out in Camden Town, preparatory to circling London in opposite directions.

Lord George Sanger is pleased. The best house he has had for many a day! He prepares to instruct it.

'Covent Garden,' he announces, pointing with his wand to a cluster of barrows, a police-station, and an Opera House.

'Vesuvius,' cries the Continental tourist, realistically banging her tambourine. 'See,' she points, 'the bloody oranges.'

'Nelly,' pleads Lord George Sanger, shocked. 'Remember your Italian!'

Cremorne is no longer safe. Our lovers seek shelter underneath the Adelphi Arches.

But what is this moustachio peering at them from the be-pigeoned dome of St. Paul's? Our lovers fly again.

They try Seven Dials. But there is Mr Pumbleberry getting his breath back. Quick to Trafalgar Square – but there, a battleship at anchor, is Mrs Marble. They flee to Chiswick Mall. Honest Ernest's pennyfarthing is blocking the way by Miss Pinkerton's Academy. Last hope – The Grand Terminus of the London, Chatham and Dover, and the London, Brighton and South Coast Railway. Useless! The Board of Directors have taken possession for an impromptu meeting.[1]

Capture is inevitable.

Despair.

But what is this muster of barrel-organs before our lovers? Hope dawns. They run quickly and, the haven reached, they heave huge sighs of relief.

Safe at last!

Lord George Sanger points his wand at Julia's bonnet. From North and South Clutterwicks and Shuttleforths crouch to leap forward.

'Saffron Hill,' announced Lord George Sanger.

From North and South Clutterwicks and Shuttleforths draw back just in time. Snobs to a man they dare not be seen in such a locality.

Why have our lovers stolen a toboggan? Why are they fleeing from their kinsmen and other well-wishers? Why do they rush so wildly around the painted diorama of our capital city and risk their respectability at Saffron Hill?

Reader, rejoice in the good news! They are eloping. Julian and Julia are going to wed. Even now the registrar is waiting for them to emerge from the suburbs.

It is indeed a daring project!

True Julia is to return to dear Mama that very afternoon (How could

---

[1] Flying Scotsman.    Peter Pan.    Snakes and Ladders.

she break her parent's heart?) And Julian must continue to reside at Number 26. (He has to consider Aunt Lobelia's failing health.) Besides, they have no money.

But Julia is confident that she can coax Papa, and Julian is sure that la Cabuchon can be swayed to his side if only to be rid of him. And once wed nothing can part them.

They are, of course, reckoning without our villain.

And though it may be weeks, months, or even years before they have their own little nest above a Pimlico Portico, they can meet secretly at night. Has not Julian his rope ladder? Has not Julia her verandah?

And no one, *no one* will ever know their secret.

They are, of course, reckoning without their authors.

The Baroness Lehzen, Governess to the Queen of England, has said good-bye to her Royal charge. Soon she will be just another old lady living with her sister in retirement, walking beneath the painted roofs of Bückeburg. Here her only link with the Court will be those rooms where the portraits of Victoria of England crowd out the pretty pattern of the wallpaper. Her only comfort the fortnightly letter from her docile charge.

Small wonder that her eyelids are red.

Outside, a landscape of luggage is en-isled upon the cab. The cabby is apprehensive. He doubts if his wilful horse will tolerate so many hat-boxes. Supposing Dobbin should refuse to move when he cracks his whip! Would that be high treason?

Along the terrace the Governesses of London are standing in a neat black line, mopping their eyes with snowy handkerchiefs. It is as though a lodestar were about to be extinguished.

But the wilful horse is unconcerned. He is looking at a lamp-post and wondering why there are no leaves on it.

Stiff as a ramrod, lonely as a widow, the Baroness Lehzen walks firmly out to the cab. The horse looks defiantly at the Baroness. Wilfully he decides to make a bolt for it. But even as he rears, the eye that has quelled a Queen of England is turned upon him. The horse thinks better of it.

The Baroness addresses the cabby.

'Take me," she says in a firm, clear voice, 'to the Grand Terminus of the London, Chatham and Dover, and the London, Brighton and

South Coast Railway.'

From the terrace the Governesses wave sodden handkerchiefs in mittened hands as the landscape of luggage bowls steadily out of sight.

Our hero and heroine are about to be wed.

What rapture! What felicity! What bliss!

True, it is to be without wedding bells, without bridesmaids, and without Mr. Mendelssohn. But to compensate for this it is to be without a choir, without second cousins and without speeches by witty Uncles pointing out that all their troubles are likely to be Little Ones.

In short, the ceremony is about to take place before the Registrar, and the only witnesses are the conniving Belinda and our Crossing Sweeper, who is always in the know.

Julia is weeping a little on dear Belinda's shoulder – but only a very little, just enough for manners. Julian looks pale and romantic and not a little like John Gielgud in the Friar's cell. The Registrar looks like Friar Lawrence.

In fact, he even talks like him.

*'Come, come,'* he says, *'and we will make short work;*
*For, by your leaves, you shall not stay alone,*
*Till Holy Church incorporate two in one.'*

'Oh, thank you,' says Julian.

He fumbles for the ring.

'Tonight, my sweet,' breathes Julian.

Julia sighs, blushes, dimples and weeps all in one.

'Very nice,' says Belinda Clutterwick briskly. 'But now you'd better run along and spin a tale to your Mrs Marble.'

\*     \*     \*

At Windsor Castle the Queen is looking out of the window at the scarlet tin soldier on guard at his box.

Dear Lehzen, kind Lehzen, leaves London today. A good counsellor and a devoted friend, thinks the Queen. What a pity she was not more tactful with dear Albert.

She takes up her quill to enter her departure in her diary. She cannot know that when dear kind Lehzen dies it will not be recorded in these pages until some days later, and that then she will write:

'Forgot to mention that my dearest, kindest friend, dear old Lehzen, expired quite peacefully on the ninth . . . After I came to the throne she got to be rather trying and especially so after my marriage, but never from evil intention. I feel much, too, that she is gone.'

* * *

It is four o'clock in the morning. Claremont Crescent is smiling in its sleep. Even Mr Purplehammer is nodding like an elderly blissful cherub as he clutches the toboggan he has taken up to bed with him.

But in Julia's casement at Number 27 a light is burning. Julian is preparing to clamber out again.

Julia lies blissfully back against her pillows.

'And to think,' she murmurs, 'that they told me this was worse than death!'

# Down the Thames, Slowly

## Jerome K. Jerome

*George is introduced to work – Heathenish instincts of tow-lines –
Ungrateful conduct of a double-sculling skiff – Towers and towed – A
use discovered for lovers – Strange disappearance of an elderly lady –
Much haste, less speed – Being towed by girls; exciting sensation – The
missing lock or the haunted river – Music – Saved!*

We made George work, now we had got him. He did not want to work,
of course; that goes without saying. He had had a hard time in the City,
so he explained. Harris, who is callous in his nature, and not prone to
pity, said:

'Ah! and now you are going to have a hard time on the river for a
change; change is good for everyone. Out you get!'

He could not in conscience – not even George's conscience – object,
though he did suggest that, perhaps, it would be better for him to stop
in the boat, and get tea ready, while Harris and I towed, because
getting tea was such a worrying work, and Harris and I looked tired.
The only reply we made to this, however, was to pass him over the tow-
line, and he took it, and stepped out.

There is something very strange and unaccountable about a tow-
line. You roll it up with as much patience and care as you would take to
fold up a new pair of trousers, and five minutes afterwards, when you
pick it up, it is one ghastly, soul-revolting tangle.

I do not wish to be insulting, but I firmly believe that if you took an
average tow-line, and stretched it out straight across the middle of a
field, and then turned your back on it for thirty seconds, that, when you
looked round again, you would find that it had got itself altogether in a
heap in the middle of the field, and had twisted itself up, and tied itself
into knots, and lost its two ends, and become all loops; and it would take

a good half-hour, sitting down there on the grass and swearing all the while, to disentangle it again.

That is my opinion of tow-lines in general. Of course, there may be honourable exceptions; I do not say that there are not. There may be tow-lines that are a credit to their profession – conscientious, respectable tow-lines – tow-lines that do not imagine they are crotchet-work, and try to knit themselves up into antimacassars the instant they are left to themselves. I say there *may* be such tow-lines; I sincerely hope there are. But I have not met with them.

This tow-line I had taken in myself just before we had got to the lock. I would not let Harris touch it, because he is careless. I had looped it round slowly and cautiously, and tied it up in the middle, and folded it in two, and laid it down gently at the bottom of the boat. Harris had lifted it up scientifically, and had put it into George's hand. George had taken it firmly and held it away from him, and had begun to unravel it as if he were taking the swaddling clothes off a new-born infant; and, before he had unwound a dozen yards, the thing was more like a badly made doormat than anything else.

It is always the same, and the same sort of thing always goes on in connexion with it. The man on the bank, who is trying to disentangle it, thinks all the fault lies with the man who rolled it up; and when a man up the river thinks a thing, he says it.

'What have you been trying to do with it, make a fishing-net of it? You've made a nice mess you have; why couldn't you wind it up properly, you silly dummy?' he grunts from time to time as he struggles wildly with it, and lays it out flat on the tow-path, and runs round and round it, trying to find the end.

On the other hand, the man who wound it up thinks the whole cause of the muddle rests with the man who is trying to unwind it.    'It was all right when you took it!' he exclaims indignantly. 'Why don't you think what you are doing? You go about things in such a slap-dash style. You'd get a scaffolding pole entangled, *you* would!'

And they feel so angry with one another that they would like to hang each other with the thing. Ten minutes go by, and the first man gives a yell and goes mad, and dances on the rope, and tries to pull it straight by seizing hold of the first piece that comes to his hand and hauling at it. Of course, this only gets it into a tighter tangle than ever. Then the second man climbs out of the boat and comes to help him, and they get in each other's way, and hinder one another. They both get hold of the same bit of line, and pull at it in opposite directions, and wonder where it is caught. In the end, they do get it clear, and then turn round and find that the boat has drifted off, and is making straight for the weir.

This really happened once to my own knowledge. It was up by Boveney, one rather windy morning. We were pulling down-stream, and, as we came round the bend, we noticed a couple of men on the bank. They were looking at each other with as bewildered and helplessly miserable expressions as I have ever witnessed on any human countenance before or since, and they held a long tow-line between them. It was clear that something had happened, so we eased up and asked them what was the matter.

'Why, our boat's gone off!' they replied in an indignant tone. 'We just got out to disentangle the tow-line, and when we looked round, it was gone!'

And they seemed hurt at what they evidently regarded as a mean and ungrateful act on the part of the boat.

We found the truant for them half a mile further down, held by some rushes, and we brought it back to them. I bet they did not give that boat another chance for a week.

I shall never forget the picture of those two men walking up and down the bank with a tow-line, looking for their boat.

One sees a good many funny incidents up the river in connection with towing. One of the most common is the sight of a couple of towers, walking briskly along, deep in an antimated discussion, while the man in the boat, a hundred yards behind them, is vainly shrieking to them to stop, and making frantic signs of distress with a scull. Something has gone wrong; the rudder has come off, or the boathook has slipped overboard, or his hat has dropped into the water, and is floating rapidly down-stream. He calls to them to stop, quite gently and politely at first.

'Hi! Stop a minute, will you!' he shouts cheerily. 'I've dropped my hat overboard.'

Then: 'Hi! Tom – Dick! Can't you hear?' not quite so affably this time.

Then: 'Hi! Confound you, you dunder-headed idiots! Hi! stop! Oh you—'

After that he springs up, and dances about, and roars himself red in the face, and curses everything he knows. And the small boys on the bank stop and jeer at him, and pitch stones at him as he is pulled along past them, at the rate of four miles an hour, and can't get out.

Much of this sort of trouble would be saved if those who are towing would keep remembering that they *are* towing, and give a pretty frequent look round to see how their man is getting on. It is best to let one person tow. When two are doing it, they get chattering, and forget, and the boat itself, offering, as it does, but little resistance, is of no real service in reminding them of the fact.

As an example of how utterly oblivious a pair of towers can be to their work, George told us, later on in the evening, when we were discussing the subject after supper, of a very curious instance.

He and three other men, so he said, were sculling a very heavily laden boat up from Maidenhead one evening, and a little above Cookham lock they noticed a fellow and a girl, walking along the tow-path, both deep in an apparently interesting and absorbing conversation. They were carrying a boat-hook between them, and attached to the boat-hook was a tow-line, which trailed behind them, its end in the water. No boat was near, no boat was in sight. There must have been a boat attached to that tow-line at some time or other, that was certain; but what had become of it, what ghastly fate had overtaken it, and those who had been left in it, was buried in mystery. Whatever the accident may have been, however, it had in no way disturbed the young lady and gentleman who were towing. They had the boat-hook and they had the line, and that seemed to be all that they thought necessary to their work.

George was about to call out and wake them up, but, at that moment, a bright idea flashed across him, and he didn't. He got the hitcher instead and reached over, and drew in the end of the tow-line; and they made a loop in it, and put it over their mast, and then they tidied up the sculls, and went and sat down in the stern, and lit their pipes.

And that young man and young woman towed these four hulking chaps and a heavy boat up to Marlow.

George said he never saw so much thoughtful sadness concentrated into one glance before, as when, at the lock, that young couple grasped the idea that, for the last two miles, they had been towing the wrong boat. George fancied that, if it had not been for the restraining influence of the sweet woman at his side, the young man might have given way to violent language.

The maiden was the first to recover her surprise, and, when she did, she clasped her hands and said, wildly:

'Oh, Henry, then *where* is auntie?'

'Did they ever recover the old lady?' asked Harris.

George replied he did not know.

Another example of the dangerous want of sympathy between tower and towed was witnessed by George and myself once up near Walton. It was where the tow-path shelves gently down into the water, and we were camping on the opposite bank, noticing things in general. By and by a small boat came in sight, towed through the water at a tremendous pace by a powerful barge horse, on which sat a very small boy. Scattered about the boat, in dreamy and reposeful attitudes, lay five fellows, the man who was steering having a particularly restful appearance.

'I should like to see him pull the wrong line,' murmured George, as they passed. And at that precise moment the man did it, and the boat rushed up the bank with a noise like the ripping up of forty thousand linen sheets. Two men, a hamper, and three oars immediately left the boat on the larboard side, and reclined on the bank, and one and a half moments afterwards, two other men disembarked from the starboard, and sat down among boat-hooks and sails and carpet-bags and bottles. The last man went on twenty yards farther, and then got out on his head.

This seemed to sort of lighten the boat, and it went on much easier, the small boy shouting at the top of his voice, and urging his steed into a gallop. The fellows sat up and stared at one another. It was some seconds before they realised what had happened to them, but, when they did, they began to shout lustily for the boy to stop. He, however, was too much occupied with the horse to hear them, and we watched them flying after him, until the distance hid them from view.

I cannot say I was sorry at their mishap. Indeed, I only wish that all the young fools who have their boats towed in this fashion – and plenty do – could meet with similar misfortunes. Besides the risk they run themselves, they become a danger and an annoyance to every other boat they pass. Going at the pace they do, it is impossible for them to get out of anybody else's way, or for anybody else to get out of theirs. Their line gets hitched across your mast and overturns you, or it catches somebody in the boat, and either throws them into the water, or cuts their face open. The best plan is to stand your ground, and be prepared to keep them off with the butt-end of a mast.

Of all experiences in connection with towing, the most exciting is being towed by girls. It is a sensation that nobody ought to miss. It takes three girls to tow always; two hold the rope, and the other one runs round and round and giggles. They generally begin by getting themselves tied up. They get the line round their legs, and have to sit down on the path and undo each other, and then they twist it round their necks, and are nearly strangled. They fix it straight, however, at last, and start of at a run, pulling the boat along at quite a dangerous pace. At the end of a hundred yards they are naturally breathless, and suddenly stop, and all sit down on the grass and laugh, and your boat drifts out to mid-stream and turns round, before you know what has happened, or can get hold of a scull. Then they stand up, and are surprised.

'Oh, look!' they say; 'he's gone right out into the middle.'

They pull on pretty steadily for a bit, after this, and then it all at once occurs to one of them that she will pin up her frock and they ease up for the purpose, and the boat runs aground.

You jump up and push it off, and you shout to them not to stop.

'Yes. What's the matter?' they shout back.

'Don't stop,' you roar.

'Don't what?'

'Don't stop – go on – go on!'

'Go back, Emily, and see what it is they want,' says one; and Emily comes back, and asks what it is.

'What do you want?' she says; 'anything happened?'

'No,' you reply, 'it's all right; only go on, you know – don't stop.'

'Why not?'

'Why, we can't steer, if you keep stopping. You must keep some way on the boat.'

'Keep some what?'

'Some way – you must keep the boat moving.'

'Oh, all right, I'll tell 'em. Are we doing it all right?'

'Oh, yes, very nicely, indeed, only don't stop.'

'It doesn't seem difficult at all. I thought it was so hard.'

'Oh, no, it's simple enough. You want to keep on steady at it, that's all.'

'I see. Give me out my red shawl, it's under the cushion.'

You find the shawl, and hand it out, and by this time another has come back and thinks she will have hers too, and they take Mary's on chance, and Mary does not want it, so they bring it back and have a pocket-comb instead. It is about twenty minutes before they get off again, and, at the next corner, they see a cow, and you have to leave the boat to chivvy the cow out of their way.

There is never a dull moment in the boat while girls are towing it.

George got the line right after a while, and towed us steadily on to Penton Hook. There we discussed the important question of camping. We had decided to sleep on board that night, and we had either to lay up just about there, or go on past Staines. It seemed early to think about shutting up then, however, with the sun still in the heavens, and we settled to push straight on for Runnymede, three and a half miles farther, a quiet wooded part of the river, and where there is good shelter.

We all wished, however, afterward, that we had stopped at Penton Hook. Three or four miles up-stream is a trifle, early in the morning, but it is a weary pull at the end of a long day. You take no interest in the scenery during these last few miles. You do not chat and laugh. Every half-mile you cover seems like two. You can hardly believe you are only where you are, and you are convinced that the map must be wrong; and, when you have trudged along for what seems to you at least ten miles, and still the lock is not in sight, you begin to seriously fear that somebody must have sneaked it and run off with it.

I remember being terribly upset once up the river (in a figurative sense, I mean). I was out with a young lady – cousin on my mother's side – and we were pulling down to Goring. It was rather late, and we were anxious to get in – at least *she* was anxious to get in. It was half past six when we reached Benson's lock, and dusk was drawing on, and she began to get excited then. She said she must be in to supper. I said it was a thing I felt I wanted to be in at, too; and I drew out a map I had with me to see exactly how far it was. I saw it was just a mile and a half to the next lock – Wallingford – and five on from there to Cleeve.

'Oh, it's all right!' I said. 'We'll be through the next lock before seven, and then there is only one more;' and I settled down and pulled steadily away.

We passed the bridge, and soon after that I asked if she saw the lock.

She said no, she did not see any lock; and I said, 'Oh!' and pulled on. Another five minutes went by, and then I asked her to look again.

'No,' she said; 'I can't see any signs of a lock.'

'You – you are sure you know a lock, when you do see one?' I asked hesitatingly, not wishing to offend her.

The question did not offend her, however, and she suggested that I had better look for myself; so I laid down the sculls, and took a view. The river stretched out straight before us in the twilight for about a mile; not a ghost of a lock was to be seen.

'You don't think we have lost our way, do you?' asked my companion.

I did not see how that was possible; though, as I suggested, we might have somehow got into the weir stream, and be making for the falls.

This idea did not comfort her in the least, and she began to cry. She said we should both be drowned, and that it was a judgement on her for coming out with me.

It seemed an excessive punishment, I thought; but my cousin thought not, and hoped it would all soon be over.

I tried to reassure her, and to make light of the whole affair. I said that the fact evidently was that I was not rowing as fast as I fancied I was, but that we should soon reach the lock now; and I pulled on for another mile.

Then I began to get nervous myself. I looked again at the map. There was Wallingford lock, clearly marked, a mile and a half below Benson's. It was a good reliable map; and, besides, I recollected the lock myself. I had been through it twice. Where were we? What had happened to us? I began to think it must be all a dream, and that I was really asleep in bed, and should wake up in a minute, and be told it was past ten.

I asked my cousin if she thought it could be a dream, and she replied that she was just about to ask me the same question; and then we both wondered if we were both asleep, and if so, who was the real one that was dreaming, and who was the one that was only a dream; it got quite interesting.

I still went on pulling, however, and still no lock came in sight, and the river grew more and more gloomy and mysterious under the gathering shadows of night, and things seemed to be getting weird and uncanny. I thought of hob-goblins and banshees, and will-o'-the-wisps, and those wicked girls who sit up all night on rocks, and lure people into whirlpools and things; and I wished I had been a better man, and knew more hymns; and in the middle of these reflections I heard the blessed strains of 'He's got 'em on', played badly on a concertina, and knew that we were saved.

I do not admire the tones of a concertina, as a rule; but oh! how beautiful the music seemed to us both then – far, far more beautiful than the voice of Orpheus or the lute of Apollo, or anything of that sort could have sounded. Heavenly melody, in our then state of mind, would only have still further harrowed us. A soul-moving harmony, correctly performed, we should have taken as a spirit-warning, and have given up all hope. But about the strains of 'He's got 'em on', jerked spasmodically, and with involuntary variations, out of a wheezy accordion, there was something singularly human and reassuring.

. The sweet sounds drew nearer, and soon the boat from which they were worked came alongside us.

It contained a party of provincial 'Arrys and 'Arriets, out for a moonlight sail. (There was not any moon, but that was not their fault.) I never saw more attractive, lovable people in all my life. I hailed them, and asked if they could tell me the way to Wallingford lock; and I had explained that I had been looking for it for the last two hours.

'Wallingford lock!' they answered. 'Lor' love you, sir, that's been done away with for over a year. There ain't no Wallingford lock now, sir. You're close to Cleeve now. Blow me tight if 'ere ain't a gentleman been looking for Wallingford lock, Bill!'

I had never thought of that. I wanted to fall upon all their necks and bless them; but the stream was running too strong just there to allow of this, so I had to content myself with mere cold-sounding words of gratitude.

We thanked them over and over again, and we said it was a lovely night, and we wished them a pleasant trip, and, I think, I invited them all to come and spend a week with me, and my cousin said her mother would be so pleased to see them. And we sang the 'Soldiers' Chorus' out of *Faust*, and got home in time for supper after all.

# A Month from the Illuminating Diary of a Professional Lady

*Anita Loos*

MAY 16TH

I really have not written in my diary for quite a long time, because Mr Eisman arrived in Paris and when Mr Eisman is in Paris we really do not seem to do practically anything else but the same thing.

I mean we go shopping and we go to a show and we go to Momart and when a girl is always going with Mr Eisman nothing practically happens. And I did not even bother to learn any more French because I always seem to think it is better to leave French to those that can not do anything else but talk French. So finally Mr Eisman seemed to lose quite a lot of interest in all of my shopping. So he heard about a button factory that was for sale quite cheaply in Vienna and as Mr Eisman is in the button profession, he thought it would be a quite good thing to have a button factory in Vienna so he went to Vienna and he said he did not care if he did not ever see the rue de la Paix again. So he said if he thought Vienna would be good for a girl's brains, he would send for Dorothy and I and we could meet him at Vienna and learn something. Because Mr Eismann really wants me to get educated more than anything else, especially shopping.

So now we have a telegram, and Mr Eisman says in the telegram for Dorothy and I to take an oriental express because we really ought to see the central of Europe because we American girls have quite a lot to learn in the central of Europe. So Dorothy says if Mr Eisman wants us to see the central of Europe she bets there is not a rue de la Paix in the whole central of Europe.

So Dorothy and I are going to take an oriental express tomorrow and I really think it is quite unusual for two American girls like I and

Dorothy to take an oriental express all alone, because it seems that in the Central of Europe they talk some other kinds of landguages which we do not understand besides French. But I always think that there is nearly always some gentleman who will protect two American girls like I and Dorothy who are all alone and who are traveling in the Central of Europe to get educated.

MAY 17TH

So now we are on an oriental express and everything seems to be quite unusual. I mean Dorothy and I got up this morning and we looked out of the window of our compartment and it was really quite unusual. Because it was farms, and we saw quite a lot of girls who seemed to be putting small size hay stacks on to large size hay stacks while their husbands seemed to sit at a table under quite a shady tree and drink beer. Or else their husbands seemed to sit on a fence and smoke their pipe and watch them. So Dorothy and I looked at two girls who seemed to be ploughing up all of the ground with only the aid of a cow and Dorothy said, 'I think we girls have gone one step to far away from New York, because it begins to look to me as if the Central of Europe is no country for we girls.' So we both became quite worried. I mean I became quite depressed because if this is what Mr Eisman thinks we American girls ought to learn I really think it is quite depressing. So I do not think we care to meet any gentlemen who have been born and raised in the Central of Europe. I mean the more I travel and the more I seem to see other gentlemen the more I seem to think of American gentlemen.

So now I am going to get dressed and go to the dining car and look for some American gentleman and hold a conversation, because I really feel so depressed. I mean Dorothy keeps trying to depress me because she keeps saying that I will probably end up in a farm in the Central of Europe doing a sister act with a plough. Because Dorothy's jokes are really very unrefined and I think that I will feel much better if I go to the dining car and have some luncheon.

Well I went to the dining car and I met a gentleman who was quite a delightful American gentleman. I mean it was quite a coinstance, because we girls have always heard about Henry Spoffard and it was really nobody else but the famous Henry Spoffard, who is the famous

Spoffard family, who is a very very fine old family who is very very wealthy. I mean Mr Spoffard is one of the most famous familys in New York and he is not like most gentlemen who are wealthy, but he works all of the time for the good of the others. I mean he is the gentleman who always gets his picture in all of the newspapers because he is always senshuring all of the plays that are not good for peoples morals. And all of we girls remember the time when he was in the Ritz for luncheon and he met a gentleman friend of his and the gentleman friend had Peggy Hopkins Joyce to luncheon and he introduced Peggy Hopkins Joyce to Mr Spoffard and Mr Spoffard turned on his heels and walked away. Because Mr Spoffard is a very very famous Prespyterian and he is really much to Prespyterian to meet Peggy Hopkins Joyce. I mean it is unusual to see a gentleman who is such a young gentleman as Mr Spoffard be so Prespyterian, because when most gentlemen are 35 years of age their minds nearly always seem to be on something else.

So when I saw no one else but the famous Mr Spoffard I really became quite thrilled. Because all of we girls have tried very hard to have an introduction to Henry Spoffard and it was quite unusual to be shut up on a train in the Central of Europe with him. So I thought it would be quite unusual for a girl like I to have a friendship with a gentleman like Mr Spoffard, who really does not even look at a girl unless she at least looks like a Prespyterian. And I mean our family in Little Rock were really not so Prespyterian.

So I thought I would sit at his table. So then I had to ask him about all of the money because all of the money they use in the Central of Europe has not even got so much sense to it as the kind of franks they use in Paris. Because it seems to be called kronens and it seems to take quite a lot of them because it takes 50,000 of them to even buy a small size package of cigarettes and Dorothy says if the cigarettes had tobacco in them, we couldn't lift enough kronens over a counter to pay for a package. So this morning Dorothy and I asked the porter to bring us a bottle of champagne and we really did not know what to give him for a tip. So Dorothy said for me to take one of the things called a one million kronens and she would take one of them called a one million kronens and I would give him mine first and if he gave me quite a dirty look, she would give him hers. So after we paid for the bottle of champagne I gave him my one million kronens and before we could do anything else he started in to grabbing my hand and kissing my hand and getting down on his knees. So we finally had to push him right out of the compartment. So one million kronens seemed to be enough. So I told Mr Spoffard how we did not know what to give the porter when he brought us our bottle of mineral water. So then I asked him to tell me all about all of the money because I told him I always seem to think that a penny earned was a penny saved. So it really was quite unusual because Mr Spoffard said that that was his favorite motto.

So then we got to talking quite a lot and I told him that I was traveling to get educated and I told him I had a girl with me who I was trying to reform because I thought if she would put her mind more on getting educated, she would get more reformed. Because after all Mr Spoffard will have to meet Dorothy sooner or later and he might wonder what a refined girl like I was doing with a girl like Dorothy. So Mr Spoffard really became quite intreeged. Because Mr Spoffard loves to reform people and he loves to sensure everything and he really came over to Europe to look at all the things that Americans come over to Europe to look at, when they really should not look at them but they should look at all of the museums instead. Because if that is all we Americans come to Europe to look at, we should stay home and look at America first. So Mr Spoffard spends all of his time looking at things that spoil peoples morals. So Mr Spoffard really must have very very strong morals or else all the things that spoil other peoples morals would spoil his morals. But they do not seem to spoil Mr Spoffards morals and I really think it is wonderful to have such strong morals. So I told Mr Spoffard that I thought that civilisation is not what it ought to be and we really ought to have something else to take its place.

So Mr Spoffard said that he would come to call on Dorothy and I in our compartment this afternoon and we would talk it all over, if his mother does not seem to need him in her compartment. Because Mr Spoffards mother always travels with Mr Spoffard and he never does anything unless he tells his mother all about it, and asks his mother if he ought to. So he told me that that is the reason he has never got married, because his mother does not think that all of the flappers we seem to have nowadays are what a young man ought to marry when a young man is full of so many morals as Mr Spoffard seems to be full of. So I told Mr Spoffard that I really felt just like his mother feels about all of the flappers because I am an old fashioned girl.

So then I got to worrying about Dorothy quite a lot because Dorothy is really not so old-fashioned that might make Mr Spoffard wonder what such an old-fashioned girl as I was doing with such a girl as Dorothy. So I told him how I was having quite a hard time reforming Dorothy and I would like to have him meet Dorothy so he could tell me if he really thinks I am wasting quite a lot of time trying to reform a girl like Dorothy. So then he had to go to his mother. So I really hope that Dorothy will act more reformed than she usually acts in front of Mr Spoffard.

Well Mr Spoffard just left our compartment so he really came to pay a call on us after all. So Mr Spoffard told us all about his mother and I was really very very intreeged because if Mr Spoffard and I become friendly he is the kind of a gentleman that always wants a girl to meet his mother. I mean if a girl gets to know what kind of a mother a gentlemans mother is like, she really knows more what kind of a conversation to use on a gentleman's mother when she meets her. Because a girl like I is really always on the verge of meeting gentleman's mothers. But such an unrefined girl as Dorothy is really not the kind of a girl that ever meets gentlemens mothers.

So Mr Spoffard says his mother has to have him take care of her quite a lot. Because Mr Spoffards mothers brains have never really been so strong. Because it seems his mother came from such a very fine old family that even when she was quite a small size child she had to be sent to a school that was a special school for people of very fine old familys who had to have things very easy on their brain. So she still has to have things very easy on her brain, so she has a girl who is called her companion who goes with her everywhere who is called Miss Chapman. Because Mr Spoffard says that there is always something new going on in the world which they did not get a chance to tell her about at the school. So now Miss Chapman keeps telling her instead. Because how would she know what to think about such a new thing as a radio, for instance, if she did not have Miss Chapman to tell her what it was, for instance. So Dorothy spoke up and Dorothy said, 'What a responsibility that girl has got on her shoulders. For instance, what if Miss Chapman told her a radio was something to build a fire in, and she would get cold some day and stuff it full of papers and light it.' But Mr Spoffard told Dorothy that Miss Chapman would never make such a mistake. Because he said that Miss Chapman came from a very very fine old family herself and she really had a fine brain. So Dorothy said, 'If she really has got such a fine brain I bet her fine old family had an ice man who could not be trusted.' So Mr Spoffard and I did not pay any more attention to Dorothy because Dorothy really does not know how to hold a conversation.

So then I and Mr Spoffard held a conversation all about morals and Mr Spoffard says he really thinks the future of everything is between the hands of Mr Blank the district attorney who is the famous district attorney who is closing up all the places in New York where they sell all of the liquor. So Mr Spoffard said that a few months ago, when Mr Blank decided he would try to get the job to be the district attorney, he put 1,000 dollars worth of liquor down his sink. So now Mr Blank says that everybody else has got to put it down their sink. So Dorothy spoke up, and Dorothy said, 'If he poured 1,000 dollars worth down his sink to get himself one million dollars worth of publicity and a good job – when we pour it down our sink, what do we get?' But Mr Spoffard is to brainy a gentleman to answer any such a foolish question. So he gave Dorothy a look that was full of dignity and he said he would have to go back to his Mother. So I was really quite angry at Dorothy. So I followed Mr Spoffard down the hall of the railway train and I asked Mr Spoffard if he thought I was wasting quite a lot of time reforming a girl like Dorothy. So Mr Spoffard thinks I am, because he really thinks a girl like Dorothy will never have any reverance. So I told Mr Spoffard I had wasted so much time on Dorothy it would really break my heart to be a failure. So then I had tears in my eyes. So Mr Spoffard is really very very sympathetic because when he saw that I did not have any handkerchief, he took his own handkerchief and he dried up all of my tears. So then he said he would help me with Dorothy quite a lot and get her mind to running on things that are more educational.

So then he said he thought that we ought to get off the train at a place called Munich because it was very full of art, which they call 'kunst' in Munich, which is very, very educational. So he said he and Dorothy and I would get off the train in Munich because he could send his mother right on to Vienna with Miss Chapman, because every place always seems to look alike to his mother anyway. So we are all going to get off the train at Munich and I can send Mr Eisman a telegram when

nobody is looking. Because I really do not think I will tell Mr Spoffard
about Mr Eisman, because, after all, their religions are different and
when two gentlemen have such different religions they do not seem to
have so much to get congeneal about. So I can telegraph Mr Eisman
that Dorothy and I thought we would get off the train at Munich to look
at all of the art.

So then I went back to Dorothy and I told Dorothy if she did not have
anything to say in the future to not say it. Because even if Mr Spoffard is
a fine old family and even if he is very Prespyterian, I and he could
really be friendly after all and talk together quite a lot. I mean Mr
Spoffard likes to talk about himself quite a lot, so I said to Dorothy it
really shows that, after all, he is just like any other gentleman. But
Dorothy says she would demand more proof than that. So Dorothy says
she thinks that maybe I might become quite friendly with Mr Spoffard
and especially with his mother because she thinks his mother and I
have quite a lot that is common, but she says, if I ever bump into Miss
Chapman, she thinks I will come to a kropper because Dorothy saw
Miss Chapman when she was at luncheon and Dorothy says Miss
Chapman is the kind of girl that wears a collar and a tie even when she
is not on horseback. And Dorothy said it was the look that Miss
Chapman gave her at luncheon that really gave her the idea about the
ice man. So Dorothy says she thinks Miss Chapman has got 3 thirds of
the brains of that trio of Geegans, because Geegans is the slang word
that Dorothy has thought up to use on people who are society people.
Because Dorothy says she thinks any gentleman with Mr Spoffards
brains had ought to spend his time putting nickels into an electric
piano, but I did not even bother to talk back at such a girl as Dorothy.
So now we must get ready to get off the train when the train gets to
Munich so that we can look at all of the kunst in Munich.

MAY 19TH

Well yesterday Mr Spoffard and I and Dorothy got off the train at
Munich to see all of the kunst in Munich, but you only call it Munich
when you are on the train because as soon as you get off of the train they
seem to call it Munchen. So you really would know that Munchen was
full of kunst because in case you would not know it, they have painted
the word 'kunst' in large size black letters on everything in Munchen,
and you can not even see a boot black's stand in Munchen that is not

full of kunst.

So Mr Spoffard said that we really ought to go to the theater in Munchen because even the theater in Munchen was full of kunst. So we looked at all of the bills of all of the theaters, with the aid of quite an intelectual hotel clerk who seemed to be able to read it and tell us what it said, because it really meant nothing to us. So it seems they were playing Kiki in Munchen, so I said, let us go and see Kiki because we have seen Lenore Ulric in New York and we would really know what it is all about even if they do not seem to talk the English landguage. So then we went to the Kunst theater. So it seems that Munchen is practically full of Germans and the lobby of the Kunst theater was really full of Germans who stand in the lobby and drink beer and eat quite a lot of Bermudian onions and garlick sausage and hard boiled eggs and beer before all of the acts. So I really had to ask Mr Spoffard if he thought we had come to the right theater because the lobby seemed to smell such a lot. I mean when the smell of beer gets to be anteek it gets to smell quite a lot. But Mr Spoffard seemed to think that the lobby of the Kunst theatre did not smell any worse than all of the other places in Munich. So then Dorothy spoke up and Dorothy said 'You can say what you want about the Germans being full of "kunst", but what they are really full of is delicatessen'.

So then we went into the Kunst theater. But the Kunst theater does not seem to smell so good as the lobby of the Kunst theater. And the Kunst theater seems to be decorated with quite a lot of what tripe would look like if it was pasted on the wall and gilded. Only you could not really see the gilding because it was covered with quite a lot of dust. So Dorothy looked around and Dorothy said, if this is 'kunst', the art center of the world is Union Hill New Jersey.

So then they started in to playing Kiki but it seems that it was not the same kind of a Kiki that we have in America, because it seemed to be all about a family of large size German people who seemed to keep getting in each others way. I mean when a stage is completely full of 2 or 3 German people who are quite large size, they really cannot help it if they seem to get in each others ways. So then Dorothy got to talking with a young gentleman who seemed to be a German gentleman who sat back of her, who she thought was applauding. But what he was really doing was he was cracking a hard boiled egg on the back of her chair. So he talked English with quite an accent that seemed to be quite

a German accent. So Dorothy asked him if Kiki had come out on the
stage yet. So he said no, but she was really a beautiful German actress
who came clear from Berlin and he said we should really wait until she
came out, even if we did not seem to understand it. So finally she came
out. I mean we knew it was her because Dorothy's German gentleman
friend nudged Dorothy with a sausage. So we looked at her, and we
looked at her and Dorothy said, 'If Schuman Heinke still has a
grandmother, we have dug her up in Munchen.' So we did not bother to
see any more of Kiki because Dorothy said she would really have to
know more about the foundations of that building before she would risk
our lives to see Kiki do that famous scene where she faints in the last act.
Because Dorothy said, if the foundations of that building were as anteek
as the smell, there was going to be a catasterophy when Kiki hit the
floor. So even Mr Spoffard was quite discouradged, but he was really
glad because he said he was 100 per cent of an American and it served
the Germans right for starting such a war against all we Americans.

MAY 20TH
Well today Mr Spoffard is going to take me all around to all of the
museums in Munchen, which are full of kunst that I really ought to look
at, but Dorothy said she had been punished for all of her sins last night,
so now she is going to begin life all over again by going out with her
German gentleman friend, who is going to take her to a house called the
Half Brow house which is the worlds largest size of a Beer Hall. So
Dorothy said I could be a high brow and get full of kunst, but she is
satisfide to be a Half brow and get full of beer. But Dorothy will really
never be full of anything else but unrefinement.

MAY 21ST
Well Mr Spoffard and I and Dorothy are on the train again and we are
all going to Vienna. I mean Mr Spoffard and I spent one whole day
going through all of the museums in Munchen, but I am really not even
going to think about it. Because when something terrible happens to
me, I always try to be a Christian science and I simply do not even think
about it, but I deny that it ever happened even if my feet do seem to hurt
quite a lot. So even Dorothy had quite a hard day in Munchen because
her German gentleman friend, who is called Rudolf, came for her at 11
o'clock to take her to breakfast. But Dorothy told him that she had had

her breakfast. But her gentleman friend said that he had had his first breakfast to, but it was time for his second. So he took Dorothy to the Half Brow house where everybody eats white sausages and pretzels and beer at 11 o'clock. So after they had their white sausages and beer he wanted to take her for a ride but they could only go a few blocks because by then it was time for luncheon. So they ate quite a lot of luncheon and then he bought her a large size box of chocolates that were full of liqueurs, and took her to the matinee. So after the first act Rudolf got hungry and they had to go and stand in the lobby and have some sandwitches and beer. But Dorothy did not enjoy the show very much and so after the second act Rudolf said they would leave because it was time for tea anyway. So after quite a heavy tea, Rudolf asked her to dinner and Dorothy was to overcome to say No. So after dinner they went to a beer garden for beer and pretzels. But finally Dorothy began to come to, and she asked him to take her back to the hotel. So Rudolf said he would, but they had better have a bite to eat first. So today Dorothy really feels just as discouradged as I seem to feel, only Dorothy is not a Christian science and all she can do is suffer.

But in spite of all my Christian science, I am really beginning to feel quite discouradged about Vienna. I mean Mr Eisman is in Vienna, and I do not see how I can spend quite a lot of time with Mr Eisman and quite a lot of time with Mr Spoffard and keep them from meeting one another. Because Mr Spoffard might not seem to understand why Mr Eisman seems to spend quite a lot of money to get me educated. And Dorothy keeps trying to depress me about Miss Chapman because she says she thinks that when Miss Chapman sees I and Mr Spoffard together she thinks that Miss Chapman will cable for the familys favorite lunacy expert. So I have got to be as full of Christian science as I can and always hope for the best.

MAY 25TH

So far everything has really worked out for the best. Because Mr Eisman is very very busy all day with the button profession, and he tells me to run around with Dorothy all day. So I and Mr Spoffard run around all day. So then I tell Mr Spoffard that I really do not care to go to all of the places that you go to at night, but I will go to bed and get ready for tomorrow instead. So then Dorothy and I go to dinner with Mr Eisman and then we go to a show, and we stay up quite late at a

cabaret called The Chapeau Rouge and I am able to keep it all up with
the aid of champagne. So if we keep our eye out for Mr Spoffard and do
not all bump into one another when he is out looking at things that we
Americans really should not look at, it will all work out for the best. I
mean I have even stopped Mr Spoffard looking at museums because I
tell him that I like nature better, and when you look at nature you look
at it in a horse and buggy in the park and it is much easier on the feet. So
now he is beginning to talk about how he would like me to meet his
mother, so everything really seems for the best after all.

But I have quite a hard time with Mr Eisman at night. I mean at
night Mr Eisman is in quite a state, because every time he makes an
engagement about the button factory, it is time for all the gentlemen in
Vienna to go to the coffee house and sit. Or else every time he makes an
engagement about the button factory, some Viennese gentleman gets
the idea to have a picknick and they all put on short pants and bare
knees and they all put a feather in their hat, and they all walk to the
Tyrol. So it really discouradges Mr Eisman quite a lot. But if anyone
ought to get discouradged I think that I ought to get discouradged
because after all when a girl has had no sleep for a week a girl can not
help it if she seems to get discouradged.

MAY 27TH

Well finally I broke down and Mr. Spoffard said that he thought a little
girl like I, who was trying to reform the whole world was trying to do to
much, especially beginning on a girl like Dorothy. So he said there was
a famous doctor in Vienna called Dr Froyd who could stop all of my
worrying because he does not give a girl medicine but he talks you out of
it by psychoanalysis. So yesterday he took me to Dr Froyd. So Dr Froyd
and I had quite a long talk in the english landguage. So it seems that
everybody seems to have a thing called inhibitions, which is when you
want to do a thing and you do not do it. So then you dream about it
instead. So Dr Froyd asked me, what I seemed to dream about. So I
told him that I never really dream about anything. I mean I use my
brains so much in the day time that at night they do not seem to do
anything else but rest. So Dr Froyd was very very surprised at a girl
who did not dream about anything. So then he asked me all about my
life. I mean he is very very sympathetic, and he seems to know how to
draw a girl out quite a lot. I mean I told him things that I really would

not even put in my diary. So then he seemed very very intreeged at a girl who always seemed to do everything she wanted to do. So he asked me if I really never wanted to do a thing that I did not do. For instance did I ever want to do a thing that was really vialent, for instance, did I ever want to shoot someone for instance. So then I said I had, but the bullet only went in Mr Jennings lung and came right out again. So then Dr Froyd looked at me and looked at me and he said he did not really think it was possible. So then he called in his assistance and he pointed at me and talked to his assistance quite a lot in the Viennese landguage. So then his assistance looked at me and looked at me and it really seems as if I was quite a famous case. So then Dr Froyd said that all I needed was to cultivate a few inhibitions and get some sleep.

MAY 29TH

Things are really getting to be quite a strain. Because yesterday Mr Spoffard and Mr Eisman were both in the lobby of the Bristol hotel and I had to pretend not to see both of them. I mean it is quite an easy thing to pretend not to see one gentleman, but it is quite a hard thing to pretend not to see two gentlemen. So something has really got to happen soon, or I will have to admit that things seem to be happening that are not for the best.

So this afternoon Dorothy and I had an engagement to meet Count Salm for tea at four o'clock, only you do not call it tea at Vienna but you seem to call it 'yowzer' and you do not drink tea at Vienna but you drink coffee instead. I mean it is quite unusual to see all of the gentlemen at Vienna stop work, to go to yowzer about one hour after they have all finished their luncheon, but time really does not seem to mean so much to Viennese gentlemen except time to get to the coffee house, which they all seem to know by instincts, or else they really do not seem to mind if they make a mistake and get there to early. Because Mr Eisman says that when it is time to attend to the button profession, they really seem to lose all of their interest until Mr Eisman is getting so nervous he could scream.

So we went to Deimels and met Count Salm. But while we were having yowzer with Count Salm, we saw Mr Spoffard's mother come in with her companion Miss Chapman, and Miss Chapman seemed to look at me quite a lot and talk to Mr Spoffards mother about me quite a lot. So I became quite nervous, because I really wished that we were not with Count Salm. I mean it has been quite a hard thing to make Mr Spoffard think that I am trying to reform Dorothy, but if I had to try to make him think that I was trying to reform Count Salm, he might begin to think that there is a limit to almost everything. So Mr Spoffards mother seems to be deaf, because she seems to use an ear trumpet and I really could not help over hearing quite a lot of words that Miss Chapman was using on me, even if it is not such good etiquet to overhear people. So Miss Chapman seemed to be telling Mr Spoffards mother that I was a 'creature', and she seemed to be telling her that I was the real reason why her son seemed to be so full of nothing but neglect lately. So then Mr Spoffards mother looked at me and looked at me, even if it was not such good etiquet to look at a person. And Miss Chapman kept right on talking to Mr Spoffards mother and I heard her mention Willie Gwynn and I think that Miss Chapman has been making some inquiries about me and I really think that she has heard about the time when all of the family of Willie Gwynn had quite a long talk with me and persuaded me not to marry Willie Gwynn for $10,000. So I really wish Mr Spoffard would introduce me to his mother before she gets to be full of quite a lot of prejudice. Because one thing seems to be piling up on top of another thing, until I am almost on the verge of getting nervous and I have not had any time yet to do what Dr Froyd said a girl ought to do.

So tonight I am going to tell Mr Eisman that I have got to go to bed early, so then I can take quite a long ride with Mr Spoffard and look at nature, and he may say something definite, because nothing makes gentlemen get so definite as looking at nature when it is moonlight.

MAY 30TH

Well last night Mr Spoffard and I took quite a long ride in the park, but they do not call it a park in the Viennese landguage but they call it the Prater. So a prater is really devine because it is just like Coney Island but at the same time it is in the woods and it is practically full of trees and it has quite a long road for people to take rides on in a horse and buggy. So I found out that Miss Chapman has been talking against me quite a lot. So it seems that she has been making inquiries about me, and I was really surprised to hear all of the things that Miss Chapman seemed to find out about me except that she did not find out about Mr Eisman educating me. So then I had to tell Mr Spoffard that I was not always so reformed as I am now, because the world was full of gentlemen who were nothing but wolfs in sheeps clothes, that did nothing but take advantadge of all we girls. So I really cried quite a lot. So then I told him how I was just a little girl from Little Rock when I first left Little Rock and by that time even Mr Spoffard had tears in his eyes. So I told him how I came from a very very good family because papa was very intelectual, and he was a very very prominent Elk, and everybody always said that he was a very intelectual Elk. So I told Mr Spoffard that when I left Little Rock I thought that all of the gentlemen did not want to do anything but protect we girls and by the time I found out that they did not want to protect us so much, it was to late. So then he cried quite a lot. So then I told him how I finaly got reformed by reading all about him in the newspapers and when I saw him in the oriental express it really seemed to be nothing but the result of fate. So I told Mr Spoffard that I thought a girl was really more reformed if she knew what it was to be unreformed than if she was born reformed and never really knew what was the matter with her. So then Mr Spoffard reached over and he kissed me on the forehead in a way that was full of reverance and he said I seemed to remind him quite a lot of a girl who got quite a write-up in the bible who was called Magdellen. So then he said that he used to be a member of the choir himself, so who was he to cast the first rock at a girl like I.

So we rode around in the Prater until it was quite late and it really was devine because it was moonlight and we talked quite a lot about morals, and all the bands in the prater were all playing in the distants 'Mama love Papa'. Because 'Mama love Papa' has just reached Vienna and they all seem to be crazy about 'Mama love Papa' even if it is not so new in America. So then he took me home to the hotel.

So everything always works out for the best, because this morning Mr Spoffard called up and told me he wanted me to meet his mother. So I told him I would like to have luncheon alone with his mother because we could have quite a little tat-atate if there was only two of us. So I told him to bring his mother to our room for luncheon because I thought that Miss Chapman could not walk into our room and spoil everything.

So he brought his mother down to our sitting room and I put on quite a simple little organdy gown that I had ripped all of the trimming off of, and I had a pair of black lace mitts that Dorothy used to wear in the

Follies and I had a pair of shoes that did not have any heels on them. So when he introduced us to each other I dropped her a courtesy because I always think it is quite quaint when a girl drops quite a lot of courtesys. So then he left us alone and we had quite a little talk and I told her that I did not seem to like all of the flappers that we seem to have nowadays, because I was brought up to be more old fashioned. So then Mr Spoffards mother told me that Miss Chapman said that she had heard that I was not so old fashioned. But I told her that I was so old fashioned that I was always full of respect for all of my elders and I would not dare to tell them everything they ought to do, like Miss Chapman seems to tell her everything she ought to do, for instants.

So then I ordered luncheon and I thought some champagne would make her feel quite good for luncheon so I asked her if she liked champagne. So she really likes champagne very very much but Miss Chapman thinks it is not so nice for a person to drink liquor. But I told her that I was a Christian science, and all of we Christian science seem to believe that there can not really be any harm in anything, so how can there be any harm in a small size bottle of champagne? So she never seemed to look at it in that kind of a light before, because she said that Miss Chapman believed in Christian science also, but what Miss Chapman believed about things that were good for you to drink seemed to apply more towards water. So then we had luncheon and she began to feel very very good. So I thought that we had better have another bottle of champagne because I told her that I was such an ardent Christian science that I did not even believe there could be any harm in two bottles of champagne. So we had another bottle of champagne and she became very intreeged about Christian science because she said that she really thought it was a better religion than Prespyterians. So she said Miss Chapman used to try to get her to use it on things, but Miss Chapman never seemed to have such a large size grasp of the Christian science religion as I seem to have.

So then I told her that I thought Miss Chapman was jealous of her good looks. So then she said that that was true, because Miss Chapman would always make her wear hats that were made out of black horses hair because horses hair does not weigh so much on a persons brain. So I told her I was going to give her one of my hats that has got quite large size roses on it. So then I got it out, but we could not get it on her head because hats are quite small on account of hair being bobbed. So I thought I would get the sissors and bob her head, but then I thought I had done enough to her for one day.

So Henry's mother said that I was really the most sunshine that she ever had in all her life and when Henry came back to take his Mother up to her room, she did not want to go. But after he got her away he called me up on the telephone and he was quite excited and he said he wanted to ask me something that was very important. So I said I would see him tonight.

But now I have got to see Mr Eisman because I have an idea about doing something that is really very very important that has got to be done at once.

MAY 31ST

Well I and Dorothy and Mr Eisman are on a train going to a place called Buda Pest. So I did not see Henry again before I left, but I left him a letter. Because I thought it would be a quite good thing if what he wanted to ask me he would have to write down, instead of asking me, and he could not write it to me if I was in the same city that he is in. So I told him in my letter that I had to leave in five minute's time because I found out that Dorothy was just on the verge of getting very unreformed, and if I did not get her away, all I had done for her would really go for nothing. So I told him to write down what he had to say to me, and mail it to me at the Ritz hotel in Buda Pest. Because I always seem to believe in the old addage, Say it in writing.

So it was really very easy to get Mr Eisman to leave Vienna, because yesterday he went out to see the button factory but it seems that all of the people at the button factory were not at work but they were giving a birthday party to some saint. So it seems that every time some saint has a birthday they all stop work so they can give it a birthday party. So Mr Eisman looked at their calendar, and found out that some saint or other was born practically every week in the year. So he has decided that America is good enough for him.

So Henry will not be able to follow me to Buda Pest because his mother is having treatments by Dr Froyd and she seems to be a much more difficult case than I seem to be. I mean it is quite hard for Dr Froyd, because she cannot seem to remember which is a dream and which really happened to her. So she tells him everything, and he has to use his judgement. I mean when she tells him that a very very handsome young gentleman tried to flirt with her on Fifth Avenue, he uses his judgement.

So we will soon be at a Ritz hotel again and I must say it will be delightful to find a Ritz hotel right in the central of Europe.

# The Macbeth Murder Mystery

## *James Thurber*

'It was a stupid mistake to make,' said the American woman I had met at my hotel in the English lake country, 'but it was on the counter with the other Penguin books – the little sixpenny ones, you know, with the paper covers – and I supposed of course it was a detective story. All the others were detective stories. I'd read all the others, so I bought this one without really looking at it carefully. You can imagine how mad I was when I found it was Shakespeare.' I murmured something sympathetically. 'I don't see why the Penguin-books people had to get out Shakespeare plays in the same size and everything as the detective stories,' went on my companion. 'I think they have different-coloured jackets,' I said. 'Well, I didn't notice that,' she said. 'Anyway, I got real comfy in bed that night and all ready to read a good mystery story and here I had *The Tragedy of Macbeth* – a book for high-school students. Like *Ivanhoe*,' 'Or *Lorna Doone*,' I said. 'Exactly,' said the American lady. 'And I was just crazy for a good Agatha Christie, or something. Hercule Poirot is my favourite detective.' 'Is he the rabbity one?' I asked. 'Oh, no,' said my crime-fiction expert. 'He's the Belgian one. You're thinking of Mr Pinkerton, the one that helps Inspector Bull. He's good, too.'

Over her second cup of tea my companion began to tell the plot of a detective story that had fooled her completely – it seems it was the old family doctor all the time. But I cut in on her. 'Tell me,' I said. 'Did you read *Macbeth*?' 'I *had* to read it,' she said. 'There wasn't a scrap of anything else to read in the whole room.' 'Did you like it?' I asked. 'No, I did not,' she said decisively. 'In the first place, I don't think for a moment that Macbeth did it.' I looked at her blankly. 'Did what?' I asked. 'I don't think for a moment that he killed the King,' she said. 'I don't think the Macbeth woman was mixed up in it, either. You suspect them the most, of course, but those are the ones that are never guilty –

or shouldn't be, anyway.' 'I'm afraid,' I began, 'that I – ' 'But don't you see?' said the American lady. 'It would spoil everything if you could figure out right away who did it. Shakespeare was too smart for that. I've read that people never *have* figured out *Hamlet*, so it isn't likely Shakespeare would have made *Macbeth* as simple as it seems.' I thought this over while I filled my pipe. 'Who do you suspect?' I asked suddenly. 'Macduff,' she said, promptly. 'Good God!' I whispered, softly.

'Oh Macduff did it, all right,' said the murder specialist. 'Hercule Poirot would have got him easily.' 'How did you figure it out?' I demanded. 'Well,' she said, 'I didn't right away. At first I suspected Banquo. And then, of course, he was the second person killed. That was good right in there, that part. The person you suspect of the first murder should always be the second victim.' 'Is that so?' I murmured. 'Oh, yes,' said my informant. 'They have to keep surprising you. Well, after the second murder I didn't know *who* the killer was for a while.' 'How about Malcolm and Donalbain, the King's sons?' I asked. 'As I remember it, they fled right after the first murder. That looks suspicious.' 'Too suspicious,' said the American lady. 'Much too suspicious. When they flee, they're never guilty. You can count on that.' 'I believe,' I said, 'I'll have a brandy,' and I summoned the waiter. My companion leaned toward me, her eyes bright, her teacup quivering. 'Do you know who discovered Duncan's body?' she demanded. I said I was sorry, but I had forgotten. 'Macduff discovers it,' she said, slipping into the historical present. 'Then he comes running downstairs and shouts, "Confusion has broke open the Lord's anointed temple" and "Sacrilegious murder has made his masterpiece" and on and on like that.' The good lady tapped me on the knee. 'All that stuff was rehearsed,' she said. 'You wouldn't say a lot of stuff like that, offhand, would you – if you had found a body?' She fixed me with a glittering eye. 'I – ' I began. 'You're right!' she said. 'You wouldn't! Unless you had practised it in advance. "My God, there's a body in here!" is what an innocent man would say.' She sat back with a confident glare.

I thought for a while. 'But what do you make of the Third Murderer?' I asked. 'You know, the Third Murderer has puzzled *Macbeth* scholars for three hundred years.' 'That's because they never thought of Macduff,' said the American lady. 'It was Macduff, I'm certain. You couldn't have one of the victims murdered by two ordinary thugs – the murderer always has to be somebody important.' 'But what about the banquet scene?' I asked, after a moment. 'How do you account for Macbeth's guilty actions there, when Banquo's ghost came in and sat in his chair?' The lady leaned forward and tapped me on the knee again. 'There wasn't any ghost,' she said. 'A big, strong man like that doesn't go around seeing ghosts – especially in a brightly lighted banquet hall with dozens of people around. Macbeth was *shielding somebody!*' 'Who was he shielding?' I asked. 'Mrs Macbeth, of course,' she said. 'He thought she did it and he was going to take the rap himself. The husband always does that when the wife is suspected.' 'But what,' I demanded, 'about the sleepwalking scene, then?' 'The same thing, only the other way around,' said my companion. 'That time *she* was shielding *him*. She wasn't asleep at all. Do you remember where it says, "Enter Lady Macbeth with a taper"?' 'Yes,' I said. 'Well, people who walk in their sleep *never carry lights!*' said my fellow-traveller. 'They have a second sight. Did you ever hear of a sleepwalker carrying a light?' 'No,' I said, 'I never did.' 'Well, then, she wasn't asleep. She was acting guilty to shield Macbeth.' 'I think,' I said, 'I'll have another brandy,' and I called the waiter. When he brought it, I drank it rapidly and rose to go. 'I believe,' I said, 'that you have got hold of something. Would you lend me that *Macbeth*? I'd like to look it over tonight. I don't feel, somehow, as if I'd ever really read it.' 'I'll get it for you,' she said. 'But you'll find that I am right.'

I read the play over carefully that night, and the next morning, after breakfast, I sought out the American woman. She was on the putting green, and I came up behind her silently and took her arm. She gave an exclamation. 'Could I see you alone?' I asked, in a low voice. She nodded cautiously and followed me to a secluded spot. 'You've found out something?' she breathed. 'I've found out,' I said, triumphantly, 'the name of the murderer!' 'You mean it wasn't Macduff?' she said. 'Macduff is as innocent of those murders,' I said, 'as Macbeth and the Macbeth woman.' I opened the copy of the play, which I had with me, and turned to Act II, Scene 2. 'Here,' I said, 'you will see where Lady Macbeth says, "I laid their daggers ready. He could not miss 'em. Had he not resembled my father as he slept, I had done it." Do you see?' 'No,' said the American woman, bluntly, 'I don't.' 'But it's simple!' I exclaimed. 'I wonder I didn't see it years ago. The reason Duncan resembled Lady Macbeth's father as he slept is that *it actually was her father!*' 'Good God!' breathed my companion, softly. 'Lady Macbeth's father killed the King,' I said, 'and hearing someone coming, thrust the body under the bed and crawled into the bed himself.' 'But,' said the lady, 'you can't have a murderer who only appears in the story once. You can't have that.' 'I know that,' I said, and I turned to Act II Scene 4. 'It says here, "Enter Ross with an old Man." Now, that old man is never identified and it is my contention he was old Mr. Macbeth, whose ambition it was to make his daughter Queen. There you have your motive.' 'But even then,' cried the American lady, 'he's still a minor character!' 'Not,' I said, gleefully, 'when you realise that he was also *one of the weird sisters in disguise!*' 'You mean one of the three witches?' 'Precisely,' I said. 'Listen to this speech of the old man's. "On Tuesday last, a falcon towering in her pride of place, was by a mousing owl hawk'd at and kill'd." Who does that sound like?' 'It sounds like the way the three witches talk,' said my companion, reluctantly. 'Precisely!' I said again. 'Well,' said the American woman, 'maybe you're right, but – ' 'I'm sure I am,' I said. 'And do you know what I'm going to do now?' 'No,' she said. 'What?' 'Buy a copy of *Hamlet*,' I said, 'and solve *that!*' My companion's eye brightened. 'Then,' she said, 'you don't think Hamlet did it?' 'I am,' I said, 'absolutely positive he didn't.' 'But who,' she demanded, 'do you suspect?' I looked at her cryptically. 'Everybody,' I said, and disappeared into a small grove of trees as silently as I had come.

# Will You Wait?

## *Alfred Bester*

They keep writing those antiquated stories about bargains with the Devil. You know . . . sulphur, spells and pentagrams; tricks, snares and delusions. They don't know what they're talking about. Twentieth Century diabolism is slick and streamlined, like jukeboxes and automatic elevators and television and all the other modern efficiencies that leave you helpless and infuriated.

A year ago I got fired from an agency job for the third time in ten months. I had to face the fact that I was a failure. I was also dead broke. I decided to sell my soul to the Devil, but the problem was how to find him. I went down to the main reference room of the library and read everything on demonology and devil-lore. Like I said, it was all just talk. Anyway, if I could have afforded the expensive ingredients which they claimed could raise the Devil, I wouldn't have had to deal with him in the first place.

I was stumped, so I did the obvious thing; I called Celebrity Service. A delicate young man answered.

I asked, 'Can you tell me where the Devil is?'

'Are you a subscriber to Celebrity Service?'

'No.'

'Then I can give you no information.'

'I can afford to pay a small fee for one item.'

'You wish limited service?'

'Yes.'

'Who is the celebrity, please?'

'The Devil.'

'Who?'

'The Devil . . . Satan, Lucifer, Scratch, Old Nick . . . The Devil.'

One moment, please.' In five minutes he was back, extremely annoyed. 'Veddy soddy. The Devil is no longer a celebrity.'

He hung up. I did the sensible thing and looked through the telephone directory. On a page decorated with ads for Sardi's Restaurant I found Satan, Shaitan, Carnage & Bael, 477 Madison Avenue, Judson 3-1900. I called them. A bright young woman answered.

'SSC&B. Good morning.'

'May I speak to Mr Satan, please?'

'The lines are busy. Will you wait?'

I waited and lost my dime. I wrangled with the operator and lost another dime but got the promise of a refund in postage stamps. I called Satan, Shaitan, Carnage & Bael again.

'SSC&B. Good morning.'

'May I speak to Mr Satan? And please don't leave me hanging on the phone. I'm calling from a – '

The switchboard cut me off and buzzed. I waited. The coin-box gave a warning click. At last a line opened.

'Miss Hogan's office.'

'May I speak to Mr Satan?'

'Who's calling?'

'He doesn't know me. It's a personal matter.'

'I'm sorry. Mr Satan is no longer with our organization.'

'Can you tell me where I can find him?'

There was muffled discussion in broad Brooklyn and then Miss Hogan spoke in crisp Secretary: 'Mr Satan is now with Beëlzebub, Belial, Devil & Orgy.'

I looked them up in the phone directory. 383 Madison Avenue, Plaza 6-1900. I dialed. The phone rang once and then chocked. A metallic voice spoke in sing-song: 'The number you are dialing is not a working number. Kindly consult your directory for the correct number. This is a recorded message.' I consulted my directory. It said Plaza 6-1900. I dialed again and got the same recorded message.

I finally broke through to a live operator who was persuaded to give me the new number of Beëlzebub, Belial, Devil & Orgy. I called them. A bright young woman answered.

'B.B.D.O. Good morning.'

'May I speak to Mr Satan, please?'

'Who?'

'Mr Satan.'

'I'm sorry. There is no such person with our organization.'

'Then give me Beëlzebub or the Devil.'

'One moment, please.'

I waited. Every half minute she opened my wire long enough to gasp: 'Still ringing the Dev —' and then cut off before I had a chance to answer. At last a bright young woman spoke. 'Mr Devil's office.'

'May I speak to him?'

'Who's calling?'

I gave her my name.

'He's on another line. Will you wait?'

I waited. I was fortified with a dwindling reserve of nickels and dimes. After twenty minutes, the bright young woman spoke again: 'He's just gone into an emergency meeting. Can he call you back?'

'No. I'll try again.'

Nine days later I finally got him.

'Yes, sir? What can I do for you?'

I took a breath. 'I want to sell you my soul.'

'Have you got anything on paper?'

'What do you mean, anything on paper?'

'The Property, my boy. The Sell. You can't expect B.B.D.O. to buy a pig in a poke. We may drink out of dixie cups up here, but the sauce has got to be a hundred proof. Bring in your Presentation. My girl'll set up an appointment.'

I prepared a Presentation of my soul with plenty of Sell. Then I called his girl.

'I'm sorry, he's on the Coast. Call back in two weeks.'

Five weeks later she gave me an appointment. I went up and sat in the photo-montage reception room of B.B.D.O. for two hours, balancing my Sell on my knees. Finally I was ushered into a corner office decorated with Texas brands in glowing neon. The Devil was lounging on his contour chair, dictating to an Iron Maiden. He was a tall man with the phoney voice of a sales manager; the kind that talks loud in elevators. He gave me a Sincere handshake and immediately looked through my Presentation.

'Not bad,' he said. 'Not bad at all. I think we can do business. Now what did you have in mind? The usual?'

'Money, success, happiness.'

He nodded. 'The usual. Now we're square shooters in this shop.

B.B.D.O. doesn't dry-gulch. We'll guarantee money, success and happiness.'

'For how long?'

'Normal life-span. No tricks, my boy. We take our estimates from the Actuary Tables. Offhand I'd say you're good for another forty, forty-five years. We can pin-point that in the contract later.'

'No tricks?'

He gestured impatiently. 'That's all bad public relations, what you're thinking. I promise you, no tricks.'

'Guaranteed?'

'Not only do we guarantee service; we *insist* on giving service. B.B.D.O. doesn't want any beefs going up to the Fair Practice Committee. You'll have to call on us for service at least twice a year or the contract will be terminated.'

'What kind of service?'

He shrugged. 'Any kind. Shine your shoes; empty ashtrays; bring you dancing girls. That can be pin-pointed later. We just insist that you use us at least twice a year. We've got to give you a quid for your quo. *Quid pro quo*. Check?'

'But no tricks?'

'No tricks. I'll have our legal department draw up the contract. Who's representing you?'

'You mean an agent? I haven't got one.'

He was startled. 'Haven't got an agent? My boy, you're living dangerously. Why, we could skin you alive. Get yourself an agent and tell him to call me.'

'Yes, sir. M-May I . . . Could I ask a question?'

'Shoot. Everything is open and above-board at B.B.D.O.'

'What will it be like for me . . . wh-when the contract terminates?'

'You really want to know?'

'Yes.'

'I don't advise it.'

'I want to know.'

He showed me. It was like a hideous session with a psychoanalyst, in perpetuity . . . an eternal, agonising self-indictment. It was hell. I was shaken.

'I'd rather have inhuman fiends torturing me,' I said.

He laughed. 'They can't compare to man's inhumanity to himself.

Well . . . changed your mind, or is it a deal?'

'It's a deal.'

We shook hands and he ushered me out. 'Don't forget,' he warned. 'Protect yourself. Get an agent. Get the best.'

I signed with Sibyl & Sphinx. That was on March 3rd. I called S&S on March 15th. Mrs Sphinx said: 'Oh yes, there's been a hitch. Miss Sibyl was negotiating with B.B.D.O. for you, but she had to fly to Sheol. I've taken over for her.'

I called April 1st. Miss Sibyl said: 'Oh yes, there's been a slight delay. Mrs Sphinx had to go to Salem for a try-out. A witch-burning. She'll be back next week.'

I called April 15th. Miss Sibyl's bright young secretary told me that there was some delay getting the contracts typed. It seemed that B.B.D.O. was re-organising its legal department. On May 1st Sibyl & Sphinx told me that the contracts had arrived and that *their* legal department was looking them over.

I had to take a menial job in June to keep body and soul together. I worked in the stencil department of a network. At least once a week a script would come in about a bargain with the Devil which was signed, sealed and delivered before the opening commercial. I used to laugh at them. After four months of negotiation I was still threadbare.

I saw the Devil once, bustling down Park Avenue. He was running for Congress and was very busy being jolly and hearty with the electorate. He addressed every cop and doorman by first name. When I spoke to him he got a little frightened; thinking I was a Communist or worse. He didn't remember me at all.

In July, all negotiations stopped; everybody was away on vacation. In August everybody was overseas for some Black Mass Festival. In September Sibyl & Sphinx called me to their office to sign the contract. It was thirty-seven pages long, and fluttered with pasted-in corrections and additions. There were half a dozen tiny boxes stamped on the margin of every page.

'If you only knew the work that went into this contract,' Sibyl & Sphinx told me with satisfaction.

'It's kind of long, isn't it?'

'It's the short contracts that make all the trouble. Initial every box, and sign on the last page. All six copies.'

I initialled and signed. When I was finished I didn't feel any

different. I'd expected to start tingling with money, success and
happiness.

'Is it a deal now?' I asked.

'Not until *he's* signed it.'

'I can't hold out much longer.'

'We'll send it over by messenger.'

I waited a week and then called.

'You forgot to initial one of the boxes,' they told me.

I went to the office and initialed. After another week I called.

'*He* forgot to initial one of the boxes,' they told me that time.

On October 1st I received a special delivery parcel. I also received a
registered letter. The parcel contained the signed, sealed and delivered
contract between me and the Devil. I could at last be rich, successful
and happy. The registered letter was from B.B.D.O. and informed me
that in view of my failure to comply with Clause 27-A of the contract, it
was considered terminated, and I was due for collection at their
convenience. I rushed down to Sibyl & Sphinx.

'What's Clause 27-A?' they asked.

We looked it up. It was the clause that required me to use the services
of the Devil at least once every six months.

'What's the date of the contract?' Sibyl & Sphinx asked.

We looked it up. The contract was dated March 1st, the day I'd had
my first talk with the Devil in his office.

'March, April, May . . . ' Miss Sibyl counted on her fingers. 'That's
right. Seven months have elapsed. Are you sure you didn't ask for *any*
service?'

'How could I? I didn't have a contract.'

'We'll see about this,' Miss Sphinx said grimly. She called B.B.D.O.
and had a spirited argument with the Devil and his legal department.
Then she hung up. 'He says you shook hands on the deal March 1st,'
she reported. 'He was prepared in good faith to go ahead with his side of
the bargain.'

'How could I know? I didn't have a contract.'

'Didn't you ask for anything?'

'No. I was waiting for the contract.'

Sibyl & Sphinx called in their legal department and presented the
case.

'You'll have to arbitrate,' the legal department said, and explained that agents are forbidden to act as their client's attorney.

I hired the legal firm of Wizard, Warlock, Voodoo, Dowser & Hag (99 Wall Street, Exchange 3-1900), to represent me before the Arbitration Board (479 Madison Avenue, Lexington 5-1900). They asked for a $200 retainer plus twenty percent of the contract's benefits. I'd managed to save $34 during the four months I was working in the stencil department. They waived the retainer and went ahead with the Arbitration preliminaries.

On November 15th the network demoted me to the mail room, and I seriously contemplated suicide. Only the fact that my soul was in jeopardy in an arbitration stopped me.

The case came up December 12th. It was tried before a panel of three impartial Arbitrators and took all day. I was told they'd mail me their decision. I waited a week and called Wizard, Warlock, Voodoo, Dowser & Hag.

'They've recessed for the Christmas holidays,' they told me.

I called January 2nd.

'One of them's out of town.'

I called January 10th.

'He's back, but the other two are out of town.'

'When will I get a decision?'

'It could take months.'

'How do you think my chances look?'

'Well, we've never lost an arbitration.'

'That sounds pretty good.'

'But there can always be a first time.'

That sounded pretty bad. I got scared and figured I'd better copper my bets. I did the sensible thing and hunted through the telephone directory until I found Seraphim, Cherubim and Angel, 666 Fifth Avenue, Templeton 6-1900. I called them. A bright young woman answered.

'Seraphim, Cherubim and Angel. Good morning.'

'May I speak to Mr Angel, please?'

'He's on another line. Will you wait?'

I'm still waiting.

# Acknowledgements

The publishers wish to thank the following for their permission to use the following material: Woody Allen and Elm Tree Books for 'Match Wits with Inspector Ford' and 'Examining Psychic Phenomena' From *Without Feathers*; Macmillan, London and Basingstoke for 'William is Hypnotised' from *William - the Outlaw* by Richmal Crompton; Hamish Hamilton Ltd and John Farquharson Ltd for an extract from *Bring on the Empty Horses* by David Niven; Florence King and Michael Joseph Ltd for two extracts from *Confessions of a Failed Southern Lady* ; Clive James, Jonathan Cape Ltd and A. D. Peters & Co Ltd for 'The Man in the Brown Paper Bag' from *Falling Towards England*; The Bodley Head and The Estate of Stephen Leacock for 'We Have With Us Tonight' from *My Discovery of England*; Alan Nelson and *The Magazine of Fantasy and Science Fiction* for 'Narapoia' © 1951 by Mercury Press, Inc.; The Trustees of the Wodehouse Trust No.3 and Century Hutchinson Ltd for 'Lord Emsworth and the Girlfriend' and 'The Amazing Hat Mystery' from *Vintage Wodehouse* by P. G. Wodehouse; Devin/Adair Co. for 'Me  Da Went off the Bottle!' from *Irish Stories and Plays* by Paul Vincent Carroll; Fran Lebowitz and Sidgwick & Jackson for 'My Day: An Introduction of Sorts', 'Plants: The Root of all Evil' and 'Digital Clocks and Pocket Calculators: Spoilers of Youth' from *Metropolitan Life*; Geoffrey Willans and The Tessa Sayle Agency for 'Ho for the Hols!' from *The Compleet Molesworth* (Pavilion Books) © 1958 by Geoffrey Willans and Ronald Searle; James Herriot and Michael Joseph Ltd for chapters 24-25 of *Vet in Harness*; Leslie Thomas and Methuen London for an extract from *The Magic Army*; A. P. Watt Ltd and the Executors of the Estate of K. S. P. McDowall for an extract from *Trouble for Lucia* by E. F. Benson; BBC Enterprises Ltd for 'The Grand Design' from *Yes, Prime Minister* by Jonathan Lynn and Anthony Jay; Malcolm Bradbury and Curtis Brown Ltd for 'Phogey!' from *All Dressed Up and Nowhere To Go* ©  1960 Malcolm Bradbury; Peter Tinniswood and Macmillan, London and Basinstoke for 'The Landfall' from *The Brigadier Down Under*; Victoria Wood and Methuen London for 'Supermarket